Glencoe Social Studies
New York Regents Rev

Global History and Geography

Dytell • Mancini • Maurer • Ponzi • Ponzi

TEACHER REVIEWERS

Robert Dytell
President, New York State Council for the Social Studies
Clifton Park, New York

Virginia Mancini
K–12 Social Studies Chairperson
Pleasantville School District
Pleasantville, New York

Carol Maurer
Social Studies Department Chairperson
Rye Neck High School
Mamaroneck, New York

Patricia H. Ponzi
Global History and AP World History Teacher (Retired)
Bay Shore High School
Bay Shore, New York
Adjunct Lecturer of Secondary Education
Dowling College
Oakdale, New York

Robert K. Ponzi
Global History and Government Teacher (Retired)
Sayville High School
West Sayville, New York
Adjunct Lecturer of Secondary Education
Dowling College
Oakdale, New York

CREDITS

TABLE OF CONTENTS

CORRELATION CHART

Correlation of Practice Test Questions to the New York State Core Curriculum
for Global History and Geography

New York Core Curriculum for Grade 10	Unit 1	Unit 2	Unit 3	Unit 4	Unit 5	Unit 6
Unit One: Ancient World—Civilizations and Religions (4000 BC–500 AD)						
A. Early Peoples	1					
B. Neolithic Revolution and early river civilizations	1					
C. Classical civilizations	2, 4, 5	6, 7				
D. The rise and fall of great empires	2, 3, 5	6, 7, 8	10, 13	16, 17		
E. The emergence and spread of belief systems	3, 5	6, 7	10, 11, 12			
Unit Two: Expanding Zones of Exchange and Encounter (500–1200)						
A. Gupta Empire (320–550 AD)	3	7				
B. Tang and Song Dynasty (618–1126 AD)		7				
C. Byzantine Empire (330–1453 AD)		8				
D. Early Russia		8	12			
E. The spread of Islam to Europe, Asia, and Africa		6, 7	10	15		
F. Medieval Europe (500–1400)		8, 9				
G. Crusades		6, 8				
Unit Three: Global Interactions (1200–1650)						
A. Early Japanese history and feudalism			13			
B. The rise and fall of the Mongols and their impact on Eurasia		6, 7, 8				
C. Global trade and interactions			10	15		
D. Rise and fall of African civilizations			10			
E. Social, economic, and political impacts of the plague on Eurasia and Africa		9				
F. Renaissance and humanism			11			
G. Reformation and Counter Reformation			11			
H. The rise and impact of European nation–states/decline of feudalism			11			
Unit Four: The First Global Age (1450–1770)						
A. The Ming Dynasty (1368–1644)				17		
B. The impact of the Ottoman Empire on the Middle East and Europe				15, 16		
C. Spain and Portugal on the eve of the encounter				15		
D. The rise of Mesoamerican empires: Aztec and Incan empires before 1500				14		
E. The encounter between Europeans and the peoples of Africa, the Americas, and Asia				15, 17	22	
F. Political ideologies: global absolutism			12			25
G. The response to absolutism: The rise of parliamentary democracy in England			12			

* numbers indicate chapters in review book

New York Core Curriculum for Grade 10	Unit 5	Unit 6	Unit 7	Unit 8
Unit Five: An Age of Revolution (1750–1914)				
A. The Scientific Revolution	18, 20			
B. The Englightenment in Europe	18			
C. Political revolutions	18, 19			
D. The reaction against revolutionary ideas	20, 23			
E. Latin America: The failure of democracy and the search for stability	18, 22			
F. Global nationalism	19, 20, 22	24, 26		
G. Economic and social revolutions	20, 21			
H. Imperialism	22, 23			
I. Japan and the Meiji Restoration	23			
Unit Six: A Half Century of Crisis and Achievement (1900–1945)				
A. World War I		24		
B. Revolution and change in Russia—causes and impacts		24, 25		
C. Between the wars		25, 26		
D. World War II—causes and impacts		25, 27		
Unit Seven: The 20th Century Since 1945				
A. Cold War balance of power			28	
B. Role of the United Nations				33
C. Economic issues in the Cold War and Post-Cold War era			28, 29, 31	
D. Chinese Communist Revolution			32	
E. Collapse of European imperialism				33
F. Conflicts and change in the Middle East			31	
G. Collapse of communism and the breakup of the Soviet Union			29	33
H. Political and economic change in Latin America			30	
Unit Eight: Global Connections and Interactions				
A. Social and political patterns and change				33
B. Economic issues				33
C. The environment and sustainability				33, 34
D. Science and technology				33, 34

* numbers indicate chapters in review book

INTRODUCING THE BOOK

This *Glencoe Social Studies New York Regents Review Series—Global History and Geography* is designed for you, the student, to help you review your Global History and Geography course. Each part of the book concentrates on the themes, issues, and facts that you will need to know to successfully take the Regents Examination in Global History and Geography.

The first part of the book familiarizes you with the kinds of questions you will see on the Regents Exam. It provides you with strategies, instructions, and tips to help you do well on the exam, using actual examples from past Regents Exams.

The second part of the book is an outline and commentary based on the student edition of *Glencoe World History*. It is organized on a unit and chapter basis, and you can use it both to review the material in your textbook and to help you prepare for the Regents Exam. In the margins next to the narrative, you will find helpful test-taking tips, key core concepts, and short anecdotes. Each unit is followed by Regents questions for practice; all answers are provided in a separate Answer Key booklet.

At the end of the book, there are three complete Regents Exams, which will provide you with total test practice, and a glossary with significant vocabulary terms.

GETTING STARTED

New York State allows three hours for you to take the Regents Exam in Global History and Geography. With proper review, this is ample time to do well on the exam. When the signal is given to begin the exam, skim the *entire* exam to get an idea of the basic content and structure of the test.

As you can see from the past Regents Examinations located at the back of this review book, the exam is composed of three parts. Part I consists of 50 multiple-choice questions. Part II consists of a Thematic Essay Question. Part III is the Document-Based Question (DBQ) portion on the exam. The DBQ has two parts: Part A requires you to answer questions about a document (there are up to nine total documents), Part B requires you to write an essay using at least five of the documents. In order to score a passing grade on the Regents Exam, you must earn a score of at least 65.

PART I   MULTIPLE-CHOICE QUESTIONS

General Strategies

Work through the multiple-choice questions the first time, and answer only those questions of which you are sure. (Remember to leave the spaces on the answer sheet blank if you have skipped a question, so you don't lose your place and can fill them in later.) Underline key words or phrases in each question, and remember to consider all of the answer choices. Then, go back and answer any questions you have not yet answered. Do not leave any spaces on the answer sheet blank. There is no penalty for guessing, but you will definitely lose points for *not* answering a question. As a final review, check your answer sheet one last time against the questions to make sure that you have marked your answers in the correct spaces on the answer sheet. (It is a good idea to circle your answers directly in the exam book so that you can cross-check them more easily.)

General Question Types

There are three general question types that usually appear on the Regents Exam: General Social Studies Questions, Regional Questions, and Cross-Regional Questions.

PREPARING FOR THE REGENTS

This entire book is set up to help you grasp the facts, main ideas, and concepts needed to do well on your Regents Exam. Notes in the margin include core concepts, test-taking tips, and more. Use blank spaces in the margins to answer questions raised in the text or to jot down key points. Before each unit of study, skim through the exams at the back of the book to develop a sense of what the Regents Exam wants you to know about your world.

- **General Social Studies Questions** This type of question tests your knowledge of general social studies concepts or key social studies vocabulary. Read through the following examples of these questions. (Answers appear on page xxv.)

1 The development of early civilizations usually depended on
  (1) the formation of democratic governments
  (2) a location near large deposits of gold and silver
  (3) the existence of large armies
  (4) a plentiful water supply and fertile land

2 Which quotation best reflects a feeling of nationalism?
  (1) "An eye for an eye and a tooth for a tooth."
  (2) "A person's greatest obligation is to the family."
  (3) "For God, King, and Country."
  (4) "Opposition to evil is as much a duty as is cooperation with good."

3 Which factor is necessary for the development of democratic institutions?
  (1) strong military forces
  (2) respect for individual rights
  (3) a one-party system
  (4) an agricultural economy

4 Which situation generally occurs in a society as a result of urbanization?
  (1) Opportunities for social mobility increase.
  (2) Ties to extended family are strengthened.
  (3) Poverty in rural areas is eliminated.
  (4) Employment opportunities in the cities decrease.

5 "In these [economic] structures, people looked to past practices plus cultural and religious beliefs to decide what to produce, how to produce it, how products would be distributed, and even when tasks should be performed."

  Which type of economy is the author of this statement describing?
  (1) command economy — all govt control
  (2) mixed economy — command + market
  (3) traditional economy — looking at the past (we
  (4) market economy — producer has control (supply + demand)

REGENTS WARM-UP

To answer question 2, you must know the definition of *nationalism:* loyalty or pride in one's nation or national group. Nationalism has been a major agent of change in the modern world.

REGENTS WARM-UP

Urbanization is the rapid growth of cities. Often, it involves the large-scale movement of people. Every region of the world is already urbanized or in the process of becoming urbanized.

nazi ger.

farming communities

6   Cultural diffusion occurs most rapidly in societies that
   (1) adhere to traditional social values
   (2) have extended families
   (3) come into frequent contact with other groups
   (4) have a strong oral history

• **Regional Questions** This type of question tests your knowledge of areas covered in the Global History and Geography curriculum. The questions are arranged on a region-by-region basis and are roughly chronological. (The early questions deal with earlier periods, and as the questions progress, they move toward more contemporary times.) The following set of questions deal with China. (Answers appear on page xxv.)

7   In ancient China, one effect on government of the teachings of Confucius was the high status of
   (1) soldiers
   (2) merchants
   (3) farmers
   (4) scholars

8   During the centuries of dynastic rule, the Chinese rejected other cultures as inferior to their own. This situation illustrates the concept of
   (1) ethnocentrism
   (2) imperialism
   (3) social mobility
   (4) cultural diffusion

9   After World War II, the Chinese Communists were successful in their revolution mainly because the
   (1) United States refused to support the Nationalists
   (2) Communists had the support of the peasants
   (3) Communists had more advanced weapons
   (4) Nationalists had been defeated by Japan

10 Which fact about China has been the cause of the other three?
   (1) The economy of China has trouble providing for all the needs of the people.
   (2) The Chinese government has set limits on the number of children families may have.
   (3) Chinese cities have a shortage of housing.
   (4) China's population exceeds one billion.

REGENTS WARM-UP

Use the regional questions in the exams at the back of the book as a study guide. If you have trouble with any of the topics, look them up in the appropriate units and chapters of this review book.

REGENTS WARM-UP

Each of the answers in question 8 is a key social studies term. Make sure you know the meaning of all four terms before taking the Regents Exam.

REGENTS WARM-UP

Question 11 focuses on the relationship between geography and history. As a tip, think of the features that all three waterways have in common.

REGENTS WARM-UP

Question 12 tests your knowledge of the key concept of political systems. Both Sparta and the Soviet Union were models of totalitarian political systems. What are some of the features of totalitarianism?

- **Cross-Regional Questions** These questions draw links between regions of the world, both in the past and in the present. Some of the questions may focus on global issues that affect the entire world. Read through the following examples of cross-regional questions. (Answers appear on page xxv.)

11 The Suez Canal, the Panama Canal, and the Straits of the Dardanelles are similar because they
   (1) are strategic waterways that have been the center of conflicts
   (2) were part of the French colonial empire
   (3) are located in regions that are rich in natural resources
   (4) were built during the time of the Roman Empire

12 The ancient Greek city-state of Sparta and the Soviet Union under Stalin were similar in that both societies
   (1) were primarily concerned with the health of their people
   (2) were powerful military states
   (3) granted universal suffrage to their people
   (4) placed great emphasis on literature and the arts

13 In the 1990s, the troubled relations between Catholics and Protestants in Northern Ireland and among Serbs, Croats, and Muslims in the Balkans helped illustrate the
   (1) difficulties of resolving ethnic and religious conflicts
   (2) inequalities created by expanding free markets and global trade
   (3) conflict created by the collapse of the Warsaw Pact
   (4) results of the failure of dictatorial governments

14 The Sepoy Mutiny in India, the Boxer Uprising in China, and the Islamic Revolution in Iran were similar in that they
   (1) restored power to the hereditary monarchies
   (2) attempted to reject traditional cultures
   (3) resisted foreign influence in these countries
   (4) reestablished the power of religious leaders

15 The North Atlantic Treaty Organization, the Cuban Missile Crisis, and the Korean War are examples of
(1) attempts to prevent the spread of communist power
(2) United States efforts to gain foreign territory
(3) the failure of capitalism and free-market economies
(4) United Nations interference in the internal affairs of member nations

16 One way in which the partition of India in 1947 and the breakup of Yugoslavia in 1992 are similar is that after each event
(1) stable democratic governments were established
(2) problems arose between ethnic and religious groups
(3) economic prosperity produced high standards of living
(4) traditional beliefs were abandoned for Western ideas

REGENTS WARM-UP

For question 16, you must draw upon your knowledge of global history. This question deals with the partition of India and the breakup of Yugoslavia. If you don't know the answer, look up these events in this review book, in your textbook, at the library, or on the Internet.

17 Modern technology has affected global society by
(1) increasing the speed and extent of cultural diffusion
(2) reducing the effects of social change
(3) reinforcing traditional values and customs
(4) preventing the spread of democratic principles to developing nations

Specific Question Types

As you have already seen, the wording and content of multiple-choice questions varies. But there are several specific types of questions, such as data-based questions and generalization questions, that reappear on most examinations. Each type involves some kind of thinking skill or interpretation of data.

- **Generalizations** A generalization is a true statement based on the available facts. Sometimes, the facts are provided by the question itself. Other times, a question challenges you to draw upon your knowledge of a global region. That is, you must recall facts that support a generalization provided in the test question. (It sometimes helps to jot down these facts next to the question.) The following questions ask you to identify or evaluate the accuracy of generalizations. (Answers appear on page xxv.)

REGENTS WARM-UP

Think of a generalization as a summary. Its main purpose is to summarize, or draw together, the facts. To allow for the addition of new facts, generalizations use such qualifying words as *most*, *usually*, *as a rule*, and so on.

18 Which generalization is best supported by a study of the history of Latin America?
   (1) Protection of human rights has been a major policy of most governments.
   (2) Foreign powers have had little influence in the area.
   (3) Political power has been concentrated in the hands of the landed elite.
   (4) Church and state have been strictly separated.

19 Which statement is a valid generalization about economic cooperation among western European nations since World War II?
   (1) Attempts at cooperative economic ventures have failed.
   (2) Efforts to achieve an economically unified western Europe have generally met with success.
   (3) The voters of western European nations have strongly opposed attempts at international cooperation.
   (4) Economic success has resulted in political instability.

Base your answer to question 20 on the following statements and on your knowledge of social studies.

- Sunnis and Shiites have different views about who should lead the Muslim faith.

- Today, some Hindus follow caste rules more closely than others do.

- Most Buddhists belong to one of two main sects.

- Christianity is practiced by both Catholics and Protestants.

20 Which generalization is supported by the information in these four statements?
   (1) In many religions, a range of beliefs often exists.
   (2) A belief in a god is common to all religions.
   (3) A hierarchy of leadership exists in all religions.
   (4) Religion is becoming less important to people.

REGENTS WARM-UP

Keep in mind that *valid* means "true or accurate." To be valid, a generalization must stand up to the known facts.

21 Which generalization is best supported by developments in trade such as Japanese investments in Southeast Asia, the sale of United States grain to Russia, and the reliance of many European nations on oil from the Middle East?

(1) Most nations are adopting socialist economies.

(2) Nations that control vital resources are no longer able to influence world markets.

(3) The goal of the world's economic planners is to decrease national self-sufficiency.

(4) The nations of the world have become increasingly interdependent.

22 Which generalization is supported by the study of the Middle East?

(1) Illiteracy has become almost nonexistent.

(2) Religious differences have led to serious conflicts.

(3) Oil wealth has led to economic inequality.

(4) Industrial development has urbanized the area.

• **Cause and Effect** History is the study of cause-and-effect relationships. As a result, you will find many questions that deal with cause and effect on the Regents Exam. A *cause* is an event or action that brings about a change. There are *immediate causes*, or events that directly trigger an event, and *underlying causes*, or developments that build up over time. An *immediate effect* directly results from a series of causes. A *long-term effect* is a lasting change that reveals itself over time. For example, if you throw a pebble in a pond, the splash of water is an immediate effect. The ripples that spread out across the pond are a long-term effect. The following are examples of cause-and-effect questions. (Answers are on page xxv.)

23 Which was a major result of the Vietnam War?

(1) North and South Vietnam were politically reunited.

(2) Relations between Vietnam and China declined significantly.

(3) The United States increased its political influence in Southeast Asia.

(4) Most Southeast Asian nations adopted a democratic form of government.

REGENTS WARM-UP

If you have trouble determining which is the most accurate generalization in question 22, review the history of the Middle East.

REGENTS WARM-UP

The word *result* is a synonym for *effect*. Notice its use in question 23. Now, read question 26 on the following page. In this case, *result* refers back to an effect—internal unrest in the Soviet Union. Your task is to determine which of the four answers produced this result (effect).

decline of church

24 In western Europe, a major immediate effect of the Reformation was a
(1) renewed domination of the Catholic Church over the German states
(2) greater tolerance of religions other than Christianity
(3) decrease in educational opportunities for the middle class
(4) decline in the religious unity and in the power of the Catholic Church

REGENTS WARM-UP

As a tip for answering question 25, remember that the Industrial Revolution and the Neolithic Revolution involved technological innovations that changed the nature of human society.

25 Which is a long-term effect of the Industrial Revolution?
(1) The nations of the world have become more interdependent.
(2) Many nations have adopted policies of isolationism.
(3) Industrialization has been limited to western European nations.
(4) Agricultural production has decreased.

26 During the 1980s, the Soviet Union experienced internal unrest mainly as a result of
(1) widespread protests against involvement in Afghanistan
(2) a lack of raw materials and natural resources
(3) a failure of modern technology in the military
(4) increased demands of minority ethnic groups in the various republics

27 What was one effect of the Russo-Japanese War (1904–1905)?
(1) Japan emerged as a major world power.
(2) Korea gained its independence.
(3) Czar Nicholas II gained power in Russia.
(4) Russia formed a military alliance with Japan.

REGENTS WARM-UP

Question 28 asks you to distinguish between cause and effect. Three of the answers are effects of one of the conditions named. This is a common question format used on the Regents Exam.

28 In Japan, which condition was the cause of the other three?
(1) Most of the nation is mountainous with little arable land.
(2) Farmland is cultivated intensely.
(3) High-rise apartments or small, crowded homes house the people.
(4) The sea is used as a source of food.

- **Comparison** Comparison involves looking for similarities and/or differences between two or more items. On the Regents Exam, you are asked to compare people, places, ideas, events, and so on. Comparison is the most common form of question used to draw cross-regional connections or to form links between historical periods. The following questions ask you to make comparisons. (Answers appear on page xxv.)

29 Compared to many Latin American nations, most western European nations have
  (1) fewer skilled workers
  (2) more investment capital
  (3) larger amounts of raw materials
  (4) fewer middle-class consumers

Europe v broken more resources + consumers

30 The early civilizations of the Nile River Valley, Mesopotamia, and the Yellow River Valley were similar because they were
  (1) industrialized societies
  (2) monotheistic
  (3) dependent on fertile land
  (4) dependent on each other for trade

31 Judaism and Christianity are similar because they
  (1) base their beliefs on the Quran
  (2) stress belief in reincarnation
  (3) are monotheistic
  (4) promote the practice of polygamy

32 What feature was typical of Greece during the Golden Age and Italy during the Renaissance?
  (1) universal suffrage *everyone votes (male + female)*
  (2) racial diversity
  (3) social equality
  (4) a questioning spirit *to improve society (philosophers)*

33 The Holocaust in Europe and the treatment of Armenians in the Ottoman Empire have both been cited as examples of
  (1) genocide
  (2) socialism
  (3) imperialism
  (4) divine right

REGENTS WARM-UP

Question 31 asks you to compare similarities between two religions. It may help to jot down features of Judaism and Christianity in the margin space.

REGENTS WARM-UP

Question 33 compares two events in history. But to answer it correctly, you also have to know the definition of the key social studies terms listed in the answers. If you don't know the meaning of any of these terms, look them up in this book, your textbook, a library reference, or on the Internet.

- **Fact and Opinion** Some questions on the Regents Exam challenge you to distinguish between facts and opinion. A *fact* is a piece of data that can be proven to be true. An *opinion* expresses a feeling or personal judgment. Others may agree with an opinion, but it cannot be proven to be absolutely true. The following questions involve identification of fact and opinion. (Answers can be found on page xxv.)

34 The economic success of Japan will most likely lead to Japan's
   (1) loss of influence in East Asia
   (2) termination of many individual freedoms
   (3) settlement of rural areas
   (4) increased power in international relations

35 Which statement about the spread of nuclear weapons is a fact rather than an opinion?
   (1) Nations possessing nuclear weapons should not have to limit the production of weapons.
   (2) The spread of nuclear weapons was a smaller problem in the 1990s than it was in the 1970s.
   (3) The United States and Russia signed the Strategic Arms Limitation Treaties during the 1970s.
   (4) Only developing nations are concerned about the spread of nuclear weapons.

- **Conclusion and Theory** A conclusion or theory is a judgment based on facts. Unlike an opinion, it is based on reason rather than emotion. As new facts become available, conclusions or theories may have to be reformed. Also, people may draw different conclusions or theories. For example, historians often come up with different interpretations of the past. To support a conclusion, a historian will list data, or facts, that support it. The following question asks you to identify or evaluate historical conclusions and theories. (Answers appear on page xxv.)

36 Which statement about ancient American civilizations expresses a historical theory rather than a historical fact?
   (1) The Incas lacked a written language.
   (2) The spread of disease caused the downfall of the Mayan Empire.
   (3) Human sacrifice was an element of Aztec religion.
   (4) The Pyramid of the Sun was located in Teotihuacán.

REGENTS WARM-UP

Question 34 calls on you to offer an opinion. The clue words within the question are "will most likely lead to . . ."

REGENTS WARM-UP

Question 36 challenges you to separate fact from theory. Three of the items can be proven to be true. If you have trouble with this question, refer to information on ancient Native American civilizations in Chapter 14.

Data-Based Questions

Quite a few questions on the Regents Exam ask you to interpret some types of data. The data may be in written form (a list or quotation) or in visual form (a map or chart). Some questions test your understanding of the data. Others involve evaluation of the data. You may be asked to form generalizations or draw conclusions. (Answers appear on page xxv.)

- **Written Sources** Sprinkled throughout past Regents Exams are various kinds of written data—quotes, mock dialogues, poems, and more. The following questions involve the interpretation of written data.

Base your answers to questions 37 and 38 on the speakers' statements below and on your knowledge of social studies.

Speaker A: "All power derives from God to his earthly representative, the king."

Speaker B: "Governments are instituted by the people to protect life, liberty, and property. People have the right to replace a government that fails to protect their rights."

Speaker C: "History is a struggle between the 'haves' and the 'have-nots.' Workers of the world will overthrow the bourgeoisie and create a classless society."

Speaker D: "Self-interest drives people to action. Government should allow each individual to pursue his or her own goals."

37 Which speaker expresses ideas similar to those of Karl Marx?
(1) A
(2) B
(3) C
(4) D

38 Which speaker is expressing ideas that derived from the laissez-faire theory?
(1) A
(2) B
(3) C
(4) D

Base your answers to questions 39 and 40 on the passage below and on your knowledge of social studies.

". . . But there are some occasions . . . when he considers certain laws to be so unjust as to render obedience to them a dishonor. He then openly and civilly breaks them and quietly suffers the penalty of their breach. . . ."

REGENTS WARM-UP

To help you get started, Speaker A is describing the principle of the divine right of kings. Speaker B is expressing the principle of consent of the governed. What principles are described by Speakers C and D?

39 This passage supports the use of
  (1) military force
  (2) civil disobedience
  (3) appeasement
  (4) retaliation

40 Which leader based his actions on the philosophy expressed in this passage?
  (1) Vladimir I. Lenin
  (2) Simón Bolívar
  (3) Yasir Arafat
  (4) Mohandas K. Gandhi

REGENTS WARM-UP

All of the individuals named in the answer choices to question 40 are key figures in history. If you do not know any of these people, look them up in this book, your textbook, at the library, or on the Internet.

Base your answer to question 41 on the passage below and on your knowledge of social studies.

> "It was a town of red brick, or of brick that would have been red if the smoke and ashes had allowed it; but as matters stood it was a town of unnatural red and black like the painted face of a savage. It was a town of machinery and tall chimneys, out of which interminable serpents of smoke trailed themselves for ever and ever, and never got uncoiled. It had a black canal in it, and a river that ran purple with ill smelling dye. . . ."
>
> —Charles Dickens, *Hard Times*

41 The author of this passage is describing conditions caused by the
  (1) Commercial Revolution
  (2) French Revolution
  (3) Industrial Revolution
  (4) Scientific Revolution

• **Maps** Often, Regents Exams include historic maps. A series of steps will help you interpret data on a map. First, you should try to identify the topic or subject of the map. Often, the title of the map provides this information. Next, you must collect the map's most important facts. The map key or written labels on the map will help you with this task. Once you have collected this information, you are ready to interpret the data. For example, you might need to figure out changes depicted on the map. Or, you might draw conclusions or generalizations based on the map's facts. The following maps and questions provide an opportunity to practice your map-reading skills. (Answers appear on page xxv.)

Base your answers to questions 42 and 43 on the maps below
and on your knowledge of social studies.

42 The boundaries of which two countries were most
changed by World War I?
(1) France and Italy
(2) Germany and Belgium
(3) Austria-Hungary and Russia
(4) Greece and Bulgaria

43 Which is the most valid conclusion that can be drawn
from the study of these maps?
(1) European boundaries more closely reflected ethnic
patterns after World War I.
(2) Communist expansion into Eastern Europe began
in 1919.
(3) The end of World War I brought military alliances.
(4) The new boundaries resulted in an end to ethnic
conflicts.

- **Political Cartoons** Political cartoons are a commonly
used data-based question type in the Regents Exam.
Political cartoons, like a newspaper editorial, express an
opinion or point of view on an issue. Base your answer
to question 44 on the cartoon on page xvii and on your
knowledge of social studies. (The answer appears on
page xxv).

REGENTS WARM-UP

Question 42 tests your
comprehension, or ability to
identify information on a map.
Question 43 calls for you to
interpret that information.

Base your answer to question 44 on the cartoon below and on your knowledge of social studies.

REGENTS WARM-UP

The figure in the front represents Mikhail Gorbachev. What do the tombstones represent? What is the cartoonist's opinion of Gorbachev's leadership? What evidence supports your answer?

44 What is the main idea of this 1991 cartoon about Mikhail Gorbachev, the former leader of the Soviet Union?

(1) He took away many freedoms.
(2) He supported the arms race and the Cold War.
(3) He encouraged many political changes.
(4) He stopped many attempts at reform.

- **Graphs** Graphs are a convenient way to compare data or show changes in data over time. To interpret graphs, follow some of the same steps used in interpreting maps. First, identify the subject or the topic of the graph, which will tell you what type of data the graph depicts. Next, determine how the data is displayed. Pie graphs use "slices" of a circle. Bar graphs use parallel bars of varying lengths. Picture graphs use pictures that represent set amounts of an item. Line graphs use indicator lines plotted along a horizontal and vertical axis. To practice reading a line graph, study the following set of graphs and sample question from past Regents. (The answers appear on page xxv.)

Base your answer to question 45 on the graphs below and on your knowledge of social studies.

BIRTH AND DEATH RATES
IN ECONOMICALLY DEVELOPED AND ECONOMICALLY DEVELOPING COUNTRIES
1850–1977

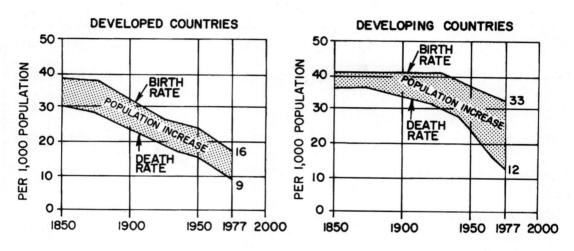

45 Which statement is best supported by the information in the graphs?

   (1) Population in both developed and developing countries increases at the same rate.

   (2) By the year 2000, the developing countries will reach the point of zero population growth.

   (3) Population growth since 1900 has largely been due to a drop in the death rate.

   (4) Population growth since 1900 has largely been due to an increase in birth rate.

- **Tables** Tables summarize and organize statistics—facts in number form—in an easy-to-read format. By arranging numerical facts into columns and rows, a table gives you an overview of a large body of information. Like other visual data, begin "reading" a table by examining its title to give you a general idea of what the numbers represent. Next, read the labels for each column and row. These headings identify the categories of information presented in the table. Once you are familiar with the table's layout, you are ready to interpret the facts.

REGENTS WARM-UP

Zero population growth occurs when the birth and death rates are equal. The population then stays constant. If you compare the figures on the two indicator lines on the graph for developing nations, you will see that a zero population growth has not occurred since around 1850. Based on this analysis, you can eliminate answer choice (2).

The following table and question from a past Regents Exam gives you a chance to analyze statistical data. (The answer appears on page xxv.)

Base your answer to question 46 on the table below and on your knowledge of social studies.

Defense Estimates of the Great Powers, 1870–1914
(in millions of pounds)

	1870	1880	1890	1900	1910	1914
Germany	10.8	20.4	28.8	41.0	64.0	110.8
Austria-Hungary	8.2	13.2	12.8	13.6	17.4	36.4
France	22.0	31.4	37.4	42.4	52.4	57.4
Great Britain	23.4	25.2	31.4	116.0	68.0	76.8
Italy	7.8	10.0	14.8	14.6	24.4	28.2
Russia	22.0	29.6	29.0	40.8	63.4	88.2

Source: A.J.P. Taylor, *The Struggle for Mastery in Europe: 1848–1918*,
Oxford University Press (adapted)

REGENTS WARM-UP

To practice forming general-izations, write statements that accurately summarize the change in expenditures for the nations listed in the table for question 46. (Write your answer in the space below.)

46 Which statement is best supported by the data contained in the table?
  (1) Austria-Hungary could not afford a large military expenditure in 1880.
  (2) France spent the greatest amount of money on defense in 1900.
  (3) Germany rapidly increased its military spending after 1890.
  (4) Great Britain attempted to prepare for a long ground war.

Answers to Sample Questions in Part I Multiple Choice

1. (4) 2. (3) 3. (2) 4. (1) 5. (3) 6. (3) 7. (4) 8. (1)
9. (2) 10. (4) 11. (1) 12. (2) 13. (1) 14. (3) 15. (1) 16. (2)
17. (1) 18. (3) 19. (2) 20. (1) 21. (4) 22. (2) 23. (1) 24. (4)
25. (1) 26. (4) 27. (1) 28. (1) 29. (2) 30. (3) 31. (3) 32. (4)
33. (1) 34. (4) 35. (3) 36. (2) 37. (3) 38. (4) 39. (2) 40. (4)
41. (3) 42. (3) 43. (1) 44. (3) 45. (3) 46. (3)

PART II THEMATIC ESSAY QUESTION

General Strategies

Each Regents Global History and Geography Exam requires you to answer a Thematic Essay Question. For this type of question, you are asked to write a well-organized essay on a given theme. For example, the theme may be "change" or "conflict." You will be given the theme and a task, which asks you to draw on your social studies knowledge to write about the given theme. You do have some choice in your essay, because you can use any examples from your study of history, including suggestions provided in the exam itself. And you are not limited to the suggestions you are given; you can choose any relevant event. This allows you to write about topics with which you are comfortable. Remember, be sure you address the theme in your essay, and address all the aspects of the task with relevant supporting information.

The example below is a Thematic Essay Question and instructions from a recent Regents examination.

In developing your answer to Part II, be sure to keep these general definitions in mind:

  (a) <u>discuss</u> **means "to make observations about something using facts, reasoning, and argument; to present in some detail"**

  (b) <u>analyze</u> **means "to determine the nature and relationship of the component elements"**

Theme: Conflict

Differences among groups that have often led to conflict

Task:

> Identify *two* ethnic, religious, political, and/or cultural conflicts and for *each*:
>
> - Discuss the historical circumstances that led to the conflict
>
> - Analyze the effect of this conflict on *two* groups involved

REGENTS WARM-UP

The Thematic Essay Question is your chance to shine! The themes presented in the exam are universal themes you have studied in your classes. And you get to pick the examples that you use, which means you can choose events with which you are most comfortable.

You may use any examples from your study of global history and geography. Some suggestions you might wish to consider include the persecution of Christians during the Roman Empire, the Reign of Terror, the Armenian massacres, the forced famine in Ukraine, the Holocaust, apartheid in South Africa, the killing fields of Cambodia, the conflict in Northern Ireland, the Sandinistas in Nicaragua, and the Tiananmen Square rebellion.

You are *not* limited to these suggestions.

Do *not* use any conflict that occurred in the United States.

Guidelines:
In your essay, be sure to:

- Develop all aspects of the task
- Support the theme with relevant facts, examples, and details
- Use a logical and clear plan of organization, including an introduction and a conclusion that are beyond a restatement of the theme

Writing the Essay

When you get ready to write your essay, be brief and to the point. Make sure your topic sentences and supporting paragraphs are clearly written.

Use the guidelines: The exam provides you with guidelines that, if followed, will help you organize and write your essay. These guidelines are called a *rubric*, and they are some of the same guidelines the exam graders will use to evaluate the content and structure of your answer. The guidelines are those that, if adhered to, would constitute the highest grade. Do not overwrite, and remember to proofread when you are finished.

When you proofread, make sure you address all of the tasks you were given and that your essay satisfactorily addresses the theme.

Write a practice essay using the sample given, and evaluate it using the scoring guidelines that appear in the question and the rubric that scorers use, provided below.

THEMATIC ESSAY GENERIC SCORING RUBRIC

Score of 5:

- Thoroughly develops all aspects of the task evenly and in depth

- Is more analytical than descriptive (analyzes, evaluates, and/or creates* information)

- Richly supports the theme with many relevant facts, examples, and details

- Demonstrates a logical and clear plan of organization; includes an introduction and a conclusion that are beyond a restatement of the theme

Score of 4:

- Develops all aspects of the task but may do so somewhat unevenly

- Is both descriptive and analytical (applies, analyzes, evaluates, and/or creates information)

- Supports the theme with relevant facts, examples, and details

- Demonstrates a logical and clear plan of organization; includes an introduction and a conclusion that are beyond a restatement of the theme

Score of 3:

- Develops all aspects of the task with little depth or develops most aspects of the task in some depth

- Is more descriptive than analytical (applies, may analyze, and/or evaluate information)

- Includes some relevant facts, examples, and details; may include some minor inaccuracies
- Demonstrates a satisfactory plan of organization; includes an introduction and a conclusion that may be a restatement of the theme

Score of 2:

- Minimally develops all aspects of the task or develops some aspects of the task in some depth
- Is primarily descriptive; may include faulty, weak, or isolated application or analysis
- Includes few relevant facts, examples, and details; may include some inaccuracies
- Demonstrates a general plan of organization; may lack focus; may contain digressions; may not clearly identify which aspect of the task is being addressed; may lack an introduction and/or a conclusion

Score of 1:

- Minimally develops some aspects of the task
- Is descriptive; may lack understanding, application, or analysis
- Includes few relevant facts, examples, or details; may include inaccuracies
- May demonstrate a weakness in organization; may lack focus; may contain digressions; may not clearly identify which aspect of the task is being addressed; may lack an introduction and/or conclusion

Score of 0:

Fails to develop the task or may only refer to the theme in a general way; *OR* includes no relevant facts, examples, or details; *OR* includes only the theme, task, or suggestions copied from the test booklet; *OR* is illegible; *OR* is a blank paper

* The term *create* as used by Anderson/Krathwohl, et al. in their 2001 revision of Bloom's *Taxonomy of Educational Objectives* refers to the highest level of the cognitive domain. This usage of *create* is similar to Bloom's use of the term *synthesis*. Creating implies an insightful reorganization of information into a new pattern or whole. While a level 5 paper will contain analysis and/or evaluation of information, a very strong paper may also include examples of creating information as defined by Anderson and Krathwohl.

PART III DOCUMENT-BASED QUESTION

General Strategies

The Document-Based Question assesses your ability to work with historical documents. You will be given eight or nine documents. For the Document-Based Question, you are asked to do two things:

(1) Answer questions about each document.

(2) Write an essay using at least five of the documents.

The questions you answer about each document will help you construct your essay in the second part of the question. You will be presented with a historical context, a task, and the documents.

The following is an example of a Document-Based Question from a recent Regents Exam. Only three of the eight documents are included in this example.

This question is based on the accompanying documents. It is designed to test your ability to work with historical documents. Some of the documents have been edited for the purposes of this question. As you analyze the documents, take into account both the source of each document and any point of view that may be presented in the document.

Historical Context: The geographic factors of location and availability of resources have affected the history of Great Britain and Japan.

Task: Using information from the documents and your knowledge of global history, answer the questions that follow each document in Part A. Your answers to the questions will help you write the Part B essay, in which you will be asked to:

> • Compare and contrast the effect of geographic factors such as location and availability of resources on the political and economic development of Great Britain and Japan

Part A Short-Answer Questions

Directions: Analyze the documents and answer the short-answer questions that follow each document in the space provided.

Document 1

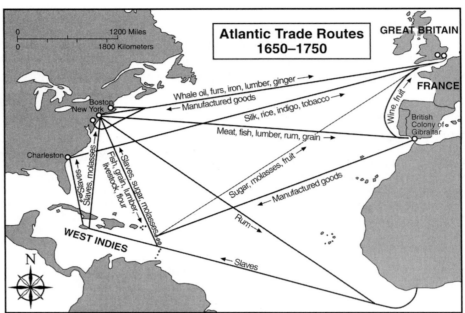

Atlantic Trade Routes 1650–1750

GREAT BRITAIN

FRANCE

Whale oil, furs, iron, lumber, ginger →

← Manufactured goods

Silk, rice, indigo, tobacco →

Meat, fish, lumber, rum, grain →

Wine, fruit

British Colony of Gibraltar

Boston

New York

Charleston

Slaves, molasses

Slaves

Fish, grain, lumber, livestock, flour

Slaves, sugar, molasses

Sugar, molasses, fruit

← Manufactured goods

Rum →

← Slaves

WEST INDIES

N

0   1200 Miles

0   1800 Kilometers

Source: Steven Goldberg and Judith Clark DuPré, *Brief Review in Global History and Geography*, Prentice-Hall (adapted)

1   What did Great Britain export along Atlantic trade routes?

_____

_____

Document 2

> In comparing the advantages of England for manufactures with those of other countries, we can by no means overlook the excellent commercial position of the country— intermediate between the north and south of Europe; and its insular situation [island location], which, combined with the command of the seas, secures our territory from invasion or annoyance. The German ocean, the Baltic, and the Mediterranean are the regular highways for our ships; and our western ports command an unobstructed [clear] passage to the Atlantic, and to every quarter [part] of the world.

2   Based on this document, identify *two* ways England has benefited from its location.

_____

_____

Document 3

... The geographical features of Japan have much in common with those of ancient Hellas [Greece]. In both there is the same combination of mountain, valley, and plain, [and] a deeply indented coastline, with its bays, peninsulas, and islands off the coast. Few places inland are far removed from the mountains, and none are really distant from the sea. . . . The land was on all sides well protected, and yet also open to the sea; and in each case, too, there was free access for commerce and civilisation from early times. . . . The deeply indented coastline of Japan provides a number of excellent harbours on the Pacific coast, and its shores abound in fish of all kinds, the rich supplies of which have for centuries constituted one of the chief articles of food of the people. The fishing industries have helped to provide Japan with a recruiting-ground for one of the strongest and most formidable navies of modern times. . . .

3   Based on this document, identify *two* ways geography has affected the development of Japan.

_____

_____

Part B   Essay

Directions: Write a well-organized essay that includes an introduction, several paragraphs, and a conclusion. Use evidence from at least *two* documents to support your response.

Historical Context: The geographic factors of location and availability of resources have affected the history of Great Britain and Japan.

Task: Using information from the documents and your knowledge of global history, write an essay in which you:

> • Compare and contrast the effect of geographic factors such as location and availability of resources on the political and economic development of Great Britain and Japan

Guidelines:
In your essay, be sure to

- Develop all aspects of the task
- Incorporate information from *at least two* documents
- Incorporate relevant outside information
- Support the theme with relevant facts, examples, and details
- Use a logical and clear plan of organization, including an introduction and conclusion that are beyond a restatement of the theme

Writing the Essay

As with the Thematic Essay Question, remember to address the task completely, and use the scoring guidelines to help you write the highest-scoring essay you can. Make sure you fully support your topic sentences and make sure your sentences are clear and to the point. Practice writing DBQs using this sample question and the sample DBQs that you can find at the end of each unit in this book. Score them according to the guidelines given in the question and the Document-Based Essay Generic Scoring Rubric given below. The rubric listed below is the actual rubric that essay graders use to score your essay.

REGENTS WARM-UP

Remember to use the information in your short answer questions to write your essay. In asking you to answer these questions, the test makers are actually helping you by providing you with the information you need to write your essay. The questions help you analyze the individual documents.

DOCUMENT-BASED ESSAY GENERIC SCORING RUBRIC

REGENTS WARM-UP

Remember, the guidelines you are given on the exam are the guidelines for the highest score. Make sure you fully address each of the guidelines given.

Score of 5:

- Thoroughly develops all aspects of the task evenly and in depth

- Is more analytical than descriptive (analyzes, evaluates, and/or creates* information)

- Incorporates relevant information from *at least* the requested number of documents

- Incorporates substantial relevant outside information

- Richly supports the theme with many relevant facts, examples, and details

- Demonstrates a logical and clear plan of organization; includes an introduction and a conclusion that are beyond a restatement of the theme

Score of 4:

- Develops all aspects of the task but may do so somewhat unevenly

- Is both descriptive and analytical (applies, analyzes, evaluates, and/or creates information)

- Incorporates relevant information from *at least* the requested number of documents

- Incorporates relevant outside information

- Supports the theme with relevant facts, examples, and details

- Demonstrates a logical and clear plan of organization; includes an introduction and a conclusion that are beyond a restatement of the theme

Score of 3:

- Develops all aspects of the task with little depth *or* develops most aspects of the task in some depth

- Is more descriptive than analytical (applies, may analyze, and/or evaluate information)

- Incorporates some relevant information from some of the documents

- Incorporates limited relevant outside information

- Includes some relevant facts, examples, and details; may include some minor inaccuracies

- Demonstrates a satisfactory plan of organization; includes an introduction and a conclusion that may be a restatement of the theme

Score of 2:

- Minimally develops all aspects of the task *or* develops some aspects of the task in some depth

- Is primarily descriptive; may include faulty, weak, or isolated application or analysis

- Incorporates limited relevant information from the documents *or* consists primarily of relevant information copied from the documents

- Presents little or no relevant outside information

- Includes few relevant facts, examples, or details; may include inaccuracies

- Demonstrates a general plan of organization; may lack focus; may contain digressions; may not clearly identify which aspect of the task is being addressed; may lack an introduction and/or a conclusion

Score of 1:

- Minimally develops some aspects of the task

- Is descriptive; may lack understanding, application, or analysis

- Makes vague, unclear references to the documents or consists primarily of relevant and irrelevant information copied from the documents

- Presents no relevant outside information

- Includes few relevant facts, examples, or details; may include inaccuracies

- May demonstrate a weakness in organization; may lack focus; may contain digressions; may not clearly identify which aspect of the task is being addressed; may lack an introduction and/or conclusion

Score of 0:

Fails to develop the task or may only refer to the theme in a general way; _OR_ includes no relevant facts, examples, or details; _OR_ includes only the historical context and/or task as copied from the test booklet; _OR_ includes only entire documents copied from the test booklet; _OR_ is illegible; _OR_ is a blank paper

* The term _create_ as used by Anderson/Krathwohl, et al. in their 2001 revision of Bloom's _Taxonomy of Educational Objectives_ refers to the highest level of the cognitive domain. This usage of _create_ is similar to Bloom's use of the term _synthesis_. Creating implies an insightful reorganization of information into a new pattern or whole. While a level 5 paper will contain analysis and/or evaluation of information, a very strong paper may also include examples of creating information as defined by Anderson and Krathwohl.

UNIT 1   THE FIRST CIVILIZATIONS AND EMPIRES, PREHISTORY–A.D. 500

PREPARING FOR THE REGENTS

This entire book is set up to help you grasp the facts, main ideas, and concepts needed to do well on your Regents Exam. Notes in the margin include core concepts, test-taking tips, and more. Use blank spaces in the margins to answer questions raised in the text or to jot down key points. Before each unit of study, skim through the exams at the back of the book to develop a sense of what your state wants you to know about your world.

Unit 1 Overview

The first humanlike creatures lived three to four million years ago. Over time, more advanced species appeared. The species *Homo sapiens sapiens* used tools, made fire, and migrated throughout the world. Civilizations arose in response to systematic agriculture followed by the rise of specialization and diversified economies.

Early civilizations included Mesopotamia, Sumeria, Egypt, Assyria, and Persia. The Indus civilization arose in India; it gradually weakened and fell to Aryan invaders. The Xia dynasty marked the beginning of Chinese civilization; it gave way to the Shang, Zhou, Qin, and Han dynasties. Ancient Greek civilization developed in many small city-states. In Athens, one of these city-states, direct democracy flourished. Alexander the Great later built an empire that spanned much of Asia and spread Greek culture, creating a blend culture called Hellenistic. The Romans built one of the greatest empires the world has ever known.

Unit 1 Objectives

After studying this unit, students should be able to

1.   explain how the first civilizations emerged;

2.   identify the similarities and differences between emerging civilizations in India and China;

3.   describe the advances made by the Greeks and reasons for the decline of the Greek empire;

4.   list and explain contributions of the Romans to Western civilization.

Section 1   **Early Humans**
Section 2   **The Neolithic Revolution and the Rise of Civilization**

Chapter Overview

Because no written records exist from the time when the earliest humans lived, anthropologists and archaeologists use fossils and artifacts to develop theories about the first humans and their ways of life. The very earliest humans were hunter-gatherers who were nomadic. They learned how to make fire and developed simple tools. Over thousands of years, they spread from their first home in Africa to locations around the globe.

The Neolithic age, the period of history from 10,000 to 4000 B.C. was a time of revolutionary change marked by the rise of systematic agriculture—the domestication of animals and the growing of crops on a regular basis. During the last stages of the Neolithic age, craftspeople discovered ways of making improved tools and weapons using copper and later bronze. Specialization of labor led to the trading of goods and a diversified economy. Civilizations emerged in response to these changes.

As you read this chapter, ask yourself these questions:
(1) What methods do scientists use to uncover evidence of early human existence?
(2) What was human life like during the Old Stone Age?
(3) What were the most important developments of the New Stone Age?
(4) What are the characteristics of a civilization?

REGENTS WARM-UP

Past Regents Exams have asked students to explain what was revolutionary about the Neolithic Revolution. They have also asked students to focus on the connections between the environment and the development of one or more aspects of human culture. As you read this chapter, focus on the core concepts of change and human-environmental interaction.

Main Ideas and Concepts

- **Movement of People and Goods** Migrations that spanned thousands of years resulted in the spread of *Homo sapiens sapiens* throughout the world by 10,000 B.C.

- **Linking Past and Present** Paleolithic peoples adapted to survive, made tools, used fire, and created art.

- **Change** The fundamental change that revolutionized life in the Neolithic period was the development of systematic agriculture.

- **Culture** As a result of the Neolithic Revolution, societies grew and became more complex, and civilizations developed.

People, Places, Terms

The following names and terms will help you to prepare for the Regents Exam in Global History and Geography. You can find an explanation of each name and term in the Glossary at the back of this book, in your textbook, or in another reference source.

archaeology	fossils	Paleolithic Age
artifacts	hierarchy	prehistory
civilization	*Homo sapiens sapiens*	surplus
culture	Neolithic Revolution	systematic agriculture
domestication	nomadic	

SECTION 1 EARLY HUMANS

Before History

Archaeology is the study of past societies through analysis of what people have left behind. Anthropology is the study of human life and culture. Archaeologists and anthropologists help us understand the existence of humans throughout history and especially during **prehistory**: the time before people kept written records. To do so, they dig up and examine **artifacts**—tools, pottery, weapons, and other objects people made—as well as **fossils**, parts of organisms or impressions of organisms that have been preserved in the earth's crust.

Dating Artifacts and Fossils Scientists use methods such as radiocarbon dating to date these objects. Microscopic and biological analyses also provide information about the lives of early peoples.

Early Stages of Human Development

The earliest humanlike creatures lived in Africa as long as three or four million years ago. Australopithecines were among the first hominids, humans and other creatures that walk upright and make simple stone tools. About 1.5 million years later, humans developed into upright beings, a species called *Homo erectus*, which made larger and more varied tools. These early humans learned how to use fire to keep warm. Around 250,000 years ago, *Homo sapiens* arose. From them came several subgroups, including *Homo sapiens sapiens*, the subspecies to which humans belong. Another group that arose from *Homo sapiens* was the Neanderthals, the first people to bury their dead. Neanderthals largely died out by 30,000 B.C.

LINKING PAST AND PRESENT

Radiocarbon dating is based on the fact that all living things absorb a small amount of radioactive carbon (C-14) from the atmosphere. After a living thing dies, it slowly loses C-14. Using radiocarbon dating, a scientist can calculate the age of an object by measuring the amount of C-14 left in it. This method is considered accurate for objects up to about 40,000 to 60,000 years old.

The Spread of *Homo Sapiens Sapiens* The search for food caused the long, slow spread of these first modern humans around the globe. Traveling at the rate of perhaps two or three miles per generation, *Homo sapiens* could be found throughout the world by 10,000 B.C.

The Hunter-Gatherers of the Old Stone Age

The term *Paleolithic Age* is used to designate the early period of human history (from approximately 2,500,000 to 10,000 B.C.) in which humans used simple stone tools. *Paleolithic* is Greek for "old stone"; this period in human history is often called the Old Stone Age.

The Paleolithic Way of Life Paleolithic peoples were **nomadic** hunter-gatherers. They moved in search of food, following animal migrations and vegetation cycles. They probably lived in small groups of perhaps twenty to thirty.

Roles of Men and Women Both men and women brought in food. Men hunted for large animals, while women often gathered. Women had responsibility for the children. Both men and women made decisions and provided for group survival.

Survival Early peoples adapted to survive. Originally, they lived in caves. Over time, they created new types of shelter, including poles or sticks covered with animal hides. They learned how to make fires for cooking, for warmth, and for protection from wild animals. Archaeologists assume that the earliest methods for making fire were based on the use of friction.

The Ice Ages Survival during the Old Stone Age was threatened by Ice Age conditions, which required people to adapt. Using fire to adapt marked a beginning in controlling the environment, a tendency of humans that would become revolutionary by the end of the last Ice Age.

Art Discoveries of cave paintings that date from as early as 25,000 B.C. show that art was part of life for the hunters and gatherers of the Old Stone Age. Paints were created from animal fat and crushed ore and applied to the walls by different methods, including the use of fingertips and brushes. Pictures show various animals and human stick figures. The purpose of the paintings may have been purposeful, religious, or for pure artistic expression.

CORE CONCEPTS: PLACES AND REGIONS

Paleolithic peoples hunted the wild animals available in the region, such as buffalo, horses, and reindeer. They gathered berries and other wild foods such as grains and nuts. In coastal areas, they fished. Over time, they developed better hunting tools such as spears and harpoons.

SECTION 2   THE NEOLITHIC REVOLUTION AND THE RISE OF CIVILIZATION

The Neolithic Revolution

The Neolithic Age is the period of human history from 8000 to 4000 B.C. The word *Neolithic is* Greek for "new stone." The Neolithic Age is far more important for agriculture than it is for stone, however. Agriculture gave humans greater control over their environment. This helped lead to the development of cities and civilization.

The **Neolithic Revolution** followed the last Ice Age. The term *revolution* refers to the fact that an entire way of life changed. Hunting and gathering as a way of life ended and **systematic agriculture**—the growing of food on a regular basis—began. The **domestication** (adaptation for human use) of animals also began.

The Growing of Crops Between 8000 and 5000 B.C., systematic agriculture developed in different areas of the world, beginning with Southwest Asia, where people grew wheat and barley and domesticated pigs, cows, goats, and sheep.

Neolithic Farming Villages The use of systematic agriculture gave rise to permanent settlements. Historians refer to these settlements as Neolithic farming villages. Neolithic villages appeared in Europe, India, Egypt, China, and Mesoamerica.

Two of the earliest and largest Neolithic farming villages arose in Southwest Asia: Jericho in Palestine and Çatal Hüyük, located in modern-day Turkey.

Consequences of the Neolithic Revolution When people began to farm systematically, their lives changed in many ways. They built permanent structures. They needed to store and protect their food and other material goods. They also began to trade with other groups. Trade, in turn, led to specialization in certain crafts. Tools became more sophisticated, and a larger number of foods came under cultivation. Because men assumed tasks that involved leaving the settlement and protecting it, they began to play a more dominant social role.

The End of the Neolithic Age Between 4000 and 3000 B.C., the Neolithic Age gave way to the Bronze Age. Even before 4000 B.C., people had begun to understand how to heat metal-bearing rocks and turn the metals into tools and weapons. The use of

CORE CONCEPTS: PLACES AND REGIONS

The cultivation of wheat and barley was established in the Nile Valley by 6000 B.C. From there, it spread to other areas of Africa. A separate system of growing tubers (root crops) also emerged in Africa. By 5000 B.C., rice was being grown in Southeast Asia. In the Western Hemisphere, Mesoamericans were growing beans, squash and maize (corn) between 7000 B.C. and 5000 B.C.

CORE CONCEPTS: CHANGE

Çatal Hüyük may have been home to 6,000 people during its high point from 6700 to 5700 B.C. Here, people cultivated at least twelve crops. This systematic agriculture resulted in the production of more crops than local people could consume, creating a **surplus**. This meant that some people did not farm; instead, they worked in trades and crafts as artisans. They made products such as weapons and jewelry and traded with neighboring peoples.

metal, in addition to advances in agriculture, helped lead to the development of more complex and wealthier societies.

The Emergence of Civilization

In general, the **culture** of a people is all the ways of life that they follow. As human groups grew into more complex societies, a new form of human existence called civilization gradually developed. A **civilization** is a complex culture in which numbers of human beings share a number of common elements, including cities, government, religion, social structure, writing, and art.

The Rise of Cities and Growth of Governments Cities are one of the chief features of civilizations. Because significant parts of civilizations lived in river valleys, cities often developed there. Governments arose to regulate human activities and to promote the smooth interaction between individuals and groups. The first civilizations were led by rulers—usually monarchs (kings or queens) who organized armies to protect their populations and made laws to regulate their subjects' lives.

The Role of Religion Religions developed to explain the workings of nature and the fact of human existence. Rituals were supervised by priests. Rulers sometimes claimed to be divine, or to have divine approval for their actions.

A New Social Structure A new social structure, or **hierarchy**, based on economic power arose, with rulers and an upper class of priests, government officials, and warriors at the top. Free people in the middle included farmers, artisans, and craftspeople. At the bottom of the social structure was a slave class.

Writing and Artistic Activity For the most part, early river civilizations developed independently. Many, but not all, depended on writing to keep records. Later, writing was used for creative expression. Artistic expression took architectural form in the construction of temples and pyramids; it also took the form of painting and sculpture.

CHAPTER 2   WESTERN ASIA AND EGYPT

Chapter Overview

The civilizations of Western Asia and Egypt emerged in the river valleys of the Tigris, Euphrates, and Nile Rivers. Farming was the economic base for the growth of these civilizations. Mesopotamia, the region between the Tigris and Euphrates Rivers, was the birthplace of several of the earliest known civilizations. Among them was Sumeria, where inhabitants engaged in widespread trade, built walled cities, created cuneiform writing, and invented tools and devices such as the wagon wheel.

Civilizations and kingdoms also developed along the Mediterranean. Throughout Western Asia, empires such as those of the Akkadians, Babylonians, and Assyrians were established and collapsed in succession. Hammurabi, the leader of the Babylonian Empire, established a central law code with sentencing guidelines that were applied across a diverse culture. After the fall of the Assyrians, Persia became the leading power in western Asia.

Egyptian civilization was remarkably stable, and ruling dynasties lasted for many centuries. Historians describe three major periods in Egyptian civilization: the Old Kingdom, the Middle Kingdom, and the New Kingdom. Egyptians created an extensive government bureaucracy and built the pyramids as tombs for mummified pharaohs. Art, science, and a form of writing called hieroglyphics flourished in Egypt.

As you read this chapter, ask yourself these questions:
(1) How did geography affect early civilizations in Western Asia and Egypt?
(2) What religions arose in these areas and what was their significance?
(3) What major laws arose?
(4) What were the first empires, and why did they decline?
(5) What was daily life like in each of these societies?
(6) What wars and conquests helped contribute to the rise and fall of these empires?
(7) Which early inventions were most important and why?

Main Ideas and Concepts

- **Environment and Society** The earliest civilizations, including those of Mesopotamia and Egypt, arose in river valleys.

- **Culture** The Sumerians created city-states and forms of communication that affect our lives today.

- **Change** As the civilizations of the Egyptians declined, new kingdoms, including that of the Israelites, emerged.

- **Diversity** The Persian Empire assimilated influences from other cultures and showed mercy to conquered cultures.

People, Places, Terms

The following names and terms will help you to prepare for the Regents Exam in Global History and Geography. You can find an explanation of each name and term in the Glossary at the back of this book, in your textbook, or in another reference source.

bureaucracy	Hammurabi's code	Nile River
city-state	hieroglyphics	Persian Empire
cuneiform	Israelites	pharaoh
empire	Mesopotamia	Phoenicians
Fertile Crescent	monotheistic	Sumerians

CORE CONCEPTS: BELIEF SYSTEMS

Because Sumerians believed that gods and goddesses owned the cities, people devoted much of their wealth to building temples, which served as the physical, economic, and political centers of their cities. The state was a theocracy, a government by divine authority, with ruling power eventually passing into the hands of kings.

SECTION 1 CIVILIZATION BEGINS IN MESOPOTAMIA

The Impact of Geography

The Greeks called the valley between the Tigris and Euphrates Rivers **Mesopotamia**, the land "between the rivers." It was part of an area known as the **Fertile Crescent**, where the land was rich enough to sustain an early civilization. The Fertile Crescent stretched from the Mediterranean Sea to the Persian Gulf. The control of water in this hot, dry land, especially for irrigation, helped lead to the development of cities.

The City-States Mesopotamian civilization included many peoples and three general areas: Assyria, Akkad, and Sumer. The people of Sumer became known as **Sumerians**. They lived in political units called **city-states**, which consisted of a city, its government, and the surrounding villages and farmlands.

Sumerian cities, which were surrounded by walls, were built from mud bricks. Using these bricks, Sumerians invented the arch and the dome and built some of the largest brick buildings in the world.

Economy and Society The economy of the city-states was based chiefly on farming but trade and industry were also important. Sumeria traded its metal work, textiles, and pottery for copper, tin, and timber. Traders traveled by land to the eastern Mediterranean in the west and by sea to India in the east. The city-states contained nobles, commoners, and slaves. Among the commoners were the farmers, who made up about 90% of the population.

Empires in Ancient Mesopotamia

To the north of the Sumerians, the Akkadians also established city-states. Their leader, Sargon, overran the Sumerian city-states to create the first empire in world history. An **empire** is a single political unit or state, usually under a single ruler, that controls many peoples or territories. Established around 2340 B.C., the Akkadian Empire came to an end by 2100 B.C., when city-states were once again at war. Hammurabi came to power in Babylon, a city-state south of Akkad, in 1792 B.C. He gained control of Sumer and Akkad, thus creating a new Mesopotamian kingdom. His empire fell to new invaders after his death, when a series of weaker kings could not keep invaders out.

The Code of Hammurabi

Hammurabi's wealth was built on trade, so he did not want war among his subjects. Laws regulated life in Mesopotamia before the time of Hammurabi, but his code, which was based on a system of strict justice, has remained memorable for many reasons. **Hammurabi's code** created one central law code for his diverse empire, which was published for all to see. It was codified, or organized, by type of law, e.g., real estate, business, or family. It made the central government, not families, responsible for enforcement, thereby reducing clan warfare. A crime against a member of the upper class by a member of a lower class was punished more severely than the same offense against a member of the lower class. Public officials were expected to catch murderers and thieves or replace the stolen property or pay fines themselves. The code also provided protections to consumers. For example, if a builder built a house that collapsed and killed the

CORE CONCEPTS: JUSTICE

Above all, Hammurabi's code is remembered for its strict, harsh punishment ("an eye for an eye, tooth for a tooth"); it might also be well remembered for how comprehensive it was in covering almost every aspect of people's lives.

owner, the builder could be put to death. If it caused the death of the son of the owner, the builder's son could be put to death.

The Importance of Religion

Mesopotamians explained natural phenomena such as storms and famine as a result of the workings of powerful spiritual beings. In their polytheistic religion, they identified almost three thousand gods and goddesses.

The Creativity of the Sumerians

Around 3000 B.C., the Sumerians created a **cuneiform** ("wedge-shaped") system of writing. They made wedge-shaped impressions on clay tablets, which were then baked in the sun. These tablets have provided great information about the culture. The writing was used primarily for recordkeeping, and becoming a scribe was the key to a successful career for boys.

One of the greatest artistic creations of the Mesopotamians is the epic known as *Gilgamesh*, a poem that records the travels of a legendary king who sets off to do great deeds. The poem reflects a universal theme—the search for immortality.

Sumerian Technology The Sumerians developed the wagon wheel. They also invented the potter's wheel, the sundial, and the arch used in construction. They were the first to make bronze out of copper and tin. They devised a number system based on 60 (from which we get our 60-minute hour and 360-degree circle), used geometry to measure fields and erect buildings, and charted the constellations. They also made accurate maps.

CORE CONCEPTS: THE USES OF GEOGRAPHY

Yearly flooding of the Nile created rich soil that made the valley prosperous. The Nile also unified Egypt by making transportation and communication easier.

CORE CONCEPTS: PLACES AND REGIONS

The Nile, along with other natural barriers such as the Red Sea to the east and the desert to the west and east, protected Egypt from invaders. Free from invasions, ancient Egyptian civilization was to develop a remarkable degree of continuity over thousands of years.

SECTION 2 EGYPTIAN CIVILIZATION: "THE GIFT OF THE NILE"

The Impact of Geography

The **Nile River** is the world's longest river. It is also unique for its delta, created at the point at which the Nile splits into two major branches. The delta is called Lower Egypt. The land to the south is called Upper Egypt.

The Importance of Religion

The Egyptians had no special word for religion because it was inseparable from daily life. They worshipped many gods, including sun, land, and river gods. Their sun god took different forms: Atum in human form and Re in the form of a human with the head of a falcon. River and land gods included Osiris and his wife, Isis. Osiris, who was associated with resurrection or rebirth, was important to the ceremonies and rites of the dead. Osiris judged whether or not a soul was worthy to enter the kingdom of the dead.

The Course of Egyptian History

Ancient Egyptian history can be divided into three major periods, known as the Old Kingdom, the Middle Kingdom, and the New Kingdom. Each of these was a period of long-term stability with a strong leader, freedom from invasion, the building of temples and pyramids, and considerable cultural activity. Between these periods were years of chaos and invasion.

The history of Egypt begins in about 3100 B.C. with the rule of Menes, who united the villages of the Upper (southern) and Lower (northern) Egypt into a single kingdom and created a dynasty, a family of rulers whose right to rule is passed on within the family.

The Old Kingdom The Old Kingdom lasted from around 2700 to 2200 B.C. At this time, the king, or **pharaoh**, possessed absolute power. A ruling bureaucracy developed which included a vizier who reported directly to the king.

The Pyramids Pyramids, tombs for the mummified bodies of pharaohs, were built during the Old Kingdom. Pyramids were part of larger cities of the dead that included not only the pharaoh's pyramid but also tombs for the pharaoh's officials and lesser pyramids for the pharaoh's family.

Pyramids contained all the objects that a person would need for the afterlife, included beds, chairs, boats, games, dishes, and foods. An Egyptian's physical body was preserved by means of mummification, which included salting the body to absorb its water before wrapping it in layers of linen soaked in resin.

The Middle Kingdom The Middle Kingdom lasted from about 2050 to 1652 B.C. During this golden age, Egypt expanded, conquering Nubia and sending armies and traders into other parts of Asia and Europe. During this period, pharaohs took greater responsibility for their subjects.

The New Kingdom The Middle Kingdom ended when it was invaded by the Hyskos, western Asians who used horse-drawn

CORE CONCEPTS: CULTURE

The largest of the pyramids, the Great Pyramid of King Khufu, was built at the time of the Old Kingdom. It covers thirteen acres and is a masterwork of precision construction. Next to the Great Pyramid at Giza is a huge statue carved from the rock known as the Great Sphinx. With its body of a lion and human head, it may have been an important guardian of the site, but there is no certain understanding of its purpose.

war chariots. From them, the Egyptians learned to use bronze for tools and weapons; they also learned military skills. Eventually, they drove out the Hyskos and reunited Egypt to follow a more militaristic path. Egypt became the most powerful and militaristic state in Southwest Asia.

During the New Kingdom, the ruler Amenhotep IV introduced the worship of the sun god Aton and eliminated the other gods. This destabilized the society, even though the changes were quickly undone after Amenhotep's death by the boy-pharaoh Tutankhamen. The instability led to a loss of empire, however. Although Ramses II made some small headway in re-establishing the empire by recapturing Palestine, the New Kingdom collapsed in 1085 B.C.

Society in Ancient Egypt

Egyptian society was organized like a simple pyramid with the king, or pharaoh, at the top. Members of the ruling class just below him ran the government. Below the upper class were merchants, artisans, scribes, and tax collectors. The largest number of people worked the land. Most of them were peasants who farmed. They paid taxes, lived in small villages, and provided military service and forced labor. The lowest class was the slave class, who worked for the state. In later times, slaves could earn their freedom by serving in the army.

Men and women married early. Men were the masters of the home, but women were respected. Women's property remained in their hands. Most careers and public offices were closed to women because education was not permitted to them, but women in the royal family could, and did, become pharaohs. Hatshepsut is the most famous example.

Writing and Education

A type of writing using pictures and abstract forms called **hieroglyphics** was developed in about 3000 B.C. It was used for writing on temple walls and other lasting monuments. A simplified version of hieroglyphics called hieratic script also came into being: it became the writing of daily life. Learning to be a scribe took many years. Since governing the country required a knowledge of reading and writing, a specialized group of educated men, known as a **bureaucracy**, came into existence.

Achievements in Art and Science

Egyptians built pyramids, temples, and other monuments and created distinctive representational art. They made advances in mathematics, calculated area and volume, and surveyed flooded land. They developed an accurate 365-day calendar. The practice of embalming also helped them to develop medical knowledge.

SECTION 3 NEW CENTERS OF CIVILIZATION

The Role of Nomadic Peoples

On the fringes of civilization were pastoral nomads, people who domesticated animals for both food and clothing. They moved along regular migratory routes to provide steady sources of nourishment for their animals. Thus they facilitated trade and helped spread new technological developments, such as the use of bronze and iron.

Among the most important nomadic peoples were the Indo-Europeans. Originally, these people probably lived north of the Black Sea or in Southwest Asia. They shared a common language. Later they moved into Europe, India, and western Asia. One group of Indo-Europeans that moved into Asia Minor and Anatolia around 1750 B.C. combined with native peoples to form the Hittite kingdom. The Hittites were the first Indo-Europeans to make use of iron.

The Chaldeans, who came from Arabia, founded the New Babylonian Empire. Their interest in astrology gave them accurate knowledge of the movements of the stars. Our knowledge of astronomy is based on astrology. To achieve accuracy in their star charts, the Chaldeans became good mathematicians, able to add, subtract, multiply, and divide.

The Phoenicians

The **Phoenicians** lived along the Mediterranean coast in the area of Palestine. They became great sea traders and created a trade empire. Their chief cities—Byblos, Tyre, and Sidon—were ports on the eastern Mediterranean. They also established colonies in the western Mediterranean. The most famous of their colonies was Carthage.

The Phoenicians invented an alphabet consisting of twenty-two signs or letters that represented speech sounds. It became the basis of the Greek alphabet, from which our own alphabet was derived.

The Israelites

Between 1200 and 1000 B.C., the **Israelites** emerged as a distinct group of people, organized in tribes, who established a united kingdom known as Israel. According to their accounts in the Hebrew Bible, they migrated from Mesopotamia to Palestine, which they called Canaan. Then they migrated to Egypt, where they were enslaved until Moses led them out. After wandering in the desert for many years, they returned to Palestine.

The Divided Kingdom Tensions between tribes eventually resulted in the division of Israel into two kingdoms: Israel in the north and Judah in the south. In 722 B.C., the Assyrians overran Israel. The kingdom of Judah remained independent until the Chaldeans conquered it, completely destroying its capital, Jerusalem, in 586 B.C. Many people of Judah were sent into captivity in Babylon. When the Persians destroyed the Chaldean kingdom, they allowed the people of Judah to return to Jerusalem and rebuild their city and temple.

CORE CONCEPTS: POWER

King Solomon, who ruled Palestine from 970 to 930 B.C., strengthened royal power, expanded the government, and encouraged trade. Under Solomon, ancient Israel was at the height of its power.

CORE CONCEPTS: IDENTITY

The people of Judah eventually gave their name to Judaism, a stateless religion based on the notion that god was not fixed to one land but was creator and lord of the whole world.

REGENTS WARM-UP

Study the chart. What kinds of laws or rules are stated in the commandments? To whom do they apply?

The Ten Commandments
1. I am the Lord thy God . . . . Thou shalt have no other gods before me.
2. Thou shalt not make unto thee any graven image . . . .
3. Thou shalt not take the name of the Lord thy God in vain . . . .
4. Remember the Sabbath day, to keep it holy.
5. Honor thy father and thy mother . . . .
6. Thou shalt not kill.
7. Thou shalt not commit adultery.
8. Thou shalt not steal.
9. Thou shalt not bear false witness against thy neighbor.
10. Thou shalt not covet . . . anything that is thy neighbor's.
Source: Exodus 20:1–17

The Spiritual Dimensions of Israel Unlike other people of western Asia and Egypt, the Jews were **monotheistic**; they believed in one god. They believed their god made a covenant with them: Yahweh promised to guide them if they obeyed the laws of God stated in the Ten Commandments. The Jews also believed their god sent prophets to guide them. The prophets brought teachings that included social justice and a vision of peace. Jews believed the knowledge of god was open to everyone who could read the Torah. They also refused to accept the gods of their conquerors and neighbors.

SECTION 4 THE RISE OF NEW EMPIRES

The Assyrian Empire

The Assyrians were a Semitic people who used iron weapons to establish an empire by 700 B.C. The Assyrian Empire included Mesopotamia, parts of the Iranian Plateau, sections of Asia Minor, Palestine, and Egypt as far as Thebes. The Assyrian army was large, well organized, disciplined, and equipped with iron weapons. It was also ruthless in conquering neighboring peoples.

The Persian Empire

After the collapse of the Assyrian Empire, the Chaldeans, under their king Nebuchadnezzar II, made Babylonia the leading state in western Asia. For a short time before it fell to Persian rule, Babylon was one of the great cities of the ancient world.

The Rise of the Persian Empire Cyrus (549–530 B.C.) unified the Persians and created the powerful **Persian Empire** that ruled from Asia Minor to western India. Unlike Assyrian leaders, Cyrus was known for his wisdom and compassion. He permitted the Jews of Babylon to return to Jerusalem. Called Cyrus "the Great," he gained a reputation for mercy. Medes, Babylonians, and Jews all accepted him as their ruler. Since his empire was so ethnically diverse, Cyrus allowed different groups to practice their own traditions and beliefs. He made use of Assyrian, Babylonian, and Egyptian designs and building methods. Cyrus's successors extended his territory.

The Structure of the Persian Empire The ruler Darius divided the empire into 20 provinces, or satrapies. Each was ruled by a governor, or satrap, who collected taxes in coin, not in goods, provided justice and security, and recruited soldiers for the royal

LINKING PAST AND PRESENT

Although the empire lasted less than one hundred years, it was well organized. The Assyrians developed an efficient system of communication consisting of a network of outposts that used relay horses to convey messages. It also established one of the world's first libraries at Nineveh.

CORE CONCEPTS: MOVEMENT OF PEOPLE AND GOODS

Roads ensured good travel and efficient communication. The Royal Road stretched from Lydia to Susa, the chief capital of the empire. Like the Assyrians, the Persians also established a series of stations that provided food, shelter, and fresh horses for the king's messengers.

army. Darius celebrated his victories by ordering an inscription in three languages. This inscription, known as the Behistun Rock, was the key to deciphering cuneiform writing.

By the time of Darius, the Persian kings had created a professional army. At its core were groups of soldiers known as Immortals because their numbers were never allowed to fall below ten thousand. When one member was killed, he was immediately replaced.

The Fall of the Persian Empire The empire was eventually weakened by the rulers' desire for greater wealth and luxury. Internal struggles over the throne also weakened the monarchy.

Persian Religion Persian religion was based on the teachings of Zoraster, a prophet born in 600 B.C. who had a vision of the one supreme being, Ahuramazda. This creator and force for good was opposed by the evil Ahriman. Humans had the power to choose between right, to follow the way of Ahuramazda, and wrong. Eventually, according to Zoraster, and the religion he founded called Zoroastrianism, good would triumph, there would be a final judgment at the end of the world, and the final separation of good and evil would occur.

Chapter Overview

Civilization in India began in the Indus River Valley. Empires weakened and gradually fell to Aryan invaders, who were the originators of Hinduism, the caste system, and the Sanskrit language. Later, Buddhism developed as a rival to Hinduism. The Mauryan dynasty, the Kushan kingdom, and the Gupta Empire flourished in succession. The Xia dynasty was the beginning of civilization in China. The Mandate of Heaven, the divine right to rule, supported the idea of the dynastic cycle. Three major Chinese philosophies, Confucianism, Taoism, and Legalism developed. During the repressive Qin dynasty under Qin Shihuangdi, the empire expanded and parts of the Great Wall were built. The ensuing Han dynasty, China's Golden Age, was more stable, and new technologies and inventions such as paper and steel, as well as trade, helped bring prosperity. It was during this period that Confucianism expanded.

As you read this chapter, ask yourself these questions:
(1) How did geography influence the development of civilizations in India and China?
(2) What were the characteristics of the early Indian and Chinese civilizations and empires?
(3) What political and social structures existed in these civilizations?
(4) What were the major religions, and what role did they play?
(5) What were the major contributions of each civilization?

Main Ideas and Concepts

- **The Uses of Geography** Early civilizations in India and China developed along river valleys.

- **Change** The Mauryan dynasty, the Kushan kingdom, and the Gupta Empire flourished in turn.

- **Belief Systems** Hinduism in India and Confucianism in China helped create social order by establishing a class hierarchy.

REGENTS WARM-UP

Past Regents Exams have tested knowledge of the general features of a traditional society. See if you can guess the answer to the question below based on this chapter.

Which generalization is characteristic of most traditional societies?

1. People move from city to city seeking jobs.
2. The same livelihood is passed down from generation to generation.
3. A high degree of social mobility exists.
4. All people have the same economic opportunity.

- **Belief Systems** Emperors in China claimed to rule by the Mandate of Heaven.

- **Conflict** The Qin Dynasty was created out of civil war, flourished briefly, and was rapidly followed by instability.

People, Places, Terms

The following names and terms will help you to prepare for the Regents Exam in Global History and Geography. You can find an explanation of each name and term in the Glossary at the back of this book, in your textbook, or in another reference source.

Aryans	Daoism	Mandate of Heaven
ascetic	enlightenment	monsoon
Buddhism	filial piety	Qin Shihuangdi
caste system	Hinduism	Silk Road
Chang Jiang	Huang He	yoga
Confucianism		

SECTION 1 EARLY CIVILIZATION IN INDIA

The Geography of India

The Indian subcontinent is shaped like a triangle hanging from the southern ridge of Asia. Its core regions include the Himalaya in the far north, the largest mountains in the world. Directly south of the Himalaya is the rich valley of the Ganges Region. To the west is the Indus River valley, which served as a cradle of Indian civilization and now helps define the modern state of Pakistan. South of the Ganges and Indus River valleys lies the Deccan, a hilly, dry, and sparsely populated plateau that extends from the Ganges Valley to the southern tip of India. Along India's eastern and western coasts are lush plains that tend to be densely populated. These coasts are separated from the Deccan by low mountain ranges called the Ghats.

India's First Civilization

Between 3000 B.C. and 1500 B.C., the valley of the Indus River supported a flourishing civilization that extended hundreds of miles from the Himalaya to the coast of the Arabian Sea. Major cities that flourished in this area are Mohenjo-Daro and Harappa. Both had between 35,000 and 40,000 inhabitants at their height, and both were carefully planned with main, broad

CORE CONCEPTS: PHYSICAL SYSTEMS

The primary feature of India's climate is the **monsoon**, a seasonal wind pattern in southern Asia. One monsoon blows warm, moist air from the southwest during the summer; it also brings heavy rains on which the farmers depend. Another monsoon blows cold, dry air from the northeast during the winter. The Himalayas protect India from the effects of these winds.

streets, large walled neighborhoods, public wells, drainage for waste water, and a system of trash collection.

Rulers and the Economy Religion and political power were closely linked. Harappan rulers based their power on a belief in divine assistance. The holy temple and the royal palace were combined in one citadel or fortress.

The economy was based on farming, but trade was also carried on with city-states in Mesopotamia. Textiles and food were imported from Sumerian city-states in exchange for copper, lumber, precious stones, cotton, and luxury goods. Much of this trade was carried by ship via the Persian Gulf.

The Arrival of the Aryans

The Indus River Valley civilization was weakened by changes in climate as well as a change in the course of the Indus River. A group of Indo-European invaders from central Asia, who were known as **Aryans**, brought the civilization to its end.

The Aryans, a nomadic people who excelled in the art of war, entered India through northwest mountain passes between 1500 and 500 B.C. They conquered the Dravidians and established the foundation of the Hindu religion. This period is known as the Vedic Age.

Aryan Ways of Life Through the use of the iron plow, along with the use of irrigation, the Aryans and their subject peoples turned the jungle growth along the Ganges into a rich farming area. Crops in the north included wheat, millet, barley, and rice. In the south, cotton, grain, vegetables, and spices such as pepper, cinnamon, and ginger were grown.

Society in Ancient India

Aryan rule resulted in a class system that persists to some degree in modern-day India called the **caste system**. It was a set of rigid categories, based in part on skin color, that determined a person's economic, social, and religious status.

The Family in Ancient India The family was the basic unit of Indian life, and the ideal was an extended family with three generations living under the same roof.

Society was patriarchal. Only males could own property, and, generally, only males could be educated. Women married early, and, in ancient times, threw themselves on their husband's funeral pyre in a ritual known as suttee. Children were expected to take care of their parents as they grew older.

CORE CONCEPTS: CULTURE

The Aryans developed their writing system, known as Sanskrit, by 1000 B.C. Some writings reveal that between 1500 and 400 B.C., India was an area of warring states in which some leaders, known as rajas, carved out small states and fought other Aryan chieftains.

CORE CONCEPTS: BELIEF SYSTEMS

In ancient times, there were five major divisions in the caste system. At the top were the Brahmins, the priestly class. The second class was the Kshatriyas, or warriors. The third class was the Vaisyas, or commoners. Most Vaisyas were merchants or farmers. Below these were the Sudras. Most Sudras were peasants who worked the land for others. They had only limited rights. The lowest level in the system were Untouchables, people who were given society's worst jobs, such as collecting trash and handling dead bodies. These people were considered subhuman.

Hinduism

Hinduism arose from the beliefs of Aryan peoples who settled India after 1500 B.C. Early Hindus believed in the existence of a single force in the universe, a form of ultimate reality or God, called Brahman. It was the duty of the individual self, called the *atman*, to seek to know this ultimate reality.

By the sixth century B.C., the idea of reincarnation, a belief that the soul is reborn in a different form after death, appeared. Karma, the force generated by a person's actions, determined how the person would be born in the next life. Dharma was the divine law that defined people's duties in life. Belief in reincarnation provided a religious basis for the rigid class divisions of the caste system. The goal of all Hindus is to achieve *moksha*, an end to the cycle of rebirth when one's atman unites with Brahman, the universal soul.

Hindus believe that oneness with god can be achieved through the practice of **yoga**. Hinduism also has many gods and goddesses; through them, individuals express their religious identity. Principal among the gods and goddesses are Brahma the Creator, Vishnu the Preserver, and Shiva the Destroyer. These, and all other deities, are a part of Brahman, the universal soul.

Buddhism

In the sixth century B.C., a new doctrine, called **Buddhism**, appeared in northern India and soon became a rival of Hinduism, although it eventually declined in India.

The Buddha The founder of Buddhism was Siddhartha Gautama, known as the Buddha, or "Enlightened One." Siddhartha began his life as the man with everything—wealth, a good family, and a throne that he would inherit. When he became aware of human suffering as a young man, however, he gave up all he had, shaved his head, and abandoned his family. At first, he tried practices of self-denial in an effort to find the true meaning of life and became an **ascetic**. Later, he tried meditation. One day, during meditation, he reached **enlightenment**. He spent the remainder of his life preaching what he had discovered.

The Basic Principles of Buddhism Gautama Buddha, as Siddhartha came to be called, preached Four Noble Truths:

1. Ordinary life is full of suffering.

2. This suffering is caused by selfish desires.

CORE CONCEPTS: INTERDEPENDENCE

Siddhartha Gautama was born in what is today Nepal. Today Nepalis practice both Buddhism and Hinduism. The practice of Buddhism ties Nepal with other Buddhist nations to the east. The practice of Hinduism ties it to India. Find Nepal on a map of Asia. How does location help explain the influence of two major world religions on Nepal?

3. The way to end suffering is to end desire for selfish goals and to see others as extensions of ourselves.

4. The way to end desire is to follow the Eightfold Path.

The Eightfold Path consists of eight steps:

1. *Right view* We need to know the Four Noble Truths.

2. *Right intention* We need to decide what we really want.

3. *Right speech* We must seek to speak the truth and to speak well of others.

4. *Right action* The Buddha gave five precepts: Do not kill. Do not steal. Do not lie. Do not be unchaste. Do not take drugs or drink alcohol.

5. *Right livelihood* We must do work that uplifts our being.

6. *Right effort* The Buddha emphasized that effort was required to follow the Way, and it must be as great as the effort of an ox that travels through deep mud carrying a heavy load.

7. *Right mindfulness* We must keep our minds in control of our senses.

8. *Right concentration* We must meditate to see the world in a new way.

Buddhism as Philosophy Siddhartha taught that all beings could reach nirvana, the end of the self and a reunion with the Great World Soul. Siddhartha urged people to follow the Middle Way—the path between a life of asceticism and a life of luxury. He accepted the idea of reincarnation but rejected the notion of castes, thus appealing to the lower end of the social scale. He also rejected the idea of gods and goddesses, although Mahayana Buddhism, which spread to East Asia, spoke of a compassionate god, and saints known as Bodhisattvas. For this reason, some see Buddhism as more of a philosophy than a religion.

SECTION 2　NEW EMPIRES IN INDIA

The Mauryan Dynasty

The Aryans occupied India, but they did not bring peace or lasting political stability. Kingdoms fought each other, and invaders came. First Persia extended its empire into western India; then Alexander the Great swept into Northwestern India in 327 B.C. His soldiers quickly left, however, making way for the rise to power of the Mauryan dynasty.

CORE CONCEPTS: INTERDEPENDENCE

Chinese merchants made huge fortunes by trading silk, spices, teas, and porcelain. Indian merchants sent ivory, textiles, precious stones, and pepper. They were exchanged for woolen and linen clothes, glass, and precious stones from the Roman Empire.

REGENTS WARM-UP

Study the map. Where did the Silk Road begin and end? What approximate distance did it cover? What happened at Antioch? How did other trade routes affect India?

Chandragupta Maurya established a highly centralized empire in northern India and ruled from 324 to 301 B.C. His empire began to flourish under the reign of his grandson, Asoka.

The Reign of Asoka Asoka is generally considered to be the greatest ruler in the history of India. Using Buddhist ideals to guide his rule, Asoka established hospitals for people and animals and he ordered that trees and shelters be placed along the road to provide shade and rest for travelers. His kingdom prospered and its role in regional trade expanded. India became a major crossroads in a vast commercial trading network stretching from the Pacific to Southwest Asia and the Mediterranean Sea. When the Mauryan kingdom declined after Asoka's death and then collapsed, India fell back into disunity.

The Kushan Kingdom and the Silk Road

New kingdoms arose after the collapse of the Mauryan Empire. They included Bactria in what is today northern Afghanistan. The Kushan Kingdom spread over northern India as far as the central Ganges Valley.

The Kushans prospered from trade on the **Silk Road**, a route between the Roman Empire and China. Part of the Silk Road passed through the mountains northwest of India.

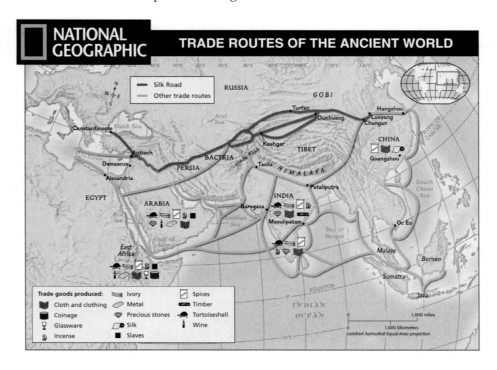

NATIONAL GEOGRAPHIC — TRADE ROUTES OF THE ANCIENT WORLD

The Kingdom of the Guptas

In the third century A.D., invaders from Persia brought the Kushan Kingdom to an end. Chandragupta (no relation to Chandragupta Maurya) and his son and successor Samudragupta established the Gupta Empire on the site of the old Mauryan Empire. It became a dominant political force in northern India and eventually gained loose control over central India as well.

Led by a series of efficient kings, the Gupta Empire, known as India's "Golden Age," actively engaged in trade with Southeast Asia, China, and the Mediterranean. Cities famous for their temples as well as for their prosperity rose along the main trade routes throughout India. Much of their wealth came from pilgrims who came to visit the major religious centers.

The Gupta rulers lived in great luxury, profiting from their gold and silver mines and vast lands. Eventually, invasions by nomadic Huns from the northwest reduced their power. After the middle of the seventh century, the empire fell completely apart, and northern India would not be reunited for hundreds of years.

The World of Indian Culture

Ancient India produced many great works of literature. The earliest known Indian literature comes from the Aryan tradition in the form of the Vedas, collections of hymns and religious ceremonies that were originally passed down orally. Two great epics that tell of legendary deeds of great warriors are the *Mahabharata*, of which the *Bhagavad Gita* forms one part, and the *Ramayana*. Both tales are strongly imbued with religious and moral lessons.

SECTION 3 EARLY CHINESE CIVILIZATIONS

The Geography of China

The **Huang He** (or Yellow River) flows more than 2,900 miles, carrying its rich yellow silt all the way from Mongolia to the Pacific Ocean. The **Chang Jiang** (or Yangtze River) flows 3,400 miles across central China before emptying into the Yellow Sea. Together, these rivers and their fertile valleys created one of the great food-producing regions of the ancient world. Only 10%

CORE CONCEPTS: SCIENCE AND TECHNOLOGY

Ancient Indians had an impressive knowledge of astronomy. They also introduced the concept of zero and had a symbol for it. A mathematician from the Gupta Empire named Aryabhata was one of the first scientists known to have used algebra.

CORE CONCEPTS: CULTURE

Three characteristic architectural forms that developed in India are the pillar, stupa, and rock chamber. Pillars were made of polished sandstone, rose as high as 50 feet, and were topped with carvings. Stupas were places of devotion for Buddhists. Rock chambers, which were carved out of rock cliffs, housed monks and served as halls for religious ceremonies.

of China's total land area, located mainly in the east, is suitable for farming, however.

The rest of China consists of mountains, deserts, and plateaus. These mountains and deserts created geographical barriers that isolated the Chinese people from peoples in other parts of Asia. Contacts with groups at China's borders has often been marked by conflict. The northern frontier of China became one of the areas of conflict as Chinese armies tried to protect their precious farmlands from invaders.

The Shang Dynasty

The history of Chinese civilization dates to the founding of the Xia dynasty over four thousand years ago. Little is known about this dynasty, which was replaced by the second dynasty, the Shang.

China under the Shang dynasty (about 1750 to 1122 B.C.) was mostly a farming society ruled by an aristocracy whose major concern was war. An aristocracy is an upper class whose wealth is based on land and whose power is passed from one generation to another. The Shang dynasty had several impressive cities. These urban centers had huge city walls, royal palaces, and large royal tombs.

Political and Social Structures The Shang king ruled from the capital city of Angyang. He controlled large armies and chose aristocratic warlords to govern his territories.

The king and his family were at the top of Shang society. Just below were a number of aristocratic families. The great majority of people were peasants who farmed the land of the aristocrats. There were also a small number of merchants, artisans, and slaves.

Religion and Culture Under the Shang The early Chinese had a strong belief in life after death. Closely linked to this belief was the practice of ancestor veneration. The Chinese believed that the souls of the dead could bring good or evil fortune to the living members of a family. Thus, it was important to treat the spirits well, and ancestral rites had to be properly performed.

The Zhou Dynasty

The Zhou dynasty lasted for almost eight hundred years (1045 to 256 B.C.), making it the longest-lasting dynasty in Chinese history. As in the Shang dynasty, the king appointed officials to

REGENTS WARM-UP

The following statement comes from a past Regents Exam: "Geographic factors have influenced the development of many nations of the world." As you read this chapter, list geographic factors that have influenced the development of China.

CORE CONCEPTS: BELIEF SYSTEMS

The Chinese believed in supernatural forces with which they could communicate. To communicate with the gods, the rulers used oracle bones. Priests scratched questions on the bones to be answered by the gods. Heated metal rods were then stuck into the bones, causing them to crack. Priests interpreted the shapes of the cracks as answers from the gods.

CORE CONCEPTS: CULTURE

The Shang dynasty is remembered for the mastery of its artisans in metal casting. These bronze objects, which often held offerings to the dead, are among the most admired creations in Chinese art.

rule over the territories, was in charge of defense, and controlled armies that served under his command throughout the country.

The Mandate of Heaven The Zhou dynasty claimed that it ruled China because it possessed the **Mandate of Heaven**. The Mandate of Heaven was based on the belief that Heaven—an impersonal law of nature—kept order in the universe through the Zhou king. Thus, he ruled over all humanity by a mandate, or authority to command, from Heaven.

The concept of a heavenly mandate became a basic principle of Chinese statecraft. If the king did not rule effectively, he could be overthrown. Therefore, the king, though serving as a representative of heaven, is not himself divine, and the people have a "right of revolution."

The Dynastic Cycle The Mandate of Heaven was closely tied to the pattern of dynastic cycles. From the beginning of Chinese history to A.D. 1912, China was ruled by a series of dynasties. Some lasted for centuries; others collapsed after a few years. No matter how long the dynasties lasted, all went through a cycle of change. A new dynasty established its power, ruled successfully for some years, and then began to decline. The power of the central government would begin to collapse, giving rise to rebellions or invasion. Finally, the dynasty collapsed and a new dynasty took over, beginning another dynastic cycle with another mandate to rule.

The Fall of the Zhou Dynasty In 403 B.C., civil war broke out in China, beginning the period known in Chinese historical records as the "Period of the Warring States." By this time, warfare had changed in China. Iron weapons came into use. Foot soldiers (infantry) and horse soldiers (cavalry) made their first appearance. The crossbow was also in use. By 221 B.C., one of the warring states, the Qin, took control.

Life during the Zhou Dynasty During the Zhou, peasants continued to work on lands owned by their lord, but they also had land of their own. Merchants and artisans lived in walled towns and operated under the direct control of the local lord. There was also a class of slaves.

Economic and Technological Growth One of the advances that occurred at this time was the use of irrigation. Large-scale water projects were set in motion to control the flow of rivers and spread water evenly across the fields. Not only irrigation but also changes in farming methods increased farm production. The use of iron plowshares had enabled the Chinese to bring more

CORE CONCEPTS: JUSTICE

Confucius, who was known to the Chinese as the First Teacher and called Master Kung by his followers, stressed duty and humanity. The concept of duty meant that all people had to subordinate their interests to the broader needs of the family and the community. Everyone should be governed by the Five Human Relationships: parent and child, husband and wife, older sibling and younger sibling, older friend and younger friend, and ruler and subject. Each person in the relationship had a duty to the other. Parents should be loving, and children should revere their parents. Husbands should fulfill their duties, and wives should be obedient. The elder sibling should be kind, and the younger sibling respectful. The older friend should be considerate, and the younger friend deferential. Rulers should be benevolent, and subjects loyal. Three of these five relationships concern the family, which shows the family's importance to Confucius: "The duty of children to their parents is the foundation from which all virtues spring."

acreage under production. Advances in farming in turn led to increases in population. Improved farming also encouraged the growth of trade and manufacturing.

The Family in Ancient China In ancient China, the family was the basic economic and social unit. The family also served as a symbol of the social order. At the heart of the concept of family in China was the idea of **filial piety**, the concept that members of a family would subordinate their needs and desires to those of the male head of the family.

The male was important as the person who ensured and provided for the well-being of others. Men worked in the fields, governed society, and were the warriors, scholars, and ministers. Women raised the children and worked at home.

The Chinese Written Language By the time of the Shang dynasty, the Chinese had begun to develop a written language. It was primarily pictographic and ideographic in form. Pictographs are picture symbols. Ideographs are characters that combine two or more pictographs to represent an idea. Today, this language has evolved so that some symbols convey phonetic information as well as meaning. Nevertheless, the pictographic and ideographic components remain fundamental to the language.

The Chinese Philosophies

Between 500 and 200 B.C., three major schools of thought about the nature of human beings emerged in China—**Confucianism**, Daoism, and Legalism. These philosophies focused on the immediate world in which people lived and on how to create a stable order in that world.

Confucianism Confucius (Kung Fu-Tzu) lived at a time of political upheaval in China. Unceasing warfare resulted in cruelty and injustice. Confucius, who was upset by the violence and moral decay of his age, emphasized social order and ethical government. His interest in philosophy was political and ethical, not spiritual. Much of his concern was with creating harmony at home and in society. He believed in a social hierarchy where people accepted their roles in society.

For Confucius, the concept of humanity meant a sense of compassion and empathy for others. One way of expressing a Confucian value is through the saying "Do not do unto others what you would not wish done to yourself."

Confucius also believed that roles in government should not be limited to those of noble birth but should be open to all men of superior talent. He traveled around China in an attempt to persuade political leaders to follow his ideas, but he was not met with much success during his own lifetime. Still, his teachings were recorded in the *Analects*, and his message eventually spread, especially during the Han dynasty. Until the twentieth century, almost every Chinese pupil studied the sayings of Confucius.

Daoism was a system of ideas based on the teachings of Laozi, who was supposedly a contemporary of Confucius. The chief ideas of Daoism are discussed in a short work known as *Tao Te Ching (The Way of the Dao)*. Like Confucianism, Daoism does not concern itself with the underlying meaning of the universe. While Confucianism emphasized man's harmony in society, Daoism stressed a relationship with nature. Harmony in nature could be achieved when the opposite forces of yin and yang were balanced. Daoists rejected government control, which they saw as unnatural.

Legalism developed from the teachings of Han Feizi during the Zhou dynasty. Unlike Confucianism and Daoism, Legalism proposed that people were evil by nature. Harsh laws and strict punishments were required to cause people to follow the correct path. The Legalists believed that a strong ruler was required to create an orderly society. The ruler was not required to show compassion for the needs of the people.

SECTION 4 RISE AND FALL OF CHINESE EMPIRES

The Qin Dynasty (221–206 B.C.)

In 221 B.C., **Qin Shihuangdi**, meaning "the first Qin emperor," defeated the last of the rivals to his dynasty and began bringing dramatic changes to China.

Changes During the Qin Dynasty Chinese politics changed dramatically at this time. Legalism became the regime's official ideology. People who opposed the government were punished or executed. Books with opposing views were publicly burned.

The Great Wall The Qin emperor's major defensive concern was in the north. There, nomadic peoples called the Xiongnu had mastered the art of fighting on horseback. They posed a threat to many communities, which began to build defensive walls in

CORE CONCEPTS: GOVERNMENT

The central bureaucracy was divided into three parts: the civil division, the military division, and the censorate. The censorate had inspectors who kept a close watch over officials to make sure they were doing their jobs. Those found guilty of wrongdoing were executed.

CORE CONCEPTS: CHANGE

Qin Shihuangdi began the wall that we know today as the Great Wall of China. However, it is not, the same wall. Rather, the Qin emperor's wall was the predecessor to the Great Wall built some 1,500 years later. The linking of the existing walls was a massive building project that required thousands of laborers. Many of them died while working on the wall.

CORE CONCEPTS: CULTURE

During the Han dynasty, the key works of the Confucian school were made into a set of classics, which became required reading for generations of Chinese schoolchildren. These works established an influential and long-lasting behavioral code.

response. Qin Shihuangdi decided to strengthen the existing walls to keep the nomads out.

The Fall of the Qin Dynasty The Qin dynasty lasted only four years past the death of its emperor, Qin Shihuangdi. A period of civil war followed.

The Han Dynasty (202 B.C.–A.D. 220)

The next dynasty was one of the greatest and longest lasting in the history of China. It was founded by Liu Bang, a man of peasant origins who did away with the harsh policies of the Qin dynasty. Confucian policies took the place of Legalism. The division of the government into three ministries, including the censorate, did, however, continue. Government officials were chosen on the basis of merit rather than birth. The Han dynasty established a civil service examination based on Confucian principles and a school to train such officials, a system that influenced Chinese civilization for two thousand years. During the Han dynasty, the population of China increased rapidly.

Expansion of the Empire Han emperors continued to expand the Chinese Empire. Han Wudi ("Martial Emperor of Han") added the southern regions below the Chang Jiang into the empire, including what is today northern Vietnam. Han armies also expanded the country westward. On the northern border, they drove back the Xiongnu, the nomads, leading the way to 150 years of relative peace in China.

Society in the Han Empire The Han dynasty was a period of great prosperity for some and was one of the golden ages of Chinese civilization. Land-owning peasants suffered, however, as surging land taxes caused many of them to sell their land and become tenant farmers. Land ownership shifted into the hands of the aristocrats, while peasants paid rents as high as half of all that they farmed on the aristocrats' land.

Technology in the Han Empire New technology led to greater economic prosperity during the Han dynasty. Technology advanced in manufacturing, water mills for grinding grain, and iron casting. Iron casting technology led to the invention of steel. Paper was also developed during the Han dynasty.

The Fall of the Han Empire The Han Empire fell gradually into decline as leaders turned their attention from governing to self-indulgence. Official corruption, the concentration of land in the hands of the wealthy, and widespread peasant unrest all led to instability and decline. Nomadic raids on Chinese territory in the north also contributed to the fall of the empire. The final blow came in 220 when China was plunged into civil war. A period of chaos ensued, lasting nearly four hundred years.

Chapter Overview

The first Greek civilization existed on the island of Crete as early as 2800 B.C. The Mycenaean culture flourished on the mainland from about 1600 to about 1100 B.C. A Dark Age followed, in which long distance trade ceased, the knowledge of writing was lost, and culture declined; then trade increased, populations grew, and many Greek city-states arose. Among them were Athens, the birthplace of democracy, and Sparta, an oligarchy and a military state. In Athens, a classical culture produced great works of art, including plays, temples, and sculpture. Great philosophers such as Socrates, Plato, and Aristotle sought to understand the meaning of the universe and answer questions of human existence.

Although Athens and Sparta were united in war against Persia, which they defeated, they eventually fought each other in the Peloponnesian War. The power of Athens declined and was later ended by Philip II, king of Macedonia. Philip's son Alexander created a vast empire by conquering Persia and large parts of southwest Asia, spreading Hellenistic culture and enabling Greece to absorb influences of other cultures.

As you read this chapter, ask yourself these questions:
(1) How did geography influence the development of the independent city-states?
(2) Why was Homer important in Greek history?
(3) What is a city-state?
(4) How did Athens and Sparta differ?
(5) How did the Persian and Peloponnesian Wars shape the course of Greek history?
(6) What were the contributions of the Greeks to Western civilization?
(7) How did Alexander the Great create his empire?

REGENTS WARM-UP

In the past, some Regents Exams have asked students to put events in chronological order. As you read, you may wish to create timelines to order major events.

Main Ideas and Concepts

- **Linking Geography to History** Minoan, and later Mycenaean, peoples established the first Greek civilizations in geographically isolated areas.

- **Government** Greek city-states arose that became the polis, or center, of Greek life.

- **Power** During Greece's classical age, which is also known as its golden age and the Age of Pericles, Athens was the center of Greek culture.

- **Culture** Greek philosophers sought reasonable explanations for the nature of the universe and the meaning of human existence.

- **Movement of People and Goods** Alexander conquered the Persian Empire and beyond, helping to bring about a Hellenistic world linked by Greek influences.

People, Places, Terms

The following names and terms will help you to prepare for the Regents Exam in Global History and Geography. You can find an explanation of each name and term in the Glossary at the back of this book, in your textbook, or in another reference source.

Aegean Sea	Athens	Plato
Age of Pericles	democracy	polis
Alexander the Great	direct democracy	Socrates
aristocracy	Hellenistic Era	Sparta
Aristotle	oligarchy	tyrant

SECTION 1 THE FIRST GREEK CIVILIZATIONS

The Impact of Geography

Greece occupies a small area that consists of a mountainous peninsula and numerous islands. The mountains and the sea helped shape Greek history. The mountains isolated Greeks from one another, causing different Greek communities to develop their own ways of life and resulting in fiercely independent groups. This independence, however, also caused that rivalry that led to warfare.

Access to the sea helped lead to a seafaring culture. Greeks sailed the **Aegean Sea**, the Mediterranean, and the Black Sea. Later, they established colonies that spread Greek civilization throughout the Mediterranean world.

The Minoan Civilization

The island of Crete was the setting of a Bronze Age civilization that developed by 2800 B.C. It flourished between 2700 and 1450 B.C. and was characterized in part by the use of metals, especially bronze, for making weapons and other items. An archaeologist named the civilization Minos after a legendary king of Crete.

The centers of Minoan civilization collapsed suddenly around 1450 B.C., perhaps either because of a tidal wave or an invasion by mainland Greeks called the Mycenaeans.

The First Greek State: Mycenae

The southern part of mainland Greece is a peninsula called Mycenae. The Mycenaean Greeks were part of the Indo-European family of peoples who spread into southern and western Europe, India, and Iran. Their civilization reached its high point between 1400 and 1200 B.C. It was made up of powerful monarchies. Each resided in a fortified palace center. These various centers of power probably formed a loose alliance of independent states.

By the late thirteenth century B.C., Mycenaean civilization weakened as states fought each other, major earthquakes caused serious damage, and invaders moved into Greece from the north. By 1100 B.C., Mycenaean civilization collapsed.

The Greeks in a Dark Age

After the collapse of the Mycenaean Empire, Greece entered a Dark Age that lasted from approximately 1100 B.C. to 750 B.C. The population declined and food production dropped. Large numbers of Greeks left the mainland and sailed across the Aegean to other islands and to the western shores of Asia Minor.

Over time, trade, economic activity, and agriculture began to revive. The use of iron tools helped bring about this change. At this time, the Greeks also adopted and simplified the Phoenician alphabet, making writing easier.

Homer   Near the end of the Dark Age, one of the greatest poets of all time created the *Iliad* and the *Odyssey*, the first great epic poems of early Greece. Their author was Homer, who used stories of the Trojan War to write his long poems. These epics told the deeds of great heroes and taught the values of heroism and honor. The *Iliad* tells the story of the Trojan war. (The word *Trojan* is an adjective formed from the name *Troy*.) According to the epic, this war occurs when Paris, a prince of Troy, kidnaps Helen, the wife of the

king of the Greek state of Sparta. The *Odyssey* tells the story of
Odysseus, a Greek hero who journeys for many years after the fall
of Troy and ultimately returns home to his wife.

SECTION 2 THE GREEK CITY-STATES

The Polis: Center of Greek Life

The Greeks called a city-state a polis. By 750 B.C., the **polis** had
become the central focus of Greek life. Our word *politics* comes
from the Greek word *polis*. In a physical sense, the polis was a
town, a city, or even a village, along with its surrounding countryside. The town, city, or village served as the center of the polis
where people met for political, social, and religious activities.
Some polises were ruled by wealthy families, **aristocrats**; others
by businessmen and landholders, oligarchies.

The polis was more than a place, however. It was a community of people who shared a common identity and common goals.
It contained citizens with political rights (adult males), citizens
with no political rights (women and children), and noncitizens
(slaves and resident aliens). Citizens had both rights and responsibilities to the polis.

A New Military System As the polis developed, so too did a
new military system. By 700 B.C., this system was based on
hoplites, heavily armed infantry or foot soldiers. They were
citizen soldiers, not professionals. Each carried a round shield, a
short sword, and a thrusting spear. They went into battle as a
unit, shoulder to shoulder in a formation known as a phalanx.
This created a wall of shields.

Greek Colonies

Between 750 and 550 B.C., large numbers of Greeks left their
homeland to settle in distant lands. New Greek colonies were
established along the coastlines of southern Italy, southern
France, eastern Spain, and northern Africa west of Egypt. The
Greeks also set up colonies in Thrace. They settled along the
shores of the Black Sea, setting up cities on the Hellespont and
the Bosporus. The most notable of these cities was Byzantium,
the site of what would become first Constantinople and later
Istanbul. In establishing these cities, the Greeks spread their
culture and political power throughout the Mediterranean. This
resulted in an expansion of wealth for trading partners on the
mainland and especially for a group of wealthy individuals in
many of the Greek city-states.

**CORE CONCEPTS:
HUMAN SYSTEMS**

The main gathering place in a
polis was usually a hill. At the
top of the hill was a fortified
area called an acropolis. It
served as a place of refuge in
an attack and sometimes was
the religious center on which
temples and public buildings
were built. Below the acropolis was an agora, an open
area for a market and
meeting place.

Tyranny in the City-States

Some wealthy individuals who wanted political power seized it by force from the aristocrats. This new group of rich men was supported by both other newly rich people and peasants who were in debt to aristocrats. They became rulers known as tyrants, although this term did not apply in the sense we use it today.

Tyrants were not necessarily wicked, but they did gain power and keep it by using hired soldiers. They also built new market-places, temples, and walls that glorified the city and added to their own popularity. Still, the tyrants, who took the law into their own hands, did not last. By the end of the sixth century B.C., tyrants had fallen out of favor.

Because the rule of tyrants ended the rule of aristocrats, it was important in the history of Greek government. When tyranny ended, many more Greeks participated in government. In some Greek city-states, this led to the development of **democracy**, which is government by the people or rule of the many. Other city-states remained committed to government by an **oligarchy**, rule by the few for the benefit of the few.

Sparta

The city-state of **Sparta** was an oligarchy headed by two kings. A group of five men known as *ephors* were elected each year and were responsible for the education of youth and the conduct of all citizens. There was also a council of elders. It included the two kings and 28 citizens over the age of 60, who decided on the issues that would be presented to an assembly made up of male citizens. This assembly did not debate; it only voted on the issues.

A Military State Between 800 and 600 B.C., Sparta was also a military state. Males were sent to military schools at age 7 and spent their childhood learning military discipline. They enrolled in military service at age 20, lived in military barracks until age 30, and stayed in the army until age 60. The two kings led the Spartan army on its campaigns. These campaigns were undertaken for defense as well as for conquest. For example, Spartans did not have enough land. They conquered their neighboring people and made those people into serfs called *helots*; because these people had once owned the land they were now forced to farm, they revolted. As a result of the slave uprising, Sparta needed to be a military state in order to keep these conquered people under control.

The lives of all Spartans were rigidly organized and tightly controlled. Males had more value than females. Physical fitness

CORE CONCEPTS: IDENTITY

Sparta turned its back on the outside world. Foreigners were discouraged from visiting, and Spartans were not allowed to travel abroad, except for military reasons. They were also discouraged from studying literature, philosophy, and the arts, subjects that might encourage new ideas. The art of war was the only Spartan ideal.

was emphasized. Infants who were not physically perfect were left to die, a practice called *infanticide*. Women also upheld strict Spartan values. Like their husbands, they were expected to exercise and remain fit. They also upheld a code of honor in which they encouraged the warlike actions of their husbands and sons.

Athens

By 700 B.C., **Athens** was a unified polis on the peninsula of Attica. It was ruled by a king. Within one hundred years, however, it had turned into an oligarchy, run by wealthy aristocrats who owned the best land.

When Athens was an oligarchy, serious economic problems led to turmoil. Many Athenian farmers who could not pay their debts were forced to become the slaves of the aristocrats. The poor wanted land and an end to their debts. Athens was on the brink of a civil war.

Draco, a judge in 621 B.C., tried to reestablish order by reforming the law code. It contained very harsh punishments, which gives us the word *draconian*. Judges were not allowed to favor their own class over the common people.

Athenian aristocrats reacted to this crisis in 594 B.C. by giving power to Solon. He freed many people who had been made slaves and cancelled land debts. He did not, however, take land from the rich and give it to the poor. He limited the amount of land that a man could own. Solon divided society into four legal groups. The groups had to contain at least two social classes. His reforms were welcome but not sufficient, and the situation led to tyranny.

Under the tyrants, trade increased. One tyrant gave some of the aristocrats' land to the poor. Rebellion ended the tyranny, however, and in 508 B.C., Cleisthenes came to power.

The Beginning of Democracy Cleisthenes built the foundations of Athenian democracy by insuring all citizens had the right to free speech and equality before the law. He created a new council of five hundred that supervised foreign affairs, oversaw the treasury, and proposed laws. The Athenian assembly, made up of all male citizens, regardless of the land they owned, debated the laws freely and openly and then voted on them. An assembly of citizens now played the central role in Athenian government. Although women, foreigners (or immigrant residents), and enslaved persons could not vote, more people had a voice in the government of Athens than in any earlier civilization.

REGENTS WARM-UP

As you read, note ways in which Sparta and Athens differed. How might geographic isolation have contributed to the fierce rivalries and extreme differences between these two city-states?

SECTION 3 CLASSICAL GREECE

The Challenge of Persia

As the Greeks spread throughout the Mediterranean, they clashed with the Persian Empire to the east. Because Greeks living on the Aegean coast objected to the Persians' control, Athens helped this colony, Ionia, to rebel against the Persians. The emperor Darius sought to punish the Greeks. In 490 B.C., the Persians invaded, landing at Marathon, only 26 miles from Athens, but they were turned back. Then the Persians gathered a much larger force. The Athenians also prepared for war and were joined by other Greek city-states, like Sparta.

When the Persian leader Xerxes invaded with a massive force at Thermopylae, a legendary battle occurred in which about 7,000 Greeks held off approximately 180,000 Persians for two days. Despite their defeat, the performance of the Spartans, who led the force and formed its heroic core, has gone down in history as a story of unparalleled valor.

After Themopylae, the Persians burned the city of Athens. The Athenians fought back at the great naval battle called Salamis, defeating the Persian navy. Eventually, the Persians returned home.

The Growth of the Athenian Empire

After the defeat of Persia, Athens took over the leadership of the Greek world. It formed a defensive alliance with the Delian League. Led by Athenians, this alliance freed Greek city-states in the Aegean Sea from Persian control. At the same time, it added to the Athenian Empire.

The Age of Pericles

Pericles was the most important person in Athenian politics between 461 and 429 B.C. Those years are known as the **Age of Pericles**: the height of power and brilliance for Athens. Pericles made reforms to democracy by paying salaries to hold office, which allowed even poor men to be elected. His influence made Athens a center of culture, art, and political growth.

At this time, Athens extended its empire abroad. Democracy also flourished at home. Athens had a **direct democracy**, in which people participated directly in government decision making through mass meetings. In Athens, every male citizen could participate in the governing assembly and vote on all

CORE CONCEPTS: DECISION MAKING

The Athenians also devised the practice of ostracism. Members of the assembly could write the name of a person they considered harmful to the city on an ostrakon, a pottery fragment. A person so named by at least six thousand members was banned from the city for 10 years.

major issues. Not all did, however. Meetings of the assembly were held every 10 days on a hillside east of the Acropolis, and the number present seldom reached six thousand (out of a possible forty-three thousand). Still, any citizen could speak, and even lower-middle class male citizens were eligible for public office. Pericles also paid people for serving on juries.

The Great Peloponnesian War

After the defeat of Persia, the Greek world was divided into the opposing states of Sparta and Athens. Athens headed the Delian League, founded by Pericles. The Delian League was an alliance of city-states. Sparta was not part of the alliance when Athens tried to extend its power onto the Peloponnesian peninsula where Sparta was located. The societies were extremely different, and neither could tolerate the other. Disputes finally led to the Great Peloponnesian War in 431 B.C.

The Spartans surrounded Athens, while Athenians chose to remain behind their city walls instead of meeting the Spartans in an open field of battle. In the second year, a plague killed more than one third of the people in the overcrowded city, and Pericles himself died the following year. The Athenians fought in these wars that lasted about 25 years.

When the Athenian fleet was destroyed, the empire fell. All the Greek states were weakened, though Sparta, Athens, and Thebes all continued to struggle against each other, ignoring the threat growing in Macedonia to the north.

Daily Life in Classical Athens

Slavery was common all over the ancient world, and Athens was no exception. Most people in Athens, except the very poor, owned at least one slave. Rich people often owned large numbers. Slaves worked in industry, in the fields, and in the home as cooks and maids. Some were owned by the state and worked on public construction projects.

The Athenian Economy The economy was based on farming and trade. Greek geography made the cultivation of grain difficult, and Athens had to import about half of its grain. This helped ensure a trading economy.

The Family and the Role of Women The Greek family's primary social function was to produce new citizens. Although considered a citizen who could take part in most religious festivals, an Athenian woman had no other role in public life.

Her chief obligation was to bear children and take care of her family and house. Women received no formal education, were married at age 14 or 15, and were strictly controlled. For example, if they left the house, they had to have a companion.

SECTION 4 THE CULTURE OF CLASSICAL GREECE

Greek Religion

Religion was a major part of Greek life, and temples dedicated to the gods and goddesses were the major buildings in Greek cities.

Greek religion focused on morality, and Greeks honored their gods in rituals. Festivals were held at special locations, such as those dedicated to the worship of Zeus at Olympia or to Apollo at Delphi. Athletic games also honored the gods, such as the first Olympic festival held in 776 B.C. Truces were declared so all the city-states could participate.

Because Greeks wanted to know the will of the gods, they often consulted oracles, earthly beings through whom gods were supposed to speak. The most famous of these oracles was at Delphi, where a priestess was thought to be inspired by Apollo.

Greek Drama

The Greeks created Western drama as we know it today. Their plays were presented in outdoor theaters (amphitheaters) as part of religious festivals. The plays were either tragedies, based on war, justice, the relationship between man and the gods; or comedies, which poked fun at philosophy or politics. Many plays dealt with how men who had too much pride were doomed to fail, a concept called *hubris*. The first Greek dramas were tragedies, which were presented in a trilogy, a related series of three plays with a common theme. The only complete trilogy known today is the *Oresteia* by Aeschylus. It tells the story of Agamemnon and his family after his return from the Trojan War.

Other great Athenian dramatists included Sophocles, the author of *Oedipus Rex* and *Antigone*, a story about a girl's fight for justice; and Euripides, a playwright who questioned traditional values and portrayed war as brutal.

CORE CONCEPTS: BELIEF SYSTEMS

Greek religion was polytheistic. Twelve chief gods and goddesses were believed to live on Mount Olympus, the highest mountain in Greece. They included Zeus, the chief god and father of the gods; Athena, goddess of wisdom and crafts; Apollo, god of the sun and poetry; Ares, god of war; Aphrodite, goddess of love; Poseidon, brother of Zeus and the god of earthquakes and the seas.

CORE CONCEPTS: CULTURE

Greek tragedies presented universal themes that are still relevant today. They examined problems such as the nature of good and evil, the rights of the individual, the nature of divine forces, and the nature of human beings. Greek comedy developed after Greek tragedy. It was used to criticize both politicians and intellectuals. The most famous Greek comic playwright is Aristophanes.

Greek Science and Mathematics

Greeks believed in investigating their world. In spite of their myths, Greeks knew that natural events had specific causes. Greeks sought to gain knowledge about their world and the heavens. They used geometry to further our knowledge. Pythagoras (560–480 B.C.) determined that the hypotenuse is equal to the squared sum of the two sides of a right triangle. Democritus taught that all matter was made of tiny particles, atoms. Hippocrates knew that disease had natural causes and he developed a system of ethics for doctors that we now call the Hippocratic Oath.

Greek Philosophy

Philosophy is an organized system of thought. Many Greek philosophers tried to explain the universe on the basis of unifying principles. For example, Pythagoras thought the essence of the universe could be found in numbers and music.

Sophists The Sophists argued that it was beyond the reach of the human mind to understand the universe. Instead, individuals should look to improve themselves. Sophists also believed there was no absolute right or wrong; the individual looked inward to perceive and pursue good. Many people viewed the Sophist philosophy as harmful to society.

Socrates Socrates taught his students by using what is now called the Socratic Method, a question-and-answer format meant to lead students to use their own reason to find answers. Real knowledge, said Socrates, is already present within each individual. Socrates questioned authority, and he taught his pupils to do the same. He wrote that the unexamined life was not worth living and that to lead a good life, one must avoid extremes. In the changed atmosphere following the Peloponnesian War, however, these attitudes were thought of as negative and corrupting to the city's youth. Socrates was sentenced by a jury to die by drinking hemlock, a poison.

Plato A pupil of Socrates, **Plato** is sometimes considered the greatest philosopher of Western civilization. He was concerned with the question of reality. For him, a world of higher, unchanging Forms has always existed, and it is the job of the trained mind to become aware of and understand these Forms. Plato also sought an ideal state. In *The Republic*, Plato suggested a state in which people were divided into three groups: philosopher-kings, who were trained to rule, at the top; warriors in the middle; and, at the bottom, the masses who are the producers of society. Plato also believed that men and women should have the same education and equal access to all positions. In his dialogues, he wrote about ethics, beauty, and logic.

Aristotle　A pupil of Plato, **Aristotle** was concerned with the analysis and investigation of the world through observation. Aristotle's interests went well beyond philosophy, however. He wrote about politics, poetry, astronomy, geology, biology, physics and more. He was also tutor to Alexander the Great. Until the seventeenth century, science in the Western world remained based largely on the ideas of Aristotle.

The Writing of History

The first western history, that is the first systematic analysis of past events, was written by Herodotus. He was the author of *History of the Persian Wars*. He was a master storyteller; in addition, he traveled widely and questioned many people to gather his information.

Many consider Thucydides, the author of *History of the Peloponnesian War*, the greatest historian of the ancient world and the first scientific historian because of his concern with getting the facts. He placed a great deal of emphasis on the accuracy of his facts. His work also contains remarkable insights into events and human motivations and interactions.

Greek Art

Western art has been greatly influenced by what is called the classical style. Classical Greek art was concerned with expressing eternal ideals: reason, moderation, balance, and harmony. The human being, presented as an object of great beauty, was often its subject matter. Greek sculptors often sculpted an idealized human body. These forms often reflected ideal proportions based on mathematical ratios found in nature and the concept of perfection.

In architecture, the most important form was the temple dedicated to a god or goddess. Temples had central rooms that housed statues of the gods. They were surrounded by a screen of columns that made Greek temples open structures. The most famous of all Greek temples is the Parthenon, built in Athens during the rule of Pericles to honor Athena and dedicated to the glory of Athens and the Athenians. It reflects the principles of classical architecture: calmness, clarity, order, and freedom from unnecessary detail.

CORE CONCEPTS: GOVERNMENT

Aristotle also studied government. For his *Politics*, he looked at 158 states and found three good forms of government: monarchy, aristocracy, and constitutional government. He regarded constitutional government as the best form for most people.

Socrates
↓
Plato
↓
Aristotle

SECTION 5 ALEXANDER AND THE HELLENISTIC KINGDOMS

The Threat of Macedonia

The Macedonians were the northern neighbors of the Greeks. By the end of the fifth century B.C., they emerged as a powerful kingdom. When Philip II took the throne of Macedonia, it became the chief power of the Greek world. He crushed resistance from Athens and other city-states and made plans for a war in which all Greeks were united against Persia. He was assassinated before his invasion could begin, however.

Alexander the Great

When Philip died, his son Alexander, who soon became known as **Alexander the Great**, moved quickly to invade Persia. He not only defeated a large Persian army but he soon had Syria, Palestine, and Egypt under his control. He built Alexandria as the Greek capital of Egypt. It became one of the most important cities in both Egypt and the Mediterranean world.

REGENTS WARM-UP

Study the map. Name ways in which geography did and did not limit Alexander's conquest.

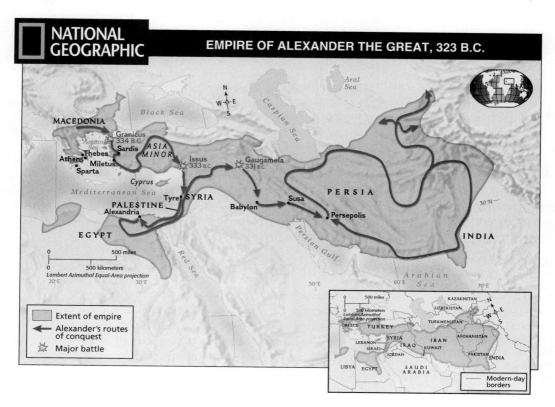

NATIONAL GEOGRAPHIC

EMPIRE OF ALEXANDER THE GREAT, 323 B.C.

Alexander continued to conquer. He took control of the Persian Empire and moved east as far as India. His exhausted soldiers refused to go farther, however. Although he planned other campaigns, he died at the age of 32. His kingdom was divided into three major kingdoms, which were ruled by his generals.

The Legacy of Alexander Through his military and leadership skills, Alexander created a vast empire. This brought large quantities of gold and silver to Greece and Macedonia, stimulating their economies.

Politically, Alexander created or left in his wake many new monarchies. Mainland Greece remained committed to the ideals of the city-state, however.

Culturally, Alexander spread Greek language, architecture, literature, and art throughout Southwest Asia and the Near East. The Greeks also absorbed aspects of the cultures they had invaded.

The Hellenistic Kingdoms

The word *Hellenistic* comes from a Greek word meaning "to imitate the Greeks." Alexander created a **Hellenistic era**, a time when Greek culture and ideas were carried to and influenced population centers. It fused Greek, Egyptian, Middle Eastern, and Asian cultures.

Eventually, four Hellenistic kingdoms emerged as the successors to Alexander: Macedonia, Syria, Pergamum, and Egypt. All of them were eventually conquered by the Romans.

Alexander had envisioned a fusion of culture with the Persians, which he hoped to achieve in part through the marriage of Greek men to Persian women. Those who succeeded Alexander, however, relied only on Greeks and Macedonians to form the new ruling class in the Hellenistic world. All business was transacted in Greek. The ruling class was determined to maintain its privileged position.

Hellenistic Culture

Alexandria became a great cultural center of the Mediterranean. Its library was the largest in ancient times, with more than five hundred thousand scrolls. Together with a museum, the library encouraged the study of literature, the study of language, and scholarly research. With the second largest library, Pergamum, the most important city in Asia Minor, also became a great cultural center of the Hellenistic world.

CORE CONCEPTS: MOVEMENT OF PEOPLE AND GOODS

Hellenistic rulers encouraged a massive spread of Greek colonists to Southwest Asia. Soldiers, administrators, architects, engineers, and actors all made their way to the new Greek cities, which included Alexandria in Egypt. It was the largest city in the Mediterranean region by the first century B.C.

Architecture and Sculpture As new cities were founded and rebuilt, buildings that were characteristic of Greece sprang up. These included baths, theaters, and temples. New Hellenistic kings patronized Greek sculptors. They brought the skill of classical Greece to their work and also added more emotional content and realism. They moved beyond sculpting perfect male figures to creating more lifelike pieces, including the Venus de Milo and the Dying Gaul.

Literature There was a great demand for literature, though little of the work from this period has survived. Appolonius of Rhodes wrote the epic poem called the *Argonautica*, which tells the story of Jason and the Golden Fleece. Theocritus wrote short poems celebrating nature. A new kind of comedy developed that avoided political content and sought to amuse. Its most famous playwright was Menander.

Science In astronomy, Aristarchus developed the theory that the sun was the center of the universe and the Earth rotated around it. Eratosthenes determined that the earth was round and calculated its diameter to within two hundred miles. Euclid wrote the *Elements*, a textbook on plane geometry used until modern times.

Archimedes not only advanced understanding of spheres and cylinders but also determined the value of pi. He is responsible for several inventions, including Archimedes' screw, a device for pumping water out of mines and for irrigation. He is also credited with shouting "Eureka" when he discovered specific gravity.

Philosophy Athens continued to be the center for philosophy in the Hellenistic world. Two new systems of thought, Epicureanism and Stoicism, were established. Epicureanism taught that happiness was the goal of life, and that human beings were free to follow their self-interest. This was achieved in emotional rather than physical ways. For example, a life could be complete when centered on the ideal of friendship. Those who followed this philosophy freed themselves from public activity.

Stoicism, which was taught by Zeno, was also concerned with how people find happiness. Happiness was gained by living in harmony with the will of god. A stoic could bear whatever life brought. Stoics were also good citizens who did not separate themselves from politics or the world.

Diogenes taught that people should practice self-control and independence. He rejected people's desire for wealth, power, and status. The word *cynic* comes from Diogenes' teachings that all people's motives are based on self-interest.

REGENTS WARM-UP

Use the margins of this Review Book or a separate sheet of paper to take notes on, or create a cluster diagram to show, the Hellenistic era.

CHAPTER 5 ROME AND THE RISE OF CHRISTIANITY

CORE CONCEPTS: TECHNOLOGY

To facilitate trade, administer their empire, and defend their territory, the Romans used their engineering skills to construct a great road system. Both goods and ideas flowed over this system, encouraging cultural diffusion.

Chapter Overview

The Romans, who once occupied only a small part of the Italian peninsula, were a great military people who eventually established one of the greatest empires the world has known. They conquered people on the Italian peninsula and then spread out around the Mediterranean, building roads that helped them organize and administrate their empire. Rome began as a republic in 508 B.C. with universal standards of justice but was undermined by civil war and internal conflict. Its decline and fall was the result of many factors, ranging from the size of its empire to the quality of its rulers.

Culturally, the Romans were greatly influenced by the Greeks, whose artistic styles they developed and spread throughout their empire. Later, during Rome's imperial period, Christianity developed. Under the Emperor Constantine, Christianity became the state religion.

As you read this chapter, ask yourself these questions:
(1) How did Rome's geography influence its development?
(2) How did Rome gain control of the lands surrounding the Mediterranean Sea?
(3) Why did the Roman republic develop?
(4) What were the chief political and economic features of the Roman Empire?
(5) What were the major aspects of Roman culture and society?
(6) How were the Greek and Roman civilizations alike and different?
(7) What were the steps in the development of Christianity?
(8) What were the major reasons for the decline and fall of Rome?

Main Ideas and Concepts

- **Human Systems** The Romans were conquerors who spread first over the Italian peninsula and then throughout the Mediterranean world.

- **Conflict** Many civil wars and changes in government resulted from the internal instability of the empire.

- **Culture** Roman culture built upon Greek culture, which the Romans spread throughout their empire.

- **Belief Systems** Christianity was carried throughout the Roman Empire and eventually became the state religion.

- **Power** Despite reforms and the division of the empire into two parts, Rome declined and eventually fell.

People, Places, Terms

The following names and terms will help you to prepare for the Regents Exam in Global History and Geography. You can find an explanation of each name and term in the Glossary at the back of this book, in your textbook, or in another reference source.

assembly	Jesus	plebeians
Augustus	Julius Caesar	republic
Constantine	patricians	senate
dictator	Paul	Twelve Tables
emperor	*Pax Romana*	

SECTION 1 THE RISE OF ROME

The Land and Peoples of Italy

Italy is a narrow peninsula jutting into the Mediterranean and other seas, centrally located between the eastern and western Mediterranean. Its mountains, the Apennines, were not sufficiently rugged to divide the peninsula into small, isolated communities. Good farmland helped Italy support a large population.

Peoples Italy's earliest peoples were Indo-European farmers and herders. One group was the Latins who lived in Latium, the area where Rome is today. Later, both the Greeks and Etruscans settled in Italy. The Greeks settled in southern Italy and Sicily, bringing with them their olives and grapes, their alphabet, and their sculpture, architecture, and literature.

The Etruscans (616–509 B.C.) settled in north-central Italy and took over Rome and most of Latium. Their dress, a toga and short cloak, was adopted by the Romans, as was the organization of their army. They were known for their metal work, which was traded throughout the Mediterranean region.

LINKING GEOGRAPHY TO HISTORY

The location of Rome was especially favorable. On the Tiber River, only eighteen miles from the Mediterranean Sea, the city was far enough inland to be safe from pirates. The seven hills on which Rome was built made it easy to defend.

The Roman Republic

In 509 B.C. the Romans overthrew the last Etruscan king and established a **republic**. In this form of government, the leader is elected and certain citizens have the right to vote.

At first, the republic was surrounded by enemies. From 343–290 B.C., Rome engaged in almost continuous warfare. It crushed the Latin states in Latium and people in the central Apennines. It also defeated Greeks and Etruscans.

It then created a Roman Confederation that gave some peoples full citizenship. Others remained free to run their communities and became allies who had a stake in Rome's success.

Why Rome Was Successful The Romans succeeded for many reasons. One reason was the leadership, courage, and discipline of many Romans. Another reason was that Romans were good diplomats. They knew how to enlist others in their own cause. They also knew how to crush rebellions when needed.

The Roman State

Early Rome was divided into two groups or orders. The **patricians**, who settled the area first, were the great landowners who became Rome's ruling class. The **plebeians** were the less wealthy landholders and tradesmen whose jobs were important. Since they were a large part of the population, they could force the patricians to extend more rights to them. Men in both groups were citizens and could vote.

The chief officers of the Roman Republic were the consuls, who ran the government and led the Roman army into battle, and the praetors, or judges, who were in charge of civil law. In times of emergency, the consuls selected a dictator who had absolute power for six months.

Rome also had a **senate** that consisted of about three hundred patricians. At first, it was an advisory body, but it gained the force of law over time. The Roman Republic also had **Assemblies**. The senate handled foreign affairs and finance.

The Struggle of the Orders The plebeians wanted political and social equality with the patricians. Their struggle for rights went on for hundreds of years. The Assembly, which consisted only of plebeians, was created in 471 B.C. New tribunes of the plebs were also created to protect the plebeians. Tribunes could veto laws passed by the consuls and senate. In 287 B.C., the Assembly

CORE CONCEPTS: IDENTITY

The Romans were also a great military people. They fought on in the face of defeat, and they were excellent strategists. They built colonies and the roads that connected them, allowing them to move quickly through their conquered territory. The Romans were also practical. They did not try to establish the ideal government. Instead, they responded well to problems as they arose.

gained the right to pass laws for all Romans: all male citizens were supposedly equal under law. Because some wealthy families continued to dominate the political offices, however, Rome was still not a democracy.

Roman Law Rome's first code of law was the **Twelve Tables**, a simple system of law that worked in a farming society. As the empire expanded and issues became more complicated, Romans established the Law of Nations. Romans regarded the Law of Nations as a type of universal law based on reason. It led to the establishment of standards of justice applicable to all people. Among these standards are principles still recognized today. For example, a person was innocent until proved otherwise. People accused of wrongdoing were allowed to defend themselves before a judge. A person had the right to know who was accusing him. A judge was expected to weigh evidence carefully before reaching a decision.

Rome Conquers the Mediterranean

The state of Carthage was a rival power to Rome. It included the coast of Northern Africa, southern Spain, Sardinia, Corsica, and western Sicily. Rich and powerful, Carthage had created an enormous trading empire in the western Mediterranean. For 120 years, Carthage and Rome were in conflict.

The First Punic War By 264 B.C., Rome and Carthage began a long struggle for control of the western Mediterranean. The first war started when Romans sent an army to Sicily to challenge Carthaginian control of part of that island. The Romans also created a navy that defeated the Carthaginian fleet. Carthage gave up its rights to Sicily, which became the first Roman province.

The Second Punic War The Second Punic War started in part because Carthage wanted revenge. It added new territory in Spain. The Romans encouraged a revolt in Spain against Carthage. Hannibal, one of the greatest Carthaginian generals, struck back. He took his massive army of men, horses, and elephants into Spain and across the Alps, where he lost most of his elephants. When the Romans met Hannibal head on, however, their power was nearly destroyed.

Over time, however, Rome gradually recovered while Hannibal was weakened. Rome then decided to invade Carthage rather than fight Hannibal in Italy. This caused the Carthaginians to call Hannibal home. In 202 B.C., the Romans crushed his forces. As a result, Carthage lost Spain, which

CORE CONCEPTS: JUSTICE

Laws in the Twelve Tables tended to favor the patricians, but the plebeians at least knew what was legal and what was not. This protected them from the arbitrary interpretation of the law by patrician judges. The Twelve Tables also took into account the laws and customs of the conquered people and the decisions made by judges in other court cases.

became a Roman province, and Rome became the dominant power in the western Mediterranean.

More Conquests When Rome fought the Third Punic War against Carthage, Carthage was completely destroyed. The city was burned, and the inhabitants were sold into slavery. It became the Roman province called Africa.

Rome also battled the Hellenistic states in the eastern Mediterranean. Macedonia became a Roman province with the remainder of Greece under its control. In 129 B.C., Pergamum became Rome's first province in Asia, making Rome master of the Mediterranean Sea.

REGENTS WARM-UP

Regents Exams often require you to summarize information or to draw conclusions about it. How would you sum up the information about the Punic Wars? Ask yourself these questions: Who fought them? What were they mainly fought for? What was lost and gained?

SECTION 2 FROM REPUBLIC TO EMPIRE

Growing Inequality and Unrest

Over time, the Roman Senate, and therefore Rome, came increasingly under the control of a small circle of wealthy and powerful families. At one time, the farmers had been the backbone of Roman society, but due to wars and heavy tax burdens many became part of a growing class of the landless poor. Two aristocrats, the brothers Tiberius and Gaius Gracchus sought to remedy this crisis by calling for the return of land from aristocrats to the landless Romans.

Most aristocrats were threatened and outraged by such a proposal. Some took the law into their own hands and killed those who suggested the idea. A new atmosphere of instability and violence characterized Rome.

A New Role for the Army

The Roman army, and especially its generals, helped bring instability, too. First, in 107 B.C., a Roman general named Marius started to recruit volunteers from the landless poor. The volunteers swore an oath of loyalty to the general—not to Rome—and were promised land in return for their service. This new system gave Roman generals enormous power. Another general, Sulla, used his military power to take control of Rome and wipe out opposition to him. He actually restored power to the Senate later, and hoped to restore a republic, but in the process, he set an example of seizing power that harmed the republic.

The plebians had nothing left except their votes, which they would sell to any politician who promised them a benefit.

Politicians gave the plebians elaborate entertainment and free bread and wine. From this, we get the phrase "bread and circuses," meaning empty promises to voters.

The Collapse of the Republic

For fifty years after Sulla, men competed for power. Then Crassus, Pompey, and **Julius Caesar** formed a triumvirate, a government of three people with equal power. When Crassus died, the Senate decided that Pompey alone should rule and that Caesar should lay down his command, which was in Gaul. Caesar refused. Instead, he kept his army and moved illegally into Italy by crossing the Rubicon, a river that formed the southern boundary of his province. (That is why the phrase "crossing the Rubicon" now means making a decision and not being able to turn back.)

Julius Caesar Caesar marched on Rome, started a civil war, defeated Pompey, and took control of the government. He was made **dictator** in 45 B.C.

Caesar gave land to the poor and increased the size of the Senate to 900, thereby decreasing the power of the original Senate. He reformed the tax system, created more jobs, and made the calendar more accurate. He had great plans for building and conquest. In 44 B.C., however, a group of leading senators assassinated him.

Antony and Octavian A second triumvirate formed after Julius Caesar's death, but it was quickly followed by a split of power by just two men. Octavian, who was Caesar's heir, took the west, and Antony, who had been Caesar's ally and assistant, took the east. They soon came into conflict.

Antony allied himself with Queen Cleopatra of Egypt. Their forces met Octavian's at the Battle of Actium in Greece. Octavian smashed Antony and Cleopatra's army and navy. Octavian took power. The civil wars were over. The republic had ended.

The Age of Augustus

Octavian became the first Roman **emperor**. The senate gave him the title of **Augustus**, meaning "the revered one." The Senator also gave him the title of *imperator*, commander in chief of the army, which is the source of our word *emperor*. Octavian also gave the Senate some powers. For the 41 years of his rule, Octavian tried to unite the empire to serve Rome. He built granaries to supply wheat to the city and established a postal

CORE CONCEPTS: POWER

Octavian, or Augustus Caesar, established a strong army, and he created a praetorian guard, which guarded the emperor. He conquered new areas for Rome. His attempt to conquer Germany failed, however.

service and a fire department for Rome. Many people gained jobs from his immense public works projects.

The Early Empire

The first four emperors after Augustus came from Augustus' natural or adopted family. They were Tiberius, Caligula, Claudius, and Nero. They took more and more powers that Augustus had given to the Senate. They also became increasingly corrupt.

At the beginning of the second century, five so-called good emperors came to power. They were Nerva, Trajan, Hadrian, Antonius Pius, and Marcus Aurelius. These emperors created a period of peace and prosperity known as the *Pax Romana*—the "Roman Peace." Under these emperors, the power of the emperor continued to expand at the expense of the Senate. Yet these emperors also did good works. Trajan created a program that gave funds to poor parents to assist them in raising and educating their children. Trajan and Hadrian were especially active in building public works such as aqueducts, bridges, and roads throughout Rome and the provinces. Marcus Aurelius was also a philosopher who believed that the ruler's life must be a model for the people.

The Height of the Roman Empire During the Early Empire, Rome continued to expand. At its height in the second century, the Roman Empire was one of the greatest states the world had ever known. It stretched from Britain in the north to Egypt in the south, and from Spain and Africa in the east to Syria in the west. It covered about three and one half million square miles.

The privileges of Roman citizenship were granted to many people throughout the empire. Cities were important to the spread of Roman culture and Roman law. Local officials often became Roman agents, administrating and collecting taxes.

Latin was spoken in the western part of the empire and Greek in the east. Roman culture spread and mixed with Greek culture. The result has been called Greco-Roman civilization.

Economic and Social Conditions The Early Empire was a period of great prosperity. Trade brought in luxury goods for the wealthy as well as plenty of grain. Farming continued to be very important within the empire and the underlying basis of Roman prosperity.

The upper classes had great leisure and luxury, but there was an enormous gap between the rich and poor. Large estates ran

CORE CONCEPTS: INTERDEPENDENCE

Language and trade became the bonds that held the empire together. Such shared experiences under Roman rule has helped define Europe as a region.

mainly on slave labor. Small farmers depended on wealthier neighbors to survive. Thousands of unemployed survived on the emperor's handouts of grain.

SECTION 3 CULTURE AND SOCIETY IN THE ROMAN WORLD

Roman Art and Architecture

Romans adopted many features of Greek art. In sculpture, they imitated the Greeks but also produced more realistic statues. In architecture, Romans used Greek features and styles such as colonnades and rectangular buildings, but they also added forms based on curved lines. The arch, the vault, and the dome were Roman features. The Romans were also the first to use concrete on a massive scale. The most impressive structures were the Pantheon, a domed structure designed to honor the gods, and the Coliseum, an amphitheater.

The Romans developed great engineering skills. They had learned about drainage and sewers from the Etruscans. They constructed a network of about 180,000 miles of roads throughout the empire. They also built bridges and aqueducts to carry water as far as 30 miles.

Roman Literature

The Augustan Age was the highpoint for Roman literature. The poet Virgil wrote his greatest work, the *Aeneid*, at this time. This epic poem portrays Aeneas, the ideal Roman, fulfilling his mission to establish the Romans in Italy and start Rome on its divine mission to rule the world.

Horace, who wrote *Satires*, pointed out the "follies and vices of his age." Livy was Rome's best-known nonfiction writer. His 142-volume *History of Rome* celebrated Rome's greatness. Though marred by some factual inaccuracy, his work was the standard history of Rome for many years.

The Roman Family

The Roman family was headed by the *paterfamilias*, the dominant male. The family included the wife, sons and their wives and children, unmarried daughters, and slaves. All Roman upper-class children, male and female, learned to read. Boys also learned skills to prepare them to be soldiers. At the age of 16, a young Roman man stopped wearing the purple-edged toga of childhood and changed to a plain white, adult toga.

Attitudes Toward Women Some families educated girls. Most girls were married at about the same age that boys began their secondary education. Throughout life, women had male guardians, which were either their father, husband, brother, or the nearest male relative.

Changing Roles By the second century A.D., roles had changed. Women no longer needed guardians. Fathers could not sell their children into slavery or have them put to death. Upper-class women could attend races, the theater, and events in the amphitheater. They could not officially participate in politics, but some influenced politics through their husbands.

Slavery

Slavery was common all over the ancient world, but no people had more slaves than the Romans. Large numbers of foreign people who had been captured in wars were brought back as slaves. Greek slaves were in demand as tutors, musicians, doctors, artists, businessmen, and craftspeople. Slaves of all nationalities were used as cooks, valets, waiters, cleaners, and gardeners. Slaves also built roads and public buildings, and they farmed the large estates of the wealthy as well as those of small Roman farmers. They often lived under harsh conditions.

Roman Economy

The Romans were heavily engaged in commerce, the business of trade. Their trade routes surrounded the Mediterranean, which they called "Mare Nostrum," or Our Sea. They linked their trade route to the major route from China, the Silk Road. Their extensive trade brought goods and also ideas, like those of the Christians, throughout the empire.

The Romans supported their empire with a huge tax system that was based on a census, counting the people and their wealth.

Slavery was one of the reasons the economy collapsed. Instead of hiring Romans to work, wealthy patricians and plebians bought slaves. That left an enormous number of Roman citizens poor and discontented.

Public Programs Rome had grand and magnificent public buildings that included temples, markets, baths, theaters, government buildings, and amphitheaters. Entertainment was

CORE CONCEPTS: HUMAN RIGHTS

Some slaves revolted against their owners. The most famous revolt was led by the gladiator Spartacus. 70,000 slaves joined in this revolt, which defeated several Roman armies. When the revolt was crushed, 6,000 followers of Spartacus were crucified.

provided in circuses. The poet Juvenal once wrote that the people, many of whom got their grain from the emperors, cared only about bread and circuses. Entertainments included chariot races, dramatic performances, and gladiatorial contests.

SECTION 4 THE DEVELOPMENT OF CHRISTIANITY

Roman Religion

The official state religion of Rome focused on the worship of a number of gods and goddesses including Jupiter, the chief god; Hera, the wife of Jupiter; Mars, the god of war; Venus, the god of love; Diana, the goddess of the hunt; and Pluto, the god of the underworld.

Jewish Unrest

The Jewish people had had considerable freedom in Hellenistic times, but Judaea came under Roman rule by A.D. 6. Reactions to that rule varied from a desire to cooperate to a desire to overthrow the Romans. The Jews, who are monotheistic, clashed with the Romans over the Romans' insistence that the emperor was a god. When a revolt against Rome began in A.D. 66, the Romans crushed the opposition and the Jewish temple at Jerusalem was destroyed in A.D. 72. Later, the Jews were expelled from Jerusalem in what is now known as the Diaspora, or the scattering.

The Rise of Christianity

A few decades before the Jewish revolt, a man named **Jesus** traveled throughout Judaea and neighboring Galilee. He preached messages of humility, charity, and love toward others, ethical concepts that would help shape the value system of Western civilization. He explained that he had come to fulfill the work of the prophets and to bring the salvation that God had promised to Israel.

Jesus eventually became a controversial figure, and some opponents turned him over to the Roman authorities. The Romans disliked his pacifist teachings, and the Jews disliked his criticism of their practices. The procurator, or the official in charge, of Judaea was Pontius Pilate. He ordered that Jesus be crucified. After that event, his followers said Jesus had risen

CORE CONCEPTS: BELIEF SYSTEMS

The Romans believed that the observation of proper rituals by state priests brought them into a right relationship with the gods. Indeed, they believed that their success in creating an empire meant that they had achieved a favored position. The Romans were tolerant of other religions as long as the followers paid taxes and would serve in the army. They allowed the worship of native gods and goddesses throughout the provinces. They even adopted some of the local gods.

CORE CONCEPTS: BELIEF SYSTEMS

The teachings of early Christianity were passed on orally. Paul and other followers also wrote letters, or epistles, outlining Christian beliefs. Accounts of the life and teachings of Jesus, written between A.D. 40 and 100, became known as the Gospels. They form the core of the New Testament, the second part of the Christian Bible.

from the dead and appeared to them. They called Jesus the Messiah, which means the "anointed one," and referred to the long-awaited savior of the Jewish people.

The Spread of Christianity After the death of Jesus, his apostles carried messages of his life and beliefs. These apostles, men who had followed or been influenced by Christ, became leaders in the spread of Christianity. Among them was Simon Peter, a leader of the apostles during Jesus' lifetime. Another was **Paul**, who joined the movement later, and who brought the message of Jesus both to the Jews and to the Gentiles (non-Jews). He traveled throughout Asia Minor and the Aegean establishing Christian communities. (The words *Christ* and *Christian* come from *Christos*, the Greek term for Messiah.)

Paul taught that Jesus was the Savior, the Son of God. His death made up for the sins of all humans. By accepting Jesus as savior, people could be saved from sin and be reconciled to God.

Roman Persecution At first the Romans paid little attention to the Christians. Later, however, they saw Christianity as harmful to the Roman state, because Christians did not worship the state gods or the emperors, who, beginning with Augustus, were officially made gods by the Roman Senate. They tried to eliminate this threat through systematic persecution.

The Triumph of Christianity

There were several reasons for the eventual rise of Christianity. First, persecution may have strengthened the religion by forcing followers to organize themselves and establish a structure. This included the clergy (the church and its leaders) and the laity (the church members).

The Christian message also had great power in contrast to the official state-based religion of Rome, which was impersonal and existed for the good of Rome. The Christian message was personal and offered salvation and eternal life to individuals. The poor and outsiders were drawn to its message of a loving god and reward in heaven for good deeds.

The Christian belief system was also familiar. Like religions that had come before, it offered immortality as the result of the sacrificial death of a savior-god.

Christianity also gave its followers a sense of belonging. Communities formed based on its values. In addition, while Christianity appealed to all classes, its message that all were

CORE CONCEPTS: CHANGE

The Romans began persecuting the Christians during the reign of Nero (A.D. 54–68). He blamed them for a fire that destroyed much of Rome and subjected them to cruel deaths. In the second century, persecution of Christians diminished. By the end of the reign of the five good emperors, Christians were a small but strong minority in the Roman world.

REGENTS WARM-UP

Past Regents Exams have included questions that require knowledge of the similarities and differences between Christianity and Judaism. Keep in mind that both are monotheistic and arose in the same place, but the belief in the arrival of the messiah is a major difference.

equal in the sight of god was especially compelling to the poor and powerless.

While some persecution still occurred in the third century, the growing force of Christianity could not be denied. Constantine became the first Christian emperor in the fourth century. In A.D. 313, he made Christianity equal to all other religions in Rome. Under Theodosius the Great, Romans adopted Christianity as their official religion.

SECTION 5 DECLINE AND FALL

The Decline

A period of conflict and confusion followed the death of the last of the five good emperors, Marcus Aurelius, in A.D. 180. Civil wars were a great problem. Those with power to seize the throne just took it. There were 22 emperors over a period of fifty years. At the same time, Persians and Germanic tribes invaded Roman territory.

Economic and Military Problems The plague, an epidemic disease, also hit the empire. Without workers, fields went untended and industry flagged. Trade declined. With all these problems, plus invaders and civil wars, armies were needed more than ever, but not enough men could be found or paid to keep them strong.

The Reforms of Diocletian and Constantine Two emperors, Diocletian and **Constantine**, restored some order to the state and began a new period of rule called the Late Roman Empire. Changes at this time included a new structure of government, a rigid economic and social system, and a new state religion, Christianity.

Because the empire was so large, Diocletian (A.D. 284–305) divided it into four units, each with its own ruler, though Diocletian claimed the highest authority. Both Diocletian and Constantine also worked to expand the Roman bureaucracy and the army.

Constantine's City Constantine's biggest project was the construction of a new capital city in the east, which was developed for defensive reasons. It was called Byzantium and later renamed Constantinople. (Today it is Istanbul.) It became the center of the Eastern Roman Empire and one of the great cities of the world.

CORE CONCEPTS: ECONOMIC SYSTEMS

Both Diocletian and Constantine also created new economic and social policies. To deal with the problem of inflation, a rapid increase in prices, Diocletian set wage and price controls. Because of the labor shortage, both emperors required that people remain in their designated vocations, so that jobs like baking became hereditary. Many policies established by the two emperors were temporarily successful, but they were also based on tight control and coercion. Ultimately, they did not save the empire and may have even worked against it.

The Fall

After Constantine, the empire continued to be divided into western and eastern parts. The capital of the Western Roman Empire remained in Rome. The capital of the Eastern Roman Empire was Constantinople.

Invading Germanic Tribes The Western Roman Empire gradually fell to invaders. When the Huns moved out of Asia and into Eastern Europe, they caused the movement of the Germanic Visigoths. In 410, the Visigoths sacked Rome. Other tribes invaded, too. The Vandals invaded Spain and Africa and also sacked Rome. The Germanic army unseated the emperor Romulus Augustus in A.D. 476 This is generally taken as the date of the fall of the Western Roman Empire. The Eastern Roman Empire, or the Byzantine Empire, continued to thrive with its center at Constantinople.

Reasons for Collapse Many factors contributed to the fall of Rome. No single reason can sufficiently explain what happened, but the empire had acquired more land than it could effectively administrate and defend. Other theories include these:

- Christianity's emphasis on a spiritual kingdom weakened Roman military virtues.

- Traditional Roman values declined as foreigners gained influence in the empire.

- Lead poisoning, through leaden water pipes and cups, caused a mental decline of the population.

- Plague wiped out one-tenth of the population.

- Rome failed to advance technologically because of slavery.

- Rome was unable to establish a workable political system.

- The size of the empire was too large to effectively protect.

- The use of mercenaries, hired soldiers rather than citizen soldiers, weakened the defense, since mercenaries had no sense of patriotism.

PRACTICING FOR THE REGENTS

Part I Multiple-Choice Questions

The following multiple-choice questions come from past Regents High School Examinations. Test your understanding of global history by answering each of these items. Circle the number of the word or expression that best completes each statement or question. Test-taking tips can be found in the margins for some questions. For additional help, see Taking the Regents Exam on pages ix–xxxv of this Review Book.

Base your answer to question 1 on the diagram below and on your knowledge of social studies.

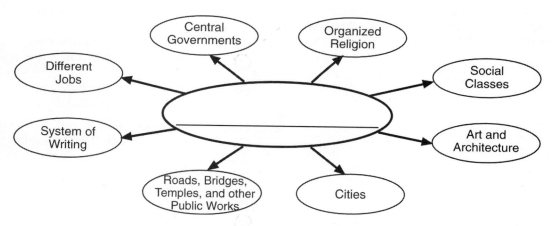

Source: *Guide to the Essentials of World History*, Prentice–Hall

1 Which title best completes this diagram?
   (1) Elements of a Civilization
   (2) Features of a Nomadic Lifestyle
   (3) Basic Components of the Paleolithic Age
   (4) Human Life 50,000 Years Ago

2 When studying ancient civilizations, a geographer would be most interested in looking at
   (1) language as a form of expression
   (2) family structure
   (3) climatic influences on food production
   (4) standards for leadership

3 Early peoples who moved frequently as they searched for the food they needed for survival are called
   (1) hunters and gatherers
   (2) village dwellers
   (3) subsistence farmers
   (4) guild members

57

REGENTS WARM-UP

Question 5 asks you to draw a cross-regional connection relating to factors that have influenced the development of ancient civilization.

4   Studying oral histories, archaeological evidence, and cultural histories are methods most often used by
(1) economists
(2) anthropologists
(3) philosophers
(4) political scientists

5   One reason the Euphrates, Indus, Nile, and Tigris valleys became centers of early civilization is that these valleys had
(1) borders and elevations that were easy to defend
(2) rich deposits of coal and iron ores
(3) the means for irrigation and transportation
(4) locations in regions of moderate climate and abundant rainfall

6   Hammurabi's Code, the Ten Commandments, and the Twelve Tables were all significant to their societies because they established
(1) democratic governments
(2) official religions
(3) rules of behavior
(4) economic systems

7   Hieroglyphic and cuneiform systems provided the basis for the development of
(1) subsistence farming
(2) painting and sculpture
(3) oral traditions
(4) recorded history

8   The history of which classical civilization was shaped by the monsoon cycle, the Himalaya Mountains, and the Indus River?
(1) Maurya Empire
(2) Babylonian Empire
(3) ancient Greece
(4) ancient Egypt

9   The terms Brahma, dharma, and moksha are most closely associated with
which religion?
    (1) Judaism   (3) Hinduism
    (2) Islam   (4) animism

Base your answers to question 10 on the diagram below and on your knowledge of social
studies.

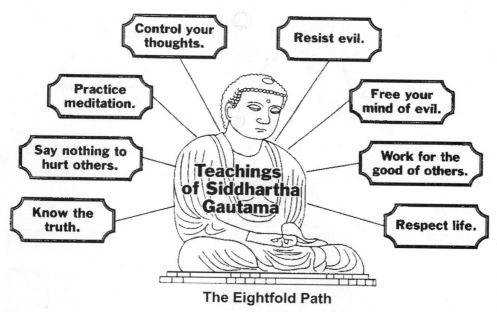

The Eightfold Path

Source: *The Human Experience*, Glencoe

10   The diagram illustrates the key concepts
of which religion?
    (1) Islam   (3) Hinduism
    (2) Christianity   (4) Buddhism

11   During the centuries of dynastic rule,
the Chinese rejected other cultures as
inferior to their own. This situation
illustrates the concept of
    (1) ethnocentrism
    (2) imperialism
    (3) social mobility
    (4) cultural diffusion

REGENTS WARM-UP

If you are not familiar with terms given in the question, you may still be able to answer it correctly. For example, in question 12, you may not be sure about either the Golden Rule or the Judeo-Christian teaching, yet still select the quotation from Confucius.

12 Which quotation from the teachings of Confucius is most similar to the Golden Rule from Judeo-Christian teaching?
(1) "If a ruler is upright, all will go well without orders."
(2) "By nature, men are pretty much alike. It is learning and practice that set them apart."
(3) "While a father or mother is alive, a son should not travel far."
(4) "Do not do to others what you do not wish for yourself."

13 The five relationships taught by Confucius encouraged people to
(1) improve their position in life
(2) maintain social and political order
(3) respect and worship nature
(4) serve the needs of religious leaders

Base your answers to questions 14 and 15 on the illustration below and on your knowledge of social studies.

Trade Routes, East to West

[Map showing trade routes from East to West with the following labels: Gobi Desert, Camels Felt, Lan-chou, Sal ammoniac, Slaves, Almonds, Jet, Tashkent, Lop Nor, Antioch, Glassware Woven goods, Samarkand, Lapis lazuli, Niva, Mediterranean Sea, Rock crystal, Khotan, Alexandria, Metals Woven goods, Bactra, Jade, TIBET, Camels Kohlrabi cabbage, Euphrates R., Taxila, Saffron, PERSIA, Nile R., Mathura, Ganges R., AFRICA, ARABIA, Spinach, Tamralipti, Amber Peacock feathers, Barygaza, Red Sea, INDIA, Jasmine Drugs Sandalwood, Bay of Bengal, Arabian Sea, Incense, Pepper, Nicobar Is. Coconuts, CEYLON Rubies; Legend: — Silk route, - - - Routes by sea, ... Overland routes, • Cities]

14 Which conclusion is supported by information provided by the map?
  (1) Traders depended mainly on rivers as avenues of transportation.
  (2) More products were carried on the ocean than across the land.
  (3) Silk was the principal product traded.
  (4) Traders often combined sea and land routes.

15 Which concept is illustrated by the map?
  (1) socialism
  (2) interdependence
  (3) self-sufficiency
  (4) cultural isolation

16 The term "subsistence farmers" refers to people who grow
  (1) enough food to feed an entire village
  (2) food to sell in village markets
  (3) just enough food to meet the needs of the immediate family
  (4) a single cash crop

17 In which region did China's earliest civilizations develop?
  (1) Gobi Desert
  (2) Himalaya Mountains
  (3) Yellow River Valley
  (4) Tibetan Plateau

18 How did geography influence the development of ancient Greece?
  (1) Rich farmland led to dependence on agriculture.
  (2) Excellent harbors encouraged seafaring trade.
  (3) Flat plains made centralized rule possible.
  (4) Tropical climate discouraged urban development.

19 The ideals developed in the Athens of Pericles and in Republican Rome influenced the development of
  (1) a parliament in Britain
  (2) military juntas in Latin America
  (3) a communist government in China
  (4) a theocracy in Iran

20 One way in which the Han dynasty and the Roman Empire were similar is that both
  (1) governed large areas around the Mediterranean Sea
  (2) created democratic societies in which people elected their government officials
  (3) developed a social system in which great equality existed
  (4) promoted unity and communication by building a strong system of roads

-5

Part II   Thematic Essay Question

The following thematic essay question comes from past Regents High School Examinations.

Directions: Write a well-organized essay that includes an introduction, several paragraphs addressing the task below, and a conclusion.

Theme: Geography

> Geographic factors have influenced historical developments and historical events of nations and regions.

Task:

> Choose *two* nations and/or regions and for each
>
> - Identify and describe *two* geographic factors in each nation and/or region
> - Explain how *each* factor has influenced the historical development or a specific historical event in each nation and/or region

You may use any nation and/or region and any geographic factors from your study of global history and geography. **Do *not* use the United States in your answer**. Some factors you might wish to consider include deserts, river valleys, or oil in the Middle East; river valleys, monsoons, or the Himalaya Mountains in India; natural resources or the island location of Japan or Great Britain; the river valley or the desert in Egypt; the regular coastline or resources in South Africa; the Amazon rain forest or the Andes Mountains in South America.

You are *not* limited to these suggestions.

Guidelines:

In your essay, be sure to

- Develop all aspects of the task

- Support the theme with relevant facts, examples, and details

- Use a logical and clear plan of organization, including an introduction and a conclusion that are beyond a restatement of the theme

Part III   Document-Based Question

This exercise is designed to test your ability to work with historical documents. It is similar to the document-based questions you will see on the Regents Examination. While you are asked to analyze three historical documents, the exercise on the actual exam will include more documents. Some of the documents have been edited for the purposes of the question. As you analyze the documents, take into account the source of each document and any point of view that may be presented in the document.

Historical Context:

> The geographic factors of location and availability of resources led to the rise of early civilizations and empires.

Task: Using information from the documents and your knowledge of global history, answer the questions that follow each document in Part A. Your answers to the questions will help you write the Part B essay, in which you will be asked to

> • Explain how geographic factors such as location and physical features influenced the political development and history of three early civilizations or empires. Explain how geography contributed to the rise of each civilization and encouraged or limited its spread

Part A Short-Answer Questions

Directions: Analyze the documents and answer the short-answer questions that follow each document in the space provided.

Document 1

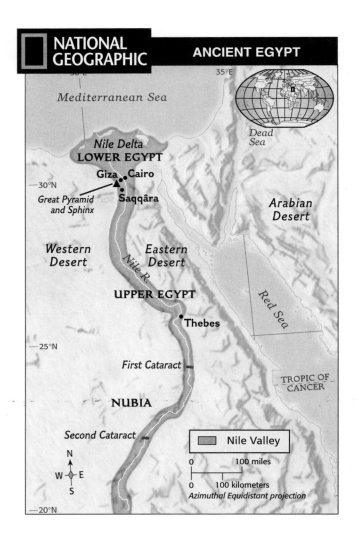

NATIONAL GEOGRAPHIC — ANCIENT EGYPT

river flows north

1a   What do the names Upper Egypt and Lower Egypt suggest about the topography of Egypt?

   lower egypt would refer to the lower elevation and upper egypt would be near mountains w/ high elevation.

b   What was the relationship between the Nile River and settlement in Ancient Egypt?

   The people of Ancient Egypt depended on the Nile River for transportation, water, and food

Document 2

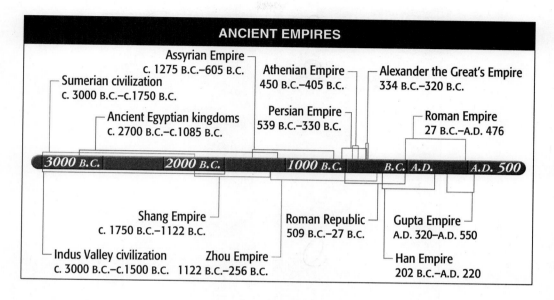

ANCIENT EMPIRES

Assyrian Empire
c. 1275 B.C.–605 B.C.

Sumerian civilization
c. 3000 B.C.–c.1750 B.C.

Ancient Egyptian kingdoms
c. 2700 B.C.–c.1085 B.C.

Athenian Empire
450 B.C.–405 B.C.

Persian Empire
539 B.C.–330 B.C.

Alexander the Great's Empire
334 B.C.–320 B.C.

Roman Empire
27 B.C.–A.D. 476

3000 B.C.   2000 B.C.   1000 B.C.   B.C. A.D.   A.D. 500

Shang Empire
c. 1750 B.C.–1122 B.C.

Indus Valley civilization
c. 3000 B.C.–c.1500 B.C.

Zhou Empire
1122 B.C.–256 B.C.

Roman Republic
509 B.C.–27 B.C.

Han Empire
202 B.C.–A.D. 220

Gupta Empire
A.D. 320–A.D. 550

2   Which empire lasted the shortest time, and which empire lasted the longest?

Alexander the Great's Empire = shortest
Ancient Egyptian Kingdoms = longest

Document 3

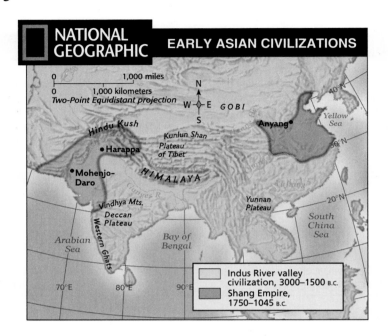

NATIONAL GEOGRAPHIC **EARLY ASIAN CIVILIZATIONS**

3a What geographic features are common to each of these civilizations?

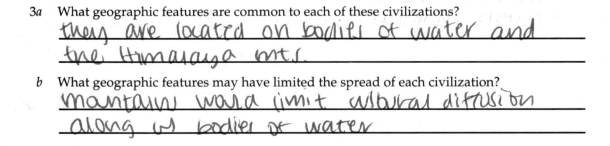

they are located on bodies of water and the Himalaya mts.

b What geographic features may have limited the spread of each civilization?

mantains would limit cultural difusion along w bodies of water

Part B   Essay

Directions: Write a well-organized essay that includes an introduction, several paragraphs, and a conclusion.

Use evidence from at least **two** documents in the body of the essay. Support your response with relevant facts, examples, and details. Include additional outside information.

Historical Context:

The geographic factors of location and availability of resources led to the rise of early civilizations and empires.

Task: Using information from the documents and your knowledge of global history and geography, write an essay in which you

- Explain how geographic factors such as location and physical features influenced the political development and history of three early civilizations or empires. Explain how geography contributed to the rise of each civilization and encouraged or limited its spread

Guidelines:

In your essay, be sure to

- Develop all aspects of the task

- Incorporate information from *at least two* documents

- Incorporate relevant outside information

- Support the theme with relevant facts, examples, and details

- Use a logical and clear plan of organization, including an introduction and conclusion that are beyond a restatement of the theme

UNIT 2 NEW PATTERNS OF CIVILIZATIONS, 500–1200

Unit 2 Overview

By the beginning of the first millennium A.D., the great states of the ancient world were mostly in decline. On the ruins of these ancient empires, new patterns of civilization began to take shape. Some of these new societies built upon elements of earlier civilizations, even as they moved in unique directions.

Religion played a large role in shaping these civilizations. The rise of Islam influenced a great number of societies as the Arab Empire reached into Africa, Asia, and Europe. Buddhism also diffused from India into China and Southeast Asia. The influence of these and other religions waxed and waned as empires came to power and then collapsed.

Societies were being increasingly linked by trade. While large sections of populations remained dependent on farming, trade between civilizations allowed cities to flourish and technological and cultural advancements to spread throughout the world.

Unit 2 Objectives

After studying this unit, students should be able to

1. identify how Arab, African, and Asian empires spread;
2. compare medieval Europe with previous civilizations;
3. describe feudalism, the influence of the Roman Catholic Church, and the impact of the Crusades.

PREPARING FOR THE REGENTS

This entire book is set up to help you grasp the facts, main ideas, and concepts needed to do well on your Regents Exam. Notes in the margin include core concepts, test-taking tips, and more. Use blank spaces in the margins to answer questions raised in the text or to jot down key points. Before each unit of study, skim through the exams at the back of the book to develop a sense of what your state wants you to know about your world.

CHAPTER 6   THE WORLD OF ISLAM

Chapter Overview

With the rise of Muhammad as a religious and political leader, the religion of Islam was born. In the years after Muhammad's death, the great Arab Empire covered parts of Africa, Asia, and Europe. The Empire's economy was based on thriving trade. As dynasties rose and fell, power shifted to different centers, including Damascus, Baghdad, and Cairo.

Overall, the period of the Arab Empire had widespread impact. Across this vast territory, Islam provided the inspiration for art, architecture, literature, and philosophy. While at its height, Islamic civilization was the source of major cultural and scientific contributions to Europe and the world.

As you read this chapter, ask yourself these questions:
(1) Who was Muhammad and what are the basic tenets of Islam?
(2) How did the Islamic religion grow and expand to other areas of the world?
(3) What events led to the division of Islam into Shiite and Sunni branches?
(4) What were the social structures in Islamic societies and how did the Arabic world contribute to the world's science and culture?

**CORE CONCEPTS:
CULTURE**

The Arab empire gave rise to a rich civilization and many advances in science, mathematics, art and literature. These advances spread new knowledge to Europe.

Main Ideas and Concepts

- **Diversity** Many different peoples and lands were ruled by the Muslims.
- **Economic Growth and Development** Trade was extremely important to the growth of the Muslim empire.
- **Culture** Muslim society contributed in many ways to the advancement of science and culture.
- **Interdependence** It was through the Muslim world that new learning was spread to Europe.

People, Places, Terms

The following names and terms will help you to prepare for the Regents Exam in Global History and Geography. You can find an explanation of each name and term in the Glossary at the back of this book, in your textbook, or in another reference source.

Abbasid dynasty	**Mecca**	**shari'ah**
Allah	**Medina**	**Shiite**
caliph	**mosque**	**sultan**
Five Pillars	**Muhammad**	**Sunni**
hajj	**Quran**	**Umayyad dynasty**

SECTION 1   THE RISE OF ISLAM

The Arabs

The Arabs were nomadic bedouins of the Arabian Peninsula who moved constantly to find water and food for their animals. Arab tribes were ruled by sheikhs. The Arabs lived as farmers, sheepherders, and later, as traders. The Arabs trace their ancestors to Abraham and his son Ishmael, who were believed to have built at **Mecca** the Kaaba, a house of worship whose cornerstone was a sacred stone called the Black Stone. Though they were polytheistic, the Arabs recognized a supreme god named **Allah**.

CORE CONCEPTS: MOVEMENT OF PEOPLE AND GOODS

The communities on the Arabian peninsula began to prosper when a new trade route from the Mediterranean through Mecca to Yemen and by ship across the Indian Ocean became more popular because of political disorder along the old route.

The Arabian Peninsula took on a new importance when political disorder in Mesopotamia and Egypt made the usual trade routes in Southwest Asia too dangerous. A safer trade route that went through Mecca to present-day Yemen and then by ship across the Indian Ocean became more popular. Communities along this route prospered. Tensions arose, however, as wealthy merchants showed little concern for the welfare of poorer clanspeople and slaves.

The Life of Muhammad   Born in Mecca around 570, **Muhammad** became troubled by the gap between the poor and the rich. Muslims believe Muhammad received revelations from God via the angel Gabriel while meditating in a cave in 610. The **Quran**, the holy book of Islam, comes from these revelations. The Quran contains an ethical code consisting of the **Five Pillars** of Islam. Those who practice the religion of Islam are called Muslims. Muhammad started preaching, but he and his followers were persecuted in Mecca. In 622, they fled to Medina and built up their power. There, Muhammad became both a religious and a political leader. This flight is called the *Hijira,* and 622 became the first year of the Muslim calendar. After eight years, Muhammad led a military force that easily conquered Mecca. Muhammad died as Islam was beginning to spread throughout the Arabian Peninsula. All Muslims are encouraged to make a pilgrimage to Mecca, called the **hajj.**

The Teachings of Muhammad Like Christianity and Judaism, Islam has only one God, Allah. Unlike Christianity, Islam does not believe its first preacher was divine. Muslims also believe that Abraham, Moses, and Jesus were earlier prophets. Muhammad is Allah's prophet. Muslims believe that those who follow the Five Pillars of Islam are guaranteed a place in eternal paradise.

The Five Pillars of Islam:

- **Belief:** Believing there is no deity but the One God, and Muhammad is his messenger

- **Prayer:** Performing the prescribed prayers five times a day

- **Charity:** Giving part of one's wealth to the poor ("giving alms")

- **Fasting:** Refraining from food and drink from dawn to sunset through the month of Ramadan

- **Pilgrimage:** Making a pilgrimage to Mecca once in a lifetime

CORE CONCEPTS: CULTURE

Islam is not just a set of religious beliefs but a way of life as well. A law code known as the **shari'ah**, based on scholars' interpretations of the Quran, applies the teachings of the Quran to daily life and provides believers with practical laws to follow.

SECTION 2 THE ARAB EMPIRE AND ITS SUCCESSORS

Creation of an Arab Empire

Muhammad died without naming a successor. Some of his closest followers chose Abu Bakr, a wealthy merchant and Muhammad's father-in-law, to be **caliph,** or successor to Muhammad.

Arab Conquest Under Abu Bakr's leadership, the Arabs expanded over Arabia and beyond. The Quran permitted jihad, or "struggle in the way of God." They defeated Byzantines to take over Syria; they also added Egypt and other parts of northern Africa to the Arab empire. The Arabs conquered the entire Persian Empire by 650.

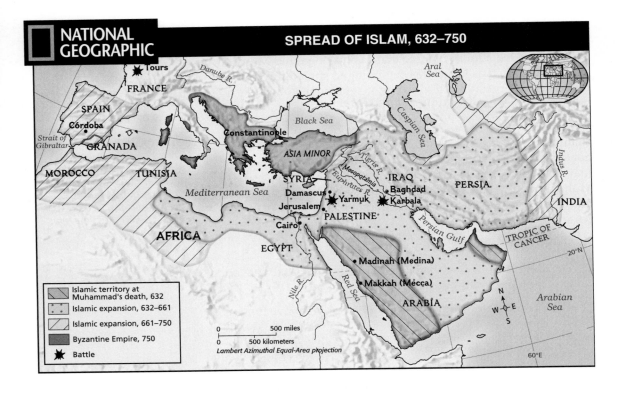

NATIONAL GEOGRAPHIC

SPREAD OF ISLAM, 632–750

Map legend:
- Islamic territory at Muhammad's death, 632
- Islamic expansion, 632–661
- Islamic expansion, 661–750
- Byzantine Empire, 750
- ✶ Battle

0 — 500 miles
0 — 500 kilometers
Lambert Azimuthal Equal-Area projection

LINKING GEOGRAPHY TO HISTORY

Study the map. Notice the directions in which the Arab empire expanded. What geographical factors affected the expansion?

Arab Rule Early caliphs ruled their far-flung empire from Medina. The problem of legitimate succession remained, however, and early caliphs, including Ali, Muhammad's son-in-law, were assassinated.

The Umayyads

In 661, Mu'awiyah, the governor of Syria and a rival to Ali, became caliph. He made the office of caliph hereditary. He also established the **Umayyad dynasty** and moved the capital of the Arab Empire from Medina to Damascus, in Syria.

Umayyad Conquests At the beginning of the eighth century, the Arab armies defeated the Berbers, a pastoral people living along the Mediterranean coast of North Africa. Around 710, combined Berber and Arab forces moved into southern Spain. By 725, most of Spain had become a Muslim state with its center at Córdoba.

In 717, a Muslim attack on Constantinople was driven back. This created an uneasy frontier in southern Asia Minor between the Byzantine Empire and the Islamic world.

A Split in Islam Many Muslims of non-Arab background did not like the way local administrators favored Arabs. In what is now Iraq, Hussein, second son of Ali, led an important revolt against Umayyad rule. Though unsuccessful, this struggle led to the split of Islam into two groups. The **Shiite** Muslims accept only the descendants of Ali as the true rulers of Islam. Today, most Shiite Muslims live in Iraq and Iran. The **Sunni** Muslims, who are today the majority, accepted the Umayyads as rulers.

The Abbasid Dynasty

Umayyad leadership was weakened by corruption and the resentment of conquered peoples. In 750, Abu al-Abbas overthrew the dynasty and set up the **Abbasid dynasty**, which lasted until 1258. ⑤ 750 - 1258

Abbasid Rule The Abbasids built a new capital at Baghdad. The move of the capital eastward increased Persian influence and encouraged a new cultural outlook. Under the Umayyads, warriors had been seen as the ideal citizens. Under the Abbasids, judges, merchants, and government officials were the new heroes. All Muslims, regardless of ethnic background, could hold both civil and military offices. Many Arabs began to intermarry with conquered peoples.

The Abbasid dynasty experienced a period of splendid rule during the ninth century. The reign of Harun al-Rashid is often called a golden age. Known for charity, Harun al-Rashid also supported artists and writers, while his son was a great patron of learning. He supported the study of astronomy and created a foundation for translating classical Greek works.

Because Arabs now controlled trade routes to the East, Baghdad became the center of an enormous trade empire that extended into Asia, Africa, and Europe, greatly adding to the riches of the Islamic world.

Decline and Division Problems of succession also plagued the Abbasids and weakened their rule. Vast wealth also gave rise to corruption. Eventually, rulers of the provinces of the Abbasid Empire began to break away from the central authority and establish independent dynasties. Spain had established its own caliphate when a prince of the Umayyad dynasty fled there in 750. Morocco became independent, and a new dynasty under the

CORE CONCEPTS: CULTURE

The Umayyads built the famous Dome of the Rock Mosque in Jerusalem. The mosque houses the rock where Muhammad reportedly ascended into heaven. It is one of the most sacred sites in Islam.

REGENTS WARM-UP

The terms *Sunni* and *Shiite* can help you explain deeply rooted conflicts in the Muslim world. Be sure you can distinguish these terms.

CORE CONCEPTS: GOVERNMENT

During the Abbasid dynasty, the caliph became more like a king, and the bureaucracy assisting the caliph became more complex. A prime minister, known as a vizier, advised the caliph. The caliph did not attend government meetings of his council, but sat behind a screen listening and whispering orders to his vizier.

Fatimids was established in Egypt, with its capital at Cairo. The Muslim Empire was now politically divided.

The Seljuk Turks

The Fatimid dynasty in Egypt soon became the dynamic center of Islamic civilization. From their position in the heart of the Nile delta, the Fatimids played a major role in the trade passing from the Mediterranean to the Red Sea and beyond. They created a strong army by hiring non-native soldiers to fight for them. One such group was the Seljuk Turks.

The Seljuk Turks were a nomadic people from central Asia. They had converted to Islam and prospered as soldiers for the Abbasid caliphate. They moved gradually into Iran and Armenia and took over the eastern provinces of the Abbasid Empire.

In 1055, a Turkish leader captured Baghdad and took command of the empire. His title was sultan—or "holder of power." The caliph was still the chief religious authority, but the Seljuk Turks had the military and political power.

By 1071, the Seljuk Turks were putting pressure on the Byzantine Empire. Soon they took over most of the Anatolian peninsula. In desperation, the Byzantine Empire turned to the West for help.

The Crusades   *1096*   *holy wars*

When Byzantine emperor Alexius I asked the Christian states of Europe for help against the Turks, many agreed. At the Council of Clermont in 1095, Pope Urban II encouraged the assembly of knights and nobles to fight against the infidels. A series of Crusades began in 1096.

At first, the Western powers conquered areas and established new crusader states. Although lasting for nearly 200 years, only the first Crusade was successful, capturing Jerusalem in 1099. The next three Crusades were failures. In 1169, Saladin, a new Muslim ruler, took control of Egypt and made himself sultan. He also got control over Syria and took the offensive against the Christian states in the area. In 1187, his army invaded the kingdom of Jerusalem and destroyed the Christian forces there. He did not, however, allow a massacre of the population. By 1291, the Muslims captured Acre, the last Christian outpost on the Mediterranean. The Crusades were military failures but had significant economic and cultural impact.

LINKING PAST AND PRESENT

In terms of political boundaries, the Crusades had little lasting influence on Southwest Asia. They did, however, help breed centuries of mistrust between Muslims and Christians.

The Mongols

The Mongols were a pastoral people who swept out of the Gobi in the early thirteenth century to seize control of much of the known world. In 1258, the Mongols seized Persia and Mesopotamia. They captured and destroyed Baghdad, burning schools, libraries, mosques, and palaces. The Mongols advanced as far as the Red Sea, but their attempt to seize Egypt failed.

Over time, the Mongol rulers converted to Islam and began to intermarry and rebuild the cities. By the fourteenth century, the Mongol Empire had begun to split into separate kingdoms. The new center of Islamic civilization became Cairo, in Egypt.

SECTION 3 ISLAMIC CIVILIZATION

Prosperity in the Islamic World

Overall, the Arab Empire was prosperous. The Arabs carried on extensive trade not only within the Islamic world but also with China, the Byzantine Empire, India, and Southeast Asia. Goods traveled by ship and camel caravans from Morocco in the far west to the countries beyond the Caspian Sea. The development of banking and the use of coins made it easier to exchange goods.

The Role of Cities Baghdad, Cairo, and Damascus were the centers of the administrative, cultural, and economic activity for their regions. During the time of the Abbasids, Baghdad, known as the City of Peace, was probably the greatest city in the empire and one of the greatest cities in the world. Islamic cities, while not regarded as especially grand, nevertheless outshone those of mostly rural Europe. At the time, Europe's two largest cities were Constantinople and the Islamic Córdoba.

Islamic cities were dominated by their palaces and mosques. There were also public buildings with fountains and secluded courtyards, and public baths. The bazaar, or marketplace, was an important part of every Muslim city or town.

The Importance of Farming The Arab world was more urban than other areas of the world during the same time period. Still, a majority of the people made their living by farming or herding animals. During the early stages of the empire, most land was owned by independent farmers. Later, landowners amassed

**CORE CONCEPTS:
INTERDEPENDENCE**

The Abbasids got gold and slaves from south of the Sahara, silk and porcelain from China, gold and ivory from eastern Africa, and sandalwood and spices from India and Southeast Asia. Within the empire, Egypt contributed grain; Iraq provided linen, dates, and precious stones; and western India supplied textile goods.

large estates. Some lands were owned by the state or court and farmed by slave labor. In the Tigris, Euphrates, and Nile River valleys, most farmers remained independent peasants.

Islamic Society

According to Islam, all people are equal in the eyes of Allah. Nevertheless, slavery was widespread in the Islamic world. Because Muslims could not be slaves, most of their slaves came from Africa or from non-Islamic populations elsewhere in Asia. Many had been captured in war. Many slaves, especially women, were used as domestic servants. Islamic law made it clear that slaves should be treated fairly, and it was considered a good act to free them.

The Role of Women The Quran granted women spiritual and social equality with men. Women had the right to own and inherit property and played prominent roles in the rise of Islam during the time of Muhammad.

Men were, however, dominant in Islamic society. Every woman had a male guardian. In an effort to expand the Muslim world, the Quran allowed Islamic men to have more than one wife, but no more than four.

After the spread of Islam, women's rights were eroded. For example, some were secluded in their homes and kept from contacts with males outside their own families.

SECTION 4   THE CULTURE OF ISLAM

Preservation of Knowledge

When most of Europe knew nothing about the ancient Greek philosophers, scholars in the Arab world were busy translating the works of Plato and Aristotle. At the same time, Muslim scholars were studying texts on mathematics from India.

Paper was introduced from China in the eighth century. Soon there were paper factories in Baghdad, followed by booksellers and libraries.

Philosophy, Science, and History

Islamic scholars made many contributions to mathematics and the natural sciences. The Muslims adopted and passed on the numerical system of India, including the use of zero. In Europe,

CORE CONCEPTS: MOVEMENT OF PEOPLE AND GOODS

It was through the Muslim world that Europeans recovered the works of Aristotle and other Greek philosophers. In the twelfth century, Arabic translations were translated into Latin, making them available to the West.

it became known as the "Arabic" system. A ninth century Arab mathematician gave shape to the mathematical discipline of algebra.

In astronomy, Muslims set up an observatory in Baghdad to study the stars. They knew that Earth was round, and they named many stars. They also perfected the astrolabe, a navigational instrument that later made it possible for Europeans to sail to the Americas.

The philosopher and scientist Ibn Sina wrote a medical encyclopedia that stressed, among other things, the contagious nature of diseases. Ibn Khaldun was a prominent Muslim historian who argued for a cyclical view of history.

Literature

Muslims regarded the Quran as their greatest literary work, but pre-Islamic traditions also influenced writers. Among the most familiar works are *The 1001 Nights* (also known as *The Arabian Nights*), which evolved from an oral tradition.

Art and Architecture

Islamic art is a blend of Arab, Turkish, and Persian influences. The best expression of Islamic art is in mosques.

The Great Mosque at Samarra in present-day Iraq was the world's largest at the time it was built: it covered 10 acres. Its most famous part is its minaret, a tower from which the muezzin, or crier, calls the faithful to prayer five times a day. Another very famous mosque is in Córdoba, Spain. Its interior has hundreds of columns that support double arches.

Palaces also reflect the glory of Islam. Beginning in the eighth century, rulers constructed large brick palaces with protective walls, gates, and baths. Designed around a central courtyard surrounded by two-story arcades and massive gate-towers, Islamic castles resembled fortresses as much as palaces.

The finest example of an Islamic palace is the fourteenth-century Alhambra in Granada, Spain. It has densely decorated, finely carved plasterwork displaying Arabic letters and abstract figures which are repeated in geometric patterns called arabesques.

CORE CONCEPTS: BELIEF SYSTEMS

No representations of the prophet Muhammad ever adorn a mosque. The Quran did not forbid this, but an early collection of the prophet's sayings warns against idolatry, any attempt to imitate God by creating pictures of living beings. As a result, figures do not appear in Islamic religious art.

CORE CONCEPTS: SCIENCE AND TECHNOLOGY

China was at the forefront of world technology during the Tang and Song dynasties. The Chinese had invented gunpowder, the printing press, and the compass. All three inventions helped change the course of world history. Knowledge of these innovations spread to other parts of the world through trade.

Chapter Overview

Between 400 and 1500, new civilizations were taking shape in a number of parts of the world, including China, India, and Southeast Asia. These societies derived wealth from farming, like the ancient societies before them, but they also witnessed a reinvigoration of trade. Through trade and conquest, these new societies exposed each other to new religions and societies resulting in significant cultural diffusion.

Innovations such as gunpowder and printing, invented during the Tang dynasty in China, and religious changes such as those that took place due to Muslim expansion, have had a lasting impact on those societies. China prospered under the Sui, Tang, and Song dynasties. Islam and Hinduism became powerful religions in the Indian subcontinent. Southeast Asia, because it was separated from the rest of Asia by mountains, plateaus, and seas, developed its own cultures.

As you read this chapter, ask yourself these questions:
(1) How did changes in the dynastic cycle bring about changes in Chinese civilization?
(2) What effect did Mongol Rule have on China?
(3) How did the decline of Buddhism and Muslim rule affect the Indian subcontinent?
(4) What geographical conditions led Southeast Asia to develop into many different countries?

Main Ideas and Concepts

- **Change** With each new dynasty, Chinese civilization experienced change.
- **Diversity** South Asian and Southeast Asian societies are characterized by great diversity in language and culture.
- **Movement of People and Goods** India, although it derived most of its wealth from farming, was a trade center between Southwest and East Asia.
- **Culture** Indian arts, most importantly architecture and prose literature, flourished between 500 and 1500.

People, Places, Terms

The following names and terms will help you to prepare for the Regents Exam in Global History and Geography. You can find an explanation of each name and term in the Glossary at the back of this book, in your textbook, or in another reference source.

agricultural society	khanate	subsistence farming
archipelago	Mahayana	Theravada
dowry	neo-Confucianism	trading society
ethnocentric	porcelain	
Genghis Khan	scholar-gentry	

SECTION 1 CHINA REUNIFIED

The Sui Dynasty

With the end of the Han dynasty, China experienced 300 years of chaos and civil war. In 581, the Sui dynasty took control of China. Although the Sui dynasty lasted only until 618, it was able to reunify China.

Sui Yangdi was the second emperor of the Sui dynasty. His major accomplishment was the completion of the Grand Canal that linked the Huang He (Yellow River) and the Chang Jiang (Yangtze River). This made it easier to ship rice from the south to the north. Sui Yangdi's use of slave labor, demands of high taxes, and military failures led to rebellion. Sui Yangdi was murdered, and his dynasty came to an end.

The Tang Dynasty

The Tang dynasty emerged soon after the Song ended, and it lasted from 618 until 907. The early rulers restored the civil service examination and gave land to peasants. The rulers also wanted to restore China to a position of power in East Asia, so they expanded their control into Tibet, the area north of the Himalayas. The Tang rulers set up trade and diplomatic relations with Southeast Asia. The dynasty ended when the Uighurs overthrew the Tang ruler.

CORE CONCEPTS: GOVERNMENT

During the eighth century, the Tang dynasty weakened. Tang rulers hired Uighurs, a northern tribal group of Turkic speaking people, to fight for the dynasty, but continued unrest led to the collapse of Tang rule in 907.

The Song Dynasty

The Song dynasty rose to power in 960. Until 1269, China experienced a period of prosperity and cultural achievement under the Song, but there were problems. From the beginning, the Song had trouble with northern neighbors who forced their way into northern China and occupied land there. This threat caused the Song leaders to move the capital farther south, from Changan to Hangzhou.

The Song dynasty was never able to overcome the trouble from the north, and within a few years, China would fall under the control of a new dynasty—the Mongol, the first foreign dynasty.

Government and Economy

From the beginning of the Sui dynasty to the end of the Song dynasty, China developed a political system based on principles developed during the Qin and Han dynasties. The government was a monarchy based on Confucian principles, and a large bureaucracy supported it. The empire was divided into provinces, districts, and villages.

Technology and Trade Chinese economy was primarily agriculturally based, but trade and manufacturing grew during this time. In addition, a number of technological developments led to the creation of new products. For example, the Chinese began to make steel, used for swords and sickles, during the Tang dynasty. Cotton and gunpowder were also introduced at this time.

These new products and developments stimulated trade. The Silk Road was renewed, and goods moved back and forth between China and Southwest and South Asia. The Chinese traded tea, silk, and porcelain in return for precious stones, exotic wood, and various tropical goods.

CORE CONCEPTS: CULTURE

In the thirteenth century, Marco Polo described Hangzhou, the Song Capital, as a place where "so many pleasures may be found that one fancies himself to be in Paradise." For the wealthy, life in many cities was good.

Chinese Society

Most people lived in villages and made their living by **subsistence farming**. The wealthy lived privileged lives in cities during the Tang and Song dynasties. There were many new forms of entertainment, including chess and cards. Block printing, invented in the eighth century, created a new way for people to communicate. Most Chinese, however, were peasants who rarely produced surplus crops.

The development of a more complete mix of landowners, free peasants, sharecroppers, and landless laborers filled the gulf between wealthy landowners and peasants. In addition, the **scholar-gentry** developed, a new class who produced most of the civil servants. The scholar-gentry replaced the old landed aristocracy and controlled much of the land in the countryside.

Unfortunately, women had a low status during this time. Female infants were not as valued as male children and were sometimes killed during a famine if food was scarce. When a girl married, her family had to pay a **dowry** (money or goods) to her husband. In some cases, poor families sold daughters to wealthy villagers.

CORE CONCEPTS: SCIENCE AND TECHNOLOGY

In the eleventh century, the Chinese improved printing with the invention of move-able type. This innovation made it possible to print hundreds of copies.

SECTION 2 THE MONGOLS AND CHINA

The Mongol Empire

The Mongols, who came from the area of modern-day Mongolia, created the largest land empire in history. The nomadic Mongols were organized into clans. They were unified under a chieftain named Temujin, who later took the name **Genghis Khan**, which means "world emperor." Under his leadership, Mongol armies traveled great distances to the west and the east. They even got as far as central Europe.

Genghis Khan died in 1227, and his death may be the only thing that kept the Mongols from attacking western Europe. His sons took over after his death and divided the empire into separate territories, with one son controlling each territory. *→ sons ruled* These territories were called **khanates**. The Mongols attacked Persia in 1231 and seventeen years later defeated the Abbasids at Baghdad. Shortly after, in the 1260s, the Mongols attacked the Song dynasty.

The Mongol Dynasty in China

Kublai Khan, one of Genghis Khan's grandsons, completed the conquest of China in 1279. He established the Yuan dynasty and ruled China until his death in 1294. He set up a capital in Khanbaliq, which would later be known as Beijing.

The Yuan (Mongol) dynasty continued to expand the empire by invading Vietman, Java, and Sumatra. But the Mongols were only able to defeat Vietnam, because their fighting tactics did not work well in tropical, hilly regions.

CORE CONCEPTS: INTERDEPENDENCE

The Chinese believed the Mandate of Heaven could be passed to foreign rulers. The Yuan dynasty exercised this right; but instead of destroying Chinese culture, they adopted many Chinese ways, contributing to China's **ethnocentric** beliefs.

CORE CONCEPTS: MOVEMENT OF PEOPLE AND GOODS

Buddhism came to China in the first century A.D. Indian merchants and missionaries brought it. Because of the instability after the collapse of the Han dynasty, both Buddhism and Daoism attracted many people, especially the ruling class, intellectuals, and the wealthy.

However, the Mongols were successful in ruling China as the first foreign dynasty. They adopted the Chinese political system and used Chinese bureaucrats, although Mongols usually held the highest bureaucratic positions. However, the Mongols and Chinese had many cultural differences, and the Mongols became a separate class with their own rules.

Many Chinese came to respect the stability and prosperity they experienced under Mongol rule. The capital, Khanbaliq, was very impressive and prosperous and many foreign visitors, such as Marco Polo, were impressed by its splendor. But the dynasty spent too much money on foreign conquests and experienced internal instability. In 1368, the Mongol dynasty was defeated and the Ming dynasty began.

Religion and Government

Confucianism was the basis for the Chinese government during the Han dynasty. Buddhism and Daoism became popular after the collapse of the Han dynasty. Buddhism was brought to China by merchants and missionaries who had traveled to India. For a while, the Tang government supported the Buddhists building monasteries, and Buddhists were even advisers to the imperial court. Gradually Buddhism fell out of favor and was criticized for being a foreign religion. In addition, the Buddhist monasteries had vast amounts of land and serfs, which led to corruption. Eventually, the government destroyed many Buddhist monasteries and forced more than 260,000 nuns and monks to return to secular life.

Neo-Confucianism After its disenchantment with Buddhism, the government turned again to Confucianism. But the new Confucianism was different from the old as practiced under the Han dynasty. The new doctrine was called **neo-Confucianism**, and it developed as a response to Buddhism and Daoism. Neo-Confucianism teaches that the world is real, not an illusion, and that fulfillment comes from participation in the world. Neo-Confucianists divide the world into material and spiritual, and they believe humans are linked with a Supreme Ultimate and should have a goal to move beyond the material world to reach union with the Supreme Ultimate.

The Golden Age of Literature and Art

Art and literature flourished in the time between the Tang and Ming dynasties. The invention of printing helped literature to grow. Poetry was the means by which Chinese of this time best expressed their literary talent. At least 48,000 poems were written by 2,200 authors during the Tang rule, and Li Bo and Duo Fu were two of the most popular poets. Landscape painting reached its high point during the Song and Mongol dynasties. Chinese painters tried to reflect ideas in their paintings, for example, portraying the "idea" of a mountain instead of painting a realistic mountain. People were painted very small in contrast to the nature around them, as painters tried to convey the idea that nature is more significant than man. Ceramics were also important as a Chinese art form. Tang artisans perfected the making of **porcelain**.

CORE CONCEPTS: CULTURE

An Arab traveler described porcelain as " . . . a very fine clay from which are made vases having the transparency of glass bottles; water in these vases is visible through them, and yet they are made of clay."

SECTION 3 INDIA AFTER THE GUPTAS

The Decline of Buddhism

Buddhism had been popular in India for hundreds of years, although it never gained the same support as Hinduism. However, there were disagreements as to the interpretation of Buddha's teachings, so the Buddhists in India split into two different sects, the Theravada and the Mahayana. The **Theravada** followed what they believed were the original teachings of Buddha, and they believed that Buddhism was a way of life, not a religion. They believed nirvana could be achieved through self-reflection and salvation. The **Mahayana** believed Buddhism was a religion, and they elevated Buddha to a divine figure. They believed nirvana was a heaven they could reach through a devotion to Buddha. However, with the revival of Hinduism and the rising popularity of Islam, neither Theravada nor Mahayana remained popular.

CORE CONCEPTS: MOVEMENT OF PEOPLE AND GOODS

Although the popularity of the Theravada and Mahayana sects dwindled in India, these groups did have a lasting effect in Asia. Monks carried Buddhism to China, Korea, Southeast Asia, and Japan, all areas in which Buddhism is still practiced today.

The Eastward Expansion of Islam

Early in the eighth century, Islam became popular in the northwestern corner of the Indian subcontinent. Today, Pakistan, in the northwest corner of the subcontinent, and Bangladesh, located in the northeast corner, are predominantly Islamic, whereas India is mostly Hindu.

Islam was successful in South Asia. India was in a state of upheaval, with no central authority to replace the collapsed Gupta Empire. When the Arab armies first came to India, they simply occupied frontier regions. But in the tenth century, a new phase of expansion began with the formation by former Turkish slaves of the new Islamic state of Ghazni, located in modern-day Afghanistan. After the death of his father, the founder of Ghazni, Mahmud, extended his rule throughout much of northern India. Rajputs (Hindu warriors) were unable to stop the invaders and by 1200, the whole plain of northern India was conquered by the Muslims, who created a Muslim state called the Sultanate of Delhi.

The Impact of Timur Lenk

The Sultanate of Delhi declined in the later half of the fourteenth century. Near the end of the century, Timur Lenk (Tamerlane), the Mongolian leader of Samarkand, invaded from the northwest via the Indus River and raided the capital of Delhi. As many as one hundred thousand Hindu prisoners were killed. Timur Lenk seized power in 1369 and during the 1380s, he conquered the entire region east of the Caspian Sea and occupied Mesopotamia. Thousands were forced to build his capital at Samarkand.

Islam and Indian Society

In India, the relationship between Muslims and Hindus was tense. The Muslims viewed themselves as conquerors and kept themselves separated from the "conquered" Hindus. There were too many Hindus to convert to Islam, but the Muslims did impose strict Islamic customs on the Indian people.

Economy and Daily Life

Between 500 and 1500, most Indians were peasant farmers who lived off the land, but many elite and wealthy people lived in cities. The farmers farmed their own tiny plots and paid a share of their harvest each year to a landlord, who in turn sent part of that payment to a local ruler. Agriculture and trade were the major sources of wealth during this time. At the time, internal trade was probably diminished due to internal conflict, but because of India's location, international trade thrived. The traders were mostly Hindu, but there were Muslim traders as well.

The Wonder of Indian Culture

Between 500 and 1500, architecture and prose literature thrived in India. The Indians built huge Hindu temples filled with extraordinary detail. As time went on, the temples became

CORE CONCEPTS: BELIEF SYSTEMS

Followers of Islam have traditionally opposed the caste system on the grounds that all people are equal before God. Muslims also reject religious images because God's spiritual nature is beyond all form. They consider the use of religious images as idolatry.

CORE CONCEPTS: CHANGE

What new ideas on government and society do you think Muslim rulers brought to India?

increasingly ornate. The Hindu Temple at Khajuraho contains many examples of the intricate, carved temple art that characterized the temples at the time. Twenty of the 80 temples built in the tenth century still stand today.

By the sixth and seventh centuries, prose literature had developed in India. This is an amazing accomplishment, considering that the first novel appeared in Japan almost three centuries later, in the tenth century. Dandin, a seventh-century author, was one of the great masters of Sanskrit prose. In his work, *The Ten Princes,* he created a fantastic world that was a combination of history and fiction.

SECTION 4 CIVILIZATION IN SOUTHEAST ASIA

The Land and People of Southeast Asia

The land and people of Southeast Asia are quite diverse in terms of religion, culture, and race, due to geographical reasons. Southeast Asia lies between China and India. It has two parts: (1) the mainland region, which extends from the border of China to the tip of the Malay Peninsula, and (2) the **archipelago**, which is a group of islands that are part of modern Indonesia and the Philippines.

The Formation of States

Between 500 and 1500, many different states formed in Southeast Asia. China and India were models for these states, but the models were adapted by each state to reflect the needs and values of its own people.

Vietnam China conquered Vietnam in 111 B.C., but was unable to make it a part of China, even though Vietnamese leaders were expected to pay tribute to the Chinese government. The Vietnamese became one of the first groups of people in Southeast Asia to form their own state. They overthrew the Chinese government in the tenth century. They called the new state Dai Viet (Great Viet). Vietnam was strongly influenced by China and adopted the Chinese model of centralized government as well as state Confucianism and the Chinese court rituals. The rulers were called emperors, and they introduced the civil service examination. By 1600, Vietnam had grown and expanded all the way to the Gulf of Siam.

CORE CONCEPTS: CULTURE

Vietnam is the nation in Southeast Asia that has been most strongly influenced by China. Contact with Confucianism has led the Vietnamese to place great value on scholarship and the written word.

CORE CONCEPTS: INTERDEPENDENCE

Contact between what is now India and Cambodia can be seen at Angkor Wat, where some styles of architecture show the influence of Hinduism. Other temples show the later contact with Buddhism.

Angkor Angkor, also called the Khmer Empire, arose in the ninth century in present-day Cambodia. Jayavarman, a powerful figure who was eventually crowned as the god-king of his people, united the Khmer people and established a capital at Angkor Thom. Angkor was one of the most powerful states in Southeast Asia until 1432, when the Thai destroyed the Angkor capital. The ruling class fled and set up a new capital in the southeast near Phnom Penh, the modern day capital of Cambodia.

Thailand The Thai conquered the Angkor capital in 1432. They were frontier people who migrated from China, beginning in the eleventh or twelfth centuries. The Mongol invasion of China spurred them on, which is how they eventually came upon the Angkor capital. The Thai set up their own capital at Ayutthaya on the Chao Phraya River. For the next four hundred years, the Thai would remain a force in the Southeast. They were influenced by India and converted to Buddhism, but they created their own unique culture, which evolved into modern day Thailand.

Burma The Burmans migrated from the Tibetan highlands in the seventh century and formed a society in the valleys of the Salween and Irrawaddy Rivers, where they soon adopted farming. In the eleventh century, they created Pagan, the first Burman state. They converted to Buddhism and adopted Indian political institutions and culture. The Mongol attack in the late thirteenth century led to the decline of Pagan.

The Malay World The Malay Peninsula and the Indonesian Archipelago had never been united as a single state, although the area had been involved in the trade that passed from East Asia to the Indian Ocean. Two states, Srivijaya, which dominated the trade route through the Strait of Malacca, and Sailendra, primarily a farming state, developed during the eighth century. Both were influenced by Indian culture. Majapahit, founded in the late thirteenth century, united most of the archipelago and possibly some of the mainland under a single rule in the mid-fourteenth century. By the fifteenth century, the Muslim state of Melaka formed on the west coast of the Malay Peninsula and eventually converted almost everyone in the region to Islam, united under the Sultanate of Melaka.

Economic Forces

The states of Southeast Asia were either **agricultural societies** or **trading societies**. Vietnam, Angkor, Pagan, and Sailendra were mostly agricultural. Srivijaya and the Sultanate of Melaka were mostly trading societies. Trade grew with a rise in demand for spices, and merchant fleets from the Arabian Peninsula and India sailed to the Indonesian islands to buy spices and exotic woods.

Social Structures

Hereditary aristocrats were socially prominent in Southeast Asia. The wealthy lived in cities and everyone else (mostly very poor rice farmers, although there were also fishermen, artisans, and merchants) lived in the country. Women enjoyed more rights than women in China and India did and were often involved in trading and farming. Customs were quite different from the rest of Asia, especially China.

Culture and Religion

Chinese and Indian culture had an impact on the states of Southeast Asia. Vietnam was mostly influenced by Chinese culture, but many other parts of Southeast Asia took influence from India. Hinduism and Buddhism were blended with old beliefs when introduced to Southeast Asia. Theravada Buddhism, introduced in Burma in the eleventh century, spread rapidly throughout southeast Asia and eventually became the religion of the masses.

CORE CONCEPTS: BELIEF SYSTEMS

Theravada Buddhism became popular because it tolerated local gods and posed no threat to established faiths. It taught that priests and rulers were not necessary to achieve nirvana—people could seek nirvana on their own.

CHAPTER 8 EMERGING EUROPE AND THE BYZANTINE EMPIRE

Section 1   **Transforming the Roman World**
Section 2   **Feudalism**
Section 3   **The Growth of European Kingdoms**
Section 4   **The Byzantine Empire and the Crusades**

CORE CONCEPTS: DIVERSITY

During this unsettled era, many vernacular, or spoken, languages began to emerge—French, Italian, Spanish, and others. This development helped foster the cultural diversity that typifies much of Europe today.

Chapter Overview

The period between 500 and 1500 is called the Middle Ages or the Medieval period. It began with the collapse of the Roman Empire, after which Europe fell subject to a series of invasions that reshaped the character and direction of European culture. Europe saw the collapse of central authority and a rise in weak local governments. This unsettled situation gave rise to new institutions, such as feudalism, that provided organization in an otherwise chaotic world.

The new European civilization was formed by the merging of Germanic tribes, the Roman legacy, and the Christian Church. During the ninth and tenth centuries, Vikings, Magyars, and Muslims invaded Europe. In the 1100s, European monarchs began to build strong states. While all of this was happening, the Byzantine Empire was creating its own civilization in the eastern Mediterranean.

As you read this chapter, ask yourself these questions:
(1) What was the role of the Catholic Church in the growth of the new European civilization?
(2) What factors helped feudalism develop in western Europe during the ninth and tenth centuries?
(3) How did centralized monarchies develop in Europe?
(4) What was the impact of the Crusades?

Main Ideas and Concepts

- **Change** The new European civilization was formed by the blending of the Germanic people, the legacy of the Roman Empire, and the Catholic Church.
- **Political Systems** Feudalism, a new political system, grew out of the collapse of central authority in Europe.
- **Power** European monarchs began to extend their power and form strong states.
- **Conflict** The Crusades saw conflict among Christians, Muslims, and Jews, which had a great impact on both eastern and western Europe.

People, Places, Terms

The following names and terms will help you to prepare for the Regents Exam in Global History and Geography. You can find an explanation of each name and term in the Glossary at the back of this book, in your textbook, or in another reference source.

chivalry	fief	patriarch
common law	infidel	pope
Crusades	knight	schism
feudal contract	Magna Carta	tournament
feudalism	monk	vassal

SECTION 1 TRANSFORMING THE ROMAN WORLD

The New Germanic Kingdoms

By the third century, Germanic people began to move into land that belonged to the Roman Empire. They were fleeing the Huns, nomadic warriors from Central Asia. Various Germanic kingdoms grew out of the merging of Romans and Germans. The Ostrogoths controlled Italy, and the Visigoths occupied Spain. The Germanic Ostrogoths and Visigoths continued to use the Roman structure of government but forbade Romans from holding power.

Germanic tribes from Denmark and northern Germany, the Angles and the Saxons, settled in Britain after the Romans abandoned it. These people eventually became the Anglo-Saxons.

The Kingdom of the Franks The kingdom of the Franks, led by military leader Clovis, was the only Germanic state to last for a significant period. Clovis converted to Christianity, which won him support from the Roman Catholic Church (formerly the Christian church in Rome). When Clovis died, his sons divided the kingdom among themselves.

Germanic Society Over time, the Germanic and Roman cultures blended through marriage, which created a new society. The concept of extended family, so important to the Germanic people, became a part of the new society. Families worked together and members protected each other. This concept of

CORE CONCEPT: POLITICAL SYSTEMS

The Frankish custom for a kingdom to be divided among the king's sons after his death helped to avoid conflicts over who would rule, since all the sons gained territory.

family affected Germanic law. Unlike Romans, who believed crimes were committed against the state, the Germanic people believed crimes were personal, an idea that could lead to blood feuds, which could be quite savage. To avoid bloodshed, they developed a system based on a fine called a wergild. Wergild was the fine paid by a wrongdoer to the family of the person he injured or killed. *Wergild* means "money for a man" and was essentially the price of one man's life. Rich people were worth more than poor people were. The Germanic people also had a means of determining guilt, called an ordeal, which was a physical trial based on the idea that divine forces would not allow an innocent person to be harmed. An accused person who was unharmed by the ordeal was considered innocent.

The Role of the Church

The Christian church developed an organizational system by the fourth century. Local Christian communities were called parishes, which were led by priests. A bishop led the group of parishes; his area of authority was called a bishopric, or diocese. Over time, the bishop of Rome claimed that he was the leader of the Roman Catholic Church. Bishops of Rome became known as **popes**. The papacy (office of the pope) gained power in the sixth century under Pope Gregory I, the leader of Rome and surrounding territories (the papal states).

Gregory I used monks to convert non-Christians in Germanic Europe to Christianity. **Monks** were men who separated themselves from society and dedicated themselves to God. Monasticism is the practice of living life as a monk. In the sixth century, Saint Benedict began a community for monks. He wrote rules for the monks that divided the day into a series of activities that emphasized prayer and manual labor. Monks lived together in monasteries and supported themselves with the land that they owned.

Monasteries were led by abbots. The first monks were men, but soon women began to follow in their path. These women were called nuns. They lived in convents run by abesses, who were often members of royal houses.

Charlemagne and the Carolingians

In the 600s and 700s, the kings of the Frankish kingdoms lost power to the chief officers of their own households, called mayors of the palace. Charles the Great, or Charlemagne, became the king of the Frankish kingdom in 768 after the death

CORE CONCEPTS: CULTURE

Monks became the new heroes of Christian society and were an important force in the new European civilization. The monastic community came to be seen as the ideal Christian society that could provide a moral example to the society around it.

CORE CONCEPTS: POLITICAL SYSTEMS

Charlemagne converted to Christianity and won the backing of the Pope. He hoped to create a Christian empire to replace Rome. When his empire fell, groups of Viking invaders again overran Europe, and feudalism took hold of the region.

of his father, Pepin, a former mayor of the palace who became king himself.

The Carolingian Empire Charlemagne ruled until 814. He expanded the Frankish kingdom and created the Carolingian Empire, which covered much of western and central Europe. Charlemagne ruled through counts (German nobles) who were representatives of the king. Charlemagne sent men, called *missi dominici*, to local districts to ensure that his orders were being carried out. In 800, Charlemagne became the Roman emperor, symbolizing the merging of the Roman, Christian, and Germanic elements of European civilization.

Although Charlemagne was possibly illiterate, his support of education led to a revival in learning and culture, sometimes called the Carolingian Renaissance. There was a revived interest in Greek and Roman works. Monks played a central role, and scriptoria, or writing rooms, were set up in monasteries where monks could copy ancient and important works.

SECTION 2 FEUDALISM

The Invaders

After Charlemagne's death, the Carolingian Empire began to disintegrate. Within thirty years, it was divided into three sections: the western Frankish lands, the eastern Frankish lands, and the Middle Kingdom. In addition, there were many invasions during the ninth and tenth centuries. The Muslims attacked southern France. The Magyars, from western Asia, settled in Hungary by the end of the ninth century. The Vikings (Northmen, or Norsemen), from Scandinavia, were responsible for the most far-reaching attacks of the time. They were great shipbuilders and sailors and great warriors. To deal with the threat, Frankish rulers tried to settle the Vikings and make them part of European civilization. One such ruler gave a band of Vikings some land in France, which would come to be known as Normandy.

The Development of Feudalism

Due to attacks from Vikings and others, people throughout Europe were frightened for their safety. They began to offer services to powerful lords in return for protection, which led to a new political and social system called **feudalism**. Germanic warriors had a personal bond with their leaders, who took care

LINKING GEOGRAPHY TO HISTORY

Europe is not the only place where a system of feudalism developed. In Japan, between 800 and 1500, a feudal system developed. And in the Valley of Mexico, the Aztec developed a political system between 1300 and 1500 that bore some similarities to European feudalism.

of the warrior's needs. A man who served in a military capacity for a lord was called a **vassal**. Vassals were given land by lords and were expected to fight for the lord in return. The land supported the vassal's family. By the ninth century, this gift of land to a vassal became known as a **fief**.

In feudal society, the chief virtue was loyalty to the lord. The relationship between a lord and vassal was an honorable relationship between two free men. However, feudalism became complicated; kings had vassals who themselves had vassals. Over time, **feudal contracts** developed, which were a set of unwritten rules concerning the relationship between lord and vassal. The vassal provided about 40 days a year of military service, gave advice to the lord when requested, and made payments to the lord on certain occasions, such as the marriage of the lord's oldest daughter. The lord, in turn, was responsible for the vassal's protection. The Roman Catholic Church exercised great authority in feudal society since many Church officials had high government positions.

During this time, the Frankish army experienced a change, as larger horses and the use of stirrups made it possible for horsemen to wear suits of mail, which formerly only foot soldiers could wear. Armies consisted of armored cavalry (soldiers on horseback) who became known as **knights**.

The Nobility of the Middle Ages

During the Middle Ages, an aristocracy formed in Europe composed of nobles that held considerable political, social, and economic power. These nobles were kings, dukes, counts, barons, and sometimes even bishops and archbishops who had large landed estates.

Within this group, warriors were united by virtue of being warriors. They were united by knighthood, but still experienced social divisions based on wealth. In the twelfth century, knights began to fight in **tournaments**, contests in which they could display their fighting skills and train for war. The joust, individual combat between two knights, became popular by the late twelfth century.

The idea of chivalry evolved in the eleventh and twelfth centuries. **Chivalry** was a code of ethics knights were to follow, which grew out of the influence of the Catholic Church. Under the code of chivalry, knights were expected to defend the Church and defenseless people and treat captives as honored

CORE CONCEPTS: POLITICAL SYSTEMS

Feudalism created a rigid class structure. Kings were at the pinnacle of society. They were served by nobles, or lords. These lords divided their land among lesser lords. Below the lords were knights. At the bottom of society were the serfs, or peasants, who worked the land and exchanged their labor for protection.

CORE CONCEPTS: CULTURE

The growth of European nobility was made visible by the growing number of castles. Castles served as both residences for nobles and their families, and servants, and as fortifications. As the Middle Ages progressed, nobles built castles with thicker walls and more elaborate decoration.

guests by not throwing them in dungeons. Chivalry also implied a desire to fight for glory, not for material reward, a concept that was not uniformly followed.

Aristocratic Women

During this time, women could hold property. However, most women remained under the control of their fathers or husbands. The lord of the manor was often not at home because he was involved in battles or in court. This left the lady of the house in charge and presented opportunities for these aristocratic women to play important roles. They had to oversee all of the workers on the estate, both officials and servants, and know how to attend to financial matters. The lady also had to make sure the household ran smoothly, from supervising servants to overseeing supplies.

Some strong women did exist, and these women often advised or even dominated their husbands. For instance, Eleanor of Aquitaine, whose first marriage was annulled, was married eights week later to a man who would become King Henry II of England. Their relationship was stormy, so Eleanor spent most of her time at home in Aquitaine, where she built a brilliant court dedicated to cultural activities.

SECTION 3 THE GROWTH OF EUROPEAN KINGDOMS

England in the High Middle Ages

King Alfred united the Anglo-Saxon kingdoms in England in the ninth century. After that, Anglo Saxons ruled England.

The Norman Conquest William of Normandy landed on the coast of England with an army of knights and defeated the Anglo-Saxon king, Harold, at the Battle of Hastings in 1066. William became the king of England. He demanded loyalty from all nobles and gave his knights fiefs. Anglo-Saxon nobility merged with the French-speaking Norman nobility, creating a new English culture. William took the first census in Europe since Roman times, which he called the Domesday Book. The census included people, manors, and farm animals. William also further developed the system of taxation and royal courts.

Henry II From 1154 to 1189, King Henry II grew the power of the English monarchy. Henry expanded the power of the king's court, which in turn expanded his own power. Under Henry, the number of criminal cases tried in the king's court increased, and he made it possible to try property cases in the royal courts. Royal courts throughout the country made possible the creation of **common law**, laws common throughout the entire kingdom. Henry also wanted to extend royal control over the Church, but he had problems. Thomas à Becket, the archbishop of Canterbury, stated that only the Church could try clerics. This angered Henry, who publicly stated that he wanted to get rid of Becket. Four of Henry's knights went to Canterbury and killed the archbishop, but public outrage forced Henry to abandon his attempts to control the clergy.

The Magna Carta and the First Parliament The power of the English king was growing, and the nobles objected. During the reign of King John, the nobles rebelled. In 1215, they forced him to accept and sign the **Magna Carta**, a document that restricted the king's use of absolute power. The Magna Carta spelled out the details of feudal relationships and said that the relationship between the king and vassals was based on mutual rights and obligations. The king's power was not supposed to be absolute.

The English Parliament emerged in the thirteenth century during the reign of Edward I. It granted taxes and passed laws. The Parliament played a vital role in the formation of representative government. Two knights from every county, two people from every town, and all nobles and bishops in England served on the Parliament. Eventually, the group split in two, with the nobles and bishops forming the House of Lords and the townspeople and knights forming the House of Commons.

The French Kingdom

The Capetian dynasty of French kings began in 987 with the death of the last Carolingian king. Hugh Capet was chosen as the new king. However, the Capetians had very little power because they only controlled the land around Paris.

From 1180 to 1223, Philip II Augustus ruled. His reign was a turning point in the French monarchy. Philip went to war with England and won back the territories of Normandy, Maine, Anjou, and Aquitaine, which had been under English control. With this, he expanded his power and the power of the French monarchy.

CORE CONCEPT: CHOICE

When King John of England put his seal on the Magna Carta, he recognized the rights of nobles, an act that kept the English monarch from becoming an absolute ruler.

LINKING PAST TO PRESENT

Today, the English Parliament is still composed of a House of Lords and a House of Commons. In addition, the development of common law led to the system of common law present in America today.

From 1285 to 1314, Philip IV, known as Philip the Fair, ruled. He expanded the royal bureaucracy, which strengthened the French monarchy. He also created a French Parliament by meeting with representatives of three estates: the clergy (first estate), the nobles (second estate), and townspeople (third estate). This meeting, held in 1302, began the Estates-General, the first French Parliament.

The Holy Roman Empire

Saxon dukes became kings of the eastern Frankish kingdom, Germany, in the tenth century. Otto I, the best known Saxon king of Germany, protected the Pope and was crowned emperor of the Romans in 962. He was the first to hold the title since Charlemagne.

The German kings tried to rule both German and Italian lands. Frederick I considered Italy the chief source of revenue and attempted to conquer northern Italy, but he encountered problems. Northern Italian cities and the Pope joined forces to defeat Frederick I in 1176. Frederick II ultimately lost the same struggle.

Effect on the Empire The German monarchy became weak as a result of clashes between emperors and popes. While the emperors were away fighting, German lords took over and created their own kingdoms in Germany. In the end, the Holy Roman Empire had no real power over either Germany or Italy. Germany and Italy did not develop national monarchies in the Middle Ages, as France and England did, and so they continued to be composed of small, independent states.

Central and Eastern Europe

The Slavic people, originally a single group in central Europe, eventually divided into three major groups: the western, the southern, and the eastern Slavs. The western Slavs formed the Polish and Bohemian kingdoms. The Czechs in Bohemia were converted to Christianity by German monks, as were the Slavs in Poland. The kingdom of Hungary was also converted to Christianity; thus, the groups of western Slavs all became part of the Roman Catholic Church.

The eastern and southern Slavs were converted by Byzantine missionaries to Eastern Orthodox Christianity, which differed from the Roman Catholic Church. Those converted included the Croats, the Serbs, and the Bulgarians. Their conversion linked these southern and eastern Slavs to Byzantine culture.

LINKING PAST TO PRESENT

Today, journalists are called the "Fourth Estate." This term grew out of the three estates of the French monarchy. In the modern world, journalists gained so much power, they were honored with their own class.

CORE CONCEPT: ENVIRONMENT

Slavic peoples traveled and traded along the so-called "River Road," a network of rivers and tributaries in eastern Europe. The Dnieper River was one of the main arteries in this network. So was the Danube, which flowed from eastern Europe into the heart of Western Europe.

The Development of Russia

Swedish Vikings moved into the areas of modern day Ukraine and Russia looking for new trade routes. There they encountered the eastern Slavs and soon dominated them. The name Russia comes from "Rus," the name given to the Viking rulers by the eastern Slavs.

Kievan Rus The Viking ruling class married Slavic wives and blended into the Slavic population. Oleg, a Viking leader, created the principality of Kiev after he settled there. His successors expanded the principality of Kiev. Orthodox Christianity became the official religion of the state in 988, when a Rus ruler, Vladimir, married the Byzantine emperor's sister and accepted Eastern Orthodox Christianity. Civil wars and invasions ended the principality of Kiev in 1169.

Mongol Rule The Mongols conquered Russia in the thirteenth century. During their occupation of Russian lands, the Mongols forced Russian princes to pay tribute to them. Alexander Nevsky, a Russian prince, defeated a German army in Russia in 1242 and was given the title of grand prince as a reward. His descendants would become the princes of Moscow, and eventually, the leaders of all of Russia.

CORE CONCEPTS: CULTURE

Grand Duchess Olga, who ruled Kiev from 945 to 955, was the first ruler to accept Christianity. However, she did not make it the state religion. Her grandson, Vladimir, accomplished this feat.

SECTION 4 THE BYZANTINE EMPIRE AND THE CRUSADES

The Reign of Justinian

In 527, Justinian became emperor of the Eastern Roman Empire. He wanted to reestablish the empire in the whole Mediterranean world and managed to do so by 552, acquiring Italy, part of Spain, North Africa, Asia Minor, Palestine and Syria. He rebuilt Constantinople after riots destroyed it in 532. Most importantly, Justinian created *The Body of Civil Law*, a simplification of Roman codes, which became the basis for much of Europe's legal system.

From Eastern Roman Empire to Byzantine Empire

Justinian died in 552, and he left the Eastern Roman Empire in serious trouble. There was too much territory to protect, no money, and new threats from outside. The Lombardis took most of Italy by 555, and other areas soon fell. Syria and Palestine were lost to Islamic forces in 636. By the beginning of the eighth century, the Eastern Roman Empire was shriveled, consisting only of the eastern Balkans and Asia minor, which historians call the Byzantine empire, which lasted until 1453.

The Byzantine empire was a mixture of Greek and Christian influences. Greek replaced Latin as the official language, but the empire was founded upon Christian faith, which many citizens shared. The Christian church became known as the Eastern Orthodox Church. The Byzantine emperor was chosen by God, and he had absolute power. The emperor controlled the Church as well as the empire because the emperor chose the **patriarch** (the head of the Eastern Orthodox Church). There were often disputes with the popes who represented the Roman Catholic Church.

Life in Constantinople

Constantinople was the largest city in Europe during the Middle Ages and was the greatest center of commerce. Constantinople was a trading hub for goods from the East, such as silk, spices, ivory, and grains. Citizens also used these goods to support their own industry. Silk was the city's most desirable product. It came from silk worms smuggled into the city from China by monks. The city included an immense palace complex, hundreds of churches, and the Hippodrome, a huge arena where gladiator fights and chariot races were held. Justinian was responsible for most of these buildings. Hagia Sophia, the Church of Holy Wisdom, was Justinian's greatest achievement, although he also built many roads, bridges, schools, courts, and churches.

New Heights and New Problems

From 867–1081, the Byzantine Empire expanded to include Bulgaria, Crete, and Syria under the reign of a new dynasty, known as the Macedonians. By 1025, the Byzantine empire was the largest it had been since the beginning of the seventh century. Constantinople flourished as the Macedonians expanded trade relations with western Europe. Unfortunately, by the late eleventh century, power struggles led to political and social disorder.

During the eleventh century, a **schism**, or separation, developed between the Roman Catholic Church and the Eastern Orthodox Church because the Eastern Orthodox Church refused

CORE CONCEPTS: MOVEMENT OF PEOPLE AND GOODS

Traders from Kiev sold furs, beeswax, and honey to Constantinople. When Muslim conquerors swept through north Africa, their ships controlled much of the Mediterranean. As a result, Byzantine merchants sent goods to Europe by a roundabout route through Kiev, which grew richer from the traffic.

CORE CONCEPT: CULTURE

According to legend, Vladimir, Grand Prince of Kiev, sent envoys to investigate both Roman and Byzantine (Eastern Orthodox) Christianity. The grandeur of Hagia Sophia so over-whelmed them that their reports convince Vladimir to convert to Eastern Orthodoxy, which he soon forced his subjects to accept, as well.

to acknowledge the Pope as the sole head of the Christian faith. In 1054, the Pope and the patriarch of the Eastern Orthodox church excommunicated each other, and the schism began. In addition to these troubles, in the eleventh century, the Seljuk Turks moved into Asia Minor and in 1071, a Turkish army defeated Byzantine forces at Manzikert.

The Crusades

From the eleventh to the thirteenth centuries, European Christians carried out the **Crusades**, which were a series of military expeditions to regain the Holy Land. They began when the Byzantine emperor, Alexius I, asked the Europeans to help him fight the Seljuk Turks, who were Muslims. Pope Urban II saw this as an opportunity to spread Catholicism and to increase his personal power. He rallied European warriors to join a holy war to liberate Jerusalem and the Holy Land (Palestine) from the Muslims. The Christians called these Muslims **infidels**, which means unbelievers.

Pope Urban II promised all warriors that they would receive immediate forgiveness for all of their sins if they died in battle. The first crusading army was composed of warriors from France and western Europe. Many knights went because of religious zeal, but some knights were simply seeking adventure or saw the opportunity to gain riches, land, and maybe even a title.

The Early Crusades The first crusade began with three bands of knights, each with several thousand cavalry members and ten thousand infantrymen. They captured Antioch in 1098 and reached Jerusalem in June 1099, taking control and massacring the inhabitants. The crusaders organized themselves into four states. Surrounded by Muslims, the states and the crusaders depended on Italian cities for supplies from Europe. This resulted in Italian port cities, such as Genoa, Pisa, and Venice, growing rich and powerful.

But life was not easy for the crusaders. By the 1140s, the Muslims began to strike back. After the fall of one of the Latin kingdoms, Saint Bernard of Clairvaux convinced King Louis VII of France and Conrad III of Germany to start a second crusade, which was a miserable failure. In 1187, Muslim forces led by Saladin took Jerusalem, and in response, a third crusade began. It was not very successful, and Richard I, the Lionhearted, came to a compromise with Saladin that would allow Christian pilgrims to come to Jerusalem.

CORE CONCEPTS: SCIENCE AND TECHNOLOGY

During the Crusades, Europeans discovered the power of gunpowder (originally invented in China). They developed cannons, which made the thick-walled castles of the Middle Ages useless for long-term defense. This use of guns and cannons would give Europeans an advantage when they edged beyond their borders during the Age of Exploration.

CORE CONCEPTS: CULTURE

The influence of religion during the Middle Ages has led historians to call it the Age of Faith.

The Later Crusades In 1193, Pope Innocent III started a fourth crusade. The crusading army became involved in a fight for control of the Byzantine throne and conquered the city in 1204. The Byzantine army would not retake the city until 1261, and by then the Byzantine empire was no longer a great power. The Ottoman Turks finally conquered the empire in 1453.

However, the crusading continued. In 1212, the Children's Crusade began in Germany. The children got all the way to Italy before being sent home by the Pope. At the same time, 20,000 French children sailed for the Holy Land to crusade, but two boats sank and the rest of the children were sold into slavery. The later adult crusades had no more success.

Religious intolerance of many Christian crusaders led to widespread attacks on Jews, since many Christians believed Jews were the "murderers of Christ."

The Crusades were one cause that led to the decline of feudalism. As kings levied taxes and raised armies, nobles sold their lands and freed their serfs in order to join the Crusades, which led to the development of true nation-states. Portugal, Spain, England, and France would emerge by the mid-1400s.

CORE CONCEPT: MOVEMENT OF PEOPLE AND GOODS

The Crusades exposed Europe to new products and goods—spices, silk, and more. European demand for these items sparked a revival of trade, which in turn stimulated the growth of towns and the use of money.

Chapter Overview

The Middle Ages, also known as the medieval period, was an important period of growth in European life. A revival of trade led to the growth of cities and towns, which would become important manufacturing centers. The Catholic Church became increasingly influential and was an important part of people's lives in the Middle Ages. Europe experienced a cultural growth, especially in the areas of art and architecture. Architectural innovations led to the creation of many of the great European Gothic cathedrals, including Notre Dame in Paris.

The Middle Ages was not without its share of problems, though. During the fourteenth and early fifteenth centuries, Europeans experienced a terrible plague, called the Black Death. Europe then became embroiled in the Hundred Years' War, and ultimately witnessed a split in Christianity.

As you read this chapter, ask yourself these questions:
(1) What were the major features of the manorial system?
(2) Why was the Catholic Church such a powerful influence in lay people's lives during the Middle Ages?
(3) What were the major cultural achievements of European civilization in the High Middle Ages?
(4) What were the economic and social results of the Black Death?

CORE CONCEPTS: CONFLICT

Tragedies such as the Black Death led to increased tensions between religious groups. Many Christians wrongly blamed the Jews for the spread of the plague, accusing them of poisoning wells. This led to persecution of the Jews.

Main Ideas and Concepts

- **Human Systems** New farming practices, the growth of trade, and the rise of cities created a flourishing European society.
- **Belief Systems** The Catholic Church played a dominant role in people's lives during the Middle Ages.
- **Culture** New technological advances in the High Middle Ages made it possible to build Gothic cathedrals, one of the greatest artistic achievements of the age.
- **Political Systems** European rulers reestablished centralized power.

People, Places, Terms

The following names and terms will help you to prepare for the Regents Exam in Global History and Geography. You can find an explanation of each name and term in the Glossary at the back of this book, in your textbook, or in another reference source.

anti-Semitism	Inquisition	relic
Black Death	interdict	sacraments
Great Schism	lay investiture	scholasticism
guild	manor	serf
heresy	money economy	theology

SECTION 1 PEASANTS, TRADE, AND CITIES

The New Agriculture

Europe had a relatively small population in the early Middle Ages, but between 1000 and 1300 (the High Middle Ages), it experienced a boom. The population almost doubled, going from 30 million to 74 million people. There were a number of factors that led to this, including increased food production, which was due to peace and stability; a change in climate conducive to growing crops; and an increased amount of land cultivated for farming. In addition, inventions such as horseshoes and horse collars made it possible for people to use horses to plow fields instead of oxen. The advent of the three-field system of farming also added to increased production, as farmers could now grow two crops at once.

In the Middle Ages, people figured out how to harness the power of wind and water to do jobs such as grinding grain, which had previously been done by humans or animals. Farming tools were made from iron mined in Europe. Iron was used to make plows that could break up heavy soil. Entire villages shared the high cost of horses and plows.

The Manorial System

Feudal estates, or **manors**, were the basic economic unit in society. Each manor was almost entirely self-supporting, producing everything from food to clothes. In earlier times, free

CORE CONCEPT: SCIENCE AND TECHNOLOGY

The watermill and windmill were the most important devices for harnessing power before the invention of the steam engine in the eighteenth century. Their spread had revolutionary consequences, enabling Europeans to produce more food and to more easily manufacture a wide array of products.

peasants had worked the land on the manors, but more and more peasants became serfs. **Serfs** were legally bound to the land and had to pay rent to the lord. They were entirely under the lord's control. In exchange for use of the land, serfs provided nobles with a share of their crops and any services the lord might require, such as building barns and digging ditches. Serfs were not slaves, just subject to a certain amount of control by the lord. Serfs could not leave the manor or marry without the lord's permission, and some lords had the power to try serfs in the lord's courts. The land given to the serfs to support themselves could not be taken away, and the lord had to protect the serfs.

Daily Life of Peasantry

Peasants in Europe led simple lives in one- or two-room wood-framed houses. The homes were constructed of wood, straw, and clay.

Women played an important but difficult role in peasant life, working in the fields with men, along with having children and managing the household. They had no property rights or freedom to marry.

Bread was the peasant's basic diet staple, but it was nutritious because it was made from wheat, rye, barley, millet, and oats. Other peasant food included vegetables, cheese, nuts, berries, and fruit. Occasionally, chickens provided eggs and meat, but meat was usually only eaten on a great feast day, like Christmas and Easter.

Most peasant activities were dictated by the seasons. September and August were harvest times. In February and March, peasants plowed their land to ready it for the next planting season in April and May. In November, peasants slaughtered excess livestock and cured the meat with salt to preserve it for the winter. Peasants also took part in feast days on such Catholic holidays as Christmas, Easter, and the Pentecost. These holidays, as well as Sunday mass, brought peasants into contact with the village church. From village priests, who were peasants themselves, the villagers learned the basic ideas of Christianity.

The Revival of Trade

In the eleventh and twelfth centuries, Europe saw a revival of trade, which brought with it a growth in cities and towns. Europe was an agricultural society, but it gradually moved

CORE CONCEPTS: CULTURE

In medieval times, books of hours were personal prayer books for the nobility that often contained calendars noting important dates of the year, such as harvest seasons and holy days. They were illustrated with scenes done in primary colors but without a sense of perspective.

CORE CONCEPT: ECONOMIC SYSTEMS

The advent of a money economy is the basis of modern economic systems. Whether communist, capitalist, or socialist, modern societies use money to buy goods.

toward trade as the Crusades introduced more products and the construction of castles revived the building trades. Venice and other northern Italian cities were bustling with trade in the Mediterranean area. The towns of Flanders were their northern trading counterparts. Flanders and Italy began trading regularly in the twelfth century, spurred on by a number of trade fairs that were organized by the counts of Champagne. As trade increased, so did the demand for gold and silver money, which led to a system of **money economy**, in which goods are exchanged for money instead of barter, an exchange of one product for another. In response to this new economy, trading companies and banking firms were established. All of these practices were part of the rise of commercial capitalism, an economic system in which people invest in trade and goods in order to make a profit.

The Growth of Cities

Cities Old and New The revival of trade caused a revival of cities. Merchants settled in old Roman cities and were soon joined by craftspeople and artisans who created goods for the merchants to sell. New cities and towns were founded, many of which were started by merchants near a castle, both because many castles were on trade routes and for the protection lords could provide. Eventually, walls were erected around cities for protection. The merchants and artisans in these cities were called burghers, or bourgeoisie, a term that stems from the German word *burg*, meaning "walled enclosure." Cities were small in comparison to modern or ancient times. A typical large trading city had about five thousand people.

City Government Townspeople wanted the right to make some of their own laws. Lords and kings granted townspeople this right in exchange for money. These rights, or charters, included the right to buy and sell property and freedom from military service. Many new towns had the right to self-government, with their own courts of law and chosen officials. These governments developed over time. Citizens (people who had been born in a city or lived there for a certain amount of time) elected officials to a city council. Elections were rigged to make sure only patricians, members of the wealthiest and most powerful families, were elected.

Daily Life in the Medieval City

Medieval cities were often not pleasant. They were crowded and surrounded by stone walls. Space was at a premium, so

CORE CONCEPT: MOVEMENT OF PEOPLE AND GOODS

Italian cities took the lead in the trade revival. Venice developed a mercantile fleet and became a major trading center by the end of the tenth century. The Italian cities traded mainly in the Mediterranean Sea. In the north, groups of merchants along the German coast organized a trade alliance known as the Hanseatic League.

CORE CONCEPT: GOVERNMENT

The new towns and cities in medieval times were a departure from manorialism. Instead of being bound to a king or lord, citizens wanted the right to dictate their own rules and laws.

streets were narrow and houses were crowded together. Fire was always a danger, since houses were wood and fire was used for light and heat. Without sewage systems, cities were often dirty and smelly, and animal and human waste abounded. In addition, rivers and streams were often polluted by tanners and slaughterhouses, forcing people to drink from wells.

Industry and Guilds

Cities and towns were centers for manufacturing. Beginning in the eleventh century, craftspeople began to organize themselves into **guilds**, or business associations. These associations dictated production quality and pricing for their respective trades. Guilds grew through the thirteenth century and determined who could enter the trades and how many could do so. To enter a trade, at a young age, a boy would become an apprentice to an experienced tradesman. In exchange for room and board, the child would learn the trade. After five to seven years, the apprentice could become a journeyman and work for other masters in the trade. Eventually, the journeyman would produce a masterpiece as an audition to join the guild and become a master himself.

SECTION 2 CHRISTIANITY AND MEDIEVAL CIVILIZATION

The Papal Monarchy

Popes were the spiritual leaders of the Catholic Church, but they were also involved in politics. They controlled the Papal States, and bishops and abbots had considerable political ties. Bishops and abbots were vassals, chosen by lords from noble families, therefore many of them were more interested in politics than spiritualism. In a practice called **lay investiture**, secular rulers chose church officials and gave them the symbols of their office, such as a ring and a staff.

Church and State Conflict Pope Gregory VII was elected in 1073. He wanted to reform the Church to free it from secular involvement in the appointment of church officials. He claimed that the pope had authority over all Church affairs and over all rulers. The pope removed from the Church all rulers who opposed his authority. Gregory wanted to eliminate lay investiture, which put him in direct conflict with the German king Henry IV. This led to the Investiture Controversy in 1075, when

LINKING THE PAST AND PRESENT

Modern unions retain some of the features of medieval guilds. Skilled craft unions today have apprentices, journeymen, and master craftsmen.

CORE CONCEPTS: ECONOMIC SYSTEMS

Each guild in a town held a monopoly on a particular trade, such as shoemaking and glass-making. Guilds were closely tied to the church and often had special saints. Because of the Christian character of the guilds, Jews were not able to join.

Gregory forbade high-ranking clergy from receiving investiture. Finally, in 1122, a new king and a new pope reached an agreement called the Concordat of Worms, under which the Church elected a German bishop who would in turn pay homage to the German king. The king invested the bishop with symbols of the worldly office and the pope invested the bishop with symbols of spiritual office.

The Church Supreme After Pope Gregory VII died, the new popes in the twelfth century did not give up his reform ideals, but they wanted to strengthen papal power. The Catholic Church reached its height of political power in the thirteenth century, under Pope Innocent III. Innocent III believed that, as pope, he had the ultimate power over European affairs. He forced the king of France to take back his wife when the king tried to annul the marriage, and he forced King John of England to accept the pope's choice for archbishop of Canterbury. Using **interdicts**, which forbid priests to give **sacraments** (Christian rites) to those who angered the pope, the pope was able to force compliance from rulers.

New Religious Orders

A New Activism Men and women increasingly joined religious orders in the late eleventh century, and more new orders arose. One of the most important to arise was the Cistercian order, founded in 1098 by some Benedictine monks seeking more discipline than could be found at their current monastery. Cistercians were strict: they ate a simple diet and had few worldly possessions; each monk had only one robe. They spent less time in services and more time praying and doing manual labor. Cistercians were new activists. Unlike Benedictine monks, they took their religion to the people outside the monastery.

Women in Religious Orders More and more women joined convents. Many were from noble families and either could not marry, did not wish to marry, or were intellectuals. The intellectuals thrived in convents, and many learned women in the Middle Ages were nuns.

The Franciscans and the Dominicans The Franciscans and the Dominicans were new religious orders that emerged in the thirteenth century and had a great impact on the lives of ordinary people. The Franciscan order was started by Saint Francis of Assisi, son of a wealthy Italian merchant. After being a prisoner of war, Saint Francis decided to give up all of his

CORE CONCEPT: POLITICAL SYSTEMS

Gregory VII and other popes believed they had power over secular monarchs because the popes were the representatives of God's power and authority, and God's power and authority outweighed human power and authority.

CORE CONCEPT: CULTURE

Female intellectuals like Hildegard of Bingen found convents a haven for their activities. Hildegard of Bingen became abbess of a convent; she was also one of the first women composers. She contributed to a genre called Gregorian chant. She was also sought out for her advice as a mystic and prophetess.

CORE CONCEPT: EMPATHY

The Franciscans became popular with the poor, among whom they lived and whom they helped. Unlike many other religious orders, the Franciscans lived in the world and undertook missionary work to aid the poor and sick and to teach the Gospels.

worldly goods and preach in poverty, even begging for food. His followers also took vows of poverty, and they lived in the world and did missionary work in Italy and even the Muslim world.

The Dominican order was founded by Dominic de Guzman, a Spanish priest, to defend Church teachings from **heresy**, or the denial of basic Church doctrines. The **Inquistion** was a court created to find and try heretics. Accused heretics who confessed to heresy were punished and forced to perform public penance. Those who would not confess were tortured and killed.

Popular Religion in the High Middle Ages

Ordinary people believed that the sacraments of the Church, like baptism and marriage, were important. People depended on the clergy to help them receive God's grace because only clergy could perform sacraments. The veneration of saints, such as the Virgin Mary or Jesus' apostles, was also important. **Relics**, bones of saints or objects connected with saints, were often worshipped as a link between God and the earthly world. People believed that relics could heal people or produce miracles. Medieval Christians also believed that pilgrimages to holy shrines produced spiritual benefits.

SECTION 3 THE CULTURE OF THE HIGH MIDDLE AGES

The Rise of Universities

CORE CONCEPTS: INTERDEPENDENCE

Universities provided the teachers, administrators, lawyers, and medical doctors for medieval society.

Universities as we know them today were created in the Middle Ages. Universities (the word comes from the Latin word for guild) grew out of educational guilds, which produced educated people. The first university was in Bologna, Italy, and the first northern European university was the University of Paris. Oxford was founded in the second half of the twelfth century by a group of students and teachers who left Paris.

Students in medieval universities studied liberal arts, which included the study of grammar, rhetoric, logic, math, music, and astronomy. Teachers taught by lectures, since books were too expensive to produce in bulk. At the end of his studies, usually four to six years, a student took an oral examination and, if he passed, received a Bachelor of Arts. He could later earn a Master of Arts. After his liberal arts curriculum was completed, a student could study law, medicine, or theology. **Theology**, the study of religion and God, was the most prestigious course of study. Students passing the oral exams at the end of their study received a doctorate and could themselves teach.

The Development of Scholasticism

Scholasticism was a philosophical and theological system that tried to reconcile faith with reason and strongly influenced the study of theology. Scholasticism tried to combine what was known through faith with what was known due to reason. The works of Aristotle, who arrived at conclusions through reason, not faith, upset many Christian theologians. In the thirteenth century, Saint Thomas Aquinas tried to reconcile Aristotle with Christian theology. In his best known work, *Summa Theologica*, Aquinas tried to reconcile the Bible and other Christian writings with knowledge learned through reason. He believed some truths were arrived at through reason and some through faith.

Literature

Latin was the universal language of medieval civilization, used in church and schools. This allowed people of different languages to communicate with one another. At this time, educated lay people began to enjoy popular literature, such as troubadour poetry. Troubadour poetry told tales of knights on quests, often inspired by a lady. The heroic epic was also popular. *The Song of Roland*, which appeared around 1100, was one of the best and most popular heroic epics.

Architecture

The eleventh and twelfth centuries saw enormous strides in building through technological and artistic advances. During this time, churches were built in the basilica shape—rectangular buildings with an arched roof instead of a flat roof. This style was known as Romanesque; it allowed for beautiful arched ceilings. Many churches had a section near the back of the church that intersected the main section, making the building shaped like a cross. Romanesque churches had little light, because heavy columns and stone walls were needed to support the high arched roofs.

In the twelfth century, a new kind of style developed, called Gothic. It was perfected in the thirteenth century. Gothic cathedrals were made possible by two innovations, ribbed vaults and flying buttresses. Ribbed vaults were created by the cross-section

CORE CONCEPTS: CULTURE

The *chanson de geste*, or heroic epic, was another type of literature. Heroic epics describe battles and poetical contests. The epic world was one of combat. Women played little or no role in this literature.

of two arches, making a kind of X. These vaults allowed for taller vertical space, because the crossed vaults provided more stability than a simple arch. Flying buttresses supported the high walls from the outside, and made it possible to distribute the weight of vaulted ceilings out and down. These innovations allowed for many windows in the church. The windows were made of stained glass and depicted religious scenes. The light filtered through the windows and the impossibly high and airy ceilings lent the Gothic cathedrals a feeling of light and spiritualism. They were referred to as "prayers built in stone."

Many of these cathedrals, such as Notre Dame and Chartres in France, stand as strongly today as in the thirteenth century, a testament to the technological architectural innovations of the Middle Ages.

SECTION 4 THE LATE MIDDLE AGES

The Black Death

CORE CONCEPTS: ENVIRONMENT

Usually, the Black Death followed trade routes. Between 1347 and 1351, it ravaged most of Europe. Possibly as many as 38 million people died in those four years out of a total population of 75 million. The Italian cities were hit hardest, losing 50 to 60 percent of their population.

The **Black Death** was a terrible plague and the worst natural disaster in European history. Bubonic plague was the most common form of the Black Death, spread by infected rats and fleas. Merchants unknowingly brought the plague from Caffa, on the Black Sea, to Sicily in 1347. The path of the plague followed trade routes, and by 1351 had spread to France, Italy, Spain, modern-day Belgium, Netherlands, and Luxembourg, Germany, England, Scandinavia, and eastern Europe.

Many believed the plague was a punishment from God. Some believed it was caused by the Devil. Unfortunately, many people accused the Jews of spreading the plague by poisoning the wells. This caused a wave of **anti-Semitism**, hatred for Jews. Jews were attacked and killed. Many Jews fled east, and many settled in Poland, where the king granted them protection. The plague caused economic devastation; trade declined and labor prices rose due to the shortages that resulted from massive deaths. Landlords were paying more for labor while incomes declined, leading some landlords to allow peasants to pay rents instead of owing services, freeing them from serfdom.

Loss of workers gave opportunities for serfs to leave for the towns, for artisans to demand higher prices, and for peasants to negotiate for lower rents. Between 1358 and 1381, there were peasant uprisings in France, England, Germany, and Italy. This would eventually lead to more centralization of political power to restore social order.

The Decline of Church Power

The Church's power declined in the fourteenth century due to a series of problems. King Philip of France had a disagreement with Pope Boniface VIII over the right of the king to tax clergy. Boniface said the clergy would only pay taxes with the Pope's consent, claiming popes ruled over the Church and the state. Philip IV refused to accept the Pope's claims and sent a force to capture him and bring him to France for trial. Boniface escaped but died soon after. Philip IV rigged the next papal election so that Clement V, a Frenchmen, won. Clement V took up residence at Avignon, France, and from 1305 to 1377, the popes lived in Avignon. That, and their lavish lifestyle there, led to much criticism.

In 1377, Pope Gregory XI returned the popes to Rome. When he died, the college of Cardinals came to Rome to elect a new pope. There, they were threatened by the Italians, who said they could not leave if they did not elect an Italian pope. They did, in the person of Pope Urban VI. Five months later, the French cardinals declared the election invalid and elected their own pope, who lived at Avignon. There were now two popes. This was called the **Great Schism**. It lasted from 1378 to 1417, and it divided Europe and the Church. In 1417, the schism was repaired and a new pope elected. But by the early 1400s, the papacy and Catholic Church had lost much of their power and authority.

The Hundred Years' War

The most violent struggle during the Middle Ages was the Hundred Years' War. It began in 1337, when King Philip VI of France took Gascony, an English possession in France. King Edward III of England declared war on Philip in retaliation. The Hundred Years' War was the first in which peasant foot soldiers armed with bows and spears, not knights, won the chief battles. In 1346, the first major battle took place at Crécy. The arrows of English soldiers, who were using longbows, devastated the French cavalry. The French were again defeated at the Battle of Agincourt in 1415 and the English now controlled northern France.

CORE CONCEPTS: CONFLICT

The Battle of Crécy was not decisive. The English did not have enough resources to conquer all of France, but they continued to try.

CORE CONCEPTS: SCIENCE AND TECHNOLOGY

The invention of the longbow greatly helped England fight France. The longbow had greater striking power, longer range, and more rapid speed of fire than the crossbow, which was formerly the weapon of choice.

All seemed hopeless for the French, but for a woman named Joan of Arc, who decided to free France. Born in 1412, Joan of Arc was deeply religious and experienced visions. In 1429, she managed to persuade the heir to the French throne to let her accompany a French army to Orleans. There, with a new confidence instilled by Joan of Arc, the French won and the heir was crowned king. Unfortunately for Joan, she was captured by the English in 1430 and tried as a witch. She was burned at the stake for her "crimes."

Political Recovery

In the fourteenth century, European rulers faced many problems, such as financial difficulties and an inability to produce male heirs. This caused rulers to fight for their position. In the fifteenth century, new rulers tried to bring back the centralized power of monarchies. Some historians call the reestablished monarchies, especially those in England, France, and Spain, new monarchies.

Western Europe The Hundred Years' War left France with a strong national spirit, which kings used to reestablish royal power. King Louis XI was key in this role, as he strengthened the use of *taille*, an annual direct tax on land, to give him a steady income and help him create a strong French monarchy and army.

England, meanwhile, experienced internal conflicts (the War of the Roses) after the Hundred Years' War, with nobles fighting to control the monarchy. In 1485, Henry VII, the first Tudor king, abolished private armies of the nobles and ended the War of the Roses. Henry worked to create a strong royal government, and he gained the support of the nobles by not overburdening them with taxes.

Muslims had conquered most of Spain by about 725. During the Middle Ages, several independent Christian kingdoms emerged as Christian rulers in Spain fought to regain their land from the Muslims. The strongest of these kingdoms were Aragon and Castile. In 1469, Isabella of Castile married Ferdinand of Aragon, which was a major step toward unifying Spain. Ferdinand and Isabella were strict Catholics, and in 1469 expelled all Jews from Spain. Muslims were asked to convert. This movement was known as the Reconquísta. In 1502, all Muslims who would not convert were expelled from Spain. Thus Spain had only one religion. Being Spanish was the same as being Catholic.

Central and Eastern Europe The Holy Roman Empire did not develop a strong monarchy. For instance, Germany was divided into hundreds of states that acted independently of the German ruler. After 1438, the Hapsburg dynasty of Austria held the position of Holy Roman Emperor. The house of Hapsburg was one of the wealthiest landholders in the empire. By the mid-fifteenth century, the Hapsburg rulers began to play a vital role in European affairs.

In eastern Europe, there was also great difficulty centralizing power, just as in Germany. Religious differences added to the problem, as Roman Catholics, Eastern Orthodox Christians, Mongols, and Muslims were in conflict. In Poland, the nobles established the right to elect their kings, which severely weakened the king's authority. In Moscow, the princes used their close relationship with Mongol khans, who had controlled Russia since the thirteenth century, to increase their wealth and power. During the reign of the great prince Ivan III of Moscow, a new Russian state was created. By 1480, the Mongols lost control of Russia.

CORE CONCEPT: POLITICAL SYSTEMS

Ivan III married the emperor's niece to establish himself as heir to the Byzantine Empire. He took the title of "czar," the Russian word for "Caesar" or "emperor." He defied Mongol rule by refusing to pay taxes. In 1480, he declared Moscow independent of the Mongols. Russians remember him as "Ivan the Great."

PRACTICING FOR THE REGENTS

Part I Multiple-Choice Questions

The following multiple-choice questions come from past Regents High School Examinations. Test your understanding of global history by answering each of these items. Circle the number of the word or expression that best completes each statement or question. Test-taking tips can be found in the margins for some questions. For additional help, see Taking the Regents Exam on pages ix–xxxv of this Review Book.

1 The phrase "from southern Spain, across northern Africa, occupying the Arabian peninsula to Southeast Asia" once described the extent of the
   (1) Aztec Empire   (3) Gupta Empire
   (2) Pax Romana   (4) Muslim world

2 • Developed a tribute system
   • Reestablished trade along the Silk Roads
   • Created an empire from Eastern Europe to the Pacific coast of Asia
   Which group was responsible for the results described above?
   (1) Huns   (3) Koreans
   (2) Japanese   (4) Mongols

3 During the early Middle Ages, western European societies were most influenced by
   (1) national monarchies
   (2) the Roman Catholic Church
   (3) elected parliaments
   (4) the Byzantine emperors

4 What is a major contribution of the Byzantine Empire to global history?
   (1) preservation of Greek and Roman culture
   (2) construction of the pyramids
   (3) expansion of equal rights
   (4) invention of writing

Base your answer to question 5 on the quotation below and on your knowledge of social studies.

> "Come then, with all your people and give battle with all your strength, so that all this treasure shall not fall into the hands of the Turks. . . . Therefore act while there is still time lest the kingdom of the Christians shall vanish from your sight . . . And in your coming you will find your reward in heaven. . . . "

5　Which event is referred to in this quotation?
(1) Enlightenment
(2) French Revolution
(3) Glorious Revolution
(4) Crusades

> "The Peace of God declared that feudal warfare could not take place on church property, and it promised sanctuary in churches and abbeys to fugitives from combat. The Truce of God forbade fighting from Wednesday evening until Monday morning, on holidays, and during the religious season of Christmas and Lent . . ."

—*Medieval and Early Modern Times*

6　This quotation implies that
(1) the church had considerable political power during this time
(2) war was limited to religious holidays
(3) religion was dictated by feudal law
(4) landlords determined when warfare took place

7　One similarity between the Gupta Dynasty (A.D. 320–550) in India and the Tang Dynasty (A.D. 618–907) in China is that each dynasty
(1) promoted equality for women
(2) made advances in the arts, sciences, and mathematics
(3) gained overseas colonies
(4) developed a representative

8　A direct result of the Crusades was that
(1) the pope lost control of the Church
(2) Europeans increased their demands for goods from the East
(3) Christians gained permanent control of the Holy Land
(4) nobles gained power over the monarchs

9　In a traditional economic system, which type of goods is most often produced?
(1) agricultural products
(2) heavy industrial machinery
(3) military supplies
(4) electronics and computers

Base your answers to questions 10 and 11 on the map below and on your knowledge of social studies.

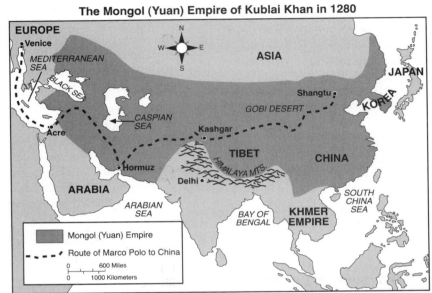

The Mongol (Yuan) Empire of Kublai Khan in 1280

Source: Henry Abraham and Irwin Pfeffer, *Enjoying Global History*, AMSCO (adapted)

10   The information provided by the map indicates that in 1280, the Mongols controlled
   (1) the areas of Africa, Asia, and Europe
   (2) territory from eastern China to eastern Europe
   (3) all of Asia
   (4) slavery

11   What was the effect of the extensive Mongol Empire on the people who lived in Europe and Asia in the 1200s?
   (1) development of common language
   (2) adoption of Confucian ideas and practices
   (3) expansion of Japanese cultural traditions
   (4) significant increases in trade and travel

12   Constantinople became the center of the Byzantine Empire because
   (1) the pope had made it the capital of the Christian world
   (2) it was a religious center for Muslims
   (3) its location made it the crossroads of Europe and Asia
   (4) it was geographically isolated from surrounding empires

13   One way the code of Chivalry in Europe and the code of Bushido in Japan were similar is that both codes
   (1) helped the ruler control his people
   (2) guide the behavior of a warrior class
   (3) benefit all the social classes
   (4) support revolutionary ideas

Base your answers to questions 14 and 15 on the following illustration and on your knowledge of social studies.

European Feudal System

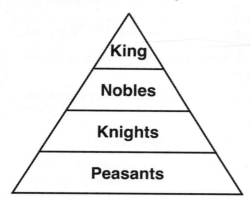

14 The illustration represents a society based on
  (1) social class
  (2) educational achievement
  (3) accumulated wealth
  (4) political ability

15 The illustration suggests that the European feudal system was
  (1) designed to promote political and economic equality
  (2) controlled by a powerful middle class
  (3) intended to provide opportunities for social mobility
  (4) supported by the labor of the peasants

16 What is a major contribution of the Byzantine Empire to global history?
  (1) preservation of Greek and Roman culture
  (2) construction of the pyramids
  (3) expansion of equal rights
  (4) invention of writing

17 Which factor contributed to the success of the vast empire created by the Mongols?
  (1) avoiding contacts with the West
  (2) paying monetary tribute to local rulers
  (3) employing superior military skills
  (4) converting conquered peoples to Confucianism

18 One result of the Crusades was an increase in trade between the Middle East and
  (1) East Asia
  (2) Africa
  (3) North America
  (4) Europe

19 The introduction of banking, letters of credit, joint stock companies, and guilds contributed to the start of the
  (1) Renaissance
  (2) Agricultural Revolution
  (3) Enlightenment
  (4) Commercial Revolution

20 The fall of the Byzantine Empire to the Ottoman Turks (1453) prompted Spain and Portugal to
  (1) seek new trade routes to East Asia
  (2) extend religious tolerance to Muslim peoples
  (3) reform their political systems
  (4) expand the Catholic Inquisition into the Middle East

Part II   Thematic Essay Question

The following thematic essay question comes from past Regents Examinations. Write your answers on a separate sheet of paper. Essay-writing tips appear in the margin. For additional help, see Taking the Regents Exam on pages ix–xxxv of this Review Book.

Directions: Write a well-organized essay that includes an introduction, several paragraphs addressing the task below, and a conclusion.

Theme: Change—Turning Points

Political, economic, and social conditions have often led to turning points that have changed the course of history for nations and people.

Task:

Identify *two* major turning points in global history and for *each*

- Describe the historical circumstances surrounding the turning point

- Explain how *each* turning point changed the course of history for nations and people

You may use any example from your study of global history. Some suggestions you might wish to consider include the Neolithic Revolution, the fall of the Roman Empire, the Crusades, the Renaissance, the Encounter, the French Revolution of 1917, World War I, creation of the modern state of Israel, Nelson Mandela elected president of South Africa, and the fall of the Berlin Wall.

Do *not* use any turning points in United States history.

You are *not* limited to these suggestions.

Guidelines:

In your essay, be sure to

- Develop all aspects of the task
- Support the theme with relevant facts, examples, and details
- Use a logical and clear plan of organization, including an introduction and conclusion that are beyond a restatement of the theme

Part III   Document-Based Question

This exercise is designed to test your ability to work with historical documents. It is similar to the document-based questions that you will see on the Regents Examination. While you are asked to analyze three historical documents, the exercise on the actual exam will include more documents. Some of the documents have been edited for the purposes of the question. As you analyze the documents, take into account the source of each document and any point of view that may be presented in the document.

Historical Context:

In early history, women had very little rights in many societies. They were controlled by men and not as valued. Throughout history, women have struggled with inequality in many ways, some successful, some not.

Task: Using information from the documents and your knowledge of Global History, answer the questions that follow each document in Part A. Your answers to the questions will help you write the Part B essay, in which you will be asked to

- Describe the change in women's attitudes from 1405 to 1842

Part A   Short-Answer Questions

Directions: Analyze the documents and answer the short-answer questions that follow each document in the space provided.

Document 1

. . . She ought to have the heart of a man, that is, she ought to know how to use weapons and be familiar with everything that pertains to them, so that she may be ready to command her men if the need arises. She should know how to launch an attack or to defend against one.

In addition she will do well to be a very good manager of the estate . . . She should often take time to visit the fields to see how the men are getting on with the work . . . She will busy herself around the house; she will find plenty of orders to give. She will have the animals brought in at the right time [and] take care how the shepherd looks after them . . .

–The Treasure of the City of Ladies, *Christine de Pizan, 1405*

1   What are some of the responsibilities of medieval gentlewomen, according to this account?

be familiar w/ and know how to use weapons, defend + launch attacks, command the men, be a manager of the estate, visit the fields, take care of the land

Document 2

> 1. Woman is born free and lives equal to man in her rights. Social distinctions can be based only on the common utility.
>
> 2. The purpose of any political association is the conservation of the natural and imprescriptible rights of woman and man; these rights are liberty, property, security, and especially resistance to oppression . . .
>
> 4. Liberty and justice consist of restoring all that belongs to others; thus, the only limits on the exercise of the natural rights of woman are perpetual male tyranny; these limits are to be reformed by the laws of nature and reason . . .
>
> 6. The law must be . . . the same for all: male and female citizens . . .
>
> 7. No woman is an exception; she is accused, arrested, and detained in cases determined by law. Women, like men, obey this rigorous law . . .
>
> 11. the free communication of thoughts and opinions is one of the most precious rights of woman, since that liberty assured the recognition of children by their fathers . . .
>
> –Declaration of the Rights of Woman and the Female Citizen, *Olympe de Gouges, 1791*

2   According to the declaration, what does liberty and justice consist of?

<u>restoring all that belongs to others</u>

Document 3

> Who has not heard of the women silkworkers' dirty, unhealthy, and badly paid work; of the women in the spinning and weaving factories working fourteen to sixteen hours (except for one hour for both meals); always standing, without a single minute for repose, putting forth an enormous amount of effort. And many of them have to walk a league or more, morning and evening, to get home. Nor should we neglect to mention the danger that exists merely from working in these large factories, surrounded by wheels, gears, enormous leather belts that always threaten to seize you and pound you to pieces.
>
> The existence of women who work as day laborers, and are obliged to abandon . . . the care of their children to indifferent neighbors is no better . . . We believe that the condition of women will never really improve until workingmen can earn enough to support their families, which is only fair. Woman is so closely linked to man that the position of the one cannot be improved without reference to the position of the other.
>
> –*from* L'Atelier, *a Parisian newspaper, 1842*

3   According to the passage, how can the condition of women improve?

<u>reduce working hours, increasing safety in machinery</u>

Part B   Essay

Directions: Write a well-organized essay that includes an introduction, several paragraphs, and a conclusion.

Use evidence from at least three documents in the body of the essay. Support your response with relevant facts, examples, and details. Include additional outside information.

Historical Context:

In early history, women had very little rights in many societies. They were controlled by men and not as valued. Throughout history, women have struggled with inequality in many ways, some successful, some not.

Task: Using information from the documents and your knowledge of global history and geography, write an essay in which you

> • Describe the change in women's attitudes from 1405 to 1842

Guidelines:

In your essay, be sure to

- Address all aspects of the task
- Incorporate information from *at least three* documents in the body of the essay
- Incorporate relevant outside information
- Support the theme with relevant facts, examples, and details
- Use a logical and clear plan of organization, including an introduction and conclusion that are beyond a restatement of the theme

UNIT 3   CONVERGING CULTURES, *1200–1650*

Unit 3 Overview

The immediate ancestors of modern human beings came from East Africa. Civilization emerged in areas where farming was mastered. Some African civilizations later became wealthy by trading ivory, gold, iron, salt, and other goods. Migration and the spread of Islam were also important.

In Europe, the Italian Renaissance introduced Europe to a secular worldview and a boom in artistic and intellectual development. These changes eventually led to the birth of Protestantism. The social upheaval led to absolutism, the complete control of government by a monarch. The works of John Locke and other Enlightenment philosophers would influence the French and American Revolutions.

Early Japanese society was made up of clans and attempts to unify the country were often thwarted by rival noble families. Japanese unification began in the mid-sixteenth century. A series of shoguns, the Tokugawa, ushered in the "Great Peace." Under Tokugawa rule, trade and manufacturing flourished. European traders and missionaries arrived. However, fear that Japanese Christians would be aligned with the pope led to the missionaries' expulsion. Japan began a period of isolation that lasted for more than two centuries.

Unit 3 Objectives

After studying this unit, you should be able to:

1.   describe important aspects of African society, such as government, the role of women, education, religion and the arts;

2.   explain the achievements of the Renaissance and the effects of the Protestant Reformation;

3.   trace the growing power of monarchs and the rise of absolutism in Europe;

4.   identify the major cultural and social elements in Japan.

Chapter Overview

The continent of Africa has played a central role in the long evolution of humankind. It was in Africa that the immediate ancestors of modern human beings—*Homo sapiens sapiens*—emerged between 200,000 and 150,000 years ago. Certainly, one of the first civilizations appeared in Africa: the kingdom of Egypt in the Nile Valley. A number of advanced societies took root in other parts of Africa as well.

The events that occurred in Africa still affect our lives today. The expansion of trade created a global society, allowing people to exchange goods, services, and ideas throughout the world. African art, music, and dance remain very influential today.

As you read through this chapter, ask yourself these questions:
(1) How did Africa's four distinct climate zones affect the development of African civilization?
(2) How did the expansion of trade lead to migration and the development of new kingdoms?
(3) What was the basis of the African family and society?

Main Ideas and Concepts

- **Physical Systems** Africa's physical features and climate have affected its cultural development.

- **Belief Systems** The coming of Islam and Christianity changed society in Africa.

- **Economic Development** African trade practices led to the development and fall of a series of kingdoms.

- **Factors of Production** Kingdoms were based on the trans-Saharan gold and salt trade.

LINKING PAST AND PRESENT

African music has greatly influenced the contemporary music scene. African music featured a strong rhythmic beat and both vocal and instrumental roles with a pattern of call and response. A leader sang a short piece, and the people would repeat it to the beat of drums. When enslaved Africans were brought to America, they often sang to lessen or lament the burden of their work days. Their music inspired jazz, gospel, ragtime, blues, rock and roll, and rap.

CORE CONCEPTS: ENVIRONMENT AND SOCIETY

The rivers of Africa have generally not been used for transportation because of the number of waterfalls and rapids on the four major rivers: the Nile, the Congo (or Zaire), the Niger, and the Zambezi. These rapids are caused by the escarpment, the sudden drop of territory to the east of Africa's plateau. They do offer the possibility of hydroelectric power for the continent. Developing hydroelectricity requires capital and technology, both of which are scarce in Africa. Only a few African nations have built dams and power facilities to produce hydroelectricity.

CORE CONCEPTS: . PHYSICAL SYSTEMS

The Great Rift Valley is one of Earth's natural wonders. A series of parallel faults or cracks in Earth's surface stretches for some 3,000 miles (4800 kilometers) from Ethiopia in the north to Kenya in the south. Due to the volcanic soil thrust up when the faults were first formed, this is one of the most fertile farming areas in Africa. Several lakes, including Lake Victoria, the world's third-largest lake, are also part of this region.

People, Places, Terms

The following names and terms will help you to prepare for the Regents Exam in Global History and Geography. You can find an explanation of each name and term in the Glossary at the back of this book, in your textbook, or in another reference source.

animism	**Great Rift Valley**	plateau
Bantu	griot	savanna
clan	lineage group	stateless society
desertification	matrilineal	subsistence farming
diviner	patrilineal	

SECTION 1 THE DEVELOPMENT OF CIVILIZATIONS IN AFRICA

The Land of Africa

Africa is the second largest continent in the world. It is nearly completely surrounded by two oceans and two seas. Its geography is very diverse. Along the northern coast are mountains. The Sahara, the largest desert on Earth, lies to the south of the mountains. The desert gradually changes to steppe (dry, largely treeless grasslands) and then high grasslands called savannas. Tropical jungles lie along the west coast but comprise less than 10 percent of Africa's total land mass. The east features snow-capped mountains, lakes, and upland plateaus. The **Great Rift Valley**, with its deep canyons surrounded by mountains, is in this region of Africa. In the south, the rain forest around the Congo River changes gradually into hills, deserts, and **plateaus.**

The Climate of Africa

The four major climate zones of Africa are Mediterranean, desert, rain forest, and savanna. The Mediterranean climate zone is along the northern coast and southern tip of the continent. Moderate rainfall and warm temperatures allow an abundance of crops to be grown. Deserts cover about 40 percent of Africa. The largest are the Sahara in the north and the Kalahari in the south. About 10 percent of Africa is made up of rain forest, located along the equator and parts of the west coast. Heavy rains and dense forests, as well as disease-bearing insects, make farming and travel difficult. The **savannas**, broad grasslands

dotted with shrubs and small trees, are found both north and
south of the rain forest. They make up another 40 percent of the
land. Although the rainfall is unreliable, there is usually enough
to farm and to herd animals.

AFRICAN TRADING EMPIRES, 1000 B.C.–A.D.1600

	Kush (Nubia) Meroë	Axum Adulis	Ghana Saleh	Mali Timbuktu	Songhai Gao
Empire					
Location	East Africa south of Egypt	East Africa (Ethiopia)	West Africa	West Africa	West Africa
Time Period	1000 B.C.–A.D. 150	A.D. 100–1400	A.D. 400–1200	A.D. 1250–1450	A.D. 1000–1600
Goods Traded	Iron products, ivory, gold, ebony, slaves	Ivory, frankincense, myrrh, slaves	Iron products, animal products, gold	Gold, salt	Gold, salt
Key Facts	Kush lost power to Axum.	Axum was founded by Arab traders; the king converted to Christianity in A.D. 324.	Ghana traded for salt from the Saharan salt mines.	Mansa Musa doubled the size of the kingdom and created a Muslim center of learning.	Songhai gained control of trade in West Africa with the conquest of Timbuktu and Jenne.

Emerging Civilization and the Rise of Islam

   People in Africa began taming animals and growing crops
around seven or eight thousand years ago. This led to the
development of the first civilizations in Africa. Egypt, Kush, and
Axum were among the earliest civilizations.

Kush Kush grew out of the region that had been known as
Nubia, located south of Egypt near the banks of the Nile. Egypt
and Nubia traded items such as ebony, ivory, leopard skins, and
frankincense. Egypt controlled Nubia until around 1000 B.C.,
which is when the area became known as Kush. For a brief time,
between 750 and 663 B.C., the Kushites ruled Egypt. They were
conquered by the Assyrians.

**CORE CONCEPTS:
ENVIRONMENT**

The growing amount of
territory that has become
desert is a cause for global
concern. Hardest hit is an
area south of the Sahara
made up of Mali, Niger,
Chad, Mauritania, Sudan, and
Ethiopia. Some causes of
desertification include
drought, overgrazing, and
deforestation.

CORE CONCEPTS: SCIENCE AND TECHNOLOGY

The Assyrians defeated the Kushites because of superior weaponry. After their defeat, the Kushites developed iron deposits in Nubia. Their new capital, Meroë, became one of the great iron-making centers of the ancient world. Ideally situated, Meroë was located on a newly opened trade route across the desert to the north.

CORE CONCEPTS: MOVEMENT OF PEOPLE AND GOODS

Through trade, Axum came into contact with Rome and Greece, the great western civilizations of the time. Either traders or missionaries brought Christianity to Africa around A.D. 100. Modern Ethiopia, which traces its heritage to Axum, is one of the oldest Christian nations in the world.

The Kushite economy was originally based on farming. After learning how to make iron tools and weapons from the Assyrians, the Kushites traded these goods with the Roman Empire, India, and Arabia. Kush flourished until about A.D. 150, when a new power known as Axum arose.

The Rise of Axum Arabs founded Axum, located in what is now Ethiopia, as a colony. Eventually, it became a state combining African and Arab cultures. On a trade route between India and the Mediterranean, it competed with Kush for control of the ivory trade. Its imports included textiles, metal goods, wine, and olive oil. It exported slaves, ivory, frankincense, and myrrh.

King Ezana, an Axumite leader, invaded and conquered Kush in the fourth century A.D. After his conversion to Christianity around A.D. 330, King Ezana made Christianity Axum's official religion.

The Coming of Islam Arab forces took control of Egypt in the seventh century. By the following century, Arabs controlled the entire North African coastal region. On the Red Sea's African coast, several Muslim trading states were established. Although Axum was a Christian state, relations were peaceful with Muslim states for hundreds of years. In the twelfth century, however, desiring control over the slave trade and ivory, Muslim states began moving inward. By the fifteenth century, Axum was in a growing conflict with the Muslim state of Adal, where the Indian Ocean and Red Sea meet.

SECTION 2 KINGDOMS AND STATES OF AFRICA

West Africa was the site of three major kingdoms: Ghana, Mali, and Songhai.

The Kingdom of Ghana

Ghana was located in the upper Nile River valley, between the Sahara and the tropical forests along the coast of West Africa. (The contemporary nation of Ghana takes its name, but not its location, from the ancient kingdom.) The kingdom of Ghana, really a loose federation of villages, emerged around A.D. 300.

The Kings of Ghana Ghana's kings relied on a large army to protect the kingdom. Strong rulers possessed great wealth as a result of the taxes collected from the trans-Saharan gold and salt trade.

Economy and Trade While most of Ghana's people were farmers, Ghana prospered because of large supplies of gold and iron ore. The gold, which was traded for metal goods, horses, textiles, and salt, made Ghana the center of a trade empire.

Much of the trade across the desert moved by camel caravans led by nomads called Berbers. Because camels could survive for days without food or water, they were crucial to Saharan trade.

The Kingdom of Mali

Mali was founded in the mid-thirteenth century by Sundiata Keita. Although located on the Atlantic coast, Mali extends far inland to its most famous city, Timbuktu.

Founding and Economy Sundiata Keita conquered the kingdom of Ghana and captured their capital in 1240. He united the people and created a strong central government. Most people farmed, growing grains such as rice, millet, and sorghum. The wealth of the kingdom was built on the salt and gold trade. People lived in villages under the rule of a religious and administrative leader. This person collected taxes and sent them to Mali's kings.

Reign of Mansa Musa One of the richest and most powerful kings of Mali was Mansa Musa. He doubled the size of the kingdom and divided it into provinces ruled by governors. A devout Muslim, he made a pilgrimage to Mecca (also spelled Makkah). When he returned, he brought architects to build a mosque and a palace. He also brought books and scholars to teach Islam to the people. Two years after his death, civil war destroyed the kingdom of Mali.

The Kingdom of Songhai

The Songhai people established their kingdom along the Niger River. Like the Nile, the Niger overflows its banks, creating rich soil for farming and tending cattle. The Dia dynasty, the first Songhai state, was established in 1009 when a ruler named Kossi converted to Islam. Because it was on the Muslim trade routes linking North Africa, West Africa, and Arabia, the Songhai kingdom prospered.

Sunni Ali began a new dynasty, the Sunni, in 1464. Songhai expanded under his leadership, gaining control of the trading empire that had made Ghana and Mali prosperous.

CORE CONCEPTS: SCARCITY

In Europe, no large gold deposits existed, so Europeans depended on the gold of West African kingdoms. The source of that gold remains a mystery. The traders exchanged gold for salt (needed in the hot climate) at a safe location outside their territories.

CORE CONCEPTS: SCARCITY

When Mansa Musa went on pilgrimage, he was accompanied by thousands of soldiers and servants and by hundreds of camels carrying gold, clothing, food, and supplies. Mansa Musa distributed gold freely during his pilgrimage. As a result, gold was devalued in Egypt for more than a decade.

The height of the Songhai Empire occurred during the reign of Muhammed Ture, who overthrew Sunni Ali's son and created the Askia dynasty. Continuing to expand, the empire eventually stretched a thousand miles along the Niger River. Muhammed Ture divided the empire into provinces ruled by governors. He used mounted soldiers and the navy to maintain peace and security. The gold and slave trade enriched the empire. Songhai declined after the death of Muhammed Ture. By the end of the sixteenth century, Moroccan forces occupied much of the kingdom.

Societies in East Africa

A number of small states grew up in East Africa. Many of them became wealthy through trade. Islam was a strong influence in many of these states.

Migration of the Bantus Farming peoples who spoke the dialect of the **Bantu** family of languages began moving from the Niger River into East Africa and the Congo River basin. Their communities were based on **subsistence farming**, with the main crops being grains, yams, beans, and melons. Both stone and iron tools were used in farming. Bantu women tended the children and fields. Men hunted, traded, or tended herds. It was the Bantu who spread iron-smelting techniques across Africa, as well as the knowledge of high-yield crops like yams and bananas.

Indian Ocean Trade and Ports Gradually, the Bantu began taking part in the regional trade along Africa's east coast. Beginning in the eighth century, Muslim traders began settling at ports along the coast. They founded the trading ports of Mogadishu, Mombasa, and Kilwa, which became wealthy. Kilwa was one of the most beautiful cities in the world. The Great Mosque and the Husuni Kubwa Palace were magnificent buildings, which the Portuguese destroyed in 1505.

A new culture known as Swahili, a mixture of African and Arabian culture, developed along the coast. Arabic architecture and the Muslim religion became a part of the area's culture. Swahili was also the name of the language, which combined Bantu and Arabic words and phrases. It is still the official language today in Kenya and Tanzania.

LINKING PAST AND PRESENT

The Bantu migration routes continue to be debated. Many historians believe they spread across one-third of the African continent. The Bantu founded Kongo (Congo), Luba, and Luanda in central Africa, as well as Tanzania, Malawi, Zambia, and Zimbabwe to the southeast. Their influence continues today through about 150 million Bantu speakers in Africa.

States and Stateless Societies in South Africa

Until the eleventh century, most of the peoples in the south-western half of Africa lived in **stateless societies**. These consisted of a group of independent villages organized by **clans** and led by a local ruler or clan head. The villages began consolidating; from these came the first states. Zimbabwe was the wealthiest and most powerful state in the region from about 1300 to 1450. Its prosperity came from the gold trade, which stretched to places as far away as China.

SECTION 3 AFRICAN SOCIETY AND CULTURE

Aspects of African Society

The center of government was the African town. The towns grew from walled villages into larger communities. Their markets were filled with goods from far regions of the world. Artisans—who were skilled in pottery, woodworking, and metalworking—lived in the towns with the merchants. Farmers, who grew crops in the nearby fields, traveled to the markets to sell their products in the towns.

King and Subject The relationship between king and subject was mutually beneficial. Merchants paid taxes to the king, and the king granted them favors. African kings, although held in high regard, were not as separated from the people as they were in many nations. Rulers sometimes held meetings to allow people to voice their complaints. Most people, however, lived in small country villages and had limited contact with leaders.

Family and Lineage The extended family was the basic level of society. Parents, children, grandparents, and other close relations lived in communities made up of other extended families known as **lineage groups**. All members of the lineage group claimed to be able to trace their ancestry to a common person. Members of extended families and lineage groups were expected to protect their members, providing many services expected from a government.

The Role of Women The women generally were subordinate to the men in Africa. Their value was in their ability to bear and

CORE CONCEPTS: SCIENCE AND TECHNLOGY

Great Zimbabwe, the kingdom's capital, was a walled city capable of housing ten thousand people. Luxury goods, including Chinese porcelain, have been found at the ruins of the city. To make the walls of Great Zimbabwe, workers stacked granite blocks, using no mortar.

CORE CONCEPTS: THE WORLD IN SPATIAL TERMS

At the northern border of Zimbabwe is the Zambezi River, which flows from its source near the Zambia-Angola border in the west to the Indian Ocean in the east. There it fans out into a delta 37 miles wide. By contrast, the delta of the Mississippi River is a mile and a half wide where it empties into the Gulf of Mexico. On the way to the sea, the river descends in many waterfalls. At Victoria Falls on the border of Zambia and Zimbabwe, it drops 355 feet (108 m). That is about twice the drop of Horseshoe Falls on the Niagara River at the Canadian-U.S. border.

raise children. Women often worked in the fields, while men hunted or tended to cattle.

In many African societies, lineage was based on the mother rather than the father. This is known as a **matrilineal** society. A **patrilineal** society is more common, when ancestry and inheritance come from the father. In a matrilineal society, husbands may be expected to move into the homes of their wives. Women were often permitted to inherit property.

Community Education and Initiation A typical village had a process to educate young people and prepare them for life in the community. Mothers taught both sons and daughters the language, songs, and family history until the children were six years old. At that point, the fathers took over the training of their sons, who learned to hunt, fish, and clear fields to grow and harvest plants. Mothers continued teaching their daughters, focusing on the domestic skills needed to run a home. At puberty, children experienced an initiation ceremony, bringing them into full community membership.

Slavery From ancient times, slavery had been practiced in Africa. Slaves included people who were captured in war, debtors, and criminals. Not all slaves were seen as inferior. Many were valued for special skills or knowledge or were trusted servants. Some became soldiers. Those who were domestic servants usually had the best lives.

Religious Beliefs in Africa

Most African societies shared some common religious ideas, including **animism**—a belief that the world was full of spirits that existed in the natural world.

Ritual, carried out by **diviners**, was one way to communicate with the gods. The diviners believed they had the power to foretell the future, usually by working with supernatural forces. The king employed many diviners to guarantee good harvests or to protect the kingdom.

Another element of African traditional religion was the importance of ancestors. Because they were believed to be closer to the gods, the ancestors had power to influence, for good or evil, the lives of their descendants. These souls lived on in an afterlife, as long as the lineage group performed the rituals and ceremonies in their name.

CORE CONCEPTS: BELIEF SYSTEMS

The initiation process involved isolating the young person from the community for a time. Youngsters were expected to show independence and great courage. Afterwards, in a ritual ceremony, they symbolically died and were reborn. This ceremony made them full adult members of the community.

CORE CONCEPTS: BELIEF SYSTEMS

The Yoruba people of Nigeria believed that their chief god sent his son, Oduduwa, to create the first humans. Oduduwa arrived by canoe. Many of the enslaved Africans of the Americas practiced the Yoruba religion.

The arrival of Islam did not always replace traditional beliefs. Islam swept across the continent's northern coast but was slower to reach the interior and was accepted more slowly in lands south of the Sahara. Progress was slower too in East Africa, particularly in Ethiopia, where Christianity was strong.

When the ideas of Islam contradicted those of traditional religion, they were sometimes ignored. For example, Islam rejected spirit worship and demanded distinct roles for men and women. Fusing native beliefs with Islam created a unique brand of Africanized Islam.

African Culture

The arts were a means of expressing religion in early Africa. Rock paintings, the most famous of which are in the Tassili Mountains of the central Sahara, were the earliest art forms. Wood carvers throughout Africa made masks and statues, often meant to represent gods, spirits, or ancestral figures. Unfortunately, much African art using wood as a medium was destroyed due to the effects of the harsh climates. In parts of Africa, metal and clay figurines and statues were also common.

The music and dance of Africa also served a religious purpose. Dances were a means of communication with spirits. The lyrics of songs conveyed religious traditions, folk legends, and historical information from one generation to another. Storytelling did the same thing. It was the job of the storyteller to keep the history of a people alive.

CORE CONCEPTS: CULTURE

During the thirteenth and fourteenth centuries, metalworkers produced beautiful statues in Ife, located in what is now southern Nigeria, and in Benin in West Africa. The artists of Ife worked in iron and bronze; those in Benin worked in bronze and may have been influenced by the Ife artists.

CORE CONCEPTS: CULTURE

Professional storytellers who were responsible for the history of a community were known as **griots**. Much of our knowledge of the founder of the kingdom of Mali, Sundiata Keita, has been passed down through the griots' oral culture.

Chapter Overview

Following the Crusades, Europe entered the modern era with a series of explosive changes. The medieval world view shattered as thinkers turned their eyes from heaven to more worldly concerns such as trade and nation-building. In the fifteenth century, intellectuals in Italy were convinced that they had entered a new age of human achievement. Today, we call this period of European history the Renaissance. A spirit of inquiry led some people to challenge the authority of the Roman Catholic Church. Leaders such as Martin Luther eventually broke away from the Church and established a new religion that came to be known as Protestantism.

As you read through this chapter, ask yourself these questions:
(1) How did the Renaissance serve as a bridge into the modern era?
(2) What was humanism and how did it transform Renaissance society?
(3) What events contributed to the religious upheavals known as the Reformation?
(4) How did the Protestant Reformation affect the Catholic Church and what actions did the church take?

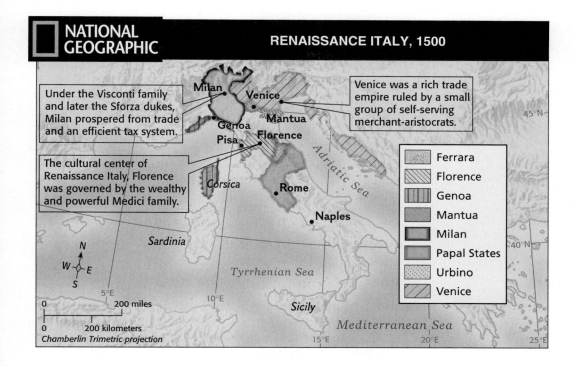

NATIONAL GEOGRAPHIC

RENAISSANCE ITALY, 1500

Under the Visconti family and later the Sforza dukes, Milan prospered from trade and an efficient tax system.

Venice was a rich trade empire ruled by a small group of self-serving merchant-aristocrats.

The cultural center of Renaissance Italy, Florence was governed by the wealthy and powerful Medici family.

Legend:
- Ferrara
- Florence
- Genoa
- Mantua
- Milan
- Papal States
- Urbino
- Venice

0   200 miles
0   200 kilometers
Chamberlin Trimetric projection

Main Ideas and Concepts

- **Culture** Cultural developments during the Renaissance represented a shift away from the medieval emphasis on the spiritual world to a greater concern with the secular, or non-spiritual world.

- **Change** The Reformation challenged a social order based upon the power and authority of the Church. In so doing, the movement ended European religious unity.

- **Technology** Technological inventions and their uses, such as the printing press, opened the way for the rapid dissemination of new ideas and increased literacy.

- **Urbanization** Powerful city-states became the centers of political, economic and social life. Within these urban societies, a new middle class was growing.

REGENTS WARM-UP

Use the map of Renaissance Italy to answer the following questions:

Venice, Milan, and Florence were the most powerful city-states in Renaissance Italy. What geographic features did they have in common?

Why were Italian city-states able to dominate trade patterns?

Which city-state was in the best location to trade by land and sea with the Byzantine Empire to the east?

People, Places, Terms

The following names and terms will help you to prepare for the Regents Exam in Global History and Geography. You can find an explanation of each name and term in the Glossary at the back of this book, in your textbook, or in another reference source.

John Calvin	indulgence	predestination
Christian humanism	justification	Renaissance
Council of Trent	Martin Luther	simony
Leonardo da Vinci	Niccolo Machiavelli	vernacular
humanism	Michelangelo	

SECTION 1 THE RENAISSANCE

The Italian Renaissance

The word *renaissance* means rebirth. In Italy between 1350 and 1550 many people believed they were witnessing a rebirth of ancient Greek and Roman knowledge. Italy was the first center of the Renaissance because of its strategic location and its Roman heritage. The cultural and political ideas and characteristics of this rebirth eventually spread throughout Europe. The Renaissance also produced an expansion of trade, exploration, and new forms of technology.

During this time, Italy and the rest of Europe were recovering from the disasters of the fourteenth century, such as the plague, political instability, and a decline in Church power. Powerful city-states were centers of cultural and political life in northern and central Italy. With this new rise of urban society came more secular views of the world, and increased wealth led to more leisure time for education, art, and the investigation of ideas.

A new view of human beings emerged as the people of the Renaissance began to emphasize individual ability and achievements. Humanism, as the movement came to be known, put importance on people improving their lives through gaining knowledge in a wide variety of subjects.

Renaissance Artists

Renaissance thinkers believed a well-rounded person could achieve success in many areas of life. **Leonardo da Vinci** was a true Renaissance man: a painter, sculptor, architect, inventor,

CORE CONCEPTS: CULTURE

The philosophy of the Renaissance was centered upon individual human potential. Renaissance values differed from Greek values with the inclusion of Christian ideas. Two leading Christian Renaissance thinkers were Desiderius Erasmus of Holland and Thomas More of England. In *Utopia*, Thomas More wrote about an ideal world free of war, ignorance, and injustice. Both criticized abuses within the Catholic Church.

engineer, and mathematician. Among his most notable works are the *Mona Lisa* and *The Last Supper*. Combining his interest in art and science, he also created sketches of flying machines and submarines centuries before these machines were actually built.

Another renowned figure was **Michelangelo**, who was an accomplished sculptor, painter, and architect. Over the course of four years (1508–1512) he painted the ceiling of the Sistine Chapel. His sculptures of the Biblical *David* and *The Pieta* showed a revival of Greek style and the introduction of realism. His works are considered some of the great masterpieces of Western art.

The Italian States

The lack of a central ruler in Italy allowed several city-states to remain independent and flourish. Expanded trade with the Byzantine and Islamic civilizations that had begun in the Middle Ages brought prosperity. Trading centers set up during the Crusades allowed merchants to bring silks, sugar, and spices back to Italy and the west. Italian trading ships also moved into the western Mediterranean and north along the Atlantic seaboard to trade in England and the Netherlands.

One of the richest city-states was Milan, located at the crossroads between Italy's coastal cities and the Alpine passes. Francesco Sforza and his band of mercenaries (soldiers who sold their services to the highest bidder) conquered the city in 1447. The rulers of Milan created a strong centralized government that was able to generate large amounts of tax revenue for the city.

Florence was governed by a small group of wealthy merchants, most notably the Medici family. The Medicis, who grew wealthy through their trading activities, dominated the politics of the city. Cosimo de' Medici and his grandson, Lorenzo de' Medici, were great patrons of the arts. The fortunes of the city eventually declined due to competition from foreign cloth manufacturers, and the Medici family was forced from power.

Machiavelli and the New Statecraft

One of the most influential books on political power was written during the Renaissance by a man named **Niccolo Machiavelli**. *The Prince* was mainly concerned with how to get and keep political power. In the book, Machiavelli wrote that leaders must be strong and ruthless to protect their states.

CORE CONCEPTS: MOVEMENT OF PEOPLE AND GOODS

The Renaissance took firmest hold in nations with commercial or urban environments. The Netherlands and Great Britain—both trading states—formed key centers of the northern Renaissance.

CORE CONCEPTS: POWER

A Dominican preacher named Girolamo Savonarola condemned the corruption and excesses of the Medici family. Florentines, frustrated by the economic downturn, backed Savonarola. However, they soon tired of his stringent regulations on swearing, gambling, and even pursuits such as painting and music. Savonarola also attacked corruption in the church, which angered the pope. In 1498, Savonarola was accused of heresy and sentenced to death. The Medici family returned to power.

Writers in the Middle Ages emphasized the importance of persons in power behaving ethically and following Christian principles. Machiavelli rejected that. He believed that a prince's behavior must be based on an understanding of human nature, which he thought was basically self-centered. A prince must be aware that people act in their own self-interest and therefore should not be guided by moral principles when making decisions in the best interest of the state. Our modern word Machiavellian means someone who is prepared to do anything to reach a goal.

Renaissance Society

Although Renaissance society was divided into three estates, or social classes, much like the Middle Ages, there were changes. Serfdom was in decline as the labor owed by a peasant to a lord was converted into rent on land paid in money. There was also a growing middle class due to increased prosperity in the urban city-states.

Nobles dominated society, although they were only a small proportion of the population. They held important political posts and served as advisors to the king.

Peasants and townspeople made up the majority of society, but their ranks became more diverse. Townspeople were divided into three classes—patricians, burghers, and the poor and unemployed.

Patricians were wealthy industrialists, bankers, and merchants. Beneath them were the burghers: shopkeepers, artisans, and guild members who provided services for the town.

The number of working poor and unemployed increased dramatically with the growth of urban society, making up about 30 to 40 percent of the population. Those in the upper reaches of society had little sympathy or patience for their situation.

Family and Marriage

Family bonds were especially important in urban Renaissance Italy, and marriages were arranged to strengthen family or business ties. The most important aspect of the upper-class marriage contract was the size of the dowry, a sum of money given by the wife's family to the husband upon marriage.

The husband-father was the most important figure in the family. He had control over the finances and made all the decisions that controlled his children's lives. Children did not become adults until their fathers went before a judge and formally freed them.

Role of Women Though still dependent on a father, brother or husband, upper-class women in the Renaissance had more educational opportunity. Some, like Artemesia Gentileschi, were taught painting. She went on to become the court artist in Spain. Christine de Pisan wrote *The City of Women*, in which she made the case for using the talents of women in society.

SECTION 2 THE INTELLECTUAL AND ARTISTIC RENAISSANCE

Italian Renaissance Humanism

A major intellectual movement of the Renaissance was **humanism**. It was based on the study of the literary classics of the Greeks and Romans and incorporated secularism and an emphasis on human characteristics. Subjects studied included grammar, rhetoric, poetry, moral philosophy, and history—what today we call the humanities.

An Italian scholar named Petrarch has been called the father of the humanist movement. He led the movement to locate and use works by Greek and Roman writers. However, humanists in Florence broke with Petrarch's views that humanists should shun family and public life. They believed instead that it was the duty of an intellectual to live an active life in service of one's state.

The Impact of Printing

In 1455, Johannes Gutenberg of Germany invented a printing press with moveable metal type that allowed for the mass production of texts. Before this invention, books had to be copied by hand, and were expensive and time-consuming to produce. Gutenberg's Bible was the first European book produced from moveable type.

The mass-production of texts encouraged scholarly research and increased people's desire for knowledge. Literacy increased and new ideas about philosophy, literature, and religion spread more rapidly. Of the almost forty thousand books printed by 1500, more than half were religious titles. These religious publications created an interest in reform both within the Catholic Church and among its opponents.

CORE CONCEPTS: SCIENCE AND TECHNOLOGY

The Chinese invented block printing around A.D. 700. Europeans learned to cast single letters on blocks in the 1400s. Most historians believe Gutenberg devised the first printing press that made use of individual, or moveable, type. The invention of printing advanced the spread of new ideas by making books more widely available at inexpensive prices.

Vernacular Literature

The emphasis on classical Roman works led to the use of Latin in many texts. However, some writers chose instead to write in the **vernacular**, the language spoken in their own regions, such as Italian, French or German. Writers such as Dante (*The Divine Comedy*) and Chaucer (*The Canterbury Tales*) wrote in their native languages.

Education in the Renaissance

Renaissance humanists believed that education could dramatically change human beings. They opened schools to share their ideas and taught various classes in liberal studies, or what we today call liberal arts. Typical subjects included history, moral philosophy, eloquence (or rhetoric), letters (grammar and logic), poetry, mathematics, astronomy, and music. Students also participated in physical activities such as archery and javelin throwing.

Females attended schools in small numbers but were excluded from mathematics and rhetoric. Religion and morals education was considered most important for "Christian ladies" so that they would become good mothers and wives.

The Artistic Renaissance

Human beings took center stage in the artistic works of the Renaissance. Renaissance art was characterized by the use of perspective, shading, and blending religious themes with natural settings. Artists were interested in re-creating nature and imbuing their pieces with a sense of reality—a break with the flat, stylized art of the Middle Ages. Although the subject matter remained largely devoted to religious subjects, Italian Renaissance artists introduced natural elements and also turned to classical mythology.

New Techniques in Painting

Masaccio was an early Florentine artist who mastered the technique of painting frescoes (water-based paints applied on fresh, wet plaster). By mastering the laws of perspective, which enabled him to create the illusion of three dimensions, Masaccio developed a new, realistic style of painting.

This mastery of perspective was key to the development of Renaissance art. Another important technical aspect was the use

CORE CONCEPTS: NEEDS AND WANTS

The purpose of a liberal education was to produce well-rounded individuals who would follow a path of virtue and wisdom and convince those around them to do the same.

REGENTS WARM-UP

Some questions in past Regents Exams have used photographs of great works of art to test your ability to recognize the values reflected in these works. Skim through a world history textbook used in your school to identify some of the great artistic works of Europe. Look for works by da Vinci, Dürer, Giotto, Holbein, and Michelangelo.

of geometry to achieve correct organization of outdoor light and space. Finally, painters were very interested in anatomy and the movement of the human body. The aim was to create as realistic a portrayal as possible, especially of the human nude.

Sculpture and Architecture Inspiration for Renaissance sculptors and architects came largely from classical Greek and Roman works. The architect Filippo Brunelleschi designed a church in Florence that was very different from the grandiose Gothic style of the Middle Ages. Using classical columns and rounded arches, the space provided comfort for worshippers instead of overwhelming them. The space was designed with the worshippers, not the worshipped, in mind.

Masters of the High Renaissance The final stage of the Renaissance, the High Renaissance, took place between 1490 and 1520. Leonardo da Vinci, Raphael, and Michelangelo are artists associated with this period. These men had mastered the realistic portrayal of the human form and were interested in creating idealized forms. Da Vinci sought to express the perfection of nature and the individual, while Michelangelo was interested in portraying divine beauty in perfectly proportioned human form.

The Northern Renaissance

The artists of northern Europe, especially the Low Countries (present-day Belgium, Luxembourg, and the Netherlands), were also interested in the realistic portrayal of the world around them. They focused on scenes of everyday life and portraits and worked on illustrating books and small panels that required a mastery of precise detail and creating objects on a small scale. Rembrandt, a Dutch painter, was very concerned with the contrast of light and shadow in his painting.

The most important northern school of art in the fifteenth century was found in Flanders. Jan van Eyck, a Flemish painter, was one of the first to use oil paint, which allowed him a wide range of colors and the ability to create fine detail, as in his work *Giovanni Arnolfini and His Bride*.

Albrecht Dürer was a German artist who incorporated both styles into his work. He learned the laws of perspective during two trips to Italy and used them, along with the minute details of northern artists, in his work *Adoration of the Magi*. Another of his works, *Melancholia*, showed a Renaissance flair for investigating the life of the mind.

SECTION 3 THE PROTESTANT REFORMATION

Erasmus and Christian Humanism

During the second half of the fifteenth century, the humanism that had such an influence on Italian Renaissance thinkers spread to northern Europe. A movement known as **Christian humanism** began. Its major goal was reform of the Catholic Church.

The Christian humanists believed in the ability of human beings to reason and improve themselves. They thought that if people studied the basic works of Christianity, they would change themselves, become more pious, and thus change society.

The best known Christian humanist was a man named Desiderius Erasmus. He called his view of religion "the philosophy of Christ." He meant that Christianity should show people how to live good lives rather than provide a system of beliefs that people have to practice to be saved. By using satire, Erasmus ridiculed superstition and prejudice, hoping that people would think about reform. Erasmus did not advocate breaking away from the Catholic Church, but he laid the groundwork for later thinkers who would.

Religion on the Eve of the Reformation

Erasmus and other reformers were concerned with corruption in the Catholic Church. Popes were accused of being more concerned with politics than spiritual matters and of using the wealth of the Church to advance themselves. The Black Death had also undermined people's faith in the Church because some priests had charged high fees for giving last rites, while others had persuaded people to leave their possessions to the Church rather than to their families.

The lack of guidance was a serious problem. Ordinary people wanted meaningful religious experience and assurance of their salvation or acceptance into heaven. Often, an **indulgence**, or forgiveness for a sin, could be purchased in the form of certificates or veneration of a relic. Critics charged that the process was driven by economic, not spiritual, concerns.

Reformers were also angered by the other practices of the Church, such as **simony**, the selling of church offices and positions, and nepotism, the employment of relatives and friends of those in positions of authority. It was this environment that allowed the ideas of reformers such as Martin Luther to take root and flourish. Those who challenged or protested the Church practices were called Protestants.

Martin Luther

Martin Luther was a monk and professor of the Bible at the University of Wittenberg in Germany. He was chiefly concerned with the certainty of salvation, a problem that had bothered him since becoming a monk. Through his study of the Bible, he believed he had found the answer.

Traditional Catholic teachings said that salvation was achieved through both faith and good works. Luther believed that faith alone was necessary to achieve salvation. He thought that people were powerless before God and could never do enough good works to attain salvation.

According to Luther, faith in God makes a person just, or worthy of salvation, and God will grant salvation because God is merciful. This idea, called **justification** (being made right before God) by faith alone, became the chief teaching of the Protestant Reformation. Because Luther came to this understanding by studying the Bible, the Bible became the sole source of religious truth for all Protestants.

The 95 Theses On October 31, 1517, Luther sent a list of Ninety-Five Theses to his church superiors, including the local bishop. In the Theses, he attacked abuses of the selling of indulgences. Pope Leo X did not take Luther seriously, however.

A Break with the Church By 1520, Luther was calling on German princes to break with the Catholic Church and establish a reformed German church. He called for the elimination of all sacraments except for baptism and the Eucharist (also known as Communion) and for the right of the clergy to marry. The Catholic Church required priests to remain celibate. Luther also continued to emphasize that salvation could be achieved through faith alone.

Luther was excommunicated, or expelled, from the Catholic Church in 1521. The emperor Charles V called him to the city of Worms to try and change his mind. Upon his failure to do so, Charles delivered the Edict of Worms, in which Luther was made an outlaw. His works were to be burned and he was to be delivered to the emperor. However, Luther's ruler, Frederick of

CORE CONCEPTS: BELIEF SYSTEMS

Luther was greatly offended by another monk, Johann Tetzel, who sold indulgences under the slogan "As soon as the coin in the coffer [money box] rings, the soul from purgatory springs." Luther's 95 Theses were a direct challenge to the Church's practice of selling indulgences, relics, and other items that would supposedly lead to salvation. He believed that people were harming their chances for salvation by purchasing these items.

Saxony, protected him. Frederick saw that he could undermine his rival, Charles V, and cut his taxes by getting rid of the Roman Catholic Church taxes.

During the next few years, Luther's movement became a revolution. German rulers took control of Catholic churches in their areas and put them under government rule. Luther designed new religious services that consisted of Bible readings, preaching the word of God, and song. This doctrine became known as Lutheranism; it was the first Protestant faith.

Politics in the German Reformation

The rise of Lutheranism was largely dependent on political affairs. Charles V was in competition with the king of France, Francis I, over a number of territories. This competition led to more than 20 years of war. Pope Clement VII was on the side of the French. Charles also faced a threat from the Ottoman Turks on the eastern part of his empire.

These distractions allowed German princes to organize against Charles and assert their own control over their lands. By the time Charles was ready to respond militarily, it was too late. He was forced to seek peace with the princes.

This peace was formalized in 1555 with the Peace of Augsburg. The agreement allowed the leaders of the German states to choose between Lutheranism and Catholicism and guaranteed Lutheran states the same rights as Catholic states. This did not mean, however, that individuals were free to choose their own religion. The people were forced to accept the religion of their ruler.

CORE CONCEPTS: CONFLICT

The Holy Roman Emperor Charles V controlled a huge empire that included Spain and its colonies, the Austrian lands, Bohemia, Hungary, the Low Countries, the duchy of Milan in northern Italy, and the kingdom of Naples in southern Italy. He hoped to preserve the unity of his empire by keeping it Catholic. However, individual rulers in the German states supported Luther as a means to assert their own authority over that of the empire. In the end, Charles abdicated his throne and divided his empire. He gave Spain and all its colonies to his son and his Austrian empire to his brother.

SECTION 4   THE SPREAD OF PROTESTANTISM AND THE CATHOLIC RESPONSE

The Zwinglian Reformation

Even before the Peace of Augsburg cemented the dissolution of Christian unity, divisions were appearing within the Protestant faith. Ulrich Zwingli, a priest in Zurich, Switzerland, led the city council to introduce religious reforms, including the abolishment of relics and the institution of new church services. Scripture reading, prayer, and sermons replaced Catholic mass.

CORE CONCEPTS: DIVERSITY

Protestant groups included Anglicans (Episcopalians), Lutherans, Calvinists, and others. The growth of many Christian churches contributed to the present-day cultural diversity of Europe.

Zwingli sought an alliance with Martin Luther as his movement grew, but they were unable to agree on the meaning of Communion. In October 1531, war broke out between the Protestant and Catholic churches in Switzerland. Zurich's army was defeated and Zwingli was killed. Leadership of the Swiss Protestants passed to John Calvin.

Calvin and Calvinism

John Calvin was born and educated in Catholic France, but was forced to flee after he converted to Protestantism. In 1536, he published *Institutes of the Christian Religion*, a summary of Protestant thought. This work established him as a Protestant leader. He also began work to reform the city of Geneva.

Calvin and his church government, which included both clergy and laity, set up a special body for enforcing moral discipline. This body was known as the Consistory. It passed down punishments for behaviors that deviated from church teachings; such acts included dancing, swearing, and playing cards.

Calvin's success in Geneva made the city a powerful center of Protestantism, and by the mid-sixteenth century Calvinism had replaced Lutheranism as the most important form of Protestantism.

The Reformation in England

In England, King Henry VIII wanted to divorce his wife, Catharine of Aragon, because she failed to give birth to a male heir. Henry needed a male heir to ensure that the Tudors would continue to rule in England. The pope was unwilling to grant an annulment declaring the marriage invalid, however, so Henry turned to England's church courts. In 1533, the archbishop of Canterbury, the highest-ranking church official in England, granted Henry the annulment.

A year later, at Henry's request, Parliament made the break with the Catholic Church official. The Act of Supremacy of 1534 declared that the king was the head of the Church of England. Henry used his new position to take control of church lands and increase his own wealth. He gave some church lands to his allies as rewards for their support. His doctrine remained close to Catholic teachings though.

CORE CONCEPTS: BELIEF SYSTEMS

Calvin agreed with Luther on many aspects of their faith. He also believed strongly in the all-powerful nature of God, which led to his ideas on **predestination**. Predestination meant that God had determined in advance who would be saved (the elect) and who would be damned (the reprobate). This belief gave Calvinists the conviction that they were doing God's work and made them determined to spread their faith to others. Missionaries trained in Geneva were sent all over Europe.

Following Henry's death in 1547, church officials who favored Protestant doctrines moved the Church of England in that direction. New laws gave clergy the right to marry and created new Protestant church services. These changes met with much opposition.

Mary, Henry's daughter by Catharine of Aragon, came to the throne in 1553. She wanted to restore England to Roman Catholicism. Her tactics included burning more than 300 Protestants as heretics. These extreme measures had the opposite effect, and at the end of her reign England was even more Protestant than it had been at the beginning.

The Anabaptists Throughout the Reformation, the state continued to play a large role in church affairs. A group of radicals known as Anabaptists disagreed with the state interfering. Anabaptists believed the true Christian church was made up of adult believers who had undergone spiritual rebirth and had then been baptized. This belief differed from Catholics and Protestants, who baptized infants. Anabaptists also advocated complete separation of church and state. They refused to hold political office or bear arms, because many took literally the biblical commandment "Thou shalt not kill." Anabaptists were considered dangerous and were persecuted by Catholics and Protestants alike.

Effects on the Role of Women

Protestantism abolished celibacy and placed the family at the center of human life. The traditional roles of men and women within the family structure did not change, however. A wife was supposed to be obedient to her husband. She was also expected to bear children—according to Calvin and Luther, that was part of the divine plan. Family life was the only destiny for most Protestant women.

The Catholic Reformation

By the mid-sixteenth century, the spread of Lutheranism and Calvinism and the English split from Rome had combined to cause the Catholic Church considerable trouble. However, the church was undergoing its own revitalization, which became known as the Counter-Reformation.

LINKING PAST AND PRESENT

Menno Simons was a popular Anabaptist leader in the Netherlands. His followers, known as Mennonites, spread from the Netherlands into Germany and Russia. In the nineteenth century, many moved to Canada and the United States, where Mennonite communities continue to flourish.

In the 1690s, another Anabaptist leader named Jacob Ammann encouraged a group of Swiss Mennonites to form their own church. They became known as the Amish. By the end of the seventeenth century, many Amish had come to the United States to practice their religion freely. Today, Amish communities can be found throughout Canada and the United States. One of the largest is in Pennsylvania. Today's Amish continue to maintain the Anabaptist way of life as it was in the sixteenth century, including their refusal to use modern devices such as automobiles and electricity.

Pope Paul III set out to deal with the corruption that plagued the papacy during the Renaissance. In 1537, he appointed a Reform Commission to institute changes. Paul III also began the **Council of Trent**. In March 1545, a group of clergy and religious leaders met in the city of Trent, on the border of Germany and Italy. The Council met off and on for the next 18 years.

The Council's final decrees confirmed the differences between Protestantism and Catholicism; specifically, that both faith and good works were necessary for salvation. The seven sacraments, the Catholic view of the Eucharist, and clerical celibacy were all upheld. Belief in indulgences was strengthened but the selling of indulgences was forbidden.

After the Council of Trent, the Catholic Church was renewed and unified under the leadership of the pope.

CORE CONCEPTS: CULTURE

In 1540, the Society of Jesus was founded by a Spanish nobleman, Ignatius of Loyola, as a small group of followers that were recognized by the pope. Known as the Jesuits, they took an oath of absolute obedience to the pope. Jesuits used education to spread their message. Their missionaries were successful in restoring Catholicism to parts of Germany and eastern Europe and in spreading their message to other parts of the world.

CORE CONCEPT: MOVEMENT OF PEOPLE AND GOODS

Russian leader Peter the Great (1682–1725) traveled to Germany, the Netherlands, England, and France to learn their technology. He brought engineers, military experts, and craftspeople back to Russia to upgrade its science and technology.

Chapter Overview

The religious upheavals of the sixteenth century left Europeans sorely divided. Wars and economic and social crises haunted Europe, making the 90 years from 1560 to 1650 an age of crisis in European life. One response to these crises was a search for order. France, Spain, Prussia and Russia centralized government's power under strong monarchs. Other states, such as England, created systems where monarchs were limited by the power of a parliament. Art, literature, and political thought were heavily influenced by changes in the wake of the Reformation. Two writers from this period, Englishman William Shakespeare and Spain's Miguel de Cervantes, are considered among the greatest writers in literature.

Political thought also evolved. Thomas Hobbes argued for absolutism, while John Locke countered that governments were formed by a contract to protect people's natural rights. Locke's ideas became important to both Americans and the French in the eighteenth century.

As you read through this chapter, ask yourself these questions:
(1) How were Spain and France's dominance of European affairs affected by their economic policies?
(2) How did European monarchs deal with religious issues and whose policies were most effective?
(3) What were the causes of the political revolutions of the 1700s?
(4) What aspects of John Locke's political theories do you recognize as influencing the political system of the United States?

Main Ideas and Concepts

- **Political Systems** In the 1500s and 1600s, the monarchies of Europe sought to centralize power in their respective political systems.

- **Power** To justify absolutism, or complete control of government, monarchs used a variety of sources. Many appealed to the theory of divine right, in which monarchs acted on behalf of God. Royal commands reflected God's wishes.

- **Human Rights** Before William and Mary ascended to the monarchy in England in 1689, Parliament required them to sign a Bill of Rights guaranteeing the civil liberties of English citizens. This document was a milestone in the protection of human rights under the law.

- **Culture** The artistic movements of Mannerism and Baroque reflected the spiritual perceptions of the time. One of the greatest dramatists ever, William Shakespeare, wrote comedies and tragedies that dealt with the human condition.

People, Places, Terms

The following names and terms will help you to prepare for the Regents Exam in Global History and Geography. You can find an explanation of each name and term in the Glossary at the back of this book, in your textbook, or in another reference source.

absolutism	Huguenots
Bill of Rights	John Locke
commonwealth	Louis XIV
constitutional monarchy	mercantilism
Oliver Cromwell	natural rights
czar	Petition of Rights
divine right of kings	Philip II
Glorious Revolution	William Shakespeare

SECTION 1 EUROPE IN CRISIS: THE WARS OF RELIGION

The French Wars of Religion

By 1560, Calvinism and Catholicism had become highly militant (combative) religions. They were aggressively trying to win converts and undermine the other's authority. These struggles led to many wars over the next several decades.

One of the most devastating conflicts was known as the French Wars of Religion (1562–1598). French kings tried to rid the country of Protestants, but were ultimately unable to stop the spread of Protestantism.

Huguenots were French Protestants who were influenced by John Calvin. Although they made up only a small portion of the population (about 7 percent), a large number of them were French nobility, as well as tradespeople and professionals. Their ranks included the house of Bourbon, which ruled the southern French kingdom of Navarre and stood next to the Valois dynasty in the royal line of succession. Huguenots became a powerful threat to the Crown.

The Catholic majority was still strong, however, and included the Valois monarchy. In addition, an extreme group known as the Ultra-Catholics had a loyal following in the north and northwest parts of the country and were strong militarily.

Battles were fought between the two sides for 30 years. Finally, in 1589, Henry of Navarre, the political leader of the Huguenots and a member of the Bourbon dynasty, succeeded to the throne as Henry IV. Upon becoming king, he converted to Catholicism because he knew France would never accept a Protestant king. Fighting ceased when he was crowned. Henry IV won over the population with his improved tax system, reconstruction of roads and bridges, and promotion of the textile trade.

In 1598, Henry aimed to end the religious problem by issuing the Edict of Nantes. The edict recognized Catholicism as the official religion of France, but gave Huguenots the right to worship and to participate in politics and education.

CORE CONCEPTS: INTERDEPENDENCE

Although the religious issue was the most important in the French civil wars, there were other factors. Towns and provinces had long been resistant to monarchical control and used the growing Protestant nobility to strengthen their position. The fact that so many nobles were Huguenots created an important base of opposition to the king.

Philip II and Militant Catholicism

Under the reign of **Philip II**, Spain was the greatest supporter of militant Catholicism in the second half of the sixteenth century. The country was also extremely powerful both politically and culturally due to the rise of its American colonies.

Philip's first goal when coming to power was to consolidate lands he had inherited from his father. These included Spain, the Netherlands, and possessions in Italy and the Americas. To achieve this, he insisted on strict conformity to Catholicism and strong monarchical control.

Philip, known as "The Most Catholic King," undertook military actions on behalf of Catholic causes. These endeavors met with mixed results. Spain led a Holy League to a stunning victory against a Turkish fleet at the Battle of Lepanto in 1571.

However, in his dealings with England and the Netherlands, Philip was not so successful. People in the Spanish Netherlands (modern Netherlands and Belgium) resented Philip's attempts to strengthen his control over the area, which was one of the richest in the empire. The Spanish controlled lucrative government positions, put troops in their towns and demanded more taxes for Phillip's projects.

When Philip tried to eliminate Calvinism in the Netherlands, Calvinists—especially nobles—resisted. Philip sent ten thousand troops in to crush the revolt but he was unsuccessful.

Philip II's reign ended in 1598. Spain had the most populous empire in the world and seemed to be the greatest power of the age. In reality, however, Spain had serious economic problems. Philip's wars and his successor's spending bankrupted the country. In addition, Spain's armed forces were badly out-of-date and the government was inefficient. The real power was shifting to England and France.

The England of Elizabeth

Elizabeth Tudor ascended to the English throne in 1558. Under her leadership, England became a leader of Protestant nations and laid the foundations for a world empire.

Elizabeth worked to keep a balance of power between Spain and France, supporting the weaker nation if the other appeared to be gaining too much. She wanted to stay out of war but ultimately could not avoid a conflict with Spain.

CORE CONCEPTS: IDENTITY

The Catholic faith was important to both Philip II and the Spanish people. During the late Middle Ages, Catholic kingdoms in Spain had reconquered Muslim areas within Spain and expelled the Spanish Jews, an event called the Reconquista. Driven by this crusading heritage, Spain saw itself as a nation of people chosen by God to save Catholic Christianity from the Protestant heretics.

CORE CONCEPTS: CHANGE

In the northern provinces, resistance was growing under the leadership of William the Silent, the prince of Orange. After a prolonged struggle, a truce was called in 1609. The provinces began to call themselves the United Provinces of the Netherlands (what is today the core of the modern Dutch state) and became an important political power. The seventeenth century has been called the Golden Age of the Dutch Republic. Despite a lack of natural resources, the Dutch made use of their coastline by becoming efficient and powerful in trade and exploration. They established colonies in Indonesia and North America, particularly in what is now New York. They were also religiously tolerant, which was unusual for the time period.

CORE CONCEPTS: CULTURE

Intelligent, careful, and self-confident, Elizabeth quickly moved to solve the divisive religious problems she inherited from her half-sister Mary Tudor. She repealed laws favoring Catholics and declared herself leader of both the state and the Church of England. Although she practiced Protestantism, it was a moderate version that most people accepted.

CORE CONCEPTS: ECONOMIC SYSTEMS

One major economic problem was inflation, or rising prices. Gold and silver imports from America were part of the problem. In addition, population growth in the sixteenth century increased the demand for land and food and drove up prices for both.

Philip II had been thinking of invading England for some time. He wanted to stop English pirate attacks on his treasure ships and to stop the spread of Protestantism. His advisors assured him that the English people would rise up against Elizabeth when the Spaniards arrived. A successful invasion would mean that England would once again be under Catholic control.

In 1588, Philip ordered an armada (a fleet of warships) to invade England. The fleet that set sail had neither the manpower nor the firepower to stand up to English warships. After being beaten badly, the armada sailed back to Spain along a northern route around Scotland and Ireland, where storms caused many of the ships to sink.

SECTION 2 SOCIAL CRISES, WAR, AND REVOLUTION

Economic and Social Crises

From 1560 to 1650, Europe suffered severe economic and social crises. Spain in particular was suffering from the cost of financing several wars, inflation, and declining silver imports. Pirates were raiding fleets and the loss of Muslim and Jewish artisans and merchants also hurt the economy. Italian economies were in decline as well.

Population shifts also caused problems. The number of people likely increased from 60 million in 1500 to 85 million in 1600. By 1620, population had leveled off and began to decline by 1650, especially in central and southern Europe. Warfare, famine, and plague all contributed to the decline.

The Witchcraft Trials

A belief in witchcraft, or magic, had been part of traditional village culture for centuries. The same zeal that led to the Inquisition soon focused on witchcraft. The fear both of witchcraft and of being accused of witchcraft increased greatly.

People accused of practicing witchcraft were often poor. More than one hundred thousand people were accused; over 75 percent were women. Most of these women were single or widowed and over 50. Under torture, these women would confess to swearing allegiance to the devil, casting evil spells on neighbors, and attending rituals at night called sabbats.

By 1650, the hysteria had begun to lessen. Stronger governments disliked disrupting society with witchcraft trials. Attitudes were changing as well. Many people found old world views about evil spirits unreasonable.

The Thirty Years' War

The Peace of Augsburg in 1555 did not end Germany's religious disputes. Part of the problem was that the agreement did not recognize Calvinism, which by the early 1600s had spread to many parts of Europe. Territorial and political motives also played an important role in the outbreak of the "last of the religious wars," the Thirty Years' War.

The war began in 1618 as a struggle between Catholics, led by the Hapsburg Holy Roman emperors, and Protestant (primarily Calvinist) nobles in Bohemia who rebelled against Hapsburg authority. The struggle soon became political, however, as Denmark, Sweden, France, and Spain got involved. Especially important was the struggle between France and the rulers of Spain and the Holy Roman Empire for European leadership.

The war was the most destructive that Europe had experienced. Germany, where most of the battles took place, was pillaged and destroyed. Villages had no protection against foreign armies.

The Peace of Westphalia ended the war in Germany in 1648. The agreement stated that all German states could choose their own religion. The states that made up the Holy Roman Empire were given the power to conduct their own foreign affairs, effectively ending the empire as a political entity. Germany would not be united for another two hundred years. Many of the countries involved gained territory and France emerged as the dominant nation in Europe.

CORE CONCEPTS: SCIENCE AND TECHNOLOGY

The Thirty Years' War was Europe's most destructive ever. The flintlock musket, soon fitted with a bayonet, was a new, accurate weapon that could be reloaded faster than earlier firearms. Increased use of firearms and greater mobility on the battlefield meant armies had to be better disciplined and trained. Governments began to support standing armies. By 1700, France had a standing army of four hundred thousand.

Revolutions in England

Seventeenth century England had to deal with internal as well as external strife. Parliament and the monarchy struggled for power and eventually England lapsed into a civil war known as the English Revolution. It would take another revolution later in the century, however, to finally resolve this conflict.

The Stuarts and Divine Right The Stuart line of rulers, beginning with James I, ascended to the throne after the death of Elizabeth I in 1603. James believed in the **divine right of kings**—that is, that kings receive their power from God and are responsible only to God. Parliament disagreed, believing that it shared power with the king.

Religion was an issue as well. Puritans, English Protestants who were inspired by Calvinist ideas, did not like James's defense of the Church of England. They wanted the church to become even more Protestant. Many Puritans were members of the well-to-do gentry class that made up the lower house of Parliament, the House of Commons.

This conflict came to a head during the reign of James's son, Charles I. Charles also believed in the divine right of kings. In 1628, Parliament passed the **Petition of Rights**. The petition prohibited passing taxes without Parliament's consent, quartering troops in private homes, and imprisoning someone without the charge being made public. After first agreeing to the petition, Charles changed his mind.

Civil War and the Commonwealth In 1642, England slipped into a civil war between the Cavaliers (supporters of the king) and parliamentary forces known as Roundheads.

Oliver Cromwell, a military genius, ultimately led the parliamentary forces to victory. His New Model Army, made up primarily of Puritan extremists called Independents, believed they were doing battle for God. The army was well disciplined and trained in new military tactics.

After his victory, Cromwell purged Parliament of all those who had not supported him. Those who were left were known as the Rump Parliament. Charles I was tried and executed and Parliament abolished the monarchy and the House of Lords. England became a republic, or **commonwealth**.

Cromwell found it difficult to work with the Rump Parliament and finally dispersed it by force. After destroying both king and Parliament, Cromwell set up a military dictatorship.

The Restoration Cromwell ruled until his death in 1658. A year later, Parliament restored the monarchy in the person of Charles II, the son of Charles I. However, Parliament kept much of its power. It passed laws restoring the Church of England as the state religion and restricting some rights of Catholics and Puritans.

In 1685, James II, an open and devout Catholic, became king. He named Catholics to high positions in government, army, navy and universities. Parliament objected but stopped short of rebellion. They knew James was an old man and his daughters, who were next in the line of succession, were Protestant. However, in 1688, his second wife, who was also Catholic, bore him a son.

A Glorious Revolution To eliminate the possibility of a Catholic monarchy, a group of English noblemen invited William of Orange, husband of James's daughter Mary, to "invade" England. An army was raised and in 1688, James and his wife

CORE CONCEPTS: CONFLICT

Charles I also tried to impose more ritual on the Church of England. The Puritans perceived this as a return to Catholicism. When Charles tried to force these changes on the Puritans, thousands chose to go to America.

and son fled to France. With almost no bloodshed, England had undergone a "**Glorious Revolution**."

In January 1689, Parliament offered the throne to William and Mary, but required them to sign a **Bill of Rights** that gave Parliament the right to pass laws and levy taxes. It also stated that standing armies could be raised only with Parliament's consent. The rights of citizens to keep arms and have a jury trial were also confirmed. The Bill of Rights helped create a system of government based on the rule of law and a freely elected Parliament. This bill laid the foundation for a limited, or **constitutional monarchy**. Parliament had destroyed the divine-right theory of kingship and asserted its right to be part of the government.

CORE CONCEPTS: JUSTICE

A legal landmark was passed in 1679. The Habeas Corpus Act gave an arrested person the right to be seen by a judge within a certain period of time to determine if a trial would be held or if the prisoner would be released.

SECTION 3 RESPONSE TO CRISIS: ABSOLUTISM

France Under Louis XIV

The belief in the divine right of kings was also present in France during the seventeenth century, where it was tied to what historians have come to call **absolutism**. Absolutism is a system in which a ruler holds total power. The reign of **Louis XIV** is regarded as the best example of absolutism. During this period, France was the dominant power in Europe and the court of Louis XIV was widely imitated.

Both Louis XIV and his predecessor, Louis XIII, were only boys when they took the throne. The French government was in turmoil during this period and was left in the hands of royal ministers. These ministers played an important role in strengthening the role of the monarchy.

Cardinal Richelieu was chief minister to Louis XIII. He took all political and military rights from the Huguenots by revoking the Edict of Nantes but allowed them religious rights. He also set up a network of spies to ferret out plots against the monarchy and executed conspirators.

Richelieu set up a system of administrators, called intendants, who controlled the military, taxes, and business. He helped to restore the economy by expanding the textile trade. Richelieu also used his role in the Thirty Years' War to make France a dominant power in Europe.

Louis XIV came to the throne in 1643 when he was only four years old. Cardinal Mazarin, his chief minister, took control of the government because of Louis's age. He had to deal with a revolt led by nobles dissatisfied with the growing power of the monarchy. After the revolt was crushed, many people believed that the best hope for stability in France lay with a strong monarch.

Louis Comes to Power When Mazarin died, Louis XIV officially took power at the age of 23. He quickly established a royal court at Versailles that served three purposes. It was his personal household and housed the chief offices of the state so that he could keep watch over them. In addition, powerful people came to find favors and offices for themselves. Louis wished to be known as the Sun King because of his lifestyle and the idea that he was the center of the French universe.

The biggest threat to Louis's rule came from very high nobles and royal princes who believed they should play a role in government. Louis dealt with them by removing them from the royal court, the chief administrative body of the king and supervisor of government. However, Louis enticed the nobles and princes to come to his court where he could keep them busy with court life.

Louis's government ministers were expected to obey his every wish. As a result, he had complete control over foreign policy, the Church and taxes. The only limits to his power were found at the local level, where nobles, local officials, and townspeople had more control over the day-to-day operation of local government. To minimize this, Louis bribed important people in the provinces to see that his policies were carried out.

The Economy and War Louis's extravagant spending on palaces, maintaining his court, and pursuing wars made finances a crucial issue for him. His controller-general of finances, Jean-Baptiste Colbert, sought to increase France's wealth by following the principles of mercantilism.

Mercantilism held that the state would be strong when exports, goods sold outside the country, exceeded imports, goods sold to the country. To accomplish this, the country built up industries and gained colonies, which were sources of raw material and markets. Mercantilism was useful to absolutism because it increased national unity.

Colbert granted subsidies to new industries with the aim of decreasing imports and increasing exports. He built roads and canals to increase communication. To decrease imports directly,

CORE CONCEPTS: POWER

Maintaining religious harmony had long been a part of monarchical power in France. Louis kept this power by attempting to convert Protestant Huguenots to Catholicism. Early in his reign, Louis ordered the destruction of Huguenot churches and the closing of their schools. As many as two hundred thousand Huguenots fled to England, the United Provinces, and the German states.

he raised tariffs on foreign goods and created a merchant marine to carry French goods. He encouraged colonization in Canada.

To ensure his domination over European affairs, Louis raised a standing army of four hundred thousand. He also waged war four times between 1667 and 1713, adding to France's territory in the northeast and establishing a member of his own Bourbon dynasty on the throne in Spain. Many nations formed coalitions against him to try and prevent him from dominating Europe.

In 1715, the Sun King died, leaving France in great debt and surrounded by enemies.

Absolutism in Central and Eastern Europe

After the Thirty Years' War, Germany was divided into more than 300 states. Two of these states, Prussia and Austria, emerged as great powers in the seventeenth and eighteenth centuries.

The Emergence of Prussia Prussia's ruler, Frederick William the Great Elector, realized that the state was vulnerable to attack. He built a standing army of forty thousand men, the fourth largest in Europe. To maintain this army, he also set up the General War Commissariat to oversee the army. The Commissariat soon became a machine for civil government as well. Many members were landed aristocracy, who were known as Junkers. In 1701, Frederick William's son Frederick became King Frederick I.

The New Austrian Empire The Austrian Hapsburgs had long been significant European leaders, but they lost their Holy Roman Empire after the Thirty Years' War. However, in the seventeenth century, they created a new empire in present-day Austria, Hungary, and the Czech Republic. After they defeated the Turks in 1587, they also took control of all of Hungary, Transylvania, Croatia, and Slavonia as well, increasing the size of their empire considerably.

The empire never became a highly centralized absolutist state, though, largely because its territory was made up of so many different national groups. No common sentiment or language tied the regions together other than the idea of service to the Hapsburgs, held by military officers and government officials.

Russia Under Peter the Great

In the sixteenth century, Ivan IV became the first ruler to take the title of **czar**, the Russian word for Caesar. Ivan expanded Russian territory eastward, defeating the Tatar khanates, and crushed the power of Russian nobility, known as boyars. Thanks to his ruthlessness (which included stabbing his own son to death), he was known as Ivan the Terrible. Ivan used his autocratic power to establish Zemsky Sobor, the Assembly of the Land. The assembly established a military force aimed at ridding the country of opposition and doubling the size of Russia's territory.

When his dynasty ended in 1598, a period of anarchy known as the Time of Troubles began and continued until the Zemsky Sobor chose Michael Romanov as the new czar in 1613. So began a dynasty that would last until 1917.

One of the most infamous Romanov czars was Peter the Great, who became leader in 1689. Like his predecessors, Peter was an absolutist monarch who claimed the divine right of kings. After a trip West, he became interested in Europeanizing Russia, especially when it came to modernizing Russia's army and navy. By the time of his death in 1725, Russia was an important European state.

Military and Governmental Changes One of Peter's first goals was to reorganize the army. He brought in both Russians and Europeans as officers and drafted peasants for 25-year stints of service. He built a standing army of 210,000 and also created the first Russian navy.

Cultural and Technological Changes After Peter returned from his trip, he instituted reforms in engineering, medicine, and science. Peter also introduced Western customs, practices, and manners. At court, nobles' beards were shorn and their coats cut off at the knees, as was the custom in Europe. Upper-class women gained much from Peter's reforms.

St. Petersburg Through his reforms, Peter desired to make Russia a great state and military power. An important part of this was finding a port with access to Europe through the Baltic Sea. At the time, Sweden controlled the Baltic.

After a long war, Peter acquired the land he needed and in 1703, he began construction of a new city on the Baltic named St. Petersburg, his "window on the west." The city remained the Russian capital until 1918.

CORE CONCEPTS: NATION-STATE

Peter aimed to effectively control Russia by dividing it into provinces. These "police states" were supposed to be well-ordered communities governed by law. In practice, few bureaucrats shared his concept of honest service and duty to the state. Peter hoped for a sense of civic duty, but his own personality created an atmosphere of fear that prevented it.

CORE CONCEPTS: CULTURE

Peter held gatherings where both sexes could mix for conversation and dancing. Also, the veils that had traditionally covered women's faces were ordered removed. The Romanov policy of westernization became linked with oppression in the minds of many Russians. As a result, later revolutionaries criticized many Western practices as "decadent," or corrupt.

SECTION 4 THE WORLD OF EUROPEAN CULTURE

Mannerism

The artistic Renaissance came to an end when a new movement, called Mannerism, emerged in Italy in the 1520s and 1530s. The turmoil of the Reformation quelled the worldly enthusiasm of the Renaissance and left people uncertain and anxious for spiritual experience.

Mannerism reflected this anxiety by ignoring High Renaissance principles such as balance, harmony, and moderation. Figures were deliberately elongated to show suffering and religious ecstasy.

A master of this new style was El Greco ("the Greek"). Originally from the island of Crete, he studied in Italy before settling in Spain. He used unusual colors in his work and often depicted elongated and distorted figures. The mood reflects well the tensions created by the religious upheavals of the period.

The Baroque Period

Mannerism was eventually replaced by another new movement—the baroque. This movement began in Italy during the last quarter of the sixteenth century and spread throughout Europe and even into Latin America.

Baroque artists tried to bring together the classical ideals of Renaissance art with the spiritual feelings of the more recent religious revival. The style was known for using dramatic effects and rich detail intended to arouse emotions. It also reflected the search for power that was such a part of the era. Baroque style was popular with kings and princes, who liked others to be in awe of their power.

One of the best Baroque artists was the Italian architect and sculptor Gian Lorenzo Bernini, who completed Saint Peter's Basilica in Rome. Action, exuberance, and dramatic effects mark the interior. The *Throne of Saint Peter* is a highly decorated cover for the pope's medieval wooden throne. It seems to hover in midair, while above the chair, rays of heavenly light drive a mass of clouds and angels toward the spectator.

A Golden Age of Literature

Literature also flourished between 1580 and 1640. Writing for the theater was marked by especially high achievement, specifically in England and Spain.

England's Shakespeare A cultural flowering took place in England during the late sixteenth and early seventeenth centuries, known as the Elizabethan Era. Of all the forms of literature, none expressed the energy of the era better than its drama and none of the dramatists is more famous than **William Shakespeare**.

Shakespeare was a "complete man of the theater" and has long been viewed as a universal genius. He was also an actor and shareholder in the chief theater company of the time. He was a master of the English language, and his language skills were matched by his insight into human psychology. Whether in his tragedies or his comedies, Shakespeare showed a remarkable understanding of the human condition.

Spanish Literature Drama flourished in Spain as well during the sixteenth century. Touring companies brought the latest Spanish plays to all parts of the Spanish empire.

One of the most prolific playwrights was Lope de Vega. He wrote almost 1,500 plays, of which almost 500 survive. They are characterized as witty, charming, action-packed, and realistic.

Another achievement of Spanish literature was the novel *Don Quixote* by Miguel de Cervantes. Cervantes presents the dual nature of the Spanish character in the novel's two main characters. Don Quixote, the knight, is a visionary with lofty ideals; his fat, earthy squire, Sancho Panza, is a realist. Each comes to see the value of the other's perspective. Both vision and hard work are necessary to the human condition.

Political Thought

The seventeenth century concerns with order and power were reflected in the political thought of the time. The English revolutions prompted two very different responses from political thinkers Thomas Hobbes and **John Locke**.

Hobbes Thomas Hobbes wrote a work called *Leviathan* (1651) to deal with the issue of disorder. Hobbes had been greatly affected by the brutality of the English Civil War. He was a tutor to the sons of King Charles I.

CORE CONCEPTS: DIVERSITY

When Shakespeare appeared in London in 1592, theater was already a very popular and successful business. The Globe theater could hold three thousand people and its admission charge of one or two pennies allowed the lower classes to attend. Other theaters catered to the well-to-do. With such diverse audiences, playwrights had to write works that would appeal to a wide audience.

Hobbes claimed that before society and politics, in what he called a "state of nature," life is brutal and violent because human nature is self-interested. Life is not guided by moral ideas, but by the desire for self-preservation. To save people from destroying one another, people must form a state by agreeing to be governed by an absolute ruler with complete power. Only in this way could social order be preserved.

Locke In his work *Two Treatises of Government* (1690), Locke argued against the absolute rule of one person. He was influenced by the success of Parliament in the Glorious Revolution. He believed that before the development of society and politics, people lived in a state of freedom and equality, not violence and war. In this state people had **natural rights**—rights with which people are born. These included the rights to life, liberty, and property.

Locke believed, however, that in the state of nature people had trouble protecting their natural rights. They agree to establish a government to secure and protect these rights. The social contract between people and government establishes mutual obligations. People should be reasonable toward government, and government should protect the people's rights. If the contract is broken, people have a right to overthrow the government.

LINKING PAST AND PRESENT

Locke's ideas were important to the American and French Revolutions. They were used to support demands for constitutional government, the rule of law, and the protection of rights. Locke's ideas are found in the American Declaration of Independence and the United States Constitution.

CHAPTER 13   EARLY JAPAN

Section 1   Early Japan
Section 2   Tokugawa Japan

Chapter Overview

The great confrontation between the newly emerging Japanese state and China was a turning point in this period of Asian history. Island societies in Japan, Korea, and Southeast Asia began to develop.

Japan's geography caused it to develop differently than other countries. Power struggles between rulers and independent families have marked Japan's history. Three powerful political figures united Japan. Many peasant uprisings occurred between 1500 and 1800.

As you read through this chapter, ask yourself these questions:
(1) Why did Japan not develop a centralized government?
(2) What economic changes took place under the Tokugawa shoguns?
(3) How did Japanese culture change during the Tokugawa era?

Main Ideas and Concepts

- **Identity** Japan's island location permitted the Japanese to develop a strong sense of identity early in their history.

- **Culture** Japan's secure boundaries as an island and its nearness to the Asian mainland allowed the Japanese to borrow selectively from other cultures without being overwhelmed by them.

- **Scarcity** Two of the most important geographic factors shaping Japanese economic foreign policy decisions have been a scarcity of arable land and a lack of industrial resources.

- **Environment** Geological instability and meteorological events—such as tidal waves and volcanic eruptions—have fostered a keen sense of the natural environment among the Japanese.

- **Culture** Japan's mountainous terrain encouraged the concentration of people along coastal plans and promoted cultural unity.

CORE CONCEPTS: THE WORLD IN SPATIAL TERMS

Japan is a country of islands. If all the islands could be compacted, they would be about the size of Montana. Most of the land is forest and mountain. Only about 11 percent of the land can be farmed. Imagine trying to feed a population of more than 125 million people farming one-tenth the land of Montana.

CORE CONCEPTS: PHYSICAL SYSTEMS

Japan has more than 50 active volcanoes and many hot springs formed from volcanic activity. Every year, more than 1,000 small earthquakes shake Japan. Undersea earthquakes or volcanic eruptions can cause massive tidal waves called tsunami, which also cause damage to buildings and loss of life. When the waves crash against the coast, they may be moving as fast as 100 miles (161 km) an hour.

CORE CONCEPTS: ENVIRONMENT AND SOCIETY

A Japanese belief is that a major earthquake occurs every 70 years. That idea seems to have some validity. A major earthquake in 1923 killed 143,000 people in the Tokyo region. In 1995, another major earthquake hit Kobe. The Japanese have developed high-tech systems for predicting earthquakes. Some scientists believe in the ability of animals to signal natural disasters. A few days before the Kobe earthquake, schools of fish that live in deep water were swimming close to the water's surface. On the morning of the earthquake itself, people noticed flocks of crows flying in odd patterns.

People, Places, Terms

The following names and terms will help you to prepare for the Regents Exam in Global History and Geography. You can find an explanation of each name and term in the Glossary at the back of this book, in your textbook, or in another reference source.

archipelago	feudal system	samurai
Bushido	han	Shinto
daimyo	hostage system	shogun
eta	Ring of Fire	Zen

SECTION 1 EARLY JAPAN

The Geography of Japan

Japan is an **archipelago,** a chain of many islands. Its total land area is about 146,000 square miles (378,000 square kilometers). Much of Japan is composed of mountains. It is located on the **Ring of Fire**, a zone of earthquake and volcanic activity surrounding the Pacific Ocean. Only about 11 percent of the total land can be farmed, but the volcanic soil is very fertile. Because of their isolation from the mainland, the Japanese developed many unique qualities. They believed that they had a destiny separate from that of the peoples on the mainland, although cultural diffusion of language, religion, and architecture did occur from China via the Korean land bridge.

The Rise of the Japanese State

The early Japanese settled in the Yamato Plain on Honshu, the largest Japanese island, in the first centuries A.D. The Yamato Plain is near the present-day cities of Kyoto and Osaka. Japanese society was made up of clans. The people were divided between a small aristocratic class and a large class of rice farmers, artisans, and servants. Eventually, one ruler of the Yamato clan became the ruler of Japan. However, other families continued to compete for power.

Chinese Influences In the early seventh century, the Yamato prince Shotoku Taishi tried to unify the clans to resist an invasion by the Chinese. He sent representatives to China to learn

how its government was organized. Then he created a centralized system of government in Japan based on the Chinese
model. He wanted to limit the powers of the aristocrats and
enhance his own authority. As a result, the ruler was portrayed
as a divine figure and the symbol of the Japanese nation. Japan
was divided into administrative districts. The village was the
basic unit of government. A new tax system was set up to pay
taxes directly to the central government rather than to local
aristocrats. All farmland belonged to the state.

The Nara Period In 622, after Shotoku Taishi's death, the
Fujiwara family gained power. A Yamato ruler was still emper-
or, but he was strongly influenced by the Fujiwara clan. The first
permanent capital, modeled after the Chinese capital, was
established at Nara in 710. The emperor began using the title
"Son of Heaven." However, the aristocrats remained powerful
enough to keep land taxes for themselves, thus weakening the
power of the central government.

The Heian Period The emperor moved the capital from Nara to
Heian, the site of present-day Kyoto, in 794. The emperor
continued to rule in name, but actual power remained in the
hands of the Fujiwara clan. The government was becoming more
decentralized. Powerful aristocrats, who began to take justice
into their own hands, dominated the rural areas. They hired
warriors called **samurai** ("those who serve") to protect their
property and security. The samurai lived by a strict code, known
as **Bushido** ("the way of the warrior"). This code was rooted in
loyalty to the lord whom the samurai served.

The Kamakura Shogunate Minamoto Yoritomo, a powerful
noble, defeated several rivals at the end of the twelfth century
and set up his power near present-day Tokyo. He created a more
centralized government under a powerful military leader known
as the **shogun** (general). The emperor remained the ruler in
name only; power was in the hands of the shogun, who supervised a system of government known as a shogunate. This
ushered in a **feudal system** similar to Europe's during the
Middle Ages. A class system based on protection for land lasted
for nearly 500 years.

The Kamakura shogunate, founded by Yoritomo, lasted from
1192 to 1333. In 1274 and again in 1281, Kublai Khan invaded
Japan. Fighting the Mongols placed a heavy strain on the government, which was overthrown by the Ashikaga family in 1333.

LINKING PAST AND PRESENT

The Japanese emperors are
the world's longest-reigning
monarchs. Akihito, the
emperor since 1989, is the
125th in an unbroken line
going back to the first century
B.C. Each new emperor
chooses a name for his reign.
Akihito's is known as the
Heisei, which means "fulfillment of peace."

CORE CONCEPTS: BELIEF SYSTEMS

According to Japanese
legend, the first emperor was
descended from the sun
goddess Amaterasu. A shrine
was established at Ise where
the emperor paid tribute to
the sun goddess.

CORE CONCEPTS: CHANGE

The development of an
intellectual class of military
rulers (the samurai) and the
rise of a merchant class
helped prepare Japan for
modernization.

CORE CONCEPTS: CONFLICT

During the 1281 invasion of Japan, Kublai Khan was defeated by the weather as much as by the Japanese. A typhoon destroyed almost the entire Mongolian fleet. The Japanese would not be subject to foreign invasion again until 1945, when Allied troops arrived near the end of World War II. Weather often controls the outcome of a battle. The Spanish Armada was defeated by a storm in the English Channel. The invasion of France on D-Day in World War II had to be timed to coincide with favorable weather.

LINKING PAST AND PRESENT

Kyoto remained the capital city until the late 1800s, when Tokyo became the capital. Kyoto had been the capital for more than 1,000 years. Today, it is perhaps best known for its gardens and temples. It has 270 Shinto shrines and more than 1,600 Buddhist temples. In 1895, a replica of the Heian Shrine, the emperor Kammu's royal palace, was built for the 1,100th anniversary of the founding of Kyoto.

Collapse of Central Rule During the fourteenth and fifteenth centuries, the power of the aristocrats grew. The heads of noble families, known as **daimyo** ("great names"), controlled large landed estates that paid no taxes. The daimyo relied on the samurai for protection. A civil war, known as the Onin War, occurred between 1467 and 1477. The capital city of Kyoto was virtually destroyed during this war and central authority disappeared. The aristocrats ruled as independent lords over large territories they seized. Almost constant warfare resulted from their rivalries.

Life in Early Japan

Farming was the basis of early Japan's economy. The Japanese people grew wet rice (rice grown in flooded fields) because of the abundant rainfall and the limited amount of farmland. In the eleventh century, foreign trade began, mainly with Korea and China. Japan exchanged raw materials, paintings, swords, and other manufactured items for books, porcelain, silk, and copper coins.

The Role of Women Women had a certain level of equality with men in early Japan. Abandoned women could divorce and remarry. However, men were allowed to divorce their wives for reasons such as illness or talking too much. Although they did not possess full legal and social rights, women played an active role in society. Aristocratic women were prominent at court. Some of them were known for their literary or artistic talents.

Religion in Early Japan The early Japanese worshipped *kami,* or spirits. They were believed to live in trees, mountains, and rivers. The Japanese also believed that their ancestors lived in the air around them. These beliefs evolved into a religion called **Shinto**, or the sacred way. Shinto is an animistic religion that has no concept of a single powerful god nor specific moral codes. In time, Shinto also included belief that the emperor was a god and that the nation of Japan was sacred. This "state Shinto" was used by the Japanese military during World War II to unify the nation. Shinto continues to be practiced today.

Chinese monks in the sixth century A.D. brought Buddhism to Japan. The most popular sect was **Zen**, which became part of the samurai's code. Zen Buddhism offers different paths to enlightenment. Some believe it can be reached suddenly, while others believe it comes only through self-discipline and meditation.

Culture in Early Japan Because many Japanese men of the aristocracy felt prose was beneath them, women were the most productive fiction writers between the ninth and twelfth centuries. Women learned to read and write at home and wrote novels, letters, and stories. Murasaki Shikibu wrote one of the world's great novels, *The Tale of Genji,* around the year 1000.

Landscape was an important means of expression in Japanese architecture and art. Built in the fourteenth century, the Golden Pavilion in Kyoto is one of the world's great treasures. A large part of its beauty is due to the harmony of the landscape, with gardens, water, and architecture surrounding it.

CORE CONCEPTS: CULTURE

The Tale of Genji is the story of a noble, Genji, who tries to remain in favor with the powerful. The novel explores different aspects of Genji's personality as he goes from youthful adventures to a life of compassion and sorrow in his later years.

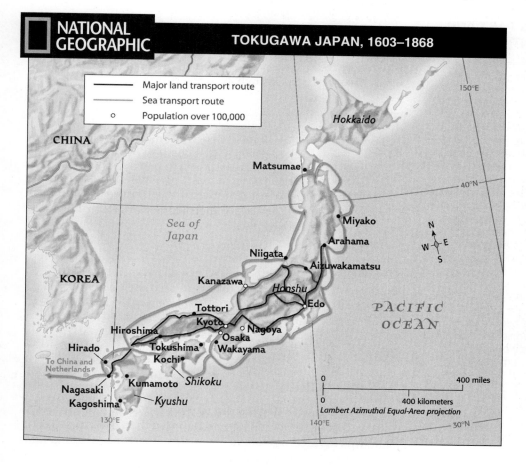

NATIONAL GEOGRAPHIC — **TOKUGAWA JAPAN, 1603–1868**

CORE CONCEPTS: BELIEF SYSTEMS

Those who practice Shinto believe that all living and nonliving things have divine spirits. This belief caused a strong reverence for nature and respect for the natural world.

LINKING PAST AND PRESENT

The Japanese regard *kami* as divine spirits. During World War II, Japanese pilots who went on suicide bombing missions were known as kamikaze pilots. The compound word means "divine wind" and was first used to describe the typhoon in 1281 that destroyed the invading Mongol fleet. The kamikaze pilots flew their planes, often packed with explosives, into American ships, killing themselves and often many Allied troops. A kamikaze force of 1,815 planes sank 32 American ships at Okinawa, killing 5,000 sailors. Before leaving for a mission, a kamikaze pilot would put on a ritual headcloth, a *hachimaki*, like those worn by the samurai warriors.

SECTION 2 TOKUGAWA JAPAN

The Three Great Unifiers

Japan was in chaos at the end of the fifteenth century. The shogunate's power had collapsed. Daimyo controlled their own lands and fought with their neighbors. After nearly 100 years of civil war, three powerful people unified Japan. Oda Nobunaga seized the imperial capital of Kyoto and placed the ruling shogun under his control. He tried to consolidate his rule throughout the central plains during the next few years.

He was succeeded by Toyotomi Hideyoshi, a farmer's son who became a military commander. He persuaded most of the daimyo to accept his authority by 1590.

After Hideyoshi's death in 1598, Tokugawa Ieyasu, the powerful daimyo of Edo, controlled Japan. He took the title of shogun in 1603. Tokugawa shoguns remained in power until 1868. Their rule was known as the "Great Peace."

Europeans in Japan

Portuguese traders were at first welcomed when they landed in 1543. European goods such as clocks and eyeglasses fascinated the Japanese. Daimyo wanted to buy European weapons.

Francis Xavier, the first Jesuit missionary, arrived in Japan in 1549. By the end of the sixteenth century, thousands of Japanese had become Christians. Fearful of western domination and angered by Jesuit destruction of shrines, Japanese leaders reacted against the missionaries. In 1587, Hideyoshi prohibited Christian activity within Japan. The edict was not strictly enforced at first, and the Jesuits continued their activity. All missionaries were expelled under Tokugawa Ieyasu, however, and Japanese Christians were persecuted. Most European merchants were also forced to leave; only Dutch ships were allowed to dock in Nagasaki once a year.

Tokugawa Rule

The Tokugawa rulers set out to establish control of the feudal system that had governed Japan for more than 300 years. The state was divided into about 250 separate territories, called **hans**, or domains. A daimyo ruled each han.

The shogunate used a **hostage system** to control the daimyo, who were required to have two residences. One was to be located on their own land and the other was in Edo, the location of the shogun's court. When the daimyo was away from his Edo residence, his family was forced to stay there, thus preventing rebellion by the daimyo. During this era, the samurai gradually became managers on the daimyo's land, rather than warriors.

Economic and Social Changes

A major economic change took place during the Tokugawa era. Trade and industry had previously been considered undesirable. Under the Tokugawa, these began to flourish. Paper money became the usual medium of exchange in business. Banking flourished and a Japanese merchant class developed.

Some farm families benefited from the growing demand for cash crops. Most peasants, however, experienced both declining profits and rising taxes and costs. Many were forced to work as hired help or become tenants. When conditions grew desperate, some peasants revolted. During the Tokugawa era, nearly 7,000 peasant revolts against high taxes occurred.

The Class System Japan's class system became rigid during this era. There were four main classes: warriors, peasants, artisans, and merchants. The emperor and imperial court were at the very top of the political and social structure. Next came the warrior class, composed of the shogun, daimyo, samurai, and ronin. The ronin were warriors without masters who traveled the countryside looking for employment. Below the warriors were the farmers, or peasants. Next was the artisan class, which included craftspeople such as carpenters and swordmakers. The merchant class was at the bottom because they profited from the labor of others. Below these classes were the **eta**, Japan's outcasts. The Tokugawa had strict laws for the eta. They regulated the eta's places of residence, dress, and even hairstyles.

The Role of Women In Tokugawa society, the role of women became somewhat more restricted. Men had broad authority over marriage, divorce, and property. Parents arranged marriages, and a wife was expected to move in with her husband's family. A wife could be divorced if she did not meet the expectations of her husband or his family. Among the common people, women were generally valued for their work as childbearers and homemakers. Both men and women worked in the fields.

CORE CONCEPTS: INTERDEPENDENCE

The Dutch were interested in trade. They did not attempt to make Christian converts. They also did not try to colonize territory. The shogun had been alarmed by Spanish aggression in the Philippines. For these reasons, for 200 years the Dutch were the only western nation permitted to trade with Japan.

CORE CONCEPTS: NEEDS AND WANTS

The daimyo were in theory independent, because they could support themselves with the taxes on their lands. However, the hostage system kept them dependent on the shogunate for safety.

CORE CONCEPTS: FACTORS OF PRODUCTION

Farmers were poor but were held in esteem because they produced rice for everyone. The shogun distributed the national rice crop. In exchange for military service, the local daimyo received land and rice from the shogun. The daimyo gave rice to the samurai, who served as advisors, castle guards, and government officials.

CORE CONCEPTS: CULTURE

Japanese poetry is based on syllable count rather than on rhyme. Haiku poetry has 17 syllables in three lines arranged 5, 7, 5. The poems are based on themes in nature and express an emotion, thought, or idea. Tanka is a five-lined poem with thirty-one syllables (5, 7, 5, 7, 7). The poems do not always have the same number of syllables when translated into English.

Tokugawa Culture

Popular literature, written by and for townspeople, began to appear in the Tokugawa era.

Literature The works of Ihara Saikaku are the best examples of the new urban fiction. His greatest novel, *Five Women Who Loved Love,* is a tragic tale. However, much of the popular literature of the time was more lighthearted. Poetry was considered serious literature. Matsuo Basho, the greatest Japanese poet, lived during the seventeenth century.

Theater and Art Kabuki theater, which is full of action, music, and dramatic gestures, began appearing in the cities. Early dramas dealt with the dance halls and teahouses. Women were forbidden to act on stage, because the government feared that these dramas would corrupt the nation's morals. This ban led to a new class of professional actors, the men who assumed female roles.

The shogun's decree that all daimyo must have homes in Edo resulted in an increase in building. Nobles competed to build the most magnificent mansions, lavishly furnished.

Other cultures influenced Japanese art. From Korea, the Japanese borrowed pottery techniques. The Japanese also studied painting styles, languages, medicine, and astronomy from Western nations. Those nations in turn wanted Japanese ceramics.

PRACTICING FOR THE REGENTS

Part I   Multiple-Choice Questions

The following multiple-choice questions come from past Regents High School Examinations. Test your understanding of World History by answering each of these items. Circle the number of the word or expression that best completes each statement or question. Test-taking tips can be found in the margins for some questions. For additional help, see Taking the Regents Exam on pages ix–xxxv of this Review Book.

1 Which statement explains a cause rather than an effect of the Bantu migration between 500 B.C. and A.D. 1500?
   (1) Techniques for herding and cultivating were spread to other peoples.
   (2) More than sixty million people now speak a Bantu language.
   (3) Trading cities developed along the coast of east Africa.
   (4) Population increases put pressure on agriculture.

2 Between A.D. 800 and 1600, the West African city of Timbuktu became prosperous with the trading of
   (1) spices and silk
   (2) iron ore and coal
   (3) gold and salt
   (4) rifles and diamonds

3 The West African kingdoms of Ghana, Mali, and Songhai experienced economic prosperity because they all
   (1) controlled vast reserves of oil and gold
   (2) traded with many other nations
   (3) maintained highly structured feudal systems
   (4) solved tribal conflicts within their empires

4 The spread of Islam into the kingdoms of Ghana and Mali resulted from
   (1) imperialism
   (2) ethnocentrism
   (3) cultural diffusion
   (4) self-determination

REGENTS WARM-UP

Question 1 tests your understanding of cause-and-effect relationships. Be sure to read the question carefully to assess which it is asking you to identify. A "cause" is an action or condition that creates certain events or outcomes.

REGENTS WARM-UP

Some multiple-choice questions compare or contrast regions. Question 3 looks for similarities in the prosperity of African kingdoms. If you have trouble answering this question, review material in Unit 3.

5   Mansa Musa commissioned great mosques to be built in Timbuktu, Mali's capital, and in other Mali cities. Under Musa's patronage, Muslim scholarship flourished, and Timbuktu began its tenure as an important center of learning. This public display of wealth and power enhanced Mali's reputation and prestige throughout the world.

Which phrase best describes Mali under the rule of Mansa Musa?
(1) a golden age
(2) a poverty-stricken era
(3) a decade of colonial unrest
(4) a period of political chaos

Base your answer to question 6 on the passage below and on your knowledge of social studies.

"[When] the legislature shall . . . grasp [for] themselves, or put into the hands of any other, an absolute power over their lives, liberties, and estates of the people, . . . they forfeit the power the people had put into their hands for quite contrary ends, and it [passes] to the people, who have a right to resume their original liberty . . . "
—John Locke, *Two Treatises of Government*

6   Which idea is expressed in this passage?
(1) The people should give up their liberty to create an orderly society.
(2) People have the right to rebel if their natural rights are denied.
(3) Governments should be obeyed regardless of their actions.
(4) Liberty can only be guaranteed in a direct democracy.

7   In Western Europe, a long-term effect of the invention of Gutenberg's printing press was that the
(1) monarchies were restored to absolute power
(2) feudal system declined
(3) literacy rate increased
(4) development of new ideas was discouraged

Base your answer to question 8 on the cartoon below and on your knowledge of social studies.

Peter the Great

Source: What is Evidence? John Murray, Ltd.

8 The cartoon is commenting on the efforts of Peter the Great to force the Russian nobility to
(1) conform to Asian social values
(2) adopt Western culture
(3) prepare for military battle
(4) bow to pressures from the Ottoman Empire

REGENTS WARM-UP

The political cartoon tests your ability to interpret a cartoonist's message or point of view. Question 8 also requires you to use your knowledge of Russian history.

9 One way Martin Luther, John Calvin, and Henry VIII were similar is that they all were
(1) Latin American revolutionary leaders
(2) Reformation leaders
(3) Impressionist painters
(4) divine right monarchs

Base your answer to question 10 on the statements below and on your knowledge of social studies.

Speaker A: "The state of monarchy is supreme on earth: for kings are not only God's lieutenants upon earth and sit upon God's throne, but even by God himself they are called gods."

Speaker B: "If government fails to fulfill the end for which it was established—the preservation of the individual's right to life, liberty, and property—the people have a right to dissolve the government."

Speaker C: "But what if the compact between the ruler and ruled is violated by the ruler? He thus becomes a tyrant, a criminal who forfeits his rights to the obedience of his subjects, who may now exercise their right to rebel and form a new compact."

Speaker D: "The ruling authority in the state, the sovereign, must have supreme power, or society will collapse and the anarchy of the state of nature will return."

10 Which two speakers would support absolutism?
(1) *A* and *D*
(2) *B* and *C*
(3) *C* and *D*
(4) *A* and *B*

REGENTS WARM-UP

Some multiple-choice questions draw connections between time periods. The purpose is to spot trends or patterns in the cultural development of the region. Question 11 is an example of such a question.

REGENTS WARM-UP

Question 13 is a data-based question. It evaluates your ability to draw inferences from a quotation. You must also draw upon your knowledge of social studies to interpret the quotation.

REGENTS WARM-UP

Question 14 evaluates your ability to identify cause-and-effect relationships. "Result" is another word for effect.

11   •   Magna Carta signed by King John
       •   Habeas Corpus Act passed during the rule of Charles II
       •   Bill of Rights agreed to by William and Mary

These events in English history were similar in that they all
(1) promoted religious freedom
(2) limited the power of the monarch
(3) provided universal suffrage
(4) supported divine right theory

12   The revival of Greek and Roman culture, the economic growth of Italian city-states in the 1400s, and the development of humanism were aspects of the
(1) Age of Revolutions
(2) Protestant Reformation
(3) spread of Islam
(4) European Renaissance

13   Which quotation was most likely made by an absolute monarch?
(1) "The government that governs best, governs least."
(2) "I am the state."
(3) "The government must be based on a sound constitution."
(4) "It is the parliament that must make the laws."

14   The Glorious Revolution in England resulted in the
(1) strengthening of divine right rule
(2) formation of a limited monarchy
(3) weakening of Parliament's power of the purse
(4) end of civil liberties guaranteed by the Petition of Right

15 In the partial outline below, which heading belongs after Roman numeral I?

> I. _____
>   A. Louis XIV
>   B. Phillip II
>   C. Henry VIII

(1) Divine Right Monarchs
(2) Supporters of Democracy
(3) Religious Reformers
(4) Leaders of the Crusades

16 In which way were the developments of the Renaissance in Italy similar to the developments of the Tang dynasty in China?
(1) The rebirth of art, technology, and learning was a central theme in both regions.
(2) Warfare and insurrection led to the devastation of both societies.
(3) Religious reform was a main focus in both regions.
(4) The peasant class was responsible for the emergence of both eras.

17 • Luther posted the Ninety-Five Theses.
   • Calvin preached the theory of predestination.
   • Henry VIII signed the Act of Supremacy.

These events occurred during the
(1) Crusades
(2) Neolithic Revolution
(3) Protestant Reformation
(4) Glorious Revolution

18 Which statement explains why the Renaissance began in Italy?
(1) Italy was not influenced by a classical heritage.
(2) The Italian city-states were wealthy centers of trade and manufacturing.
(3) Italy was politically unified by a strong central government.
(4) The Catholic Church did not have any influence in Italy.

19 One similarity between the rule of Peter the Great of Russia and that of Akbar the Great of India was that both leaders
(1) implemented strict religious codes of conduct within their nations
(2) modernized and expanded their empires using ideas from other cultures
(3) relied on peaceful resolutions of conflicts with neighboring peoples
(4) introduced democratic ideas into their political systems

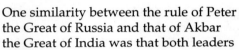

Therefore, the Parliament declares:
    That the [king's] pretended power of suspending laws . . . without consent of Parliament is illegal. That levying money [taxes] for or to the use of the crown [king] . . . without grant [consent] of Parliament . . . is illegal.

20 This 17th-century excerpt is found in the
(1) English Bill of Rights
(2) Declaration of the Rights of Man and the Citizen
(3) Napoleonic Code
(4) Balfour Declaration

21   The primary goal of most of Europe's
     absolute monarchs was to
     (1) support political freedom for the
          new middle classes
     (2) prevent contact with areas beyond
          Europe's borders
     (3) centralize their political control over
          their nations
     (4) maintain peaceful relations with
          neighboring nations

22   • Sale of indulgences authorized by
        Pope Leo X to raise money to build
        St. Peter's Basilica in Rome (1515)
     • Ninety-Five Theses posted (1517)
     • Hearing held at Worms, Germany
        (1521)

     These events are most closely associated
     with
     (1) Charles V and absolutism
     (2) Martin Luther and the Protestant
          Reformation
     (3) John Locke and the Enlightenment
     (4) Karl Marx and scientific socialism

23   Niccolo Machiavelli in *The Prince* and
     Thomas Hobbes in *Leviathan* both
     advocated that a ruler should
     (1) obtain power from a social contract
          with the governed
     (2) place the needs of subjects first
     (3) apply Christian teachings to all
          decisions
     (4) employ absolute power to maintain
          order in the areas under their rule

24   Carefully drawn calligraphy, Zen
     gardens, and the tea ceremony are
     examples of
     (1) artifacts of Mansa Musa's Timbuktu
     (2) the accomplishments of the
          Protestant Reformation
     (3) early Japanese culture
     (4) the achievements of Renaissance
          Florence

Base your answer to question 25 on the
quotation below and on your knowledge of
social studies.

     "Harmony should be valued and
quarrels should be avoided. Everyone
has his biases, and few men are far
sighted. Therefore some disobey their
lords and fathers and keep up feuds
with neighbors. But when the superiors are in harmony with each other
and inferiors are friendly, then the
affairs are discussed quietly and the
right view of matters prevails."
     —Prince Shotoku of Japan (A.D. 604)

25   Prince Shotoku's statement indicates the
     influence of the ideas of
     (1) Confucius
     (2) Muhammad
     (3) Genghis Khan
     (4) Emperor Hirohito

26   One similarity between Japanese
     Shintoism and African animism is the
     belief that
     (1) everything in nature has a spirit and
          should be respected
     (2) only one God exists in the universe
     (3) people's moral conduct determines
          their afterlife
     (4) religious statues should be erected
          to honor the gods

Part II   Thematic Essay Question

The following thematic essay question comes from past Regents Examinations. Write your answers on a separate sheet of paper. Essay-writing tips appear in the margin. For additional help, see Taking the Regents Exam on pages ix-xxxv of this Review Book.

Directions: Write a well-organized essay that includes an introduction, several paragraphs addressing the task below, and a conclusion.

Theme: Change

> Individuals have brought about great changes in history. These individuals have had positive and/or negative effects on nations or regions.

Task:

> Choose *two* individuals from your study of global history and geography and for *each* individual chosen
>
> - Discuss *two* specific changes made by the individual in a specific nation or region
> - Evaluate whether these changes have had a positive or a negative effect on that nation or region

You may use any example from your study of global history and geography. Some suggestions you might wish to consider include Elizabeth I, Genghis Khan, Muhammed, Martin Luther, Napoleon Bonaparte, Toussaint L'Overture, Nelson Mandela, Fidel Castro, Boris Yeltsin, Deng Xiaoping, and Yasir Arafat.

You are *not* limited to these suggestions.

Do *not* use an individual from the United States in your answer.

Guidelines:

    In your essay, be sure to

- Develop all aspects of the task
- Support the theme with relevant facts, examples, and details
- Use a logical and clear plan of organization, including an introduction and conclusion that are beyond a restatement of the theme

Part III   Document-Based Question

This exercise is designed to test your ability to work with historical documents. It is similar to the document-based questions that you will see on the Regents Examination. While you are asked to analyze three historical documents, the exercise on the actual exam will include more documents. Some of the documents have been edited for the purposes of the question. As you analyze the documents, take into account the source of each document and any point of view that may be presented in the document.

Historical Context:

Both Africa and Japan have faced scarcity of resources. Each region has responded in creative ways to the difficulties created by climate and geography.

Task: Using information from the documents and your knowledge of global history, answer the questions that follow each document in Part A. Your answers to the questions will help you write the Part B essay, in which you will be asked to

> • Compare and contrast the effect of geographic resources on the development of Africa and Japan. You may wish to consider climate, location, resources, and landforms.

Part A   Short-Answer Questions

Directions: Analyze the documents and answer the short-answer questions that follow each document in the space provided.

Document 1

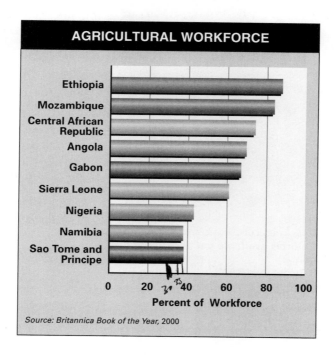

AGRICULTURAL WORKFORCE

Ethiopia
Mozambique
Central African Republic
Angola
Gabon
Sierra Leone
Nigeria
Namibia
Sao Tome and Principe

0   20   30 35 40   60   80   100

Percent of Workforce

Source: Britannica Book of the Year, 2000

1a   What nation on the graph has the highest percentage of agricultural workers?

  Ethiopia has the largest percent of workers

b   What is the least percentage of agricultural workers represented on the graph?

  Sao Tome and Principe have the least amt of workforce

~37%

Document 2

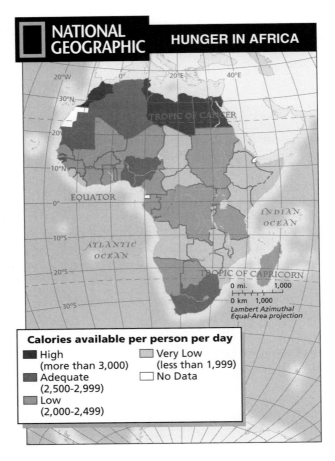

2a   What generalization can you make about the calories available to people living in most of central and west Africa?

<u>In central parts of Africa less calories are</u>
<u>available to the people</u>

b   Based on your knowledge of history, why do you think the highest number of calories per person is located where it is?

<u>they are near more urban areas, or near</u>
<u>water so they can trade</u>

Document 3

> The land was on all sides well protected, and yet also open to the sea; and . . . there was free access for commerce and civilisation from early times. . . .
>
> The deeply indented coastline of Japan provides a number of excellent harbors on the Pacific coast, and its shores abound in fish of all kinds, the rich supplies of which have for centuries constituted one of the chief articles of food of the people. The fishing industries have helped to provide Japan with a recruiting ground for one of the strongest and most formidable navies of modern times. . . .
>
> Walter Weston, *"The Geography of Japan in Its Influence on the Character of the Japanese People," in* The Japan Society of London, *Transactions and Proceedings, XX (1922–1923)*

3 Based on this document, identify **two** ways that geography affected the development of Japan.

land that was landlocked was harder to get to and land near ports can trade and fish to help the development of an area

Part B   Essay

Directions: Write a well-organized essay that includes an introduction, several paragraphs, and a conclusion.

Use evidence from at least **two** documents in the body of the essay. Support your response with relevant facts, examples, and details. Include additional outside information.

Historical Context:

Both Africa and Japan have faced scarcity of resources. Each region has responded in creative ways to the difficulties created by climate and geography.

Task: Using information from the documents and your knowledge of global history and geography, write an essay in which you

> • Compare and contrast the effect of geographic resources on the development of Africa and Japan. You may wish to consider climate, location, resources, and landforms.

Guidelines:

In your essay, be sure to

- Develop all aspects of the task
- Incorporate information from *at least two* documents in the body of the essay
- Incorporate relevant outside information
- Support the theme with relevant facts, examples, and details
- Use a logical and clear plan of organization, including an introduction and conclusion that are beyond a restatement of the theme

UNIT 4   THE MODERN WORLD
1450–1770

PREPARING FOR THE REGENTS

This entire book is set up to help you grasp the facts, main ideas, and concepts needed to do well on your Regents Exam. Notes in the margin include core concepts, test-taking tips, and more. Use blank spaces in the margins to answer questions raised in the text or to jot down key points. Before each unit of study, skim through the exams at the back of the book to develop a sense of what the Regents wants you to know about the world.

Unit 4 Overview

Several powerful empires—Maya, Aztec, and Inca—controlled civilizations in Mesoamerica and South America for centuries before the arrival of Europeans. Beginning in the late fifteenth century, Europeans engaged in a vigorous period of exploration. The result was a new era of discovery, trade, and colonization. Also during this period, two Islamic empires, the Ottoman in Turkey and the Safavids in Persia, arose in Southwest Asia. A third Islamic empire, the Mogul, unified and ruled the Indian subcontinent. Under these Muslim empires, trade and the arts flourished. China and Japan in East Asia were least affected by European expansion.

Unit 4 Objectives

After studying this unit, you should be able to:

1.   describe the similarities between and differences among the Native American cultures in North America;

2.   explain the accomplishments of the Maya, Aztec, and Inca civilizations;

3.   summarize the fifteenth century European voyages of discovery and their results;

4.   analyze the effects of European expansion on Africa and Southeast Asia;

5.   discuss the role of religion in the Muslim Empires of Arabia and East Asia.

CHAPTER 14   THE AMERICAS

Chapter Overview

The first organized societies had begun to take root in Mexico and Central America by 1200 B.C. One key area of development was on the plateau of central Mexico. Another was in the lowland regions along the Gulf of Mexico and extending into modern-day Guatemala. Civilizations also thrived in the central Andes. Other societies were emerging in the river valleys and the great plains of North America.

The events occurring during this time period continue to affect our lives. In the southwestern United States, the Anasazi culture and the Anasazi's descendants influenced adobe dwellings and handcrafted pottery made today. The Iroquois League provided a model of confederation for the British colonies in North America. Compulsory military service, which has been used in the United States and other parts of the world, was also part of the Incan Empire.

As you read through this chapter, ask yourself these questions:
(1) Who were the first inhabitants of the Americas?
(2) What are the principal cultural developments of the Mayan civilization?
(3) What method did the Inca use to enlarge their empire?

Main Ideas and Concepts

- **Change** The voyages of exploration and European colonization increased interdependence among four continents—North America, South America, Europe, and Africa.

- **Identity** Common cultural characteristics helped form the Americas as a region.

- **Technology** The ancient civilizations of the Americas demonstrated technological achievements, such as a knowledge of mathematics and astronomy and the ability to construct massive architectural works.

People, Places, Terms

The following names and terms will help you to prepare for the Regents Exam in Global History and Geography. You can find an explanation of each name and term in the Glossary at the back of this book, in your textbook, or in another reference source.

adobe	Hernán Cortés	*quipu*
Andes	hieroglyph	tepee
Bering Strait	maize	tribute
clan	Francisco Pizarro	
conquistadors	pueblo	

SECTION 1 THE PEOPLES OF NORTH AMERICA

The Lands of the Americas

The Americas cover an enormous land area, from the Arctic Ocean in the north to Cape Horn at the tip of South America. Over this huge region, there are many different landscapes: ice-covered lands, dense forests, fertile river valleys, coastlines, tropical forests, hot deserts, and mountain ranges.

On the western side of the Americas, there are two major mountain ranges, the Rocky Mountains in North America and the **Andes** in South America. Lower mountain ranges run along the eastern coasts. Between the mountain ranges there are valleys with rich farmland through which great rivers flow. The two largest are the Mississippi in North America and the Amazon in South America.

The First Americans

No one is certain when the first human beings began living in the Americas. Scholars do know that between 100,000 and 8,000 years ago, the last Ice Age produced low sea levels. The low sea levels created a land bridge in the **Bering Strait** between Asia and North America. Historians believe that small groups of people from Asia crossed the Bering Strait into North America. They were probably hunters who were following herds of bison and caribou. They may have become the first Americans.

CORE CONCEPTS: PHYSICAL SYSTEMS

The Andes are the world's longest mountain range, stretching 4,500 miles (7,242 km) along the western coast of South America. It is also one of the highest systems, with several peaks more than 20,000 feet (6,096 m) above sea level. Several ranges of mountains run parallel to one another like the folds in a carpet. These parallel ranges are known as *cordillera*.

The Peoples of North America

North America is a large continent, with varying geographical features and climate. Various peoples made their homes in these different regions.

Arctic and Northwest: The Inuit A group of people called the Inuit moved into North America about 4000 B.C. They settled along the coasts of the tundra, a treeless area south of the Arctic. They learned how to survive in such a cold environment. They hunted caribou, seal, and fish, which were used for both food and clothing. Their homes were made of stone and turf.

Eastern Woodlands: The Mound Builders Farming villages developed in the Eastern Woodlands around 1000 B.C. This region is in eastern North America, from the Great Lakes to the Gulf of Mexico. The people of the Eastern Woodlands were farmers but also continued gathering plants for food.

The Hopewell people, also known as the Mound Builders, are the best known of this group. They lived in the Ohio River valley, eventually extending their culture as far as the Mississippi River. Their earth mounds were used for tombs or for ceremonies.

About A.D. 700, the people began farming full-time. Corn, squash, and beans were their most common crops. Cities began appearing, the most famous of which was Cahokia. Between A.D. 850 and A.D. 1150, Cahokia, located near present-day East St. Louis, was the seat of government for much of the Mississippi culture. Archaeologists have found a burial mound more than 98 feet (30 m) high nearby. Its base is larger than Egypt's Great Pyramid. Cahokia died out in the thirteenth century, for unknown reasons.

Eastern Woodlands: The Iroquois Northeast of the Mississippian culture, the Iroquois peoples lived. Their villages were in present-day Pennsylvania, New York, and southern Canada.

Wars were common until an elder known as Deganawida worked to form an alliance known as the Iroquois League. With Hiawatha, a member of the Onondaga group, he created the Great Peace. A council of representatives known as the Grand Council met to settle differences among the groups. Although the representatives were men, the women selected them. Groups of related families, known as **clans**, in turn made up each Iroquois group. The women of the clan chose one woman as the clan mother. It was the responsibility of the clan mothers to choose the members of the Grand Council.

Peoples of the Great Plains The Plains Indians lived west of the Mississippi River. Like the Iroquois, they grew corn, beans, and squash. The men hunted buffalo in the summer, using various parts of the animal for food, clothing, and tools. They stretched buffalo skins over wooden poles to make their circular tents, known as **tepees**.

Peoples of the Southwest: The Anasazi In the present area of New Mexico, Utah, Arizona, and Colorado, the Anasazi civilization developed. Although the area is dry, in some regions there is enough rain to farm. The Anasazi used canals and dams to turn parts of the desert into gardens between A.D. 500 and 1200. From stone and sun-dried brick known as **adobe**, they built **pueblos**, multi-storied structures that housed many people. The Anasazi made beautiful baskets and pottery. Large communities developed at Chaco Canyon in northwestern New Mexico and at Mesa Verde in southern Colorado. Both communities were eventually abandoned because of drought.

SECTION 2 EARLY CIVILIZATIONS IN MESOAMERICA

CORE CONCEPTS: CHOICE

Some historians believe that Benjamin Franklin later used the Iroquois Confederation as the democratic model for a Plan of Union for the British colonies.

CORE CONCEPTS: SCIENCE AND TECHNOLOGY

Pueblo Bonito was a tenth-century village built in Chaco Canyon. It had about 800 rooms and was five stories tall in some places. Across the canyon and desert, the inhabitants built a 400-mile road system that was 30 feet wide.

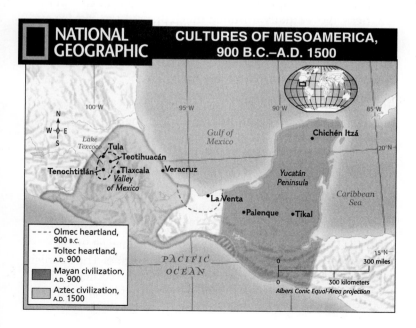

NATIONAL GEOGRAPHIC

CULTURES OF MESOAMERICA, 900 B.C.–A.D. 1500

- - - - Olmec heartland, 900 B.C.
- - - - Toltec heartland, A.D. 900
Mayan civilization, A.D. 900
Aztec civilization, A.D. 1500

Albers Conic Equal-Area projection

The Olmec and Teotihuacán

The Olmec civilization appeared around 1200 B.C. in Mesoamerica, the name used for areas of Mexico and Central America already civilized before the arrival of the Spanish. The Olmec peoples, who were farmers, lived in the swampy, hot lowlands along the coast of the Gulf of Mexico.

The Olmec had large cities that were centers for their religious rituals. Talented artists helped construct the earliest religious buildings in the region. In one of these cities, La Venta, was a huge pyramid. The Olmec carved large heads, probably meant to represent their gods. Their civilization declined and collapsed around 400 B.C.

Teotihuacán was the first major city in Mesoamerica. Its name means "Place of the Gods." The city was the capital of an early kingdom, near present-day Mexico City, that existed from about 250 B.C. until about A.D. 800. Temples and palaces lined its main street, which was called the Avenue of the Dead. The Pyramid of the Sun, which was built in four tiers that reached over 200 feet (60 m) high, was also there.

The Maya and Toltec

The Mayan civilization flourished on the Yucatán Peninsula between A.D. 300 and 900. One of the most sophisticated in the Americas, it eventually included much of southern Mexico and Central America.

Political and Social Structures Mayan cities were constructed around a pyramid topped with a shrine to the gods, with other temples and palaces built nearby. Some of these cities were home to more than 100,000 people. Tikal, the largest Mayan city, gained most of its wealth from trade with other civilizations in the region.

City-states, which were often at war, made up Mayan civilization. Rulers of these city-states claimed to be descended from the gods. They were assisted by nobles and a class of scribes, who may also have functioned as priests. Artisans, merchants, officials, and peasant farmers made up the rest of the society.

Writings and Calendar The Maya developed a system of writing known as **hieroglyphs**, or picture writing. The Spanish made no effort to understand the writing or the contents of books, which they burned. Only four have survived, written on bark with plaster covers. Their contents were a mystery to

**CORE CONCEPTS:
PLACES AND REGIONS**

Palenque is a ruin deep in the Mexican peninsula's jungle. There, archaeologists have found a large collection of Mayan hieroglyphs in a royal tomb. They tell of the deeds of the ruler Pacal, who was buried in the tomb.

**CORE CONCEPTS:
BELIEF SYSTEMS**

The Maya believed that all life was in the hands of the gods. Their chief god was Itzamna, which means Lizard House. Some of the gods, such as the jaguar god of night, were evil. Captured enemy soldiers were sometimes used for human sacrifices, which were designed to appease the gods or to celebrate special occasions.

scholars until someone noticed that the symbols corresponded to dates on the Long Count, a Mayan calendar. The Long Count was based on a cycle of creation and destruction.

The Maya developed two different calendars. One was a solar calendar of 365 days, divided into 18 months of 20 days each, with an extra five days at the end. The other was a sacred calendar of 260 days, divided into 13 weeks of 20 days. Only priests could use these to foretell the future.

The Toltec For several centuries beginning around A.D. 900, the Toltec controlled the upper Yucatán Peninsula. The Toltecs were builders of palaces and pyramids as well as warriors. The center of the empire was Tula, northwest of present-day Mexico City. They had a second capital at Chichén Itzá. Their control extended into the Mayan lands of Guatemala and the northern Yucatán. Their civilization declined about 1200.

The Aztec

Aztec origins are uncertain. Sometime during the twelfth century A.D. they migrated to the Valley of Mexico. Their capital was Tenochtitlán, on an island in the middle of Lake Texcoco.

Rise of the Aztec The Aztec chose their capital based on a legend that said when they saw an eagle sitting on a cactus growing out of a rock, they would be at their journey's end. Under attack from another group, they were driven into Lake Texcoco's swamps and islands around 1325. There, they saw the promised sign. For the next century, they built the capital, Tenochtitlán, on the site of present-day Mexico City. In addition to the palace, public buildings, and homes, they built causeways linking the islands to the mainland. During this time they also consolidated their rule over much of what is now central Mexico. The kingdom was made up of territories ruled by a local lord. The Aztec ruler supported the lords in return for **tribute**, which is money or goods paid by a conquered people to the conqueror.

Political and Social Structures The Aztec were a warlike people with a strict class structure. The Aztec ruler claimed to be descended from the gods. A council of lords and government officials assisted him in his rule. The rest of the people were commoners, indentured workers, and slaves. Indentured workers did not own land, but contracted to work on the nobles' estate. Those who were captured in war became slaves. Most common people were farmers or merchants.

CORE CONCEPTS: CULTURE

The Mexican government issued a challenge to artists in 1920. Having come through a successful revolution, the new rulers wanted Mexicans to have more pride in their heritage. Diego Rivera, one of the nation's foremost artists, accepted the challenge. He created a series of murals on the sides of schools and government buildings, depicting the Aztec civilization. He worked on these idealized murals for thirty years, from 1920 until 1950.

CORE CONCEPTS: POWER

The Aztec proved to be harsh rulers over those they conquered. As a consequence, when the Spaniards arrived, many of the native people joined with them to overthrow the Aztec.

LINKING PAST AND PRESENT

Present-day Central Americans find a common heritage in the Mayan civilization. Several countries in the region are joining together to construct the Maya route, *La Ruta Maya*, linking ancient Mayan sites.

CORE CONCEPTS: BELIEF SYSTEMS

Another important god was the feathered serpent, Quetzalcoatl. An Aztec legend said that he had left centuries before, but would return in triumph. Stories of a Toltec prince who would return from exile when an arrow pierced a sapling also shaped the Aztec beliefs. When they saw the sign of the cross on the breastplates of Spanish soldiers, they thought they saw an arrow piercing a sapling. They believed the Spaniards were representing Quetzalcoatl.

CORE CONCEPTS: MOVEMENT OF PEOPLE AND GOODS

Hernán Cortés first tasted a drink called *xocoatl* at the court of Montezuma. Made from cacao seeds, with spiced chili peppers added, it was somewhat bitter. Cortés took some of the cacao seeds back to Europe, where the Spanish altered the recipe. They added sugar, vanilla, and cinnamon to create a sweet drink. For nearly 80 years, they kept their new beverage a secret. But a chocolate craze swept Europe when the word got out.

Although women were not considered equal to men, they were allowed to own and inherit property and enter into contracts. They were also permitted to become priestesses. They were expected to remain at home, weaving textiles and caring for the children.

Religion and Culture The Aztec religion was supported by a priest and warrior class. Like the Maya, the Aztec were polytheistic. The most important god was the god of sun and war. Aztec religion was based on belief in a struggle between good and evil forces. Aztec believed that an earthquake would destroy the world. They tried to delay this by sacrificing to the sun god. At the top of the pyramids they built were shrines to the gods and altars for human sacrifices.

The Destruction of Aztec Civilization A Spanish army under the command of **Hernán Cortés** landed at Veracruz on the Gulf of Mexico in 1519. He and succeeding waves of **conquistadors** went to the new world for "Gold, God, and Glory." On his march to Tenochtitlán, Cortés made alliances with city-states that wanted freedom from Aztec rule. Montezuma, the ruler of the Aztec, welcomed Cortés to the capital.

Tensions arose between the Spanish and the Aztec; a year after the Spanish arrived, they were driven from the city. However, the Aztec had been infected with diseases from Europe to which they had no immunity. With fresh soldiers and Indian allies who resented Aztec influence, Cortés besieged the city, which surrendered after four months. The Spanish destroyed the city, using the stones of palaces, temples, and pyramids to build churches and government buildings. They also filled in the canals and rivers.

SECTION 3 EARLY CIVILIZATIONS IN SOUTH AMERICA

Early Civilizations

Caral, located in the Supe River valley of Peru, was the oldest major city in the Americas. Its stone buildings included apartment buildings and large homes, as well as buildings for officials. By diverting a river into their fields, the people of Caral developed a system of irrigation. The city was abandoned sometime between 2000 and 1500 B.C.

Another civilization appeared near the Pacific coast, south of the border of present-day Ecuador, around 200 B.C. The capital of this state was Moche, located in the valley of the Moche River. Farmers used the river to irrigate their fields, growing maize, peanuts, potatoes, and cotton. The power of the Moche rulers extended far along the coast. Although the people of Moche left no written language, scholars study their pottery to learn about the culture. The pottery indicates that warfare was a central feature of their lives. Both pottery and paintings depict prisoners, warfare, and human sacrifices. This civilization ended around A.D. 700.

The Inca

A new power arose about three hundred years after the end of the Moche civilization. Known as the kingdom of Chimor, it controlled the region for about four centuries. The Inca finally destroyed it. In the late 1300s, the Inca were only a small community in the area of Cuzco, which was a city located in the southern Peruvian mountains. Under the leadership of the ruler Pachacutí, the Inca began in the 1440s to conquer the entire region. The "children of the sun" were empire builders who relied on a common language and road system to unify their empire.

Political Structures Pachacutí created a centralized state. His successors, Topa Inca and Huayna Inca, extended the boundaries of the Incan Empire as far as Ecuador, central Chile, and the edge of the Amazon Basin.

Because the Incan state was built on war, all young men had to serve in the Incan army. The army had two hundred thousand soldiers. Llamas carried supplies, because the Inca did not use the wheel.

Once an area came under Incan control, the people were taught the Quechua language. A noble was sent out to govern the new region. Local leaders could keep their posts as long as they were loyal to the Inca ruler. Pachacutí divided the empire into four regions, each ruled by a governor. The quarters were further divided into provinces, also ruled by governors. Each province was supposed to contain about ten thousand people. The emperor, believed to be descended from the sun god Inti, was at the top of the entire system.

All Incan subjects were required to perform labor for the state, generally for several weeks each year. Laborers were moved

LINKING PAST AND PRESENT

Descendants of the Inca still live and farm in the Andean highlands from Ecuador to Brazil. These people are known as the Quechua, after their language, which was adapted from that of the Inca. They have been the subjects of many studies about the effects of living at high altitudes.

from one part of the country to another to take part in building projects. Incan buildings and monuments were constructed of close-fitting stones without mortar. This helped them to withstand the area's earthquakes. The Incas also built a road system 24,800 miles (about 40,000 km) long. Along the roads were rest houses and storage depots. The Inca built bridges over waterways and ravines.

Social Structures Incan society was highly regimented. Men and women selected a marriage partner from within their own social groups. Women were to raise children and weave cloth. Some young girls served as temple priestesses.

In rural areas, the people lived mainly by farming. In the mountains of those areas, farmers built terraces, which were watered by irrigation systems. They planted corn, potatoes, and other crops. The farmers' houses were made of adobe or stone and located near the fields. In a form of early socialism, all land belonged to the Inca in common, although the government allocated crops from harvests to groups of people and stored some to be used during famines.

Building and Culture The Inca were great builders. The building in the capital of Cuzco dazzled European visitors. The ruins of the abandoned city Machu Picchu show architectural genius. The small city of about two hundred buildings was located on mountain peaks far above the Urubamba River. In one section, a long stairway leads to an elegant stone, which the Inca called "the hitching post of the sun." This may have been used as a solar observatory. People gathered there to chant to the sun god during sun festivals.

The Inca used a system of knotted strings called the *quipu* instead of a writing system. Other cultural achievements included a tradition of court theater, with both tragic and comic works. Poetry was recited, often to the musical accompaniment of reed instruments.

Conquest and Culture The Incas were in the midst of a bloody civil war between their ruler, Atahuallpa, and his brother when **Francisco Pizarro** arrived in 1531 with soldiers, steel weapons, horses, and gunpowder.

After Atahuallpa defeated his brother's army, Pizarro captured and killed Atahuallpa and his followers, who could not compete with the superior technology of the Spanish conquistadors. The Spanish then captured Cuzco and set up a new capital at Lima in 1535.

CORE CONCEPTS: CULTURE

The *quipu* was useful for recording anything that could be counted, such as number killed in battle or number of speeches the emperor had given. Because it could not record any prose text, the Inca created poems and stories which they committed to memory to preserve their history.

CHAPTER 15 THE AGE OF EXPLORATION

Chapter Overview

At the beginning of the sixteenth century, European adventurers launched their small fleets into the vast reaches of the Atlantic Ocean. They were hardly aware that they were beginning a new era, not only for Europe but also for the peoples of Asia, Africa, and the Americas. These European voyages marked the beginning of a process that led to radical changes in the political, economic, and cultural life of the entire non-Western world.

The events that occurred during this time period continue to affect our lives today. European trade was a factor in producing a new age of commercial capitalism that was one of the first steps toward today's world economy. The consequences of slavery continue to impact our lives. The Age of Exploration led to a transfer of ideas and products, many of which are still important in our lives.

As you read through this chapter, ask yourself these questions:
(1) What impact did European expansion have on the conquerors and the conquered?
(2) How were the African states structured politically?
(3) How did the power shift from the Portuguese to the Dutch in the control of the spice trade?

Main Ideas and Concepts

- **Technology** Widespread use of new technological inventions opened the way for the expansion of European ideas and power.

- **Power** The Age of Exploration marked the end of European isolation and the start of European domination of much of Latin America, Africa, Southeast Asia, and China lasting into the twentieth century.

- **Political Systems** In the 1500s and 1600s, the monarchies of Europe sought to centralize power in their respective political systems.

People, Places, Terms

The following names and terms will help you to prepare for the Regents Exam in Global History and Geography. You can find an explanation of each name and term in the Glossary at the back of this book, in your textbook, or in another reference source.

balance of trade	conquistador	Middle Passage
bureaucracy	*encomienda*	plantation
colony	mainland states	triangular trade
Columbian Exchange	mercantilism	

SECTION 1 EXPLORATION AND EXPANSION

Motives and Means

During the fifteenth century, Europeans began to sail all over the world. Because of the conquests by Ottoman Turks in the fourteenth century, Europeans could no longer travel to the East by land, as Marco Polo had done in the thirteenth century. This problem made Europeans attempt to reach Asia by sea. They had three main reasons for undertaking these dangerous voyages. The first motive was economic. The Crusades had shown the variety of goods and spices available in the East. The Europeans had come to need these goods. The second motive was religious. Many Europeans believed that it was their duty to convert other peoples to Christianity. The third motive was a desire for glory and adventure. These three motives were summarized by the Spanish as "God, glory, and gold."

Not only did the Europeans of the fifteenth century have motives for exploration, but they also had means that they had not possessed before. By the second half of the fifteenth century, European monarchies had increased both their power and their resources and were thus able to sponsor voyages. Europeans had also reached a level of technology that made the voyages possible.

The Portuguese Trading Empire

Beginning in 1420, Portuguese fleets began to explore the western coast of Africa. These fleets were sponsored by Prince Henry the Navigator. In Africa, the Portuguese discovered a new

CORE CONCEPTS: MOVEMENT OF PEOPLE AND GOODS

Many Europeans read with fascination the account that Italian Marco Polo wrote of his travels. With his father and an uncle, Polo had traveled to the court of the Mongol ruler Kublai Khan. Christopher Columbus was one of the people influenced by the book.

source of gold. The southern coast of West Africa became known to Europeans as the Gold Coast.

Portuguese sea captains heard about a route to India around the southern tip of Africa. In 1488, Bartholomeu Dias rounded the tip, called the Cape of Good Hope. Later, Vasco da Gama went around the Cape and cut across the Indian Ocean to the coast of India. There he took on a cargo of spices. After he returned to Portugal, he made a profit of several thousand percent.

Portuguese fleets returned to the area to gain control of the spice trade, which had been controlled by the Muslims. In 1509, a Portuguese fleet defeated a fleet of Turkish and Indian ships off the coast of India. A year later, Admiral Afonso de Albuquerque set up a port at Goa, on the western coast of India.

The Portuguese then began to search for the source of the spice trade. Albuquerque gained control of Melaka, which was a thriving port for the spice trade. From Melaka, the Portuguese made expeditions to China and the Spice Islands. They signed a treaty with a local ruler for the purchase and export of cloves. This treaty gave the Portuguese control of the spice trade. They now had a trading empire, but they did not try to colonize the Asian regions.

Navigational Technology

From earlier contacts with the Chinese and the Arabs, European sailors created working compasses and more accurate star charts. The invention of the astrolabe and sextant made it possible to sail in open waters without getting lost. The ships were larger, which made it possible to carry more cargo and withstand rougher seas. Advances in sails and rigging made steering the ship and adjusting to changes in wind conditions more efficient. Besides these innovations, the Europeans had expanded their use of gunpowder weapons, making their ships seagoing forts.

Voyages to the Americas

The Portuguese sailed eastward through the Indian Ocean to reach the source of the spice trade. The Spanish tried to reach it by sailing westward across the Atlantic Ocean.

The Voyages of Columbus Christopher Columbus, an Italian, believed that he could reach Asia by sailing west, instead of east around Africa. He persuaded Queen Isabella of Spain to finance

CORE CONCEPTS: SCIENCE AND TECHNOLOGY

Europeans were able to make the advances they did because of technologies borrowed from the Arab world. Arab navigators and mathematicians had created charts known as *portolani*, which recorded the shapes of coastlines and distances between ports. Arabs had invented both the compass and the astrolabe, which allowed sailors to determine their direction and latitude. In addition, Arab sailors used lateen, or triangular sails, which made ships easier to maneuver.

CORE CONCEPTS: POWER

With their long Atlantic-facing coastlines, Spain, Portugal, England, and the Netherlands wrested control of trade from Italy, which was centered in the Mediterranean. Many Italian sea captains sought employment from the Atlantic coast countries.

an expedition. In October 1492, he reached the Americas. He believed that he had reached India. He made three more voyages to try to find a route through the islands to the Asian mainland. In his four voyages, he reached all of the major islands of the Caribbean and the Central American country of Honduras. Still convinced that he was in Asia, he called the islands the Indies.

A Line of Demarcation By the 1490s, both Spain and Portugal had explored and claimed new lands. Both countries were afraid that the other might claim some of its newly discovered territories. In 1494, they signed the Treaty of Tordesillas. It created an imaginary line that extended from north to south through the Atlantic Ocean and the easternmost part of South America. Portugal would control unexplored territories located east of the line, while Spain controlled those west of the line. The treaty gave Portugal control over its route around Africa. It gave Spain rights to almost all of the Americas.

Race to the Americas Many countries in Europe began to sponsor expeditions to the Americas. A Venetian seaman, John Cabot, explored the New England coastline for England. The Portuguese sea captain Pedro Cabral landed in South America in 1500. Amerigo Vespucci went along on several voyages and wrote letters describing what he saw. His letters led to using America as the name for the new lands. Europeans called these lands the New World, but they were new only to the Europeans. They already had flourishing civilizations when the Europeans arrived.

In 1519, Ferdinand Magellan tied together the work of Portugal's Henry the Navigator and Spain's Balboa, the first European to see the Pacific. Magellan's fleet was the first to circumnavigate the globe.

The Spanish Empire

The Spanish conquerors of the Americas were known as **conquistadors**. Their guns and horses brought them success. The forces of Hérnan Cortés took only three years to overthrow the Aztec Empire in Central America. By 1550, the Spanish had gained control of northern Mexico. In South America, Francisco Pizarro led an expedition that took control of the Inca Empire.

By 1535, the Spanish had created a system of colonial administration in the Americas. Queen Isabella declared that the Native Americans were her subjects. She granted Spanish settlers *encomienda* (the right to use Native Americans as laborers). The

CORE CONCEPTS: IMPERIALISM

The Treaty of Tordesillas explains why Portuguese, not Spanish, is the official language of Brazil, the largest and most eastern South American nation.

Spanish settlers were supposed to protect Native Americans, but few did. Instead, they put them to work on sugar plantations and in gold and silver mines.

Forced labor, starvation, and disease took a terrible toll on Native American lives. The native peoples had little resistance to European diseases, and 30 to 40 percent of them died from smallpox, measles, and typhus. In the early years of the conquest, Catholic missionaries forcibly converted and baptized hundreds of thousands of native peoples. Native American social and political structures were torn apart and replaced by European systems of religion, language, culture, and government.

Economic Impact and Competition

Wherever they went, Europeans looked for gold and silver. Along with those precious metals, sugar, cotton, dyes, vanilla, and animal hides soon flowed into Europe from the Americas. Agricultural products such as potatoes, coffee, corn, and tobacco were also shipped to Europe. This exchange of plants and animals is known as the **Columbian Exchange**. Because of its trading posts in Asia, Portugal soon became the chief entry point for the trade in spices, jewels, silks, carpets, ivory, leather, and perfumes.

New Rivals Enter the Scene By the end of the 1500s, several European countries were vying for the eastern trade. Ferdinand Magellan, a Portuguese explorer who was financed by the king of Spain, sailed around the tip of South America and crossed the Pacific Ocean to the Philippines. Spanish ships carried silver from Mexico to the Philippines and returned to Mexico with silk and other luxury goods.

Trying to find a northern passage to India, John Cabot, an Italian sailing for England, explored the waters off Canada. From the mid to late 1500s, Spain was harassed by English attacks on its treasure fleet. At the beginning of the 1600s, an English fleet landed on the northwestern coast of India. The English established trade relations with the people there and trade flourished.

The first Dutch fleet arrived in India in 1595. Shortly after, the Dutch formed the East India Company and began competing with the English and the Portuguese.

The Dutch also formed the West India Company to compete in the Americas. They established the Dutch colony of New Netherlands in the Hudson River valley.

CORE CONCEPTS: IDENTITY

The ruler of Spain presented a special gift to the captain of the only ship from Magellan's voyage that actually encircled the globe and returned to Spain. The gift was a globe, with the words *Prius circumdedisti me* inscribed on it. The words, which mean "You were the first to encircle me," were added to the captain's coat of arms.

However, the English seized the colony and renamed it New York. They also founded Virginia and the Massachusetts Bay Colony. By 1700 the English had established a colonial empire along the eastern seaboard of North America.

The French were also interested in the Americas and colonized parts of present-day Canada and Louisiana. An Italian, Giovanni da Verrazano, surveyed the Atlantic coast for France. Jacques Cartier's investigation of the St. Lawrence River led to the establishment of their first colony in Canada.

Trade, Colonies, and Mercantilism

In the 1500s and 1600s, European nations established trading posts and colonies in the Americas and the East. A **colony** is a settlement of people living in a new territory, linked with the parent country by trade and direct government control.

Colonies played a role in the theory of **mercantilism**, a set of principles that dominated economic thought in the seventeenth century. According to mercantilists, the prosperity of a nation depended on a large supply of gold and silver. To bring in gold and silver, nations tried to have a favorable **balance of trade**. The balance of trade is the difference in value between what a nation imports and what it exports over time. When the balance is favorable, the goods exported are of greater value than those imported.

To encourage exports, governments stimulated export industries and trade. They granted subsidies, or payments, to new industries and improved transportation systems. They tried to keep foreign goods out of their own countries by placing high tariffs (taxes) on these goods. Colonies were important because they were sources of raw materials and markets for finished goods.

SECTION 2 AFRICA IN AN AGE OF TRANSITION

The Slave Trade

Slavery had been practiced in Africa since ancient times. As had been done in other parts of the world, African governments sold criminals, debtors, and prisoners of war as slaves. African slaves were occasionally freed by their masters. Freed slaves held the same rights in the community as the rest of the people. Slavery also existed in some European countries. The demand for slaves increased dramatically with the discovery of the Americas in the 1490s.

During the sixteenth century, **plantations** (large agricultural estates) growing sugar cane were set up in Brazil and on islands in the Caribbean. Much labor is required to grow sugar cane. Because many of the Native Americans had died of disease, African slaves were shipped to Brazil and the Caribbean to work on the plantations.

Growth of the Slave Trade A Spanish ship carried the first boat filled with slaves directly from Africa to the Americas in 1518. During the following two centuries, the trade in slaves grew dramatically and became part of the **triangular trade**. In that trade system, European ships carried manufactured goods, such as cloth and guns, to Africa, where they were traded for a cargo of slaves. The slaves were then shipped to the Americas and sold. Europeans then bought tobacco, molasses, sugar, and raw cotton and shipped them back to Europe. As many as ten million African slaves were brought to the Americas between the early sixteenth and late nineteenth centuries.

The journey from Africa to the Americas was known as the **Middle Passage**, the middle portion of the triangular trade route. Many slaves died on the journey. Even those who arrived in the Americas often died because they had little or no immunity to diseases.

Sources of Slaves

Before Europeans became involved in the slave trade, most slaves in Africa were prisoners of war. Slaves were sold at slave markets on the coasts. At first, African slave traders got their supplies of slaves from coastal areas nearby. As the demand for slaves increased, they began to move farther inland to find their victims.

Many local rulers traded slaves, viewing them as a source of income. Many sent raiders into defenseless villages. Some local rulers became concerned about the effect of the slave trade on their societies, but Europeans, Arabs, and other Africans generally ignored their protests.

CORE CONCEPTS: INTERDEPENDENCE

The Europeans referred to different sections of Africa according to the products for which they were most noted. In addition to a Gold Coast, there was also a Slave Coast, a Grain Coast, and an Ivory Coast. European trade with Africa fostered interdependence between the two regions. The trade, however, worked largely to Europe's favor rather than to Africa's. Africa supplied products not available in Europe. For example, Europeans called African pepper the "grain of heaven," hence the name Grain Coast.

CORE CONCEPTS: EMPATHY

One Dutch trader lamented the effect of the slave trade on Africa. "From us," he said, "they have learned strife, quarreling, drunkenness, trickery, theft, unbridled desire for what is not one's own, misdeeds unknown to them before, and the accursed lust for gold."

Effects of the Slave Trade

In some areas, the slave trade led to depopulation. It also took the youngest and strongest men and women from many communities. The West African communities became dependent on the metal, cloth, and guns traded from Europe, negatively affecting their economy. The need to provide a constant supply of slaves led to increased warfare in Africa. Coastal leaders increased their raids on neighboring peoples using guns they obtained in trade from Europeans.

The slave trade also had a devastating effect on some African states. In Benin, for example, the slave trade caused a drop in population and increased warfare. Over time, the people of Benin lost faith in their gods, their art deteriorated, and human sacrifice became more common.

Political and Social Structures

In general, the European influence in Africa did not extend beyond the coastal regions. Only in a few areas, such as South Africa and Mozambique, were there signs of a permanent European presence.

Traditional Political Systems In most places, traditional African political systems continued to exist. By the sixteenth century, monarchy had become a common form of government throughout Africa. Some kingdoms were highly centralized, but others were more like collections of small principalities knit together by ties of kinship or other loyalties. Many Africans continued to live in small political units in which a village leader exercised authority.

Europeans caused other changes. In the western Sahara, trade routes shifted toward the coast because of trade with the Europeans. This shift led to a weakening of the old Songhai trading empire. It also helped a new Moroccan dynasty to emerge in the late 1500s. In 1591, Moroccan forces defeated the Songhai army and then occupied the city of Timbuktu. Eventually, the Moroccans were forced to leave, but Songhai was never the same.

Foreigners also influenced African religious beliefs, although Europeans had less influence than Islamic culture. In North Africa, Islam continued to spread. It also expanded into the states of West Africa. The Portuguese engaged in some Christian missionary activity in Africa, but the French and Dutch did little to spread the Christian message. The spread of Christianity was limited mainly to South Africa and Ethiopia.

CORE CONCEPTS: CULTURE

The state of Ashanti, on Africa's Gold Coast, is a good example of a nation bound by kinship ties. To demonstrate their unity, each local ruler was given a ceremonial seat of office. The king had a golden seat that symbolized the unity of the entire state.

SECTION 3 SOUTHEAST ASIA IN THE ERA OF THE SPICE TRADE

Emerging Mainland States

In 1500, mainland Southeast Asia was a relatively stable region. Kingdoms with their own ethnic, linguistic, and cultural characteristics were being formed. Conflicts, such as the bitter one between the Thai and the Burmese, eventually erupted among the emerging states. In 1767, a Burmese army sacked the Thai capital. This forced the Thai to create a new capital at Bangkok, farther south. By the end of the fifteenth century, the Vietnamese had subdued the state of Champa and gradually took control of the Mekong delta from the Khmer. By 1800, the Khmer monarchy had virtually disappeared.

In the Malay Peninsula and the Indonesian Archipelago, Muslim merchants in search of spices caused changes. New states arose along the trade route that the Muslims created. In the fifteenth century, the sultanate of Melaka became the leading power in the region owing to its location and to the rapid growth of the spice trade.

LINKING GEOGRAPHY TO HISTORY

The Khmer built an empire based in present-day Cambodia that extended deep into Thailand. The empire reached its peak between A.D. 800 and 1430. The capital, Angkor Wat, was the center of Buddhist and Hindu influence in Southeast Asia.

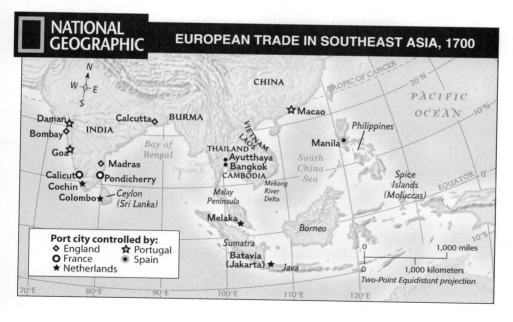

NATIONAL GEOGRAPHIC EUROPEAN TRADE IN SOUTHEAST ASIA, 1700

Port city controlled by:
◇ England   ☆ Portugal
O France   ● Spain
★ Netherlands

The Arrival of Europeans

In 1511, the Portuguese seized Melaka and soon occupied the Moluccas, known to the Europeans as the Spice Islands. These islands were the chief source of the spices that had originally attracted the Portuguese to the Indian Ocean. Not having the resources to set up colonies in the region, the Portuguese instead created small settlements, which they used as trading posts.

A Shift in Power Circumstances changed with the arrival of the English and Dutch traders. In the early 1600s, the Dutch gradually pushed the Portuguese out of the spice trade. They took over most of the Portuguese forts along the trade route, including Melaka. The Dutch traders also drove the English traders out of the spice market. The English were left with a single port on the southern coast of Sumatra. The Dutch tried to dominate the clove trade by limiting the growing of cloves to one island. They also established a fort on the island of Java, at Batavia, in 1619. They gradually took control of the entire island.

Impact on the Mainland The arrival of Europeans had less impact on Southeast Asia. The Portuguese had limited trade relations with several **mainland states**, including Thailand, Burma, and Vietnam. (Mainland states are part of the continent, rather than peninsulas or islands.) These states had strong monarchies that resisted foreign intrusion. When other European nations began competing for trade and missionary privileges in the area, the mainland states united and drove them out.

In Vietnam, a civil war temporarily divided the country into two separate states. When the Europeans arrived in the mid-seventeenth century, they began building trading posts and taking sides in Vietnamese politics. By the end of the seventeenth century, however, most of the trading posts were abandoned after it became clear that economic opportunities in the area were limited. French missionaries who tried to stay were blocked by Vietnamese authorities, who saw Catholicism as a threat to the Vietnamese emperor's prestige.

Religious and Political Systems

During the period from 1500 to 1800, religious beliefs changed in Southeast Asia. Both Islam (in Malaysia and Indonesia) and Christianity were beginning to attract converts, especially in the non-mainland states and the Philippines. Buddhism was advancing on the mainland, becoming dominant from Burma to Vietnam. Traditional beliefs still survived, however, and influ-

CORE CONCEPTS: DIVERSITY

The present-day nation of Nepal practices both Hinduism and Buddhism. The tolerance of both religions encourages people to take part in the ceremonies of each faith, often as national holidays.

enced the new religions. Hinduism survived in parts of Indonesia.

Political systems in Southeast Asia evolved into four main styles of kingship: Buddhist kings, Javanese kings, Islamic sultans, and Vietnamese emperors. All of these styles adapted European models of government to local circumstances.

The Buddhist style of government was the main form of government in Laos, Thailand, Burma, and Cambodia. In this style, the king was considered superior to other human beings. He served as a link between humans and the universe.

The Javanese style was based on political traditions of India and resembled the Buddhist system in many ways. Javanese kings were believed to have a sacred quality. They maintained the balance between the sacred and material worlds.

The Islamic style was found on the Malay Peninsula and in the small states on the Indonesian Archipelago. In this style, the head of state was a sultan, viewed as mortal, but with some special qualities. He defended the Islamic faith and staffed his **bureaucracy** (a body of nonelected government officials) mainly with aristocrats.

Kingship in Vietnam followed the Chinese model. The emperor ruled according to the teachings of Confucius. He was viewed as a mortal appointed by heaven to rule because of his talent and virtue. He was also the intermediary between heaven and Earth.

Chapter Overview

During Europe's age of exploration, between 1500 and 1800, the world of Islam experienced new life with the rise of three great Muslim empires. A military adventurer named Babur created one of them—the Mogul Empire—in India. Along with the Ottomans and the Safavids, the Moguls dominated Southwest Asia and the South Asia subcontinent. For about two hundred years, these three powerful Muslim states brought stability to a region that had been in turmoil for centuries.

The events that occurred during this time period still impact our lives today. Muslim art and architectural forms have endured, and examples can be found throughout the world. Since the territory once occupied by the Ottoman and Safavid dynasties produces one-third of the world's oil supply, these regions continue to prosper.

As you read through this chapter, ask yourself these questions:
(1) What were the major events in the growth of the Ottoman Empire?
(2) What events led to the creation and growth of the Safavid dynasty?
(3) How did Mogul rulers develop the empire's culture?

Main Ideas and Concepts

- **Environment** The physical environment of the Middle East is rich in oil but poor in water.

- **Technology** Since the beginning of human settlement in the Muslim regions, people have used technology to make the region's environment more habitable.

- **Identity** The religious beliefs and values of a people play a major role in shaping their cultural identity.

- **Culture** In South Asia, religious beliefs and social organization are closely related.

- **Change** Islam arrived in South Asia through conquest. Differences between the Hindu and Islamic world views brought changes to the subcontinent that can still be felt today.

People, Places, Terms

The following names and terms will help you to prepare for the Regents Exam in Global History and Geography. You can find an explanation of each name and term in the Glossary at the back of this book, in your textbook, or in another reference source.

Akbar	harem	shah
anarchy	Istanbul	Sikhs
caliph	janissary	sultan
chartered companies	orthodoxy	suttee
gunpowder empire	pasha	zaminder

SECTION 1 THE OTTOMAN EMPIRE

Rise of the Ottoman Turks

In the late thirteenth century, a new group of Turks began to build power in the northwest corner of the Anatolian peninsula. The name of the leader of this group of Turks was Osman. As the Seljuk Empire began to decline in the early fourteenth century, the Osman Turks began to expand. This was the beginning of the Ottoman dynasty.

The Ottomans expanded westward and eventually controlled the Bosporus and the Dardanelles. These two straits (narrow passageways) connect the Black and Aegean Seas. The Byzantine Empire had previously controlled this area. In the fourteenth century, the Ottoman Turks expanded into the Balkans. The Ottoman rulers took the title of **sultan** and began to build a strong military by developing an elite guard called **janissaries**. They were taken at a young age from Christian communities, converted to Islam, and taught to be loyal to the sultan.

The Ottomans also began to master firearms. The Ottomans defeated the Serbs at the Battle of Kosovo in 1389. During the 1390s, they took over Bulgaria.

CORE CONCEPTS: PLACES AND REGIONS

The Dardanelles Strait, the Sea of Marmara, and the Bosporus Straits not only connect the Black and Aegean Seas, they are also the dividing point of Europe and Asia, and are therefore of strategic importance. Rich in oil resources, especially on the Black Sea, they retain their importance today.

CORE CONCEPTS: CONFLICT

The Ottomans took 80,000 troops to battle against Constantinople's mere 7,000. Cannons offered the Ottomans a further advantage. The cannons had 26-foot (8-m) barrels that could launch stone balls each weighing up to 1,200 pounds (545 kg).

CORE CONCEPTS: MOVEMENT OF PEOPLE AND GOODS

Because Muslims were not allowed to enslave other Muslims, the Ottomans occasionally traveled the empire in search of Christian boys, usually from the Balkans, to recruit as a special class of slaves. This was known as the *Devshirme*, the boy levy. Levy means not only a tax, but also enlistment of people for military service. The boys ranged from 10 to 20 in age. They went to Constantinople for training, where they attended palace schools and were converted to Islam. At 25, the young men were assigned different tasks: janisseries, guards, cavalry members, or government officials.

Expansion of the Empire

Ottoman rule expanded to include large areas of Western Asia, North Africa, and Europe during the next three hundred years.

The Fall of Constantinople Under the leadership of Mehmet II, the Ottomans moved to end the Byzantine Empire. They attacked its capital, Constantinople. Although the Byzantines fought for almost two months to save their city, the Ottomans finally conquered it. The Byzantine emperor died in the final battle.

Western Asia and Africa The Ottomans used Constantinople, later renamed **Istanbul**, as their capital. Now the Ottomans dominated the Balkans and the Anatolian Peninsula. Between 1514 and 1517, Sultan Selim I took control of Mesopotamia, Egypt, and Arabia. He now controlled several of Islam's holy cities, including Jerusalem, Mecca, and Medina. Selim declared himself to be the new **caliph**, defender of the Islamic faith and successor to Muhammad. Ottoman forces then moved westward along the African coast, eventually reaching almost to the Strait of Gibraltar. Wherever possible, the Ottomans preferred to use local rulers to administer their conquered lands. These appointed officials, known as **pashas**, collected taxes, maintained law and order, and were responsible to the sultan's court.

Europe Following their conquest of Constantinople, the Ottomans attempted to take the rest of the Balkan region. They traveled up the Danube and took Belgrade under Süleyman I. At the Battle of Mohacs in 1526, the Ottomans won a major victory over the Hungarians.

They then conquered most of Hungary and moved into Austria, advancing as far as Vienna, where they were defeated in 1529. They also extended their power in the Mediterranean until 1571, when the Spanish destroyed a large Ottoman fleet. For the next century, the Ottomans did not attempt to conquer any more territory in eastern Europe.

In the second half of the seventeenth century, however, they again went on the offensive. By mid-1683, the Ottomans had marched through the Hungarian plain and attacked Vienna, but an army of Europeans forced their retreat, and they were pushed out of Hungary. Never again would they be a threat to central Europe.

The Nature of Ottoman Rule

The Ottoman Empire is often called a **"gunpowder empire."** Gunpowder empires were formed by outside conquerors who unified the regions that they conquered. The success of these empires was based mainly on the use of gunpowder and firearms.

The sultan was at the head of the Ottoman system. He was the supreme authority in both a political and military sense. The position of the sultan was hereditary, although the eldest son did not automatically inherit the throne. As the empire expanded, the status and prestige of the sultan increased. The sultan controlled his bureaucracy through an imperial council that met four days a week. A chief minister, known as the grand vizier, led these meetings. The empire was divided into provinces and districts, each governed by officials. The sultan gave land to senior officials, who were then responsible for collecting taxes and supplying armies for the empire.

Because of the administrative system, the sultan became increasingly isolated in his palace. The private domain of the sultan was known as the **harem** ("sacred place"). The sultan and his wives resided there. When a son became sultan, his mother was known as the queen mother and acted as a major adviser to the throne.

Religion in the Ottoman World

The Ottomans were Sunni Muslims. The Ottoman sultans had since the early sixteenth century claimed the title of caliph. In theory, they were responsible for guiding the Muslims in their empire and maintaining Islamic law. In practice, they gave their religious duties to a group of religious advisers known as the ulema. The ulema administered the legal system and schools for educating Muslims.

The Ottoman system was usually tolerant toward non-Muslims. Each religious group was organized into administrative units called millets. The non-Muslims had to pay a special tax but were not required to serve in the military. Most people in the European areas of the empire remained Christian. In some areas, such as present-day Bosnia, many people converted to the Islamic faith.

CORE CONCEPTS: SCIENCE AND TECHNOLOGY

The Chinese discovered gunpowder during the eighth century. Two centuries later, they were using gunpowder in fireworks and weapons. The Chinese invented guns, rockets, mines, and bombs.

Ottoman Society

Ottomans were divided by occupational groups. In addition to the ruling class, there were four other major classes: peasants, artisans, merchants, and pastoral peoples (nomadic herders). Except for the ruling class, merchants were the most privileged class in Ottoman society. They were largely exempt from government regulations and taxes, often amassing large fortunes.

Women in the Ottoman Empire had the same restrictions as women in other Muslim societies, although their position was somewhat better. They were allowed to own and inherit property. They could not be forced into marriage and in some cases could seek a divorce. They could testify in court cases. A few women even served as senior officials, such as governors of provinces.

Problems in the Ottoman Empire

The Ottoman Empire reached its high point under Süleyman the Magnificent, who ruled from 1520 until 1566. After the death of Süleyman, sultans became less involved with government and allowed their ministers to exercise more power. The sons of the elite received senior positions. Members of the elite soon formed a privileged group seeking wealth and power. The central bureaucracy became less connected with rural areas. As a result, local officials grew corrupt, and taxes rose.

Officials and merchants began to imitate European habits and lifestyles. They wore European clothes, bought Western furniture and art objects, and ignored Muslim rules against drinking alcohol.

Ottoman Art

During the period from Mehmet II to the early eighteenth century, the arts flourished in the Ottoman Empire. The sultans were enthusiastic patrons of the arts. By far the greatest contribution of the Ottoman Empire to the world of art was in architecture. The mosques of the last half of the sixteenth century were magnificent. During that time, Sinan, the greatest of all Ottoman architects, began to build the first of 81 mosques. One of Sinan's masterpieces, the Suleimaniye Mosque, is in Istanbul.

Exquisite textiles and rugs were also made at this time. Factories produced silks for wall hangings, sofa covers, and especially court costumes. Rugs made of wool and cotton were a peasant industry. Different regions had their own distinctive designs and color schemes.

CORE CONCEPTS: MOVEMENT OF PEOPLE AND GOODS

Coffee was introduced into Ottoman society during the sixteenth and seventeenth centuries and from there spread to Europe. Europeans decorated their homes with tiles, tulips, pottery, and rugs of the Ottoman world. They also borrowed their military technology.

CORE CONCEPTS: CULTURE

Ottoman Turks modeled their mosques on the Byzantine church in Constantinople known as Hagia Sophia, which means "Holy Wisdom." That building, which is still standing despite earthquakes, fires, and war, features a large open central area under a large dome. The walls are filled with mosaics, generally figures of saints. The church was completed in 537.

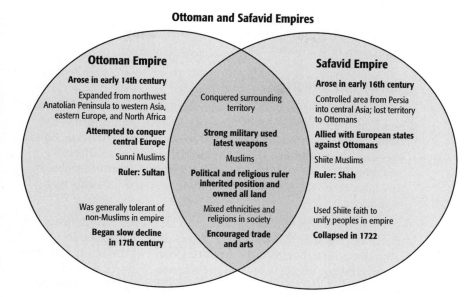

Ottoman and Safavid Empires

Ottoman Empire

Arose in early 14th century

Expanded from northwest Anatolian Peninsula to western Asia, eastern Europe, and North Africa

Attempted to conquer central Europe

Sunni Muslims

Ruler: Sultan

Was generally tolerant of non-Muslims in empire

Began slow decline in 17th century

Conquered surrounding territory

Strong military used latest weapons

Muslims

Political and religious ruler inherited position and owned all land

Mixed ethnicities and religions in society

Encouraged trade and arts

Safavid Empire

Arose in early 16th century

Controlled area from Persia into central Asia; lost territory to Ottomans

Allied with European states against Ottomans

Shiite Muslims

Ruler: Shah

Used Shiite faith to unify peoples in empire

Collapsed in 1722

SECTION 2 THE RULE OF THE SAFAVIDS

Rise of the Safavid Dynasty

After the collapse of the empire of Tamerlane (Timur Lenk) in the early fifteenth century, Persia fell into disorder and lawlessness, or **anarchy**. At the beginning of the sixteenth century, a new dynasty, known as the Safavid, took control. It was founded by Ismail, the descendant of an earlier leader named Safi-al-Din. (The word *Safavid* comes from his name.) Ismail seized much of present-day Iran and Iraq in 1501. He called himself the **shah**, or king, of a new Persian state.

The Safavids were devout Shiite Muslims. Ismail sent Shiite preachers into Anatolia to convert members of Turkish tribes in the Ottoman Empire. He also ordered the massacre of Sunni Muslims in 1508 when he conquered Baghdad. The Ottoman sultan, Selim I, was alarmed and attacked the Safavids in Persia. Although he won a major battle near Tabriz, Ismail regained the city a few years later.

Like the Ottoman sultan, the shah claimed to be the spiritual leader of all Islam. This tactic was in part an attempt to unify the empire. In the 1580s, the Ottomans again attacked. They gained

CORE CONCEPTS: BELIEF SYSTEMS

The division between Sunni and Shiite Muslims developed after Muhammad's death. Shiites believed that only Muhammad's son Ali and his descendants should be rulers in the Muslim world. Sunni Muslims were willing to follow leaders who were not related to Muhammad. Shiite Muslims believe that only the ayatollahs, experts on Islamic law, can impart knowledge of Islam. Sunni Muslims do not believe in a central Muslim authority; however, they believe all Muslims are united by a common faith and custom.

control of Azerbaijan and the Caspian Sea. This forced the new Safavid shah, Abbas, to sign a peace treaty in which he lost a great deal of territory.

Glory and Decline

Under Shah Abbas, who ruled from 1588 to 1629, the Safavids reached their high point. In the early seventeenth century, the Shah moved against the Ottomans to regain lost territory. Abbas created a new military style combining cavalry—soldiers on horseback—with infantry armed with gunpowder weapons. In 1612, a peace treaty returning Azerbaijan to the Safavids was signed.

After the death of Shah Abbas in 1629, the Safavid dynasty declined. Most of the successive rulers did not have Shah Abbas's political skills or talent. The power of the Shiite religious groups began to increase. The pressure to conform to traditional religious beliefs, known as religious **orthodoxy,** also increased. Persian women were now forced into seclusion and were required to wear a veil in public.

During the reign of Shah Hussein in the late eighteenth century, Afghan peoples invaded and seized the capital of Isfahan. The Safavid ruling family was forced to retreat to Azerbaijan. The Turks took advantage of the situation to seize territories along the western border. Persia sank into a long period of social and political anarchy.

Political and Social Structure

Under the Safavids, Persia was a mixed society. The Safavids had come to power with the support of nomadic Turkish groups, but the majority of the people were Persian. Most of them were farmers or townspeople. The combination of Turkish and Persian elements affected nearly all aspects of Safavid society.

The Safavid's political system, like that of most empires, could be represented by a pyramid. At the top was the shah. The bureaucracy and landed classes were in the middle, and at the bottom were the common people.

The Role of the Shah The Safavid rulers were supported by Shiites, who believed that Shah Ismail, the founder of the empire, was one of the prophet Muhammad's direct descendants. The shahs declared Shia Islam to be the state religion.

LINKING PAST AND PRESENT

Horses from the Middle East were prized by the British. Soldiers returned from battles with admiration for the horses' speed when running in sand. Male horses from the Middle East were purchased and taken to England, where they mated with British mares. The result was a leaner and faster horse that has come to be called a Thoroughbred.

Shahs were more available to the people than many other rulers were. People were appointed to senior positions based on merit rather than on birth. To avoid competition between Turkish and non-Turkish people, Shah Abbas hired a number of foreigners for government positions.

Economy and Trade The shahs played an active role in trade and manufacturing. There was also a large urban middle class involved in trade. Most goods traveled by camel caravans or by horse, using public resting places the government provided. In times of strong rulers, the roads were kept fairly clear of thieves.

Safavid Culture

From 1588 to 1629, during the reign of Shah Abbas, the arts flourished. The Shah's capital at Isfahan was a planned city with wide spaces and a sense of order. It even included polo grounds. Carpet weaving and silk weaving based on new techniques both flourished. Stimulated by Western demand for Persian carpets, that industry expanded. Persian painting during this period featured soft colors and flowing movement.

SECTION 3 THE GRANDEUR OF THE MOGULS

The Mogul Dynasty

By 1500, the Indian subcontinent was still divided into a number of Hindu and Muslim kingdoms. However, the Moguls (Mughals) established a new dynasty and brought a new era of unity to the region.

Babur was the founder of the Mogul dynasty. His father was a descendant of Tamerlane, and his mother was descended from Genghis Khan. Babur inherited part of Tamerlane's empire. While still a young man, he commanded a group of warriors who seized Kabul in 1504. Thirteen years later, his forces crossed the Khyber Pass to India. Babur captured Delhi and established his power in the plains of North India, where he continued his conquests until his death in 1530.

In Babur's time, the **Sikh** religion was established. Sikhs believe in one god, stressing that mankind's goal is unity with the deity. Their leader, Nanak, and those who followed him,

LINKING PAST AND PRESENT

Today, Isfahan is a major city in the west-central part of Iran, still known for its textiles, handcrafts, tiles, rugs, and cotton fabrics. Recovery of the city, which had declined greatly since Shah Abbas's time, began in the second quarter of the twentieth century.

CORE CONCEPTS: INTERDEPENDENCE

Through trade and conquest, the system of numbers originally invented in India traveled to the Middle East and from there to Europe. The Europeans found the numbers much easier to use than the old Roman system of numerals. Today in mathematics class, you use the symbols invented in India. Indian mathematicians also invented the concept of zero.

were called gurus. Since Muslims believe there can be no prophets after Muhammad, they clashed with the Sikhs. The Sikh response was to become militaristic, always carrying weapons for defense.

The Reign of Akbar

Babur's grandson **Akbar** was only fourteen when he came to the throne with the goal of extending his rule. By 1605, he had brought most of India under Mogul rule. To overpower the stone fortresses of their enemies, his armies used heavy artillery. After conquest, Akbar treated his former enemies well so that the hostility between the Moguls and the people they conquered would end and peace would prevail. Akbar created the greatest Indian empire since the Mauryan dynasty two thousand years earlier.

Akbar is best known for the humane character of his rule. Although a Muslim, he was tolerant of other religions. He invited representatives of all religions to his court to understand their teachings. He even tried to establish a new religion blended from what he learned.

The upper ranks of his government were filled with non-native Muslims, but many of the lower officials were Hindu. Giving these local officials, known as **zamindars**, plots of farmland was common practice. The zamindars kept part of the local taxes as their salaries, forwarding the remainder to the central government. All Indian peasants were required to pay about one-third of their annual harvest to the state. The system was fairly administered; when bad weather struck in the 1590s, taxes could be reduced or suspended.

Foreign trade prospered in the Akbar era. Indian goods, including textiles, tropical food products, spices, and precious stone, were exported in exchange for gold and silver.

Decline of the Moguls

Akbar died in 1605 and was succeeded by his son Jahangir. During the early years of his reign, Jahangir continued to strengthen the central government's control of the empire. His control began weakening when he fell under the control of one of his wives. The empress used her position to enrich her own family and arranged the marriage of her niece to her husband's son, Shah Jahan.

CORE CONCEPTS: BELIEF SYSTEMS

Akbar truly practiced his ideals of religious tolerance. Jesuits were welcomed as advisers to his court. He also chose a Hindu princess as his wife.

Shah Jahan ruled from 1628 to 1658. He maintained the Mogul political system and expanded the boundaries of the empire. However, he failed to deal with growing domestic problems. He had inherited a nearly empty treasury. His military campaigns and building projects put heavy strains on the imperial finances and forced him to raise taxes, while most of his people lived in poverty.

When Shah Jahan became ill in the mid-1650s, two of his sons struggled for power. One of them, Aurangzeb, had his brother put to death and imprisoned his father. He then crowned himself emperor in 1658.

Aurangzeb (1658–1707) is one of the most controversial rulers in the history of India. He tried to eliminate what he saw as the evils of India. He forbade both the levying of illegal taxes and the Hindu custom of **suttee** (cremating a widow on her husband's funeral pyre). A devout Muslim, he reversed many of the Mogul policies of religious tolerance. The building of new Hindu temples was prohibited, and Hindus were forced to convert to Islam.

These policies led to Hindu protests. Revolt broke out in provinces throughout the empire. With no strong central ruler after Aurangzeb, the maharajahs, rulers of small principalities, broke from the Moguls. India became divided and vulnerable to attack. In 1739, the Persians sacked Delhi and left it in ruins.

The British in India

The arrival of the British hastened the decline of the Mogul Empire. In 1650, the British established trading forts at Surat, Fort William, and Chennai. From Chennai, British ships carried Indian-made cotton goods to the East Indies, the area around present-day Indonesia, where they were traded for spices.

The French established their own forts at Pondicherry, Surat, and in the Bay of Bengal. They even captured the British fort at Chennai.

The British eventually were able to restrict the French to the fort at Pondicherry and a few other territories on the southeastern coast. This was largely due to the efforts of Sir Robert Clive. Clive became the chief representative in India of the British East India Company. The British Crown had given the company the power to act on its behalf. It was Clive's job to fight any force, French or Indian, that threatened the power of the East India Company. In 1757, Clive led a small British force to victory over

CORE CONCEPTS: CONFLICT

France and Great Britain were global rivals. The battles that the two nations fought over control of South Asia spilled over into North America, triggering the so-called French and Indian War.

a Mogul-led army more than ten times its size. The Mogul court was then forced to give the British East India Company the power to collect taxes from lands in the area surrounding Calcutta.

In the late eighteenth century, the East India Company moved inland from the coastal cities. British expansion made many British merchants and officials wealthy. British officials discovered that they could obtain money from local rulers by selling trade privileges. The British were in India to stay.

Society and Daily Life in Mogul India

The Moguls were foreigners in India. They were Muslims ruling a largely Hindu population. The Mogul attitudes toward women affected Indian society.

Women had long played an active role in Mogul society; some even fought on the battlefield alongside men. Women from aristocratic families were permitted to own land and take part in business activities.

At the same time, Moguls placed certain restrictions, based on their interpretation of Islamic law, on women. The practice of isolating women was compatible with Hindu customs and was adopted by many upper-class Hindus. In other ways, Hindu practices continued despite Mogul rule. The customs of suttee and child marriages continued.

Mogul Culture

The Moguls brought together Persian and Indian influences in a new and beautiful architectural style, best symbolized by the Taj Mahal. Considered the loveliest building in India, if not the world, it was built by Shah Jahan in memory of his wife. The government raised land taxes, driving many Indian peasants into complete poverty, to build it.

Another major artistic achievement of the Mogul period was in painting. The "Akbar style" combined Persian and Indian elements. Akbar encouraged his artists to imitate European art forms, including the use of perspective and lifelike portraits. The Mogul emperors were dedicated patrons of the arts. Painters, poets, and artisans from many other countries had a goal of going to India. Moguls were said to reward a good poet with his weight in gold.

CORE CONCEPTS: ECONOMIC SYSTEMS

For much of eighteenth century Europe, **chartered companies** were the main instruments of imperial expansion. These private companies were granted certain royal privileges, such as monopolies, that brought their rulers military and territorial dominance even as they sought commercial gains. Not all chartered companies prospered, however. The French East India Company, for example, did not survive.

CHAPTER 17   THE EAST ASIAN WORLD

Section 1   **China at Its Height**
Section 2   **Chinese Society and Culture**

Chapter Overview

Between 1500 and 1800, China's empire expanded yet it continued its ethnocentric policy of limited Western influence. In 1514, Portuguese ships arrived on the coast of China. At first, the new arrivals were welcomed. During the seventeenth century, however, most of the European merchants and missionaries were forced to leave. Chinese leaders adopted a "closed country" policy to keep out foreign ideas and protect their values and institutions. Until 1800, China was little affected by events taking place outside the region.

The events that occurred during this time period still impact our lives today. China today exports more goods than it imports. Chinese porcelain is admired and collected throughout the world. The Forbidden City in China is an architectural wonder that continues to attract people from around the world. Relations with China still require diplomacy and skill.

As you read through this chapter, ask yourself these questions:
(1) What was remarkable about the naval voyages under Emperor Yong Le?
(2) How did the Manchus gain the support of the Chinese?
(3) Why did commercial capitalism not develop during this period?

Main Ideas and Concepts

- **Political System** Under the dynastic cycle and the Mandate of Heaven, a ruling family held power only as long as they remained responsible to the needs and wants of Chinese society.

- **Change** Throughout Chinese history, a change in dynasty brought a change in leadership but not a significant change in Chinese values.

- **Identity** In traditional Chinese society, the interest of the group prevailed over the interest of the individual.

- **Justice** Within Chinese society, women were denied most of the basic rights provided to men.

People, Places, Terms

The following names and terms will help you to prepare for the Regents Exam in Global History and Geography. You can find an explanation of each name and term in the Glossary at the back of this book, in your textbook, or in another reference source.

Beijing	Imperial City	queue
clan	Manchu	Zheng He
commercial capitalism	Ming dynasty	
ethnocentrism	porcelain	

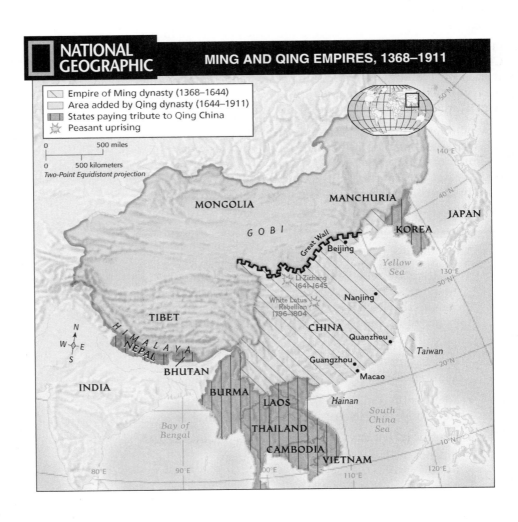

NATIONAL GEOGRAPHIC

MING AND QING EMPIRES, 1368–1911

Empire of Ming dynasty (1368–1644)
Area added by Qing dynasty (1644–1911)
States paying tribute to Qing China
Peasant uprising

0   500 miles
0   500 kilometers
Two-Point Equidistant projection

SECTION 1 CHINA AT ITS HEIGHT

The Ming Dynasty

The **Ming dynasty** began with the overthrow of the Mongols in China in 1368. The Ming period lasted until 1644. China extended its rule into Mongolia and central Asia and briefly reconquered Vietnam under the Ming emperors.

Ming rulers ran an effective government using a centralized bureaucracy staffed with officials who had taken the civil service examination. Ming emperors set up a national school system based on Confucian ideas. They completed the Grand Canal, on which grain was shipped south to north in China. The Ming dynasty was a period of significant economic and cultural progress.

The Voyages of Zheng He Emperor Yong Le began building the **Imperial City**—known as the Forbidden City today—in **Beijing** in 1406. The Imperial City remained the home of China's emperors for nearly 500 years.

Led by the court official **Zheng He**, China made seven voyages of exploration between 1405 and 1433. On the first, almost 28,000 men sailed on 62 ships. The fleet visited the western coast of India and city-states of East Africa. The voyages produced great profits, which alarmed Confucian traditionalists who regarded trading as an unworthy activity. The voyages halted after Yong Le's death in 1424.

First Contacts with the West A Portuguese fleet arrived off the coast of China in 1514. The emperor was unimpressed with the Europeans, whom he considered barbarians. He viewed foreign rulers as "younger brothers" of the Chinese emperor, who was viewed as the Son of Heaven. After outraging the Chinese with their behavior, the Portuguese were expelled from Guangzhou (Canton) but were allowed to occupy Macao.

Jesuit missionaries also made the trip to China, impressing the emperor with western inventions such as eyeglasses and clocks. The Jesuits in turn were impressed by Chinese architecture, the teachings of Confucius, and the printing of books. More importantly, both sides benefited from the exchange of ideas.

Fall of the Ming Dynasty The Ming dynasty declined due to a series of weak rulers, corrupt government, high taxes, low crop yields, peasant unrest, and a major epidemic in the 1630s. The

CORE CONCEPTS: SCIENCE AND TECHNOLOGY

On his first voyage, Zheng He commanded a fleet of 317 ships crewed by 27,870 men. No other fleet in the world could match China's at this time. The sailing ships, known as *junks*, could carry up to 1500 tons. They were five times larger than the ships that Vasco da Gama commanded around the Cape of Good Hope seventy years after Zheng He's voyages. The Chinese also invented the magnetic compass and star charts, which allowed Chinese sailors to go into deep water rather than risk shipwreck by staying near the coastlines.

CORE CONCEPTS: MOVEMENT OF PEOPLE AND GOODS

Farmers on the eastern plains of China developed better agricultural methods, including fertilization techniques, that allowed enough food to be grown to feed a large population. Food production was further improved by the introduction of corn and sweet potatoes from the Americas in the 1500s.

CORE CONCEPTS: CULTURE

The term *martial arts* refers to arts of combat and self-defense. They are a significant part of Asian history and culture. Chinese martial artists were highly visible already during the Han dynasty. Later, in 495, a Zen Buddhist monastery began developing methods of physical training known today as kung fu. Westerners have become interested in many forms of Asian martial arts, in part due to films that feature these movements.

suffering from the epidemic in part caused the peasant revolt led by Li Zecheng in 1644. He occupied Beijing, the capital, and the last Ming emperor committed suicide.

The **Manchus**, a farming and hunting people who lived in the area now known as Manchuria, pushed through the Great Wall and conquered Beijing. They created the Qing ("pure") dynasty, which remained in power until 1911.

The Qing Dynasty

The Chinese at first resisted the new Manchu rulers. Rebels seized the island of Taiwan. To more easily identify the rebels, the government ordered all Chinese men to adopt Manchu dress and hairstyles. Under penalty of death, they were to shave their foreheads and braid their hair into a pigtail called a **queue**.

The Manchus were gradually accepted, especially by the scholar-officials, who were impressed that the Manchu leaders adopted the Confucian examination system and government bureaucracy. The Qing dynasty flourished. A series of strong emperors corrected social and economic ills, and restored peace and prosperity.

Qing Adaptations Although the Qing preserved their own identities by having a different legal status, maintaining large landholdings, and forming separate Manchu military units known as banners, they brought the Chinese into the top ranks of the imperial administration, demonstrating a willingness to share power.

Reign of Kangxi Perhaps the greatest emperor of China, Kangxi ruled from 1661 to 1722. Highly disciplined and intelligent, he calmed unrest along the frontiers and won the support of scholars through his championing of arts and letters.

Kangxi was tolerant of Christians. Christian missionaries were quite active, and hundreds of Chinese officials became Catholics. His successors suppressed Christianity in China.

Westerners in China The first signs of internal decay of the dynasty occurred during the reign of Qianlong (1736–1795). Corrupt officials and high taxes led to rural unrest, while an expanding population created hardship for the peasants. The White Lotus Rebellion (1796–1804), a peasant revolt, was suppressed but at great financial expense, creating a strain on the imperial treasury.

The decline occurred just as Western nations were seeking trade partners. The Qing government sold trade privileges to the Europeans. However, to limit contact between the Chinese and foreigners, they confined the traders to a small island and limited their stays.

In 1793, Lord George Macartney led a British mission trying to win more liberal trade policies. The emperor wrote King George III that China had no need of "your country's manufactures." China would later pay for this rejection during its century of humiliation in the 1800s, as China was divided into spheres of influence.

SECTION 2 CHINESE SOCIETY AND CULTURE

Economic Changes

Between 1390 and the end of the 1700s, the population of China grew from 80 to 300 million people. One reason was the long period of peace and stability. Another was an increased food supply due to a faster-growing species of rice.

China's economy was changing from 1500 to 1800. There was less land for each family. By the 1700s nearly all available farmland was being cultivated. Shortages led to unrest.

Manufacturing and trade increased during this period. Nonetheless, China did not develop the **commercial capitalism** (private business based on profit) that the European nations did because merchants were less independent in China. The government controlled trade and manufacturing, levying high taxes on it.

Daily Life

The Confucian emphasis on family remained strong and contributed to the stability of Chinese society.

The Chinese Family The family met the needs of its members, and those members were expected to sacrifice their individual desires for the good of the entire family. The ideal family in Qing China was the extended family, with as many as four generations. Sons brought their wives to live in the home, where unmarried daughters remained. The Confucian concept of filial piety, love and respect, for parents was key to the Chinese family system.

CORE CONCEPTS: CULTURE

From ancient times, China thought of itself as the Middle Kingdom, that is, the center of the world. The Chinese believed that their culture was superior to others. This belief is known as **ethnocentrism**. It led the Chinese to reject influence from other cultures while at the same time attempting to exert influence on other cultures.

CORE CONCEPTS: HUMAN SYSTEMS

Many areas of the world experienced a population boom during the seventeenth century. In Europe, for example, the population increased during the 1700s from 120 to 200 million people. In addition to increased food supply and a greater variety of foods, people were less likely to die of disease. Also, because nations could control larger segments of land, there was less likelihood of violence and death.

The elderly were highly respected and cared for and the spirits of ancestors were honored as a method of linking the past to the present and ensuring good fortune to the family.

The **clan** of up to hundreds of related families was also important. A clan council and religious and social activities linked the families. Wealthier families helped poorer families within the clan.

The Role of Women Women were considered inferior to men. Only males could be educated and have careers. The wife was to be subordinate to the husband. Wives had no power to inherit property or to initiate a divorce. Husbands could divorce wives who did not bear sons.

The practice of footbinding restricted the mobility of women. Bound feet were a status symbol and made getting married easier, lending an economic incentive to the practice. Up to two-thirds of Chinese women bound their feet. The process was painful, and women with bound feet could not walk. Women who worked in the fields did not bind their feet.

Cultural Developments

Under the Ming and Qing dynasties, traditional Chinese culture reached new heights.

The Chinese Novel A new literary form developed during the Ming dynasty. Many consider *The Golden Lotus*, with its criticisms of the wealthy and powerful, to be the first realistic social novel. *The Dream of the Red Chamber*, written by Cao Xuegin and published in 1791, is still considered China's best popular novel. It tells of a tragic love between two young people.

Ming and Qing Art The Imperial City in Beijing is the most outstanding example of the period's architecture. Emperor Yong Le began construction of the complex of palaces and temples in 1406. The Imperial City is an immense walled compound with a maze of apartments, offices, and stately halls. It became known as the Forbidden City because commoners could not enter.

The most famous decorative art of the Ming era was blue-and-white **porcelain**. From the fifteenth century onwards, Europeans collected it and other Chinese pottery enthusiastically.

CORE CONCEPTS: CULTURE

In addition to the famous blue-and-white porcelain, the Chinese are also known for "three-color" pottery. Created during the Tang dynasty (A.D. 618–906), it created bold patterns using three colors of lead glaze. China's high-quality ceramics are due in part to the deposits of porcelain stone and good clay available.

PRACTICING FOR THE REGENTS

Part I   Multiple-Choice Questions

The following multiple-choice questions come from past Regents High School Examinations. Test your understanding of World History by answering each of these items. Circle the number of the word or expression that best completes each statement or question. Test-taking tips can be found in the margins for some questions. For additional help, see Taking the Regents Exam on pages ix-xxxv of this Review Book.

1   The global transfer of foods, plants, and animals during the colonization of the Americas is known as the
   (1) Scientific Revolution   (3) Columbian Exchange
   (2) New Imperialism   (4) Middle Passage

2   One similarity of the Aztec, Maya, and Inca empires is that they
   (1) developed in fertile river valleys
   (2) maintained democratic political systems
   (3) coexisted peacefully with neighboring empires
   (4) created complex civilizations

3   Inca terrace farming and Aztec floating gardens are examples of
   (1) the ability of civilizations to adapt to their region's physical geography
   (2) slash-and-burn farming techniques
   (3) Mesoamerican art forms symbolizing the importance of agriculture
   (4) colonial economic policies that harmed Latin American civilizations

Base your answer to question 4 on the map below and on your knowledge of social studies.

South American Cultures 100–1535

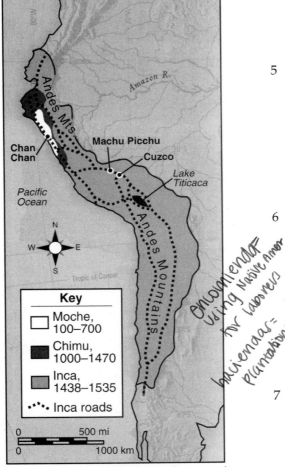

Key

- ☐ Moche, 100–700
- ■ Chimu, 1000–1470
- ▨ Inca, 1438–1535
- •⁚•⁚• Inca roads

0   500 mi
0   1000 km

Source: *World History: Patterns of Interaction,* McDougal Littell

4 Which conclusion about Incan society could be drawn from the map?
  (1) An extensive road system connected all parts of the Empire for trade.
  (2) Their trade depended on many seaports.
  (3) Tropical climatic conditions existed throughout the empire.
  (4) A similar language unified the Inca civilization.

5 A direct result of the conquest of Tenochtitlán by Hernán Cortés in 1521 was the
  (1) expulsion of Jews and Muslims from Spain
  (2) establishment of Portuguese trade routes around Africa
  (3) fall of the Aztec Empire
  (4) conquest of the Kush Kingdom

6 Which statement about the encomienda system during the 16th and 17th centuries is accurate?
  (1) Aztec and Inca civilizations prospered.
  (2) Life expectancy among Native American populations increased.
  (3) Spanish influence declined in its colonies.
  (4) Many Native Americans were forced to labor on large estates.

7 One way in which the encomienda system and European feudalism were similar is that both
  (1) encouraged social mobility
  (2) created a class structure in which landowners held the power
  (3) resulted from the growth of the African slave trade
  (4) depended on extensive trade routes

8 "In three or four months . . . more than
   seven thousand children died of hunger,
   their fathers and mothers have been taken to
   the mines . . . Thus they [Spaniards] ruined
   and depopulated all this island [Cuba]."
   —*Bartolome de Las Casas, 1552,*
   The Brief Account of the Destruction of the
   Indies

   The event described in the quotation
   illustrates
   (1) a result of the "Encounter"
   (2) the forced migration of Native
       Americans to Spain
   (3) the dangerous effects of mining
       without proper equipment
   (4) an impact of Enlightenment
       philosophers

9 • Smallpox outbreak spreads through-
      out Mexico.
   • Many Incas convert to Christianity in
      ceremonies in Lima, Peru.
   • Spanish and Portuguese are intro-
      duced to chocolate, peanuts, toma-
      toes, and corn.
   • Cortés brings Aztec gold and silver
      treasures to Spain.

   Which situation is illustrated in these
   statements?
   (1) empathy of Europeans for Native
       American Indian civilizations
   (2) triangular trade and its effects on
       agrarian economies
   (3) the relatively high costs of
       colonialism
   (4) the impact of contact between
       different peoples

10 A major reason for the end of the Aztec
   Empire was
   (1) the refusal of the people to obey
       their leaders
   (2) a conflict with the Inca Empire
   (3) the technology of the Spanish
       conquistadors
   (4) political corruption and an unstable
       government

11 Which economic theory, developed in
   the 17th century, supported European
   colonialism?
   (1) socialism
   (2) mercantilism
   (3) bartering
   (4) feudalism

12 • Invention of the compass
   • European dependence on spices
      from Asia
   • Rise of nation-states in Europe

   These developments influenced the start
   of the
   (1) Crusades
   (2) Renaissance
   (3) Reformation
   (4) Age of Exploration

   take from the colonies then sell it back

13 The term "mercantilism" is defined as
   an economic system in which
   (1) prices are determined by the laws of
       supply and demand *= capitalism / free market*
   (2) colonies exist for the <u>benefit</u> of the
       <u>colonial power</u>
   (3) factors of production are owned by
       the government *= command economy*
   (4) the proletariat benefit at the expense
       of the bourgeoisie *= communism*

Adam Smith = Wealth of Nations

14 Which statement best illustrates the concept of European mercantilism during the Age of Exploration?
    (1) England encouraged free trade among its colonies.
    (2) Spain reduced exports to its South American colonies.
    (3) Portugal sought trade benefits from its colonial possessions.
    (4) France refused to give financial support to weak national industries.

15 The journals of early travelers such as Ibn Battuta of Morocco, Zheng He of China, and Mansa Musa of Mali are examples of
    (1) primary sources describing observations of the travelers
    (2) works of fiction intended to describe the adventures of the travelers
    (3) secondary sources that record the travelers' interpretations of history
    (4) outdated resources for historical research

Base your answer to question 16 on the map below and on your knowledge of social studies.

Voyages of Zheng He During the Ming Dynasty of China

Source: Harriett Geller and Erwin M. Rosenfeld, *Global Studies, Volume I, Asia, Africa, and Latin America,* Barrons Educational Services, Inc. (adapted)

16 Which conclusion can be made about the Ming dynasty of China as a result of the travels of Zheng He?
    (1) China profited more from African trade than from Asian trade.
    (2) Islam became the dominant religion of China.
    (3) The Ming dynasty established trade routes to Europe.
    (4) Advanced navigation technology was available in China.

Base your answers to questions 17 and 18 on the map and on your knowledge of history.

The Mongol Empire 1300

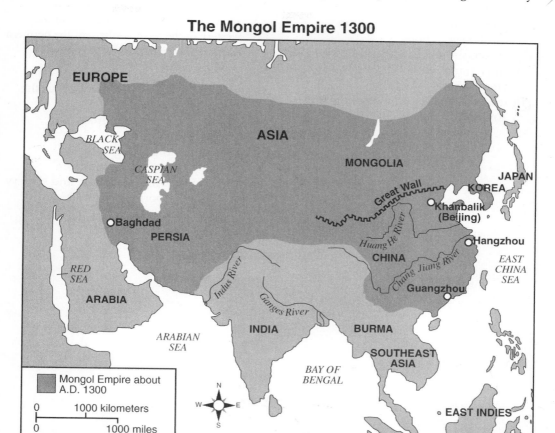

Source: H. Braun, L. Forman, H. Brodsky, *Reviewing Global History and Geography*, AMSCO (adapted)

17 The purpose of the Great Wall was to
(1) protect the Chinese from nomadic tribes of northern and central Asia
(2) supply food from the south to Khanbalik (Beijing)
(3) control the flood waters of the Huang He and Chang Jiang rivers
(4) protect the port city of Guangzhou

18 Which statement is best supported by the information on this map?
(1) By 1300, the Mongol Empire had reached the Red Sea.
(2) The Mongol Empire controlled India and Japan by 1300.
(3) By 1300, most of Europe had been conquered by the Mongols.
(4) The Mongol Empire controlled a large portion of Asia by 1300.

19 The success of the triangular trade
    system depended on increasing
    (1) political independence of the
         Caribbean nations
    (2) emphasis on free trade in Europe
    (3) slave trade in the Western
         Hemisphere
    (4) industrialization of the South
         American colonies

20 "The countries beyond the horizon and from
    the ends of the Earth have all become
    subjects and to the most western of the
    western or the most northern of the northern
    countries however far away they may be."
    —*Ming dynasty official*

    The intent of this statement about the
    Ming dynasty was to
    (1) demonstrate supremacy and
         strength in China
    (2) control the Mongols
    (3) stop European imperialism
    (4) impose Chinese culture and slavery
         on neighboring countries

Base your answers to questions 21 and 22 on the map below and on your knowledge of social studies.

A Comparison of Chinese and Portuguese Expeditions Until 1514

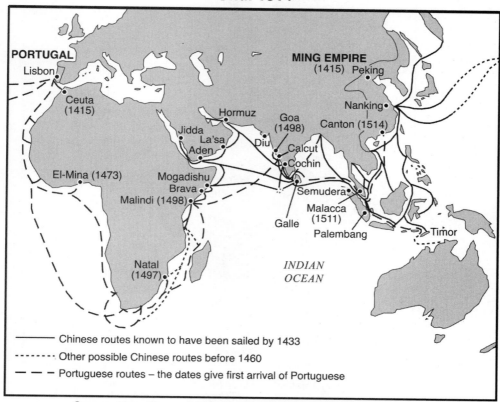

Source: Yong Yap and A. Cotterell, *Chinese Civilization from the Ming Revival to Chairman Mao*, St. Martin's Press (adapted)

21 Which statement can best be supported by the information on the map?
  (1) The Portuguese taught the Chinese their sailing knowledge.
  (2) Portugal and China practiced isolationism during the 15th century.
  (3) Only the Portuguese explored the east coast of Africa.
  (4) The Portuguese and the Chinese were active explorers.

22 Which explorers are associated with the travels shown on the map?
  (1) Ferdinand Magellan and Matthew Perry
  (2) Christopher Columbus and Genghis Khan
  (3) Vasco da Gama and Zheng He
  (4) Francisco Pizarro and Marco Polo

Base your answer to question 23 on the map below and on your knowledge of social studies.

SPAIN AND PORTUGAL IN THE AMERICAS (1600)

Spanish Settlement

Portuguese Settlement

Source: Henry Abraham and Irwin Pfeffer, *Enjoying Global History*, AMSCO (adapted)

23 Which conclusion regarding early European settlements is best supported by the information on the map?
   (1) Portugal became the dominant colonial power in South America by 1600.
   (2) Geography made the interior of South America easy to explore.
   (3) Neither the Spanish nor the Portuguese developed major urban centers in Latin America.
   (4) In 1600, most of the land in South America was not settled by Europeans.

24 The geographic isolation of a society most often leads to the
   (1) development of trade
   (2) strengthening of traditional culture
   (3) promotion of cultural diffusion
   (4) growth of international alliances

Part II Thematic Essay Question

The following thematic essay question comes from past Regents Examinations. Write your answers on a separate sheet of paper. Essay-writing tips appear in the margin. For additional help, see Taking the Regents Exam on pages ix-xxxv of this Review Book.

Directions: Write a well-organized essay that includes an introduction, several paragraphs addressing the task below, and a conclusion.

Theme: Geography and Society

> At various times in global history, human activity has altered or changed the land people live on and their surrounding environment. These changes in physical geography have affected society.

Task:

> Select *two* changes that a society or two different societies have made to their land or surrounding environment, and for *each* change
>
> - Identify the society in which the change took place
> - Describe how the physical environment was changed by human activity
> - Discuss how the change in the physical environment affected society

You may use any *two* examples from your study of global history and geography. Some suggestions you might wish to consider include irrigation systems, terrace farming, road systems, canal systems, burning of fossil fuels, or the use of nuclear power.

REGENTS WARM-UP

Read the directions in Regents essay questions carefully so that you carry out all operations. In the Thematic Essay, you are asked to respond with information about two different changes.

You are *not* limited to these suggestions.

Do *not* use any environmental change that occurred in the United States in your answer.

Guidelines:

In your essay, be sure to

- Develop all aspects of the task

- Support the theme with relevant facts, examples, and details

- Use a logical and clear plan of organization, including an introduction and conclusion that are beyond a restatement of the theme

Part III   Document-Based Question

This exercise is designed to test your ability to work with historical documents. It is similar to the document-based questions that you will see on the Regents Examination. While you are asked to analyze three historical documents, the exercise on the actual exam will include more documents. Some of the documents have been edited for the purposes of the question. As you analyze the documents, take into account the source of each document and any point of view that may be presented in the document.

Historical Context:

> A *turning point* is defined as a period in history when a significant change occurs. Three of these turning points were the *Neolithic Revolution*, the *Age of Exploration*, and the *collapse of communism in the Soviet Union*.

Task: Using information from the documents and your knowledge of global history, answer the questions that follow each document in Part A. Your answers to the questions will help you write the Part B essay, in which you will be asked to

> Choose *two* of these turning points and for *each*
>
> - Explain why it is considered a turning point
> - Evaluate whether the impact of the turning point has been positive or negative

Part A   Short-Answer Questions

Directions: Analyze the documents and answer the short-answer questions that follow each document in the space provided.

Document 1

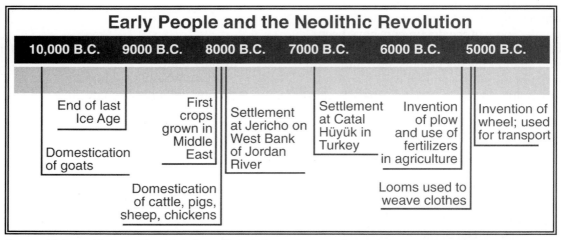

Early People and the Neolithic Revolution

10,000 B.C.	9000 B.C.	8000 B.C.	7000 B.C.	6000 B.C.	5000 B.C.

End of last Ice Age

Domestication of goats

First crops grown in Middle East

Domestication of cattle, pigs, sheep, chickens

Settlement at Jericho on West Bank of Jordan River

Settlement at Catal Hüyük in Turkey

Invention of plow and use of fertilizers in agriculture

Looms used to weave clothes

Invention of wheel; used for transport

Source: Vivienne Hodges, *New York State Global History Regents Coach*, Educational Design, Inc. (adapted)

1   Based on this time line, identify two ways that people's lives changed during the Neolithic Revolution.

(1) ___Invention of the wheel for transportation___

(2) ___invention of the plow and use of fertilizers in agriculture___

Document 2

> To achieve his overall objective of making the Soviet Union a more open society, Gorbachev has formulated and is in the process of implementing a strategy of radical reform consisting of ten specific strategies:
>
> 1. Economy: Decentralization of decision making of state-owned enterprises including such decisions as product mix, prices, output, wage, employment, investment, research and development, domestic and internal sales and marketing, and incentives. Creation of new financial institutions to finance the expansion of Soviet enterprise. Authorization of private enterprises in the service sector of the economy.
>
> 2. Agriculture: Decentralization of state-owned farms and strengthening of agricultural cooperatives. Greater use of market incentives and an increase in the number of private farms. . . .
>
> 6. Democratization: Decentralization of the Communist party, the Soviet government, and the Soviet economy. Increased democracy in the workplace. Greater freedom of political dissent. Improved possibilities to emigrate from the Soviet Union.
>
> –*Thomas H. Naylor. The Gorbachev Strategy, D. C. Heath and Co.*

2   Based on the document, identify two changes proposed by Gorbachev's program.

(1) _He wanted to decentralize decision making of companies that are state owned_

(2) _increase the number of private farms_

Document 3a

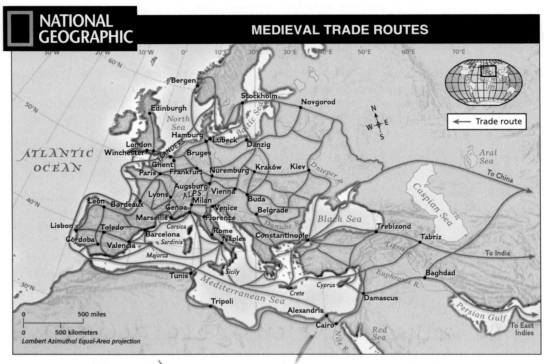

NATIONAL GEOGRAPHIC — MEDIEVAL TRADE ROUTES

You can cite only 3a or 3b for essays (in direction)

Document 3b

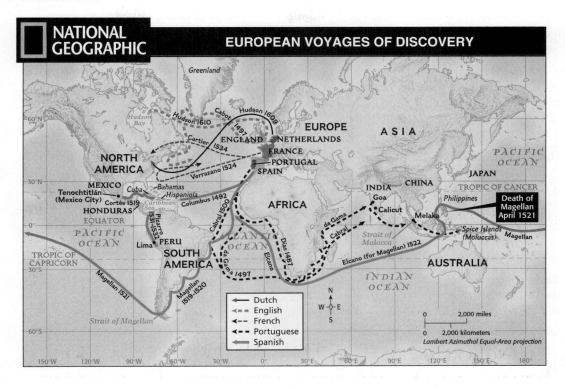

NATIONAL GEOGRAPHIC   **EUROPEAN VOYAGES OF DISCOVERY**

3   According to the maps, how did the early voyages of discovery change European trade routes?

different countries started trading and cultural diffusion began

able to use more waterways

→ trade leads to all over world

Part B Essay

Directions: Write a well-organized essay that includes an introduction, several paragraphs, and a conclusion.

Use evidence from at least *two* of the documents in the body of the essay. Support your response with relevant facts, examples, and details. Include additional outside information.

Historical Context:

> A *turning point* is defined as a period in history when a significant change occurs. Three of these turning points were the *Neolithic Revolution*, the *Age of Exploration*, and the *collapse of communism in the Soviet Union*.

Task: Using information from the documents and your knowledge of global history and geography, write an essay in which you:

Choose *two* of these turning points and for *each*

- Explain why it is considered a turning point
- Evaluate whether the impact of the turning point has been positive or negative

---

Guidelines:

In your essay, be sure to

- Develop all aspects of the task
- Incorporate information from *at least two* documents in the body of the essay.
- Incorporate relevant outside information
- Support the theme with relevant facts, examples, and details
- Use a logical and clear plan of organization, including an introduction and a conclusion that are beyond a restatement of the theme

UNIT 5   AN ERA OF EUROPEAN IMPERIALISM, *1750–1914*

Unit 5 Overview

During the eighteenth and nineteenth century, Europe was transformed by revolutions. The Scientific Revolution led to an examination of social order in the Enlightenment. Those ideas led, in turn, to ideas reflected in both the American and French Revolutions. Revolutions continued with the Industrial Revolution, which began in Great Britain, and a number of political revolutions. Later in the century, the Second Industrial Revolution resulted in the growth of prosperity and the emergence of a mass society, while other factors combined to dismantle views of a more orderly and rational universe.

In the nineteenth century, a new imperialism emerged in Africa and Asia: Africa came almost completely under Western control, while the British ruled India. European control over Latin America, however, was overthrown. In East Asia, the Qing dynasty declined, and civil war followed. Japan was forced to open to the West, and the Meiji Restoration brought reform and industrialization as well as a new Japanese imperialism.

PREPARING FOR THE REGENTS

This entire book is set up to help you grasp the facts, main ideas, and concepts needed to do well on your Regents Exam. Notes in the margin include core concepts, test-taking tips, and more. Use blank spaces in the margins to answer questions raised in the text or to jot down key points. Before each unit of study, skim through the exams at the back of the book to develop a sense of what your state wants you to know about your world.

Unit 5 Objectives

After studying this unit, students should be able to

1.   explain how the Scientific Revolution and Enlightenment changed the way people viewed their world;

2.   compare the causes and evaluate effects of the English, French, and American Revolutions;

3.   describe the revolutionary and reform movements of the 1800s—such as the Industrial Revolution—that reshaped life and politics in Europe and the Americas;

4.   explain how nationalists unified Italy and Germany and challenged autocracy in Russia and Austria-Hungary;

5.   discuss the effects of imperialism in Asia, Africa, and Latin America.

Chapter Overview

The Scientific Revolution changed the way people viewed the universe and their place within it. It also established a new emphasis on the scientific method and the use of reason. The philosophes in France and elsewhere used the ideas of the Scientific Revolution, and especially those of Newton and Locke, to re-examine all aspects of life. New ideas about economics, justice, the rights of the individual, women, and religion developed. The rococo style developed in art. Some believed at the time that enlightened absolutism also developed, but only Joseph II of Austria sought truly radical changes based on Enlightenment ideas. During the eighteenth century, vast colonial empires were developing in North America and in Latin America. British colonies in North America eventually declared their independence, fulfilling, in some ways, the political dreams of the Enlightenment.

As you read this chapter, ask yourself these questions:
(1) What were the major scientific advances, and what impact did they have?
(2) What conditions led to the Enlightenment?
(3) What philosophies and social changes arose during the Enlightenment?
(4) What caused the War of the Austrian Succession and the Seven Years' War?
(5) What was the impact of European colonization in North America, Central America, and South America?

Main Ideas and Concepts

- **Change** The Scientific Revolution changed people's concepts of the universe and their place within it.

- **Civic Values** The philosophes formed ideas that included natural rights and suggested that society could be changed for the better, especially through the use of reason.

- **Change** Enlightenment ideas affected the politics, music, art, architecture, and literature of Europe.

- **Conflict** The colonies in North America and Latin America developed political ideas that differed from their mother countries.

People, Places, Terms

The following names and terms will help you to prepare for the Regents Exam in Global History and Geography. You can find an explanation of each name and term in the Glossary at the back of this book, in your textbook, or in another reference source.

capitalism
Catherine the Great
checks and balances
Creoles
René Descartes
encomienda
enlightened
 absolutism
Galileo Galilei

laissez-faire
line of
 demarcation
John Locke
mestizos
Montesquieu
natural rights
Isaac Newton
peninsulares

philosophe
Jean-Jacques Rousseau
scientific method
separation of powers
Adam Smith
social contract
Maria Theresa

SECTION 1 THE SCIENTIFIC REVOLUTION

Background to the Revolution

During the Middle Ages, people with an interest in the world around them had looked to a few ancient authorities, especially Aristotle, for their scientific knowledge. During the Renaissance, however, scholars gained access to works that showed other theories, began solving technical problems that brought them new knowledge, and used mathematics to develop new theories. The Renaissance scientists put an emphasis on observation and experimentation as the true basis for science.

A Revolution in Astronomy

Discoveries in astronomy were a major part of the Scientific Revolution. They helped change people's ideas of the universe and their place within it.

REGENTS WARM-UP

Past Regents questions have asked not only about political revolutions but also about revolutions in ways of life and ideas. As you read, think about what kind of revolution occurred as scientific thinkers developed new theories about the world and how this revolution changed people's lives.

The Ptolemaic System Ptolemy lived in the second century A.D. He constructed a theory of the universe that was geocentric: Earth was at its center and was motionless. Around the Earth were many spheres, one inside the other. The rotation of the spheres made the heavenly bodies (the moon, Mercury, Venus, the sun, Mars, Jupiter, Saturn, and fixed stars) rotate around Earth and move in relation to one another. The last sphere in this system was the "prime mover," which moved itself and gave motion to the other spheres.

Renaissance Science

Copernicus and Kepler In 1543, the Polish mathematician Nicholas Copernicus published *On the Revolutions of the Heavenly Spheres*. It proposed a heliocentric, or sun-centered, conception of the universe. Mercury, Venus, Earth, Mars, Jupiter, and Saturn revolved around the sun. The moon revolved around the Earth. Copernicus also explained that the apparent movement of the sun around Earth was actually caused by the daily rotation of the Earth on its axis as well as the Earth's yearly revolution around the sun.

Using a chart developed by Tycho Brahe, a Danish astronomer, the German mathematician Johannes Kepler confirmed that the sun was at the center of the universe and also showed that the orbits of the planets were not circular but elliptical, with the sun toward the end of the ellipse instead of at the center.

Galileo The Italian mathematician **Galileo Galilei** was the first European to make regular observations using a telescope. He discovered mountains on the moon, four moons revolving around Jupiter, and sunspots. His observations also showed that other planetary bodies were composed of material substance, just as Earth is. Galileo published his observations in *The Starry Messenger*.

Newton Until the mathematician **Isaac Newton** (1642–1727) explained motion in the universe, nothing really tied together the theories proposed by Copernicus, Kepler, and Galileo. In his major work, known as *Principia*, Newton explained the laws that govern natural forces. Crucial to his argument was the universal law of gravitation, which explains why planetary bodies do not go off in straight lines but have elliptical orbits. The law states that every object in the universe is attracted to every other object by a force called gravity. Newton's work also included the development of calculus.

CORE CONCEPTS: SCIENCE AND TECHNOLOGY

Kepler established the three laws of planetary motion: a. the paths were elliptical; b. each had a different speed; and c. speed was determined by distance from the sun.

CORE CONCEPTS: BELIEF SYSTEMS

The Catholic Church was threatened by Galileo's findings and the Copernican worldview. Their theories suggested that the heavens weren't a spiritual place but a world of matter. Humans were not at the center of the universe, and God was not in a fixed placed. Therefore, the Church put Galileo on trial and under threat of death ordered him to abandon the Copernican idea.

Newton's ideas created a new picture of the universe. It was now seen as one huge, regulated, uniform machine that worked according to natural laws (a mechanistic worldview).

Breakthroughs in Medicine and Chemistry

The Greek physician Galen lived in the second century A.D. Galen, who dissected animals, was the authority on medicine until the Renaissance, when Andreas Vesalius (1536–1562) became the first person to dissect humans and carefully and accurately examine the individual organs and general structure of the human body. Vesalius is known as the founder of modern scientific anatomy because of his use of first-hand observation.

Both Galen and Vesalius believed there were two kinds of blood flowing in arteries. Their ideas were dispelled in 1628 by William Harvey. Harvey showed, for the first time, that the heart was the beginning point of circulation of blood in the body. He also proved that blood flows in both veins and arteries and makes a complete circuit as it passes through the body.

In the mid-1600s, chemist Robert Boyle was one of the first scientists to conduct controlled experiments. Boyle's Law states that the volume of a gas varies with the pressure exerted on it. Boyle also determined that air is a mixture of gases. In the eighteenth century, Antoine Lavoisier invented a system for naming the chemical elements, much of which is still used today.

Women and the Origins of Modern Science

Among the women who participated in the Scientific Revolution was Margaret Cavendish. Her work suggested that humans were not the masters of nature but merely a "small part" of it.

The Scientific Method

An English philosopher named Francis Bacon pioneered the **scientific method,** a systematic procedure for collecting and analyzing evidence. He thought the method should be inductive, beginning with systematic observations and carefully controlled experiments. These would lead to hypotheses, and not vice versa. Bacon saw the systematic investigation of the physical universe as a means of gaining control over nature.

CORE CONCEPTS: SCIENCE AND TECHNOLOGY

Because his ideas changed the existing worldview and dominated it until the twentieth century, Newton is considered the greatest genius of the Scientific Revolution. His view of the world as a machine which could be understood rationally led other philosophers to apply reason to the study of the nature of man.

CORE CONCEPTS: DIVERSITY

Between 1650 and 1710, women made up about 14 percent of all German astronomers. The most famous was Maria Winkelmann, who discovered a comet. Still, the work of scientists was considered chiefly for males, and Winkelmann was denied a position at the Berlin Academy.

Descartes and Reason   *opinion = fact* (handwritten)

French philosopher **René Descartes** was initially preoccupied with the ideas of doubt and uncertainty. The one thing he found beyond doubt was his own existence. Emphasizing the importance of the mind, he went on to assert "I think, therefore I am." He argued that because "the mind cannot be doubted but the body and material world can, the two must be radically different." From this came the principle of mind and matter; therefore, matter was detached and could be investigated independently through reason. Descartes came to be called the father of modern rationalism. This system of thought is based on the belief that reason is the chief source of knowledge. Descartes laid the basis for deductive reasoning by emphasizing the importance of questioning all established knowledge and the importance of solid evidence.

SECTION 2 THE ENLIGHTENMENT

Path to the Enlightenment

The Enlightenment was an eighteenth-century philosophical movement of intellectuals who were impressed with the achievements of the Scientific Revolution. They hoped to use the scientific method to make progress toward a better society. *Reason*, *natural law*, *hope*, and *progress* were words these philosophers used frequently.

Enlightenment thinkers were especially influenced by the ideas of Isaac Newton and **John Locke**. Newton's view of the world as a kind of orderly machine governed by natural laws led these thinkers to believe that they could discover the natural laws that governed human society. John Locke believed that every person was born with natural rights to life, liberty, and the pursuit of happiness. Locke's theory that everyone was born with a blank mind, or *tabula rasa*, and therefore could be changed by the right environment, also inspired them with a confidence that society could be changed for the better.

Philosophes and Their Ideas

The intellectuals of the Enlightenment were known by the French name **philosophe**. They believed the purpose of philosophy was to change the world. They championed reason, and wanted to apply it to everything, including religion and politics. French philosophes Montesquieu and Voltaire dominated Enlightenment thought.

(handwritten in left margin) John Locke = born good + became evil

REGENTS WARM-UP

As you read, think about how the ideas of Montesquieu and Voltaire differed and how they were alike.

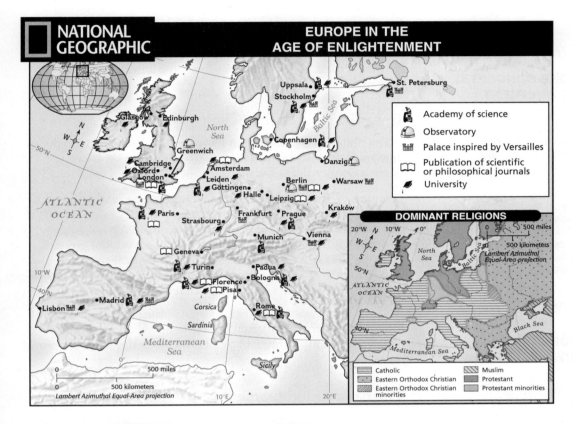

NATIONAL GEOGRAPHIC

EUROPE IN THE AGE OF ENLIGHTENMENT

Academy of science
Observatory
Palace inspired by Versailles
Publication of scientific or philosophical journals
University

DOMINANT RELIGIONS

Catholic
Eastern Orthodox Christian
Eastern Orthodox Christian minorities
Muslim
Protestant
Protestant minorities

Montesquieu **Montesquieu** used the scientific method to identify the natural laws that govern social and political relationships. In *The Spirit of Laws*, he identified three basic kinds of government—republics, despotism, and monarchies. When he studied England's government, he identified three branches—executive, legislative, and judicial. He believed the government functioned through a **separation of powers.** In this separation, the three branches limit and control each other in a system of **checks and balances.** This system provides both freedom and security from dictatorship by preventing any one person or group from gaining too much power.

Voltaire The greatest figure of the Enlightenment was François-Marie Aouet, known simply as Voltaire. Known for his pamphlets, plays, letters, essays, and histories, Voltaire believed in deism, an eighteenth-century religious philosophy based on reason and natural law. It was based on the Newtonian worldview, and suggested that a mechanic (God) had created the universe, which was like a clock. God had

CORE CONCEPTS: GOVERNMENT

Montesquieu's work greatly influenced the structure of the government of the United States.

CORE CONCEPTS: GOVERNMENT

In *The Wealth of Nations*, Adam Smith argued that government had only three basic roles: protecting society from invasion; defending citizens from injustice; and keeping up certain public works, such as roads and canals. His ideas had great influence on the development of **capitalism**, the foundation of the American economic system.

CORE CONCEPTS: CIVIC VALUES

Mary Wollstonecraft was an Enlightenment thinker who is often viewed as the founder of the women's rights movement. She is the author of *A Vindication of the Rights of Women*, a book which pointed out contradictions in the views of Enlightenment thinkers, especially Rousseau. First, she proposed, if Enlightenment thinkers could say that the arbitrary power of monarchs over people was wrong, then the arbitrary power of men over women was wrong, too. Second, she suggested, if Enlightenment thinkers believed in reason in all beings, women have reason, so they are entitled to the same rights as men.

created it, set it in motion, and allowed it to run without his interference, according to its own natural laws. Voltaire supported John Locke's view of man's inherent natural rights. He also criticized governments that prohibited freedom of religion.

Toward a New Social Science

The philosophes' belief that there are natural laws that govern human society led to the development of the social sciences (areas such as economics and political science).

Economics The Physiocrats and **Adam Smith** are considered the founders of the social science of economics. They believed that if individuals are free to pursue their own economic self-interest, all society ultimately benefits. They also believed that government should not interrupt the free play of natural economic forces. This doctrine became known by its French name, **laissez-faire**, meaning to "let (people) do what they want."

hands off

Adam Smith was a big critic of mercantilism because it gave too much control to government. He believed the natural laws of competition and supply and demand were better ways to control business.

The Later Enlightenment

The most famous philosophe of the later Enlightenment was **Jean-Jacques Rousseau**. One idea Rousseau suggested was that people had adopted laws and government in order to protect their private property. His most famous work was *The Social Contract*. He explained a **social contract** as an agreement in which an entire society agrees to be governed by the general will. Individuals who wish to follow their own self-interest are forced to abide, instead, by the general will.

Unlike many Enlightenment thinkers, Rousseau believed that emotions, as well as reason, were important to human development. He sought a balance between emotions and reason.

Social World of the Enlightenment

Enlightenment ideas did not belong only to nobles and aristocrats. Nevertheless, most common people, and especially peasants, were not aware of this movement.

The Growth of Reading and Salons During the eighteenth century, a new middle class reading public arose that included women and urban artisans. Daily newspapers and magazines for the general public were published. Enlightenment ideas were also spread in the salon—elegant drawing rooms of the urban upper classes where people gathered to discuss the new ideas of the philosophes.

Religion in the Enlightenment

Although many philosophes attacked Christianity, most Europeans were still Christians, and the need and desire for spiritual experience still ran deep. Many people sought a deeper personal devotion to God.

In England, the most famous new religious movement was Methodism, founded by John Wesley. Many of Wesley's converts joined Methodist societies in which they helped each other do good works. They influenced the abolition of the slave trade in the early 1800s.

SECTION 3 THE IMPACT OF THE ENLIGHTENMENT

Enlightenment and Enlightened Absolutism

The philosophes believed in **natural rights** for all people. These rights included equality before the law; freedom of religious worship; freedom of the press; and freedom to assemble, and hold property. Philosophes also believed that the people had to be governed by enlightened rulers. Such rulers must obey the rules themselves and enforce them fairly.

Many historians once assumed that a new type of monarchy, called **enlightened absolutism**, or enlightened despotism, emerged in the eighteenth century. This monarchy had royal powers but enlightened principles. Yet, of all the monarchs, only Joseph II of Austria made truly radical changes based on Enlightenment ideas.

CORE CONCEPTS: HUMAN RIGHTS

Frederick the Great made some enlightened reforms. He abolished the use of torture except in treason and murder cases. He also granted limited freedom of speech and press and greater religious toleration. However, he did not abolish serfdom or the rigid social structure in Prussia.

CORE CONCEPTS: HUMAN RIGHTS

Catherine the Great did consider the idea of a new law code that would recognize the equality of all people. In the end, however, she did nothing because she knew that her success depended on the support of the Russian nobility.

Prussia: Army and Bureaucracy Two Prussian kings, Frederick William I and Frederick II, made Prussia a major European power in the eighteenth century. Frederick William I doubled the size of the army, making it the most important institution in Prussia. Frederick II (also called Frederick the Great) was cultured and well informed about the ideas of the Enlightenment. He, too, enlarged the Prussian army, and he kept a strict watch over the bureaucracy.

The Austrian Empire By the beginning of the eighteenth century, the Austrian Empire had become one of the great European states. It was difficult to rule, however, because it was made up of many different nationalities, languages, religions, and cultures. Empress **Maria Theresa**, who inherited the throne in 1740, worked to centralize the Austrian Empire and strengthen the power of the state. Her successor was Joseph II. He was determined to make changes. He abolished serfdom, eliminated the death penalty, established the principle of equality of all before the law, and enacted religious reforms. Most of his reforms failed, however. He upset the nobles by freeing the serfs. The Catholic Church was unhappy with his religious reforms. Even the serfs were unhappy, because they were confused by the drastic changes in his policies. Joseph's reforms were reversed by his successors.

Russia under Catherine the Great Catherine II (also known as **Catherine the Great**) ruled Russia from 1762 to 1796. She was an intelligent woman who was familiar with the works of the philosophes, but she thought many of their ideas were impractical. Her policies led to worse conditions for the Russian peasants and eventually to rebellion. The rebellion spread across southern Russia, but soon collapsed. Catherine took stronger measures against the peasants. All rural reform was halted, and serfdom was expanded into new parts of the empire. Under Catherine, Russia spread southward to the Black Sea. To the west, Russia gained about 50 percent of Poland's territory.

War of the Austrian Succession

Austria and Great Britain fought Prussia and France in a war that started when Maria Theresa assumed the Austrian throne. Believing Maria Theresa weak, Prussia seized Austrian Silesia and France occupied the Austrian Netherlands. France also took Madras in India from the British. The British took the French fort of Louisbourg in North America. The war went on for seven years. A treaty then returned all the occupied territories except Silesia.

The Seven Years' War

Maria Theresa could not accept the loss of Silesia. She worked diplomatically to separate France from its ally, Prussia. Rivalries shifted in Europe as first France allied with Austria and then Russia followed. Britain, the enemy of France in North America, allied itself with Prussia. This shift in alliances was known as the diplomatic revolution of 1756. It led to war in three major areas: Europe, India, and North America.

The War in Europe In Europe, the British and Prussians clashed with the Austrians, Russians and French. Frederick the Great of Prussia had the military advantage and early success. The tide turned, however, and eventually there was a desire for peace. The European war ended in 1763. All occupied territories were returned to their original owners, and Austria officially recognized Prussia's permanent control of Silesia.

The War in India France and Britain continued to struggle in India. At the Battle of Plassey (1757), a British force under the leadership of Robert Clive defeated a much larger native force directed by the French. This led to British control of Bengal. Successive British victories on land and at sea pushed the French out of India militarily and politically. After the Treaty of Paris (1763), Britain continued to expand its political influence in India.

The War in North America The greatest conflicts of the Seven Years' War took place in North America. There, the French had thinly populated territories in what became Canada and Louisiana. The British had thirteen prosperous and growing colonies on the east coast of the future United States. The French and British fought over the waterways of the Gulf of the St. Lawrence and over the Ohio River valley. In the valley, the French allied themselves with the Native Americans and achieved a number of victories.

When the British began concentrating on a naval strategy, the tide of war turned for them. One decisive victory occurred in 1759 when General Wolfe defeated the French under General Montcalm on the Plains of Abraham, outside Quebec. The British went on to seize Montreal, the Great Lakes area, and the Ohio River valley. By the terms of Treaty of Paris, the French transferred Canada and the lands east of the Mississippi to England. Their ally Spain transferred Spanish Florida to British control. In return, the French gave their Louisiana territory to the Spanish. By 1763, Great Britain had become the world's greatest colonial power.

REGENTS WARM-UP

As you read, summarize. Answer these questions: What was the Seven Years' War? Where was it fought? What global results did it have? How did it affect Britain in particular?

SECTION 4 COLONIAL EMPIRES AND THE AMERICAN REVOLUTION

Colonial Empires in Latin America

Spain and Portugal competed for influence in the new world. To prevent conflict, Pope Alexander VI established a **line of demarcation** in 1493, providing Spain trade and exploration rights in lands west of the line, and giving Portugal rights east of the line. Portugal eventually dominated Brazil as a result of the exploration of Cabral in 1500.

Spain established an enormous colonial empire that included parts of North America, Central America, and most of South America. In Central and South America, a new civilization arose, which we call Latin America. Mexico and the Caribbean region are included in this region.

Latin America was a multiracial society. The **peninuslares**, leaders born in the Iberian peninsula, and **Creoles**, American-born descendants of the settlers, dominated Latin American society. The offspring of Europeans and Native Americans were called **mestizos**. Over three centuries, about 8 million African slaves were brought to work on Spanish and Portuguese plantations. Another racial group arose, the offspring of Africans and Europeans, called mulattoes.

Economic Foundations The Spanish and Portuguese took gold and silver from their colonies. They also took sugar, tobacco, diamonds and animal hides, which they traded for their own manufactured goods. At first, they tried to keep other countries out of this trade.

Farming was also a source of prosperity for the Spanish and Portuguese. They established immense estates with dependent peasants. As part of an **encomienda** system of forced labor, many natives became peons, tenant farmers indebted to landlords. This system has been a lasting feature of Latin American society.

State and Church Spanish and Portuguese rulers were determined to Christianize the native peoples. This policy gave the Catholic Church an important role in the Americas. There were conflicts within the church hierarchy over treatment of the natives, resulting in the "new laws of the Indies" in 1542, requiring better conditions for the farmers. Unfortunately, most of these laws were not enforced.

peninsulares
creoles
mestizos
mulattoes

CORE CONCEPTS: POWER

The exploitation of gold and silver mines in New Spain made Spain one of the richest and most powerful countries in Europe. Spain's hold on the Americas was finally broken in 1588 when the Spanish Armada suffered a terrible defeat at the hands of the English.

CORE CONCEPTS: MOVEMENT OF PEOPLE AND GOODS

The Catholic Church also built cathedrals, hospitals, orphanages, and schools in the colonies. It provided the choice of entering the convent to women who did not wish to marry.

Missionaries went to different parts of the Spanish Empires. To make their efforts easier, they brought Native Americans together into villages, or missions, where the native peoples could be converted, taught trades, and encouraged to grow crops. The missions made it possible for the missionaries to control the lives of the Native Americans.

Britain and British North America

The United Kingdom of Great Britain came into existence when the governments of England and Scotland were united in 1707. The term *British* came to refer to both the English and the Scots.

In eighteenth-century Britain, the monarch and the parliament shared power, with parliament gradually gaining power. In 1714, a new dynasty, the Hanoverians, was established when Queen Anne died without an heir and her nearest relatives were the Protestant rulers of the German state of Hanover. The first two Hanoverian rulers, George I and George II, let their ministers handle parliament.

The American Revolution

After the Seven Years' War, Britain wanted more money from its colonies. In 1765, it passed the Stamp Act, a tax on printed materials, and other unfair tax laws. Colonists protested this "taxation without representation."

In 1770, the crises escalated at the Boston Massacre, when British soldiers killed five protesting colonists. Tension increased further in 1773 when colonists dumped British tea into the Boston Harbor to protest a tax on tea.

The War Begins To counteract British actions, the colonies organized the First Continental Congress. It met in Philadelphia in 1774. Fighting erupted between the colonies and the British army in April 1775 in Lexington and Concord, Massachusetts. On July 4, 1776, the Second Continental Congress approved a declaration of independence written by Thomas Jefferson. The declaration incorporated the Enlightenment idea of John Locke that people have the right to rebel against an unjust government.

Foreign Support and British Defeat The French supplied arms and money to the colonies. Spain and the Dutch Republic also gave support. When the army of General Cornwallis was forced to surrender to Washington at Yorktown in 1781, the British

CORE CONCEPTS: IDENTITY

During this time, Britain's empire expanded. In North America, the colonies grew and became prosperous. The states established their own legislatures and became accustomed to acting independently.

REGENTS WARM-UP

Regents questions often probe cause-effect relationships. What effect did the Seven Years' War have on Britain's actions toward its North American colonies?

decided to end the war. The Treaty of Paris, signed in 1783, recognized the independence of the colonies. It also gave the Americans control of the western territory from the Appalachians to the Mississippi River.

The Birth of a New Nation

CORE CONCEPTS: GOVERNMENT

Some eighteenth-century intellectuals saw the American Revolution as the embodiment of the Enlightenment's political dreams. The premises of the Enlightenment seemed confirmed.

The Constitution After the weak federal government created under the Articles of Confederation failed to solve the nation's problems, it was replaced. The new plan for government was the Constitution. It created a federal system in which power would be shared between the national government and state governments. The national government was divided into three branches: the executive (the president); the legislative (the Senate and House of Representatives); and the judicial (the Supreme Court and other courts).

The Bill of Rights The adoption of the Constitution hinged, in part, on the addition of a Bill of Rights. It guaranteed freedom of religion, speech, press, petition, and assembly. It also gave the right to bear arms, to be protected against unreasonable searches, and arrest. It guaranteed trial by jury, due process of law, and the protection of property rights. It echoed ideas developed by eighteenth-century philosophes.

Chapter Overview

The French Revolution had many causes, including social inequality in a society that was divided into estates. The revolution was also caused, in part, by short-term financial difficulties. The revolution began with the storming of the Bastille and a declaration of rights. It shifted quickly toward radicalism, however, and soon called for the execution of the king. The Reign of Terror followed, which eventually gave way to the establishment of a new government that included the Directory. In 1799, Napoleon Bonaparte led a coup d'état that overthrew the Directory. He made himself emperor, made peace with the Catholic Church, and established laws. He also preserved some basic rights while taking away others. He then built an empire across Europe that lasted only a few years. Defeats in Russia and later at Waterloo ended his power.

As you read this chapter, ask yourself these questions:
(1) What were the causes of the French Revolution?
(2) How did the French Revolution lead to the end of the old regime?
(3) What were the causes of the Reign of Terror?
(4) What was the Age of Napoleon, and what brought it about?
(5) Why did Napoleon's empire collapse?

CORE CONCEPTS: CHANGE

The French Revolution has been seen as a major turning point in European political and social history. As you read, think of reasons that support this claim.

Main Ideas and Concepts

- **Needs and Wants** Both social inequality and economic problems helped cause the French Revolution.

- **Power** Radical groups took control of the government and a Reign of Terror followed.

- **Nationalism** Results of the revolution in France included increased nationalism and Napoleon's rise to power.

People, Places, Terms

The following names and terms will help you to prepare for the Regents Exam in Global History and Geography. You can find an explanation of each name and term in the Glossary at the back of this book, in your textbook, or in another reference source.

Napoleon Bonaparte
bourgeoisie
coup d'état
Declaration of
　the Rights of
　Man and Citizen

estates
Louis XVI
Napoleonic Code
nationalism

Reign of Terror
Maximilien
　Robespierre

SECTION 1　THE FRENCH REVOLUTION BEGINS

Background to the Revolution

The French Revolution resulted from both long-range problems and immediate causes. A divided French society was one of the long-range problems.

CORE CONCEPTS: ECONOMIC SYSTEMS

Economic inequality, including an extremely unequal tax burden, was a key cause of the French Revolution.

The Three Estates　Before the revolution, French society was based on inequality. France was divided into three social classes, or **estates**. The First Estate was the clergy. The Second Estate, the nobility, held many of the leading positions in the government, military, courts, and higher church offices.

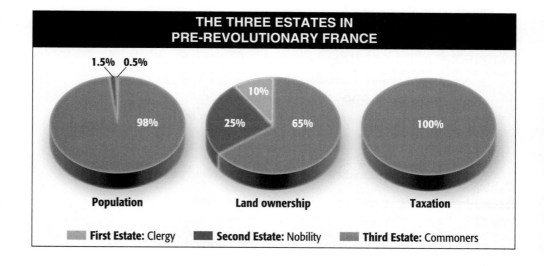

THE THREE ESTATES IN PRE-REVOLUTIONARY FRANCE

1.5%　0.5%　98% — Population

10%　25%　65% — Land ownership

100% — Taxation

First Estate: Clergy　Second Estate: Nobility　Third Estate: Commoners

The Third Estate, commoners, made up the majority of the French population and were mostly peasants. They had little or no land, but they still had to pay fees to local landlords to use things like village flourmills and ovens. The Third Estate also included skilled craftspeople, shopkeepers, and other wage earners in the cities. The **bourgeoisie**, or middle class, was another part of the Third Estate. It was about 8 percent of the population that owned about 20 to 25 percent of the land.

Members of the middle class resented the privileges of the nobility and yet had a great deal in common with the nobility. The merchants, bankers, doctors, lawyers, and writers of the bourgeoisie could become part of the nobility by obtaining public office. Like the nobility, they were influenced by the ideas of the Enlightenment.

Financial Crisis An immediate cause that led to the French Revolution was the collapse of government finances. Bad harvests in 1787 and 1788 and a slowdown in manufacturing led to food shortages, rising prices for food, and unemployment in the cities. The number of poor reached crisis proportions. At the same time, the French government continued to spend an enormous amount of money on wars and luxuries. The queen, Marie Antoinette, was known for her extravagance. On the verge of a complete financial collapse, the government of **Louis XVI** was forced to call a meeting of the Estates-General, the French parliament, that had not met since 1614.

From the Estates-General to National Assembly

The Estates-General was a representative body, but the First and Second Estates, which represented a minority, had as many deputies, or representatives, as the Third Estate. When the Estates-General met on May 5, 1789, to try to solve the financial problems, the Third Estate wanted each deputy to have one vote. This would have allowed them, with a little help from the clergy and nobility, to outvote the First and Second Estates. The king disagreed.

The Third Estate then called itself a National Assembly and decided to draft a constitution on its own that would set up a constitutional government and abolish the tax exemptions of the clergy and nobility. When they arrived at their meeting place three days later, however, they found the doors locked. Taking what is called the Tennis Court Oath, they swore they would continue to meet until they had produced a French constitution.

CORE CONCEPTS: CONFLICT

Revolution and rebellion spread throughout France. A panic called the Great Fear spread. Citizens began to form militia, because they were afraid that they would be invaded by foreign troops that supported the French monarchy.

CORE CONCEPTS: DIVERSITY

The guarantee of equal rights did not include women. In response, Olympe de Gouges, a female author, wrote *Declaration of the Rights of Woman and the Female Citizen*. In it, she insisted that women should have the same rights as men. The National Assembly ignored her demands.

CORE CONCEPTS: CHANGE

As you read, consider how the revolution, which started out voicing Enlightenment ideals, moved farther and farther away from them.

Louis XVI began planning to use force against the Third Estate, but before he could do so, a mob of Parisians stormed the Bastille, an armory and prison in Paris. On July 14, 1789, they tore it apart, brick by brick. (July 14 is now a French national holiday as a result of the storming of the Bastille.) The rebels gained control of Paris.

The Destruction of the Old Regime

Soon the National Assembly moved to abolish aristocratic privileges, including the rights of landlords, as well as the financial privileges of nobles and clergy.

Declaration of the Rights of Man The National Assembly adopted the **Declaration of the Rights of Man and Citizen**. Reflecting Enlightenment thought, it proclaimed freedom and equal rights for all men, access to public office based on talent, and an end to exemptions from taxation. All citizens were to have the right to take part in the making of laws. Freedom of speech and the press were affirmed.

The King Concedes At first, Louis XVI refused to accept the National Assembly's new decrees. He remained at Versailles. However, thousands of Parisian women armed with pitchforks, swords, and whatever else was at hand, marched on Versailles. The royal family journeyed to Paris and accepted the new decrees. In Paris, the royal family became virtual prisoners.

Church Reforms The National Assembly seized and sold the lands of the Church. It also put into effect a new Civil Constitution of the Clergy that said bishops and priests were to be elected by the people and paid by the state. The French government now controlled the Church.

A New Constitution and New Fears The National Assembly created a new constitution that set up a limited monarchy. It included a king, but the legislature made the laws. It allowed all males over 25 who paid a certain amount in taxes to vote, ensuring that only affluent members of society would be elected.

The new constitution was not radical enough for some people who wanted stronger reforms. Catholic priests, nobles, and other people who had been hurt by the revolution also opposed the new Constitution.

War with Austria Fearful that revolutions would spread to their own countries, the leaders of Austria and Prussia tried to restore Louis XVI to power. The new government of France declared war on Austria in response. This resulted in more suffering for many people.

SECTION 2 RADICAL REVOLUTION AND REACTION

The Move to Radicalism

The Legislative Assembly called a National Convention. Radicals took control and took revenge on people who had supported the king or resisted the revolution by arresting or killing them. New leaders encouraged the poor to use violence to get what they needed.

The Fate of the King When the newly elected National Convention began to meet, their first major step was to abolish the monarchy and establish the French Republic. The National Convention did not rule all of France, however. Peasants in western France and people in France's major provincial cities refused to accept the authority of the National Convention.

The National Convention split into factions (dissenting groups) over the fate of the king. Two factions were the Girondins, who represented the provinces, and the Mountain, which represented Paris radicals. The Mountain won at the beginning of 1793 when they convinced the National Convention to condemn Louis XVI to death.

Crises and Response The execution of the king outraged the royalty of most of Europe. An informal coalition of Austria, Prussia, Spain, Portugal, Britain, and the Dutch Republic took up arms against France. By spring of 1793, they were ready to invade. To meet this crisis, the National Convention gave broad powers to a special committee of twelve known as the Committee of Public Safety. It was dominated at first by Georges Danton, then by **Maximilien Robespierre.**

The Reign of Terror

When the Committee of Public Safety took control between 1793 and 1794, it acted to defend France from foreign enemies. It also set in motion an effort that came to be known as the **Reign of Terror**. During the Reign of Terror, nearly 40,000 people were killed. Most executions were held in places that had openly rebelled against the authority of the National Convention.

CORE CONCEPTS: SCIENCE AND TECHNOLOGY

Louis XVI, as well as about 16,000 other victims of the revolution, was sent to the guillotine. This relatively new device was thought to be the most humane choice for capital punishment because it was fast and efficient.

CORE CONCEPTS: ECONOMIC SYSTEMS

The Committee tried to provide some economic controls by establishing price limits on goods considered necessities, such as food, fuel, and clothing. The controls failed, however, because the government could not enforce them.

CORE CONCEPTS: BELIEF SYSTEMS

Dechristianization never took hold in France because the country was still overwhelmingly Catholic.

People from all classes were killed. About 15 percent of the victims came from the clergy and nobility; the rest were from the bourgeoisie and peasant classes.

The Republic of Virtue The Committee of Public Safety also took steps to create a new order, or what Robespierre called the "Republic of Virtue." In this new republic, men and women were no longer called "mister" and "madame" but "citizen" and "citizeness." A law aimed at primary education for all passed but was not widely implemented. Slavery was abolished in France's colonies.

The Committee also pursued a policy of dechristianization. The word *saint* was removed from street names, churches were pillaged or closed, and priests were encouraged to marry. A new calendar was adopted in which years were no longer numbered from the birth of Christ but from September 22, 1792, the first day of the French Republic. Sundays and church holidays were eliminated.

A Nation in Arms

During this time, France was threatened by external forces. To save the republic from its foreign enemies, the Committee decreed a universal mobilization (*levée en masse*) of the nation on August 23, 1793. In less than a year, the French revolutionary government had raised a huge army. At its peak, it numbered over one million and it soon pushed back invading armies. By summer 1794, France had defeated most of its foreign enemies.

The French revolutionary army was an important step in the creation of modern nationalism. Previously, wars had been fought between governments or ruling dynasties by relatively small armies of professional soldiers. The new French army was the creation of a people's government. Its wars were people's wars. When dynastic wars became people's wars, however, warfare became more destructive.

End of the Terror Because many members of the National Convention feared Robespierre, a vote was eventually taken to execute him. After his death, more moderate leaders took control, and the Reign of Terror ended.

The Directory

The National Convention reduced the power of the Committee of Public Safety. The churches were allowed to reopen. A new constitution in 1795 created a legislative assembly consisting of a Council of Elders and a Council of 500. The Council of Elders elected five directors to act as the executive committee, or Directory. Together with the legislature, the Directory ruled the country.

The period of government under the Directory (1795–1799) was a time of corruption. Enemies of the directory included Royalists who wished to restore the monarchy and radicals who were unhappy with the more moderate path of the government. Economic problems remained unsolved.

In 1799, a **coup d'état** (a sudden overthrow of the government) ended the Directory. The coup d'état was led by the successful and popular general **Napoleon Bonaparte**.

SECTION 3 THE AGE OF NAPOLEON

The Rise of Napoleon

Napoleon, who was born in 1769 on the island of Corsica, studied in France. After he became a lieutenant in the French army, he rose rapidly through the ranks. By 1796, he was commander of the French armies in Italy, where he won many victories. In 1797, he returned to France as a hero. He was given command of an army training to invade Britain. Knowing the French were not ready to invade, he proposed to strike indirectly at Britain by taking Egypt and threatening India. The British, who controlled the seas, cut off Napoleon's army in Egypt. Napoleon abandoned his army and returned to Paris.

Consul and Emperor After the coup d'état, a new government called the consulate was proclaimed. As First Consul, Napoleon controlled the entire government. He appointed members of the bureaucracy, controlled the army, conducted foreign affairs, and influenced the legislature. In 1802, he was made consul for life. Two years later, he crowned himself Emperor Napoleon I.

Napoleon's Domestic Policies

One of Napoleon's actions at home was to return the people's Catholic religion to them. In 1801, Napoleon made an agreement with the pope that recognized Catholicism as the religion of the majority. In return, the pope agreed not to ask for

CORE CONCEPTS: POWER

Napoleon dominated French and European history from 1799 to 1815. Political instability following the French Revolution made his rise possible.

the return of the church lands seized in the revolution. This agreement was popular both with Catholics and with people who had bought Church lands during the revolution.

Codification of the Laws Napoleon's most famous domestic achievement was his codification of the laws. Before the revolution, France had almost 300 different legal systems. Napoleon completed seven codes of law. The most important of these was the Civil Code, or **Napoleonic Code**. It recognized the principle of equality of all citizens before the law and the right of the individual to choose a profession. It included religious toleration and the abolition of serfdom and feudalism. Property rights were protected, but when women married, their property was under the control of their husbands. In lawsuits, women were treated as minors.

A New Bureaucracy Napoleon developed a bureaucracy in which promotion was based on ability, not rank or birth. He also created a new aristocracy based on merit in the civil or military service.

Preserver of the Revolution? Napoleon claimed to have preserved the gains of the revolution. The Civil Code did preserve the equality of all citizens. Opening government careers to more people was another gain. On the other hand, Napoleon destroyed some revolutionary goals. Liberty suffered. He also eliminated freedom of the press by shutting down 60 of France's 73 newspapers and requiring that all manuscripts be approved before publication. Even the mail was opened by government police.

Napoleon's Empire

Napoleon began building an empire soon after he came to power. From 1807 to 1812, Napoleon was the master of Europe. His Grand Empire was composed of three parts: the French Empire, dependent states, and allied states.

NATIONAL GEOGRAPHIC — NAPOLEONIC EUROPE

French Empire, 1812
Dependent states, 1812
States allied with Napoleon, 1812
States allied against Napoleon, 1812

300 miles
300 kilometers
Lambert Azimuthal Equal-Area projection

CORE CONCEPTS: THE USES OF GEOGRAPHY

Study the map. Where were the states located that were allied against Napoleon in 1812? What geographic factors would have helped these states remain independent of Napoleon's control?

Spreading the Principles of the Revolution Within his empire, Napoleon tried to spread some of the principles of the French Revolution, including legal equality, religious toleration, and economic freedom. In many areas, the nobility and clergy lost their special privileges.

The European Response

Napoleon's Grand Empire collapsed almost as quickly as it had been formed. There were two main reasons for this: the survival of Great Britain and the force of nationalism.

Britain's Survival Sea power saved Britain. The British navy defeated a combined French-Spanish fleet at Trafalgar in 1805. When invasion did not work, Napoleon turned to his Continental System to defeat Britain. Its goal was to prevent British goods from reaching the European continent. The System failed because allied states resented being told that they could not trade with Britain. Some began to cheat. New markets in the Middle East and in Latin America gave Britain other outlets for its goods. By 1809–1810, British exports were at near-record highs.

Nationalism The second key factor in Napoleon's defeat was **nationalism**, the unique cultural identity of a people based on common language, religion, and national symbols. Napoleon's spread of the principles of the French Revolution beyond France indirectly aroused nationalism as well. First, other countries hated the French as oppressors and felt more patriotic toward their own countries. Second, the French showed the people of Europe what nationalism was and what a nation in arms could do.

The Fall of Napoleon

The beginning of Napoleon's downfall came in 1812 with his invasion of Russia. Within only a few years, the fall was complete.

Russia Because the Russians refused to remain in the Continental System, Napoleon had little choice but to invade them. In June 1812, a Grand Army of over 600,000 men entered Russia. Napoleon's hopes for victory depended on a quick defeat of the Russian armies, but they refused to fight. Instead, they retreated, burning their own villages and countryside to keep Napoleon's army from finding food. This is referred to as a "scorched earth" policy.

The Great Retreat When the Grand Army arrived in Moscow, they found it on fire. Without food and supplies, Napoleon abandoned Moscow and began the "Great Retreat" across Russia. Less than 40,000 of the original army made it back to Poland. This military disaster led other European states to attack the French army. Paris was captured in March 1814, and Napoleon was sent into exile on the island of Elba. The Bourbon monarchy was restored to France, and Louis XVIII became king.

The Final Defeat The new king had little support, and Napoleon was able to slip back into France. When troops were sent to capture him, they went over to his side. Napoleon entered Paris in triumph on March 10, 1815. He raised another army and moved to attack the nearest allied forces in Belgium. At Waterloo in Belgium on June 18, 1815, Napoleon met his final defeat at the hands of a combined British and Prussian army under the Duke of Wellington. Napoleon was then exiled to St. Helena, a small island in the South Atlantic.

CORE CONCEPTS: PLACES AND REGIONS

Ask yourself why the Russian strategy worked so well. Refer to the map on page 255 as needed.

REGENTS WARM-UP

To sum up this chapter, make a two-column chart like the one below in which you show some of Napoleon's greatest accomplishments and greatest defeats.

Napoleon's Rise and Fall

Rise ↑ | | | \ Fall

CHAPTER 20   INDUSTRIALIZATION AND NATIONALISM

Chapter Overview

The Industrial Revolution began in Britain when machines changed the way cotton was produced. It led to a movement from the farm to the city and an economy based on manufacturing. Meanwhile, even though the Great Powers worked to maintain a conservative order in Europe, the forces of liberalism and nationalism undermined their efforts. Nationalism was evident in the unification of both Italy and Germany

As you read this chapter, ask yourself these questions:
(1) How did industrialization change the Western world?
(2) How did the popular appeal of the liberal, conservative, and national movements change?
(3) What were reasons for revolution and reform in Europe?
(4) What events led to the unification of Italy and Germany?
(5) What were the characteristics of romanticism and realism?
(6) What developments shaped the new age of science?

Main Ideas and Concepts

- **Urbanization** Cities grew as people moved from the country to work in factories.

- **Change** The forces of nationalism and liberalism grew in Europe, challenging the conservative order and leading to revolutions.

- **Nationalism** Nationalism led to the unification of Italy as well as to the creation of a new, unified, and militaristic Germany.

- **Culture** In the arts, Romanticism arose as a reaction to the art forms and ideas of the Enlightenment. At the same time, new developments in science as well as social conditions led to the realist movement.

People, Places, Terms

The following names and terms will help you to prepare for the Regents Exam in Global History and Geography. You can find an explanation of each name and term in the Glossary at the back of this book, in your textbook, or in another reference source.

Agrarian Revolution	liberalism	Romanticism
capitalism	militarism	secularization
conservatism	nationalism	socialism
Crimean War	realism	**Otto von Bismarck**
kaiser		

SECTION 1 THE INDUSTRIAL REVOLUTION

REGENTS WARM-UP

List three main reasons why the Industrial Revolution began in Britain.

The Industrial Revolution in Great Britain

The Industrial Revolution, which began in Great Britain in the 1780s, was caused, in part, by changes in agriculture, referred to as an "Agricultural or **Agrarian Revolution**." Factors such as expansion of farmland, good weather, improved transportation, and new crops had led to a dramatic increase in the food supply. Increase in supply meant lower prices. Now British families could use some of their money to buy things other than food. In addition, abundant food supplies led to an increase in population. A large labor force was created.

Another cause of the Industrial Revolution in Britain was Britain's ready supply of capital, or money, to invest in the new machines and factories. Natural resources were also plentiful in Britain. The country's many rivers provided waterpower and transportation. Britain also had abundant supplies of coal and iron ore, needed for manufacturing.

Finally, Britain had the markets in which to sell goods. Britain had a huge empire and ships to sail the goods. With an increased population, it also had a growing market at home.

Changes in Cotton Production Making cotton started out as a cottage industry in England; it was done by individuals in their homes. Inventions changed that. The flying shuttle made weaving faster. In fact, cloth could be made faster than spinners could spin the thread needed to make it. Next, the spinning jenny came along. Soon thread was being made faster than it could be woven. Then the water-powered loom made weaving faster.

The water-powered loom also caused people to move, as workers needed to be brought to the machines. The machines needed to be located near streams and rivers. When steam engines began to power machinery, the need to have workers in the same place increased. Workers no longer had to be next to water, however, as steam engines were fired by coal.

Soon, cotton was Britain's most valuable product. British cotton goods were sold everywhere in the world and were produced mainly in factories.

The Coal and Iron Industries The success of the steam engine increased the need for coal and led to an expansion in coal production. New processes using coal led to the expansion of another industry—iron.

Railroads In 1804, the first steam locomotive ran on an industrial line in Britain. In a short period of time, better locomotives were developed that could pull heavier loads at faster rates of speed. As locomotives improved, Britain laid down more and more track. Soon railroads were moving goods and resources efficiently and contributing to the success of the Industrial Revolution.

The New Factories The factory created a new labor system. Machines could run constantly, so workers began working in shifts. Workers had to learn to keep regular hours and do the same work over and over.

The Spread of Industrialization

By the mid-nineteenth century, Great Britain had become the world's first and richest industrial nation. It produced one-half of the world's coal and manufactured goods.

Europe The Industrial Revolution spread to the rest of Europe at different times and speeds. First to be industrialized in continental Europe were Belgium, France, and the German states. In these places, the government encouraged industrialization by funding the building of roads, canals, and railroads.

Social Impact in Europe

The Industrial Revolution drastically changed the social life of Europe and the world. This was most evident in the growth of cities and in the emergence of two new social classes: the industrial middle class and the industrial working class.

CORE CONCEPTS: SCIENCE AND TECHNOLOGY

One of Britain's natural resources was iron ore. A new process for developing high-quality iron was developed by Henry Cort using coke, which is derived from coal. Britain soon began producing more iron than the rest of the world combined. The high-quality iron was used to build new machines, especially new means of transportation.

CORE CONCEPTS: ECONOMIC SYSTEMS

The industrial economy created a cycle of economic growth. Building railroads created new jobs. Less expensive transportation led to lower-priced goods, thus creating larger markets. More sales meant more factories and more machinery. With the profits, business owners could reinvest in new equipment and more railroad track.

CORE CONCEPTS: URBANIZATION

A massive growth in population as well as a shift in population from the farms to the cities provided labor for an ever-growing number of factories.

Growth of Population and Cities Between 1750 and 1850, the population of Europe nearly doubled. This growth was the result of a decline in diseases, wars, and death rates. It was also the result of an increase in food production.

An exception was the Irish potato famine (1845–1850). The Irish depended on the potato crop for food, and when a fungus infected the crops, almost a million people died. A million more emigrated, many to the United States.

Cities and towns in Europe grew dramatically during the first half of the nineteenth century. By 1850, especially in Great Britain and Belgium, cities were becoming home to many industries. People moved from the country to the cities to find work.

The Industrial Middle Class With the Industrial Revolution came the rise of industrial capitalism, an economic system based on industrial production. It produced the new industrial middle class. This class was made up of the people who built the factories, bought the machines, and figured out where the markets were. They had great drive, great vision, and, often, a heightened sense of greed.

The Industrial Working Class Industrial workers faced terrible conditions. They worked 12–16 hour days, six days a week. There was no minimum wage and no job security. Conditions were worst in the cotton mills, which were hot, dirty, dusty, dangerous, and unhealthy. Conditions in the coal mines were also harsh. Cave-ins, explosions, and gas fumes were a way of life.

By 1830, women and children made up two-thirds of the cotton industry's workforce in Britain. A reformer and former member of Parliament, Michael Sadler, published a report in 1833 detailing the horrible conditions of factory workers, especially children. His report led to the Factory Act of 1833, which set minimum age requirements and limits on the number of hours they could work. After this law passed, more and more women, who were paid half as much as men, filled the gaps left by children.

Early Socialism The social conditions of the Industrial Revolution led to the rise of socialism. **Socialism** is a system in which society, usually in the form of the government, owns and controls some means of production, such as factories and utilities. Early socialists believed in the equality of all people and wanted to replace competition with cooperation in industry.

CORE CONCEPTS: ECONOMIC SYSTEMS

Capitalism—an economic system in which goods and services are produced, exchanged and owned by individuals with minimal governmental regulation—was replacing mercantilism as the dominant economic system.

CORE CONCEPTS: MOVEMENT OF PEOPLE AND GOODS

The rapid growth of cities led to bad living conditions. Calls for reform began, but they were not answered until the second half of the nineteenth century.

SECTION 2 REACTION AND REVOLUTION

The Congress of Vienna

After the defeat of Napoleon, Great Britain, France, Austria, Prussia, and Russia (the Great Powers) met at the Congress of Vienna in 1814. They wanted to arrange a peace. They also wanted to keep any one power from dominating Europe. (This is referred to as a "balance of power" concept.) This meant balancing political and military forces. For their leader, Klemens von Metternich, from Austria, it also meant that the lawful monarchs from the royal families that had ruled before Napoleon came to power would be restored to their positions. This was believed to be a sure route to peace and order in Europe.

The Conservative Order

Metternich believed in the political philosophy called **conservatism**. It is based on tradition and social stability. The rulers being restored to power were also conservative in their outlook. They believed the forces of change that had led to the French Revolution needed to be stopped. Instead, obedience to political authority and organized religion would restore order.

The Great Powers agreed to meet in conference to take steps to maintain peace in Europe. These meetings came to be called the Concert of Europe. The Great Powers also established a principle of intervention. They would step in to put down revolutions that occurred in Europe and to restore the monarchy. Britain refused to accept this principle, but the other powers acted on it.

The Forces of Change

Conservatives were not alone in Europe. Forces of change, in the form of liberalism and nationalism, were also about.

Liberalism **Liberalism** is a political philosophy that states that people should be as free as possible from government restraint, including government interference in the economy. In large part, this meant that civil liberties, such as freedom of assembly, speech, and press, as well as equality before the law, should be guaranteed to all. Most nineteenth-century liberals also wanted religious tolerance, as well as separation of church and state. They also believed that laws should be made by a representative assembly.

CORE CONCEPTS: POLITICAL SYSTEMS

Liberals did not believe in a democracy that gave everyone the right to vote. Instead, they favored a constitutional monarchy, in which the actions of a king or queen are controlled by a written constitution and the rights of individuals are preserved. Liberalism grew out of a middle-class concern for itself: these people wanted voting rights for themselves and the opportunity to share power with the landowning classes. They did not advocate the same privileges for the lower classes.

Nationalism Nationalism was an even stronger force than liberalism during the nineteenth century in Europe. **Nationalism** is the unique cultural identity of a people based on common language, religion, and national symbols. Nationalism often results in particular nationalities wanting to be separate nations. For example, in the 1800s, Hungary wished to break off from Austria. In some cases, people of the same nationality who exist in separate states, such as the Germans did in the early 1800s, express a nationalistic desire for unity.

Revolutionary Outbursts Revolutions began in Europe in 1830. The French established a constitutional monarchy. Belgium rebelled against being part of the Dutch Republic and formed its own nation. Revolutions in Poland and Italy were less successful, in part because armies from other countries helped put them down.

The Revolutions of 1848

Severe economic problems in France were the spark for yet another revolution there, which began in 1846. In 1848, the monarchy (which had been restored after Napoleon) was overthrown. A temporary republican government was established. It called for the election of representatives to a Constituent Assembly. The job of the Constituent Assembly was to write a new constitution. Election to the assembly was by universal male suffrage—all adult males could vote.

The new constitution set up a republic called the Second Republic. It had a legislature and a president elected by universal male suffrage.

At this time, the 38 independent German states also attempted unification. An all-German parliament called the Frankfurt Assembly was held. It was composed of elected representatives who drafted a constitution. It had no means of enforcement, however, and unification was not achieved.

Revolutions in Central Europe At this time, Austria was a multinational state, a collection of different peoples. In 1848 in Vienna, liberals took control of the capital and demanded a liberal constitution. Over the next several months, however, the Austrian government crushed rebellions that plagued it.

Revolts in the Italian States The Congress of Vienna had established nine states in Italy. In 1848, revolutionaries revolted against Austrian control in Lombardy and Venetia. Other revolutionaries fought to unify the states but were also defeated.

CORE CONCEPTS: NATIONALISM

The desire for new and separate nation-states in Europe was a threat to the existing political order. Conservatives tried to repress nationalism. Liberals joined with the nationalists, however. How were liberal ideals closer to nationalist ideals than to conservative ideals?

Throughout Europe in 1848, popular revolts challenged conservative governments. Conservative governments prevailed, though the forces of nationalism and liberalism continued to influence political events.

SECTION 3 NATIONAL UNIFICATION AND THE NATIONAL STATE

NATIONAL GEOGRAPHIC

EUROPE AFTER THE CONGRESS OF VIENNA, 1815

German Confederation

Breakdown of the Concert of Europe

In the nineteenth century, the Ottoman Empire was in decline. At the same time, Russia wanted to expand its territory into the Balkans.

The Crimean War In 1853, the Russians invaded the Turkish Balkan provinces of Moldavia and Walachia. In response, the Ottoman Turks declared war on Russia. Great Britain and

LINKING GEOGRAPHY TO HISTORY

In particular, Russia sought access to the Mediterranean via the Dardanelles. Control of this area would make Russia the major power in Eastern Europe and a challenge to British naval control.

France, who feared the increased power of Russia, declared war on Russia also. The conflict came to be called the **Crimean War**.

The war ended the Concert of Europe, which had been upheld primarily by Russia and Austria. Austria had refused to support Russia in the Crimean War, however, because it had interests of its own in the Balkans. Russia withdrew from European affairs for the next 20 years. Austria was now without friends among the Great Powers.

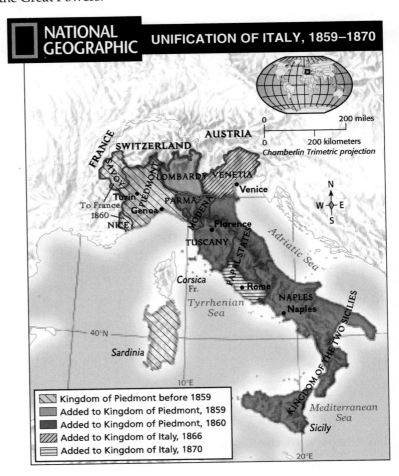

NATIONAL GEOGRAPHIC — **UNIFICATION OF ITALY, 1859–1870**

Kingdom of Piedmont before 1859
Added to Kingdom of Piedmont, 1859
Added to Kingdom of Piedmont, 1860
Added to Kingdom of Italy, 1866
Added to Kingdom of Italy, 1870

REGENTS WARM-UP

To review, make a sequence chain showing the major steps in the process of Italian unification.

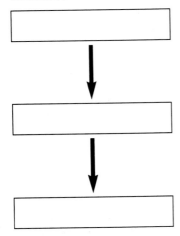

Italian Unification

A series of wars and negotiations led to Italian unification (1859–1870). The prime minister of the northern state of Piedmont, Camillo di Cavour, pursued economic policies that allowed the Kingdom of Piedmont to equip a large army.

Cavour wanted to overthrow Austria, but he knew that despite their bigger army, Piedmont couldn't do it alone. He made an alliance with the French. As a result of war with the Austrians, Piedmont got Lombardy. Cavour's success in Piedmont led revolutionaries in Parma, Modena and Tuscany to overthrow their government and join up with Piedmont.

Giuseppe Mazzini, a revolutionary and supporter of unification, founded a group called Young Italy, which organized uprisings against Austrian rule. In southern Italy, Giuseppe Garibaldi's revolutionary army took control of Sicily and Naples. King Victor Emmanuel II then proclaimed a new kingdom of Italy.

NATIONAL GEOGRAPHIC

UNIFICATION OF GERMANY, 1866–1871

Legend:
- Prussia before 1866
- Added 1866–1867 as the North German Confederation
- Added in 1871
- Annexed in 1871 after the Franco-Prussian War
- Battle

German Unification

The German states looked to Prussia for aid with unification (1866–1871). Prussia was strong and prosperous. It was known for its **militarism**, or reliance on military strength.

King William I of Prussia wanted a large army. He appointed **Otto von Bismarck** as prime minister, who strengthened the

CORE CONCEPTS: POWER

German unity had come from Prussia, and Prussian militaristic values were now fundamental to the new German state. This military might would combine with its industrial resources to make it the strongest power on the European continent.

REGENTS WARM-UP

Compare the policies of
Camillo di Cavour with those
of Otto von Bismarck.

**CORE CONCEPTS:
NATIONALISM**

British nationalism was
reflected in the reign of
Queen Victoria from 1837 to
1901. Her sense of duty and
moral responsibility was
reflected in the attitudes of
what has come to be known
as the Victorian Age.

**CORE CONCEPTS:
CHANGE**

Napoleon III also accom-
plished many things. Among
them:

- expanded the French
  economy

- created infrastructure
  of roads, canals, and
  railroads

- vastly rebuilt Paris,
  including new, broad
  boulevards, spacious
  buildings, public squares,
  an underground sewage
  system, a public water
  supply, and gaslights

army and, in general, acted without the approval of the parliament of Prussia.

Bismarck organized the German states north of the Main River
into a North German Confederation. When tensions between
Prussia and France led to the Franco-Prussian War (1870–1871),
the French lost the states of Alsace and Lorraine to the new
German nation. Even before the end of the war, the southern
German states decided to enter the North German
Confederation. In 1871, William I of Prussia was proclaimed
kaiser, or emperor, of the Second German Empire.

Nationalism and Reform in Europe

Great Britain In 1832, Parliament passed a bill that decreased
the strength of the aristocratic landowning classes by increasing
the number of male voters. These new voters were chiefly
members of the industrial middle class.

Extension of the vote together with continuing economic
growth helped insulate Britain from revolution. By 1850, the
British middle class was already prosperous as a result of the
Industrial Revolution. After 1850, the working classes began to
share in some of this prosperity as real wages for laborers
increased more than 25 percent between 1850 and 1870.

Ireland Nationalism was a growing force in Ireland during the
second half of the nineteenth century. Various groups in Ireland
and the United States advocated for independence from Great
Britain. Their protests, which were at times violent, were ultimately unsuccessful.

France Although Louis-Napoleon had been elected as a president in 1848, only four years later, he asked the people of France
to restore the empire. In a popular vote, or plebiscite, 97 percent
voted yes. In 1852, Louis-Napoleon became Napoleon III,
Emperor of France. This began the Second Empire.

Napoleon III completely controlled the government and
limited civil liberties. When opposition to Napoleon III arose in
the 1860s, he gave the legislature more power. The people never
overthrew their emperor. Instead, the Second Empire ended
with the defeat of France in the Franco-Prussian War.

The Austrian Empire After Austria was defeated by the Prussians
in 1866, it made concessions to the fiercely nationalistic Hungarians
within its state. It created the dual monarchy of Austria-Hungary.
Each had its own constitution, legislature, government bureaucracy,
and capital (Vienna for Austria and Budapest for Hungary). They

shared one monarch (Francis Joseph), one army, their foreign policy, and their system of finances.

Russia In the first half of the nineteenth century, Russia was rural, agricultural, and autocratic. The czar had unlimited power.

After Russia suffered a humiliating defeat to the Ottoman Turks, Great Britain, and France in the Crimean War, many Russians realized that Russia was falling behind the western European powers. Czar Alexander II, who was greatly influenced by Enlightenment ideals, decided to make reforms. In 1861, he issued an emancipation edict that freed the serfs. Before this time serfs had not been able to own land or marry as they chose. Now, the government provided land for peasants. The new land system, however, created huge problems, as the landowners had kept the best land for themselves, and the newly freed serfs found they could not make a living on the land they had received.

Nicholas II, who ruled from 1894 to 1917, completed the Trans-Siberian Railroad, which connected the European parts of Russia with its Asian sections. Before this, the only Russians who settled Siberia were convicts, explorers, and traders. With the completion of the railroad, industrial towns sprung up along its route.

CORE CONCEPTS: CONFLICT

Alexander II attempted other reforms, but discontent grew both from the conservatives, who thought Russia was changing too much or too fast, and from the peasants, who did not gain sufficient benefits. A group of radicals assassinated Alexander II in 1881. Alexander III brought back many of the old methods of repression.

SECTION 4 CULTURE: ROMANTICISM AND REALISM

CROSS-CULTURAL CONNECTIONS

Abraham Lincoln's Emancipation Proclamation of 1863 freed the slaves in the Confederate states of the United States.

Romanticism

During the Enlightenment, intellectuals had stressed reason as the way to discover truth. In the nineteenth century, a new intellectual movement arose called **Romanticism**. It emphasized feelings, emotions, and imagination as sources of knowing.

Visual Arts Artists at this time, such as J.M.W. Turner and John Constable in England and French painter Eugene Delacroix, abandoned pure reason and filled their canvases with warmth and emotion. They didn't just paint what they saw but instead infused the artist's feelings and imagination into the canvas. Landscape paintings showing the power of nature were popular as well.

Music Music, too, began to probe human emotions. At this time, it lost some of its orderliness and predictability. Ludwig van Beethoven was the bridge between the classical and romantic periods in music. He brought powerful feelings and dramatic intensity to music.

A New Age of Science

The Industrial Revolution brought a heightened interest in scientific research. Soon science came to have a greater and greater impact on people's lives. At this time, Louis Pasteur proposed the germ theory of disease, which was crucial to the development of modern medical practices. Dmitry Mendeleyev developed the periodic table in chemistry. Michael Faraday created a primitive generator that laid the foundation for the use of electric current.

Science Undermines Religion The new and dramatic material benefits of science caused people to have more faith in science and less faith in religion. The nineteenth century was a time of increasing **secularization** (indifference to or rejection of religion). No one did more to create this feeling than Charles Darwin (1809–1882).

Darwin was influenced by an English economist named Thomas Malthus. Malthus's most influential work, *Essay on the Principle of Population*, put forth the theory that population increases more rapidly than food supply, and that wars and disease would have to kill off the extra population. Malthus's ideas helped Darwin establish a relationship between progress and natural selection.

In his work *Origin of the Species* (1859), Darwin proposed and presented a compelling body of scientific evidence for a process called organic evolution. It meant that each kind of plant and animal had evolved over a long period of time from earlier and simpler forms of life. In a process called natural selection, only those forms of life best suited for survival endured over generations. This theory came to be known as "survival of the fittest."

CORE CONCEPTS: IDENTITY

Darwin's work threatened people's sense of themselves and their world. Some people were outraged by Darwin's suggestion that God had not created every species, and especially human beings, just as they were. Others questioned whether there was any moral value in a world in which only the "fittest" could survive.

Realism

The new scientific outlook was expressed, in part, through realism. **Realism** is the belief that the world should be reviewed realistically. In art, realism took the form of showing real life, including real places, real people, and real events. Ordinary people took the place of romantic heroes.

In literature, realist writers preferred the novel to poetry. The books they wrote examined social issues. Gustave Flaubert blazed the way with the novel *Madame Bovary,* which criticized small-town life and values in France. Charles Dickens followed with novels that described with vivid realism the urban poor and the brutal life they led. French journalist Emile Zola worked to portray the lives of ordinary people in his novel *Germinal.*

Section 1   **The Growth of Industrial Prosperity**
Section 2   **The Emergence of Mass Society**
Section 3   **Toward the First World War**

Chapter Overview

During the Second Industrial Revolution, production rose sharply and consumer products became more available. A mass society emerged with an improved standard of living, and the middle class expanded and become more literate. Political democracy expanded in Great Britain and France, but not all countries experienced increases in civil liberties. Extreme nationalist thinkers used the ideas of Social Darwinism to put forth racist ideas. The Zionist movement began. Writers, artists, and musicians rebelled against traditional literary and artistic styles with a heightened emotionalism and somber realism.

As you read this chapter, ask yourself these questions:
(1) What changes occurred during the Second Industrial Revolution?
(2) What roles did technological innovations, such as electricity and the telephone, play in this revolution?
(3) How did new ideas such as socialism, modern physics, and psychology affect people's lives?
(4) What were the most important cultural developments between 1870 and 1914?

Main Ideas and Concepts

- **Change** The Second Industrial Revolution led to changes in standards of living, a mass society, and the formation of socialist parties.

- **Needs and Wants** A middle class that could meet its needs and satisfy some of its wants emerged in Victorian England.

- **Power** The emergence of new political parties and labor unions challenged the governments of Western Europe.

- **Change** New political and social ideas forced a rethinking of Enlightenment ideas and created new social structures.

People, Places, Terms

The following names and terms will help you to prepare for the Regents Exam in Global History and Geography. You can find an explanation of each name and term in the Glossary at the back of this book, in your textbook, or in another reference source.

command economies
Karl Marx
socialism

SECTION 1 THE GROWTH OF INDUSTRIAL PROSPERITY

The Second Industrial Revolution

Westerners in the late 1800s worshiped progress. The first Industrial Revolution had given rise to textiles, railroads, iron, and coal. In the Second Industrial Revolution, steel, chemicals, electricity, and petroleum led the way to new industrial frontiers.

New Products An important shift was from iron to steel. Steel was used to build lighter, smaller, and faster machines and engines, as well as railways, ships, skyscrapers and weapons.

Electricity became a major new form of energy. It could easily be converted into other forms of energy, such as heat, light, and motion. It gave birth to a series of inventions. The light bulb, the telephone, and the radio were direct and revolutionary product offshoots.

The development of the internal combustion engine gave rise to new ocean liners, the airplane, and automobile.

New Patterns Industrial production grew at a rapid pace due to increased sales. Europeans could afford to buy more products because many were making higher wages. In addition, the costs of the products dipped as transportation costs went down.

Not all nations benefited from the Second Industrial Revolution. Great Britain, Belgium, France, the Netherlands, Germany, the western part of the Austro-Hungarian Empire, and northern Italy made up an advanced industrial core. They had a high standard of living and decent transportation systems.

CORE CONCEPTS: SCIENCE AND TECHNOLOGY

Electricity also improved transportation, as streetcars and subways appeared. Electricity transformed factories by powering conveyor belts and providing light 24 hours a day.

CORE CONCEPTS: FACTORS OF PRODUCTION

Soon the first department stores appeared in the cities. They offered products ranging from clocks and bicycles to electric lights and typewriters.

Other parts of Europe remained largely agricultural. They included southern Italy, most of Austria-Hungary, Spain, Portugal, the Balkan kingdoms, and Russia.

Toward a World Economy With the growth of transportation and industry, a world economy grew. Europeans bought products ranging from wool and sugar to coffee and iron ore from Asia, Australia, South America, and Africa. In turn, they invested their capital abroad and also sold goods to foreign countries.

Responses to Industrialization

The difficult working conditions of the era led to many different attempts at reform.

The word **socialism** was first used in the early 1800s. Early socialists, known as Utopian Socialists, saw the factory system as unfair to the average worker and looked to change the way workers were treated. A Utopian and factory owner, Robert Owen, established a model society in the village of New Lanark in Scotland. There he was able to institute labor reforms in his factories and raise living conditions while still making a profit.

British economist David Ricardo also influenced socialist thinkers. Ricardo's labor theory of value stated that the value of a commodity (good) was a function of the labor needed to produce it. According to this theory, a watch costing $10 required ten times as much labor for its production as did a piece of paper costing $1. Karl Marx later used this theory in his own work, determining that factory owners were exploitative because only the labor done by workers adds value to a product.

Marx's Theory The ideas of socialism were based on *The Communist Manifesto*, which had been written by **Karl Marx** and Friedrich Engels in 1848. They were reacting to the horrible conditions in factories of their times, which they blamed on industrial capitalism. They proposed a new social system of **command economies** that would eventually be called communism.

Marx believed that world history was a "history of class struggles." These struggles were between the "haves," who owned the land, raw materials, money, and so forth, and the "have-nots." Government was seen as an instrument of the oppressors or ruling class. In his own times, Marx saw the middle class, or bourgeoisie, as the "haves." He called the "have-nots" the proletariat.

CORE CONCEPTS: ECONOMIC SYSTEMS

Among Marx's beliefs:

- the "haves" exploited the proletariat
- the workers of the world would rise up, revolt and take over (revolution was inevitable)
- a classless society would evolve in which all would share wealth and power
- this new society would own the means of production and distribution and replace capitalism

Socialist Parties Working-class leaders formed socialist parties based on Marx's ideas. The most important was the German Social Democratic Party. It called for revolution. At the same time, it competed in German parliament elections. Party members who won seats worked to improve working conditions. By 1912, it was the largest single party in Germany.

Other European nations also had socialist parties. They varied in their goals. Pure Marxists thought, as Marx had, that capitalism would be overthrown in a violent revolution. Other Marxists, called revisionists, suggested that workers organize and even work with other political parties to effect change. As workers received the right to vote, they could achieve their aims by working within democratic systems.

Trade Unions Trade unions were a force for evolutionary rather than revolutionary change. They gained the right to strike in Britain in the 1870s. (A strike is a work stoppage called by members of a union to pressure an employer into meeting their demands.) Soon after, workers in factories were organized into trade unions so they could use strikes to achieve reforms. Trade unions grew rapidly in Great Britain. In other nations, they had varying degrees of success.

SECTION 2 THE EMERGENCE OF MASS SOCIETY

The New Urban Environment

CORE CONCEPTS: URBANIZATION

Urban populations also grew as conditions in cities improved and people could survive in cities longer.

More and more people lived in the cities. In the early 1850s, urban dwellers made up about 40 percent of the English, 15 percent of the French, 10 percent of the Prussian, and 5 percent of the Russian population. By 1890, those numbers had increased to 60 percent in England, 25 percent in France, 30 percent in Prussia, and 10 percent in Russia.

Urban areas grew because the jobs were there. People left the countryside to find jobs in the factories and, later, the service trades and professions.

Social Structure of Mass Society

The Elite

- landed aristocrats
- industrialists
- bankers
- merchants

The Middle Class

- lawyers
- doctors
- members
  of the civil service
- business managers
- accountants
- chemists

- shopkeepers
- traders

- salespeople
- bookkeepers
- telephone operators
- secretaries

The Working Class

- landholding peasants
- sharecroppers
- domestic servants
- semi-skilled and unskilled laborers
- farm laborers
- skilled artisans

At the top of European society was a new elite. Made up of about 5 percent of the population, it controlled between 30 and 40 percent of the wealth. Members of the elite became leaders in the government and military.

The Second Industrial Revolution produced a new group of white-collar workers between the lower middle class and lower classes. The European middle classes believed in hard work. They were also regular churchgoers who believed in the good conduct associated with Christian morality. The Second Industrial Revolution also allowed people to pursue new forms of leisure.

Almost 80 percent of Europeans were working class. Unskilled laborers included large numbers of domestic servants.

The Industrial Revolution also caused millions of Europeans to move to other nations. As many as 55 million immigrated to the United States and South American countries, such as Brazil and Argentina, in search of better jobs and land. Others left their home countries to move within Europe.

The Experiences of Women

The Second Industrial Revolution created new job opportunities for women. A demand for relatively low-paid white-collar workers, together with a shortage of male workers, led employers to hire women.

For most women, marriage and family remained the ideal, if not the only honorable option. One important change did occur, however. Throughout the 1800s, the number of children born to the average woman began to decline—the most significant development in the modern family. The decline was tied to improved economic conditions as well as to increased use of birth control. With fewer children, women could devote more time to caring for the children they had and domestic leisure.

Working class women had very different lives, however. Most had to earn money to help support their families. For their children, childhood ended at age nine or ten, when children became apprentices or were employed in odd jobs. Between 1890 and 1914, however, this pattern began to change. Higher paying jobs in industry made it possible for working class families to depend on the income of the husband alone.

Movement for Women's Rights Feminism, the movement for women's rights, began during the Enlightenment, when some women advocated equality based on the concept of natural rights. Olympe de Gouges wrote *Declaration of the Rights of Woman and the Female Citizen,* demanding that women have the same rights as men. The strongest statement for the rights of women was advanced by the English writer Mary Wollstonecraft. Many see her as the founder of the modern European and American movement for women's rights. In *A Vindication of the Rights of Women,* Wollencraft took issue with Enlightenment thinkers who argued that a monarch's power over their subjects was wrong. She pointed out that the power of men over women was equally wrong.

One of the first significant changes for women in the 1800s was gaining the right to hold property in England in 1870. At this time, some women also fought for and gained the right to enter universities.

CORE CONCEPTS: DIVERSITY

The British women's movement was the most active in Europe. British activist Emmeline Pankhurst and others used unusual stunts, such as chaining themselves to lampposts and throwing eggs, to gain rights for women. In 1848 in the United States, Elizabeth Cady Stanton penned the *Declaration of Sentiments*, modeled after the Declaration of Independence. By 1914, however, women had the right to vote only in a few nations like Norway and Finland, and in a few American states.

Universal Education

Universal education was a product of the mass society of the late nineteenth and early twentieth centuries. In most Western governments, education shifted from being for the elite and wealthier middle class to being for everyone between the ages of six and 12.

One reason for the shift to universal education was that the businesses of the Second Industrial Revolution needed trained, skilled labor. The chief motive, however, was political. Primary schools instilled patriotism.

Compulsory education created a demand for teachers, most of whom were women. The first female colleges were really teaching training schools.

SECTION 3 TOWARD THE FIRST WORLD WAR

International Rivalries

Because Otto Von Bismarck feared that France might try to establish an anti-German alliance, he created a defensive alliance with Austria-Hungary in 1879. In 1882, the addition of Italy created the Triple Alliance.

In 1890, Emperor William II fired Bismarck and embarked on an activist policy dedicated to increasing German power. He dropped a treaty that had been established earlier with Russia, thus bringing France and Russia closer together. German policies caused Great Britain to lean away from Germany and by 1907, it joined with France and Russia to form the Triple Entente (an entente is an informal alliance between countries). Between 1907 and 1913, relations between the two alliances became more and more strained.

CORE CONCEPTS: NEEDS AND WANTS

The most important result of public education was an increase in literacy. In western and central Europe, most adults could read by 1900. Some countries lagged seriously behind, however. Nearly 79 percent of the adults in Serbia and Russia could not read by 1900. With the rise of literacy came the rise of newspapers. Millions of copies were sold each day.

CORE CONCEPTS: ENVIRONMENT

The rain forests of Southeast Asia provide ideal conditions for growing rubber and hardwood trees. Both of these natural resources have led outside powers to exploit the region through conquest and imperialism.

Chapter Overview

During the nineteenth century, a wave of "new imperialism" took the form of total control over vast territories. The British and Dutch carved out large portions of Southeast Asia for their plantations, while almost all of Africa fell under the control of Western colonial powers. Some advocates of imperialism had humanitarian intentions, and some believed in a racial justification, but in general, imperialists exploited local people and their resources.

In Latin America, a wave of nation building began in the nineteenth century as leaders such as Simón Bolívar and José de San Martín led South American nations to independence, and revolts and revolution occurred in Mexico. In general, prosperity increased as a result, but the new middle class sector was generally conservative and allied itself with landholding elites, thereby helping to maintain inequality.

As you read this chapter, ask yourself these questions:
(1) How did colonial powers take over and rule other territories?
(2) How did Western nations impose their values and institutions?
(3) How did nationalism give subject peoples a means for seeking their freedom?
(4) How did colonies provide raw materials and new markets for industrialized nations?
(5) What social divisions existed in colonies between the colonizers and the colonized?

Main Ideas and Concepts

- **Imperialism** The "new imperialism" took the form of total control over vast territories.

- **Places and Regions** Almost all of Africa came under colonial control.

- **Imperialism** British rule in India created some benefits, including political stability, but had many costs, including the destruction of local industries.

- **Factors of Production** For the benefit of the colonizing nations, raw materials flowed out of the colonies and manufactured goods flowed into them.

People, Places, Terms

The following names and terms will help you to prepare for the Regents Exam in Global History and Geography. You can find an explanation of each name and term in the Glossary at the back of this book, in your textbook, or in another reference source.

annex	indirect rule	sepoy
Creole	mestizo	Social Darwinism
direct rule	peninsulare	Suez Canal
Mohandas Gandhi	pogroms	Zionism
imperialism	protectorate	

SECTION 1 COLONIAL RULE IN SOUTHEAST ASIA

The New Imperialism

In the nineteenth century, European nations began to view Asian and African societies as a source of industrial raw materials and as a market for Western manufactured goods. The products of European factories were sent to Africa and Asia in return for oil, tin, rubber, and other resources needed to fuel European industries.

Beginning in the 1880s, European countries began an intense scramble for overseas territories. **Imperialism**, the extension of a nation's power over other lands, was not new. In the past, Europeans had set up colonies in North and South America and trading posts around Africa and the Indian Ocean.

The new imperialism was different. Now European countries wanted nothing less than total control over vast territories. The reasons for the new imperialism were both economic and political. Economically, the countries wanted raw materials and markets. Politically, they wanted to gain an advantage over their rivals.

Colonies were also a source of prestige; some felt they contributed to a nation's greatness. **Social Darwinism** gave legitimacy to the new imperialism by suggesting that some races were inferior.

CORE CONCEPTS: NATIONALISM

The combination of nationalism and racism was especially apparent in Germany. Some people believed that Germans were the only pure successors of the Aryans, who were portrayed as the original creators of Western culture. The Jews were singled out as their racial enemy.

Social Darwinism and Racism

Scientific theories could be applied for negative purposes. This was the case with Darwin's theories.

A British philosopher named Herbert Spencer and others created a school of thinking called Social Darwinism. It suggested that since the fit, or strong, advanced while the weak declined, then Darwin's theory explained why some people gained success in the world and others did not. The successful person was, they said, fit and energetic; the unsuccessful person, lazy. In extreme circumstances, these ideas were used to defend negative social conditions and racism.

Religious and humanitarian reasons were also given to justify imperialism. Some Europeans thought the whites had a moral responsibility to civilize primitive people, who were the "white man's burden." Some believed they must bring the Christian message to the "heathen masses." Others thought they had to extend the benefits of Western democracy and capitalism.

Anti-Semitism and Zionism

Anti-Semitism, hostility against Jews, was not new. Since the Middle Ages, Jews had been portrayed as murderers of Christ and subjected to mob violence. Their rights had been restricted, and they had been required to live in areas of cities known as ghettos.

In the nineteenth century, Jews had been granted legal equality in many European cities. Many had assimilated into the cultures around them. Anti-Semitism was still a strong force, however.

The worst persecution occurred in Russia. Russian Jews were forced to live in certain regions of the country. Persecutions and **pogroms** (organized massacres) were widespread. This caused hundreds of thousands of Jews to emigrate. Many came to the United States. Others moved to Palestine, which became home for a Jewish national movement called **Zionism.**

Palestine, the land of ancient Israel, had long been the land of dreams for many Jews. They hoped to make it a Jewish state.

The Colonial Takeover of Southeast Asia

By 1900, almost all of Southeast Asia was under Western rule.

Great Britain Great Britain began the process of colonization in Southeast Asia when it founded Singapore on the tip of

Malaysia. It was a major stopping point for traffic going to or from China. Soon the British expanded into Burma (modern Myanmar). This led to the collapse of the Burmese monarchy.

France At first, France had only missionaries in Vietnam. Internal rivalries divided that country into two separate governments in the north and the south. Worried that the British might monopolize trade, France forced its protection on Vietnam in 1857. Over time, the French seized the country and made the Vietnamese Empire a French **protectorate**—a political unit that relies on another government for its protection.

In the 1880s, France extended its control over neighboring Cambodia, Annam, Tonkin, and Laos. By 1887, France included all of its possessions in a new Union of French Indochina. Among Southeast Asian states, only Thailand did not come under colonial rule.

The United States During the Spanish-American War, United States naval forces defeated the Spanish fleet in Manila Bay. President McKinley decided to turn the Philippines into an American colony. The islands were a convenient jumping-off point for American trade with China. American takeover also prevented Japan from gaining control of the islands.

American motives mixed idealism with profits. The Filipinos agreed with neither. Under their guerilla leader and self-proclaimed president Emilio Aguinaldo, they fought bitterly for independence. The United States defeated the guerilla forces and hung on.

Colonial Regimes in Southeast Asia

The goals of the colonial powers were to exploit natural resources and open up markets. They justified their rule by speaking of the blessings of Western civilization that they were bringing to their subjects.

Indirect and Direct Rule Rule of colonies was direct or indirect. **Indirect rule** was achieved through cooperation with local political elites. Local rulers maintained positions of authority, making it easier and cheaper for Western powers to gain access to natural resources. Indirect rule also had less effect on local culture.

Indirect rule was not always possible, however. In some cases, local rulers resisted the colonial powers. Such was the case in Burma. Therefore, Great Britain established **direct rule:** it

CORE CONCEPTS: IMPERIALISM

The following excerpt is from a poem written in 1899 by Rudyard Kipling. It is often quoted on Regents exams.

The White Man's Burden

"Take up the White Man's
     burden—
Send forth the best ye breed—
Go bind your sons to exile
To serve your captives'
     need;
To wait in heavy harness,
On fluttered folk and wild—
Your new-caught sullen
     peoples,
Half-devil and half-child. . . .
Take up the White Man's
     burden—
And reap his old reward:
The blame of those ye better,
The hate of those ye guard—
The cry of hosts ye humour
(Ah, slowly;) toward the light:—
'Why brought he us from
     bondage,
Our loved Egyptian night?' "

REGENTS WARM-UP

As you read this chapter, note how the United States practiced many of the same imperialist policies as European nations.

CORE CONCEPTS: IMPERIALISM

France used both direct and indirect rule to control Vietnam. It imposed direct rule on the south and used indirect rule in the north.

REGENTS WARM-UP

To review, create a cause-and-effect diagram to show some of the effects of colonial rule.

administered the country directly through its own colonial rule in India.

Colonial Economies The colonial powers did not want their colonists to develop their own industries and instead stressed the export of raw materials. Often, this led to the establishment of plantation agriculture, in which peasants worked as wage laborers on plantations owned by foreign investors. Wages were often at poverty level and conditions so unhealthy that many workers died. These workers were also taxed. Colonial economies did bring some benefits, however. Colonial governments built railroads and highways. In some countries, small growers of rubber, palm oil, coffee, tea, and spices were able to benefit from the development of an export market.

Resistance to Colonial Rule

Many colonists resisted colonial rule. At first, resistance came from the ruling classes, but peasants also revolted, often when they were driven off land to make way for plantations. Early resistance movements failed.

A new kind of resistance based on nationalism began to emerge at the beginning of the twentieth century. It was organized by a class that had emerged as a result of colonialism: new urban intellectuals who had been exposed to Western ideals. At first, these leaders sought to defend the economic interests and religious beliefs of the natives. Over time, these resistance movements would begin to demand independence.

SECTION 2 EMPIRE BUILDING IN AFRICA

West Africa

In 1874, Great Britain **annexed,** or incorporated a country within a state, the west coastal states of Africa as the first British Colony of Gold Coast. It also established a protectorate over warring groups in Nigeria. Soon after, France established French West Africa.

Europe's first interest in West Africa had been slavery. When slavery was finally abolished in all major countries by the 1890s, Europe's interest in other forms of trade increased. Europeans sold textiles and other manufactured goods for such West African natural resources as peanuts, timber, hides, and palm oil.

North Africa

When the **Suez Canal,** connecting the Mediterranean and Red Seas, was completed in 1869, Britain grew interested in the canal as a "lifeline to India." In 1875, Britain bought Egypt's share in the canal. It made Egypt a protectorate in 1914. This lasted until 1956.

Central Africa

Explorer David Livingstone and later, journalist Henry Stanley, helped create interest in Central Africa. King Leopold II of Belgium was led to claim vast territories in the Congo. France also occupied some areas north of the Congo River.

THE USES OF GEOGRAPHY

Study the map. Identify the two independent countries in Africa in 1914. Sum up where the British, French, Germans, and Belgians had most of their claims.

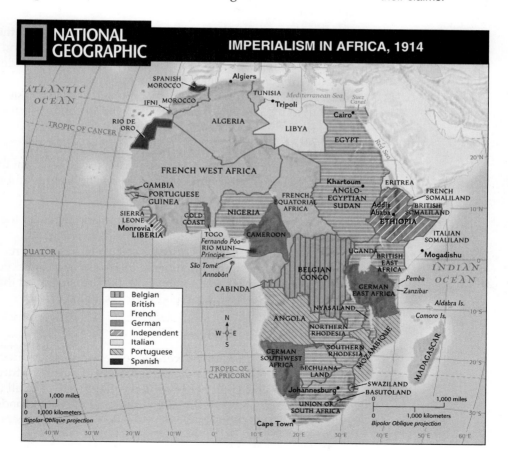

IMPERIALISM IN AFRICA, 1914

East Africa

Germany tried to develop colonies in East Africa. Most of East Africa had not yet been claimed by any other power. However, the British were also interested in the area because control of East Africa would connect the British Empire in Africa from South Africa to Egypt. To settle the conflicting claims, the Berlin Conference met in 1884 and 1885. Both British and German claims to this area were recognized. Portugal received a claim on Mozambique. No Africans were present at the conference.

South Africa

Dutch settlers had occupied Cape Town and surrounding areas in South Africa since the seventeenth century. Their descendants were the Boers, or Afrikaners. During the Napoleonic Wars, the British seized these lands and created the Cape Colony.

The Dutch went north to form the Orange Free State and the Transvaal. There, they put native peoples on reservations and battled the Zulu people. In the early nineteenth century, under the leadership of their ruler Shaka, the Zulu carved out an empire for themselves. They remained powerful after Shaka's death, but in the late 1800s, became involved in conflicts with the British. The British defeated the Zulu.

Rhodesia Cecil Rhodes, who founded diamond and gold companies, gained control of an area north of the Transvaal that he called Rhodesia, after himself. Rhodes had enormous ambition for the British colonization of Africa.

The Boer War Eventually the British fought and defeated the Boers in the Boer War (1899–1902). The British created an independent Union of South Africa, a self-governing nation within the British Empire. To appease the Boers, who believed white superiority was ordained by God, the British agreed that only whites, with a few propertied Africans, could vote.

Colonial Rule in Africa

Most of the British colonies were governed through indirect rule. One benefit of this was the preservation of native culture. African leaders and elites held positions of authority, but all they were expected to do was enforce the rules and decisions made by the British. One problem of indirect rule was that by keeping the old elite in power, class and tribal tensions grew, many of which erupted after independence came during the twentieth century.

Most other European nations governed through a form of direct rule. The French ideal was to assimilate African subjects into French culture rather than preserve native traditions. Africans were, however, eligible to run for office and even serve in the French National Assembly.

Rise of African Nationalism

Through imperialism, Africans were introduced to Western ideas and institutions. Some of these they regarded as positive and worthy of adopting. They saw, however, that while Westerners exalted democracy, equality, and political freedom, they did not apply these values in the colonies. A mixture of factors, including a determination to assert their own nationality and cultural identity, eventually resulted in organized political parties and movements to end foreign rule.

SECTION 3 BRITISH RULE IN INDIA

The Sepoy Mutiny

During the eighteenth century, the British East India Company became actively involved in India's political and military affairs. Its own soldiers, in addition to Indian soldiers known as **sepoys**, helped them protect the company's interests.

In 1857, the sepoys revolted in what Indians call the First War of Independence and what British call the Sepoy Mutiny. Although the British eventually crushed the uprising, it led the British Parliament to transfer the powers of the East India Company directly to the British government. Queen Victoria was called the Empress of India, and India was her "jewel in the crown."

Colonial Rule

Britain ruled India through a viceroy, or governor, and a large civil service staff. It brought some benefits to India, including political stability, a new school system, railroads, the telegraph, and a postal service.

CORE CONCEPTS: CULTURE

During the Sepoy Mutiny, rumors spread that the British had greased rifle cartridges with beef fat (a violation of Hindu beliefs) and pork fat (a violation of Muslim beliefs). As a result both Hindu and Muslim sepoys joined in the rebellion.

Among the many costs of British rule was the destruction of local industries. Policies related to business and taxation brought economic hardship to millions. By discouraging farming, the British helped ensure that food supplies could not keep up with the growing population. Racist attitudes and arrogance degraded and humiliated the Indian people.

An Indian Nationalist Movement

In 1885, reformers established the Indian National Congress (INC). It called for a share in the governing process rather than for immediate independence. The movement lacked unity, however, as its largely Hindu goals did not reflect Muslim concerns. In 1915, **Mohandas Gandhi** became active in the movement that would eventually lead to Indian independence.

SECTION 4 NATION BUILDING IN LATIN AMERICA

Nationalist Revolts

In Latin America, **peninsulares,** Spanish and Portuguese officials who lived temporarily in Latin America for economic or political gain, had all the power. Next in the social order were the **Creoles,** descendants of Europeans who lived permanently in Latin America. Peninsulares regarded the Creoles as second-class citizens, and Creoles deeply resented them. The largest part of the population consisted of **mestizos** (people of European and native descent) and natives, who worked as servants or laborers.

peninsulares
Creoles
mestizos
Indians
slaves

Change and Revolution The Creole elites denounced Spanish and Portuguese rule. When Napoleon's wars weakened these rulers, a series of revolts enabled most of Latin America to become independent.

Haiti In 1804, slaves led by François-Dominique Toussaint-Louverture seized control of all of the island of Hispaniola. The western part, Haiti, announced its freedom and became the first independent state in Latin America.

Mexico Miguel Hidalgo led Indians and mestizos in Mexico to revolt against Spain in 1810. This unsuccessful revolt threatened both the peninsulares and Creoles. Conservative elites then overthrew Spanish rule in 1821. Agustín de Iturbide declared himself emperor in 1822 but was deposed in 1823. Mexico then became a republic.

South America José de San Martín of Argentina liberated Argentina from Spanish authority by 1810. He then went on to liberate Chile. Meanwhile, Simón Bolívar was leading revolts in Venezuela, Colombia, and Ecuador. In Peru, San Martín and Bolívar joined forces to crush the Spanish army. By the end of 1824, all Central and South American states had become independent, including Brazil, which had declared its independence from Portugal in 1822.

Difficulties of Nation Building

The wars for independence resulted in the loss of people, property, and livestock. The new nations went to war to settle border disputes. They did not have the transportation or communication systems to help their nations develop.

In many new states, strong leaders called *caudillos* rose to power. They ruled by military force. Some modernized and built. Others were destructive. In Mexico, Antonio López de Santa Anna created chaos. American settlers in the state of Texas revolted against him. Later, in a war between Mexico and the United States, Mexico lost about half its territory to the United States.

The rule of Benito Juárez followed. He brought liberal reforms including the separation of church and state, education, and land distribution to the poor.

A New Imperialism Soon Great Britain dominated the Latin American economy. Just as before, Latin America exported raw materials and imported finished products, which ensured the ongoing domination of the Latin American economy by foreigners. Latin American countries remained economic colonies of Western nations, even though they were no longer political colonies.

Persistent Inequality Land remained the basis of wealth, and only a few elites owned most of the land. These landed elites ran government, controlled courts, and used a system of inexpensive labor. They made enormous profits while the masses experienced dire poverty.

Political Change in Latin America

After 1870, most Latin American governments wrote constitutions similar to those of the United States and European democracies. They limited voting rights, however.

CORE CONCEPTS: POWER

When European powers favored the use of troops to reestablish Spanish control in Latin America, the U.S. and Britain disagreed. The U.S. president James Monroe issued the Monroe Doctrine, guaranteeing the independence of the new Latin American nations and warning against European intervention in Latin America. Meanwhile, more significantly, Britain possessed the naval power to keep European powers from interfering with its trade in Latin America.

Revolution in Mexico When Porfirio Díaz rose to power, a conservative, centralized government favored large landowners and the Catholic Church. The poor owned almost no land.

Emiliano Zapata led a call for reform. The peasants began to seize the land of wealthy landowners. Mexican general Francisco "Pancho" Villa led a peasant army to many victories against government forces. Between 1910 and 1920, the Mexican revolution caused great damage to Mexico's economy. In 1917, a new constitution set up a government led by a president and established land-reform policies. It helped to put the nation back on track.

Economic Change in Latin America

Export of some basic items, such as wheat and beef from Argentina, coffee from Brazil, and silver from Peru, combined with some industrialization, did bring a new prosperity. Middle sectors of the population grew. In general, this group sought liberal reform but not revolution. Once they had the right to vote, they often sided with the landholding elites.

CHAPTER 23   EAST ASIA UNDER CHALLENGE

Chapter Overview

Pressures from the West and internal problems, such as corruption and a rapidly growing population, combined to undermine the Qing dynasty and eventually cause its collapse. The weakened dynasty underwent civil wars and rebellions, including the Tai Ping Rebellion and the Boxer Rebellion. Sun Yat-sen worked to establish what became the nationalist party, but uprisings led only to further instability. During the same years, the Open Door policy was established and China was flooded with Western ideas.

Under military pressure from Matthew Perry's fleet, Japan established diplomatic ties and trade with the United States. Samurais forced the shogun from power, and the Meiji Restoration began. It initiated a program of democratic change as well as imperialism.

As you read this chapter, ask yourself these questions:
(1) What changes led to the decline of the Qing dynasty?
(2) What reforms did the Qing dynasty attempt?
(3) How did Sun Yat-sen propose to reform China's government?
(4) What effects did Western trade have on the Chinese economy?
(5) What was the new political system in Japan?
(6) How did Western culture influence the Japanese?

Main Ideas and Concepts

- **Power** Pressure from the West helped lead to the decline of the Qing dynasty and increased Western economic involvement in China.

- **Change** The establishment of a nationalist party, as well as Western influences, helped bring political and social change to China.

- **Movement of People and Goods** After Western intervention opened Japan to trade, a modern industrial society developed there.

People, Places, Terms

The following names and terms will help you to prepare for the Regents Exam in Global History and Geography. You can find an explanation of each name and term in the Glossary at the back of this book, in your textbook, or in another reference source.

extraterritoriality	Matthew Perry	Sun Yat-sen
Hong Kong	spheres of influence	Treaty of Nanjing
Open Door policy		

SECTION 1 THE DECLINE OF THE QING DYNASTY

Causes of Decline

The Qing dynasty collapsed for several reasons. One was intense pressure from the modern West. Other reasons included corruption, peasant unrest, and a growing population that faced serious food shortages.

The Opium Wars At first, Europeans were restricted to a small trading outlet at Guangzhou, or Canton. The British did not like this arrangement. They also had an unfavorable trade arrangement with China, from which they imported a great deal of tea and luxury goods. They began illegally importing opium into China.

When Britain refused to halt its activity, the Chinese tried to blockade Guangzhou. The British responded with force, starting the First Opium War (1839–1842).

China lost the First Opium War. The **Treaty of Nanjing** opened five coastal ports to British trade, limited taxes on imported British goods, and paid for the costs of the war. It also gave British the island of **Hong Kong**. After the Second Opium War China was forced to open more ports and offer trading concessions to other Western nations.

The Tai Ping Rebellion

The Tai Ping Rebellion (1850–1864) was a peasant revolt that became a civil war. It appealed to many people because it called for social reforms, including holding lands and farms in common and treating women as the equals of men.

CORE CONCEPTS: INTERDEPENDENCE

Great Britain secured the opium from poppies grown in India—one of the imperialist holdings within the British Empire.

CORE CONCEPTS: IDENTITY

In the ports, British lived in their own areas and did not have to follow Chinese laws, a practice known as **extraterritoriality**.

Determined to destroy the Qing dynasty, the rebels seized
Nanjing and massacred 25,000 men, women, and children.
Europeans eventually came to the aid of the Qing dynasty.

Efforts at Reform

Reform-minded officials called for the adoption of Western
technology. The government tried to modernize China's military
forces and build up industry without touching the basic elements
of Chinese civilization, such as Confucian values and institutions. Railroads, weapons factories, and shipyards were built.

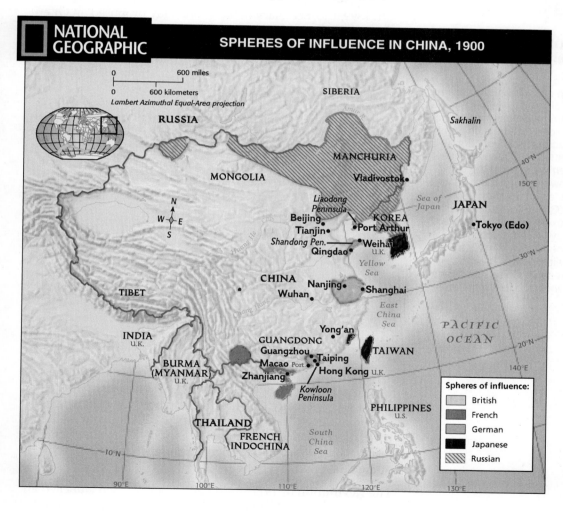

NATIONAL GEOGRAPHIC

SPHERES OF INFLUENCE IN CHINA, 1900

The Advance of Imperialism

Soon European powers began to create **spheres of influence**, areas where the imperial powers had exclusive trading rights. They got them by negotiating directly with local warlords. At the same time, both Russia and Japan took over some Chinese territory, and Tibet separated itself from China. Finally, Empress Ci Xi helped bring about the overthrow of the Qing by her unwillingness to make reforms.

Opening the Door to China

In 1899, U.S. Secretary of State John Hay proposed an **Open Door policy**, in which all nations had equal access to Chinese markets. This reduced imperialist hysteria over access to the China market.

The Boxer Rebellion

The so-called Boxers, members of a secret organization, were upset by the foreign takeover of Chinese lands. They wanted to destroy the foreigners, including the missionaries who seemed to threaten Chinese traditions. When they began to kill missionaries and businessmen, a Western allied army attacked and restored order. The army also demanded more concessions from the Chinese government.

SECTION 2 REVOLUTION IN CHINA

The Fall of the Qing

By the time Empress Ci Xi began to embrace reforms in education, administration, and the legal system, it was too little too late. Resentment grew.

The Rise of Sun Yat-sen Sun Yat-sen (Sun Yixian) believed the Qing dynasty could no longer govern, but he also knew that China was not ready for immediate democracy. He proposed reform in stages. In 1905, he formed the Revolutionary Alliance, which later became the Nationalist Party (or *Guomindang*). It promoted nationalism, democracy, and the people's right to pursue their own livelihoods.

The Revolution of 1911 Followers of Sun Yat-sen launched an uprising in central China in 1911. A member of the old army, General Yuan Shigai, took power. Yuan did not embrace the new

CORE CONCEPTS: IMPERIALISM

The United States feared that the other imperialist powers might partition China in the same way that they had divided up Africa. In 1899, Secretary of State John Hay issued an "Open Door" note demanding that the world powers respect the principle of "equal trading opportunity" in China. In 1900, after the Boxer Rebellion broke out, Hay issued a second "Open Door" note. In this way, the United States tried to preserve Chinese independence and its own interests.

ideas of the reformers. When Yuan dissolved the new parliament, the Nationalists launched a rebellion. The rebellion failed, and Sun Yat-sen fled to Japan.

When Yuan died in 1916, chaos followed. Warlords seized power, and soldiers caused massive destruction.

Chinese Society in Transition

Westerners affected the Chinese economy in three ways: (1) the introduction of modern means of transportation and communication; (2) creation of an export market; and (3) integration of Chinese markets into the nineteenth-century world economy. These changes were beneficial to some. They also had costs as Chinese local industry was largely destroyed. Also, many profits of the new Chinese economy left the country.

China's Changing Culture

The introduction of Western ideas and the growth of a new economy broke down traditional culture, especially in the cities, where Confucian social ideals were declining rapidly. Western books, paintings, music, and ideas were introduced.

SECTION 3 RISE OF MODERN JAPAN

An End to Isolation

The United States was the first foreign power to break through Japanese isolation. In 1853, Commodore **Matthew Perry** arrived with warships and a letter from the president. It urged better treatment of U.S. sailors shipwrecked on Japanese islands (who had been mistreated in the past) and requested the opening of foreign trade relations between the U.S. and Japan. When Perry returned with an even bigger fleet of warships, the Japanese signed the Treaty of Kanagawa, which provided for the opening of two ports to Western traders, the return of shipwrecked American sailors, and the establishment of a U.S. consulate in Japan.

Resistance to the New Order

Many Japanese, and especially the samurai, strongly resisted the opening of relations with Western powers. They restored the authority of the emperor. Shortly after, the shogunate system collapsed. Meiji ("enlightened") rule began.

CORE CONCEPTS: ECONOMIC SYSTEMS

At the beginning of the twentieth century, the pace of change quickened. Chinese investors began to develop new ventures. Major industrial and commercial centers developed. The middle class and an industrial working class grew.

REGENTS WARM-UP

As you read, compare and contrast the Japanese response to contacts with the Western imperialist powers with the Chinese response.

The Meiji Restoration

Meiji reformers set out to create a modern government based on the Western model. The Meiji government spent years studying Western political systems. A group called the Progressives eventually took control of the Meiji government, and the constitution that was adopted in 1889 gave most of the authority to the executive branch. Power remained in the hands of a ruling oligarchy.

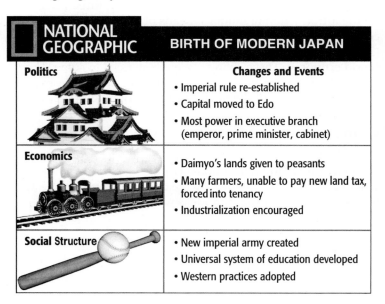

NATIONAL GEOGRAPHIC · BIRTH OF MODERN JAPAN

Politics	Changes and Events
	• Imperial rule re-established • Capital moved to Edo • Most power in executive branch (emperor, prime minister, cabinet)
Economics	• Daimyo's lands given to peasants • Many farmers, unable to pay new land tax, forced into tenancy • Industrialization encouraged
Social Structure	• New imperial army created • Universal system of education developed • Western practices adopted

Joining the Imperialist Nations

The Japanese believed that Western nations had become wealthy not only because of their democratic, economic, and educational systems but also because of their colonies.

Following suit, Japan claimed control of the Ryukyu Islands, which had long been subject to the Chinese Empire. Two years later, Japan forced Korea to open its ports to Japanese trade. The Chinese had long controlled Korea and were concerned with Japan's growing influence there. In 1894, the two nations went to war. The first Sino-Japanese War ended with China ceding (transfering) Taiwan and the Liaodong Peninsula, with its strategic naval base at Port Arthur, to Japan and recognizing the independence of Korea.

Relations between Russia and Japan were also strained because of concerns over influence in Korea. In 1904, Japan launched a surprise attack on a Russian naval base at Port Arthur. (The Russians had taken it from the Chinese.) Japanese forces were victorious on land and in the sea. The Russians agreed to a peace in 1905 and ceded territory to Japan. The Japanese victory stunned the world. Japan had become one of the world's great powers.

During the next few years, Japan consolidated its position in northeastern Asia. In 1910, Japan annexed Korea outright.

PRACTICING FOR THE REGENTS

Part I   Multiple-Choice Questions

The following multiple-choice questions come from past Regents High School Examinations. Test your understanding of global history and geography by answering each of these items. Circle the number of the word or expression that best completes each statement or question. Test-taking tips can be found in the margins for some questions. For additional help, see Taking the Regents Exam on pages ix-xxxv of this Review Book.

Base your answers to questions 1 and 2 on the drawing below and on your knowledge of social studies.

Source: *The Way We Saw It: ...,* Highsmith, Inc., 1998

1   This drawing illustrates conditions that contributed primarily to the beginning of the
    (1) Protestant Reformation
    (2) French Revolution
    (3) Napoleonic Wars
    (4) European Renaissance

2   Which conclusion can be drawn from this drawing?
    (1) One group paid heavy taxes that supported the other two groups.
    (2) Hard work, prayer, and a good example allowed for a stable government in France.
    (3) Peasants and professionals in this society were gaining political and economic power.
    (4) French society emphasized the importance of natural law and social equality.

3   "When the legislative and executive powers are united in the same person, or in the same body of magistrates [government officials], there can be no liberty; because apprehensions [fears] may arise, lest the same monarch or senate should enact tyrannical laws to execute them in a tyrannical manner . . . "
    —*Baron de Montesquieu*, Spirit of the Laws

    Which solution would Baron de Montesquieu offer to avoid the enactment of tyrannical laws?
    (1) granting freedom of speech
    (2) reinstating absolute monarchies
    (3) limiting natural laws
    (4) separating the branches of government

4   "If man in the state of nature is free, if he is absolute lord of his own person and possessions, why will he give up his freedom? Why will he put himself under the control of any person or institution? The obvious answer is that rights in the state of nature are constantly exposed to the attack of others. Since every man is equal and since most men do not concern themselves with equity and justice, the enjoyment of rights in the state of nature is unsafe and insecure. Hence each man joins in society with others to preserve his life, liberty, and property."
    —*John Locke*, Two Treatises of Government, *1690*

    This statement provides support for the
    (1) elimination of laissez-faire capitalism
    (2) formation of government based on a social contract
    (3) continuation of absolute monarchy
    (4) rejection of the natural rights philosophy

5   The main cause of the mass starvation in Ireland during the 19th century was the
    (1) British blockade of Irish ports
    (2) failure of the potato crop
    (3) war between Protestants and Catholics in northern Ireland
    (4) environmental damage caused by coal mining

Base your answers to questions 6 and 7 on the passage below and on your knowledge of social studies.

    "It was a town of red brick, or of brick that would have been red if the smoke and ashes had allowed it; but as matters stood it was a town of unnatural red and black like the painted face of a savage. It was a town of machinery and tall chimneys, out of which interminable serpents of smoke trailed themselves for ever and ever, and never got uncoiled. It had a black canal in it, and a river that ran purple with ill-smelling dye. . . . "
    —*Charles Dickens*, Hard Times

6   The author of this passage is describing conditions caused by the
    (1) Commercial Revolution
    (2) French Revolution
    (3) Industrial Revolution
    (4) Scientific Revolution

7   Which problem is the subject of this passage?
    (1) economic inequality
    (2) urban pollution
    (3) lack of child labor laws
    (4) poor transportation systems

8   Developments in World History
     A   Protestant Reformation
     B   Feudal Period
     C   Industrial Revolution
     D   Neolithic Revolution

     Which set of events is listed in the
     correct chronological order?
     (1) $C \rightarrow A \rightarrow B \rightarrow D$
     (2) $D \rightarrow C \rightarrow B \rightarrow A$
     (3) $B \rightarrow D \rightarrow A \rightarrow C$
     (4) $D \rightarrow B \rightarrow A \rightarrow C$

9   The needs of the Industrial Revolution
     in 19th-century Europe greatly con-
     tributed to the
     (1) growth of overseas empires
     (2) beginning of the triangular trade
     (3) development of international
          peacekeeping organizations
     (4) promotion of political and economic
          equality in Asia and Africa

10   Which statement is supported by the
     ideas of Karl Marx?
     (1) Private ownership of businesses
          helps workers.
     (2) Industrialization benefits the
          wealthy and exploits the poor.
     (3) Countries should benefit from the
          wealth of their colonies.
     (4) Industrial capitalism allows workers
          and employers to work together for
          a common purpose.

Base your answer to question 11 on the
excerpt below and on your knowledge of
social studies.

     Take up the White Man's burden–
     Send forth the best ye breed–
     Go bind your sons to exile
     To serve your captives' need;
     To wait in heavy harness
     On fluttered folk and wild–
     Your new-caught sullen peoples,
     Half-devil and half-child.
     — Rudyard Kipling, 1899

11   The message of this poem was used by
     many Europeans to justify
     (1) industrialism
     (2) feudalism
     (3) imperialism
     (4) fascism

12   Which 19th-century ideology led
     to the unification of Germany and of
     Italy and to the eventual breakup of
     Austria-Hungary and of the Ottoman
     Empire?
     (1) imperialism
     (2) nationalism
     (3) liberalism
     (4) socialism

13   One way in which Simón Bolívar,
     Camillo di Cavour, and Ho Chi Minh
     were similar is that they
     (1) encouraged a spirit of nationalism
          among their people
     (2) enlisted the support of European
          nations to achieve their goals
     (3) opposed territorial expansion of
          their nations
     (4) followed the ideas of Thomas
          Hobbes in establishing systems of
          government

14   Which event was an example of
     Asian reaction to European
     imperialism?
     (1) Boxer Rebellion
     (2) Glorious Revolution
     (3) Boer War
     (4) Congress of Berlin

15   What was one effect of the Russo-
     Japanese War (1904–1905)?
     (1) Japan emerged as a major world
          power.
     (2) Korea gained its independence.
     (3) Czar Nicholas II gained power in
          Russia.
     (4) Russia formed a military alliance
          with Japan.

16 The Meiji Restoration in Japan was prompted in part by
  (1) a fear that Japan would be colonized by Western nations
  (2) the failure of Japanese expansion
  (3) the Shogun's conversion to Christianity
  (4) a desire to stay isolated

17 One similarity in the actions of Simón Bolívar and Napoleon Bonaparte is that both leaders
  (1) encouraged nationalism
  (2) relied on diplomatic negotiations
  (3) established a representative form of government
  (4) rebelled against imperialism

18 The Sepoy Mutiny in India and the Boxer Rebellion in China were similar in that they
  (1) restored power to the hereditary monarchies
  (2) attempted to reject traditional values
  (3) resisted foreign influence
  (4) reestablished the power of religious leaders

REGENTS WARM-UP

Question 18 asks you to draw a cross-regional connection between India and China. If you have trouble answering this question, review information on the events in chapters 22 and 23.

19 One of the most important motives for the European "Scramble for Africa" in the late 1800s was that Africa provided a source of   → beginning of imperialism → gaining resources for industry ↳ build up military
  (1) raw materials used in industry ←
  (2) religious inspiration
  (3) free labor for the Americas
  (4) technologically innovative practices

Base your answers to questions 20 and 21 on the map below and on your knowledge of social studies.

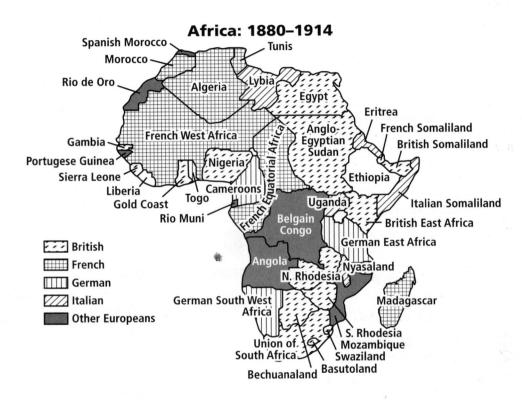

Africa: 1880–1914

Spanish Morocco
Morocco
Rio de Oro
Tunis
Lybia
Algeria
Egypt
Eritrea
French Somaliland
Anglo-Egyptian Sudan
British Somaliland
Gambia
Portugese Guinea
Sierra Leone
French West Africa
Nigeria
French Equatorial Africa
Ethiopia
Liberia
Gold Coast
Togo
Cameroons
Rio Muni
Uganda
Belgain Congo
Italian Somaliland
British East Africa
German East Africa
Angola
Nyasaland
German South West Africa
N. Rhodesia
Madagascar
S. Rhodesia
Union of South Africa
Mozambique
Swaziland
Bechuanaland
Basutoland

British
French
German
Italian
Other Europeans

20 According to the information provided by the map, which European nation controlled the Union of South Africa?
(1) Germany
(2) France
(3) Great Britain
(4) Italy

21 Another title for this map could be
(1) European Imperialism
(2) African Nationalism
(3) The Growth of Islam
(4) Cold War Politics

22 Which social class controlled most of the political, economic, and social power in colonial Latin America?
(1) peninsulares
(2) mestizos
(3) Creoles
(4) native people

23 "Americans today and perhaps to a greater extent than ever before, who live within the Spanish system, occupy a position in society no better than that of serfs destined for labor, or at best they have no more status than that of mere consumers. . . . "

This quotation, written in September 1815, represents the view of
(1) Martin Luther
(2) Simón Bolívar
(3) Catherine the Great
(4) Adam Smith

24 A lasting result of colonial rule in many Latin American nations has been the
(1) elimination of national debts
(2) control of power by wealthy landowners
(3) decrease in the power of the Catholic Church
(4) creation of industrial economics

REGENTS WARM-UP

Question 23 is a data-based question. It evaluates your ability to draw inferences from a quote. You must also draw upon your knowledge of social studies to interpret data in the quote.

Karl Marx

· Communist Manifesto
· 1848
· format socialism
· no classes
· abolish private ownership
· make it happen
· proletariat vs bourgeois
· works only in small communities

Part II   Thematic Essay Question

The following thematic essay question comes from past Regents Examinations. Write your answers on a separate sheet of paper. Essay-writing tips appear in the margin. For additional help, see Taking the Regents Exam on pages ix-xxxv of this Review Book.

Directions: Write a well-organized essay that includes an introduction, several paragraphs addressing the task below, and a conclusion.

Theme: Change Throughout history, political revolutions had many causes. These revolutions affected society and led to many changes. The changes may or may not have resolved the problems that caused the revolutions.

Task:

Choose *one* political revolution from your study of global history and geography and

- Explain the *causes* of the revolution
- Describe the *effects* this political revolution had on society
- Evaluate whether the *changes* that resulted from the political revolution resolved the problems that caused it

You may use any example from your study of global history, but **do *not* use the American Revolution**. Some suggestions you might wish to consider include the French Revolution (1789), Mexican Revolution (1910), Russian Revolution (1917), Chinese Revolution (1949), Cuban Revolution (1959), or Iranian Revolution (1979).

You are *not* limited to these suggestions.

Guidelines:

In your essay, be sure to

- Develop all aspects of the task
- Support the theme with relevant facts, examples, and details
- Use a logical and clear plan of organization, including an introduction and a conclusion that are beyond a restatement of the theme

Part III   Document-Based Question

This exercise is designed to test your ability to work with historical documents. It is similar to the document-based questions you will see on the Regents Examination. While you are asked to analyze three historical documents, the exercise on the actual exam will include more documents. Some of the documents have been edited for the purposes of the question. As you analyze the documents, take into account the source of each document and any point of view that may be presented in the document.

Historical Context:

The late eighteenth and nineteenth centuries were a time of great political, social, and economic change.

Task: Using information from the documents and your knowledge of global history, answer the questions that follow each document in Part A. Your answers to the questions will help you write the Part B essay, in which you will be asked to

- Discuss a way in which *two* nations attempted to bring about economic, political, or social reform during the nineteenth century
- Evaluate the impact of the reform in *each* nation

Part A   Short-Answer Questions

Directions: Analyze the documents and answer the questions that follow each document in the space provided.

Document 1

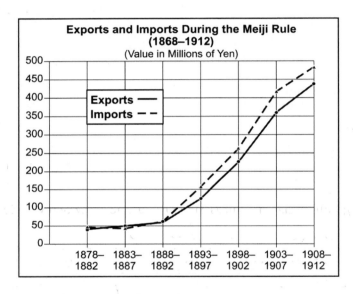

Exports and Imports During the Meiji Rule (1868–1912)
(Value in Millions of Yen)

Handwritten annotation: Value of ↑ imports exports increased

1   According to this graph, what economic change occurred during the Meiji rule?

Handwritten answer: during the meiji rule, they had more exports than imports which means they were making more money (spending more out than taking in) (buying)

Document 2

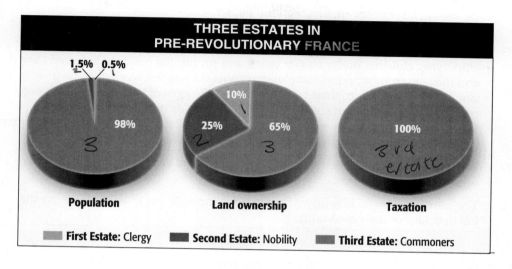

**THREE ESTATES IN
PRE-REVOLUTIONARY FRANCE**

1.5% 0.5%

98%

3

Population

10%

25%   65%

2   3

Land ownership

100%

3rd
estate

Taxation

First Estate: Clergy   **Second Estate:** Nobility   **Third Estate:** Commoners

2   Based on the graphs, what inferences can you draw about why revolution occurred in
    France?

the commoners were the largest group of
people but only owned 65% of the land
and the only taxes were for the
commoners; the ~~clergy~~ nobility was a~~tax~~ small amount
amt., had alot of land, but were not taxed

Document 3

British Factory Legislation

1833   Parliament passed a Factory Act, which forbade nearly all textile mills from employing children under eleven years, and prohibited children between eleven and thirteen from working more than forty-eight hours a week, or nine in a single day. It also prohibited youths between the ages of thirteen and eighteen from working more than sixty-nine hours a week, or twelve in a single day. These work periods were to include an hour and a half for meals. Children under thirteen were required to have two hours of schooling per day.

1847   The Ten Hours Act limited the workday to ten hours for women and children who worked in factories.

1880   The first Employers' Liability Act granted compensation to workers for on-the-job injuries not their own fault.

3   Identify two actions taken by the government to reform economic policy.

The 10 hours act limited the work day to ten hours for women + children in factories; and the first employers' liability act gave compensation to workers who got injured while working.

Part B   Essay

Directions: Write a well-organized essay that includes an introduction, several paragraphs, and a conclusion.

Use evidence from the documents in the body of the essay. Support your response with relevant facts, examples, and details. Include additional outside information.

Historical Context: The late eighteenth and nineteenth centuries were a time of great political, social, and economic change.

Task: Using information from the documents and your knowledge of global history and geography, write an essay in which you

> • Discuss a way in which *two* nations attempted to bring about economic, political, or social reform during the nineteenth century
> • Evaluate the impact of the reform in *each* nation

Guidelines:

In your essay, be sure to

- Develop all aspects of the task
- Incorporate information from *at least two* of the documents in the body of your essay
- Incorporate relevant outside information
- Support the theme with relevant facts, examples, and details
- Use a logical and clear plan of organization, including an introduction and conclusion that are beyond a restatement of the theme

UNIT 6   THE TWENTIETH-CENTURY CRISIS, 1900–1945

Unit 6 Overview

Nationalism, militarism, and a system of alliances led to World War I. A total war followed in which millions died. After the war, inflation and the Great Depression created conditions in which people turned to extremist political parties and dictators. Benito Mussolini took power in Italy and Adolph Hitler ruled Germany. Authoritarian regimes arose in Latin America. Bolsheviks took power in Russia. New nations emerged from the collapse of the Ottoman Empire. Meanwhile, African nations and India began a push for independence. Japan militarized, and Communist ideas spread through Asia. In China, Nationalists and Communists fought each other.

Hitler's many acts of aggression during the 1930s were met by appeasement until the Nazis marched into Poland. Soon the Allied Powers fought the Axis Powers in a war that was waged in Europe, North Africa, and across the Pacific. Millions also died in the Holocaust. Germany's surrender came after defeats in the Soviet Union as well as the D-Day invasion. Japan's surrender followed the dropping of the atomic bomb on Hiroshima and Nagasaki.

Unit 6 Objectives

After studying this unit, students should be able to

1. describe the causes and impact of World War I;

2. trace the growth of Fascist and Communist dictatorships in Italy, Germany, and the Soviet Union;

3. explain the upsurge of nationalism in Asia, Africa, and Latin America;

4. trace the events that led to World War II;

5. describe major events and turning points of World War II;

6. describe events that took place during the Holocaust;

7. describe the impact of World War II on civilians.

PREPARING FOR THE REGENTS

This entire book is set up to help you grasp the facts, main ideas, and concepts needed to do well on your Regents Exam. Notes in the margin include core concepts, test-taking tips, and more. Use blank spaces in the margins to answer questions raised in the text or to jot down key points. Before each unit of study, skim through the exams at the back of the book to develop a sense of what your state wants you to know about your world.

CHAPTER 24   WAR AND REVOLUTION

Chapter Overview

Growing nationalism and militarism, along with a system of alliances, helped lead to World War I. When the archduke of Austria-Hungary was assassinated, countries quickly lined up to fight. All expected a fast war, but trench warfare on the Western Front turned the fight into a war of attrition. The war was also a total war in which citizens became involved and in which governments gained increasing control over their citizens. Enormous losses of men and property led to the desire for harsh terms of peace, which included Germany's loss of its military, reparations, and acceptance of blame for the war.

Enormous war losses for Russia increased the political unrest that eventually led to Russia's withdrawal from the war and its own civil war. The monarchy was toppled by a provisional government, which was in turn toppled by the Bolsheviks. In the ensuing civil war, the victory of the Bolsheviks (Red forces) over their adversaries (White forces) led to a Communist regime.

As you read this chapter, ask yourself these questions:
(1) What were the Triple Alliance and the Triple Entente?
(2) What were the causes of World War I?
(3) Why was there a stalemate on the Western Front, and what happened on the Eastern Front?
(4) What innovations changed warfare at this time?
(5) What is "total war"?
(6) What events led to the fall of czarist Russia and the rise of the Communists?
(7) Why did the Allies win World War I?
(8) What were the major provisions of the Treaty of Versailles?

Main Ideas and Concepts

- **Nationalism** Militarism, nationalism, and alliances were all underlying causes of World War I.

- **Science and Technology** New kinds of warfare, including the use of trenches, proved deadly and lengthened the war.

- **Change** In a weakened Russia, the czarist regime fell, the Bolsheviks grabbed power, and civil war followed.

- **Nation-States** Peace settlements embittered the German people and redrew the map of Eastern Europe, creating fresh territorial tensions.

People, Places, Terms

The following names and terms will help you to prepare for the Regents Exam in Global History and Geography. You can find an explanation of each name and term in the Glossary at the back of this book, in your textbook, or in another reference source.

armistice	**propaganda**	**Triple Alliance**
Bolsheviks	**reparations**	**Triple Entente**
V. I. Lenin	**total war**	**Woodrow Wilson**
mobilization	**Treaty of Brest-Litovsk**	
planned economies	**trench warfare**	

SECTION 1 THE ROAD TO WORLD WAR I

The United States

Between 1870 and 1914, the United States became an industrial power with a foreign empire.

Expansion Beginning in the middle of the nineteenth century, the United States began to expand. It bought Alaska from Russia. It gained the Samoan islands and later Hawaii. After defeating Spain in the Spanish-American War, it acquired Puerto Rico, Guam, and the Philippines.

Nationalism and the System of Alliances

The system of nation-states that emerged in Europe during the last half of the nineteenth century led to competition. Rivalries over colonies and trade grew during an age of frenzied nationalism and imperialist expansion. At the same time, Europe's great powers had been divided into two loose alliances. Germany, Austria-Hungary, and Italy formed the **Triple Alliance** in 1882. Great Britain, France, and Russia formed the **Triple Entente** in 1907.

REGENTS WARM-UP

As you read, make a list of the factors that led to World War I.

NATIONAL GEOGRAPHIC   **ALLIANCES IN EUROPE, 1914**

Triple Alliance
Triple Entente
Balkans

In the early years of the twentieth century, a series of crises tested these alliances and intensified rivalries. At the same time, forces of division existed in those who yearned for nation-states but had not yet achieved them, such as Slavic minorities in the Balkans.

Internal Dissent

Labor strife and class division led to socialist labor movements and strikes. Some conservative leaders who were alarmed by these movements were willing to avert what they saw as possible revolution through the use of military might.

Militarism

European armies doubled in size between 1890 and 1914. In part, this was due to conscription, or a military draft, which had been established in most Western countries (although not Britain

CORE CONCEPTS: THE USES OF GEOGRAPHY

Study the map. What geographic factors would make it more difficult for Germany to overrun Britain than to overrun any other European country?

and the United States) before 1914. Militarism—the aggressive preparation for war—was also growing. Military leaders became more and more powerful.

The Serbian Problem In 1914, Serbia, supported by Russia, was determined to create a large, independent Slavic state in the Balkans. Austria-Hungary was equally determined to prevent this from happening.

Assassination in Sarajevo The spark that finally led to the outbreak of war came on June 28, 1914. Archduke Francis Ferdinand, the heir to the throne of Austria-Hungary, was assassinated by a Bosnian Serb while visiting the Bosnian city of Sarajevo. Austria-Hungary declared war on Serbia, and the system of alliances in place created a domino effect of nations declaring war on other nations.

Russia Mobilizes The czar of Russia was determined to support Serbia because of Slavic identity. He ordered partial mobilization of Russia's army against Austria-Hungary. **Mobilization** is the process of assembling troops and supplies and making them ready for war. In 1914, mobilization was considered an act of war. Germany warned Russia to stop mobilization within 12 hours. When Russia ignored the warning, Germany declared war.

Germany declared war on France and demanded to pass through Belgium, a neutral country, as it put its war plans into action.

Britain then declared war on Germany, stating its reason as the violation of Belgian neutrality. Nevertheless, Britain had its own interests, as well as its alliance with France and Russia, to protect. By August 4, 1914, all the great powers of Europe were at war.

SECTION 2 THE WAR

1914 to 1915: Illusions and Stalemate

Illusions helped lead to World War I. In part, they were formed by a genuine belief of so many people that their own nation's cause was just. Some of these feelings had been created through **propaganda**—ideas spread in order to influence public opinion. Furthermore, almost everyone believed in August 1914 that the coming war would be brief. Soldiers and public alike expected an end by Christmas.

The Western Front The Germans moved quickly into France but were stopped at Marne. There, a new kind of fighting called **trench warfare** began. It involved both sides digging systems of trenches for shelter and defense. Soon, two lines of trenches stretched from the English Channel to the frontiers of Switzerland. These trenches kept both sides in almost the same geographic position for four years.

The Eastern Front On the Eastern Front, the war began in Germany, where the Germans won battles against the Russians. The Austrians, however, suffered some defeats by the Russians. To make matters worse, the Italians betrayed their allies in the Triple Alliance by attacking Austria in 1915. Italy joined France, Britain, and Russia in what had been called the Triple Entente, but was now called the Allied Powers, or Allies.

Soon, however, Germany and Austria combined forces to push Russia and Serbia out of the war. They also gained a new ally in Bulgaria.

1916 to 1917: The Great Slaughter

The development of trench warfare challenged military leaders, who were used to movement on open fields. At times, they ordered artillery offensives meant to weaken the other side and allow for an open assault. When soldiers tried to cross to enemy trenches, however, they stood little chance of success thanks to machine guns. Millions of young men died attempting these crossovers. This turned World War I into a war of attrition, a war based on wearing the other side down by constant attack and heavy losses.

The War in the Air During World War I, airplanes appeared in battle for the first time. At first, planes were used to spot an enemy's position, but soon they were also used to bomb targets on the ground. Then fights with handheld pistols and, later, machine guns occurred in the air. The use of poison gas, or "mustard gas" caused horrible new injuries and suffering. Tanks, which were used for the first time in World War I, helped to break the stalemate of trench warfare.

Widening of the War

The Ottoman Empire had entered the war on the side of Germany in 1914. In 1915, the Allies landed at Gallipoli in the Ottoman Empire, south of Constantinople. There, Germany, Austria-Hungary, and Bulgaria, called the Central Powers, forced the Allies to withdraw.

CORE CONCEPTS: HUMAN SYSTEMS

The lines of trenches for both sides were protected by barbed wire entanglements up to 5 feet high and 30 yards wide, concrete machine-gun nests, and other gun batteries, supported farther back by heavy artillery. Troops lived in holes in the ground, separated from each other by a strip of territory known as no-man's-land.

CORE CONCEPTS: SCIENCE AND TECHNOLOGY

The Germans also used giant airships called zeppelins to bomb London and eastern England. These airships caused little damage but great fear. They were, however, very dangerous when hit by antiaircraft guns, because they exploded into infernos.

Entry of the United States

The United States tried to remain neutral during the war, but the use of unrestricted submarine warfare by the Germans eventually led the nation into the conflict. American passions were aroused when the Germans sunk the passenger ship *Lusitania* in 1915. There were about 1,100 civilians on this British ship, including more than 100 Americans. For a while, the Germans stopped using unrestricted submarine warfare. When they resumed in 1917, however, the United States entered the conflict.

United States troops did not reach Europe in large numbers until 1918. Still, the entry of the United States into the war gave the Allies a great psychological boost. The United States also brought a major new source of money and war goods.

The Home Front: The Impact of Total War

As World War I dragged on, it became a **total war**, involving a complete mobilization of resources and people. It affected the lives of all citizens in the warring countries. The home front rapidly became a cause for as much effort as the war front.

Increased Government Powers When the war stretched on longer than anyone had anticipated, governments expanded their powers to meet the needs for more men and supplies. Countries drafted tens of millions of men. Governments also set up **planned economies**, which created price, wage, and rent controls; rationed foods supplies and materials; and regulated imports and exports.

Manipulation of Public Opinion The length of the war and the enormous casualties also caused public support to wane. War governments, however, fought back against growing opposition to the war. Authoritarian regimes, such as those of Germany, Russia, and Austria-Hungary, relied on force to subdue their populations. Democratic states also expanded police powers to stop internal dissent. The British government passed an act that allowed the government to arrest protestors as traitors. Newspapers were censored.

Governments also made use of propaganda. The British and French exaggerated German atrocities in Belgium. Ad campaigns were often aimed at motivating youth. Popular songs and literature aimed to boost morale.

Total War and Women World War I created new roles for women by opening up jobs that had not been available to them before. With so many men at war, women took jobs as truck drivers, farm laborers, and factory workers. Nevertheless, as soon as men returned home after the war, women were quickly unemployed or saw their pay reduced. Still, the role played by women in World War I gave a boost to the women's movement. British women gained the right to vote in 1918; Germany, Austria, and the United States gave women the right to vote shortly after World War I. Through their roles in the workplace, women had also gained a greater sense of independence.

REGENTS WARM-UP

Sum up some of the effects of World War I on those who remained at home.

SECTION 3 THE RUSSIAN REVOLUTION

Background to Revolution

Czar Nicholas II took control of Russia in 1894. He faced much internal dissent, and Russia's defeat in the Russo-Japanese War made him even more vulnerable.

Several groups, including peasants and the intellectual elite, came together to protest. On January 22, 1905, a protest march in St. Petersburg ended with more than 1,000 people dead or injured after they were attacked by the military. By the end of the year, Nicholas had signed documents creating a state assembly (the Duma), granting basic civil rights, and allowing the formation of political parties.

Russia was not prepared militarily or technologically for World War I. It did not have good military leaders, and its troops did not have basic supplies. It suffered enormous losses.

Beginnings of Upheaval Military and economic problems caused the Russian people to become more and more upset with their czarist regime.

The March Revolution Economic problems led to a series of strikes led by working-class women in 1917. The price of bread skyrocketed, and the government began bread rationing in Petrograd. On March 8, 10,000 women marched through the streets demanding "Peace and Bread." On March 10, they called for a general strike, which shut down all the factories. In response, Nicholas ordered troops to break up the crowd by shooting them if necessary. Soon, however, soldiers joined the demonstrators. The czar's orders could not be carried out.

On March 12, the Duma established a provisional government. Nicholas stepped down on March 15, ending the 300-year-old Romanov dynasty. Alexander Kerensky, head of the provisional government, decided to remain in World War I, an error that alienated him from the people.

The provisional government was then undermined by the soviets. These were councils that represented workers and soldiers. They had sprung up not only in Petrograd (still called St. Petersburg in 1917), but in army units, factory towns, and rural areas. They were made up largely of socialists.

The Rise of Lenin

Vladimir Ilyich Ulianov, who became known to the world as **V. I. Lenin**, believed that the provisional government should be overthrown and that the soviets should take power. Lenin was the leader of the **Bolsheviks**, a small faction of the Marxist party called the Russian Social Democrats. The Bolsheviks became dedicated to a violent revolution that would destroy the capitalist system.

The Bolsheviks reflected the discontent of the Russian people. They promised an end to the war, the redistribution of all land to the peasants, the transfer of factories and industries from capitalists to committees of workers, and the transfer of government power from the provisional government to the soviets. Lenin's slogan was "Peace, Land, and Bread."

The Bolsheviks Seize Power

On November 6, Bolshevik forces seized control of the provisional government. After the government fell, Lenin passed power to the Congress of Soviets. The real power, however, was in the hands of the Council of People's Commissars, headed by Lenin.

The Bolsheviks soon renamed themselves the Communists. One of Lenin's first acts was to sign the **Treaty of Brest-Litovsk** (1918), ending Russian participation in the war and giving up huge tracts of land to Germany. Peace did not come to Russia, however, because the country was soon engaged in civil war.

Civil War in Russia

The new Communist, or Bolshevik, regime had many enemies, both within and outside Russia. The Allies sent help to anti-Communist forces, but these forces were ultimately repelled. Over time, the Communist regime also regained control over the independent nationalist governments in Georgia, Russian Armenia, and Azerbaijan.

Triumph of the Communists

By 1921, the Communists were in total command of Russia. How had they triumphed? One reason was that their opposition

CORE CONCEPTS: POLITICAL SYSTEMS

Lenin's adaptation of Marxism became known as "Leninism." This system of thought introduced the idea of dictatorship by the Communist party. Lenin argued that a band of seasoned revolutionaries needed to rule until the peasants were ready to take over the reins of government. That time never came.

CORE CONCEPTS: POWER

The royal family had been taken into captivity after the czar stepped down. The czar and his family were assassinated in 1918 by members of a local soviet.

was fragmented. Those who wanted to restore the monarchy did not wish to join forces with liberals or others with political differences.

The Communists were also able to translate their revolutionary faith into practical instruments of power. They used a policy of war communism to get supplies for the Red Army. They controlled the banks and most industries. They seized grain from peasants and centralized the power of the state under their own control.

By 1921, Russia had become a single state dominated by a single party. The state was hostile to the Allied powers that had opposed it.

REGENTS WARM-UP

Compare the causes of the French Revolution to the causes of the Russian Revolution of 1917.

SECTION 4 END OF THE WAR

The Last Year of the War

When the Russians withdrew from World War I, the Germans gained new hope for success. With victory on the Eastern Front, they decided to launch a grand offensive on the Western Front. By April 1918, however, the German offensive was ended. Allies then began a steady advance toward Germany.

In September 1918, the German government was informed by the military that the war was lost. However, the Allies were unwilling to make peace with the autocratic government. Although reform efforts were begun, it was too late. German citizens rose up in protest, and in November, William II left the country. On November 11, 1918, the new government signed an **armistice**, an agreement to end the fighting.

The Peace Settlements

When European nations had gone to war in 1914, it had largely been for territorial gains. When the representatives of the 27 victorious Allied nations met for the final settlement of the war, they expressed new reasons for having fought World War I.

Wilson's Proposals United States President **Woodrow Wilson** portrayed World War I as a people's war against "absolutism and militarism." He thought these enemies of liberty could be eliminated if a general association of nations, which Wilson called a League of Nations, worked together against them. This proposal was one of Wilson's "Fourteen Points" for a just and lasting peace.

The Paris Peace Conference When the peace conference was held in 1919, however, it was clear that nations brought various other aims to the table. British prime minister David Lloyd George was determined that the Germans should pay for the war. French premier Georges Clemenceau also wanted Germany to pay **reparations** to cover the costs of war. The French also wanted Germany to be stripped of all its weapons and to create a separate Rhineland state as a buffer between France and Germany.

The Treaty of Versailles The final peace settlement took the form of five different treaties with the defeated nations. The Treaty of Versailles with Germany was by far the most important.

NATIONAL GEOGRAPHIC

EUROPE, 1923

The treaty ordered Germany to pay reparations for all the damages to the Allied Powers. It required Germany to reduce its army and navy and eliminate its air force. Germany had to give Alsace and Lorraine, which it had taken in 1871, back to France. Sections of Germany were given over to a new Polish state. Land along the Rhine River was turned into a demilitarized zone. There was also a War Guilt Clause, which greatly angered the German people. It said Germany and Austria were responsible for starting the war. Germany complained, but it had little choice but to accept the treaty.

A New Map of Europe World War I resulted in a redrawing of the map of Eastern Europe. Both the Germans and Russians lost a great deal of territory. The war also led to the breakup of the Austro-Hungarian Empire. It was replaced by the independent republics of Austria, Hungary, and Czechoslovakia, along with the large state called Yugoslavia. Almost every eastern European state was left with ethnic minorities: Germans in Poland; Hungarians, Poles, and Germans in Czechoslovakia; Hungarians in Romania; and Serbs, Croats, Slovenes, Macedonians, and Albanians in Yugoslavia. Rivalries among these nations would weaken Europe for the next 80 years.

The breakup of the Ottoman Empire also resulted in the creation of new states, which the Allies had promised to recognize. Once the war ended, however, the Western nations changed their minds. France took control of Lebanon and Syria, and Britain received Iraq and Palestine: acquisitions that were officially called mandates.

The War's Legacy Almost 10 million people died in the war. There was enormous destruction. Faith in a rational world and in progress was undermined.

Because World War I was a total war, it increased the powers of government over its citizens. The war made strong central authority a way of life.

The breakup of old empires and the creation of new states also led to new problems. Greater insecurity reigned. The hope that Europe and the rest of the world would return to normalcy was soon dashed.

REGENTS WARM-UP

Regents questions often probe cause-effect relationships. What effect did World War I have on political boundaries in Eastern Europe and elsewhere?

Section 1	The Futile Search for Stability
Section 2	The Rise of Dictatorial Regimes
Section 3	Hitler and Nazi Germany
Section 4	Cultural and Intellectual Trends

Chapter Overview

REGENTS WARM-UP

Past Regents Exams have asked students to explain cause-and-effect relationships between economic and social conditions and political events. As you read, note the relationship between economic factors, such as inflation and the Great Depression, and political events.

Peace and prosperity were short-lived after World War I. Although industries and the middle class grew in Western Europe and the United States during the 1920s, the Great Depression created mass suffering. In Europe, dictatorships arose, which took the form of both authoritarian regimes, such as Franco's government in Spain, and totalitarian regimes, such as Benito Mussolini's Fascist Italy and Hitler's Nazi Germany. In the Soviet Union, Stalin took control after the death of Lenin, collectivizing farms, initiating programs of heavy industrialization, and dealing ruthlessly with political opponents. Meanwhile, advances in mass communications, such as the discovery of radio waves and the development of motion pictures, helped advance both mass communication and propaganda.

As you read this chapter, ask yourself these questions:
(1) What were the weaknesses of the League of Nations?
(2) What factors led to the Great Depression?
(3) How did Great Britain, France, Germany, and the United States respond to economic hardship?
(4) How are a dictatorship and a totalitarian government different?
(5) How did Mussolini, Stalin, Franco, and Hitler rise to power?
(6) What were Hitler's anti-Semitic policies and activities?
(7) What were the major developments in literature and science during this time period?

Main Ideas and Concepts

- **Economic Systems** A global depression weakened Western economies and helped create political instability and change.

- **Power** Mussolini created a modern totalitarian state in Italy, while Stalin collectivized farms, instituted programs of industrialization, and eliminated threats to his regime.

- **Nationalism** Hitler and the Nazi party took over the German government to create a new totalitarian state based on principles of national superiority, anti-Semitism, and militarism.

- **Science and Technology** Radio and motion pictures were used to spread political messages.

- **Culture** Works of art and literature reflected the uncertainties and despair of the times.

People, Places, Terms

The following names and terms will help you to prepare for the Regents Exam in Global History and Geography. You can find an explanation of each name and term in the Glossary at the back of this book, in your textbook, or in another reference source.

collectivization
concentration camp
Dawes Plan
depression
fascism
Adolf Hitler

Benito Mussolini
New Economic Policy
Franklin Delano Roosevelt
Joseph Stalin
totalitarian state

SECTION 1 THE FUTILE SEARCH FOR STABILITY

Uneasy Peace, Uncertain Security

The end of World War I created an uneasy peace. Germans resented the Treaty of Versailles, while other nations resented new boundaries. Also, the United States never ratified the Treaty of Versailles. Among other things, this meant that the United States did not join the League of Nations, thereby weakening the organization.

French Demands Tensions quickly arose again between France and Germany. France became outraged by Germany's failure to pay war reparations and sent troops to occupy the Ruhr Valley, Germany's chief industrial and mining center. France was determined to collect its own reparations by operating and using the Ruhr mines and factories.

CORE CONCEPTS: ECONOMIC SYSTEMS

In 1914, 4.2 German marks equaled 1 U.S. dollar. By November 1, 1923, it took 130 billion marks to equal 1 U.S. dollar. By the end of November, it took 4.2 trillion marks.

Inflation in Germany The German government adopted a policy of passive resistance to French occupation. The workers went on strike, and the government paid them by printing more paper money. This added to the inflation (rise in prices) that had already begun in Germany at the end of the war. Soon there was runaway inflation in Germany. As money became worthless, both France and Germany sought a way out of the disaster.

In 1924, an international commission produced the **Dawes Plan**. It coordinated Germany's annual payments with its ability to pay. It also granted a huge loan for German recovery. This resulted in a brief period of European prosperity.

The Treaty of Locarno In 1925, France and Germany signed the Treaty of Locarno, which guaranteed Germany's new western borders with France and Belgium. Then Germany joined the League of Nations in March 1926. Nations did not cut back on their weapons, however.

The Great Depression

The brief period of economic prosperity soon collapsed, followed by the Great Depression. A **depression** is a period of low economic activity and rising unemployment.

Causes of the Depression In the United States, people were investing in the stock market and "buying on the margins." This practice allowed people to buy stocks for a fraction of their actual worth and sell the stock when the price increased. This system worked as long as the stock price went up, but in 1928, United States investors began pulling money out of the stock market, and in 1929, the market crashed.

In the mid-1920s, many nations were already experiencing downturns in their economies. American investors pulled money out of Germany and other European funds. This weakened European banks and even caused collapse.

Responses to the Depression By 1932, approximately one in every four British workers was out of work. In Germany, the unemployment rate was about 40 percent. The unemployed and homeless filled the streets.

Governments did not know how to deal with the crisis. They tried traditional solutions such as lowering costs by lowering wages and raising tariffs. These measures only made the economic crisis worse.

The Depression had several serious effects. One was the direct participation of the government in the economy. Another was a suspicion of capitalism, which seemed to have self-destructed, just as Marx had predicted. Communism became more popular both among workers and among intellectuals. Finally, people began to turn to leaders who offered simple solutions.

Democratic States after the War

In the 1920s, Europe seemed to be returning to the political trends of the prewar era—parliamentary regimes and the growth of civil liberties. This was not an easy process, however, after four years of total war and in the midst of postwar turmoil.

Germany Imperial Germany came to an end when Germany was defeated in 1918. The new German state, the Weimar Republic, was born. The republic faced problems from the outset, including weak leadership, inflation and high unemployment. As the middle class floundered economically, political parties that were hostile to the republic flourished.

France Political chaos followed the Great Depression. By 1936, a coalition of leftist parties—Communists, Socialists, and Radicals—formed the Popular Front. It started a program for workers that has been called the French New Deal, but failed to solve the problems of the depression.

Great Britain In 1931, a new Conservative government took credit for leading Britain out of the worst stages of the Depression using traditional policies of balanced budgets and protective tariffs.

The United States After Germany, no Western nation was more affected by the Great Depression than the United States. President **Franklin Delano Roosevelt** began a policy of active government intervention known as the New Deal. It included an increased program of public works, as well as social legislation that began the U.S. welfare system. This social revolution may have saved the country from political revolution. It did not, however, solve the problem of unemployment. Only World War II and the growth of the weapons industries brought the country back to full employment.

SECTION 2 THE RISE OF DICTATORIAL REGIMES

CORE CONCEPTS: POWER

The totalitarian states that emerged had a single leader and a single political party. Individual freedoms were subordinated to the collective will of the masses, but that collective will was organized and determined by one leader and one party.

The Rise of Dictators

By 1939, only two major European states—Great Britain and France—remained democratic. Italy, the Soviet Union, Germany, and many other states had dictatorial regimes.

A new form of dictatorship arose, the totalitarian state. A **totalitarian state** is a government that aims to control the political, economic, social, intellectual, and cultural lives of its citizens.

Totalitarian states wanted more than obedience; they wanted utter control of the people's minds and hearts. Technology helped them achieve the spread of their propaganda.

Fascism in Italy

In the early 1920s, **Benito Mussolini** established the first European fascist state in Italy. **Fascism** is a political philosophy that glorifies the state above the individual by emphasizing the need for a strong central government led by a dictatorial ruler. In a fascist government, all opposition is repressed.

Rise of Fascism After World War I, Italy experienced the hardships of the depression. Inflation grew, and socialists talked about revolution. The middle class feared the kind of communist takeover that had occurred in Russia.

In 1920 and 1921, Mussolini formed bands of armed Fascists called Blackshirts. They used force to disrupt strikes. They also attacked socialist offices and newspapers. Large landowners and industrialists who feared middle-class strikes began to support the Blackshirts.

In 1922, Mussolini and the Fascists threatened to march on Rome if they were not given power. King Victor Emmanuel III made Mussolini prime minister. Mussolini used his position to create a Fascist dictatorship. Mussolini could now make laws by decree, and the police could arrest and jail anyone for political or nonpolitical crimes. By 1926, Mussolini had outlawed all other political parties. He ruled Italy as *Il Duce*, "The Leader."

The Fascist State Both propaganda and organizations were used to promote the ideals of fascism and control the population.

Fascist youth groups included 66 percent of the population between the ages of 8 and 18

Although the Fascists spoke of creating a nation of fit, disciplined, and war-loving people, traditional society stayed in place. Women were to be homemakers and mothers. Victor Emmanuel continued to be king. Catholicism also stayed central to people's lives.

A New Era in the Soviet Union

Drought and a great famine between 1920 and 1922 led to an industrial collapse in Russia and great suffering. In response, the peasants began to sabotage the communist program by hoarding food. They also grew to distrust Lenin.

Lenin's New Economic Policy In response, Lenin established a **New Economic Policy** (NEP) that was a modified version of the old capitalist system. Peasants could sell their own produce, and small businesses could be privately owned and operated. Heavy industry, banking, and mines, however, remained under state control. By 1922, a good harvest brought an end to famine. Together with the NEP, it put the government back on track.

The Rise of Stalin The Politburo had become the leading policy-making body of the Communist Party. When Lenin died in 1924, its seven members argued over the future direction of the Soviet Union. An intense rivalry arose between two Politburo members: Leon Trotsky and **Joseph Stalin**. Because Stalin was general secretary of the party, he was able to gain control. Soon, he eliminated the Bolsheviks of the revolutionary era from the Politburo.

Five-Year Plans In many ways, the Stalinist Era was a period of more sweeping change than the revolutions of 1917. One dramatic shift was economic. Stalin established his Five-Year Plans, which set economic goals for five-year periods. Their purpose was to transform the country almost overnight from an agricultural to an industrial economy.

The shift to industrialization had great costs for the people. There was a rapid movement to the cities, where housing was inadequate. Consumer goods, such as food, clothing, and shoes, were sacrificed in order to concentrate on heavy industry. Real wages also declined significantly. To keep workers content, government propaganda stressed the need for sacrifice to create the new socialist state.

CORE CONCEPTS: NATION-STATE

In 1922, Lenin and the Communists formally created a new state called the Union of Soviet Socialist Republics, which is also known as the USSR (by its initials) and the Soviet Union (as a shortened form).

CORE CONCEPTS: ECONOMIC SYSTEMS

The new production emphasis of the Stalinist Era was on capital goods: heavy machines that could produce other goods, such as tractors, trucks, and armaments. The production of heavy machinery and steel increased dramatically between 1928 and 1937, the period of the first two five-year plans.

At this time, private farms were also eliminated in a process called **collectivization**. Now the government owned all the land, and the peasants worked it.

Costs of Stalin's Programs Peasants resisted collectivization, often by hoarding food and slaughtering livestock. Widespread famine killed millions in 1932 and 1933. Ukraine was hit particularly hard by a famine that was forced by Stalin's policies. In 1932, in an attempt to force farmers to collectivize, Stalin ordered a grain quota that was impossible for farmers to meet, leaving them no grain to feed themselves. Soldiers were sent in to assure that no one was hoarding grain. About a million people starved to death over a two-year period.

Authoritarian States in the West

Some states were not totalitarian but authoritarian. Their goal was to preserve the existing social order rather than to create a mass society. They used only some of the methods of the totalitarian state, such as police powers.

Spain In 1936 in Spain, General Francisco Franco led military forces to revolt against the democratic government. A civil war began. The Fascist regimes of Italy and Germany aided Franco's forces. The capture of Madrid by Franco's forces in 1939 brought the war to an end.

SECTION 3 HITLER AND NAZI GERMANY

Hitler and His Views

Adolf Hitler was born in Austria, where he developed the views he held for the rest of his life. Chief among them were racism, especially anti-Semitism, and nationalism.

By 1921, Hitler took control of the German Workers' Party, a small, right-wing extremist party, which became the National Socialist German Worker's party (NSDAP), or Nazi for short.

Overconfident in his power, Hitler staged an uprising against the government in 1923. This landed him in jail, where he wrote *Mein Kampf*, or *My Struggle*, an account of his movement and its basic ideas.

CORE CONCEPTS: POWER

Stalin was also ruthless about dissent. He instituted a policy of Russification to "assimilate" ethnic minorities within Russia. Only the Russian language was allowed to be spoken and Russian history and culture were promoted. Ethnic minorities were often denied basic human rights. Those who resisted his ideas were sent to forced labor camps in Siberia, where they were executed or from which they never returned. Stalin's regime also overturned much of the progressive social legislation enacted in the early 1920s.

CORE CONCEPTS: IDENTITY

Mein Kampf links extreme German nationalism, anti-Semitism, and anti-communism. It uses Social Darwinism to suggest a struggle of the fittest. It upholds the right of superior nations and superior individuals to gain leadership over others.

Rise of Nazism

Hitler expanded the Nazi party to all parts of Germany. By 1932, it had become the largest party in the Reichstag, the German parliament. In 1933, the president allowed Hitler to become chancellor and create a new government. His power became complete with the Enabling Act, which allowed government to ignore the constitution while it issued laws to deal with the country's problems.

Victory of Nazism

The Nazis moved quickly to bring all institutions under their control. Jews and democratic elements were purged from the civil service. Large prison camps called **concentration camps** were set up for those who opposed the regime.

The Nazi State, 1933–1939

Hitler's broadest goal was the development of an Aryan racial state that would dominate Europe and even the world for generations to come. Hitler believed the Germans were the true descendants and leaders of the Aryans and would rule the world as the Romans had. He believed there had already been two German empires or Reichs: the Holy Roman Empire and the German Empire of 1871 to 1918. Hitler's goal was to create a Third Reich, the empire of Nazi Germany.

The State of Terror Nazi Germany used terror freely. The *Schutzstaffeln*, known simply as the SS, was originally created as Hitler's personal bodyguard. Secret police, criminal police, concentration camps, and later, execution squads and death camps were all used to meet the goal of establishing an Aryan master race.

Economic Policies Hitler put people back to work on public works projects and in private industry. A massive rearmament program was, however, the key to solving the unemployment problem. The renewed economy that resulted helped create public support for Hitler.

Spectacles and Organizations Mass demonstrations and spectacles were used to create enthusiasm and extend control. Schools, churches, and universities were all brought under the control of the state.

CORE CONCEPTS: NATIONALISM

Germany's economic problems were a crucial factor in the Nazi rise to power. Unemployment had risen dramatically. Hitler's appeals to national pride, national honor, and traditional militarism also moved audiences and brought them to his side.

CORE CONCEPTS: IDENTITY

Aryan was a term that linguists used to identify speakers of Indo-European languages. The Germans misused the term, identifying it with the ancient Greeks and Romans, as well as with twentieth-century Germans and Scandinavians.

Women and Nazism Nazi ideals taught that men were warriors and political leaders while women were destined as bearers of children to bring about the great Aryan race. While allowing women to be nurses and social workers, Nazis generally promoted a campaign against working women.

Anti-Semitic Policies In September 1935, the Nazis announced the Nuremberg Laws. They excluded Jews from German citizenship and forbade marriages between Jews and German citizens. In 1941, Jews were required to wear yellow Stars of David and to carry identification cards saying they were Jewish.

More repression soon followed. Jews were barred from all public transportation and buildings. They couldn't own, manage, or work in stores. They were also encouraged to emigrate.

SECTION 4 CULTURAL AND INTELLECTUAL TRENDS

Mass Culture: Radio and Movies

The discovery of wireless radio waves helped lead to a revolution in mass communication. The mass production of radios, as well as the development of full-length feature films as a regular source of middle-class entertainment, revolutionized both information and leisure.

Both the radio and movies were used for propaganda purposes. The Nazi regime encouraged radio listening by urging manufacturers to produce inexpensive radios that could be bought on an installment plan. They knew Hitler's speeches carried very well on radio waves.

More Goods, More Leisure

During the 1920s, assembly-line production made more goods available, and increased income as well as credit meant that more people could buy them. By 1920, the eight-hour workday had become the norm for many people, and there was now time for leisure activities. These ranged from sporting events to travel.

Artistic and Literary Trends

World War I had left many people in a state of despair. They questioned Western values; they also questioned whether the world was a rational place after all. They also responded to the political and economic uncertainties that developed as dictatorships arose and the Great Depression scarred the lives of millions. A group of writers known as the "Lost Generation" used naturalistic techniques to express these uncertainties.

Literature: The Search for the Unconscious The interest in the unconscious also surfaced in literature. Writers created a "stream of consciousness," used to report the innermost thoughts and responses of their characters. The most famous example of this technique appeared in *Ulysses* by James Joyce, which tells the story of one day in the life of an ordinary man and others in Dublin.

The Heroic Age of Physics

The prewar revolution in physics continued in the 1920s. Newtonian physics, which suggested that all phenomena could be defined and predicted, was shaken by the uncertainty principle. Its foundation was the unpredictability of subatomic particles. The theory's emphasis on randomness presented a new worldview that mirrored the uncertainties of the years between the wars.

CORE CONCEPTS: CULTURE

A German teacher and writer, Erich Maria Remarque, wrote a partly autobiographical novel about his experiences as a soldier in World War I called *All Quiet on the Western Front*. It reflected his depression about his experiences and described the horrors of war from the perspective of ordinary soldiers. It became a bestseller in Europe. The Nazis banned the book, and Remarque was persecuted and forced into exile.

Chapter Overview

After the fall of the Ottoman Empire, Kemal Atatürk helped establish the Turkish Republic and, as president, modernized Turkey. In Persia, a nationalist movement led to the rise of the Pahlavi dynasty and the modern state of Iran. Ibn Saud united Arabs in the northern part of the Arabian peninsula to form Saudi Arabia, while tensions and violence flared in Palestine as Britain declared support for a Jewish homeland and more and more Jews emigrated. People in Africa and Asia also began to create independence movements, including Gandhi's movement in India.

Japan became a more aggressive military state, and Soviet agents spread their influence to colonial societies around the world. In China, the Nationalists and Communists briefly joined forces; then Nationalist Party leader Chiang Kai-shek (Jiang Jieshi) took control of a weakened, divided nation.

In Latin America, the greed of foreign investors, notably the United States, and the impact of the Great Depression, led to the rise of dictators as well as some efforts at reform. Many major industries, such as oil and steel, came under government control.

As you read this chapter, ask yourself these questions:
(1) How did the forces of nationalism affect events in the Middle East, Africa, Asia, and Latin America?
(2) What roles did individual leaders play in the struggle for national independence?
(3) How did the creation of modern states include modernizing the economy?
(4) How did lower classes play a role in bringing about social changes?

REGENTS WARM-UP

Past Regents Exams have probed the relationship between economic conditions and political events. As you read, note how the Great Depression, as well as shifting economies, affected choices about governments and political systems.

Main Ideas and Concepts

- **Nationalism** Nationalism led to the creation of the modern states of Turkey, Iran, and Saudi Arabia.

- **Places and Regions** Throughout Asia and Africa, colonized people began to be influenced by nationalist ideas and to create movements for independence.

- **Conflict** In China, nationalist forces briefly triumphed over Communist forces but faced enormous obstacles in creating a new government.

- **Change** In Latin America, resentment of foreign interests, as well as economic instability resulting from the Great Depression, led to the rise of military dictatorships and government-owned industries.

People, Places, Terms

The following names and terms will help you to prepare for the Regents Exam in Global History and Geography. You can find an explanation of each name and term in the Glossary at the back of this book, in your textbook, or in another reference source.

Amritsar Massacre	genocide	Palestine
Atatürk	Chiang Kai-shek	Salt March
Balfour Declaration	Reza Khan	Ibn Saud
Mohandas Gandhi	mandates	Mao Zedong

SECTION 1 NATIONALISM IN THE MIDDLE EAST

Decline and Fall of the Ottoman Empire

The Ottoman Empire had been growing steadily weaker since the eighteenth century and had lost much of its European territory.

In 1876, a new constitution had been adopted and then suspended. The suspension became a symbol of change to a group of reformers named the Young Turks. They forced the restoration of the constitution in 1908 and deposed the sultan the following year.

Impact of World War I The final blow to the Ottoman Empire occurred during World War I, when the British sought to undermine the Ottomans by supporting nationalist activities in the Arabian Peninsula.

Massacre of the Armenians The Christian Armenian minority had been pressing the Ottoman government for its independence for years. In 1915, the government reacted violently to an

CORE CONCEPTS: LINKING PAST AND PRESENT

In the Bosnian War of 1993 to 1996, a practice that was much like the genocide of the Armenians would be labeled ethnic cleansing.

Armenian uprising. It left an estimated one million Armenians dead. They were the victims of **genocide**, the deliberate mass murder of a particular racial, political, or cultural group. By 1918, another 400,000 Armenians had been massacred.

Emergence of the Turkish Republic By the end of World War I, only the present-day area called Turkey remained under Ottoman control. Then Greece invaded Turkey and seized the western parts of the Anatolian peninsula. The forces of war hero Colonel Mustafa Kemal drove the Greeks out. Kemal also summoned a national congress calling forth the creation of an elected government and a new Republic of Turkey.

The Modernization of Turkey

CORE CONCEPTS: ECONOMIC SYSTEMS

Atatürk also took steps to modernize the Turkish economy. A five-year plan emphasized industry. He also tried to modernize agriculture but had little success.

President Kemal was now popularly known as **Atatürk**, or "Father Turk." His goal was to modernize Turkey. He put a democratic system in place, although he did not tolerate opposition and harshly suppressed his critics.

Atatürk's most significant goal may have been the desire to make Turkey a secular state. The caliphate was formally abolished in 1924. Men were forbidden to wear the fez, the brimless cap worn by Turkish Muslims. Women were forbidden to wear the veil. New laws gave women marriage and inheritance rights equal to men's.

The changes went beyond politics. Many Arabic letters were eliminated from the alphabet. People were forced to adopt last names, in the European style. Popular education was introduced.

Not all of these reforms were widely accepted. However, most of Atatürk's changes were kept after his death in 1938.

The Beginnings of Modern Iran

CORE CONCEPTS: IDENTITY

The name *Pahlavi*, which Reza Khan chose for the new dynasty, was the name of the ancient Persian language.

The discovery of oil in the southern part of Persia in 1908 increased foreign interest there. Oil exports increased rapidly, and most of the profits went to British investors.

A native Persian nationalist movement arose. In 1921, **Reza Khan** led a military mutiny that seized control of Tehran, the capital city. In 1925, Reza Khan made himself shah, or king, and was called Reza Shah Pahlavi.

Like Atatürk, Reza Shah Pahlavi introduced many reforms aimed at modernizing the government, the economy, and the military. He urged the creation of a Western-style educational system. He also forbade women to wear the veil. In 1935, the modern state of Iran was created.

Unlike Atatürk, Reza Shah Pahlavi did not try to reduce the power of traditional Islamic beliefs. Angered by foreign demands, he drew closer to Nazi Germany. During World War II, he stepped down in protest because the British and Soviets sent troops into Iran when he refused to expel Nazis. His son Mohammad Reza Pahlavi became king.

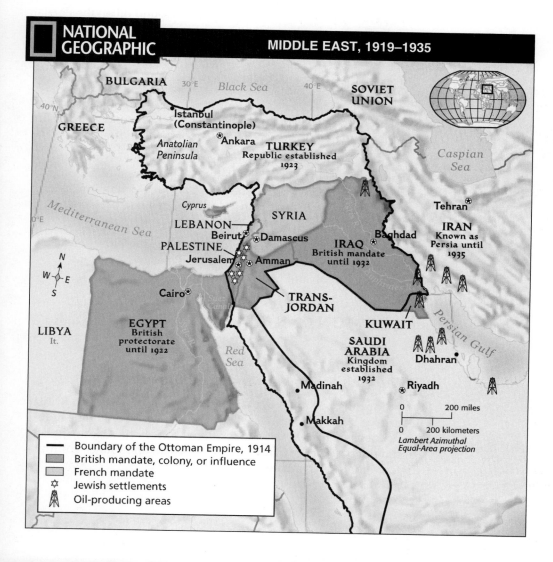

NATIONAL GEOGRAPHIC

MIDDLE EAST, 1919–1935

— Boundary of the Ottoman Empire, 1914
British mandate, colony, or influence
French mandate
✡ Jewish settlements
Oil-producing areas

Arab Nationalism

After World War I, Britain made an agreement with France to create **mandates** (nations governed by other nations on behalf of the League of Nations) in former Ottoman territories. For the most part, the Europeans created the states, dividing people or placing them within borders regardless of national or ethnic identity. Great Britain governed Iraq, Jordan, and Palestine. France governed Syria and Lebanon.

In the early 1920s, a reform leader, **Ibn Saud**, united Arabs in the northern part of the Arabian Peninsula. He established the kingdom of Saudi Arabia in 1932. At first, the new kingdom was desperately poor. Then U.S. prospectors found oil on the Persian Gulf. The isolated kingdom was suddenly flooded with Western oil industries.

The Problem of Palestine

The Jews had once called **Palestine** home, but not since the first century A.D. Although a Jewish presence remained, Muslim Arabs made up 80 percent of the region's population.

The Zionist movement, which called for a Jewish state in Palestine, began in the 1890s. Jews began to migrate. During World War I, the British issued the **Balfour Declaration**, stating support for a Jewish state in Palestine. They had previously supported an Arab state in the same area.

More Jews migrated. Then, during the 1930s, Nazi policies caused the migration of more Jews to Palestine. Tensions between Jewish and Muslim inhabitants grew.

SECTION 2 NATIONALISM IN AFRICA AND ASIA

Movements Toward Independence in Africa

Africans had fought in World War I in the French and British armies. After the war, they hoped their reward would be independence. This did not happen. Even the colonies Germany lost did not become free. Instead, Great Britain and France administered them as mandates.

African Protests After World War I, Africans became more active politically. Their experience and education had helped them see the wide gulf between Western ideals and practices.

Reform movements took different forms. In Kenya, Harry Thuku and the Young Kikuyu Association protested taxes. Their demands ended in violence and Thuku's exile. In Libya, Omar Mukhtar led guerrilla insurgents in a revolt against Italian rule. A violent Italian response and the death of Mukhtar ended the revolt. In some countries, Westerners began to make reforms. They were, however, too few and too late.

New Leaders In Africa, various leaders appeared. Jomo Kenyatta of Kenya argued that British rule was destroying the traditional culture. Léopold Senghor organized an independence movement in Senegal. Nnamdi Azikiwe of Nigeria urged nonviolence as a method for gaining independence.

The Movement for Indian Independence

Mohandas Gandhi had become active in the movement for Indian independence before World War I. The people of India referred to him as India's Great Soul, or Mahatma.

Protest and Reform Gandhi began to organize mass protests that involved civil disobedience—the refusal to obey laws considered to be unjust. In 1919, British soldiers killed hundreds of unarmed protestors in the **Amritsar Massacre**. Gandhi briefly retreated from active politics. When he returned, he was arrested and spent several years in jail. In 1935, Britain did, however, expand the role of Indians in the governing process. This included a legislative role as well as the right of a very small part of the population to vote.

A Push for Independence When Gandhi renewed his political activity, he called for nonviolence and noncooperation. He told people to protest against the salt tax and restrictions on the Indian manufacture or harvest of their own salt. Gandhi led supporters on a march that came to be known as the **Salt March**, in which thousands participated in nonviolent protest.

New Leaders and New Problems In the 1930s, a split in the movement occurred between traditionalists and those who were more Western and secular in their beliefs. Another rift that had always existed was the split between Hindu and Muslim. By the 1930s, the Muslim League was beginning to believe in the creation of a separate Muslim state of Pakistan.

CORE CONCEPTS: MOVEMENT OF PEOPLE AND GOODS

Some young African leaders were influenced by African American W. E. B. Du Bois, who tried to make all Africans aware of their cultural heritage. Others were influenced by Jamaican American Marcus Garvey, who called for the unity of all Africans, a movement known as Pan-Africanism.

CORE CONCEPTS: HUMAN RIGHTS

Marcus Garvey's *Declaration of the Rights of the Negro Peoples of the World* had a strong impact on later African leaders.

The Rise of a Militarist Japan

During the first two decades of the twentieth century, Japanese society developed along a Western model. A modern industrial and commercial sector brought increasing prosperity.

A Zaibatsu Economy Single family-controlled enterprises called *zaibatsu* arose in Japan. These firms were vast companies that controlled major segments of the Japanese industrial sector.

The concentration of wealth in these companies meant economic inequality. Other problems at this time included inflation and a rapid increase in population, which led to food riots. Citizens called for Japan to use its own strength to solve its problems and dominate Asia.

Japan and the West Like Western nations, Japan needed sources of raw materials as well as markets for its goods. Before World War I, Japan had seized territories to solve this problem. As a result, the United States worried about its own trading interests in the Pacific. With eight other nations, it established trading rules, but the terms proved too difficult for a country that desperately needed resources not found in abundance in Japan.

The Rise of Militarism By the end of the 1920s, militant groups had emerged in Japan's political system. Civilians also began to form extremist patriotic organizations. One group of middle-level army officers invaded Manchuria without government approval in the autumn of 1931. Shortly, all of Manchuria had been conquered.

Nationalism and Revolution in Asia

Before World War I, most Asian societies had no interest in Marxism. After all, most Asian societies were still agricultural.

The Spread of Communism Communism spread to Asia. Communists were against the West. One such leader was Ho Chi Minh in Vietnam.

SECTION 3 REVOLUTIONARY CHAOS IN CHINA

Nationalists and Communists

On May 4, 1919, students gathered to protest the settlement of the Treaty of Versailles. The May Fourth Movement, as it came to be known, began a patriotic outburst against foreign imperialists and warlords and signaled the beginning of Chinese nationalism. By 1920, two political competitors had emerged in China: the Nationalists and the Communists.

When the Communist party formed, Comintern agents advised it to join the Nationalists in their anti-imperialist struggle. (Comintern was an international Communist organization founded by Stalin.) At the time, Nationalist leader Sun Yat-sen (Sun Yixian), who had alienated the West, welcomed the Communists and Soviet support. By spring 1927, they had control of all of China south of the Chiang Jiang.

Tensions inevitably arose between the different parties, however. When Sun Yat-sen died in 1925, he was succeeded by **Chiang Kai-shek** (Jiang Jieshi). In 1927, Chiang Kai-shek and his supporters killed thousands of Communists in what is now called the Shanghai Massacre.

The Communists in Hiding

After the massacre, some Communist Party members went into hiding in Jiangxi Province south of the Chiang Jiang. Their leader was **Mao Zedong**. Unlike other leading members of the Communist Party, Mao was convinced that a Chinese revolution would be driven by the poverty-stricken peasants in the countryside rather than by the urban working class. Mao's forces, though much smaller, fought effectively against the Nationalists using guerrilla tactics.

The Long March

When Chiang Kai-shek's forces finally surrounded the Communist base in Jiangxi, the People's Liberation Army began its Long March. It traveled almost 6,000 miles to reach the last surviving Communist base in northwest China. Of the 90,000 troops that started out, 9,000 arrived. Starvation and freezing claimed the others. During this march, Mao Zedong became the sole leader of the Chinese Communist Party.

The New China of Chiang Kai-shek

Chiang Kai-shek believed China had to gradually transition to a constitutional government. Chiang Kai-shek's support came mainly from the middle class and landed gentry, who would object to his programs that aimed at redistribution of wealth, the shifting of wealth from a rich minority to a poor majority.

Chiang Kai-shek also had to be wary of building a modern state that appeared Western. He tried to bring together modern innovations with traditional Confucian values of hard work, obedience, and integrity.

SECTION 4 NATIONALISM IN LATIN AMERICA

The Latin American Economy

At the beginning of the twentieth century, the Latin American economy was based largely on the export of foodstuffs (cash crops) and raw materials. For most countries, the returns were small.

Role of the United States Beginning in the 1920s, the United States began to replace Britain as the foremost investor in Latin America. American firms gained control of the copper-mining industry in Chile and Peru, as well as the oil industry in Mexico, Peru, and Bolivia.

U.S. control of Latin American companies angered many Latin Americans. Furthermore, some profits were used to keep ruthless dictators in power. For example, in Venezuela, U.S. oil companies had a close relationship with dictator Juan Vicente Gómez. The United States had also intervened militarily in Latin American affairs for years. This was especially true in Central America and the Caribbean.

Impact of the Great Depression During the Great Depression, the U.S. demand for Latin American foodstuffs and raw materials dropped drastically. Countries that relied on the export of single foods, such as coffee, meat, and sugar, were especially hard hit. Without selling their own products, these countries could not buy manufactured goods. The only benefit of this problem was that some countries did begin to develop their own industry. In some cases, however, the industries were government-run (an example of economic nationalism), such as the oil business in Mexico and the steel industries in Chile and Brazil.

The Move to Authoritarianism

Although most Latin American countries had republican forms of government, small groups of church officials, military leaders, and large landowners had most of the power. The military was often used to support these special-interest groups. In the economic hard times of the 1930s, authoritarianism increased. Many military dictatorships began to develop, especially in Brazil and Mexico.

During World War II, a second generation of military officers, known as the Group of the United Officers, would overthrow the Argentine government and establish the presidency of Juan Perón.

Mexico After the Mexican Revolution during the early part of the twentieth century, Mexico had a relatively stable political order. Although its government was democratic in form, one party, the Institutional Revolutionary Party, or PRI, controlled major groups in the society and chose the presidential candidate, who was always elected.

From 1934 to 1940, 44 million acres of land were redistributed to the landless Mexican peasants. The government also seized control of foreign oil fields in Mexico. U.S. oil companies were furious and wanted President Franklin Roosevelt to send troops in response. He refused. Eventually, the Mexican government did pay the oil companies for their property. It then set up PEMEX, a national oil company, to run its oil industry.

CHAPTER 27 WORLD WAR II

Chapter Overview

Hitler's first acts of military buildup and aggression were met by appeasement. The Allies declared war in 1939, following the invasion of Poland. Soon Germany had control of most of continental Europe. Japan, which became an Axis power along with Italy, bombed the United States, thereby drawing it into the war, and waged war in the Pacific. During the war, Germany carried out resettlement in the East and genocide of the Jewish and Roma people. On the home front, total war existed with extensive economic mobilization and the relocation and bombing of civilian populations. The peace negotiated at the end of the war divided Europe into East and West and dramatically revealed the tensions between the Soviet Union and the West.

As you read this chapter, ask yourself these questions:
(1) What steps did Germany and Japan take that led to the beginning of World War II?
(2) What were Germany's and Japan's successes in the early part of the war?
(3) What were the major events of the last years of the war?
(4) What were the causes and effects of the Holocaust?
(5) What were the conditions of the peace settlement?
(6) How did the peace settlement help bring about the Cold War?

Main Ideas and Concepts

- **Imperialism** Both Germany and Japan followed a policy of aggressive expansion that led to war.

- **Choice** Allied perseverance and efficient military operations, as well as Axis miscalculations, brought an end to the war.

- **Power** Hitler's theories of racial superiority were carried out in practices ranging from resettlement to the physical extermination of Jews and others.

- **Environment** Civilian populations were deeply affected by this war in which they were bombed, resettled, and economically mobilized.

- **Science and Technology** New weaponry was developed with the use of the blitzkreig, sonar, radar, walkie-talkies, atomic bombs, nuclear weapons, and aircraft carriers.

People, Places, Terms

The following names and terms will help you to prepare for the Regents Exam in Global History and Geography. You can find an explanation of each name and term in the Glossary at the back of this book, in your textbook, or in another reference source.

appeasement	**Adolf Hitler**	**Nuremburg Trials**
blitzkrieg	**Holocaust**	**Franklin D. Roosevelt**
Winston Churchill	**iron curtain**	**Joseph Stalin**
Final Solution	**Chiang Kai-shek**	
Hiroshima	**Benito Mussolini**	

SECTION 1 PATHS TO WAR

The German Path to War

World War II had its beginnings in the ideas of **Adolf Hitler**. He believed that the great Aryan race would spread out on land to the east—in the Soviet Union. The Third Reich, he believed, would dominate Europe for one thousand years.

The First Steps In direct violation of the Treaty of Versailles, Hitler began to build up Germany's military. France, Great Britain, and Italy condemned this action and warned against future aggressive steps. In 1936, Hitler sent German troops into the Rhineland, a part of Germany that was a demilitarized area. France wanted to meet this action with military force, but would not act without Britain. Britain responded with a policy of **appeasement**, satisfying reasonable demands so that dissatisfied countries would be content and peace and stability could be maintained in Europe.

New Alliances Italy's fascist leader **Benito Mussolini** also had dreams of empire, and in 1936, invaded Ethiopia. Mussolini welcomed Hitler's support. In 1936, both Italy and Germany sent

**CORE CONCEPTS:
IMPERIALISM**

Western nations were also in the midst of the Great Depression, and greatly distracted by the problems it brought. This was just one reason why Hitler was not stopped.

troops to help General Francisco Franco in the civil war. Later that year, Italy and Germany created the Rome-Berlin Axis. In the same year, Germany and Japan signed the Anti-Comintern Pact, promising a common front against communism.

Union with Austria By threatening Austria with invasion, Hitler achieved another goal: union with Austria. In March 1938, Hitler annexed Austria to Germany.

Demands and Appeasement Hitler's next objective was Czechoslovakia. He demanded that Germany be given the Sudetenland, an area in northwestern Czechoslovakia inhabited largely by Germans. At a hasty conference in Munich, Britain, France, Germany, and Italy gave in to Hitler's demands.

Great Britain and France React In March 1939, Hitler invaded and took control of western Czechoslovakia. Finally, the Western powers saw the danger. Britain offered to protect Poland in the event of war. France and Britain also began political and military negotiations with **Joseph Stalin**, the Soviet dictator, in hopes of containing Nazi aggression.

Hitler and the Soviets Fearing a Western alliance with the Soviets, Hitler made his own pact with Stalin. In the Nazi-Soviet Nonaggression pact, both sides agreed not to attack the other. To get Stalin to agree, Hitler offered Stalin control of eastern Poland and the Baltic states. Hitler did not keep his promises.

On September 1, German forces invaded Poland. Two days later, Britain and France declared war on Germany.

The Japanese Path to War

In September 1931, Japan seized Manchuria from China. The League of Nations condemned this action, so Japan withdrew from the League. It then strengthened its hold on Manchuria, renaming it Manchukuo, and began to expand into North China.

War with China At first, **Chiang Kai-shek** tried to appease Japan by allowing it to govern areas in North China. The Japanese moved southward, however, and by July 1937, Chiang formed a united military front with the Chinese Communists against them. By December 1937, the Japanese had seized the Chinese capital of Nanjing. Chiang Kai-shek refused to surrender and moved his capital.

CORE CONCEPTS: POWER

The Munich Pact was the high point of Western appeasement. Through it, the British prime minister, Neville Chamberlain, thought he had achieved "peace for our time." Hitler, after all, had promised that he would make no more demands.

REGENTS WARM-UP

Practice your skills at relating cause and effect:

What was a major reason for Japan's invasion of Manchuria in 1931?

(1) The province of Manchuria was originally a Japanese territory.

(2) The government of Japan admired Manchurian technical progress.

(3) The people of Manchuria favored Japanese control.

(4) Japan needed Manchuria's natural resources.

The New Asian Order Japanese leaders had hoped that Chiang Kai-shek would agree with a New Order in East Asia that would comprise Japan, Manchuria, and China. Japan hoped to seize Soviet Siberia, with its rich resources, as part of this plan, and it had first believed it would have the assistance of Nazi Germany in doing so. With the signing of the Nazi-Soviet Nonaggression Pact, Japanese aims shifted to Southeast Asia. When Japan began to make demands for the resources of Southeast Asia, the United States objected. It threatened sanctions, restrictions intended to enforce international law. Japan needed raw materials from Southeast Asia, but it also needed the oil and scrap iron it had been getting from the United States. After many debates, Japan decided to launch a surprise attack on U.S. and European colonies in Southeast Asia.

SECTION 2 THE COURSE OF WORLD WAR II

Europe at War

Hitler's attack on Poland in September 1939 was fast and efficient. His **blitzkrieg**, or "lightning war," used armored columns of tanks and troops supported by airplanes. Within four weeks, the Polish army surrendered. Britain and France declared war and World War II began.

Hitler's Early Victories In April 1940, another blitzkrieg was launched against Denmark and Norway. One month later, Germany attacked the Netherlands, Belgium, and France. The main attack through the Ardennes Forest took the French and British forces by surprise and split the Allied armies. French forces and the entire British army were trapped on the beaches of Dunkirk. Only through a desperate and heroic effort did the British Navy and civilians save them by evacuating them to Britain.

The French signed an armistice on June 22. Germany now occupied about three-fifths of France. An authoritarian regime under German control was set up over the remainder of the country. It was known as Vichy France and was led by Marshal Henri Pétain.

Britain remained undefeated. It asked the United States for help. President **Franklin D. Roosevelt** denounced the aggressors, but the United States followed a policy of isolationism. Neutrality acts passed in the 1930s prevented U.S. involvement. Roosevelt was convinced that these acts actually encouraged Axis aggression. They were gradually relaxed as the United States supplied food, ships, weapons, and planes to Britain.

The Battle of Britain Germany's next move was to attack Britain from the air. It began by hitting military targets but was soon bombing British cities, hoping to break the will of the British people. Britain's great wartime leader, **Winston Churchill**, rallied his people.

Attack on the Soviet Union Hitler was convinced that defeating the Soviets would break Britain's will to continue. He also believed the Soviets could be defeated quickly.

On June 22, 1941, Hitler invaded the Soviet Union. The massive attack spread out along a front of some 1,800 miles. The troops advanced rapidly, capturing two million Russian soldiers. By November, one German army group had swept through Ukraine. A second army was besieging Leningrad, while a third approached within 25 miles of Moscow.

An early winter halted the Germans, however. The troops had no winter uniforms. For the first time in the war, German armies had been stopped. A counterattack by the Soviets in December 1941 made it clear that the Germans might be stopped after all.

Japan at War

On December 7, 1941, Japanese aircraft attacked the U.S. naval base at Pearl Harbor in the Hawaiian Islands. Japan launched assaults on the Philippines and Malaya on the same day. Soon after, it invaded and occupied other Pacific islands. In some cases, resistance was fierce; nevertheless, almost all of Southeast Asia and much of the western Pacific was in Japanese hands by the spring of 1942.

The attack on Pearl Harbor unified American opinion about becoming involved in the war. The United States now joined with European nations and Nationalist China in a combined effort to defeat Japan. Believing American involvement in the Pacific would make the United States ineffective in Europe, Hitler declared war on the United States four days after Pearl Harbor. Another European conflict had turned into a global war.

CORE CONCEPTS: IMPERIALISM

The Japanese not only believed that their attack on Pearl Harbor would destroy the U.S. fleet but that it would lead to American acceptance of Japanese dominance in the Pacific. They believed the American people had been made soft by material indulgence.

The Allies Advance

The three major Allies—Great Britain, the United States, and the Soviet Union—agreed to stress military operations and ignore political differences. The Allies also agreed to fight until the Axis Powers—Germany, Italy, and Japan—surrendered unconditionally, or without any conditions that were in any way favorable to them.

The European Theater Until late 1942, it still appeared as if Germany might win the war. In North Africa, the Afrika Korps, German forces under General Erwin Rommel, broke though British defenses in Egypt and advanced toward Alexandria. A renewed German offensive in the Soviet Union led to the capture of the entire Crimea.

By 1943, however, the tide was turning. British and American troops forced the surrender of German and Italian troops in North Africa in May 1943. In what was perhaps the most terrible battle of the war, the Soviets cut off Nazi supply lines in frigid winter conditions. The entire German Sixth Army was lost. It became clear that the Germans would not defeat the Soviet Union.

The Asian Theater In 1942, a Japanese invasion in the Philippines overpowered American and Filipino troops and forced them to surrender. Approximately 70,000 American and Filipino prisoners of war were forced to march for several days without food or water to a prison camp. Many were tortured or shot for falling behind. About 10,000 perished in the Bataan Death March.

The turning point of the war in Asia came at the Battle of Midway Island, where the United States established naval superiority in the Pacific. U.S. forces were also gathering for new operations. One, led by General Douglas MacArthur, would move into the Philippines and the South Pacific Islands. The other would island-hop across the South Pacific to Japan.

Last Years of the War

By the beginning of 1943, the tide of battle had turned against Italy, Germany, and Japan.

The European Theater German forces liberated Mussolini, who had been arrested by Victor Emmanuel III, the king of Italy. Mussolini set up a puppet German state in northern Italy, and German troops moved into and occupied much of Italy. Rome did not fall until June 1944. By that time, the Allied forces opened their long-awaited second front in western Europe.

On June 6, 1944, Allied forces under U.S. general Dwight D. Eisenhower landed on the Normandy beaches. This day, known as D-Day, was history's greatest naval invasion. The Allies fought their way past underwater mines, barbed wire, and machine gun fire to set up a beachhead. Within three months, the Allies had landed two million men and a half-million vehicles. Allied forces then pushed inland and broke through German defensive lines.

From Normandy, Allied forces fanned out. Some reached Paris, where resistance fighters rose up against the occupying Germans to liberate Paris with the Allies. Others linked up with the Soviets in northern Germany.

On April 30, 1945, Hitler committed suicide, just two days after Mussolini had been shot by resistance fighters in Italy. On May 7, 1945, German commanders surrendered, ending the war in Europe.

The Asian Theater The U.S. advance across the Pacific had been slow and bloody. As the Allied advance drew closer to the main Japanese islands in the first months of 1945, President Harry S. Truman had to decide whether to use newly developed atomic weapons. Truman and his advisers believed that Allied losses would be very great if they invaded Japan. Yet no one knew for sure how effective the new bombs would be.

The first atomic bomb was dropped on the city of **Hiroshima** on August 6. Three days later a second bomb was dropped on Nagasaki. Both cities were leveled. Thousands died immediately; thousands more died later from radiation. On September 2, 1945, Japan signed an unconditional surrender to the United States aboard the *USS Missouri*.

LINKING PAST AND PRESENT

After defeating the Germans at Stalingrad and also at the Battle of Kursk, Soviet forces had reoccupied the Ukraine and moved into the Baltic states. They had also occupied Warsaw; swept through Hungary, Romania, and Bulgaria; and entered Berlin. Their conquest of these areas would figure heavily in postwar political divisions.

CORE CONCEPTS: CONFLICT

All told, seventeen million soldiers died in battle during World War II. Perhaps twenty million civilians also perished.

SECTION 3 THE NEW ORDER AND THE HOLOCAUST

The New Order in Europe

In 1942, the Nazi regime stretched across continental Europe. Mainly, it was organized in two ways. Some areas, such as western Poland, were annexed directly and made part of Germany. Most of occupied Europe, however, was run by German officials with the help of local people who were willing to collaborate with the Nazis.

Resettlement in the East Hitler viewed conquered lands to the east as living areas for German expansion. He viewed Slavic peoples as racially inferior and sought to move them out of the east and replace them with Germans. Heinrich Himmler, the leader of the SS, was put in charge of Hitler's resettlement plans.

As part of this resettlement, over one million Poles were uprooted and moved to southern Poland. By 1942, more than two million Germans had been resettled in the Poles' place.

The invasion of the Soviet Union made the Nazis even more excited about German colonization in the east. In Hitler's plan for a colossal social engineering project, millions of Poles, Ukrainians, and Russians would be removed from their lands and become slave labor for the Germans. German peasants would then settle on the abandoned lands and "germanize" them.

Slave Labor in Germany Labor shortages in Germany led to the rounding up of seven million foreign workers. They made up 20 percent of Germany's labor force. Another seven million workers were forced to labor for the Nazis in their own countries on farms, in industries, and even in military camps.

The Holocaust

Hitler's racial ideas led to the **Final Solution**: the genocide, or physical extermination, of the Jews. Himmler and the SS, who closely shared Hitler's views of the Jews as parasites intent on destroying the superior Aryans, carried out this extermination.

In June 1941, mobile killing units followed the regular army's advance into the Soviet Union. They rounded up Jews in their villages, executed them, and buried them in mass graves. Often the victims had to dig the graves themselves before they were shot.

The Death Camps Soon Jews were rounded up, packed into freight trains, and shipped to Poland where six extermination centers had been built. The largest of them was Auschwitz. Most people who arrived at Auschwitz went to the gas chambers. About 30 percent were sent to a labor camp to be starved or worked to death. Some arrivals were subjected to cruel and painful "medical" experiments.

In the death camps, first priority was given to the Jews of Poland. By 1942, Jews were also shipped from France, Belgium, and Holland. Later they came from Greece and Hungary. Even when the Germans were facing defeat at the end of the war, the Final Solution had priority in using railroad cars to ship Jews to death camps.

The Death Toll The Germans killed between five and six million Jews, about half of them in death camps. Overall, the **Holocaust**, or mass slaughter of the Jews, was responsible for the death of nearly two out of every three Jews in Europe. The Nazis were also responsible for the deliberate death by shooting, starvation, or overwork of at least another nine to ten million non-Jewish people. The Roma (sometimes known as the Gypsies), like the Jews, were also considered an inferior race and rounded up for mass killing. Leading citizens of the Slavic peoples—clergy, intellectuals, civil leaders, judges, and lawyers—were arrested and killed. About four million Poles, Ukrainians, and Belorussians lost their lives as slave laborers for Nazi Germany. The Germans also killed three to four million Soviet prisoners of war.

The New Order in Asia

Japan organized its new possessions in Asia into the Greater East-Asia Co-prosperity Sphere. This economic community was supposedly designed for mutual benefits of the occupied areas and the home country.

Japanese Policies Japan conquered Southeast Asia under the slogan "Asia for the Asiatics." They appealed to anticolonial feelings, but subordinated the lives and resources of the natives to Japanese goals. In some cases, this brought extreme hardship, as in Vietnam, where the use of rice for the Japanese caused more than one million Vietnamese to starve to death between 1944 and 1945.

Japanese Behavior At first, many Southeast Asian nationalists, such as those in Burma, agreed to cooperate with their new masters. Japanese attitudes toward the locals soon became apparent, however, as, for example, Buddhist pagodas in Burma were used as latrines.

Far worse was disrespect for human life. In Nanjing, China, in 1937, Japanese forces killed, raped, and looted. They sent almost

CORE CONCEPTS: CONFLICT

Many resisted the Final Solution. Jews in and out of the camps made both individual and organized attempts at resistance. Foreign diplomats tried to save Jews by issuing exit visas. The nation of Denmark saved almost its entire Jewish population.

800,000 Korean people to Japan as forced laborers. They used local people as well as prisoners of war as labor forces, often under appalling working conditions that included almost no food.

Some occupied peoples turned against the Japanese. Some, for whom colonial powers were an even greater evil, did nothing.

SECTION 4 THE HOME FRONT AND THE AFTERMATH OF THE WAR

The Mobilization of Peoples: Four Examples

Even more than World War I, World War II was a total war. It covered most of the world.

The Soviet Union In Leningrad, which was under siege for 900 days, people became so desperate for food that they ate dogs, cats, and mice. Probably 1.5 million people died there.

Soviet women played a major role in the war effort. The number working in industry increased 60 percent. Some women dug air-raid ditches. Others served in battle as snipers and in the aircrews of bomber squadrons.

The United States The United States did not fight the war at home but became the arsenal of the Allies, producing six ships a day and 96,000 planes in 1943.

Economic mobilization brought social turmoil. New factories created boomtowns with shortages of houses and schools. Millions moved, and some frequently, for military or work reasons.

On the West Coast, 110,000 Japanese Americans, 65 percent of whom had been born in the United States, were forcibly resettled. Their resettlement in camps with barbed wire was said to be necessary for security reasons.

African Americans also moved. A mass migration from the rural South to the cities of the North and West was prompted by jobs in industry. The new presence of African Americans in some American cities led to tensions and, in some places like Detroit, prompted race riots. Meanwhile, one million African Americans enrolled in the military. They were segregated in their own battle units.

Germany Hitler wanted the support of his home front, so he adopted economic policies that may have cost Germany the war. He refused to cut consumer goods production for the sake of armaments production until the German defeats on the Russian front. Between 1942 and 1943, the production of armaments tripled. A total mobilization of the economy was put into effect in 1944, closing schools, theaters, and cafes, but it was too late to save Germany from defeat.

Nazi attitudes toward women changed as the war progressed. Women were encouraged to become working and fighting comrades. Still, the number of working women increased only slightly.

Japan Wartime Japan was a highly mobilized society. The government created a planning board to control prices, wages, labor, and resources. It used traditional habits of obedience and hierarchy to encourage work for the national cause. Calls for sacrifice reached their high point near the end of the war when young Japanese were encouraged to serve as pilots in suicide missions against U.S. ships at sea. These pilots were known as kamikaze, or "divine wind."

Japan resisted mobilizing women. Female employment increased during the war, but only in areas where women had traditionally worked, such as the textile industry and farming. Instead of using women to meet labor shortages, the Japanese brought in Korean and Chinese laborers.

NATIONAL GEOGRAPHIC

EUROPE AFTER WORLD WAR II

- Area of Soviet influence
- Area of Western influence

Lambert Azimuthal Equal-Area projection

Peace and a New War

Real peace did not follow the Allies' victory in World War II. Instead, the Cold War, an ideological conflict primarily between the United States and the Soviet Union, started.

The Tehran Conference Stalin, Churchill, and Roosevelt were the leaders of the Big Three: the Soviet Union, Great Britain, and the United States. They met in Tehran in November 1943 to decide the future course of the war. They planned an American-British invasion through France. This plan meant that Eastern Europe would likely be liberated by Soviet forces. The Allies also agreed to a partition of postwar Germany.

The Yalta Conference The Big Three met again in Yalta, Ukraine in February 1945. Stalin was deeply suspicious of the Western powers. He wanted to establish pro-Soviet governments along the border of the Soviet Union to protect it from possible future Western aggression. Roosevelt felt that liberated countries should hold free elections to determine their political systems. Stalin agreed to free elections in Poland. He also agreed that

Germany would be divided into four zones occupied and governed by the United States, Great Britain, France, and the Soviet Union. The issue of free elections for Eastern Europe could not be resolved, however.

Roosevelt also wanted the Big Three to pledge to be part of a new United Nations. Both Stalin and Churchill agreed to this.

The Potsdam Conference At Potsdam, Germany in July 1945, Truman, who had succeeded Roosevelt, demanded free elections again. The Soviets, who had lost more people in the war than any other nation, would not agree.

A New Struggle The war left the Soviet Union and Britain and the United States bitterly divided. The West thought Soviet policy was part of a worldwide Communist conspiracy. The Soviets viewed Western, and especially American, policy as capitalist expansionism. In March 1946, Winston Churchill declared that an "**iron curtain**" had "descended across the continent." Stalin said Churchill's speech was a "call to war with the Soviet Union."

CORE CONCEPTS: JUSTICE

At Potsdam, the Allies agreed that trials should be held for leaders who had committed crimes against humanity during the war. In 1945 and 1946, Nazi leaders were tried and condemned at the **Nuremburg Trials** in Germany. Trials were also held in Japan and Italy.

PRACTICING FOR THE REGENTS

Part I Multiple-Choice Questions

The following multiple-choice questions come from past Regents High School Examinations. Test your understanding of global history and geography by answering each of these items. Circle the number of the word or expression that best completes each statement or question. Test-taking tips can be found in the margins for some questions. For additional help, see Taking the Regents Exam on pages ix-xxxv of this Review Book.

1   Which statement explains the decline in unemployment rates in Britain between 1914 and 1918?
  (1) World War I generated jobs at home in England and in the military.
  (2) Many new jobs were available in Britain's African colonies.
  (3) Assembly-line production of consumer goods required more workers.
  (4) The British were buying huge amounts of war materials from the United States.

2   The Treaty of Versailles contributed to the economic collapse of Germany after World War I by
  (1) mandating economic reforms in Germany
  (2) requiring that Germany pay for war damages
  (3) placing a quota on goods exported from Germany
  (4) devaluing German currency

3   "A civilized, international dress is worthy and appropriate for our nation, and we will wear it. Boots or shoes on our feet, trousers on our legs, shirt and tie, jacket and waistcoat—and of course, to complete these, a cover with a brim on our heads. I want to make this clear. This head-covering is called 'hat.' "
  —*Kemal Atatürk*

  The clothing rules established by Kemal Atatürk indicated that he wanted Turkey to
  (1) retain its traditional culture
  (2) westernize its society
  (3) give women equal rights
  (4) establish Islamic fundamentalism

4   During World War II, which event occurred last?
  (1) German invasion of Poland
  (2) Russian defense of Stalingrad
  (3) United States bombing of Hiroshima and Nagasaki
  (4) Japanese invasion of Manchuria

5 During World War II, the Allied invasion of France on D-Day (June 6, 1944) was significant because it
(1) demonstrated the power of the atomic bomb
(2) resulted in a successful German revolt against Hitler and the Nazi Party
(3) led to the immediate surrender of German and Italian forces
(4) forced Germans to fight a two-front war

Base your answers to questions 6 and 7 on the maps below and on your knowledge of social studies.

Source: *Regional Extensions*, 1999

6   In 1919, European boundaries were changed in an attempt to
    (1) satisfy the demands for self-determination by ethnic nationalities
    (2) allow for communist expansion in Eastern Europe
    (3) establish a European common market
    (4) balance economic needs and natural resources

7   Which nation lost the most territory as a result of World War I?
    (1) Belgium   (3) Austria-Hungary
    (2) France   (4) Germany

8   The Japanese, the Germans, and the Italians pursued a policy of expansionism before World War II to gain
    (1) natural resources
    (2) warm-water ports
    (3) manufacturing plants
    (4) freedom of the seas

9   The Japanese invasion of Manchuria in 1931 and Hitler's rebuilding of the German military in 1935 demonstrate the
    (1) success of defensive alliances
    (2) fear of communist expansion
    (3) support for the Treaty of Versailles
    (4) failure of the League of Nations

10 Which action illustrates the concept of genocide?
    (1) the British negotiating peace with Adolf Hitler during the 1938 Munich Conference
    (2) Adolf Hitler and Joseph Stalin signing a nonaggression pact in 1939
    (3) the Nazi armies eliminating the Jews and other groups as part of Adolf Hitler's Final Solution
    (4) German generals plotting against Adolf Hitler

11 In Russia, the events of Bloody Sunday, the heavy casualties during World War I, and the ineffective leadership of the czar led directly to the
    (1) Revolution of 1917
    (2) German defeat at Stalingrad
    (3) signing of the Munich Pact
    (4) creation of the Warsaw Pact

12 One characteristic of a totalitarian state is that
    (1) minority groups are granted many civil liberties
    (2) several political parties run the economic system
    (3) citizens are encouraged to criticize the government
    (4) the government controls and censors the media

13 Which statement is the most appropriate heading for the partial outline below?

    I. _____
        A. Oil discovered in 1908
        B. Nationalist movement arises
        C. Reza Shah Pahlavi gains power
        D. Modernization of government and economy

    (1) Beginnings of Modern Iran
    (2) Islamic Fundamentalism Increases
    (3) Mandates in the Middle East
    (4) Beginnings of Modern Saudi Arabia

Base your answers to questions 14 and 15 on the statements below and on your knowledge of social studies.

Speaker A: "What was actually happening on the battlefield was all secret then, but I thought that the Greater East Asia Co-prosperity Sphere would be of crucial importance to backward races."

Speaker B: "We Nazis must hold to our aim in foreign policy, namely to secure for the German people the land and soil to which they are entitled . . ."

Speaker C: "The Munich Pact saved Czechoslovakia from destruction and Europe from Armageddon."

Speaker D: "We shall defend our island, whatever the cost shall be. We shall fight on the beaches, we shall fight on the landing grounds, we shall fight in the fields and in the streets. . . . We shall never surrender."

14 The common theme in the statements of Speakers *B* and *D* is
(1) colonialism
(2) containment
(3) nationalism
(4) reparations

15 The clearest example of the policy of appeasement is in the statement made by Speaker
(1) *A*
(2) *B*
(3) *C*
(4) *D*

16 During World War II, which geographic features contributed most to the Soviet Union's defense against the German invasion?
(1) deposits of many natural resources
(2) size and climate
(3) Atlantic ports and rivers
(4) mountainous territory and desert areas

17 One way in which Chiang Kai-shek (Jiang Jieshi) of China, Ho Chi Minh of Vietnam, and Jomo Kenyatta of Kenya were similar is that they all
(1) supported close ties with their former colonial powers
(2) opposed United Nations membership for their governments
(3) led nationalistic movements
(4) resisted attempts to modernize their nation's political and social institutions

18 Kemal Atatürk's efforts to modernize Turkish culture were most strongly opposed by
(1) Indian nationalists
(2) republicans
(3) industrialists
(4) religious forces

19 Lenin's promise of "Peace, Land, Bread" during the Bolshevik Revolution of 1917 was made in an effort to
(1) end France's occupation of Russia
(2) gain popular support to overthrow the government
(3) restore Czar Nicholas II to power
(4) resolve conflicts between farmers of diverse ethnic backgrounds

20   "Don't pay your taxes or send your
     children to an English supported
     school. . . . Make your own cotton cloth
     by spinning the thread at home, and
     don't buy English-made goods. Provide
     yourselves with homemade salt, and do
     not buy government-made salt."
     —*Mohandas Gandhi*

     In this statement, Gandhi was express-
     ing his commitment to
     (1) armed rebellion
     (2) civil disobedience
     (3) criminal acts
     (4) guerrilla tactics

21   Which situation was a direct result of
     the Holocaust and other atrocities
     committed by the Nazis during World
     War II?
     (1) development of the Cold War
     (2) war crimes trials in Nuremberg
     (3) formation of the League of Nations
     (4) separation of Germany into Eastern
         and Western zones

Base your answer to question 22 on the diagram below and on your knowledge of social
studies.

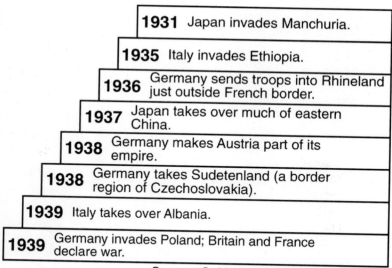

1931 Japan invades Manchuria.

1935 Italy invades Ethiopia.

1936 Germany sends troops into Rhineland just outside French border.

1937 Japan takes over much of eastern China.

1938 Germany makes Austria part of its empire.

1938 Germany takes Sudetenland (a border region of Czechoslovakia).

1939 Italy takes over Albania.

1939 Germany invades Poland; Britain and France declare war.

Source: *Guide to Essentials*, Prentice Hall

22   Based on the information provided by
     the diagram, which statement is a valid
     conclusion about the 1930s?
     (1) The United States led international
          peace-keeping efforts.
     (2) Aggression led to the start of World
          War II.
     (3) The actions of Italy, Germany, and
          Japan united Europe.
     (4) Economic and social upheaval led to
          the rise of democracy in Asia.

23   Joseph Stalin's rule in the Soviet Union
     was characterized by the
     (1) introduction of democratic political
          institutions
     (2) encouragement of religious beliefs
     (3) development of a market economy
     (4) establishment of a totalitarian
          dictatorship

Part II   Thematic Essay Question

The following essay question comes from questions from past Regents Examinations. Write your answers on a separate sheet of paper. Essay-writing tips appear in the margin. For additional help, see Taking the Regents Exam on pages ix-xxxv of this Review Book.

Directions: Write a well-organized essay that includes an introduction, several paragraphs addressing the task below, and a conclusion.

Theme: Conflict

> Differences among groups have often led to conflict.

Task:

> Identify *two* ethnic, religious, political, and/or cultural conflicts and for *each*
>
> - Discuss the historical circumstances that led to the conflict
> - Analyze the effect of this conflict on *two* groups involved

You may use any examples from your study of global history and geography. Some suggestions you might wish to consider include the persecution of Christians during the Roman Empire, the Reign of Terror, the Armenian massacres, the forced famine in Ukraine, the Holocaust, Apartheid in South Africa, the Killing Fields of Cambodia, the conflict in Northern Ireland, the Sandinistas in Nicaragua, and the Tiananmen Square rebellion.

You are *not* limited to these suggestions.

Guidelines:

   In your essay, be sure to

- Develop all aspects of the task
- Support the theme with relevant facts, examples, and details
- Use a logical and clear plan of organization, including an introduction and a conclusion that are beyond a restatement of the theme

Part III   Document-Based Question

This exercise is designed to test your ability to work with historical documents. It is similar to the document-based questions you will see on the Regents Examination. While you are asked to analyze three historical documents, the exercise on the actual exam will include more documents. Some of the documents have been edited for the purposes of the question. As you analyze the documents, take into account the source of each document and any point of view that may be presented in the document.

Historical Context:

The Allied victory in World War II was by no means assured. In the beginning of war, it appeared as if Germany might achieve its goals.

Task: Using information from the documents and your knowledge of global history and geography, write an essay in which you

- Discuss how and when the tide of war changed for the Axis Powers, especially Germany and Japan
- Include an explanation of at least three major battles or offensives that significantly altered the course of the war

Part A   Short-Answer Questions

Directions: Analyze the documents and answer the short-answer questions that follow each document in the space provided.

Document 1

NATIONAL GEOGRAPHIC   **ALLIANCES IN EUROPE, 1914**

Legend:
- Axis Powers
- Axis-controlled area, November 1942
- Farthest Axis advance, December 1941
- Vichy France and territories
- Allied Powers
- Allied-controlled area, November 1942
- Neutral nations
- ★ Major battle with date

Lambert Azimuthal Equal-Area projection

1a   Summarize the Axis control of Europe by November 1942.

controled the soviet union, libya, the UK, Germany, ~~Italy~~, Greece, most of northeastern europe

b   What was the first Allied-controlled area?

southern france

Document 2

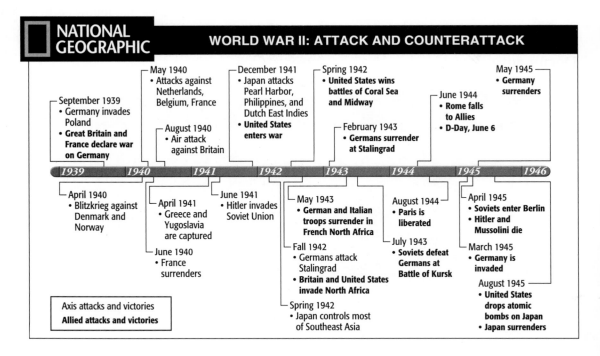

NATIONAL GEOGRAPHIC

WORLD WAR II: ATTACK AND COUNTERATTACK

September 1939
• Germany invades Poland
• **Great Britain and France declare war on Germany**

May 1940
• Attacks against Netherlands, Belgium, France

August 1940
• Air attack against Britain

December 1941
• Japan attacks Pearl Harbor, Philippines, and Dutch East Indies
• **United States enters war**

Spring 1942
• **United States wins battles of Coral Sea and Midway**

February 1943
• **Germans surrender at Stalingrad**

June 1944
• **Rome falls to Allies**
• **D-Day, June 6**

May 1945
• **Germany surrenders**

1939   1940   1941   1942   1943   1944   1945   1946

April 1940
• Blitzkrieg against Denmark and Norway

April 1941
• Greece and Yugoslavia are captured

June 1940
• France surrenders

June 1941
• Hitler invades Soviet Union

May 1943
• **German and Italian troops surrender in French North Africa**

Fall 1942
• Germans attack Stalingrad
• **Britain and United States invade North Africa**

Spring 1942
• Japan controls most of Southeast Asia

August 1944
• **Paris is liberated**

July 1943
• **Soviets defeat Germans at Battle of Kursk**

April 1945
• **Soviets enter Berlin**
• Hitler and Mussolini die

March 1945
• **Germany is invaded**

August 1945
• **United States drops atomic bombs on Japan**
• Japan surrenders

Axis attacks and victories
Allied attacks and victories

2a   During what years did most of Europe surrender?

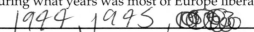

1940, and 1945 and 1943

b   During what years was most of Europe liberated?

1944, 1945, ⊘⊘⊘

Document 3

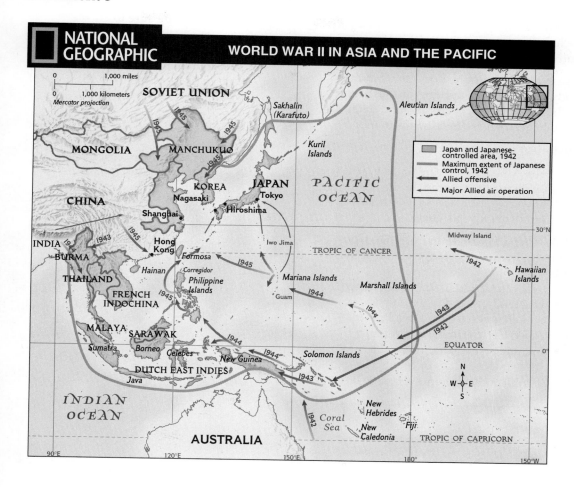

NATIONAL GEOGRAPHIC — **WORLD WAR II IN ASIA AND THE PACIFIC**

3   Describe the area of Japanese control in 1942.

near water ports for trade routes
in pacific ocean

Part B   Essay

Directions: Write a well-organized essay that includes an introduction, several paragraphs, and a conclusion.

Use evidence from the documents in the body of the essay. Support your response with relevant facts, examples, and details. Include additional outside information.

Historical Context:

> The Allied victory in World War II was by no means assured. In the beginning of war, it appeared as if Germany might achieve its goals.

Task: Using information from the documents and your knowledge of global history and geography, write an essay in which you

- Discuss how and when the tide of war changed for the Axis Powers, especially Germany and Japan
- Include an explanation of at least three major battles or offensives that significantly altered the course of the war

Guidelines:

In your essay, be sure to

- Develop all aspects of the task

- Incorporate information from *at least two* of the documents in the body of your essay

- Incorporate relevant outside information

- Support the theme with relevant facts, examples, and details

- Use a logical and clear plan of organization, including an introduction and conclusion that are beyond a restatement of the theme

UNIT 7   TOWARD A GLOBAL CIVILIZATION

Unit 7 Overview

The end of World War II led immediately to the Cold War (so-called because it did not lead to fighting, or a "hot" war). Russia and the United States, the two superpowers, tried to check each other's influence while engaging in an arms race. Shifting polices and reforms in the Soviet Union led to its sudden collapse, and Communist regimes throughout Eastern Europe soon fell. In Latin America, economic crises following World War II led to political upheavals, include military rule and revolution. In Africa, newly independent nations struggled with dictators, economic challenges, and violence, while in the Middle East, the creation of Israel led to ongoing conflicts with the Palestinians and neighboring Arab states.

Mao Zedong made many reforms in an effort to turn the People's Republic of China into an ideal communist state, but new leaders have moved the country toward capitalism and democracy. India was divided into Hindu and Muslim states, though religious conflict, along with poverty, still troubled the nation. In Southeast Asia, newly independent states also faced challenges, but Japan, Singapore, Hong Kong, South Korea, and Taiwan all managed to create successful industrial economies.

Unit 7 Objectives

After studying this unit, you should be able to

1.   summarize the causes and impact of the Cold War;

2.   describe conflicts in Asia and the region's emergence as an economic powerhouse;

3.   analyze the legacy of colonial rule in Africa and the challenges facing that continent;

4.   examine the rival nationalistic movements in the Middle East and the region's search for peace;

5.   identify political and economic trends in Latin America;

6.   analyze factors that are leading toward globalization.

PREPARING FOR THE REGENTS

This entire book is set up to help you grasp the facts, main ideas, and concepts needed to do well on your Regents Exam. Notes in the margin include core concepts, test-taking tips, and more. Use blank spaces in the margins to answer questions raised in the text or to jot down key points. Before each unit of study, skim through the exams at the back of the book to develop a sense of what your state wants you to know about your world.

Chapter Overview

At the end of World War II, the United States and the Soviet Union were the world's two competing superpowers. They became locked in the Cold War, a generally bloodless battle in which both sought to maintain their own power and political ideology. After Stalin's death, a more moderate regime under Nikita Khrushchev took control. In Europe, postwar societies rebuilt their economies with the help of the Marshall Plan. West Germany experienced rapid economic growth, while Great Britain, forced by economic necessity that resulted mainly from its building of a welfare state, gave up its empire. The market economies of Western countries flourished, while Cold War countries maintained command economies. In the United States, New Deal promises evolved into gains for the civil rights movement. Shifting social structures in both the United States and Europe included a larger middle class and a more economically empowered lower class. These changes, along with new inventions, helped lead to social upheaval that included the women's movement and student protests.

As you read this chapter, ask yourself these questions:
(1) How did the Cold War, the Cuban missile crisis, and the Vietnam War develop?
(2) Who were Stalin and Khrushchev?
(3) How did Soviet power spread?
(4) What were the most significant developments in postwar Western societies?

REGENTS WARM-UP

Questions on past Regents Exams have explored how events or policies in one part of the world have affected regions elsewhere. As you read this chapter, identify ways in which Soviet policies affected European development during the two decades that followed World War II.

Main Ideas and Concepts

- **Conflict** After World War II, the two superpowers, the United States and the Soviet Union, engaged in a cold war that included suspicions, alliances, and an arms race.

- **Conflict** The Soviet Union faced revolts and protests in its attempt to gain and maintain control over Eastern Europe.

- **Economic Systems** Postwar western societies rebuilt their economies.

- **Change** A change in the social structure that included a larger middle class and a better-off lower class helped lead to social upheaval.

- **Science and Technology** The arms race between the Soviet Union and the United States led to the development of hydrogen bombs, sophisticated intercontinental missiles, and nuclear weapons.

- **Economic Systems** The United States and its supporters in the Cold War pushed for capitalism, while the Soviet Union and its supporters advocated a command economy.

People, Places, Terms

The following names and terms will help you to prepare for the Regents Exam in Global History and Geography. You can find an explanation of each name and term in the Glossary at the back of this book, in your textbook, or in another reference source.

arms race	**Marshall Plan**	**satellite state**
bloc	**NATO**	**Warsaw Pact**
Nikita Khrushchev	**policy of containment**	**welfare state**
Mao Zedong		

SECTION 1 DEVELOPMENT OF THE COLD WAR

Confrontation of the Superpowers

After World War II, the United States and the Soviet Union became rivals who were suspicious of each other's every move. Between 1945 and 1949, these two superpowers (countries whose military power is combined with political influence) opposed each other in a number of events in what was to be called the Cold War.

Rivalry in Europe The United States and Great Britain believed the people of Eastern Europe should freely determine their own governments. Stalin opposed this idea. Because the Soviet army had freed this area from the Nazis, its army remained there. The countries of Eastern Europe became economically dependent **satellite states** of the Soviet Union.

A civil war in Greece in 1946 became another area of conflict for the superpowers. Great Britain originally supported anticommunist forces, but facing its own economic problems, had to withdraw.

The Truman Doctrine The British withdrawal and possibility of Soviet expansion into the Mediterranean led to the Truman Doctrine in 1947. The United States stated it would provide money to countries (in this case, Greece) threatened by Soviet expansion. President Truman argued that if the Soviets were not stopped in Greece, the United States would have to face the spread of communism throughout the world.

Marshall Plan Later in 1947, the United States issued the **Marshall Plan**, which was similar in strategy to the Truman Doctrine. Secretary of State George C. Marshall believed that communism was successful in countries with economic problems. Therefore, the Marshall Plan provided $13 billion to rebuild war-torn Europe. The Soviets saw the Marshall Plan as an attempt to buy the support of countries.

As the split between the United States and the Soviet Union became a fact of life, George Kennan, a well-known diplomat, argued for a **policy of containment**. It aimed at keeping communism within its existing boundaries and preventing its further spread.

The Division of Germany At the end of World War II, the Allied Powers had divided Germany into four zones, each occupied by one of the Allies—the United States, the Soviet Union, Great Britain, and France. Berlin, located deep within the Soviet zone, was also divided into four zones. By 1948, after failing in their attempts to establish a unified Germany because of Soviet opposition, the United States, Great Britain, and France wished to unify their sections into West Germany. The Soviets mounted a blockade (sealing off of a place to prevent people and goods from entering or leaving) of West Berlin to prevent this. Food and supplies could not reach the 2.5 million people in the city's three Western zones. The West did not want to start a war, so it airlifted supplies into Berlin. For ten months, British and American planes delivered more than two million tons of supplies. The Soviets, who also did not want a war, lifted the blockade in 1949. Shortly after, the Federal Republic of Germany, or West Germany, was created. Its capital was Bonn. The Soviets, in return, set up the German Democratic Republic, the East German state, with East Berlin as its capital. Berlin was now divided into two parts.

NATIONAL GEOGRAPHIC

DIVIDED GERMANY AND THE BERLIN AIR LIFT

The Berlin Wall Prosperity was greater in West Berlin than in the East German areas surrounding it, and many East Germans fled. To prevent that, the East German government began to construct a wall separating East Berlin and West Berlin. Begun in 1961, it eventually became a massive barrier with barbed wires, floodlights, machine gun towers, minefields, and dog patrols.

The Spread of the Cold War

In 1949, Communists under Mao Zedong took control of the government in China. Also the United States and the Soviet Union became involved in an **arms race**, a competitive buildup of armies and weapons. Each side believed that only by building

CORE CONCEPTS: SCIENCE AND TECHNOLOGY

The Soviet Union set off its first atomic bomb in 1949. In the early 1950s, both superpowers developed the even more deadly hydrogen bomb. Soon both also had intercontinental ballistic missiles (ICBMs) capable of sending bombs anywhere.

up their arsenals could they prevent the other side from attacking. Nuclear weapons became increasingly destructive. Each side believed that an arsenal of nuclear weapons would prevent war, because if one nation attacked with nuclear weapons, the other could respond and devastate the attacker.

The launching of the Soviet satellite *Sputnik I* in 1957 initiated a space race between the U.S. and the Soviet Union. Three years later, the U.S. launched three satellites.

New Military Alliances The search for security led to the formation of alliances. The North Atlantic Treaty Organization (**NATO**) was formed in 1949. Belgium, Luxembourg, France, the Netherlands, Great Britain, Italy, Denmark, Norway, Portugal, the United States, and Canada all pledged mutual help if any one of them was attacked. Later, West Germany, Turkey, and Greece joined NATO too.

In 1955, the Soviet Union joined with Albania, Bulgaria, Czechoslovakia, East Germany, Hungary, Poland, and Romania in a formal military alliance known as the **Warsaw Pact**.

SECTION 2 THE SOVIET UNION AND EASTERN EUROPE

The Reign of Stalin

Because the Soviet Union's economy had been devastated by World War II, Joseph Stalin initiated a program of economic recovery that emphasized the building of new power plants, canals, factories, and heavy industry (the manufacture of machines and equipment for factories and mines).

This new emphasis raised industrial production dramatically, but it created shortages of consumer goods. People also suffered from a shortage of housing. Meanwhile, until Stalin's death in 1953, repression and political terror were used against the Soviet people.

The Khrushchev Era

The new Soviet leader, **Nikita Khrushchev,** took steps to undo some of the worst features of Stalin's regime. This process became known as de-Stalinization. It included lifting bans from literary works. Khrushchev also tried to put more emphasis on increasing consumer goods and agriculture. Unfortunately, not all of his intentions brought success. The industrial growth rate slowed, and foreign policy failures damaged his reputation. He was forced into retirement.

Eastern Europe: Behind the Iron Curtain

Between 1945 and 1947, Soviet-controlled communist governments became firmly entrenched in East Germany, Bulgaria, Romania, Poland, and Hungary. In 1948, the Soviets seized control of Czechoslovakia.

The satellite states followed Soviet models by instituting five-year plans with emphasis on heavy industry rather than consumer goods. They collectivized agriculture, eliminated all noncommunist parties, and set up secret police and military forces.

Challenges to Soviet Power Many Eastern European peoples resented the economic exploitation and bad living conditions under Soviet control. In the 1950s and 1960s, when the Soviet Union made it clear that it would not allow its satellite states to become independent, protests erupted.

In Hungary, economic problems and unrest led to calls for revolt. The Hungarian leader, Imre Nagy, declared Hungary a free nation on November 1, 1956. Three days later, the Soviet army attacked Budapest and reestablished Soviet control.

In Czechoslovakia, when Alexander Dubček started democratic reforms such as freedom of speech and press, a period of euphoria broke out that became known as "Prague Spring." In response, the Soviet Army invaded Czechoslovakia in August 1968 and crushed the reform movement.

Role of Non-Aligned Nations Newly independent nations often relied on economic assistance from industrialized countries. They often turned to their former colonizing powers for help. Their need for loans and trade with these countries made them vulnerable to foreign influence, and some leaders were wary of a new kind of economic colonialism. However, some countries learned to play Cold War powers against each other while maintaining a nonaligned status. Leaders such as India's Jawaharlal Nehru believed that nonaligned nations could form a powerful political bloc in their own right.

SECTION 3 WESTERN EUROPE AND NORTH AMERICA

Western Europe: Recovery

With the help of the Marshall Plan, the countries of Western Europe recovered rapidly. The 1950s and 1960s were a period of dramatic growth and prosperity in Europe with nearly full employment.

The Economic Miracle of West Germany Chancellor Konrad Adenauer led the new Federal Republic of Germany to an "economic miracle" with record levels of employment. In fact, West Germany eventually brought in thousands of "guest" workers on visas from Italy, Spain, Greece, Turkey, and Yugoslavia. In the mid-1960s, an economic downturn led to a party change. Willy Brandt, leader of the Social Democrats, became the new chancellor.

The Decline of Great Britain The war left Great Britain with massive economic problems, leading to the defeat of Churchill's Conservative Party. The new Labour government under Clement Attlee set out to create a **welfare state**—a state in which the government takes responsibility for providing citizens with services.

The costs of World War II and of building a welfare state at home led to the dismantling of the British Empire. Economic necessity forced Britain to give in to the demands of its many colonies for national independence.

Western Europe: The Move Toward Unity

After the war, many Europeans saw the need for unity. France, West Germany, the Netherlands, Belgium, Luxembourg, and Italy formed an economic union called the European Economic Community (EEC), also known as the Common Market. The EEC was a free-trade area; they did not impose any tariffs (import changes) on one another's goods. By 1960, the EEC had become the world's largest exporter and purchaser of raw materials.

Postwar United States

Between 1945 and 1970, Franklin D. Roosevelt's New Deal largely determined American domestic politics. Changes included an increase in the role and power of the federal government, the rise of organized labor as a significant force in the economy and

CORE CONCEPTS: GOVERNMENT

In 1946, the British government passed the National Insurance Act and the National Health Service Act. The insurance act provided government funds to help the unemployed, the sick, and the aged. The health act created a system of socialized medicine that ensured medical care for everyone.

politics, the beginning of a welfare state, and a realization of the need to deal fairly with minorities, especially African Americans.

An economic boom followed World War II. Between 1945 and 1973, real wages (the actual purchasing power of income) grew an average of 3 percent a year, the most prolonged advance in American history.

The Emergence of a New Society

After World War II, Western societies experienced rapid change. New inventions such as televisions, computers, and jets changed the pace and nature of life.

A Changing Social Structure Changes in the middle class were especially noticeable. It expanded to include managers and technicians as well as businesspeople, lawyers, doctors, and teachers. Changes also occurred in the lower classes. The number of farmers and industrial class workers declined, and the number of white-collar workers increased. An increase in real wages gave them some of the buying power of the middle class. This led to a consumer society, a society preoccupied with buying goods. Buying on credit also became widespread during the 1950s.

Women in the Postwar World Women's roles also changed. Many governments had given women voting rights after World War I. During World War II, women had entered the workforce in huge numbers. At the end of the war, may of them were let go to provide jobs for returning soldiers. Birthrates rose, creating a "baby boom" in the late 1940s and 1950s.

By the end of the 1950s, birthrates fell and the number of women in the workforce increased in Europe and the United States. Women earned less than men and also tended to be restricted to traditionally female jobs. These inequalities led to renewed interest in feminism, or the women's liberation movement.

Student revolts also rocked both Europe and the United States in the 1960s. Some of the most notable were in Berkeley, California, and at the Sorbonne in Paris. University enrollments had shifted as students from the middle and lower classes began to attend. Many European university classrooms were overcrowded, however, and many professors paid little attention to their students. This led to a student attempt to reform the universities. By the early 1970s, however, the movement had largely disappeared.

CORE CONCEPTS: CONFLICT

Prosperity was not the only characteristic of the 1950s, however. Cold War struggles, as well as the war in Korea, led to widespread fear of Communists having infiltrated the United States. This climate of fear produced a dangerous political agitator, Senator Joseph R. McCarthy, who helped create a massive "Red Scare."

CHAPTER 29   THE CONTEMPORARY WESTERN WORLD

Chapter Overview

Reforms made by Mikhail Gorbachev helped lead to the break-up of the Soviet Union. They also helped lead to the fall of communism throughout Eastern Europe and the end of the Cold War. When Yugoslavia underwent a political metamorphosis, complex relationships among its republics and ethnic groups led to war and NATO intervention. Changes in the economies of Canada, the United States, and European nations brought shifts in their economic policies to both the right and the left. Society changed as more and more women entered the workplace. Technological innovation helped lead to a more global society, and the United States became the leading exporter of popular culture.

As you read this chapter, ask yourself these questions:
(1) Why did communism as an economic system collapse in the Soviet Union?
(2) What role did nationalism play in the collapse of communism and the breakup of the Soviet Union?
(3) What problems does Russia face as it moves toward capitalism?
(4) What events led to German reunification?
(5) What changes occurred in Eastern Europe?
(6) How were Western European economies unified?
(7) What were the motivating factors for European unity?
(8) What recent changes have occurred in women's roles, science, and technology?

Main Ideas and Concepts

- **Change** The policies of Mikhail Gorbachev helped bring about the disintegration of the Soviet Union.

- **Nationalism** Massive demonstrations ended some Communist regimes, while violence ended others.

- **Economic Systems** European nations moved to unite their economies after 1970.

- **Science and Technology** Technological and scientific advances have created an interdependent global society.

People, Places, Terms

The following names and terms will help you to prepare for the Regents Exam in Global History and Geography. You can find an explanation of each name and term in the Glossary at the back of this book, in your textbook, or in another reference source.

Bosnia	ethnic cleansing	perestroika
Leonid Brezhnev	glasnost	Vladimir Putin
Chechnya	Mikhail Gorbachev	Lech Walesa
détente	Václav Havel	Boris Yeltsin
dissident	Kosovo	

SECTION 1 DECLINE OF THE SOVIET UNION

From Cold War to Post–Cold War

By the 1970s, American-Soviet relations had entered a new phase known as **détente,** which was marked by a relaxation of tensions and improved relations between the two superpowers. The United States began to sell grain and consumer goods to the Soviet Union.

The Cold War Intensifies Détente collapsed in 1979 when the Soviet Union invaded Afghanistan. President Jimmy Carter stopped the shipment of grain to the Soviet Union. He also would not allow Americans to participate in the 1980 Olympic Games, which were held in Moscow.

The Cold War worsened when Ronald Reagan was elected president in 1980. He called the Soviet Union an "evil empire." He set up the "Star Wars" program of military defense against ballistic missile attacks and gave military aid to the Afghan rebels.

End of the Cold War When **Mikhail Gorbachev** became leader of the Soviet Union in 1985, changes began that eventually ended the Cold War. Gorbachev made an agreement with the United States in 1987 to eliminate intermediate-range nuclear weapons. Gorbachev also stopped giving military support to Communist governments in Eastern Europe. This opened the door to the overthrow of Communist governments in these countries. A

CORE CONCEPTS: ECONOMIC SYSTEMS

Both the United States and the Soviet Union had reasons to slow down the arms race. Gorbachev wanted to make economic and other reforms in the Soviet Union. The national debt in the United States had tripled, and the United States had moved away from being a creditor nation to being the world's biggest debtor nation. By 1990, both countries knew they had to cut military budgets to solve domestic problems.

revolutionary movement swept through Eastern Europe in 1989. Germany was reunified on October 3, 1990. In 1991, the Soviet Union was dissolved. The Cold War had ended.

Upheaval in the Soviet Union

What had happened to cause such drastic change in the Soviet Union?

The Brezhnev Era After Khrushchev was removed from office, **Leonid Brezhnev** became the dominant leader of the Soviet Union. He was determined to keep Eastern Europe in Communist hands and was not interested in reform. His policy, called the Brezhnev Doctrine, insisted on the right of the Soviet Union to intervene if communism was threatened in another Communist state. Under his regime, the government did allow more access to Western styles of music, dress, and art. **Dissidents** (those who spoke out against the regime) were still punished, however. At this time, there were many problems in the Soviet economy, including a huge bureaucracy, a declining economy, rising alcoholism, and poor working conditions. These and other problems led to the emergence of a small group of reformers, including Mikhail Gorbachev.

Gorbachev and Perestroika Gorbachev, who saw the need for reform, began a new era of **glasnost**, or openness in public discussions of Soviet problems. He preached radical reforms, the basis of which was **perestroika** (restructuring). At first, this meant restructuring economic policy. He wanted to start a market economy, in which consumers influence what is produced. Gorbachev realized that political reform had to precede economic reform. He established a new Soviet parliament, the Congress of People's Deputies. It met for the first time in 1989. In 1990, Gorbachev allowed noncommunist political parties to organize.

The End of the Soviet Union As Gorbachev loosened the control of the Communist Party, nationalist movements emerged throughout the republics of the Soviet Union. Communist Party officials became worried. On August 19, 1991, a group of conservatives arrested Gorbachev and tried to seize power. The attempt failed, however, when **Boris Yeltsin**, president of the Russian Republic, and thousands of Russians resisted the rebel forces in Moscow.

CORE CONCEPTS: POLITICAL SYSTEMS

Gorbachev also strengthened his own power by creating the office of president. In 1990, Gorbachev became the Soviet Union's first and last president.

REGENTS WARM-UP

List four actions taken by Gorbachev that led to the end of the Soviet Union.

CORE CONCEPTS: NATION-STATE

Before its breakup, the Soviet Union had united within its borders 92 ethnic groups and 112 languages.

The Soviet republics now moved for complete independence. Ukraine voted for independence on December 1, 1991. A week later, the leaders of Russia, Ukraine, and Belarus announced that the Soviet Union had "ceased to exist." Gorbachev resigned, and Boris Yeltsin became president of the new Russia.

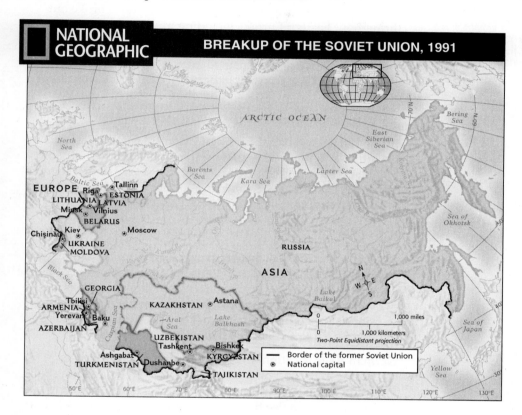

NATIONAL GEOGRAPHIC   **BREAKUP OF THE SOVIET UNION, 1991**

— Border of the former Soviet Union
⊛ National capital

The New Russia Boris Yeltsin was committed to introducing a free market economy as quickly as possible, but organized crime and the problems of the Chechens, who wanted to secede and create their own state, slowed the transition. At the end of 1999, **Vladimir Putin** replaced Yeltsin, vowing to return **Chechnya** to Russian authority. He also began economic reforms such as allowing the free purchase and sale of land, tax cuts, and efforts to join the World Trade Organization.

REGENTS WARM-UP

Study the map. Name the independent states that arose in 1991.

SECTION 2 EASTERN EUROPE

REGENTS WARM-UP

Past Regents Exams have asked students to draw conclusions over periods of time. In the thirty years following World War II, which area of the world was most influenced by the Soviet Union?

Revolutions in Eastern Europe

After Gorbachev made it clear that the Soviet Union would not interfere militarily in its republics, revolutions broke out throughout Eastern Europe, including in Poland, Czechoslovakia, and East Germany.

Poland In 1980, a worker named **Lech Walesa** had organized a national trade union called Solidarity. It gained the support of both workers and the Roman Catholic Church. In 1988, the Polish government agreed to hold free parliamentary elections— the first free elections in Eastern Europe in 40 years. A new government was elected, ending 45 years of Communist rule in Poland. When Walesa became president, his program of rapid free-market reforms led to discontent and severe unemployment. In 1995, Aleksandr Kwasniewski, a former Communist, became the new president.

Czechoslovakia In Czechoslovakia, mass demonstrations took place in 1988 and 1989. In December 1989, the Communist government collapsed. **Václav Havel**, a writer who had played an important role in bringing down the Communists, became the new president. His government faced old ethnic conflicts, so the two national groups, Czechs and Slovaks, agreed to a peaceful division of the country. On January 1, 1993, Czechoslovakia split into the Czech Republic and Slovakia.

German Reunification In East Germany, Erich Honecker became head of the Communist Party in 1971. He used the Stasi, the secret police, to rule for the next 18 years. In 1989, many East Germans began to flee their country. In the fall of the same year, mass demonstrations broke out. The Communist government gave in and opened its border with the West. Thousands of East Germans rushed across it, and people on both sides began tearing down the Berlin Wall. During East Germany's first free elections in March 1990, the Christian Democrats won almost 50 percent of the vote. They supported reunification with Germany, which took place on October 3, 1990.

The Disintegration of Yugoslavia

Although Yugoslavia had a Communist government, it was never a satellite state. The country had remained under Communist rule after the death of Tito in 1980. By 1990, however, new parties had emerged, and the Communist Party lost power.

Calls for Independence Tensions between ethnic groups in the republics go back hundreds of years. In 1990, the Yugoslav republics of Slovenia, Croatia, Bosnia-Herzegovina (often called **Bosnia**), and Macedonia began to push for independence. Slobodan Milosevic, who became the leader of Serbia in 1987, wanted to draw borders to include the Serb minorities in all the republics in a new Greater Serbian state. In June 1991, Slovenia and Croatia declared their independence. In September, the Yugoslavian army, dominated by Serbia, began a full assault against Croatia. Before a cease-fire was arranged, Serbian forces captured one-third of Croatia's territory.

The War in Bosnia In 1992, the Serbs began an assault on Bosnia-Herzegovina. By mid-1993, Serbian forces held 70 percent of Bosnian territory. The Serbs carried out a policy they called **ethnic cleansing** (killing or forcibly removing people from their lands) toward Bosnia's Muslim populations. By 1995, 250,000 Bosnians had been killed, and two million were homeless. Then, with support from NATO, Bosnians regained much of their land. Serbs signed a peace treaty agreeing to split Bosnia into a loose union of a Serb republic and a Muslim-Croat federation. NATO sent a force to monitor the area.

The War in Kosovo In 1974, Tito had made **Kosovo** a self-governing province in Yugoslavia. Kosovo's inhabitants were mainly ethnic Albanians with their own language and customs. In 1989, Slobodan Milosevic had taken self-government away from Kosovo. Some Albanians then formed the Kosovo Liberation Army and began a campaign against Serbian rule. In response, Serb forces began to massacre Albanians. In 1999, Albanians in Kosovo regained self-government.

Elections held in 2000 ended Milosevic's rule, and he was brought to trial for his role in the bloodshed in the Balkans. In 2003, Serbia and Montenegro formed a union and stopped using the name *Yugoslavia*.

REGENTS WARM-UP

How was Yugoslavia like other states that achieved independence as a result of the breakup of the Soviet Union? How was it different?

REGENTS WARM-UP

Did the nationalistic feelings of the various ethnic groups in Yugoslavia help or hinder the development of this area after the fall of communism?

REGENTS WARM-UP

Some Regents Exam
questions will ask you to
make comparisons. How
were the EEC and the EU
alike?

REGENTS WARM-UP

The main purpose of the
European Union (EU) and the
North American Free Trade
Agreement (NAFTA) is to

(1) reduce the spread of
     nuclear weapons
(2) address the problem of
     international political
     corruption
(3) increase educational
     opportunities for under-
     developed countries
(4) stimulate economic
     growth for participating
     countries

CORE CONCEPTS: DIVERSITY

In 1972, Brandt signed a
treaty with East Germany that
led to greater cultural,
personal, and economic
contacts. For this, he
received the Nobel Peace
Prize in 1971.

SECTION 3 EUROPE AND NORTH AMERICA

Winds of Change in Western Europe

An economic downturn, caused in part by the dramatic rise in
the price of oil, hit Europe in the mid-1970s and early 1980s.
Socialist programs in Britain and France were not working.
Inflation and unemployment rose dramatically. Economies
recovered later in the 1980s, but problems remained.

The Western European nations moved toward a greater union
of their economies after 1970. Steps were taken for free movement
of goods, services, money, and travel among member nations.
The European Economic Community (EEC) expanded to include
nine new nations by 1995. The European Union (EU) evolved out
of the EEC. One of its first goals was to establish a common
European currency, the euro. The euro proved to be so strong
that most EU nations gave up their currency in favor of the euro
by January 1, 2002.

NAFTA In 1993, Mexico, the United States, and Canada
approved NAFTA (the North American Free Trade Agreement),
which established guidelines for making trade better. Unlike the
EU, NAFTA does not establish any governmental bodies or laws
that supersede those of the participating nations.

From West Germany to Germany In West Germany, the Social
Democrats, a moderate socialist party, replaced the Christian
Democrats as the leading party in 1969. Their chancellor was
Willy Brandt.

In 1982, power in West Germany shifted to the conservative
Christian Democratic Union of Helmut Kohl. When reunification
occurred in 1990, Germany became the leading power in Europe.
Many problems came with unification, however, including the
collapse of the East German economy. One result of this was that
the Social Democrats were returned to power in 1998. Tensions
existed between Germans and immigrant groups who had
entered the country looking for work under Germany's liberal
immigration policies after World War II. Some Neo-Nazi groups
attacked foreigners, especially Muslims.

SECTION 4 WESTERN SOCIETY AND CULTURE

Changes in Women's Lives

Since 1970, more and more women have entered the workforce in Western countries. Nevertheless, women continue to receive lower wages than men for the same work, and they have fewer opportunities to reach top positions. In 1963, the United States passed the Equal Pay Act. This law gave legal support to equal pay for equal work for women.

In the 1990s, some women wanted legitimacy returned for a woman to choose a traditional role as housewife and mother. Other women tried to redefine the term *feminism* as the struggle to balance career, family, and personal goals.

Science and Technology

The most famous product of wartime research was the atomic bomb. After the war, wartime technology was adapted for peacetime uses. Computers and jet airplanes are two examples. In addition, a new scientific establishment that had been forged between the government and private enterprise continued to operate. Massive government funding enabled the United States to land astronauts on the moon in 1969.

In the 1960s and 1970s, people began to worry that technological advances were damaging the environment. Chemical fertilizers, for example, helped farmers grow more crops but also destroyed the ecological balance of streams, rivers, and woodlands.

Chapter Overview

Economic crises after World War II resulted in political upheavals, including military rule and revolution. Some revolutions and civil wars were leftist or communist. Fidel Castro's Communist Party took power in Cuba. The United States helped crush leftist guerrillas in El Salvador. Marxist Sandanistas overthrew the Somoza family dictatorship in Nicaragua. Some changes brought dictators to power, such as Alberto Fujimori in Peru and Augusto Pinochet in Chile. These dictatorships were often upheld not only by the military but also by the landed aristocracy. Finally, some changes in Latin American governments were primarily constitutional, such as the defeat of the PRI and the system of one-party power in Mexico. Economically, the countries of the region tended to industrialize, but dependence on the advanced industrial nations did not end.

GLOBAL CONCEPTS: PLACES AND REGIONS

The landed aristocracy and military were aided in their bid for power by a lack of education among the mass of people and physical features that promoted regionalism.

As you read this chapter, ask yourself these questions:
(1) What political and economic changes did Latin America experience after 1945?
(2) What were the chief features and impact of the Cuban Revolution?
(3) What is the future of communism and Castro in Cuba?
(4) In what ways were dictatorships an oppressive consequence of political and economic instability?
(5) How has the role of the Catholic Church changed in Latin America?
(6) How have Latin American countries become more democratic?

Main Ideas and Concepts

- **Economic Systems** Economies built on the export of raw materials and the import of manufactured goods faced economic and political upheaval.

- **Power** The United States feared the spread of communism in Central America, which led to active American involvement in the region.

- **Government** Democracy has advanced in South America since the late 1980s.

People, Places, Terms

The following names and terms will help you to prepare for the Regents Exam in Global History and Geography. You can find an explanation of each name and term in the Glossary at the back of this book, in your textbook, or in another reference source.

Fidel Castro	**multinational corporations**	**PRI**
contras	**oligarchy**	**privatization**
encomienda	**Juan Perón**	**Sandinistas**

SECTION 1 GENERAL TRENDS IN LATIN AMERICA

Economic and Political Developments

Since the nineteenth century, Latin America has exported raw materials and imported manufactured goods from industrialized countries. When exports declined during the Great Depression and Latin American countries lacked money for imports, they developed industries to produce their own goods. By the 1960s, however, Latin American countries were still dependent on the United States, Europe, and Japan for the technology needed for modern industries. Many Latin American countries also had trouble finding markets for their manufactured goods.

In the 1960s, military governments in Chile, Brazil, and Argentina returned to export-import economies. They also encouraged **multinational corporations,** companies with divisions in more than two countries, to come to Latin America. In the 1970s, Latin American countries became even more dependent as they tried to maintain their weak economies by borrowing money. Wages fell while inflation and unemployment skyrocketed.

To get new loans, the countries had to make basic reforms. The debt crisis brought a movement toward democracy. Many people realized that military power alone could not build a strong state. By the mid-1990s, several democratic governments had been created. This trend was fragile, however.

CORE CONCEPTS: INTERDEPENDENCE

The multinational corporation embodies the growing interdependence between more developed and less developed nations. In this case, technological superiority based on extensive capital sometimes gives multinationals power to affect the economies of underdeveloped nations. Some multinationals boast larger incomes than the GNP of some developing countries.

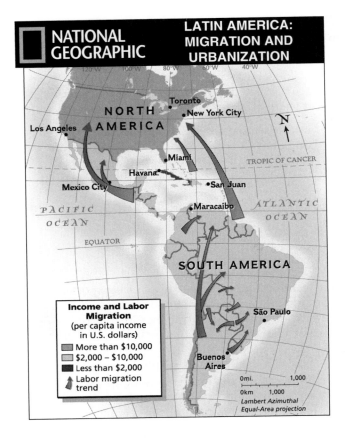

Latin American Society

Dramatic population growth intensified Latin America's economic problems. Cities grew rapidly and by 2000, 50 cities in Latin America and the Caribbean had more than one million people. Slums and shantytowns were found in many cities. The gap between rich and poor remained huge. Landholding and urban elites owned huge estates and businesses while the poor struggled just to survive. The international drug trade also brought crime and corruption to some Latin American countries.

The United States and Latin America

The United States has long played a role in Latin America. For years, the United States sent troops to protect United States interests and to help dictators that were friendly to the United States. In 1948, the Organization of American States (OAS) called for an end to the involvement of one state in the affairs of any other state in the Western Hemisphere. Still, in the era of the Cold War, the United States remained involved. It took action whenever it believed that Soviet agents were trying to establish communist governments. The United States also provided huge amounts of military aid to anticommunist governments.

Latin American Culture

Writers and artists have often been accorded higher status in Latin America than in other areas of the world. Among Latin America's greatest writers are two Nobel Prize winners, Gabriela Mistral and Gabriel García Márquez. García Márquez is known for his use of magic realism, a style that mixes real and fantastic settings and events.

The Changing Role of the Catholic Church

Most Christians in Latin America are Roman Catholics, and Roman Catholic traditions influence daily life in the region. Since colonial times, Church leaders have played an important role in politics. When the call for independence came, Church officials backed the wealthy and powerful classes.

During the late 1990s, however, Roman Catholics in Latin America began to support the concerns of the poor and oppressed. In recent years, many Roman Catholic clergy and laypeople have opposed dictatorships and worked to improve the lives of disadvantaged groups. For example, the Church has been active in movements for land reform and for improvements in education and health care.

Immigration to the United States

Growing numbers of Latin Americans have migrated abroad, especially to the United States. Many of these migrants have come to the United States to find a better way of life, some entering without visas. Others are well-educated people or skilled workers who could make important contributions to their home countries. For example, if scientists or researchers leave Latin America, its countries may ultimately lack the human resources necessary to solve environmental problems. To stem this out-migration, Latin American leaders are seeking to create jobs for their people by attracting more foreign investment.

Latin American migrants, meanwhile, have brought many changes to the United States. Immigration from Latin America has made the United States the country with the fifth-largest Spanish-speaking population in the world. Latin Americans have contributed much to the many communities in which they have settled—Mexicans in Texas, California, and Illinois; Cubans in Florida; and Puerto Ricans and Dominicans in New York.

SECTION 2 MEXICO, CUBA, AND CENTRAL AMERICA

The Mexican Way

The official political party of Mexico, the **PRI** (Institutional Revolutionary Party) dominated Mexican politics for decades. Its presidential candidate was always elected.

During the 1950s and 1960s, economic growth led to real gains in wages for more and more people in Mexico. At the end of the 1960s, however, students began to protest the one-party system. When university students gathered in Mexico City in protest, police forces opened fire and killed hundreds. People were now concerned about the need for change. The next two presidents made political reforms and opened the door to new political parties. Greater freedom of debate in the press and universities was allowed.

In the late 1970s, vast new reserves of oil were discovered in Mexico. The sale of oil abroad increased dramatically, and the government became more dependent on oil revenues. When oil prices dropped in the mid-1980s, Mexico could not make the payments on its foreign debt. The government was forced to adopt new economic policies. One new policy was **privatization** (the sale of government-owned companies to private firms). The debt crisis and rising unemployment caused support for the PRI to drop. In 2000, Vicente Fox defeated the PRI candidate for the presidency.

The North American Free Trade Agreement (NAFTA) has helped boost Mexican exports and created thousands of new jobs. Mexican workers are generally paid less than workers in the United States. Some American companies are wary of relocation, however, because certain costs, such as electricity, are higher in Mexico.

The Cuban Revolution

Fulgencio Batista ruled Cuba for 25 years after leading a coup in 1933. He ended all political opposition and allowed foreign businesses, especially in the United States, to come and get wealthy off of the resources of Cuba.

In the 1950s, **Fidel Castro** led a movement to overthrow Batista's government. Many Cubans who disagreed with Castro fled to the United States. When Cuba began to receive aid and arms from the Soviet Union, its relationship with the United States deteriorated. In October 1960, the United States declared a trade embargo and broke all diplomatic relations with Cuba.

Tensions intensified when President John F. Kennedy tried to overthrow Castro's new government by means of the Bay of Pigs invasion. The Soviet Union began placing missiles in Cuba, which led to the Cuban missile crisis.

Over time, Castro, who had declared himself a Marxist, lost faith in the Soviet Union and hoped to start a social revolution in the rest of Latin America, but this failed. In Cuba, his government provided some benefits to the Cuban people, including free medical services and the elimination of illiteracy.

The Cuban economy relied on the production and sale of sugar. Economic problems forced Castro's government to depend on Soviet aid and the purchase of Cuban sugar by Soviet bloc countries. After the collapse of these governments in 1989, economic conditions steadily declined, but Castro managed to remain in power.

Upheaval in Central America

Central America includes seven countries: Costa Rica, Nicaragua, Honduras, El Salvador, Panama, Belize, and Guatemala. It has depended economically on the export of bananas, coffee, and cotton. Varying prices for these products have created economic crises from time to time. A huge gulf between the wealthy elite and poor peasants has also created instability in these countries. Fear of communism has often led the United States to support repressive regimes in this area.

Nicaragua In Nicaragua, the Somoza family took control of the government in 1937 and kept control for the next 42 years. The Somozas, who got rich at the nation's expense and used murder and torture against their opponents, generally had the support of the United States government. By 1979, the United States was no

CORE CONCEPTS: MOVEMENT OF PEOPLE AND GOODS

The Cuban Revolution reduced the power of the upper and middle classes, the traditional property and business owners. Many of these people fled to Florida. Today, so many Cubans live in Miami that a section of the city has been nicknamed "Little Havana."

CORE CONCEPTS: INTERDEPENDENCE

The collapse of Soviet communism severely affected Cuba. In the 1960s and 1970s, Cuba served as a base for exporting communism— and revolution—to the rest of Latin America. By the 1990s, Cuba found itself isolated from the Latin American community of nations.

CORE CONCEPTS: INTERDEPENDENCE

The civil war in Nicaragua spread turmoil to other nations in the region as guerrillas crossed borders seeking safe havens. Costa Rica tried to stay out of the conflict by following a policy of neutrality.

longer willing to support the Somoza government. In the same year, Marxist guerrilla forces, known as the **Sandinista** National Liberation front, won a number of victories against government forces and gained control of the country. Soon a group called the **contras,** who were opposed to the Sandinistas' policies, began to the overthrow the new government. The Reagan and Bush administrations supported the contras because they were worried about the Sandinistas' ties with the Soviet Union. The Sandinistas lost support and agreed to free elections. They lost the elections that followed but remained one of the strongest political parties in Nicaragua.

Panama Panama became a nation in 1903 when the United States helped it break away from Colombia. In return for this help, the United States was able to build the Panama Canal. The United States also had a great deal of influence over the government and economy of Panama. After 1968, political power rested in the hands of Panama's National Guard. One member of the guard, Manuel Noriega, took control of Panama in 1983. At first, the United States supported Noriega, but his brutality and involvement with the drug trade turned American leaders against him. In 1989, President George Bush sent United States troops to Panama. Noriega was arrested and sent to prison in the United States on charges of drug trafficking.

A major issue for Panamanians was finally settled in 1999 when Panama took control of the canal. The terms for this change of control had been set in a 1977 treaty with the United States.

Guatemala A majority of Guatemalans are indigenous peoples descended from the Maya. The **encomienda** system's effects on the native population can still be felt today. Less than 1 percent of the population controls 75 percent of the best land in the country. This inequality in land ownership has forced the indigenous peoples to work for small wages doing seasonal work.

In the 1960s, a Castro-backed rebellion set off a 36-year civil war between the military government and leftist guerrillas, including forces sympathetic to native peoples. Massacres were common and more than 200,000 indigenous people were killed.

CORE CONCEPTS: SCIENCE AND TECHNOLOGY

Although the Panama Canal remains important for naval traffic, the development of airplanes and rockets has reduced its strategic importance in terms of war. This technological change helped influence the United States' decision to turn the canal over to Panama in 2000.

allowing Slavery

CORE CONCEPTS: INTERDEPENDENCE

The Great Depression and World War II left much of Europe in economic ruins. As a result, the United States became the dominant economic power in Latin America.

SECTION 3 SOUTH AMERICA

Argentina

Argentina is Latin America's second largest country. For years, it was ruled by a powerful **oligarchy**. In 1943, military officials overthrew the oligarchy and **Juan Perón** became the new labor secretary. He won the support of the workers by increasing job benefits and encouraging them to join labor unions. In 1946, he was elected president of Argentina.

Perón's main support came from the urban middle classes. To please them, he increased industrialization and tried to free Argentina from foreign investors. The government bought the railways and took over the banking, insurance, shipping, and communications industries.

Perón's regime was authoritarian. He created Fascist gangs modeled after Hitler's Brownshirts. They used violence against Perón's opponents. Fearing his power, the military overthrew Perón in 1955 but eventually brought him back when they were overwhelmed by the nation's problems. Perón was reelected president in 1973 but died one year later.

In 1976, the military took over again. Approximately 36,000 people were killed at this time by a regime that allowed no opposition. A human rights group, the Mothers of the Plaza de Maya, have been active for more than twenty-five years. The group is made up of mothers whose children disappeared and were likely tortured and murdered during the military's war against the Left from 1976 to 1983. The Mothers continue to ask the government to account for those who disappeared and to fight against repression in Argentina.

When serious economic problems arose, the military tried to divert people's attention by invading the Falkland Islands off the Argentine coast, which Great Britain had controlled since the nineteenth century. Great Britain sent troops and took the island back. The loss discredited the military and opened the door to civilian rule.

In 1983, Raúl Alfonsín was elected president and worked to restore democratic practices. In 1989, the Perónist Carlos Saúl Menem won the presidential election. This peaceful transfer of power made many people hopeful that Argentina was moving on a democratic path.

CORE CONCEPTS: POWER

Perón's wife Eva (Evita), who grew up in poverty, was the darling of the working classes. While she had hospitals, schools, and orphanages built and pushed for women's rights, she also lived lavishly.

CORE CONCEPTS: FACTORS OF PRODUCTION

Like parts of Latin America, Africa still suffers from a lack of industrial development and an over-reliance on single cash crops. As you read, watch for how imperialism as well as other factors of production affected the region's economies.

Chapter Overview

Independence from colonial rule followed World War II for most African nations. Democracy did not also follow as hoped, however, because ethnic divisions, economic challenges, and other problems made the transition difficult. Nevertheless, some democratic change has occurred, as in South Africa, where apartheid was abolished. Today's Africa is, in general, a land of contrasts between modern and traditional, rich and poor, urban and rural.

In the Middle East, a period of conflict followed World War II. Israel became a nation in 1948, and wars and tensions have followed ever since. A revolution in Iran ended American ties and led to an Islamic republic. Afghanistan was invaded by the Soviets, then taken over by the Taliban. Iraq has been both an invading and an invaded nation. Conservative Muslims have increasingly enforced Islamic beliefs throughout the Middle East.

As you read this chapter, ask yourself these questions:
(1) How have independent nations emerged in Africa?
(2) What ethnic, cultural, environmental, and economic challenges face African nations?
(3) How did the Cold War and nationalism affect politics in the Middle East?
(4) What steps and people have been involved in the Middle East peace process?
(5) What steps led to the end of apartheid in South Africa?

Main Ideas and Concepts

- **Political Systems** With independence came the hope for democracy in African states, but many new nations became military regimes and one-party states.

- **Culture** A tension between the modern and traditional, rural and urban, exists in Africa today.

- **Human Rights** In many areas in Africa and the Middle East, people continue to struggle for basic human rights.

- **Conflict** Political instability in many areas in the Middle East has led to armed conflict and the need for outside mediation and intervention.

- **Culture** An Islamic revival has influenced political and social life.

People, Places, Terms

The following names and terms will help you to prepare for the Regents Exam in Global History and Geography. You can find an explanation of each name and term in the Glossary at the back of this book, in your textbook, or in another reference source.

ANC	F.W. de Klerk	PLO
apartheid	Nelson Mandela	Saddam Hussein
Yasir Arafat	OPEC	Sinai Peninsula
Camp David Accords	Pan-Africanism	Desmond Tutu
Ayatollah Khomeini	Pan-Arabism	West Bank

SECTION 1 INDEPENDENCE IN AFRICA

The Transition to Independence

After World War II, Europeans decided that colonial rule would have to end. In the 1950s and 1960s, most African nations gained their independence. In 1957, the former British colony of the Gold Coast was the first to gain independence. It became Ghana. Nigeria, the Belgian Congo (renamed Zaire), Kenya, and others followed. Seventeen new African nations emerged in 1960. Another eleven followed between 1961 and 1965.

After a series of guerrilla wars, the Portuguese finally gave up their colonies of Mozambique and Angola in the 1970s. In North Africa, the French gave Morocco and Tunisia their independence in 1956. After a guerilla war by Algerian nationalists against the French, Algeria was granted independence in 1962.

In South Africa, the situation was more complicated. A system of racial segregation known as **apartheid** had developed. Blacks had no political power or right to vote. They were required to have passes to travel around the country and were forced to ride on separate trains. Land, jobs, schools, and even ambulances were segregated. The African National Congress (**ANC**) was formed in 1912, but it had little success.

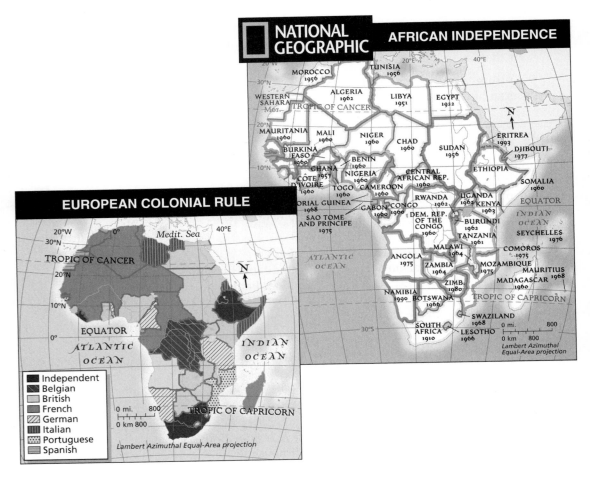

NATIONAL GEOGRAPHIC   **AFRICAN INDEPENDENCE**

EUROPEAN COLONIAL RULE

Legend:
- Independent
- Belgian
- British
- French
- German
- Italian
- Portuguese
- Spanish

Lambert Azimuthal Equal-Area projection

CORE CONCEPTS: POWER

Four other nations in southern Africa had large white-settler populations: Angola, Mozambique, Namibia, and Rhodesia. In 1980, Rhodesia was renamed Zimbabwe. Communist-backed rebels in Angola and Mozambique ousted the Portuguese. Namibia came under South African control at the end of World War I. South Africans withdrew in 1990.

By the 1950s, South African whites had strengthened the laws separating whites and blacks. In 1960, police opened fire on people who were leading a peaceful march, killing 69. After the arrest of ANC leader **Nelson Mandela** in 1962, members of the ANC called for armed resistance to the white government.

Mandela spent 26 years in prison for his activities in the ANC. Archbishop **Desmond Tutu** and others worked to free him and to end apartheid in South Africa. Worldwide pressure on the government of South Africa also helped lead to reforms and the end of apartheid laws. Bowing to internal unrest and international pressure, Mandela was released from prison and the government of President **F.W. de Klerk** lifted the ban on the ANC in 1990. In 1993, the government agreed to hold democratic elections—the first in the nation's history. In 1994, Nelson Mandela became South Africa's first black president.

The New Nations

Independence went hand in hand with dreams of stable governments and economic prosperity. Most of these dreams have yet to be realized.

New African Leaders Most leaders of the newly independent African nations came from the urban middle class, were Western-educated, and believed in democracy. Economically, however, their views were diverse. Some believed in Western-style capitalism. Others wanted an African form of socialism based on African traditions of community. Some African leaders believed in the dream of **Pan-Africanism**, the unity of all black Africans, regardless of national boundaries. Leaders who believed in Pan-Africanism included Léopold Senghor of Senegal, Kwame Nkrumah of Ghana, and Jomo Kenyatta of Kenya. The Organization of African Unity (OAU), founded in 1963, resulted from the belief in Pan-Africanism. In 2002, the African Union (AU) replaced the OAU. Its aims are to promote democracy and economic growth in the region.

Economic Problems Independence did not bring economic prosperity. Most countries still relied on the export of a single crop or natural resource, and most still had to import manufactured goods. Often, nations depend on their former colonial countries for economic support and on already established trading ties.

New states also created some new problems. In some cases, officials were corrupt. In other cases, scarce national resources were spent on expensive consumer goods or military equipment instead of on building foundations for an industrial economy.

The Democratic Republic of Congo (formerly Zaire) is an example of an African nation that is rich in natural resources but has yet to capitalize on that wealth. Corrupt leadership and political instability has chased away crucial foreign investment.

The high rate of African population growth, droughts, and famine crippled some efforts to build economies. In recent years, the spread of AIDS has also hurt economies.

Because of all these problems, poverty is widespread in Africa, especially among the three-quarters of the population still living off the land. Cities have grown rapidly and are surrounded by massive slums. Rapid urbanization has overwhelmed sanitation and transportation systems.

The United Nations has played a large role in Africa since its inception. In 1977, it urged nations to enforce sanctions and an arms embargo on South Africa until apartheid was ended. It has also undertaken peacekeeping missions, sent food and supplies to drought-stricken countries, and provided relief to refugees of civil and tribal wars.

Political Challenges Many people had hoped that independence would lead to stable political systems based on "one person, one vote." They were soon disappointed. Democratic government gave way to military regimes and one-party states. Between 1957 and 1982, over 70 leaders of African nations were violently overthrown.

Nigeria An example of ethnic conflict is in Nigeria. In 1914, the British formed the colony of Nigeria from several smaller ethnic territories. As a result, many different ethnic and religious groups lived within Nigeria's boundaries. Despite their differences, Nigerians came together to resist colonial rule. In 1960, the colony of Nigeria became independent.

The ethnic and religious differences of the past soon erupted in civil war, however. When northerners began to kill the Ibo people, thousands fled to the eastern part of the country. There, the Ibo organized a resistance and declared the eastern region of Nigeria an independent state called Biafra. After two and a half years of bloody civil war, Biafra surrendered and accepted the authority of the government of Nigeria.

Rwanda and Burundi Hutu and Tutsi people lived peacefully in this region of Central Africa for centuries. However, colonial powers Germany and Belgium both viewed the Tutsi as a superior people and promoted them in society. Most Hutu were exploited and denied positions of authority.

The violence began with a Hutu uprising in 1959. When Rwanda and Burundi gained independence in 1962, Hutu and Tutsi groups began to struggle for control of the two countries. Since the 1960s, more than a million Hutu and Tutsi people have been killed and millions more have been driven from their homes. Both nations are still working toward stable, democratic governments, but there has been no end to the violence.

New Hopes

In recent years, demonstrations have led to the rise of democracies in several countries. In Uganda, for example, Idi Amin

CORE CONCEPTS: NATION-STATES

The concept of nationhood in new African states was undermined by warring ethnic groups. This resulted from the arbitrary drawing of borders by colonial powers.

had ruled by terror throughout the 1970s, but he was deposed in 1979. Dictatorships also came to an end in Ethiopia, Liberia, and Somalia. In these cases, however, civil war followed later.

Society and Culture in Modern Africa

Africa is a study in contrasts. Old and new, native and foreign, live side by side. Constant tension exists between traditional ways and Western culture.

City and Countryside Most African cities look like cities elsewhere in the world. They have high-rise apartments, neon lights, movie theaters, and traffic jams. Outside the major cities, where about three-quarters of the people of Africa live, modern influence has had less impact. Millions of people live much as their ancestors did, in thatched dwellings without modern plumbing and electricity. They farm, hunt, or raise livestock by traditional methods. Many urban dwellers see rural people as backward. Rural people see the cities as corrupting and destructive to traditional African values and customs.

Women's Roles After independence, women were allowed to vote and run for political office. Women dominate some professions, such as teaching, child care, and clerical work, but they do not have the range of choices that men do. Most African women are employed in low-paid positions. In many rural areas, traditional attitudes toward women, including arranged marriages, still prevail.

CORE CONCEPTS: IDENTITY

More than 200 million Africans still practice traditional African religions. About 150 million follow Islam, while another 130 million follow some form of Christianity.

SECTION 2 CONFLICT IN THE MIDDLE EAST

The Middle East after World War II

The continued rise of nationalism after World War I and II gradually ended direct colonial rule. By the 1960s, most areas had achieved political freedom. Even after gaining independence, regional economies often remained under colonial control. Leaders in Iran, Iraq, and Libya placed foreign-owned oil companies under state control.

Various nations have fought each other over land and water resources. Because water is scarce, people have settled over the centuries along seacoasts, rivers, and other areas where water is readily available. Desert areas remain largely uninhabited, except where oil is abundant.

The region is growing rapidly. Many citizens, especially in North Africa, are unable to find work and must migrate to other countries. Large urban areas have experienced explosive growth and struggle to keep up with housing and transportation needs. As in many other parts of the world, this rapid urbanization has resulted in pollution and poverty for many urban dwellers.

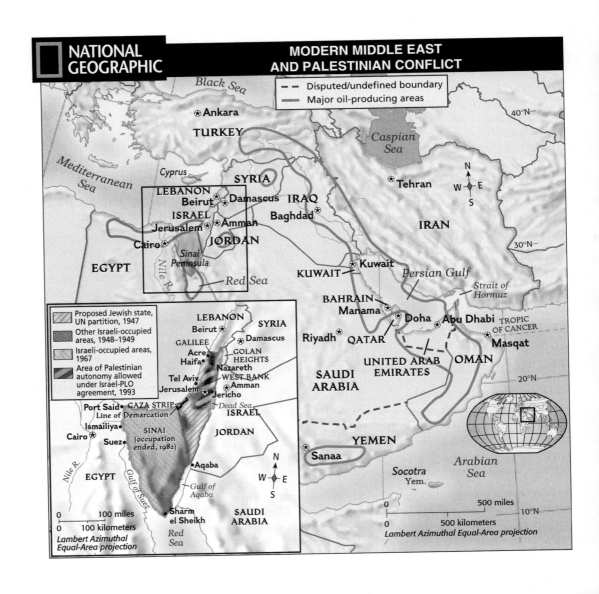

NATIONAL GEOGRAPHIC

MODERN MIDDLE EAST AND PALESTINIAN CONFLICT

- – – Disputed/undefined boundary
- —— Major oil-producing areas

The Question of Palestine

Before World War II, Great Britain ruled Palestine under a United Nations mandate and limited Jewish migration. As a result of the Holocaust, however, sympathy grew for a Jewish state and many Jews emigrated to Palestine. In 1948, a United Nations resolution divided Palestine into a Jewish state and an Arab state. Jews in Palestine proclaimed the state of Israel on May 14, 1948. Arab nations saw the new state as a betrayal of the Palestinian people, most of whom were Muslim. Several Arab countries invaded Israel. The invasion failed, but the Arab states still refused to recognize Israel's right to exist. As a result of the division of Palestine, hundreds of thousands of Palestinians fled to neighboring countries. Other Palestinians came under Israeli rule.

Nasser and Pan-Arabism

In the early 1950s, Colonel Gamal Abdel Nasser took control of the Egyptian government. In 1956, Nasser seized the Suez Canal Company, which had been under French and British control. The attack by Great Britain, France, and Israel on Egypt started the Suez War of 1956. The United States and the Soviet Union supported Nasser and forced Britain, France, and Israel to withdraw their troops from Egypt.

Nasser emerged from the conflict as a powerful leader. He began to promote **Pan-Arabism** (Arab unity). In 1958, Egypt united with Syria to form the United Arab Republic (UAR). Nasser was named the first president. Egypt and Syria hoped that the union would eventually include all Arab states, but many were suspicious of Pan-Arabism. Oil-rich states were concerned they would have to share oil revenues with poorer states. In 1961, military leaders took over Syria and withdrew the country from its union with Egypt.

The Arab-Israeli Dispute

During the 1950s and 1960s, tensions increased between Israel and the other states in the Middle East. In 1967, Nasser imposed a blockade against Israeli shipping through the Gulf of Aqaba and proclaimed readiness to confront Israel. Fearing attack, Israel launched air strikes against Egypt and several of its Arab neighbors. Israeli planes wiped out most of the Egyptian air force. They also broke through the blockade and occupied the **Sinai Peninsula.** They seized territory on the **West Bank** of the Jordan River, occupied Jerusalem, and took control of the Golan Heights. During this Six-Day War, Israel tripled the size of its territory.

CORE CONCEPTS: IDENTITY

Syria left the alliance to avoid Egyptian domination. After the split, however, both Egypt and Syria kept the words "Arab Republic" in their names—Syrian Arab Republic and Arab Republic of Egypt. The purpose was to underscore the Arab identity of each nation.

Over the next few years, Arab states demanded the return of the occupied territories. Israeli Prime Minister Golda Meir refused to stop the expansion of settlements in the new territories.

Nasser died in 1970 and was succeeded by Anwar el-Sadat. In 1973, Arab forces led by Sadat launched a new attack against Israel. An attack on the country by Egypt and Syria on Yom Kippur, 1973, took their defenses by surprise and led to the eventual resignation of Meir. A cease-fire agreement negotiated by the United Nations ended this conflict in 1974.

The war had indirect effects on Western nations. A number of Arab oil-producing states formed the Organization of Petroleum Exporting Countries (**OPEC**) in 1960 to gain control over oil prices. During the 1973 war, some OPEC nations announced large increases in the price of oil to foreign countries. The price hikes and cuts in oil production led to oil shortages in the United States and Europe. The United States was eager for a resolution and brought the leaders to Camp David, the presidential retreat. In March 1979, Sadat and Begin signed the **Camp David Accords**, an agreement to sign an Israeli-Egyptian peace treaty. It ended the war between Egypt and Israel. The Camp David Accords failed, however, because the premises that it was built upon failed.

The PLO and the *Intifada*

In 1964, the Egyptians took the lead in forming the Palestine Liberation Organization (**PLO**) to represent the interests of the Palestinians. The PLO believed that only the Palestinian people had the right to create a state in Palestine. A guerrilla movement headed by PLO leader **Yasir Arafat** began to launch terrorist attacks on Israeli territory. During the early 1980s, Palestinian Arabs became even more militant. The *intifada* ("uprising") among PLO supporters living in Israel began.

Peace talks in the early 1990s led to an agreement in 1993 between Israel and the PLO. The Oslo Accords called for Palestinian autonomy in certain areas. In return, the PLO recognized the Israeli state. Yasir Arafat became the head of the semi-independent area known as the Palestinian authority.

Arafat and Israeli prime minister Yitzhak Rabin were awarded the Nobel Peace Price in 1994 for their roles in creating the accords. Rabin was assassinated in 1995.

REGENTS WARM-UP

Practice for the Regents by using test-taking tips, such as eliminating answers you are sure are wrong, to answer this question:

In 1979, the signing of the Camp David Accords by Egypt and Israel indicated that

(1) nationalism was no longer a force in Middle Eastern politics
(2) the differences between Shiite and Sunni Muslims had been settled
(3) former political enemies were able to negotiate
(4) the Soviet Union dominated Middle Eastern affairs

Revolution in Iran

The autocratic, Western-leaning leadership of Shah Mohammad Reza Pahlavi and revenue from oil helped Iran to become a rich country. Millions of Muslims disliked the new Iranian state, however, which they felt was based on greed and materialism, and this was attributed to American influence. Leading the opposition to the shah was the Ayatollah Ruhollah Khomeini, a member of the Muslim clergy. In 1979, the shah's government collapsed and was replaced by an Islamic republic led by Khomeini. It began to restore Islamic law. After the death of Khomeini in 1989, a new government under President Hashemi Rafsanjani began to loosen control over personal expression and social activities. A new wave of government repression began in the mid-1990s.

Iraq's Aggression

Although Iran and Iraq are neighbors, the Iranians are mainly Shiite Muslims and the Iraqis are mainly Sunnis. Iran and Iraq have had many disputes over territory, especially the Strait of Hormuz, which connects the Persian Gulf and the Gulf of Oman. In 1980, President **Saddam Hussein** of Iraq launched an attack on Iran. Poison gas was used against civilians, and children were used to clear minefields. A cease-fire was finally arranged in 1988.

In 1990, Iraqi troops moved across the border and occupied Kuwait. This sparked the Persian Gulf War. The United States led an international force that freed Kuwait and destroyed a large part of Iraq's armed forces. In 2003, the United States with some allies again attacked the region. This time the government of Saddam Hussein was toppled. An interim government was formed but some religious groups and terrorist fighters have kept up attacks on this government.

Kurds

Most Kurds are Muslim. They live in the border areas of Turkey, Iraq, Iran, Syria, and the Caucasian republics, in an area sometimes called Kurdistan. However, the Kurds have no country of their own. Their efforts to win self-rule have been repeatedly crushed by their Turkish and Arab rulers. During the war with Iran, Saddam Hussein used chemical weapons against the Kurds, killing thousands.

CORE CONCEPTS: IDENTITY

At the time of the revolution, anti-American feelings led to the taking of 52 American hostages from the United States embassy in Iran. In this way, the new government asserted its distance from and power over the United States. They were held for over a year.

CORE CONCEPTS: POWER

The military actions of Saddam Hussein realigned power relationships among Middle Eastern nations who favored regional peace. The coalition in the Persian Gulf War against Iraq succeeded largely through the support of Turkey and Saudi Arabia.

Islamic Fundamentalism

In recent years, conservative religious forces have tried to replace Western cultural influence with Islamic beliefs and values. This movement is called Islamic fundamentalism. For most Muslims, it is a reassertion of Islamic law, cultural identity, religious observance, family values, and morality. As Islamic identity grew in popularity, many Arab leaders, such as Libya's Muammar Qaddafi appealed to Islam to enhance their authority and gain political support.

Some Turkish Muslims have pushed for a greater role for religion in society. The secular establishment that is the legacy of Kemal Atatürk is carefully guarded, however.

In Algeria, the failure of the National Liberation Front (the party that won independence from France) to solve the country's social and economic problems led to the rise of Islamist political parties. When these parties won a majority in local and parliamentary elections, however, they were outlawed and many of their leaders arrested, sparking a civil war.

Islamic Militants The goal of Muslim extremists is to remove all Western influence in Muslim countries. The movement to return to pure ideals began in Iran, under Ayatollah Khomeini. In revolutionary Iran, the return to traditional Muslim beliefs affected clothing styles, social practices, and the legal system. In Egypt, militant Muslims assassinated President Sadat in 1981.

Terrorism

Acts of terrorism have become part of modern society. Terrorists kill civilians, take hostages, and hijack airplanes to draw attention to their demands or to achieve their goals. Some terrorists are militant nationalists who wish to create separate states.

State-sponsored terrorism is another form of terrorism. Some militant governments have provided support to terrorist organizations; Iraq, Syria, Cuba, and North Korea are some examples.

Afghanistan and the Taliban

After World War II, the king of Afghanistan developed close ties with the Soviet Union in order to gain economic assistance for his country. After the king was overthrown, new leaders attempted to create a Communist government, but groups

CORE CONCEPTS: POLITICAL SYSTEMS

The Sunni Muslims do not have a priesthood or clergy. They believe the Quran should be studied by all believers. The Shiites, however, believe the interpretation of the Quran belongs to special teachers known as imams. The most powerful imams are called ayatollahs, one of the most influential groups in present-day Shiite nations.

wanting to create an Islamic state opposed them. The Soviets then launched a full-scale invasion of Afghanistan in 1979. They occupied the country for ten years until they were forced to withdraw by anticommunist forces supported by the United States and Pakistan. Various Islamic groups began to fight for control. One of them, the Taliban, seized power.

The Taliban was condemned for its human rights abuses and harsh social policies. It was also suspected of sheltering Osama bin Laden and his al-Qaeda organization. In 1990 and 2000, the United Nations Security Council demanded that the Taliban hand over bin Laden for trial, but it refused.

September 11, 2001

One of the most destructive acts of terrorism occurred on September 11, 2001. Four groups of terrorists hijacked four commercial U.S. jets. Three of the airplanes were flown into buildings in New York City and Washington, D.C. The fourth plane was diverted in Pennsylvania by heroic passengers who forced the plane to crash in an isolated area. Thousands of people were killed.

The U.S. government gathered evidence that indicated the acts had been carried out by al-Qaeda. President George W. Bush began military action against Afghanistan. In 2001, the Taliban was driven out of Kabul by rebel forces and American bombers.

CHAPTER 32   ASIA AND THE PACIFIC

Chapter Overview

In mainland China, Mao Zedong sought to create an ideal socialist state by launching programs such as the Great Leap Forward and the Cultural Revolution. After his death, Deng Xiaoping and others brought some of Mao's more destructive policies to an end, and a limited movement toward capitalism began.

After its independence, the Indian subcontinent was divided into Muslim Pakistan and Hindu India. In India, the government continued to struggle with ethnic conflict as well as problems of overpopulation and poverty. In Southeast Asia, colonies gained their independence after World War II but were not able to establish democracies for many years.

Japan was occupied after World War II by U.S. forces and began a program of political and social change. Economically, it rebuilt itself into an industrial giant. Other nations in the Pacific also created successful industrial societies, including South Korea, Taiwan, Singapore, and Hong Kong.

As you read this chapter, ask yourself these questions:
(1) What economic and political changes occurred in China?
(2) What are some characteristics of China's changing culture?
(3) What was China's role in the Cold War and Korean War?
(4) How did India change, and how were Pakistan and Bangladesh formed?
(5) What is religious, social, and cultural life like in India?
(6) What are the independent states of Southeast Asia, and what is life like there?
(7) What social and political changes occurred during the Allied occupation of Japan?
(8) How has Japan changed since 1945?

Main Ideas and Concepts

- **Political Systems** Mao Zedong launched ambitious programs to create an ideal communist state, but many of them proved disastrous for the Chinese people.

- **Economic Systems** After the death of Mao Zedong, Deng Xiaoping established capitalist policies to create economic growth.

- **Conflict** Economic problems and political conflicts hampered the growth of democracy in newly created countries in South and Southeast Asia.

- **Economic Systems** Japan and other nations of the Pacific have built successful industrial economies.

People, Places, Terms

The following names and terms will help you to prepare for the Regents Exam in Global History and Geography. You can find an explanation of each name and term in the Glossary at the back of this book, in your textbook, or in another reference source.

Bangladesh	Mao Zedong	per capita
Cultural Revolution	Ho Chi Minh	Singapore
Deng Xiaoping	occupied	Taiwan
domino theory	Pakistan	Tiananmen Square
Hong Kong		

SECTION 1 COMMUNIST CHINA

With the beginnings of communism, China developed command economies, or government-controlled economies. Government controls were used to boost industrial output.

Much of China is rural, and a majority of its people were farmers. Large numbers of people were needed to work the land because many farmers used (and still do use) traditional tools.

Despite large oil and coal deposits in the western part of China, development has proceeded slowly because of the lack of transportation. China's rivers provide important routes inland from seaports.

Civil War and the Great Leap Forward *china*

By 1945, there were two Chinese governments. The Nationalist government of Chiang Kai-shek was based in southern and central China. The United States supported it. The Communist government under **Mao Zedong** was based in North China. In 1945, war broke out between the Nationalists and the

REGENTS WARM-UP

Essay questions on past Regents Exams have asked how the ideas or actions of an individual have shaped history. Underline the information in this chapter that shows how Mao Zedong changed the course of Chinese history.

Communists. Many peasants joined Mao's People's Liberation Army, attracted by the promises of land. By the spring of 1949, the People's Liberation Army had defeated the Nationalists. Chiang Kai-shek and his followers fled to the island of **Taiwan**.

China was now ruled by the Communist Party and called the People's Republic of China. In 1955, the government began a program to build a socialist society. Land was taken away from wealthy landlords and given to poor peasants. About two-thirds of the peasants received land under the program. Most industry and commerce was nationalized, and most farmers were urged to collectivize. Chinese leaders hoped collective farming would increase the food supply and allow more people to work in industry, but this did not happen.

To speed up economic growth, Mao began a radical program, known as the Great Leap Forward. Collective farms were combined into vast communes, each with thirty thousand people who lived and worked together to meet newly imposed government quotas. Peasant resentment of the new system, combined with bad weather, led to the starvation of almost 15 million people. Two years later, the government began to break up the communes.

The Cultural Revolution

Mao still dreamed of a classless society. He believed that only permanent revolution, an atmosphere of constant revolutionary fervor, would lead to this goal. In 1966, he launched the Great Proletarian **Cultural Revolution**. (*Proletarian* means "related to the working class.")

To promote the Cultural Revolution, Red Guards were formed. These revolutionary groups, made up primarily of young people, were sent throughout the country to eliminate the "Four Olds"—old ideas, old culture, old customs, and old habits. Using a collection of Mao's thoughts called "The Little Red Book" as their guide, the Red Guards destroyed temples, books written by foreigners, and foreign music.

Vicious attacks were made on individuals who had supposedly deviated from Mao's plan. Intellectuals and artists with pro-Western ideas and others who did not follow Mao's plan were attacked. Key groups, such as Communist Party members and military officers, did not share Mao's desire for permanent revolution. Opposition to Mao began to grow.

CORE CONCEPTS: HUMAN RIGHTS

Like other totalitarian governments, the People's Republic made use of secret police to crush opposition. In 1956, Mao relaxed state control and urged people to discuss Communist policies. Using words from Confucius, he said, "Let a hundred flowers bloom; let a hundred schools of thought contend." However, instead of praising communism, many people criticized it. Mao swiftly canceled the "Hundred Flowers" campaign and silenced free speech.

Chinese Society Under Communism

The Chinese Party wanted to create a new kind of citizen who would put the society ahead of all other loyalties. To do so, it attacked the old Confucian order, including family loyalty, which Communists felt undermined the state. During the Great Leap Forward and the Cultural Revolution, children were encouraged to spy on their parents and report any criticism. Women's roles also changed: they could now take part in politics, and a new marriage law in 1950 gave them equal rights with men. Even clothing changed, as people wore only "Mao suits." After Mao, there was a shift back to family traditions, as well as to jeans, sneakers, and sweat suits.

China After Mao

When Mao died in 1976, a group of reformers led by **Deng Xiaoping** seized power and brought the Cultural Revolution to an end.

Policies of Deng Xiaoping Under Deng Xiaoping, the government followed a policy called the Four Modernizations, which focused on four areas—agriculture, industry, technology, and national defense—and took steps to speed up the modernization process. For more than 20 years, China had been isolated from the technological advances taking place around the world. To catch up, the government invited foreign investors to China and sent students abroad to study. The government also allowed limited privatization of agriculture and industry.

China also started a new agricultural policy, known as the responsibility system, which allowed peasant families to lease land and sell anything they produced that was beyond the amount they paid for rent. Communes were dismantled. Overall, this plan for modernization worked. Industrial output skyrocketed and **per capita** (per person) income doubled during the 1980s. The standard of living increased for most people.

Movement for Democracy Students who went abroad learned about Western society and began to call for a fifth modernization, democracy. The Communist Party did not allow criticism, however, and those calling for democracy could be sent to prison. In the late 1980s, problems of inflation and corruption erupted in student protests. These massive protests, held in Tiananmen Square in Beijing, were supported by many people in the cities. When Deng Xiaoping saw that the demonstrators were calling for the end of the Communist Party, he ordered tanks and troops into Tiananmen Square to crush the demonstrators. Hundreds were killed.

REGENTS WARM-UP

The ideas and actions of Deng Xiaoping redirected the course of the Chinese revolution. As your read, underline ways in which Deng's policies differed from those of Mao Zedong. This will help you to answer Regents Exam questions that deal with the programs undertaken by each leader.

CORE CONCEPTS: HUMAN RIGHTS

Throughout the 1990s, China's human rights violations and its determination to unify with Taiwan strained its relationship with the West.

China and the Cold War: The Cold War in Asia

When Communists gained power in China, American fears about the spread of communism intensified. When China signed a pact of friendship with the Soviet Union in 1950, Westerners worried about communist world domination. But Mao and Stalin disagreed on communist ideology and there were many border disputes between China and the Soviet Union. In 1960, the alliance between the two countries ended.

The Korean War Korea was a part of the Japanese Empire from 1905 to 1945. In August 1945, the Soviet Union and the United States agreed to divide Korea into two zones at the 38th parallel.

North Korean troops invaded South Korea on June 25, 1950. U.S. President Harry Truman, with the support of the United Nations, sent U.S. troops to fight the North Koreans. When United Nations forces (mostly Americans) pushed north of the 38th parallel, the Chinese sent thousands of troops into Korea to push them back. Fighting went on for three more years with no clear victory. The war was brutal, and atrocities were committed on both sides. An armistice was signed in 1953.

Comparison of Germany and Korea Like Korea, Germany was divided into two distinct entities, one with a Communist government (East Germany) and one a democratic republic. However, Germany was reunited in 1989 after widespread protests in East Germany against the Communist government. North and South Korea are still two separate states, and, although democracy has come to the South, the North remains under the firm grip of Communist dictator Kim Jong-Il. Like families in Germany, many Korean families have been separated for decades. North Koreans have suffered through shortages of food, electricity, and other basic needs under the regime. However, because of strict control on information, it is impossible to precisely determine the extent of North Korea's problems.

CORE CONCEPTS: THE WORLD IN SPATIAL TERMS

The 38th parallel remains the boundary line between North and South Korea.

SECTION 2 INDEPENDENT STATES IN SOUTH AND SOUTHEAST ASIA

Before World War II, the Indian independence movement, under the leadership of Mohandas Gandhi, had used civil disobedience to protest colonial British laws it considered unjust. A split in the movement occurred when Jawaharlal Nehru, who

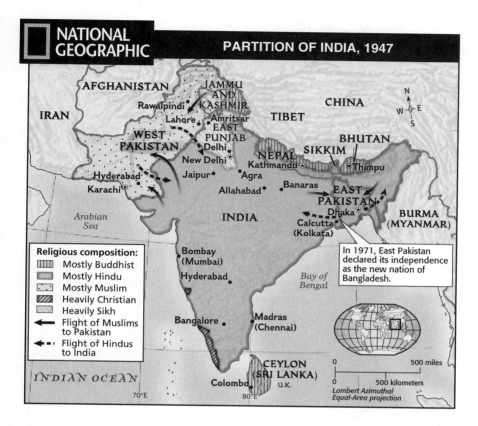

NATIONAL GEOGRAPHIC

PARTITION OF INDIA, 1947

AFGHANISTAN

JAMMU AND KASHMIR

Rawalpindi

Lahore

Amritsar

EAST PUNJAB

WEST PAKISTAN

Delhi

New Delhi

Jaipur

Agra

Hyderabad

Karachi

Arabian Sea

CHINA

TIBET

NEPAL

Kathmandu

SIKKIM

BHUTAN

Thimpu

Banaras

Allahabad

EAST PAKISTAN

Dhaka

Calcutta (Kolkata)

BURMA (MYANMAR)

INDIA

IRAN

In 1971, East Pakistan declared its independence as the new nation of Bangladesh.

Religious composition:
- ▥ Mostly Buddhist
- ▨ Mostly Hindu
- ⬚ Mostly Muslim
- ▨ Heavily Christian
- ▨ Heavily Sikh
- ⬅ Flight of Muslims to Pakistan
- ⬅- Flight of Hindus to India

Bombay (Mumbai)

Hyderabad

Bay of Bengal

Bangalore

Madras (Chennai)

INDIAN OCEAN

CEYLON (SRI LANKA) U.K.

Colombo

70°E   80°E

0   500 miles
0   500 kilometers
Lambert Azimuthal Equal-Area projection

pushed for more Western-style reforms, entered the movement. Tensions between Muslims and Hindus, which had existed for centuries, were also growing. Muslims were upset over Hindu dominance of the independence movement.

India Divided

At the end of World War II, British India's officials came to the conclusion that India would have to be divided into two countries, one Hindu (India) and one Muslim (Pakistan). Pakistan consisted of two regions separated by India. One part, West Pakistan, was to the northwest of India. The other part, East Pakistan, was to the northeast. On August 15, 1947, India and Pakistan became independent. Violence broke out, and more than one million people were killed. One of those killed was Mohandas Gandhi. Millions of Hindus and Muslims fled across the new borders—Hindus to India and Muslims to Pakistan.

CORE CONCEPTS: MOVEMENT OF PEOPLE AND GOODS

The mass dislocation of people because of political or economic hardship or change is a major theme in world history and geography. What other major world events and changes have caused mass relocation or dislocation?

The New India

The Indian National Congress, now renamed the Congress Party, began to rule with Jawaharlal Nehru as prime minister. His vision of the new India combined a parliamentary form of government with a moderate socialist structure. The government took over the ownership of major industries, utilities, and transportation. Farming remained private, as did business at the local level. Industrial production tripled between 1950 and 1965.

Nehru died in 1964. Congress Party leaders selected Nehru's daughter, Indira Gandhi, as the new prime minister in 1966. During her terms in office until 1984, India experienced many problems, including huge population growth, worsening poverty, slums, and ethnic and religious conflict.

A key principle of India's foreign policy has been nonalignment. A policy of neutrality made sense given India's history of colonial domination and civil disobedience. It also allowed India to act as a Third World leader during the Cold War period and kept influence from its former colonial power, Britain, at a minimum.

One great ethnic problem arose with the Sikhs who lived in the northern Punjab province and agitated for an independent state. Gandhi refused their appeal for independence and, in 1984, used military force against Sikh rebels who had taken refuge in the Golden Temple, one of the Sikhs' most holy places. More than 450 Sikhs were killed. Later that year, two Sikh bodyguards of Gandhi assassinated her in retaliation.

Gandhi's successors have continued to emphasize free market enterprise and privatization. This has led to the growth of India's middle class. The Congress Party has remained the leading party, but new parties have competed for control. Tensions between Hindus and Muslims continue to disturb India's stability.

Kashmir Religious differences also fueled a long-term dispute between India and Pakistan over Kashmir, a territory between the two nations. Today, Pakistan controls one-third of Kashmir, and the rest is held by India. Troops from both countries patrol the border between the two areas. The danger from this conflict escalated in 1998 when both India and Pakistan tested nuclear warheads.

Pakistan

The division between East and West Pakistan quickly became a source of conflict for the newly created state of Pakistan. Because the government was based in West Pakistan, many in East Pakistan felt it ignored their needs. In 1971, East Pakistan

REGENTS WARM-UP

Regents Exam questions often pose cause-effect relationships:

During the 1980s, national unity in India was hindered by

(1) a foreign policy of nonalignment
(2) continued fear of attack from the Soviet Union
(3) political interference from China
(4) conflicts with Sikhs, Hindus, and Muslims

declared its independence. After a brief civil war and with military help from India, it became the new nation of **Bangladesh**.

Bangladesh and Pakistan have both had problems establishing stable governments. In both nations, military officials have often seized control of the government. Both nations are also very poor and are dealing with issues of rapid population growth, urbanization, and environmental problems.

Southeast Asia

Southeast Asian colonies gained independence after World War II.

Independence In 1946, the United States granted total independence to the Philippines. As Great Britain ended its colonial rule, Burma became independent in 1948 and Malaya in 1956. Although the Dutch at first tried to suppress it, a new Indonesian republic was granted independence in 1949. In Vietnam, the situation was very different. In 1945, the Vietminh, forces under the Communist Party, seized power. Ho Chi Minh became the first president. France, however, refused to accept the new government and seized the southern part of the country.

The Vietnam War France fought the Vietminh for control of Vietnam but did not succeed. After a great defeat at Dien Bien Phu, it agreed to a peace settlement in 1954. The country was divided into two parts. In the north, Communists were based in Hanoi. In the south, noncommunists were based in Saigon. Both sides agreed to hold elections in two years to create a single government. When the conflict continued, the United States provided aid to South Vietnam. In spite of this aid, the Viet Cong, South Vietnamese guerrillas supported by North Vietnam, were on the verge of seizing control of the entire country by early 1965.

Vietnam and the Domino Theory

In 1965, President Lyndon Johnson sent troops to Vietnam. The United States became involved in Vietnam in order to keep the Communist regime of North Vietnam from gaining control of South Vietnam. It saw the conflict in terms of the **domino theory**: if the Communists succeeded in South Vietnam, the argument went, other countries in Asia would also fall (like dominoes in a line) to communism.

Despite massive advantages in equipment and firepower, the United States failed to defeat the North Vietnamese under the leadership of **Ho Chi Minh**. American public opinion turned against the war. President Richard Nixon reached an agreement with Vietnam in 1973 that allowed the United States to withdraw its forces. Two years later, Vietnam had been forcibly united by Communist armies from the North. The domino theory, however, proved unfounded. One reason was that communism was not a single force directed by Moscow; instead, Communist China and the Soviet Union had different philosophies and agendas.

The reunification of Vietnam under Communist rule had an immediate impact on the region. By the end of 1975, both Laos and Cambodia had Communist governments. In Cambodia, a brutal revolutionary regime under Pol Pot, leader of the Khmer Rouge, massacred more than one million Cambodians.

Government in the Independent Nations Newly formed independent nations hoped for democratic governments. Weak economic growth derailed these hopes. Military and one-party regimes took control. In recent years, however, some Southeast Asian societies have moved toward greater democracy. In the Philippines, an uprising forced the corrupt Ferdinand Marcos to leave the country. In 1986, Corazon Aquino, the wife of a man who had opposed Marcos, became president and worked for democratic reforms. In Burma, activist Aung San Suu Kyi has worked for democratic reforms and has been subject to house arrest repeatedly by the military government.

SECTION 3 JAPAN AND THE PACIFIC

The Allied Occupation

From 1945 to 1952, Japan was an **occupied** country—its lands were held and controlled by U.S. forces.

The Japanese Miracle

After World War II, Japan quickly became an economic giant. This dramatic recovery from the war, the "Japanese miracle," was due to many factors including Japan's new constitution, which created a stable democratic society. It was also due to the government's role in the economy, which has been described as a system of "state capitalism." During the occupation of Japan, a land reform program created a strong class of farmers.

Cultural factors also help explain Japan's success. The Japanese are group oriented and cooperate well with one

REGENTS WARM-UP

The Pol Pot regime has been examined on past Regents Exams as an example of one of the worst abuses of human rights in this century. Like Hitler, Pol Pot embarked upon a program of genocide, or mass murder.

CORE CONCEPTS: ECONOMIC SYSTEMS

Japan was for a long time the greatest exporting nation in the world. It still has one of the highest per capita incomes.

another. They are a hardworking people who are inclined to save rather than to buy. High savings rates and high labor productivity have been good for the economy.

Other reasons for Japan's success include the fact that Japan's industries were destroyed in World War II. As a result, Japan built entirely new, modern factories. Also, Japanese workers spend considerably more time at their jobs than workers in other countries do. Corporations reward innovations and maintain good management-labor relations. Finally, some people believe that Japan uses unfair trading practices such as selling some goods below cost to break into foreign markets and preventing foreign goods from coming to market in Japan.

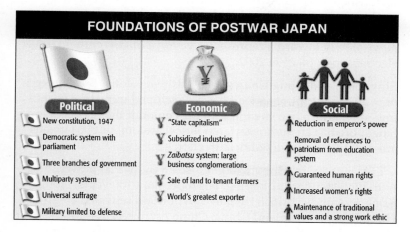

FOUNDATIONS OF POSTWAR JAPAN

Political	Economic	Social
New constitution, 1947	"State capitalism"	Reduction in emperor's power
Democratic system with parliament	Subsidized industries	Removal of references to patriotism from education system
Three branches of government	*Zaibatsu* system: large business conglomerations	Guaranteed human rights
Multiparty system	Sale of land to tenant farmers	Increased women's rights
Universal suffrage	World's greatest exporter	Maintenance of traditional values and a strong work ethic
Military limited to defense		

REGENTS WARM-UP

Study the chart. How are Japan's postwar characteristics different from those of China?

Social Changes Major social and cultural changes occurred in Japan after the war. A new educational system removed all references to patriotism and loyalty to the emperor. It also stressed individualism. Women were given the right to vote and encouraged to enter politics. Still, many values persisted, such as a strong work ethic. The subordinate position of women has also not been entirely eliminated.

Culture Postwar Japanese writers created a somber picture of loss and despair. Since the 1970s, increasing wealth and high literacy rates have created a massive outpouring of books. By 1975, Japan produced twice as much fiction as the United States. Contemporary Japanese authors deal with the same concerns as authors in other wealthy industrial nations do. Haruki Marukami is one of Japan's most popular writers.

CORE CONCEPTS: IDENTITY

In modernizing Japan, the Japanese sought to compete with the West rather than to mimic its culture. Whenever possible, they adapted borrowed practices or ideas to fit the Japanese identity.

CORE CONCEPTS: LINKING PAST AND PRESENT

Unification remains a major issue for Taiwan because the Communist People's Republic of China on the mainland is still committed to this goal. The United States supports self-determination for the people of Taiwan.

CORE CONCEPTS: MOVEMENT OF PEOPLE AND GOODS

The British decision to return Hong Kong to China in 1997 led to a large-scale migration of people. Many Chinese from Hong Kong have sought shelter in Canada, changing the ethnic composition of that nation. Prior to the Chinese-British agreement, Canada had only a small Asian population.

The "Asian Tigers"

Several Asian nations have imitated Japan's industrial success. Sometimes called the "Asian tigers," they are South Korea, Taiwan, Singapore, and Hong Kong.

South Korea After the war ended in 1953, Korea suffered several years of harsh autocratic rule and government corruption. Although the economy experienced growth, protest was suppressed. Opposition grew, and democracy finally came in the 1990s. Elections held in 1997 brought the reformer Kim Tae-jung to the presidency.

Taiwan: The Other China Chiang Kai-shek and his followers established a capital at Taipei. The new government built a modern industrialized society, but other political parties were not allowed. After the death of Chiang in 1975, Taiwan began to move slowly toward a representative form of government. Free elections took place in 2002.

Singapore and Hong Kong Once a British colony, **Singapore** is now an independent state. It has a developed industrial economy and has also become the banking center of the region. Singapore has an authoritarian political system, but its citizens are demanding more political freedoms.

Like Singapore, **Hong Kong** is also an industrial powerhouse with high standards of living. For more than 150 years, Hong Kong was under British rule. In 1997, Britain returned control of Hong Kong to mainland China. China promised that for the next 50 years, Hong Kong would enjoy a high degree of economic freedom under a capitalist system. Hong Kong's future, however, remains uncertain.

PRACTICING FOR THE REGENTS

Part I Multiple-Choice Questions

The following multiple-choice questions come from past Regents High School Examinations. Test your understanding of global history and geography by answering each of these items. Circle the number of the word or expression that best completes each statement or question. Test-taking tips can be found in the margins for some questions. For additional help, see Taking the Regents Exam on pages ix–xxxv of this Review Book.

1 The purpose of the Marshall Plan was to
   (1) restore Japanese economic development
   (2) provide military aid to Middle Eastern allies
   (3) assure nationalist success in the Chinese civil war
   (4) provide for economic recovery in Western Europe

2 Mikhail Gorbachev instituted the policies of glasnost and perestroika to
   (1) reinforce the basic economic principles of communism
   (2) bring the Soviet Union into the European Economic Community
   (3) reform the Soviet Union politically and economically
   (4) gain acceptance for free political elections

3 The Boxer Rebellion, the Salt March, and the Iranian Revolution were reactions against
   (1) Mongol rule
   (2) rapid industrialization
   (3) Western influence
   (4) economic depression

Base your answer to question 4 on the statements below, which appeared in a newspaper in 1998.

> "In response to the nuclear tests, people in New Delhi took to the streets lighting firecrackers, thanking Hindu gods, and crying out, 'Bharat Mata Jai!' (Victory to Mother India)."

> "President Bill Clinton decided tonight to impose economic sanctions on India's government for detonating three underground nuclear explosions."

4   Which statement is supported by these two news excerpts?
   (1) India is falling behind in the race to develop nuclear weapons.
   (2) The United States officially supports India's nuclear weapons program.
   (3) People in India and the United States have reacted very differently to India's nuclear test.
   (4) India's development of nuclear weapons will improve chances for peace in the region.

5   A key principle of the economic theory of communism is
   (1) restoration of a bartering system
   (2) organization of workers' unions
   (3) government ownership of property
   (4) privatization of business

Base your answers to questions 6 and 7 on the map below and on your knowledge of social studies.

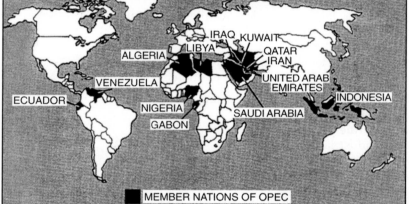

Member Nations of OPEC

Source: Killoran, Zimmer, and Jarret, *The Key to Understanding Global History*,
Jarret Publishing

6   According to the map, which region of the world has the greatest number of nations belonging to the Organization of Petroleum Exporting Countries (OPEC)?
   (1) Middle East
   (2) Southern Africa
   (3) North America
   (4) Southeast Asia

7   The potential power of the member nations in OPEC lies in their
   (1) political influence in tropical regions
   (2) control of access to important religious sites
   (3) military control over strategic waterways
   (4) economic influence over industrialized nations

8   The Truman Doctrine, Korean War, crisis in Guatemala, and Soviet invasion of Afghanistan were all
- (1) reasons for the Industrial Revolution
- (2) examples of Japanese imperialism
- (3) events of the Cold War
- (4) causes of World War II

9   Which development took place in China under Mao Zedong?
- (1) The family became the dominant force in society.
- (2) The Four Modernizations became the basis for economic reform.
- (3) The people adopted the practice of ancestor worship.
- (4) Communist teachings became required learning in all schools and universities.

10   One way in which the partition of India in 1947 and the breakup of Yugoslavia in 1992 are similar is that after each event
- (1) stable democratic governments were established
- (2) problems arose between ethnic and religious groups
- (3) economic prosperity produced high standards of living
- (4) traditional beliefs were abandoned for Western ideas

11   Several historic events are listed below.
- (A) Partition of India and Pakistan
- (B) Establishment of the caste system
- (C) British colonization of the Indian subcontinent
- (D) Gandhi's Salt March

What is the correct chronological order of this set of events?
- (1) A → B → C → D
- (2) B → C → D → A
- (3) C → D → A → B
- (4) D → B → A → C

12   Mahatma Gandhi and Jomo Kenyatta were similar in that both
- (1) supported colonial policies
- (2) sought to gain independence from Great Britain
- (3) led a worldwide boycott of British goods
- (4) used violent revolution to achieve their aims

Base your answer to question 13 on the graphs below and on your knowledge of social studies.

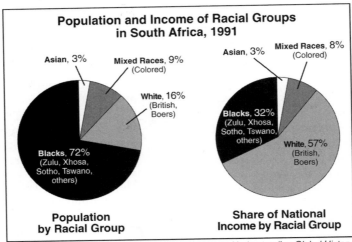

Population and Income of Racial Groups in South Africa, 1991

Asian, 3%

Mixed Races, 9% (Colored)

White, 16% (British, Boers)

Blacks, 72% (Zulu, Xhosa, Sotho, Tswano, others)

Population by Racial Group

Asian, 3%

Mixed Races, 8% (Colored)

Blacks, 32% (Zulu, Xhosa, Sotho, Tswano, others)

White, 57% (British, Boers)

Share of National Income by Racial Group

Source: Killoran, Zimmer, and Jarrett, *The Key to Understanding Global History*, Jarrett Publishing Co.

13   The best conclusion that can be drawn from these graphs is that in 1991
     (1)   the Boers outnumbered the British in South Africa
     (2)   the black population has decreased due to emigration
     (3)   Asians controlled a greater proportion of income in comparison to their population
     (4)   whites continued to control the largest amount of income after the end of apartheid

Base your answers to questions 14 and 15 on the map below and on your knowledge of social studies.

MEMBERS OF NATO AND THE WARSAW PACT

☐ MEMBERS OF NATO
☒ MEMBERS OF WARSAW PACT

FINLAND

NORWAY

NORTHERN IRELAND

North Sea

SWEDEN

IRELAND   GREAT BRITAIN

DENMARK

NETH.

English Channel

EAST GER.

POLAND

SOVIET UNION

BEL.   WEST

Bay of Biscay

LUX.

GERMANY

CZECHOSLOVAKIA

FRANCE

SWITZ.   AUSTRIA   HUNGARY

RUMANIA

ITALY

Black Sea

PORTUGAL

SPAIN

YUGOSLAVIA

BULGARIA

ALBANIA

TURKEY

GIBRALTAR

Mediterranean

GREECE

Sea

AFRICA

Source: *The Key to Understanding Global History*, Killoran

14   Both alliances shown on the map were formed after World War II primarily to
(1) increase military defense
(2) promote democracy in Europe
(3) compete in the global economy
(4) expand trade between the members

15   Which of these countries was not a member of either the North Atlantic Treaty Organization (NATO) or of the Warsaw Pact?
(1) East Germany
(2) Great Britain
(3) Rumania
(4) Austria

16   Which newspaper headline illustrates a policy of appeasement?
(1) "Dien Bien Phu Falls; French to Leave Vietnam"
(2) "Chamberlain Agrees to German Demands: Sudetenland to Germany"
(3) "Marshall Plan Proposes Economic Aid Program for Europe"
(4) "Soviet Troops and Tanks Crush Hungarian Revolt"

Base your answers to questions 17 and 18 on the document below and on your knowledge of social studies.

Article 3: Everyone has the right to life, liberty and security of person. . . .
Article 5: No one shall be subjected to torture or to cruel, inhuman or degrading treatment or punishment. . . .
Article 9: No one shall be subjected to arbitrary arrest, detention or exile.
Article 19: Everyone has the right to freedom of opinion and expression; this right includes freedom to hold opinions without interference and to seek, receive and impart information and ideas through any media regardless of frontiers.
   —*Universal Declaration of Human Rights*

17   In which time period of Western history did thinkers first express these ideas in written form?
(1) Renaissance
(2) Reformation
(3) Enlightenment
(4) Middle Ages

18   Which pair of 20th century leaders most clearly violated these principles?
(1) Anwar Sadat and Charles DeGaulle
(2) Corazon Aquino and Margaret Thatcher
(3) Jawaharlal Nehru and Reza Pahlavi
(4) Pol Pot and Joseph Stalin

Base your answer to question 19 on the time line below and on your knowledge of social studies.

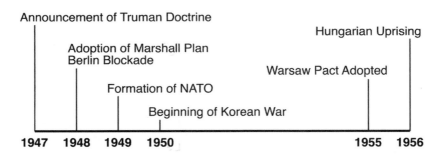

Announcement of Truman Doctrine

Adoption of Marshall Plan
Berlin Blockade

Formation of NATO

Beginning of Korean War

Hungarian Uprising

Warsaw Pact Adopted

1947   1948   1949   1950   1955   1956

19 All the events on the time line show actions taken during the
(1) policy of appeasement
(2) Cold War
(3) decline of nationalism
(4) Green Revolution

20 Since the 1980s, Chinese leaders have tried to improve China's economy by implementing a policy of
(1) isolation
(2) collectivization
(3) limited free enterprise
(4) representative government

21 During the Cold War, the Soviet Union and the democracies in the West competed for influence in the Middle East because of its
(1) strategic location and valuable resources
(2) vast fertile farmlands and rivers
(3) large well-educated population
(4) industrial potential

22 Which type of economic system was used by both Joseph Stalin and Mao Zedong to accelerate the economic growth of their respective nations?
(1) mixed
(2) market
(3) command
(4) traditional

23 Which statement describes the economic history of Japan since World War II?
(1) Japan has been limited in industrial development by the occupation of the United States.
(2) Japan has developed a strong economic base built on the export of manufactured goods.
(3) Japan has withdrawn from the world economic community and has practiced economic self-sufficiency.
(4) Japan has concentrated on rebuilding its defense industries.

24 Which term is often used to describe the actions of Adolf Hitler in Germany and Pol Pot in Cambodia?
(1) nonalignment
(2) neocolonialism
(3) scorched-earth policy
(4) genocide

25 One way in which the Boxers in China and the Islamic fundamentalists in revolutionary Iran were similar is that each group attempted to
(1) encourage cultural and economic ties with Western nations
(2) eliminate foreign influence in their nations
(3) establish national religious movements
(4) expand overseas colonies

Base your answers to questions 26 and 27 on the chart below and on your knowledge of social studies.

Date	Event
1948	South Africa introduces apartheid policies.
1956	Sudan is proclaimed an independent republic.
1957	Ghana becomes independent.
1960	Belgian Congo is granted full independence and becomes Zaire.
1962	Algeria gains independence from France.
1963	African nations form Organization of African Unity (OAU).
1967	Civil war breaks out in Nigeria.
1975	Civil war breaks out in Angola.
1990	Repeal of apartheid laws begins in South Africa.
1994	African National Congress wins South Africa's first open, multiracial elections.

26 Which statement can be supported by the information provided on this chart?
   (1) South Africa has supported a policy of apartheid since before World War II.
   (2) Algeria was the first nation in Africa to gain its independence since the end of World War II.
   (3) Independence for African nations has been smooth and orderly.
   (4) Since 1990, South Africa has been moving toward a more democratic society.

27 Which is the best title for this chart?
   (1) Living Standards Improve
   (2) Industrialization of Developing Nations
   (3) The Decline of Imperialism and its Aftermath
   (4) United Nations Membership Grows

Part II   Thematic Essay Question

The following thematic essay question comes from past Regents Examinations. Write your answers on a separate sheet of paper. Essay-writing tips appear in the margin. For additional help, see Taking the Regents Exam on pages ix–xxxv of this Review Book.

Directions: Write a well-organized essay that includes an introduction, several paragraphs addressing the task below, and a conclusion.

Theme: Economic Change

> Since the 19th century, industrialization has had positive and negative effects on the lives of workers.

Task:

> - Define the term "industrialization"
> - Select *one* nation you have studied and discuss *two* specific examples of the ways in which industrialization changed the lives of workers in that nation
> - Discuss the response of the workers, reformers, and/or government to these changes

You may use any nation from your study of global history *except the United States*. Some suggestions you might wish to consider include: Great Britain (19th century), Japan (19th or 20th century), Russia (19th or 20th century), Korea (post–World War II), and Brazil (20th century).

You are *not* limited to these suggestions.

Guidelines:

In your essay, be sure to

- Develop all aspects of the task
- Support the theme with relevant facts, examples, and details
- Use a logical and clear plan of organization, including an introduction and a conclusion that are beyond a restatement of the theme

Part III   Document-Based Question

This exercise is designed to test your ability to work with historical documents. It is similar to the document-based questions you will see on the Regents Examination. While you are asked to analyze three historical documents, the exercise on the actual exam will include more documents. Some of the documents have been edited for the purposes of the question. As you analyze the documents, take into account the source of each document and any point of view that may be presented in the document.

Historical Context:

> Despite the horrors of the Holocaust, abuses of human rights have continued in the post–World War II era.

Task: Using information from the documents and your knowledge of global history and geography, answer the questions that follow each document in Part A. Your answers to the questions will help you write the Part B essay, in which you will be asked to

- Describe examples of human rights abuses in the post–World War II era
- Discuss efforts that the world community has made to eliminate these human rights abuses

Part A   Short-Answer Questions

Directions: Analyze the documents and answer the short-answer questions that follow each document in the space provided.

Document 1

Universal Declaration of Human Rights

Article 1 —	All human beings are born free and equal in dignity and rights.
Article 3 —	Everyone has the right to life, liberty and security of person.
Article 4 —	No one shall be held in slavery or servitude; slavery and the slave trade shall be prohibited in all their forms.
Article 5 —	No one shall be subjected to torture or to cruel, inhuman or degrading treatment or punishment.
Article 9 —	No one shall be subjected to arbitrary arrest, detention or exile.
Article 13 —	1. Everyone has the right to freedom of movement and residence within the borders of each State.
	2. Everyone has the right to leave any country, including his own, and to return to his country.
Article 14 —	Everyone has the right to seek and to enjoy in other countries asylum from persecution.
Article 15 —	Everyone has the right to a nationality.
Article 18 —	Everyone has the right to freedom of thought, conscience and religion.
Article 19 —	Everyone has the right to freedom of opinion and expression.
Article 20 —	Everyone has the right to freedom of peaceful assembly and association.
Article 21 —	Everyone has the right to take part in the government of his country, directly or through freely chosen representatives.

1   State *two* human rights listed in this document.

(1) _everyone is born free and equal in dignity and rights_

(2) _everyone has the right to freedom of opinion and expression_

Document 2

> From the middle of 1975 to the end of 1978, between one million and three million Cambodians, out of a population of about seven million, died at the hands of Pol Pot's Khmer Rouge. Former government employees, army personnel, and "intellectuals" were executed in the hundreds of thousands. Others were killed by disease, exhaustion, and malnutrition during forced urban evacuations, migrations, and compulsory labor. Families were broken apart and communal living established; men and women were compelled to marry partners selected by the state. Education and religious practices were proscribed [forbidden].
>
> —*David Hawk, "The Killing of Cambodia,"* The New Republic, *1982*

2   Identify *two* human rights violations carried out by the Khmer Rouge.

(1) _executions of government empolyees, army personel, and "intellectuals"_

(2) _education + religious practices were forbidden_

Document 3

Statute of Amnesty International

Object and Mandate

1. The object of Amnesty International is to contribute to the observance throughout the world of human rights as set out in the Universal Declaration of Human Rights. . . .

   Recognizing the obligation on each person to extend to others rights and freedoms equal to his or her own, Amnesty International adopts as its mandate:

   - To promote awareness of . . . the Universal Declaration of Human Rights and other internationally recognized human rights instruments, . . . and the indivisibility and interdependence of all human rights and freedoms;
   - To oppose grave violations of the rights of every person freely to hold and to express his or her convictions and to be free from discrimination and of the right of every person to physical and mental integrity. . . .

Methods/Actions

2. In order to achieve the . . . object and mandate, Amnesty International shall: . . .

   - Promote as appears appropriate the adoption of constitutions, conventions, treaties and other measures which guarantee the rights contained in the provisions referred to in Article 1; . . .
   - Publicize the cases of prisoners of conscience or persons who have otherwise been subjected to disabilities in violation of the . . . provisions;
   - Investigate and publicize the disappearance of persons where there is reason to believe that they may be victims of violations of the rights set out in Article 1;
   - Oppose the sending of persons from one country to another where they can reasonably be expected to become prisoners of conscience or to face torture or the death penalty;
   - Send investigators, where appropriate, to investigate allegations that the rights of individuals under the . . . provisions have been violated or threatened.

3 Identify *two* actions taken by Amnesty International to protect human rights.

(1) _publicize the cases of prisoners_

(2) _send investigators to investigate it_
provision have been violated/threatened

Part B   Essay

Directions: Write a well-organized essay that includes an introduction, several paragraphs, and a conclusion.

Use evidence from the documents in the body of the essay. Support your response with relevant facts, examples, and details. Include additional outside information.

Historical Context:

Despite the horrors of the Holocaust, abuses of human rights have continued in the post–World War II era.

Task: Using information from the documents and your knowledge of global history and geography, write an essay in which you

- Describe examples of human rights abuses in the post–World War II era
- Discuss efforts that the world community has made to eliminate these human rights abuses

Guidelines:

In your essay, be sure to

- Develop all aspects of the task
- Incorporate information from *at least two* of the documents in the body of your essay
- Incorporate relevant outside information
- Support the theme with relevant facts, examples, and details
- Use a logical and clear plan of organization, including an introduction and conclusion that are beyond a restatement of the theme

UNIT 8 GLOBAL INTERACTIONS

Chapter 33   **The World Today**
Chapter 34   **Challenges for the Global Community**

Unit 8 Overview

Although great diversity characterizes the world's many cultures, all regions share the same global environment. In recent decades, modern technology and world trade patterns have increased global interdependence and speeded the process of cultural diffusion. Today people are more keenly aware than ever before of their membership in one global community.

Many of the issues that face the world today are not new. Some issues—such as war and peace—have existed throughout history. Others—such as industrial pollution—are a product of the modern era.

Today's world faces the challenges of protecting and preserving the environment, addressing economic and social changes, implementing new technologies, resolving political conflicts, and eliminating international terrorism. The world's inhabitants must adopt a cooperative global vision to address the problems that confront all humankind. More and more, people are coming to understand that destructive forces unleashed in one part of the world soon affect the entire world. Today, conflicts rarely stay within national boundaries. All these issues make us aware of the global nature of contemporary problems.

Unit 8 Objectives

After studying this unit, students should be able to

1.   identify the challenges that face the world in the twenty-first century;

2.   describe the advances of the technological revolution and identify its problems;

3.   identify environmental issues facing the world and how they are being dealt with;

4.   identify the causes and effects of regional conflicts around the globe.

PREPARING FOR THE REGENTS

This entire book is set up to help you grasp the facts, main ideas, and concepts needed to do well on your Regents Exam. Notes in the margin include core concepts, test-taking tips, and more. Use blank spaces in the margins to answer questions raised in the text or to jot down key points. Before each unit of study, skim through the exams at the back of the book to develop a sense of what the Regents wants you to know about your world.

Section 1   Social and Political Patterns and Change
Section 2   Economic Issues

Chapter Overview

The twenty-first century is a time of challenge and opportunity. Although scientific and technological progress continues, many nations remain mired in poverty and disease. Developing nations struggle to balance modern and traditional ways. Women and children continue to be at risk in many nations, despite progress in the West. Religious and ethnic conflicts persist in many places around the world.

As you read this chapter, ask yourself these questions:
(1) How have population patterns changed in recent times?
(2) What economic differences separate the industrial and developing nations?
(3) How do various cultures seek to address the balance of tradition and modernity?
(4) How have science and technology assisted in solving modern problems?
(5) What problems are created because of new technologies?
(6) What are some of the most pressing concerns facing women and children?
(7) What is the purpose, and what have been the major accomplishments, of the United Nations?

Main Ideas and Concepts

- **Scarcity** Developing nations continue to struggle to feed and care for their people.

- **Science and Technology** Despite rapid advances in science and industry, technology has not solved the problems of disease, hunger, or poverty.

- **Movement of People and Goods** Patterns of migration in the late 20th and early 21st centuries have involved both voluntary and forced movement.

- **Human Rights** Women and children still face economic, political, and social barriers.

- **Decision Making** Organizations have been created to respond to global issues.

People, Places, Terms

The following names and terms will help you to prepare for the Regents Exam in Global History and Geography. You can find an explanation of each name and term in the Glossary at the back of this book, in your textbook, or in another reference source.

AIDS	free trade	population growth
birthrate	human rights	standard of living
ethnic cleansing	migration	United Nations
ethnic group	outsourcing	urbanization

SECTION 1 SOCIAL AND POLITICAL PATTERNS AND CHANGE

Human and Physical Geography

The cultural and technological developments since World War II have increasingly broken down the barriers between peoples and countries. A five-fold increase in population occurred during the past three centuries, from 500 million people in 1650 to 2.5 billion in 1950. Growing numbers of people interacting with the physical environment require global solutions to a number of problems.

REGENTS WARM-UP

Past Regents Exams have asked students to compare human-environmental interaction in several regions of the world. Look at the sample Regents Exams at the back of this text for essay questions that focus on the connections between the environment and the development of some aspect of human culture.

Population by Continent, 2003	
Asia	3,857,719,000
Africa	879,855,500
Europe	721,573,500
North America	494,093,100
South America	370,773,700
Australia/Oceania	31,528,600

Source: *The World Gazetteer*, 2003
Note: Populations are estimates.

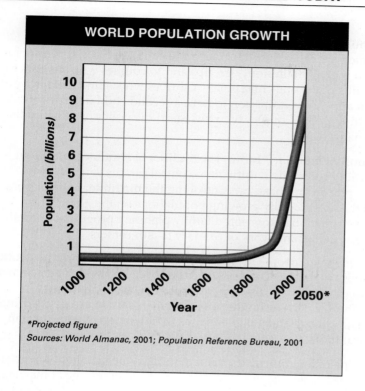

WORLD POPULATION GROWTH

*Projected figure
Sources: World Almanac, 2001; Population Reference Bureau, 2001

CORE CONCEPTS: HUMAN SYSTEMS

The increase in population is due to a number of factors: improved infant mortality rates, better nutrition and antibiotics to fight disease, and improved crop yields and water supplies.

Population Pressures and Poverty

A serious problem in developing countries is **population growth**. The current world population is 6.2 billion. Rapidly growing populations have caused many people to move to cities to find jobs. Millions of people in cities in developing countries live in terrible conditions.

An increasing population, particularly in developing nations in the Southern Hemisphere, creates pressures on food and land supplies. This increase in population is rooted in several factors: (1) traditionally high value placed on children, (2) lack of information about family planning, (3) religious beliefs emphasizing the importance of having many children, and (4) the need for many children to help work.

One-Child Policy—China In 2002, China enacted the Population and Family Planning Law. Parts of the law had already been in practice for thirty years. "One child per family" has been China's approach to controlling population growth. However, this does not reflect the more complicated realities of

REGENTS WARM-UP

Human rights is one of the key world issues studied in New York. The issue of human rights cuts across regions and time periods. Be sure to review examples of human rights violations before taking the Regents Exam.

family planning in a country as large and diverse as China, which has more than 2,000 separate counties. Special consideration is given to minority groups and to couples who are both the results of the one-child policy. Couples whose first child is a girl can apply for permission to have a second child in hopes of getting a son. Couples who disregard the policy are financially penalized.

Family Planning—India The traditional Hindu emphasis on fertility has made it difficult to control population in India. Despite an emphasis on controlling the **birthrate**, India has one of the most rapidly growing populations on the globe. The government has sponsored family planning programs in rural areas, using a network of primary health centers.

However, people in rural areas tend to resist education about family planning. This resistance has been met with a government program to organize women's clubs encouraging lower birthrates. This technique offers women empowerment to bring about change and a higher status than women often receive in rural India.

One of the difficulties faced in India is the fact that women still marry at a young age. Eighteen was the average age at marriage in the mid-1990s. Another concern is the deeply held preference for sons, who are thought to be more help financially and as farm labor and for whom no marriage dowry is required. The infant mortality rate for girls is slightly higher than that for boys. As a result of poor care of females born, the nation has a deficiency of females in all but one state of India. Some experts believe that India's population will not stabilize until 2060.

Mother Teresa One of the most remarkable efforts at caring for the poor came from an Albanian nun. Mother Teresa, who was awarded a Nobel Prize for Peace in 1979 for her work in Kolkata (Calcutta), went to India in 1931 as a Roman Catholic missionary. She took her final vows as a nun in Calcutta, where she taught high school until 1948.

The poverty and disease around the convent where she lived caused her to devote her life to the poorest of the poor. In 1950, she founded the order of The Missionaries of Charity, which now has branches in more than 40 countries. More than a million co-workers assist the nuns and brothers in their work. Mother Teresa died in 1997 and has been declared a saint by the Roman Catholic Church.

Cycles of Poverty and Disease Disease and poverty move together. In poor areas of the world, human and industrial wastes are not processed, leading to water-borne diseases such as hookworms, cholera, hepatitis, and dysentery. Intestinal parasites infect one-third of the developing world's poor people each year. In addition, medical care is absent or overburdened in regions of poverty, so that illnesses are often untreated and viruses spread.

Because businesses are unlikely to operate in regions that suffer from disease, the poorest communities cannot afford to finance schools or to treat water and sewage. Information about controlling disease is distributed through education, so funding schools is a crucial step.

Migration

The movement of people from one place to another is as old as humanity. **Migration** can be internal, the flow of people from rural to urban societies in the same country, or external, the movement across international borders, usually involving long distances.

Migration can be sparked by push factors, such as lack of resources, or pull factors, such as hope for better employment or educational opportunities. Today, the largest migrations are from rural to urban locations, leading, in many parts of the world, to rapid urbanization.

Urbanization As people seek to escape poverty, they often migrate to urban areas, creating slum areas such as Brazil's *favelas*. In the slums, people lack basic resources such as medical care, electricity, and clean drinking water. Disease and malnutrition are additional problems for those who remain unemployed or underemployed. Several nations have tried to address these concerns through national social policies.

In many developing nations, **urbanization** is taking place at a rapid speed. For example, Latin American cities have grown nearly twice as fast as cities in the rest of the world since World War II. Latin America has three of the twelve largest urban areas of the world: Mexico City, São Paulo, and Buenos Aires. However, there are not enough industrial jobs for all the rural people who come to the cities, most of whom end up doing a number of odd jobs to earn money for food and housing.

CORE CONCEPTS: ENVIRONMENT

Urbanization is the rapid growth of cities, often involving the large-scale movement of people. Every region in the world is already urbanized or in the process of becoming urbanized.

REGENTS WARM-UP

Some essay questions on past Regents Exams have asked students to compare the effects of urbanization and modernization in various developing regions. India and Southeast Asia, Africa, Latin America, and the Middle East would be regions to study. Before taking the Regents Exam, review the effects of urbanization and/or modernization on each of these areas. Ask yourself, "What strategies are different nations taking to deal with the negative effects of overpopulation and urbanization?"

The growth of cities creates pressure on resources such as clean drinking water, electricity, and transportation systems. The scarcity of housing means that available housing is too expensive for newcomers, many of whom live on the streets or in slum areas. For example, in 1990, the government of India estimated nearly 49 million people were living in the slums of Indian cities. Particularly in hot climates, disease spreads rapidly through these slums because of the lack of proper sanitation.

Geographic mobility also disrupts traditional patterns of family life, making the nuclear family more common than the extended family or clan. It also breaks down geographic loyalties, so that people think of themselves as citizens of a nation rather than of a village or province.

Developed nations are also dealing with the issue of suburbanization—regional residential areas outside of major cities and urban areas. Lower rent and land costs allowed middle class citizens to move out of congested urban centers into new suburban developments, where crime rates were generally lower and there was more open space. However, concerns have arisen about the sprawl and environmental impact of suburban development.

Global Migration Because of the improvements in communications and travel, migration at the beginning of the twenty-first century had reached levels not seen for a century. Approximately 150 million people live outside the nation in which they were born.

International migration occurs for several reasons. In some cases, migration results from persecution, whether religious or political. People are often attempting to escape poverty. Some governments actively recruit workers with skills needed by that nation. Newly industrialized nations, especially in East and Southeast Asia, face shortages of both skilled and unskilled labor. Taiwan, for example, is the site of both illegal immigration from mainland China and legal importing of inexpensive labor from other nearby nations.

Europe and America are home to more than forty percent of the current migration. Germany is one example of the post-World War II need for workers. During the 1950s and 1960s, like other nations of northwest Europe, Germany made bilateral agreements with Turkey and Italy that allowed guest workers into Germany. These workers were sent back to their native lands during the recession of the 1970s. However, during the 1980s, much of the migration involved families rather than specific workers.

CORE CONCEPTS: MOVEMENT OF PEOPLE AND GOODS

Britain's decision to return Hong Kong to China in 1997 led to a large-scale migration of people. Many Chinese from Hong Kong have sought shelter in Canada, changing the ethnic composition of that nation. Prior to the Chinese-British agreement, Canada had only a small Asian population.

During the 1980s and 1990s, much of the international migration was due to individuals seeking political asylum or to refugees. More than 16 million people were refugees by the mid-1990s, two-thirds of them in the Middle East and Africa. Ethnic cleansing became a renewed problem in the Balkan states, creating more refugees.

Modernization/Tradition—Finding a Balance

As nations begin to industrialize, they seek to find a balance between modern technology and ideas and the more familiar, traditional approaches to life. Several nations continue to struggle for the ideal balance, as the following examples demonstrate.

REGENTS WARM-UP

Along with other students, divide the regions discussed in this section and research current issues in that area of the world. Share the information each of you finds in a Regents review session.

Japan   After World War II ended, the United States attempted to help Japan rebuild. A 1952 mutual defense treaty contained the provision that Japan could spend no more than one percent of its gross national income on defense. Japan's leaders thus had an incentive for economic development.

Burdened by a large population, a lack of natural resources, and the loss of its overseas empire, Japan nevertheless accomplished what some have called an economic miracle. The island nation has a gross national product larger than that of France and Great Britain combined.

This growth was due in part to the traditional Japanese emphasis of a strong work ethic, reinforced in the educational system. Japan's workforce was willing to accept wages and working conditions that most in the West would not agree to, giving Japan an advantage, despite the need to import most raw materials. The nation is now known for its automobiles, computer technology, and televisions.

Women in Japan, although legally protected from workplace discrimination, continue to play a subordinate role. During the Allied occupation, women were given the right to vote and urged to enter politics. However, women appear content with traditional female roles.

Although they comprise more than 40 percent of the workforce, they earn about 60 percent of men's wages, since they work largely in retail and service positions. Patriotism remains strong in the Japanese national character, even though all references to emperor worship and patriotism were removed from textbooks after World War II ended.

Middle East The conservative Islam movement in many Middle Eastern nations has caused a severe strain on efforts to modernize. Islamic extremists have called for a return to traditional values and culture. Men are required to grow untrimmed beards and give up neckties and other Western dress. However, the situation is particularly difficult for women, who must remain covered in the traditional *burka* when in public and who are denied employment and education.

Africa In 1963 the Organization of African Unity was founded to promote the idea of Pan-Africanism, the unity of all black Africans. That organization was superseded by the African Union in 2002, a 53-member group trying to promote economic growth and democracy.

The region is hindered by a traditional dependence on exporting a single natural resource or crop. Most African nations must import manufactured goods and technology from Western nations. The nations of Africa also struggle due to scarce resources spent on military buildup, bribery and corruption, and population growth, as well as widespread poverty caused by drought.

African national boundaries were drawn by European colonial powers, which ignored ethnic, linguistic, and territorial groups. Because of this, ethnic wars have continued to erupt.

Western influence has been greatest in the cities, where the colonial presence was strongest. Life there appears similar to that in cities throughout the world. Rural people continue to migrate to cities in hopes of a better life, despite some people's views of cities as corrupt and opposed to traditional African values and customs.

Seventy-five percent of African people still make their living from the land. They live as traditional people always have, in huts with thatched roofs without electricity or plumbing. Traditional clothing, methods of farming, and religious beliefs remain in place. Rural women in Africa produce more than 70 percent of Africa's food. Although women have been allowed to vote and run for political office, they are generally in low-paying positions such as servants, farm workers, and factory workers. Traditional attitudes toward women, including arranged marriages, are common throughout Africa.

CORE CONCEPTS: CHANGE

Urbanization is occurring so rapidly in Kenya that a huge makeshift slum has formed in the Mathare Valley, a mile north of Nairobi. Here more than 100,000 people have set up homes as they leave rural areas looking for work in the nation's capital.

Latin America The family, which can include three or more generations, is the most important unit in Latin American tradition. Parents play a key role in the lives of their children. "Family" also extends to godparents, who sponsor the children in religious activities and care for them if something happens to their parents.

Women are gaining political power throughout Latin America, where they have voting rights in every nation and have held office in several. This new political equality has eroded the traditional power of *machismo*, an attitude glorifying male dominance. In rural communities, however, progress is slow.

Latin American nations are also trying to find a balance as North American culture enters through Music Television (MTV) Latino. While some people in Latin America resent the influence of the United States, protesting against the mixture of Spanish and English used by Latin video deejays, others welcome the cultural sharing.

CORE CONCEPTS: CULTURE

Marriage partners are still often determined by parents. Most Latin Americans are opposed to marriages between social classes. To indicate the high status of each of their parents' families, many aristocrats use two last names.

Scientific and Technological Advances

Modern medicine and advances in science and technology have improved lives around the globe. Although a cure for AIDS has not been found and treatment is expensive, other diseases have been all but eliminated.

Treatment of Infectious Diseases In 1978, the United Nations called for the elimination of all infectious diseases by the year 2000. This ambitious goal was not realistic and was not met, despite major victories against diphtheria, smallpox, and polio. Diseases once thought to be under control, such as tuberculosis and malaria, are on the increase.

AIDS, the acquired immunodeficiency syndrome, was first identified in 1981. The disease, once thought to be confined to the homosexual male population, quickly spread to epidemic proportions, especially in Africa south of the Sahara, where an estimated 25 million children, women, and men are infected. Since the start of the epidemic, nearly 22 million people have died of AIDS.

Improved Standard of Living The term *standard of living* refers to having basic needs met, as well as available comforts and luxuries. These basic needs include shelter, safe drinking water, and food.

CORE CONCEPTS: DIVERSITY

Southeast Asia is a region in which the variety of family patterns is influenced, in part, by the many different religions practiced in the area.

CORE CONCEPT: CHANGE

Daw Aung San Suu Kyi was awarded the Nobel Peace Prize in 1991, but could not attend the ceremony. The Myanmar government had placed her under house arrest because of her call for a nonviolent revolution against the government. The arrest lasted from 1989 to 1995. Suu Kyi and her party won a landslide victory in the 1990 elections, but were not permitted to take power. She developed a new form of public meeting, the gateside meeting, at which she spoke to her followers from behind the gates of her home.

Status of Women and Children

Economic Issues In Western countries, the gaps between men and women in the workplace have been steadily decreasing. The number of women in the workforce continues to increase, along with the number of women university graduates. Many countries have passed laws requiring equal pay for equal work. A number of Western countries also have laws that prohibit sex discrimination.

Women in developing countries, on the other hand, often remain bound to their homes and families and are subordinate to their fathers and husbands. They continue to face problems in obtaining education, property rights, and decent jobs.

Around the world, particularly in South and Southeast Asia, more than 250 million children between the ages of five and fourteen work. Approximately 50 million children work in India alone, often in conditions that are unsafe or harmful to their emotional well-being. It is difficult to enforce laws against this exploitation of children, since the work most often takes place in family businesses, domestic service, agriculture, and the sex trade.

Social Issues Women in less developed nations have been expected to remain at home, isolated and uneducated. Women are twice as likely as men to be illiterate in Arab and Muslim countries.

One of the problems in South Asian nations is the custom of dowry deaths. If the dowry paid to the groom's family is thought to be inadequate or if the new bride displeases her husband, she is doused with kerosene and set on fire, and her death is explained as a cooking accident. More than 700 cases of dowry death were reported in Delhi alone in 1983. Between 1994 and 1997, more than 500 Pakistani men set fire to their wives. Activists in India and Pakistan have begun to challenge this custom and to set up shelters for women who survive this ordeal.

Political Issues Most women around the world can vote, although they do not have the political power that men do. In several nations, women have held high office. India, Pakistan, and Sri Lanka have all had women rulers in recent decades.

In 1975, the United Nations initiated a Decade for Women and has regularly held global conferences on women's status since then.

Ethnic and Religious Tensions

Regional, ethnic, and religious differences continue to create conflict around the world. In Europe, Yugoslavia has been torn apart by ethnic divisions. In the Middle East, the conflict between Israelis and Palestinians continues to produce acts of violence. Conflicts between **ethnic groups** in Africa have led to massacres of hundreds of thousands of people.

Northern Ireland Since the early 1970s, Northern Ireland has been the scene of intermittent violence between Protestant and Catholic Christians. This tension is fueled in part by Catholics who have joined the Irish Republican Army (IRA). The group is dedicated to joining the Republic of Ireland, which gained independence in 1949, and Northern Ireland, which is still ruled by Great Britain.

Balkans After World War I, the Allies redrew the map of Europe. They disregarded ethnicities in doing so, leaving ethnic minorities in nearly every state in Eastern Europe.

Dictator Josep Tito held together six republics and two provinces that made up Yugoslavia after World War II. Although a Communist state, Yugoslavia was not a Soviet satellite. At the end of the 1980s, Yugoslavia was part of the revolutionary movement in Eastern Europe, and the nation split into several independent states, such as Slovenia and Croatia.

Aided by Serbian minorities in Croatia, the Yugoslav army attacked Croatia in 1991, gaining a third of the territory. The Serbs next turned to Bosnia-Herzegovina, capturing 70 percent of Bosnian territory by 1993.

At the same time, the Serbs were following a policy of **ethnic cleansing**, killing or removing Muslims from the land. A quarter million Bosnians, most of them civilians, had been killed and another two million were left homeless by 1995.

Three years later, after NATO air strikes and a treaty ended fighting in Bosnia, new violence erupted in Kosovo, where Serbs began a massacre of Albanians. NATO again intervened and new republics formed as Yugoslavia disintegrated.

Indonesian Christians Violence against the minority Christians in Indonesia led to at least a thousand dead during 1999–2000. Despite a Muslim-Christian peace accord signed in 2001, at the end of 2003, the violence continued in several separate attacks. Extremist Muslim groups are suspected of the violence, which

CORE CONCEPTS: NATIONALISM

The Irish Republican Army (IRA) is an example of a militant nationalist group. Its goal is to unite Northern Ireland, which is ruled by Great Britain, with the Irish Republic. Since the 1970s, IRA terrorists have been responsible for the deaths of thousands of people.

included direct attacks, churches and homes destroyed, and bombs planted in churches. Although authorities responded with arrests of suspects, some believe that the attackers had weapons usually reserved for the police force.

East Timor East Timor was annexed by Indonesia after declaring its independence in 1975. After a long and bloody guerilla war, the United Nations supervised elections in which the people of East Timor again asserted their independence. However, anti-independence forces (with help from the Indonesian military) began a series of violent uprisings. U.N. peacekeepers were called in and independence was finally recognized in 2002.

China-Tibet In 1950, the Chinese took control of Tibet by force. More than a decade later, fighting broke out between China's People's Liberation Army (PLA) and Tibet. Once a free nation, Tibet is now part of China's borderlands, governed by Beijing.

The people of Tibet have their own literature, language, and religion. Tibetan Buddhism focuses on the person of the Dalai Lama, a term meaning "Ocean of Wisdom." The present Dalai Lama fled Tibet, along with 80,000 others who went to India and Nepal to escape China.

CORE CONCEPTS: BELIEF SYSTEMS

Before the Communist invasion, Tibet was an example of a theocracy, or a country in which religious leaders exercise political power. To break the authority of the Tibetan monks, the Chinese reduced their numbers (through law and death) from 3,000 in 1950 to about 500 in 1990.

SECTION 2 ECONOMIC ISSUES

World's Richest Countries

Country	Gross National Product, per Capita (in U.S. dollars)
Luxembourg	45,360
Switzerland	44,355
Japan	41,010
Liechtenstein	40,000
Norway	34,515

Source: World Development Indicators 2000, World Bank.

World's Poorest Countries

Country	Gross National Product, per Capita (in U.S. dollars)
Mozambique	80
Congo, DNC	100
Eritrea	100
Ethiopia	100
Somalia	100

Source: World Development Indicators 2000, World Bank.

North/South Dichotomy: Issues of Development

The nations of the Northern Hemisphere enjoy a higher standard of living than do people of the Southern Hemisphere. For example, the annual wage in the United States in 1999 averaged $33,900. In Central America, the range of annual wage varied between $2,050 in Honduras and $7,600 in Panama. This kind of gap means basic services are often not available to those living in the Southern Hemisphere. After the 1970s, both African and Latin American nations faced similar problems: rising import costs, falling commodity prices, and huge foreign debt.

Africa The nations of Africa gained independence from colonial powers in record numbers during and after the 1960s. The quest for national unity was difficult, however, complicated by the colonial divisions, which ignored ethnic and economic divisions. A number of military coups occurred following independence, such as the one in Zaire (now the Democratic Republic of the Congo) in the early 1960s. Because of the extreme poverty, particularly in nations south of the Sahara, basic civil services such as sewage treatment, education, and welfare programs are absent.

While Africa contains 10 percent of the world's population, it produces only 1 percent of the world's industrial output. Lacking managerial expertise, foreign investment and markets, capital, and technology, Africa is unable to benefit fully from its rich agricultural products, raw materials, and mineral resources.

Latin America Political instability has plagued the newly independent nations of Latin America as well as those that won their freedom during the nineteenth century. Democracy is slowly taking root among people more accustomed to military dictatorships.

The continent shares some of the same difficulties as Africa. Regional differences and high foreign debt have prevented economic gains, despite trade organizations such as the Central American Common Market. Between 26 percent and 45 percent of the people of Latin America earn less than $2 per day.

Several factors have inhibited industrial growth in Latin America. The region as a whole, with the exception of Venezuela and Mexico, lacks fossil fuels and must import energy sources. Most people cannot support economic expansion through consumer purchases. The area lacks the necessary infrastructure, such as adequate highway systems, for development. Local companies cannot compete with multinational corporations that have established businesses in the region.

Korea's Economic Miracle

At the end of the war in 1953, Korea was divided and exhausted. North Korea was a Communist state. With the coup and subsequent election of Chung Hee Park in 1961, South Korea's economy began to grow stronger. Peasants received land after Park instituted land reforms and promoted new industries. Gradually, South Korea became a major industrial power in East Asia, particularly in chemicals, textiles, automobiles, and shipbuilding.

Park ruled as an autocrat. Democracy came slowly to South Korea, but in 1997, an economic crisis and new elections brought Kim Tae-jung, a reformer, to the presidency.

Economic Interdependence

In the current global economy that emerged after the collapse of communism in the 1990s, nations are interdependent. Deregulation, privatizing formerly state-held enterprises, unrestricted trade, and foreign investments have shaped the economic interdependence that is best symbolized by large global companies. These companies place a small staff in a central location, but most functions are sent out to the most competitive location. About 50,000 of these global companies have come into existence in the past two decades.

Organizations such as the World Trade Organization, a federation of more than 100 countries, work to eliminate barriers to **free trade** and to settle disputes over trade agreements.

The new system is not without controversies. By moving functions out of a nation in search of the cheapest labor and production costs, companies avoid paying taxes and supporting the social fabric of the home country. The federal tax portion of United States corporations has shrunk from 30 percent to 12 percent.

Outsourcing Outsourcing has also become an issue of economic interdependence. Outsourcing is the reassignment of work to subcontractors or outside workers. It often means that the work is being sent overseas to workers who do not make as much money to perform the same job. India and China, particularly, are taking advantage of this trend, especially in technology-driven areas, such as software development and technical support.

CORE CONCEPTS: INTERDEPENDENCE

Multinational businesses reflect the growing interdependence between more developed and less developed nations. In the case of Latin America, technological superiority based on extensive capital sometimes gives multinational companies the power to affect the economies of underdeveloped nations. Some businesses have a larger income than the gross national product of the less developed nations.

World Hunger

Hunger has also become a staggering problem. Every year, more than 8 million people die of hunger. The United Nations estimates that 840 million people in the world are undernourished, 799 million of them in the developing world. More than 153 million of the malnourished are children under the age of five. The intellectual development and physical growth of these malnourished children will be affected as a result of lack of food. Fifty-four nations, most of them in Africa south of the Sahara, do not grow enough food to meet the needs of their population.

Most of the hunger is caused by deeply-rooted poverty. Between five and ten percent of the hunger in the world is caused by natural catastrophes, such as floods or droughts, or by economic and political factors. Rapid population growth and poor soil also contribute to widespread hunger.

The United Nations

Representatives of Allied forces founded the **United Nations** (UN) in 1945 in San Francisco. The United Nations had two main goals: peace and human dignity. The General Assembly of the United Nations is made up of representatives of all member nations. It has the power to discuss any question of importance to the organization and recommend the action to be taken. The secretary-general, whose offices are located in New York City, supervises the day-to-day administrative business of the UN.

The most important advisory group of the UN is the Security Council. It has five permanent members (the United States, Russia, Great Britain, France, and China) and ten members chosen by the General Assembly to serve limited terms. The Security Council decides what actions the UN should take to settle international disputes. On various occasions, the United Nations has also provided peacekeeping forces (military forces drawn from neutral member states) to help settle conflicts and supervise truces.

Until recently, the basic weakness of the United Nations was that, throughout its history, it had been subject to the whims of the two superpowers, the Soviet Union and the United States. With the end of the Cold War, the United Nations has played a more active role in keeping alive a vision of international order.

CORE CONCEPTS: SCARCITY

Civil wars have created severe food shortages. In Sudan, civil war broke out in the 1980s. Both sides refused to allow food to be sent to their enemies. As a result, 1.3 million people had died from starvation in Sudan by the early 1990s.

CORE CONCEPTS: NEEDS AND WANTS

Several specialized agencies function under the direction of the United Nations. These include the United Nations Educational, Scientific, and Cultural Organization (UNESCO), the World Health Organization (WHO), and the United Nations International Children's Emergency Fund (UNICEF). All of these agencies have been successful in helping to address economic and social problems.

CHAPTER 34　CHALLENGES FOR THE GLOBAL COMMUNITY

Section 1	The Environment and Sustainability
Section 2	Science and Technology

Chapter Overview

The world has seen stunning developments in science, technology, and agriculture, including travel into space, high-speed communication, and a green revolution. Nevertheless, technological progress has brought serious environmental issues as well as the potential for the misuse of ever more hazardous weapons.

As you read this chapter, ask yourself these questions:
(1) What environmental issues challenge all nations of the world?
(2) What are the costs and benefits of the technological revolution?

Main Ideas and Concepts

- **Environment and Society** The world faces environmental problems that cut across national borders.

- **Science and Technology** The technological revolution has brought both costs and benefits.

- **Places and Regions** Environmental and nuclear concerns threaten various regions, especially in the Southern Hemisphere.

- **Change** People must respond to ever more rapid changes and increased data in the information age.

People, Places, Terms

The following names and terms will help you to prepare for the Regents Exam in Global History and Geography. You can find an explanation of each name and term in the Glossary at the back of this book, in your textbook, or in another reference source.

acid rain	disarmament	nuclear proliferation
deforestation	ecology	ozone layer
desertification	greenhouse effect	

SECTION 1 THE ENVIRONMENT AND SUSTAINABILITY

The Environmental Crisis

When American scientist Rachel Carson wrote *Silent Spring*, she warned that the use of pesticides was having deadly results. Her warnings helped lead to a new field of science called **ecology**, the study of the relationship between living things and their environment.

Impact of Population Growth There are many threats to the environment. Rapid population growth could result in more people than the world's resources can support. **Deforestation**, the clearing of forests, is one result of the growing population. Forests and jungles have been cut down to provide farmland and firewood, resulting in the loss of habitats for plants and animals and upsetting a balance on which human life depends.

CORE CONCEPTS: ENVIRONMENT

The loss of tropical rain forests has been of special concern. They support about 50 percent of the world's species of plants and animals.

REGENTS WARM-UP

Study the map. Name the continent with the largest area of rain forests. Name the area in which the most rain forest acreage has been lost.

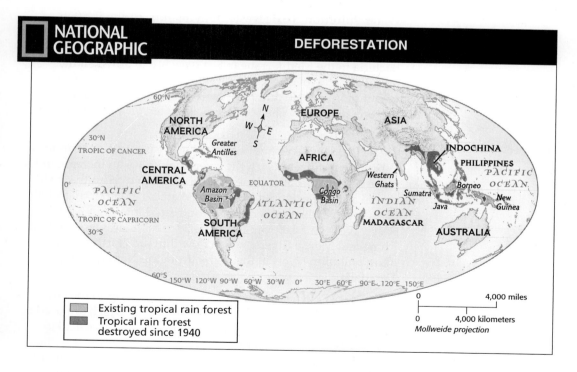

NATIONAL GEOGRAPHIC — DEFORESTATION

Existing tropical rain forest
Tropical rain forest destroyed since 1940

0 — 4,000 miles
0 — 4,000 kilometers
Mollweide projection

Pollution

Air Pollution Air quality has become a major concern in recent decades. Factories and vehicles emit greenhouse gases, which trap solar energy in the form of heat. This in turn creates global warming, which has been linked to changes in weather and in species survival.

The nations of Europe struggle with air pollution caused by factory emissions and traffic exhaust. People in the Netherlands drive the highest number of cars per square mile in Europe. High levels of air pollution affect health in the region. Swiss researchers in 2000 suggested that approximately 6 percent of the deaths across France, Switzerland, and Austria were the result of vehicle pollution.

The countries of Eastern Europe are among the most polluted nations in the world. Factories that were built during the Communist era pollute the air, in turn poisoning crops, causing increased incidence of cancer, and lowering life expectancy in nations such as Poland, the Czech Republic, and Romania.

Water Pollution Toxic waste from manufacturing is often dumped in waterways, causing fish and plants to die. The Mediterranean region of Europe is facing these problems. Bacteria in the Mediterranean Sea once broke down all the pollution. However, a growing population and tourism has meant more people dumping more trash—too much for the bacteria to handle. The Mediterranean now takes a century to renew itself.

The Danube River has been affected by agricultural runoff. When the fertilizers reach the river, they cause an increase in the algae population. The algae require so much oxygen that fish die. In another example, the city of Warsaw, Poland, treats half of its sewage; the rest is dumped untreated into the Vistula River. Western European industries deposit their wastes into the Rhine and Meuse Rivers, which flow into the North Sea, doubling pollution levels in the region from the Netherlands to Denmark.

Chemical Wastes and Disasters Another danger to the environment is chemical waste. Chlorofluorocarbons, which are used in aerosols, air conditioning, and refrigerators, are a particular concern. Scientists warn that chlorofluorocarbons destroy the **ozone layer**, a thin layer of gas in the upper atmosphere that shields Earth from the sun's ultraviolet rays. Scientists have also proposed a **greenhouse effect**, global warming caused by the buildup of carbon dioxide in the atmosphere. Another problem is **acid rain**, the rainfall that results when sulfur from factories mixes with moisture in the air. Acid rain has killed forests in both North America and Europe.

Major ecological disasters have occurred during the last 20 years. The oil spill of the tanker *Exxon Valdez* graphically illustrated the effects of water pollution. In 1989, the oil tanker ran aground in Alaska; the oil spill destroyed local animals and polluted fishing grounds.

In 1987, representatives of 43 nations met in Montreal. They agreed to protect Earth's ozone layer by reducing the use of chlorofluorocarbons. In 1992, an Earth Summit in Rio de Janeiro looked at the challenges to the environment and proposed new solutions. At the 1997 conference in Kyoto, the delegates of 159 nations agreed to cut greenhouse gas emissions believed to cause global warming. In 1999, members of the European Union agreed to guidelines that increased protection from industrial waste, protected endangered species, and prevented ships and airplanes from dumping pollution into the Mediterranean.

Deforestation

As people move into areas surrounding cities, they clear the land of trees. The wood is used for firewood and for building homes; the cleared land can be used for grazing animals or for farming. In addition, industrialists tap trees, such as rubber trees, for their organic compounds. But the loss of trees further harms the environment.

Tropical rain forests, located near the Equator, cover only 6 percent of Earth's surface. However, that region accounts for 50 percent of the animal and plant species of the planet. Some scientists believe that rain forest plants may have potential as medicines. In addition, rain forests remove carbon dioxide from the atmosphere and provide it with oxygen.

One of the most serious losses of forest is occurring in the Amazon Basin of Brazil. Brazil has begun encouraging development in the interior regions, where the Amazon River, the world's second-largest, provides an east-west waterway across South America. The Brazilian government has also begun extracting minerals, such as tin, copper, iron, and petroleum, from the rain forest. Thirteen percent of the rain forest in Brazil has already been cleared.

CORE CONCEPTS: ENVIRONMENT

Mismanagement of the environment has been one of the harshest legacies of Soviet communism. A path of pollution and toxic wastes stretches from nuclear test sites in Siberia to the poisoned rivers of Eastern Europe.

CORE CONCEPTS: IMPERIALISM

Rain forests in Southeast Asia offer ideal growing conditions for hardwoods and rubber trees. Both of these natural resources have led outside powers to exploit the region through conquest and imperialism.

CORE CONCEPTS: ENVIRONMENT

About 150 acres (61 ha) of rain forest are destroyed every minute, losing untold riches. A few acres of rain forest may contain 450 different species of trees. A single tree may be home for 650 types of bees. Rain forest plants offer food, medicine, and chemical substances.

Experts urge sustainable development, economic and technological growth that does not deplete the natural and human resources of an area. Balancing the need to improve the standard of living for many people with preserving wilderness creates an ongoing tension.

Desertification

In West Africa, the Sahel region—a semi-arid land—is increasingly becoming desert land. Bordering the Sahara, the Sahel stretches across the northern section of the area. Nomads once grazed their herds in the region; the animals fertilized the soil, and farming was possible. Now, **desertification** has spread into the nations of Mali, Mauritania, Chad, and Sudan.

Droughts have always been part of the area's natural history. Since the 1960s, however, severe droughts have turned the farmland into a wasteland. The United Nations Food and Agriculture Organization in 2000 warned that famine may become a concern in central Africa due to the unpredictable weather and large numbers of refugees in the area.

Weapons The technological revolution has also led to the development of nuclear, biological, and chemical weapons. Although the end of the Cold War reduced the chances of a major nuclear war, there is still concern that nuclear materials (bombs or radioactive matter) will be obtained and used by terrorists. Biowarfare (the use of disease and poison against civilians and soldiers in wartime) is not new. Chemical weapons were used in World War I and in the Iran-Iraq War in the 1980s. Japan used biological weapons on China and Manchuria in the 1930s and 1940s. Governments have made agreements to limit the research, production, and use of biological and chemical weapons, but these agreements have not prevented terrorists from practicing bioterrorism (the use of biological and chemical weapons in terrorist attacks).

Nuclear Safety

From 1949 until 1987, the Soviet Union set off more than 600 nuclear explosions. They developed and stockpiled nuclear weapons. During the Cold War, the Soviet Union generated electricity through nuclear power. Producing nuclear power creates nuclear waste, some of which can remain radioactive for

CORE CONCEPTS: HUMAN SYSTEMS

Proposed solutions to the problem of desertification include crop rotation, soil conservation, and planting trees. However, these solutions may interfere with traditional tribal and nomadic life. The Maasai people, for example, might stop herding in favor of fenced-in farms or might reduce the size of their herds, but this would change Maasai culture.

thousands of years. Most of these wastes were placed in storage, but some were dumped directly into Russia's northern waters.

Trying to keep pace with the West led to poorly trained workers who ignored proper safeguards at substandard nuclear plants and reactors. The nuclear explosion at Chernobyl in 1986 highlighted the dangers of such an approach. Tons of radioactive particles were released into the air and carried by the wind to other countries.

Because the Soviets did not alert the public or evacuate people quickly, thousands of people were exposed to radiation. More than 8,000 people had died by the mid-1990s as a result. In Russia alone, more than 30 million people lived in the 19,300 square miles (50,000 sq. km) affected by radiation.

Endangered Species

From the armadillo in South America to the zebra in South Africa, many animals and plants are endangered or threatened. Decreasing numbers may be due to hunting, loss of habitat, or environmental changes.

Africa's elephants, placed on the endangered species list in 1989, are one example of the dilemma. Tens of thousands of the animals were slaughtered during the nineteenth century for sport, for meat, and especially for the ivory tusks that both male and female elephants grow. The ivory was carved into everything from piano keys to jewelry. From 1930 to 1979, biologists estimate that the African elephant population dropped from 5 to 10 million to 1.3 million, decreasing to 600,000 by the late 1980s.

The efforts of several countries to save and encourage growth in endangered species appear to be working. In the United States, 27 species were removed from the Endangered Species list, including the bald eagle. In Africa, Zimbabwe has set up a successful program to reduce poaching by consulting with local communities.

CORE CONCEPTS: ENVIRONMENT AND SOCIETY

Efforts are underway in Europe to reintroduce the wolf, a species that keeps down the numbers of elk, reindeer, and musk oxen. The number of wolves tripled in northwest Spain. Wolves have been reintroduced in the Carpathian Mountains of Romania.

SECTION 2 SCIENCE AND TECHNOLOGY

The Technological Revolution

Many changes since World War II have combined to create a technological revolution.

Transportation, Communications, and Space Modern transportation and communication systems are transforming the world. Jumbo jets, the Internet, satellites, cable television, fax machines, and cellular telephones are some examples. American astronauts have landed on the moon, and space probes have increased our understanding of distant planets. Satellites provide information about weather and transmit signals for radio, television, and telephone communications.

Information Age

The end of the twentieth century saw a revolution in communication. Computers, first developed during the 1940s for the United States Army, became smaller and faster, as well as affordable. The ability to transfer information globally within seconds became a reality with the Internet and the World Wide Web.

English has been the dominant language of this global communication device. However, many nations have adapted modern technology for their own purposes. In much of the world, for example, television stations are state-controlled. Broadcasting is used to promote state building and to distribute propaganda.

Green Revolution

In agriculture, the Green Revolution has promised huge returns. The Green Revolution refers to the development of new strains of rice, corn, and other grains that have greater yields. It was promoted as the technological solution to feeding the world's growing population. But immense amounts of chemical fertilizers and pesticides are needed to grow the new strains. Many farmers cannot afford the fertilizers, and the pesticides create environmental problems.

CORE CONCEPTS: SCIENCE AND TECHNOLOGY

The first all-electronic computer was named ENIAC, electronic numerical integrator and calculator. Designed in 1946, it had thousands of vacuum tubes and weighed 30 tons. The tubes got hot and needed to be cooled down on a regular basis. Small moths tended to get into the machine and stop its calculations. Scientists had to debug the computer regularly, adding a new word to our vocabulary.

Space Exploration

The Soviet launch of *Sputnik I* in 1957 initiated a space race between that nation and the United States. A Soviet craft also made the first successful moon landing, although the United States is the only nation to have sent people to the moon. Twelve American astronauts landed on the moon from 1969 until 1972, in six different Apollo missions. Most commonly, robotic devices explore the universe, sending back photographs.

Impact of Satellites

Nearly a thousand satellites orbit a few thousand miles above Earth. Many of these are communication satellites, making it possible for us to use telephones, television, and the Global Positioning Systems (GPS). Other satellites photograph the ozone layer, the movement of migratory birds, the growth of crops, oil spills, and weather patterns.

CORE CONCEPTS: SCIENCE AND TECHNOLOGY

Animals are often used to attempt new feats in space. The Soviets first sent up a dog, Laika, in 1957. Dogs have respiration and blood circulation patterns similar to humans. Chimpanzees, whose genetic makeup is similar to that of humans and who can be trained, also are used.

Communication around the World

Country	Daily newspaper circulation per 1,000 persons	Radios per 1,000 persons	Televisions per 1,000 persons	Telephone main lines per 1,000 persons	Cellular phone subscribers per 1,000 persons	Estimated personal computers per 1,000 persons
Canada	158	1,067	710	677	285	39
China	n/a	335	321	111	66	2
Cuba	118	352	239	44	1	1
France	218	946	595	580	494	30
Germany	311	948	567	601	586	34
Italy	104	880	528	474	737	21
Japan	578	956	686	653	526	32
Mexico	97	329	272	125	142	5
Russia	105	417	410	218	22	4
South Africa	34	355	134	114	12	6
United Kingdom	331	1,443	521	557	670	34
United States	212	2,116	806	700	365	59

Sources: United Nations and International Telecommunications Union, 2001.

Literacy and Education

The idea of universal education came about in the late nineteenth and early twentieth centuries. Literacy had always been a mark of privileged people. For example, when the British Empire stretched across India, illiteracy rates remained at about 90 percent; Indians were not to be educated, but used as human capital. In a more extreme instance, teaching enslaved Africans in America to read was a crime in some places.

Most Western nations made a commitment to universal primary education following the Second Industrial Revolution, when an educated workforce became desirable. Also, offering universal suffrage meant the need for an educated voting population.

Throughout central and western Europe, by 1900 most adults could read. At the same time in Russia and Serbia, the illiteracy rate was 79 percent.

Medical Breakthroughs

In the field of health, new technologies have enabled doctors to perform "miracle" operations. Mechanical valves and pumps for the heart and organ transplants have allowed people to live longer lives. Technological changes in the health field have also raised new concerns. For example, genetic engineering is a new scientific field that alters the genetic information of cells to produce new variations. Some people worry that the new variations could be deadly. The overuse of antibiotics has already created "supergerms" that do not respond to treatment with available antibiotics. The issues of stem-cell research and human cloning have also created intense debates.

CORE CONCEPTS: LINKING PAST AND PRESENT

Nearly 22 million people have already died of AIDS. This figure equals that from the flu pandemic of 1918–1919, which killed between 20 and 40 million people, more than died during World War I.

Epidemics

Despite progress in eradicating life-threatening diseases, public health officials are concerned about new diseases such as the Ebola fever and the acquired immunodeficiency syndrome (AIDS) virus. The latter is fatal, due to the human immunodeficiency virus (HIV), which attacks and kills the cells of the immune system, leaving the body vulnerable to disease. When these diseases arise, AIDS, the final stage of HIV, occurs.

The disease first reached epidemic proportions in Africa south of the Sahara. As of December 2000, more than 25.3 million cases had been identified in Africa, 5.8 million in Asia, and 1.4 million in South America. World totals were 36.1 million infected persons.

The situation in Africa is critical. Life expectancy is expected to decline from 59 to 45 between 2005 and 2010 because of the epidemic. Eighty percent of the children with HIV/AIDS live in Africa; ten million children are orphaned because of the disease. Some successful programs have begun, most notably in Uganda.

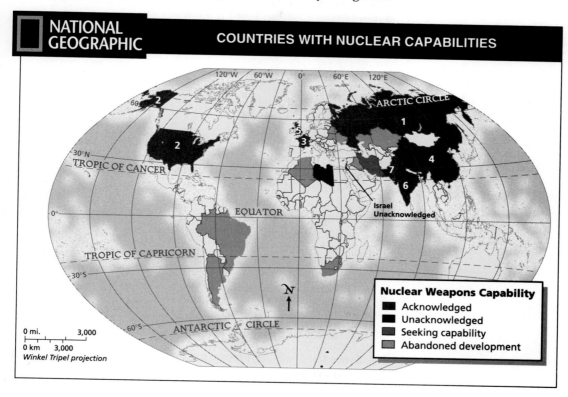

NATIONAL GEOGRAPHIC

COUNTRIES WITH NUCLEAR CAPABILITIES

Nuclear Weapons Capability
- Acknowledged
- Unacknowledged
- Seeking capability
- Abandoned development

Winkel Tripel projection

Nuclear Proliferation

According to one estimate, the Commonwealth of Independent States and the United States possess a combined total of 23,000 strategic nuclear warheads, a grim legacy from the Cold War years. This figure does not include the nuclear weapons owned by other nations. Efforts at limiting **nuclear proliferation** and at encouraging **disarmament** have had moderate success.

Some nations are suspected of having nuclear arms, but are unwilling to allow neutral inspections. Some of those nations have a record of terrorist activities or support. The proliferation of nuclear weapons increases the likelihood of a third world war, in which the planet's ecological system could well be destroyed.

PRACTICING FOR THE REGENTS

Part I   Multiple-Choice Questions

The following multiple-choice questions come from past Regents Examinations. Test your understanding of global history and geography by answering each of these items. Circle the number of the word or expression that best completes each statement or question. Test-taking tips can be found in the margins for some questions. For additional help, see Taking the Regents Exam on pages ix-xxxv of this Review Book.

1   I.   _____
    A. Mass starvation in Ireland (1845–1850)
    B. Partition of India (1947)
    C. Latin Americans seeking jobs in the United States (post World War II)
    D. Ethnic cleansing in the Balkans (1990s)

Which title best completes this partial outline?
(1) Causes of Industrialization
(2) Causes of Global Migrations
(3) Reasons for Colonialism
(4) Reasons for Cultural Borrowing

2   During the 20th century, in which area did deforestation become a serious problem?
    (1) Great European Plain
    (2) Deccan Plateau
    (3) Amazon Basin
    (4) Great Rift Valley

3   Since the 1960s, famine in many parts of the world has been reduced by
    (1) increased urbanization
    (2) global warming
    (3) laissez-faire capitalism
    (4) the Green Revolution

4   Since the late 1970s, which measure has the Chinese government taken to reduce the effects of overpopulation?
    (1) supported a policy of forced migration to other nations
    (2) reduced food production
    (3) emphasized the teachings of Confucius
    (4) imposed a one-child policy that limits family size

Base your answer to question 5 on the cartoon below and on your knowledge of social studies.

(adapted)

5   This 1998 cartoon depicts religious tensions in which nation?
(1) Israel
(2) Ireland
(3) Iran
(4) India

6   The problems created by the deterioration of the Earth's ozone layer and increases in the amounts of acid rain suggest a worldwide need for
(1) rapid industrialization of developing economies
(2) better health-care programs
(3) nuclear-powered electric generating facilities
(4) stricter pollution regulations

7   During the late 1990s, the Sahel region of Africa has been faced with problems resulting from
(1) increasing desertification
(2) the lack of rainfall from the monsoons
(3) the effects of acid rain
(4) water pollution

8   In the 1990s, the troubled relations between Catholics and Protestants in Northern Ireland and between Serbs, Croats, and Muslims in the Balkans helped illustrate the
(1) difficulties of resolving ethnic and religious conflicts
(2) inequalities created by expanding free markets and global trade
(3) conflict created by the collapse of the Warsaw Pact
(4) results of the failure of dictatorial governments

"Famine seems to be the last, the most dreadful resource of nature. The power of population is so superior to the power in the earth to provide subsistence for man, that premature death must in some shape or other visit the human race. . . ."

—*Thomas Malthus, "Essay on Population," 1798*

This prediction proved to be wrong in part because of increases in
(1) ethnic cleansing
(2) farm productivity
(3) the number of wars
(4) the number of droughts

10 In the 1990s, what was the most severe threat to the physical environments of Brazil, Costa Rica, and the Democratic Republic of the Congo (Zaire)?
(1) spread of urban centers
(2) nuclear waste disposal
(3) increased immigration
(4) destruction of the rain forests

Base your answer to question 11 on the document below and on your knowledge of social studies.

Universal Declaration of Human Rights
Article 2: Everyone is entitled to all the rights and freedoms set forth in this declaration, without distinction of any kind, such as . . . colour, sex, language, . . . national or social origin, property, birth or other status.
Article 5: No one shall be subjected to torture or to cruel, inhuman or degrading treatment or punishment.
Article 9: No one shall be subjected to arbitrary arrest, detention or exile.
Article 13: Everyone has the right to leave any country, including his own, and to return to his country.
Article 18: Everyone has the right to freedom of thought, conscience and religion. . . .
Article 20: Everyone has the right to freedom of peaceful assembly and association.
Article 21: Everyone has the right to take part in the government of his country, directly or through freely chosen representatives.
—United Nations, December 10, 1948

11 The ideas expressed in the United Nations Universal Declaration of Human Rights most closely reflect the political philosophy of the
(1) Scientific Revolution
(2) Age of Enlightenment
(3) Commercial Revolution
(4) Middle Ages

Base your answer to question 12 on the cartoon below and on your knowledge of social studes.

Source: Schot/Algemeen, *World Press Review*

12 The cartoon implies that economic refugees will
   (1) be able to solve problems in their own regions
   (2) not seek refuge in the United States and Canada
   (3) not be admitted to Europe
   (4) be accepted by the members of the European Union

13 • Nuclear accident at Chernobyl in the former Soviet Union
   • Dumping of toxic waste in the ocean
   • Cutting down the rain forest in Africa and South America

Which conclusion can be drawn from these situations?
   (1) Environmental problems need global solutions.
   (2) The fall of the Soviet Union has caused severe environmental hazards.
   (3) Technology has helped the world stop polluting the environment.
   (4) Only nations that create environmental problems will suffer from them.

14 In India, the population movement from rural to urban areas has resulted in
   (1) a revival of interest in traditional values
   (2) the weakening of the nuclear family
   (3) the end of hostilities between Hindus and Muslims
   (4) a decrease in rigid class distinctions

15 Which issue continues to raise concern from the world community regarding the nations of India, Iraq, Pakistan, and North Korea?
   (1) overpopulation
   (2) ethnic cleansing
   (3) desertification
   (4) nuclear proliferation

Base your answer to question 16 on the chart below and on your knowledge of social studies.

United Nations (1945–1995)

Year	Members	Annual Operating Budget	Peacekeeping Missions
1945	51	$147 million	0
1961	58	$177 million	4
1988	158	$258 million	8
1995	185	$1.3 billion	16

Source: *The New York Times*, 10/22/95

 16 An analysis of this chart shows that the United Nations
(1) expects individual nations to solve their own problems
(2) is very much like the League of Nations and does not have the resources to enforce its decisions
(3) relies on the United States to carry out its peacekeeping missions
(4) faces an increasing financial burden as it deals with a growing number of crises

17 "My village is changing. A straight road was built in the mid-1960s to carry iron ore from the mines to the port of Paradip, 40 miles away. . . . Nylon, stainless steel, plastic, [soft] drinks have reached the village. Electricity has come too. . . . There is a cinema and video hall."

Which conclusion can be drawn from this quotation?
(1) Roads in most villages today have fallen into disrepair.
(2) New technologies will have little effect on village life.
(3) Modernization often changes village life.
(4) The best jobs can be found in cities.

18 The Green Revolution of the 1960s resulted in
(1) the destruction of large industrial enterprises
(2) an increase of food output in many developing nations
(3) a decrease in world agricultural output
(4) improvements in human genetic engineering

19 During the 20th century, one effect of industrialization on the culture of India was the
(1) strengthening of cottage industries
(2) reduction of social class mobility
(3) increased internal migration
(4) decline in the political and economic power of women

 20 During the last two decades, a problem that slowed industrialization in many developing nations was the
(1) limited supply of labor
(2) shortage of money for capital investment
(3) rapid decline in population growth
(4) refusal of these nations to make trade agreements with other nations

Base your answers to questions 21 and 22 on the chart below and on your knowledge of social studies.

Socioeconomic Status of Asian Countries			
Country	Per Capita GDP	Life Expectancy	Infant Mortality (per 1,000 births)
Bangladesh	200	55	107
India	270	58	78
Philippines	860	63	51
Japan	19,800	79	4
Thailand	1,800	68	37
Country	Percent Urban Population	Percent Literate	Birthrate (per 1,000 people)
Bangladesh	14	47	35
India	26	48	28
Philippines	44	88	27
Japan	77	99	10
Thailand	19	89	19

Source: *The World Almanac Book of Facts, 1995*

 21 According to the chart, which of these Asian nations is the least urbanized and the least industrialized country?
(1) Bangladesh
(2) India
(3) Philippines
(4) Thailand

 22 Which statement about Japan's socioeconomic status is an opinion?
(1) Japan's gross domestic product (GDP) is high and its birthrate is low.
(2) Japan has the most efficient educational system and the best culture in Asia.
(3) Japan's infant mortality rate is low and its life expectancy is high.
(4) Japan has a high percentage of urban population and a high rate of literacy.

Base your answer to question 23 on the table below and on your knowledge of social studies.

Health Statistics of Selected Countries, 1996					
Country	Population (thousands)	Life Expectancy at Birth (male/female)	Hospital Beds (per 1,000 people)	Physicians (per 1,000 people)	Infant Mortality (deaths per 1,000)
Argentina	34,673	68/75	4.4	2.7	28
Australia	18,261	76/83	5.0	2.3	6
Guatemala	11,278	63/68	*	0.8	51
Myanmar	45,976	55/58	0.6	0.3	81
Netherlands	15,568	75/81	5.7	2.6	5
Zaire	46,498	45/49	2.1	0.1	108

*Data unavailable   Source: *World Almanac and Book of Facts*

23 Which conclusion can be drawn from the table?
  (1) Women live longer than men only when the infant mortality rate is low.
  (2) Infant mortality increases as the number of hospital beds increases.
  (3) The size of the population is directly related to the infant mortality rate.
  (4) There is a relationship between the level of health care and life expectancy.

24 Which statement about the spread of nuclear weapons is a fact rather than an opinion?
  (1) Nations possessing nuclear weapons should not have to limit the production of weapons.
  (2) The spread of nuclear weapons was a smaller problem in the 1990s than it was in the 1970s.
  (3) The United States and Russia signed the Strategic Arms Limitation Treaties during the 1970s.
  (4) Only developing nations are concerned about the spread of nuclear weapons.

Base your answer to question 25 on the graph below and on your knowledge of social studies.

Moving Goods: Expansion of Global Trade, 1960–1993

25 What is a major reason for the trend
illustrated by the graph?
(1) the fall of communist governments
in Eastern Europe
(2) the formation of oil cartels, such as
the Organization of Petroleum
Exporting Countries (OPEC)
(3) an increase in global interdependence resulting from modern
technology and expanded trade
agreements
(4) a general decline in the standard of
living for people in developing
countries

Part II   Thematic Essay Question

The following thematic essay question comes from questions from past Regents Examinations. Write your answers on a separate sheet of paper. Essay-writing tips appear in the margin. For additional help, see Taking the Regents Exam on pages ix–xxxv of this Review Book.

Directions: Write a well-organized essay that includes an introduction, several paragraphs addressing the task below, and a conclusion.

Theme: Geography

> Geographic features can positively or negatively affect the development of a nation or region.

Task:

> Select *one* geographic feature from your study of global history and geography and
>
> - Explain how this geographic feature has had an effect on the historical development of *two* nations or regions

Be sure to include specific historical examples in your essay.

You may use any geographic feature from your study of global history and geography. Some suggestions you might wish to consider include: river valley, mountain, desert, island, rain forest, and climate. Do *not* use the United States in your answer.

You are *not* limited to these suggestions.

Guidelines:

In your essay, be sure to

- Develop all aspects of the task
- Support the theme with relevant facts, examples, and details
- Use a logical and clear plan of organization, including an introduction and a conclusion that are beyond a restatement of the theme

Part III   Document-Based Question

This exercise is designed to test your ability to work with historical documents. It is similar to the document-based questions you will see on the Regents Examination. While you are asked to analyze three historical documents, the exercise on the actual exam will include more documents. Some of the documents have been edited for the purposes of the question. As you analyze the documents, take into account the source of each document and any point of view that may be presented in the document.

Historical Context:

Throughout global history, people have migrated as a result of political, social, and economic conditions.

Task: Using information from the documents and your knowledge of global history, answer the questions that follow each document in Part A. Your answers to the questions will help you write the Part B essay, in which you will be asked to

- Discuss the political, social, and/or economic reasons for the mass movement of peoples throughout global history

Do *not* use examples from the United States in your answer.

Part A   Short-Answer Questions

Directions: Analyze the documents and answer the short-answer questions that follow each document in the space provided.

Document 1

> . . . Hundreds of thousands of Hindus and Sikhs who had lived for centuries on the Northwest Frontier [of India] abandoned their homes and fled [the riots] toward the protection of the predominantly Sikh and Hindu communities in the east. They traveled on foot, in bullock carts, crammed into [trucks], clinging to the sides and roofs of trains. Along the way— . . . at crossroads, at railroad stations—they collided with panicky swarms of Muslims fleeing to safety in the west. The riots had become a rout.
>
> By the summer of 1947, when the creation of the new state of Pakistan was formally announced, ten million people—Muslims, Hindus and Sikhs—were in flight.
>
>   —*Khushwant Singh*, Train to Pakistan

1   According to the document, why did Hindus, Sikhs, and Muslims abandon their homes during this period?

the were leaving because of the riots

Document 2

> The Nazi Holocaust, which engulfed millions of Jews in Europe, proved anew the urgency of the re-establishment of the Jewish State, which would solve the problem of Jewish homelessness by opening the gates to all Jews and lifting the Jewish people to equality in the family of nations.
>
>   — *David Ben-Gurion, "Declaration of the State of Israel" (1948)*

2   Why did many Jews move to Israel (Palestine) after World War II?

they wanted to form their own state for protection and equality

Document 3

> When I was in the Sinai with Anwar [Sadat], I was shocked by what I saw. The war had left its mark on everything and everyone. Wherever I went I saw Palestinians who had been forced from their homeland by the creation of Israel and the fighting that had ensued [followed] in 1948. Dressed in black, mothers with their children squatted silently alongside the roads, in the towns. . . . More than one million Arabs had suddenly become homeless, depending on the United Nations Relief Fund for subsistence. . . . Refugee camps lined the roads, the tents so close they seemed like a canvas city.
>
> "Is your family faring well?" I asked our cook, a Palestinian woman from one of the refugee camps.
>
> She dropped her eyes. "It is not like before," she said quietly. . . . "From the camp we can see the tops of the lemon and orange trees on our old farm," she said slowly, as if reluctant to remember. "On our land it was always green and warm, but here in the desert it is very cold. . . ."
>
> . . . "Tell me about your husband," I pressed. "What work does he do? "
>
> The woman's eyes dropped even lower. "At home he was a farmer. Here in the desert there is nothing for him. . . ."
>
> — *Jehan Sadat*, A Woman of Egypt

3   According to the document, state one reason Palestinians were forced into refugee camps in the Sinai.

Palestinians ; forced out ot their homes
because ot the war

Part B   Essay

Directions: Write a well-organized essay that includes an introduction, several paragraphs, and a conclusion.

Use evidence from the documents in the body of the essay. Support your response with relevant facts, examples, and details. Include additional outside information.

Historical Context:

> Throughout global history, people have migrated as a result of political, social, and economic conditions.

Task: Using information from the documents and your knowledge of global history and geography, write an essay in which you

- Discuss the political, social, and/or economic reasons for the mass movement of peoples throughout global history

Do *not* use examples from the United States in your answer.

Guidelines:

In your essay, be sure to

- Develop all aspects of the task
- Incorporate information from *at least two* of the documents in the body of your essay
- Incorporate relevant outside information
- Support the theme with relevant facts, examples, and details
- Use a logical and clear plan of organization, including an introduction and conclusion that are beyond a restatement of the theme

GLOSSARY/GLOSARIO

A

absolutism   a political system in which a ruler holds total power

acid rain   precipitation carrying large amounts of dissolved acids which damages buildings, forests, and crops, and kills wildlife

adobe   sun-dried brick

Age of Pericles   the period between 461 and 429 B.C. when Pericles dominated Athenian politics and Athens reached the height of its power

agricultural society   a group of people whose economy is largely based on farming

AIDS (auto-immune deficiency syndrome) a disease of the human immune system that is caused by infection with HIV

anarchy   political disorder; lawlessness

animism   a belief in the existence of spirits separable from bodies

annex   incorporate territory into an existing political unit, such as a city or country

anti-Semitism   hostility toward or discrimination against Jews

apartheid   "apartness," the system of racial segregation in South Africa from the 1950s until 1991

appeasement   satisfying demands of dissatisfied powers in an effort to maintain peace and stability

archaeology   the study of past societies through an analysis of the items people left behind them

archipelago   a chain of islands

aristocracy   an upper class whose wealth is based on land and whose power is passed on from one generation to another

armistice   a truce or agreement to end fighting

absolutismo   un sistema politico en el cual la autoridad tiene el poder total o absoluto

lluvia ácida   precipitación que lleva grandes cantidades de ácidos disueltos, los cuales dañan los edificios, los bosques y las cosechas y matan la fauna

adobe   ladrillo secado al sol

Era de Pericles   la época durante el cual Pericles dominó la política en Atenas, entre los años 461 y 429 antes de Cristo y durante el cual Atenas alcanzó la cúspide de su poder

sociedad agrícola   un grupo de personas cuya economía se basa en gran medida en la agricultura

EL SIDA   o Síndrome de Inmunodeficiencia Adquirida es una enfermedad causada por el virus de la inmunodeficiencia humana (VIH)

anarquía   ausencia de autoridad política

animismo   una creencia en la existencia de seres espirituales

anexar   incorporar territorios a una unidad política ya existente, como una cuidad o un país

antisemitismo   hostilidad hacia los judíos o discriminación hacio los judíos

segregación racial   "separación," el sistema de segregación racial aplicado en Sudáfrica desde la década de 1950 hasta 1991

apaciguamiento   satisfacción de las demandas razonables de poderres insatisfechos en un esfuerzo por mantener la paz y la estabilidad

arqueología   el estudio de sociedades pasadas a través de un análisis de los artículos que la gente ha dejado

archipiélago   una cadena de isles

aristocracia   una clase alta cuya riqueza está basada en tierras y cuyo poder pasa de una generación a otra

armisticio   una tregua o acuerdo para dar fin a una guerra

arms race   building up armies and stores of weapons to keep up with an enemy

carrera armamentista   constitución de ejércitos y acopio de armas mantenerse a la par conun enemigo

artifacts   tools, pottery, paintings, weapons, buildings, and household items left behind by early people

artefacto   herramientas, artículos de alfarería, pinturas, armas, edificaciones, y artículos para el hogar dejados por pueblos antiguos

Aryans   used in Nazism to designate a supposed master race of non-Jewish Caucasians having especially Nordic features

arios   termino que fue usado por los Nazis para designar una raza como superior con derecho al exterminio de las razas débiles como la judia

ascetic   a person who practices self-denial to achieve an understanding of ultimate reality

asceta   una persona que practica la abnegación para alcanzar un entendimiento de la realidad última

assembly   a legislative body; specifically the lower house of a legislature

asamblea   un grupo legislativo, especialmente la cámara baja legislative

B

balance of trade   the difference in value between what a nation imports and what it exports over time

balanza commercial   la diferencia en valor entre lo que una nación importa y lo que exporta en un período de tiempo

Bantu   a family of languages spoken in central and southern Africa; a member of any group of the African peoples who speak that language

bantú   una familia de idiomas hablados en el centro y sur de África; un miembro de cualquier grupo de los pueblos africanos que hablan dicho idioma

Bill of Rights   the first 10 amendments to the United States Constitution

Bill of Rights   las diez primeras enmiendas de la constitución estadounidense

birthrate   the number of births per year of every 1,000 people

indice de natalidad   el número de nacimientos por año por cada 1000 personas

Black Death   a form of bubonic plague, spread by fleas carried by rats

peste negra   peste bubónica, contagiada por las pulgas con la ayuda de las ratas

blitzkrieg   German for "lightning war," a swift and sudden military attack; used by the Germans during World War II

guerra relámpago   término alemán para "guerra relámpago," una táctica utilizada por los alemanes durante la Segunda Guerra Mudial

bloc   a group of nations with a common purpose

bloque   un grupo de naciones con un objetivo en común

Bolsheviks   a revolutionary group in Russia led by Vladimir Ilyich Lenin

Bolcheviques   un grupo revolucionario en Rusia dirigido por Vladimir Ilyich Lenin

bourgeoisie the middle class, including merchants, industrialists, and professional people

Buddhism a religious doctrine introduced in northern India in the sixth century B.C. by Siddhartha Gautama, known as the Buddha, or "Enlightened One"

bureaucracy an administrative organization that relies on nonelective officials and regular procedures

Bushido "the way of the warrior," the strict code by which Japanese samurai were supposed to live

burguesía la clase media

budismo una doctrina religiousa introducida en el norte de la India en el siglo sexto A.C. por Siddhartha Gautama, conocido como Buda (o "el Iluminado")

burocracia una organización administrative con funcionarios y procedimientos habituales

bushido "el código del guerrero," el estricto código según el cual debían vivir los samurai japoneses

C

caliph a successor of Muhammad as spiritual and temporal leader of the Muslims

capitalism an economic system based on private property and free enterprise

caste system a set of rigid categories in ancient India that determined a person's occupation and economic potential as well as his or her position in society, based partly on skin color

chartered companies private companies granted certain royal privileges, such as monopolies, that brought rulers territorial and military dominance while they achieved commercial success

checks and balances the system in which each branch of government has a check on the other branches so that no one branch becomes too powerful

chivalry in the Middle Ages, the ideal of civilized behavior that developed among the nobility; it was a code of ethics that knights were supposed to uphold

califa un sucesor de Mahoma como líder espiritual y temporal de los musulmanes

capitalismo un sistema económico basado enla propiedad particular y la empresa libre

sistema de castas un conjunto de categories rígidas en la Antigua India que determinaba la ocupación de una persona y su potencial económico, así como también su posición en la sociedad, parcialmente sobre la base de del color de la piel

compañias colegiadas compañías particulares que recibieron ciertos privilegios, como monopolios, que otorgaron a los gobenantes dominio territorial y militar al mismo tiempo que lograban éxito comercial

restricciones y equilibrios el sistema en el cual cada rama del gobierno refrena las otras ramas para que ninguna rama se vuelva demasiado poderosa

caballerosidad en la Edad Media, el ideal de conducta civilizada que se desarrolló entre la nobleza; fue el código de ética que los caballeros debían mantener

Christian humanism   a movement that developed in northern Europe during the Renaissance combining classical learning (humanism) with the goal of reforming the Catholic Church

city-state   a city with political and economic control over the surrounding countryside

civilization   a complex culture in which large numbers of people share a number of common elements such as social structure, religion, and art

clan   a group of related families

collectivization   a system in which private farms are eliminated and peasants work land owned by the government

colony   a settlement of people living in a new territory, linked with the parent country by trade and direct government control

Columbian exchange   exchange of goods, ideas, and people between Europe and the Americas

command economy   an economic system in which decisions are made by government planners who determine what sorts of goods and services to produce and how they are to be allocated

commercial capitalism   economic system in which people invest in trade or goods to make profits

common law   a uniform system of law that developed in England based on court decisions and on customs and usage rather than on written law codes; replaced law codes that varied from place to place

commonwealth   a republic

humanismo cristiano   un movimiento que se desarrolló en el norte de Europa durante el Renacimiento que combinaba el aprendizaje clásico (humanismo) con el objetivo de reformar la Iglesia Católica

ciudad-estado   una ciudad con control político y económico sobre el campo alrededor

civilización   una compleja cultura en la que grandes números de personas comparten un gran número de elementos tales como la estructura social, la religion, y el arte

clan   un grupo de familias relacionadas

colectivización   un sistema en el cual se eliminan las fincas privadas y los campesinos trabajan la tierra que es la propiedad del gobierno

colonia   un asentamiento de personas que está viviendo en un nuevo territorio, enlazado a la madre patria por el comercio y el control directo del gobierno

Cambio Colombiano   el cambio de productos, ideas, y personas entre Europa y las Américas

economia de mandato   un sistema económico en el cual proyectistas del gobierno toman decisiones acerca de la producción de mercancías y servicios y de cómo se deben distribuir

capitalismo commercial   un sistema económico en la cual la gente invertía en comercio y mercancía con el fin de obtener ganancias

derecho consuetudinario   sistema de leyes desarrollado en Inglaterra y que era uniforme en todo el país; reemplazó los códigos legales que variaban de lugar en lugar

namcomunidad   nación o estado gobernando por el pueblo o representantes del mismo

concentration camp a camp where prisoners of war, political prisoners, or members of minority groups are confined, typically under harsh conditions

Confucianism the system of political and ethical ideas formulated by the Chinese philosopher Confucius toward the end of the Zhou dynasty; it was intended to help restore order to a society that was in a state of confusion

conquistador a Spanish conqueror of the Americas

conservatism a political philosophy based on tradition and social stability, favoring obedience to political authority and organized religion

constitutional monarchy a system of government that has a monarch at its head, but whose powers are limited by a constitution

contras rebels financed by the United States who began a guerrilla war against the Sandinista government in Nicaragua

coup d'etat a sudden overthrow of the government

Creole a person of European descent born in the New World and living there permanently

Crusades military expeditions carried out by European Christians in the Middle Ages to regain the Holy Land from the Muslims

culture the way of life a people follows

cuneiform "wedge-shaped," a system of writing developed by the Sumerians using a reed stylus to create wedge-shaped impressions on a clay tablet

czar Russian for "Caesar," the title used by Russian emperors

campo de concentración un campo donde se confina a prisioneros de guerra, prisioneros politicos, o miembros de grupos minoritarios, típicamente bajo condiciones duras

confucianismo el sistema de ideas políticas y éticas formuladas por el filósofo chino Confucio hacia fines de la dinastía Zhou; fue concebido para restaurar el orden en una sociedad que estaba en estado de confusión

conquistador uno de los conquistadores españoles de las Américas

conservatismo una filosofía política basada en la tradición y estabilidad social sobre la base de la obediencia a la autoridad política y la religion organizada

monarquía constitucional un sistema de gobierno que tiene a un monarca como dirigente, pero su poder se limita por una constitución

contras rebeldes financiados por los Estados Unidos que empezaron una guerra guerrillera contra el gobierno sandinista en Nicaragua

golpe de estado un súbido derrocamiento del gobierno

criollo descendiente de europeos nacido en el Nuevo Mundo

Cruzadas expediciones militares llevadas a cabo por cristianos europeos para conquistar la Tierra Santa de las manos de los musulmanes

cultura forma de vida de las personas

cuneiforme "forma de cuña," sistema de escriturra desarrollado por los sumerios utilizando un punzón de lengüeta para crear impresiones con forma de cuña en una tableta de arcilla

zar (de "caesar") titulo adoptado por los gobernantes de Rusia desde finales del siglo XV

D

daimyo "great names," heads of noble families in Japan who controlled vast landed estates and relied on samurai for protection

Daoism a system of ideas based on the teachings of Laozi; teaches that the will of Heaven is best followed through inaction so that nature is allowed to take its course

deforestation the clearing of forests

democracy "the rule of the many," government by the people, either directly or through their elected representatives

depression a period of low economic activity and rising unemployment

desertification process in which arable land is turned into desert

détente a phase of relaxed tensions and improved relations between two adversaries

dictator an absolute ruler

direct democracy a system of government in which the people participate directly in government decision making through mass meetings

direct rule colonial government in which local elites are removed from power and replaced by a new set of officials brought from the mother country

disarmament a limit or reduction of armed forces and weapons

dissident a person who speaks out against the regime in power

diviner a person who is believed to have the power to foretell events

divine right of kings the belief that kings receive their power from God and are responsible only to God

domestication adaptation of plants and animals for human use

daimyo "grandes nombres," líderes de familias nobles en Japón, quienes controlaban vastas propiedades y confiaban su proteción a los samurai

Daoísmo sistema de ideas basado en la doctrina de Laozi; enseña que la verdadera manera de seguir la voluntad del Cielo es inacción—permiter que la naturaleza tome su curso

deforestación la tala de bosques

democracia literalmente, el gobierno de muchos, bajo el cual los ciudadanos eligen quién los gobernará

depression un período de baja actividad económica y aumento del desempleo

desertificación proceso en el cual la tierra arable se vuelve desierto

disminución una fase de relajamiento de relaciones o tensiones entre dos adversaries

dictador un líder que goza de poder absoluto

democracia directa un sistema de gobierno en que las personas participan directamente en la toma de decisions del gobierno a través de asambleas

dominio directo gobierno colonial en el que las elites locales son removidos del poder y reemplazadas por un nuevo grupo de oficiales traídos desde la madre patria

desarme un límite o reducción de las fuerzas armadas y del armamento

disidente una persona que critica abiertamente al regimen que tiene el poder

adivino una persona de quien se cree tiene el poder de predecir eventos

derecho divino de reyes la creencia de que los reyes reciben su poder de parte de Dios y de que son responsables solo ante Dios

domesticar adiestrar animals o adaptar plantas para satisfacer necesidades humanas

domino theory   idea that if one country falls to communism, neighboring countries will also fall

dowry   a gift of money or property paid at the time of marriage, either by the bride's parents to her husband or, in Islamic societies, by a husband to his wife

Duma   the Russian legislative assembly

teoría domino   la idea de que si un país cae ante el comunismo, los países colindantes también lo harán

dote   dinero o bienes pagados por los padres de una novia a su esposo al casarse ella

Duma   la asamblea legislative rusa

E

ecology   the study of the relationships between living things and their environment

emperor   the sovereign or supreme male monarch of an empire

empire   a large political unit, usually under a single leader, that controls many peoples or territories

encomienda   system of rewarding conquistadors with tracts of land and the right to tax and demand labor from Native Americans who lived on the land

enlightened absolutism   a system in which rulers tried to govern by Enlightenment principles while maintaining their full royal powers

Enlightenment   a movement during the 1700s emphasizing the importance of reason and questioning traditions and values

estates   the three classes into which French society was divided before the revolution: the clergy (first estate), the nobles (second estate), and the townspeople (third estate)

eta   Japan's outcast class, whose way of life was strictly regulated by the Tokugawa

ethnic cleansing   a policy of killing or forcibly removing an ethnic group from its lands, used by the Serbs against the Muslim minority in Bosnia

ecología   el estudio de las relaciones entre cosas vivas y su ambiente

emperador   un soberano o monarca masculino supremo de un imperio

imperio   una grande unidad política, normalmente bajo un solo líder, y que controla a mucha genta o territorios

encomienda   sistema de recompensar a los conquistadores con extensions de tierra y el derecho de recaudar impuestos y exigir mano de obra a los Nativos Americanos que vivían en la tierra

absolutimo ilustrado   un sistema en el cual los gobernantes trataban de gobernar por medio de principios de Ilustración mientras mantenían sus poderes reales totales

Iluminación   un movimiento durante principios de los 1700 que enfatizaba la importancia de la razón y cuestionaba las tradiciones y valores

estado   las tres clases en las que se dividía la sociedad francesa medieval: el clero (primer estado), los nobles (segundo estado), y la plebe (tercer estado)

eta   la case más baja de la sociedad japonesa, cuya forma de vida era estrictamente regulada por el Tokugawa

purificación étnica   una política de matar o remover por la fuerza a un grupo étnico desde sus territorios

ethnocentric characterized by or based on the attitude that one's own ethnic group is superior

extraterritoriality living in a section of a country set aside for foreigners but not subject to the host country's laws

etnocéntrico caracterizado por la actitud de un grupo étnico que se considera superior

extraterritorialidad vivir en una sección de un país apartada para extranjeros pero no sujeta a las leyes del país anfitrión

F

fascism a political philosophy, movement, or regime that exalts nation and race above the individual and stands for a centralized autocratic government headed by a dictatorial leader, severe economic and social regimentation and forcible suppression of opposition

feudal contract under feudalism, the unwritten rules that determined the relationship between a lord and his vassal

feudalism (feudal system) political and social system that developed during the Middle Ages, when royal governments were no longer able to defend their subjects; nobles offered protection and land in return for service

fief under feudalism, a grant of land made to a vassal; the vassal held political authority within his fief

filial piety the duty of family members to subordinate their needs and desires to those of the male head of the family, a concept important in Confucianism

Final Solution the Nazi program for extermination of all Jews in Europe

fossil remnants or impressions of an organism from a past geologic age that has been preserved in the earth's crust

free trade the removal of trade barriers so that goods can flow freely between countries

fascismo una filosofía política, un movimiento o régimen que exalta la nación y la raza sobre el individuo y es representado por un gobierno autocrático centralizado con un líder dictatorio, organización económica y social muy rígida y supresión forzado de la oposición

contrado feudal bajo el feudalismo, las reglas no escritas que determinaban la relación entre un señor y su vasallo

feudalismo (sistema feudal) sistema politico y social que se desarrolló durante la Edad Media cuando gobiernos reales ya no podían defender a su pueblo; los nobles ofrecían protección y tierras a cambio de servicio

feudo bajo el feudalismo, una concesión de tierras hecha a un vasallo el vasallo tenía autoridad política dentro de su feudo

piedad filial el deber de los miembros de la familia de subordinar sus necesidades y deseos a aquellos del líder de la familia, un concepto importante en el Confucianismo

Última solución el programa de los Nazis para la exterminación de los judíos en Europa

fósil pinturas hecha en yeso fresco y húmedo con pinturas a base de agua

comercio libre la eliminación de barreras comerciales para que las mercancías puedan circular libremente entre países

G

genocide   the deliberate mass murder of a particular racial, political, or cultural group

glasnost   Russian term for a new "openness;" part of Mikhail Gorbachev's reform plans

Great Schism   a split in the Catholic Church that lasted from 1378 to 1418, during which time there were rival popes in Rome and in the French city of Avignon. France and its allies supported the pope in Avignon, while France's enemy England and its allies supported the pope in Rome

greenhouse effect   global warming caused by the buildup of carbon dioxide in the atmosphere

griot   a special class of African storytellers who help keep alive a people's history

guild   a business association associated with a particular trade or craft; guilds evolved in the twelfth century and came to play a leading role in the economic life of medieval cities

gunpowder empire   an empire formed by outside conquerors who unified the regions that they conquered through their mastery of firearms

genocidio   la matanza masiva de un grupo racial, politico o cultural en particular

glasnost   término ruso para una nueva "apertura;" parte de los planes de reforma de Gorbachev

Gran Cisma   una division en la Iglesia Católica que duró desde 1378 hasta 1418, durante la cual hubo papas rivales en Roma y en la ciudad francesa de Aviñón. Francia y sus aliados respaldaban al papa de Aviñón, mientras que el enemigo de Francia, Inglaterra y sus aliados respaldaban al papa de Roma

efecto invernadero   calentamiento global causado por la acumulación de dióxido de carbono en la atmósfera

griot   un tipo especial de narradores de historias africanos que contribuían a mantener viva la historia de un pueblo

gremio   una asociación comercial relacionada con un oficio o artesanía en particular; los gremios evolucionaron en el siglo XII y pasaron a tenere un papel importante en la vida económica de las ciudades medievales

imperio de pólvora   un imperio formado por conquistadores del exterior que unieron las regiones que conquistaron por medio del dominio de armas

H

hajj   a pilgrimage to Mecca, one of the requirements of the Five Pillars of Islam

han   one of the approximately 250 domains into which Japan was divided under the Tokugawa

harem   "sacred place," the private domain of an Ottoman sultan, where he and his wives resided

hajj   una peregrinación a La Meca; uno de los requitos de los Cinco Pilares del Islam

han   uno de los aproximadamente 250 dominios independientes en los que se dividió Japón bajo Tokugawa

harén   "lugar sagrado," el dominio privado de un sultán, en donde residía él y sus esposas

Hellenistic Era the age of Alexander the Great; period when the Greek language and ideas were carried to the non-Greek world

heresy the denial of basic church doctrine

hierarchy the classification of a group of people according to ability or economic, social, or professional standing

hieroglyph a picture or symbol used in a hieroglyphic system of writing

hieroglyphics "priest-carving" or "sacred writings," a complex system of writing that used both pictures and more abstract forms; used by the ancient Egyptians and Mayans

Hinduism the major Indian religious system, which had its origins in the religious beliefs of the Aryans who settled India after 1500 B.C.

Holocaust the mass killings of 6 million Jews by Germany's Nazi leaders during World War II

Homo sapiens sapiens "wise, wise human being," a species that appeared in Africa between 150,000 and 200,000 years ago; they were the first anatomically modern humans

hostage system a system used by the shogunate to control the daimyo in Tokugawa Japan; the family of a daimyo lord was forced to stay at their resident in the capital whenever the lord was absent from it

Huguenots French Protestants who were influenced by John Calvin

Era Helenística la era de Alejandro el Grande de Grecia, durante la cual el idioma griego y las ideas griegas fueron llevados al mundo no-griego

herejía desacuerdo con las enseñanzas básicas de la iglesia

jerarquía la clasificación de un grupo de personas conforme a su capacidad o posición económica, social, o profesional

jeroglífico un retrato o símbolo usado en el sistema de escritura jeroglífica

jeroglíficos "grabados sacerdotales" o "escrituras sagradas," un complejo sistema de escritura del antiguo Egipto que utilizaba tanto imagines como formas más abstractas

hinduismo el mayor sistema religiouso de la India, que tuvo sus orígenes en las creencias religiosas de los arios que se establecieron en la India después del año 1500 A.C.

Holocausto el asesinato masivo de 6 milliones de judíos por los líderes Nazi de Alemania durante la Segunda Guerra Mundial

Homo sapiens sapiens "ser humano sabio, sabio," una especie que apareció en África entre 150.000 y 200.000 años atrás; fueron los primeros humanos anatómicamente modernos

sistema de rehén un sistema utilizado por el shogun para controlar el daimyo en Tokugawa Japón; cada daimyo tenía que mantener dos residencies, una en su propia tierra y una en la capital, donde se encontraba la corte del shogun; la familia daimyo estaba obligada a permanecer en la residencia del shogun cuando él estaba ausente

hugonote protestantes franceses que fueron influenciados por Juan Calvin

humanism an intellectual movement of the Renaissance based on the study of the humanities, which included grammar, rhetoric, poetry, moral philosophy, and history

human rights rights regarded as belonging to all persons, such as freedom from unlawful imprisonment, torture, and execution

humanismo un moviemiento intellectual del Renacimiento basado en el estudio de las humanidades, que incluía gramática, retórica, poesía, filosofía moral, e historia

derechos humanos derechos, tal como la libertad de encarcelamiento illegal, tortura, y ejecución, considerados como pertenecientes a todas las peronas

I

imperialism the extension of a nation's power over other lands

indirect rule colonial government in which local rulers are allowed to maintain their positions of authority and status

indulgence a release from all or part of punishment of sin by the Catholic Church, reducing time in purgatory after death

infidel an unbeliever, a term applied to the Muslims during the Crusades

Inquisition a court established by the Catholic Church in 1232 to discover and try heretics; also called the Holy Office

interdict a Roman Catholic censure withdrawing most sacraments and Christian burial from a person or district

intifada "uprising," militant movement that arose during the 1980s among supporters of the Palestine Liberation Organization living in Israel

Iron Curtain the political and military barrier that isolated Soviet-controlled countries of Eastern Europe after World War II

Israelites a native or inhabitant of the ancient northern kingdom of Israel

imperialismo la extensión del poder de una nación hacia otras tierras

dominio indirecto gobierno colonial en el que los gobernantes locales pueden mantener sus posiciones de autoridad y estatus

indulgencia perdón de todo o parte de un castigo por pecados otorgado por la Iglesia Católica, reduciendo el tiempo en el purgatorio tras la muerte

infiel un no-creyente, un término aplicado a los musulmanes durante las Cruzadas

Inquisición un tribunal establecido por la Iglesia Católica en 1232 para descubrir y someter a juicio a los herejes; también llamado el Santo Oficio

interdicción una censura papal que prohibía a los sacerdotes impartieran los sacramentos de la iglesia y un entierro cristiao a una persona o un distrito

intifada "levantamiento," un movimiento que surgió durante la década de 1980 entre quienes respaldaban a la Organización Para la Liberación de Palestina que vivían dentro de Israel

cortina de hierro la barrera política y militar que aisló a los países de Europa Oriental controlados por los soviéticos después de la Segunda Guerra Mundial

israelitas un nativo o habitante del reino antiguo del norte de Israel

J

janissary   a soldier in the elite guard of the Ottoman Turks

jenízaro   un soldado de la guardia de élite del imperio turco otomano

justification   the act, process, or state of being justified by God

justificación   el acto, proceso o el estado de ser justificado por Dios

K

kaiser   German for "Caesar," the title of the emperors of the Second German Empire

káiser   término alemán para "césar," el título de los emperadores del Segundo Imperio Alemán

khanate   one of the several separate territories into which Genghis Khan's empire was split, each under the rule of one of his sons

kanato   uno de los diversos territorios independientes en los que se dividió el imperio de Genghis Khan, cada uno bajo el gobierno de uno de sus hijos

knight   under feudalism, a member of the heavily armored cavalry

caballero   bajo el feudalismo, un miembro de la caballería fuertemente blindada

L

laissez-faire   literally, "let [people] do [what they want]," the concept that the state should not impose government regulations but should leave the economy alone

laissez-faire   literalmente, "dejar [a las personas] hacer [lo que quieran]," el concepto de que el estado no debe imponer regulaciones gubernamentales si no que debe dejar la economía sola

language family   group of related languages that have all developed from one earlier language

familia de lenguajes   grupo de lenguajes relacionados que se desarrollaron de un lenguaje anterior

lay investiture   the practice by which secular rulers both chose nominees to church offices and gave them the symbols of their office

invesetidura secular   el costumbre en cual los líderes seculares elegían candidatos a cargos en la iglesia y los investían con los símbolos de su oficio

liberalism   a political philosophy originally based largely on Enlightenment principles, holding that people should be as free as possible from government restraint and that civil liberties—the basic rights of all people—should be protected

liberalismo   una filosofía política originalmente basada principalmente en principios de la Época de las Luce , que mantenía que las personas deberían ser lo más libres posible a pesar de las restricciones gubernamentales y que las libertades civiles—los derechos básicos de las personas—deberían ser protegidos

lineage group   an extended family unit that has combined into a larger community

grupo de linaje   una unidad extendida de una familia que se ha combinado en una comunidad mayor

line of demarcation   an imaginary line running down the middle of the Atlantic Ocean from the North Pole to the South Pole dividing the Americas between Spain and Portugal

línea de demarcación   una línea imaginaria a lo largo del medio del Océano Atlántico desde el Polo Norte hasta el Polo Sur para dividir las Américas entre España y Portugal

M

Magna Carta   the "great Charter" of rights, which King John was forced to sign by the English nobles at Runnymede in 1215

Carta Magna   la Gran Cédula de derechos, que el Rey Juan Sin Tierra fue obligado a firmar por los nobles ingleses en Runnymede en 1215

Mahayana   a school of Buddhism that developed in northwest India, stressing the view that nirvana can be achieved through devotion to the Buddha; its followers consider Buddhism a religion, not a philosophy, and the Buddha is a divine figure

Mahayana   una escuela de budismo que se desarrolló en el noroeste de la India y que enfatiza la vision de que se puede alcanzar el nirvana a través de la devoción al Buda; sus seguidores consideran al Budismo una religion, no una filosofía, y a Buda como una figura divina

mainland states   part of the continent, as distinguished from peninsulas or offshore islands

estados continentales   parte del continente, diferente de las penínsulas o islas

maize   corn

maiz   el maíz nativo de la América

mandate   a nation governed by another nation on behalf of the League of Nations

mandato   una nación gobernada por otra nación en nombre de la Liga de Naciones

Mandate of Heaven   claim by Chinese kings of the Zhou dynasty that they had direct authority from heaven to rule and to keep order in the universe

Madato del Cielo   la reclamación por parte de los reyes de la dinastía Zhou de China que ellos tenían la autoridad para gobernar y mantener el universo en orden directamente por derecho celestial

manor   in medieval Europe, an agricultural estate run by a lord and worked by peasants

palacete   en la Europa medieval, una propiedad agrícola administrada por un señor y trabajada por campesinos

matrilineal   tracing lineage through the mother rather than the father

línea maternal   que traza el linaje por medio de la madre y sus ancestors, no a través del padre

mercantilism   a set of principles that dominated economic thought in the seventeenth century; it held that the prosperity of a nation depended on a large supply of gold and silver

mestizo   a person of mixed European and native American Indian descent

Middle Passage   the journey of slaves from Africa to the Americas, so called because it was the middle portion of the triangular trade route

migration   the movement of people from place to place

militarism   reliance on military strength

mobilization   the process of assembling troops and supplies and making them ready for war

modernism   a movement in which writers and artists between 1870 and 1914 rebelled against the traditional literary and artistic styles that had dominated European cultural life since the Renaissance

money economy   an economic system based on money rather than barter

monk   a man who separates himself from ordinary human society in order to dedicate himself to God; monks live in monasteries headed by abbots

monotheistic   having one god

monsoon   a seasonal wind pattern in southern Asia that blows warm, moist air from the southwest during the summer, bringing heavy rains, and cold, dry air from the northeast during the winter

mosque   a Muslim house of worship

multinational corporations   a company with divisions in more than two countries

mercantilismo   un conjunto de principios que dominaban el pensamiento económico en el siglo XVII; mantenía que la prosperidad de una nación dependía de tener grandes cantidades de oro y plata

mestizo   la progenie de europeos e americanos indígenas

paso central   seción intermedia del comercio triangular, en el cual los africanos esclavizados eran traídos a las Américas por barco

migración   el movimiento de gente de un lugar a otro

militarismo   política nacional basada en la fuerza miltar y la glorificación de la guerra

movilzación   el proceso de agrupar tropes y suministros y prepararlos para la guerra

modernismo   un movimiento en cual escritores e artistas se rebelaron entre 1870 y 1914 en contra de los estilos literarios y artísticos tradicionales que habían dominado la vida cultural europea desde el Renacimiento

economía monetaria   un sistema económico basado en el dinero y no en el trueque

monje   un hombre que se separa de la sociedaad humana con el fin de dedicarse a Dios; los monjes viven en monasterios liderados por abades

monoteísta   con un solo dios

monzón   un patrón de viento en el sur de Asia que sopla aire cálido y húmedo desde el suroeste durante el verano, trayendo fuertes lluvias, y aire frío y seco desde el noreste durante el invierno

mezquita   casa de veneración de los musulmanes

compañía multinacional   una compañía con divisions en más de dos países

N

nationalism   the unique cultural identity of a people based on common language, religion, and national symbols

NATO (North Atlantic Treaty Organization)   an international organization created in 1949 by the North Atlantic Treaty for purposes of collective security

natural rights   rights with which all humans are supposedly born, including the rights to life, liberty, and property

neo-Confucianism   a revised form of Confucianism that evolved as a response to Buddhism and held sway in China from the late Tang dynasty to the end of the dynastic system in the twentieth century

Neolithic Revolution   the shift from the hunting of animals and gathering of food to the keeping of animals and the growing of food on a regular basis that occurred around 8000 B.C.

New Economic Policy (NEP)   a modified version of the old capitalist system adopted by Lenin in 1921 to replace war communism in Russia; peasants were allowed to sell their produce, and retail stores and small industries could be privately owned, but heavy industry, banking, and mines remained in the hands of the government

nomadic   moving from place to place with no permanent home

nuclear proliferation   the spreading development of nuclear arms

Nuremberg Trials   two sets of trials of Nazis involved in World War II and the Holocaust

nacionalismo   la singular identidad cultural de un pueblo basada en un idioma, religion, y símbolos nacionales en común

OTAN   una organización internacional creada en 1949 por el Tratado del Atlántico Norte para la seguridad colectiva

derechos naturales   derechos con los que todos los humanos supuestamente nacen, incluyendo el derecho a la vida, la libertad y la propiedad

neo-confucianosmo   una forma modificada de confucianismo que evolucionó como respuesta al Budismo y mantuvo su dominio en China desde el fin de la dinastía Tang hasta fines del sistema de dinastías en el siglo XX

Revolución Neolítica   el cambio de la caza de animales y recolección de alimentos a el mantenimiento de animales y el cultivo de alimentos que ocurrió alredededdor del 8000 antes de cristo

Nueva Política Económica   una versión modificada del sistema capitalista antíguo adoptado por Lenin en 1921 para reemplazar el comunismo de guerra en Rusia; se permitía a los campesinos vender sus productos, y las tiendas y pequeñas industrias podían ser privadas, pero la gran industria, la banca y las minas permanecieron en manos del gobierno

nómada   que se mueve de un lugar a otro sin hogar permanente

proliferación nuclear   la extensión del desarrollo de armas nucleares

juicios de Nuremberga   dos series de juicios de Nazis involucrados en la Segunda Guerra Mundial y el Holocausto

O

occupied   held by a foreign power

oligarchy   "the rule of the few," a form of government in which a small group of people exercises controls

OPEC   (Organization of Petroleum Exporting Countries)   an organization of countries formed in 1961 to agree on a common policy for the production and sale of petroleum

Open Door policy   a policy that allowed each foreign nation in China to trade freely in the other nations' spheres of influence

orthodoxy   traditional beliefs, especially in religion

outsourcing   the practice of subcontracting manufacturing work to outside companies, especially foreign and nonunion companies

ozone layer   a thin layer of gas in the upper atmosphere that shields Earth from the sun's ultraviolet rays

ocupado   país cuyas tierras son poseídas por un poder extranjero

oligarquía   literalmente, "el gobierno de unos pocos," en el cual un pequeño grupo de personas controla el gobierno

OPEP   Organizacion Paises Exportadores de Petróleo   una organización de paises que se formo en 1961 para estableier una politica en comun acerca la prodution y venta de petróleo

política de Puerta Abierta   una política que permitía a cada nación extranjera en China que comerciara libremente en las esferas de influencia de las otras naciones

ortodoxia   creencias tradicionales, especial-mente religiosas

recurso de afuera   la práctica de subcon-tratar la fabricación a compañías de afuera, especialmente extranjeras o compañías que no ocupan obreros sindicalizados

capa de ozono   una capa de gas delgada en la atmósfera superior que protégé a la Tierra de los rayos ultravioleta provenientes del sol

P

Paleolithic Age   from the Greek for "Old Stone," the early period of human history, from approximately 2,500,000 to 10,000 B.C., during which humans used simple stone tools; sometimes called the Old Stone Age

Pan-Africanism   the unity of all black Africans, regardless of national boundaries

Pan-Arabism   Arab unity, regardless of national boundaries

Era Paleolítica   del griego "Piedra Antigua," el antiguo periodo de la historia humana, desde aproximadamente el 2.500.000 al 10.000 A.C., durante el cual, los humanos utilizaban simples herramientas de piedra; algunas veces se le conoce como Edad de Piedra

Panafricanismo   movimiento que promo-ciona la unidad de todos los africanos por todo el mundo

Panarabismo   política que promueve la unidad árabe internacional

pasha   an appointed official in the Ottoman Empire who collected taxes, maintained law and order, and was directly responsible to the sultan's court

patriarch   the head of the Eastern Orthodox Church, originally appointed by the Byzantine emperor

patricians   great landowners, they formed the ruling class in the Roman Republic

patrilineal   tracing lineage through the father

peninsular   a person born on the Iberian Peninsula; typically, a Spanish or Portuguese official who resided temporarily in Latin America for political and economic gain and who then returned to Europe

per capita   per person

perestroika   Mikhail Gorbachev's plan to reform the Soviet Union by restructuring its economy

pharaoh   the most common of the various titles for ancient Egyptian monarchs; the term originally meant "great house" or "palace"

philosophe   French for "philosopher;" applied to all intellectuals—i.e., writers, journalists, economists, and social reformers—during the Enlightenment

planned economies   an economic system directed by government agencies

plantation   a large agricultural estate

plateau   a relatively high, flat land area

plebeians   in the Roman Republic, a social class made up of minor landholders, craftspeople, merchants, and small farmers

PLO (Palestine Liberation Organization) political and paramilitary organization dedicated to the establishment of a Palestinian state

pogrom   organized persecution or massacre of a minority group, especially Jews

pachá   official designado en el Imperio Otomano que cobraba impuestos, mantenía la ley y el orden y era directamente responsible ante la corte del sultan

patriarca   el líder de la Iglesia Ortodoxa Oriental, originalmente designado por el emperador bizantino

patricios   grandes terratenientes, formaban la clase dominante en la República Romana

patrilieal   que viene de la línea paterna

peninsular   persona nacida en la peninsula ibrica; normalmente, un oficial español o portugués que vivía temporalmente en Latinoamerica para obtener ganancia politica y economica y luego regresaba a Europa

per cápita   por persona

perestroika   plan de Mikhail Gorbachev para reformar la URSS, reestructurando su economía

faraón   el más común de los diversos títulos que existían para los monarcas del antiguo Egipto; el término originalmente significaba "gran casa" o "palacio"

filosofío   término francés para "filosofío;" se aplicaba a todos los intelectuales— escritores, periodistas, economistas y reformadores sociales—durante la Ilustración

economias planificadas   sistema económico dirigido por agencias gubernamentales

plantación   una propiedad agrícola grande

altiplanide   región relativamente llana más elevada que el área circundante

plebeyo   en la República de Roma, una clase social compuesta de terratenientes menores, artesanos, mercaderes y pequeños granjeros

PLO   organización política y paramilitar dedicada al establecimiento de un estado palestino

pogrom   persecución organizada de un grupo minoritario, usualmente judíos

policy of containment a plan to keep something, such as communism, within its existing geographical boundaries and prevent further aggressive moves

polis the early Greek city-state, consisting of a city or town and its surrounding territory

pope the bishop of Rome and head of the Roman Catholic Church

population growth increase in the number of people who inhabit a territory or state

porcelain a ceramic made of fine clay baked at very high temperatures

predestination the belief that God has determined in advance who will be saved (the elect) and who will be damned (the reprobate)

prefecture in the Japanese Meiji Restoration, a territory governed by its former daimyo lord

prehistory the period before writing was developed

privatization the sale of government-owned companies to private firms

propaganda ideas spread to influence public opinion for or against a cause

protectorate a political unit that depends on another government for its protection

pueblo a multistoried structure of the Anasazi that could house up to 250 people

política de contención plan para matener algo, como por ejemplo el comunismo, dentro de sus fronteras geográficas existentes e impedir mas movimientos agresivos

polis la ciudad-estado de la Antigua Grecia, que constaba de una cuidad o pueblo y el territorio de sus alrededores que existe como entidad política

papa el obispo de Roma y líder de la Iglesia Católica Romana

crecimiento de la población crecimiento del número de personas que habitan un territorio o estado

porcelana cerámica hecha de arcilla fina horneada a temperatures muy altas

predestinación la creencia de que Dios ha determinado anticipadamente quién se salvará (el elegido) y quien se condenará (el réprobo)

prefectura en la Restauración Meiji japonesa, un territorio gobernado por su anterior señor daimyo

prehistoria el periodo anterior a que se creara la escritura

privatización la venta de companies del Estado a firmas privadas

propaganda ideas que se difunden para influir la opinion pública a favor de una causa o en contra de ella

protectorado unidad política que depende de otro gobierno para su protección

pueblo estructuras de multiples pisos de Anasazi que podían albergar hasta 250 personas

Q

queue the braided pigtail that was traditionally worn by Chinese males

quipu a system of knotted strings used by the Inca people for keeping records

Quran the holy scriptures of the religion of Islam

coleta trenza de pelo única en la parte posterior de la cabeza tradicionalmente en hombres chinos

quipu un sistema de cuerdas con nudos usado por los incas para mantener registros

Corán las escrituras sagradas de la religion del Islam

R

realism mid-nineteenth century movement that rejected romanticism and sought to portray lower- and middle-class life as it actually was

relic bones or other objects connected with saints; considered worthy of worship by the faithful

Renaissance in Europe, a 300-year period of renewed interest in classical learning and the arts, beginning in the 1300s

reparations payments made to the victors by the vanquished to cover the costs of a war

republic a form of government in which the leader is not a king and certain citizens have the right to vote

Ring of Fire a zone of earthquake and volcanic activity surrounding the Pacific Ocean

rococo an artistic style that replaced baroque in the 1730s; it was highly secular, emphasizing grace, charm, and gentle action

romanticism an intellectual movement that emerged at the end of the eighteenth century in reaction to the ideas of the Enlightenment; it stressed feeling, emotion, and imagination as sources of knowing

realismo movimiento a medianos del Siglo XIX que rechazo el romanticismo y trató de describir la vida de las clases bajas y medias del momento

reliquia huesos o otros objetos relacionados con santos que se consideraban dignos de adoración por los fieles

Renacimiento en Europa, un período de renovado interés por las enseñanzas y artes clásicas que comenzó cerca del 1300 y duró 300 años

reparacións pago hecho a los victoriosos por los derrotados para cubrir los costos de una guerra

república forma de gobierno en la cual el líder no es un rey y ciertos ciudadanos tienen derecho a votar

círculo de fuego una zona de actividad volcánica y de terremotos alrededor del Océano Pacífico

rococó un estilo artístico que reemplazo al estilo barroco por 1730; era muy mundano, acentuando la gracia, el encanto, y la acción suave

romanticismo un movimiento intelectual que surgió e finales del siglo XVIII en reacción a las ideas de la Ilustración, daba énfasis a los sentimientos, la emoción y la imaginación como fuentes del conocimiento

S

sacraments Christian rites

samurai "those who serve," Japanese warriors similar to the knights of medieval Europe

Sandinistas Marxist guerrilla forces who came to control Nicaragua in the late 1970s

satellite state a country that is economically and politically dependent on another country

sacramento ritos cristianos

samurai "aquellos que sirven," guerreros japoneses similares a los caballeros de la Europa medieval

Sandinistas guerrilleros marxistas que controlaron Nicaragua a finales de 1970

estado satélite un país que depende económicamente y políticamente de otro país

savanna broad grassland dotted with small trees and shrubs

schism the separation between the two great branches of Christianity that occurred when the Roman Pope Leo IX and the Byzantine patriarch Michael Cerularius excommunicated each other in 1054

scholar-gentry in China, a group of people who controlled much of the land and produced most of the candidates for the civil service

scholasticism a medieval philosophical and theological system that tried to reconcile faith and reason

scientific method a systematic procedure for collecting and analyzing evidence that was crucial to the evolution of science in the modern world

secularization indifference to or rejection of religion or religious consideration

senate in the Roman Republic, a select group of about 300 patricians who served for life; originally formed to advise government officials, it came to have the force of law by the third century B.C.

sepoy an Indian soldier hired by the British East India Company to protect the company's interests in the region

serf in medieval Europe, a peasant legally bound to the land who had to provide labor services, pay rents, and be subject to the lord's controls

shah king (used in Persia and Iran)

shari'ah a law code drawn up by Muslim scholars after Muhammad's death; it provided believers with a set of practical laws to regulate their daily lives

Shiite a Muslim group that accepts only the descendants of Muhammad's son-in-law Ali as the true rulers of Islam

sabana amplias tierras con pequeños árboles y arbustos

cisma la separación entre dos grandes divisions de la cristiandad que tuvo lugar cuando el papa romano León IX y el patriarca bizantino Miguel Cerularius se excomulgaron mutuamente en el año 1054

erudito en China, un grupo de personas que controlaba gran parte de la tierra y producía la mayoría de los candidatos para el servicio civil

escolástica sistema filosófico y teológico medieval que trató de conciliar la fe y la razón

método científico procedimiento sistemático para colectar y analizar evidencia que fue crucial para la evolución de la ciencias en el mundo moderno

secularización indiferencia a o rechazo de la religión o consideraciones religiosas

senado en la República de Roma, un grupo selecto de alrededor de 300 patricios que trabajaban por vida; formado originalmente para aconsejar a los oficialies del gobierno, llegó a tener la fuerza de la ley durante el siglo III

cipayo soldado Indio contratado por la British East India Company para proteger los intereses de la compañía en la region

siervo en la Europa medieval, un campesino obligado legalmente a la tierra y que tenía que proporcionar servicios de manos de obra, pagar rentas y estar sujeto al control del señor

sha rey (se usa en Persia e Irán)

shari'ah código legal formulado por eruditos musulmanes después de la muerte de Mahoma; le entregó a los creyentes un conjunto de leyes practices para regular sus vidas diarias

chiíta un grupo musulmán que solo acepta a los descendientes de Ali, yerno de Mahoma, como los verdaderos gobernantes del Islam

Shining Path a radical guerrilla group in Peru with ties to Communist China

Shinto "the Sacred Way" or "the Way of the Gods," the Japanese state religion; among its doctrines are the divinity of the emperor and the sacredness of the Japanese nation

shogun "general," a powerful military leader in Japan

Sikhs followers of Sikhism, a religious faith originating in Punjab

Silk Road a route between the Roman Empire and China, so called because silk was China's most valuable product

simony the buying or selling of a church office

social contract the concept proposed by Rousseau that an entire society agrees to be governed by its general will, and all individuals should be forced to abide by the general will since it represents what is best for the entire community

Social Darwinism the theory that social progress came from "the struggle for survival" as the "fit"—the strong—advanced while the weak declined; often used by extremists to justify imperialism and racism

socialism a system in which society, usually in the form of the government, owns and controls the means of production

solidarity unity that produces or is based on a community of interests, objectives, and standards

spheres of influence areas in which a foreign power has been granted exclusive rights and privileges, such as trading rights and mining privileges

Sendero Luminoso grupo radical de guerrilleros en Perú con nexos a la China comunista

sintoísmo "el Camino Sagrado" o "el Camino de los Dioses," un tipo de religion del estado que se practica en Japón; sus doctrinas incluyen la divinidad del emperador y la santidad de la nación japonesa

shogun "general," líder militar muy poderoso en Japón

siks seguidores de Sikkim, una fe religiosa que se originó en Punjab

Ruta de la Seda ruta entre el Imperio Romano y China, se llamaba así porque la seda era el producto más valioso de China

simonía la compra y venta de una oficina de la iglesia

contrado social el concepto propuesto por Rousseau de que una sociedad completa accede a ser gobernada por la volutad general y que todos los individuos deben ser forzados a soportar el deseo general, porque representa lo mejor para la comunidad completa

darvinismo social la teoría que explicaba que el progreso social venia de la "lucha por la sobrevivencia" ya que los acaudalados—los más fuerte—avanzaban mientras los más débiles iban descendiendo; muchas veces se usó por los extremistas para justificar el imperialismo y el racismo

socialismo sistema en el cual la sociedad, por lo general en la forma del gobierno, posee y controla el medio de producción

solidaridad unidad que produce o esta basada en una comunidad de intereses, objetivos, y normas

esfera de influencia area en la que se le ha garantizado a una potencia extranjera derechos y privilegios exclusivos, tales como derechos de comercio y privilegios de minería

standard of living   a measure of people's overall wealth and quality of life; a minimum of necessities and luxuries that a group is accustomed to

stateless society   a group of independent villages organized into clans and led by a local ruler or clan head without any central government

subsistence farming   the practice of growing just enough crops for personal use, not for sale

sultan   "holder of power," the military and political head of state under the Seljuk Turks and the Ottomans

Sunni   a Muslim group that accepts only the descendants of the Umayyads as the true rulers of Islam

surplus   excess; amount left over after necessary expenses are paid

suttee   the Hindu custom of cremating a widow on her husband's funeral pyre

systematic agriculture   the keeping of animals and the growing of food on a regular basis

norma de vivir   una medida de calidad comprensiva de vida y riqueza de la gente; el mínimo de las necesidades y lujos a los cuales un grupo está acostumbrado

sociedad apátrida   grupo de aldeas independientes organizadas por clanes y lideradas por un soberano local o líder de un clan sin un gobierno central

agricultura de subsistencia   la práctica de sembrar solo las cosechas suficientes para uso personal, no para la venta

sultan   "poseedor del poder," el líder militar y politico del estado bajo los turcos Seljuk y otomanos

sunnita   un grupo musulmán que solo acepta a los descendientes de los Omeya como los verdaderos gobernantes del Islam

superávit   exceso; la cantidad que sobra después de pagar los gastos necesarios

suttee   la costumbre hindú de incinerar a la viuda en la pira funeral del esposo

agricultura sistemática   el mantenimiento de animales y la siembra de alimentos regularmente

T

tepee   a circular tent made by stretching buffalo skins over wooden poles

theology   the study of religion and God

Theravada   "the teachings of the elders," a school of Buddhism that developed in India; its followers view Buddhism as a way of life, not a religion centered on individual salvation

totalitarian state   a government that aims to control the political, economic, social, intellectual, and cultural lives of its citizens

tepee   tienda circular hecha de pieles de búfalo estiradas sobre postes de madera

teología   el estudio de la religion y Dios

Theravada   "las enseñanzas de los ancianos," escuela del budismo que se desaroyó en la India; sus seguidores consideran al budismo como un estilo de vida, no una religion centrada en la savación del individuo

estado totalitario   gobierno que se apunta a controlar no solo el lado político de la vida, sino también la vida económica, social, intelectual y cultural de sus ciudadanos

total war   a war that involves the complete mobilization of resources and people, affecting the lives of all citizens in the warring countries, even those remote from the battlefields

tournament   under feudalism, a series of martial activities, such as jousts, designed to keep knights busy during peace time and help them prepare for war

trading society   a group of people who depend primarily on trade for income

trench warfare   fighting from ditches protected by barbed wire, as in World War I

triangular trade   a pattern of trade that connected Europe, Africa, and the American continents; typically, manufactured goods from Europe were sent to Africa, where they were exchanged for slaves, who were sent to the Americas, where they were exchanged of raw materials that were then sent to Europe

tribute   goods or money paid by conquered people to their conquerors

tyrant   an absolute ruler unrestrained by law or constitution

guerra total   guerra que implica la movilización completa de recursos y personas, afecta las vidas de todos los ciudadanos en los países en guerra, incluso aquellos alejados de los campos de batalla

torneo   bajo el feudalismo, una serie de actividades marciales, tal como justas, diseñadas para mantener a los caballeros ocupados durante los tiempos de paz y ayudarlos a preparase para la guerra

sociedad comerical   grupo de personas que dependen principalmente del comercio para sus ingresos

guerra de tincheras   pelea desde trincheras protegidas por alambres de púa, como en la Primera Guerra Mundial

comercio triangular   ruta de tres direcciones entre Europa, África y América en el Siglo XVII

tributo   mercancías o dinero pagado por pueblos conquistados a sus conquistadores

tirano   una regla absoluta sin límite por ley o constitución

U

United Nations   intergovernmental organization established in 1945 as a successor to the League of Nations

urbanization   the movement of people from rural areas into cities

Organización de las Naciones Unidas   una organización intergubernamental establecida en 1945 como sucesora de la Sociedad de las Naciones

urbanización   el movimiento de personas de las areas rurales a las ciudades

V

vassal   under feudalism, a man who served a lord in a military capacity

vernacular   the language of everyday speech in a particular region

vasallo   bajo el feudalismo, un hombre que servía a un señor en una capacidad militar

vernacular   el lenguaje que se habla diariamente en una región particular

W

welfare state   a state in which the government takes responsibility of providing citizens with services such as health care

estado benefactor   estado en el cual el gobierno tiene responsabilidad de entregarle a los ciudadanos servicios tal como los de la salud

Y

yoga   a method of training developed by the Hindus that is supposed to lead to oneness with God

yoga   método de entrenamiento desarrollado por los hindúes que se supone conduce a la unidad con Dios

Z

zaminder   a local official in Mogul India who received a plot of farmland for temporary use in return for collecting taxes for the central government

Zen   a sect of Buddhism that became popular with Japanese aristocrats and became part of the samurai's code of behavior; under Zen Buddhism, there are different paths to enlightenment

Zionism   an international movement originally for the establishment of a Jewish national or religious community in Palestine, and later, for the support of modern Israel

zamindar   un oficial local en la India Mogol que recibía una parcela de tierra para su uso temporal a cambio de cobrar impuestos para el gobierno central

Zen   secta del budismo que se hizo popular entre los aristócratas japoneses y se volvió parte del código de conducta de los samurai; según el budismo Zen, existen diferentes vías para llegar a la ilustración

sionismo   un movimiento internacional originalmente para el establecimiento de una comunidad nacional o religiosa judía en Palestina y más tarde para el apoyo del Israel moderno

The University of the State of New York

REGENTS HIGH SCHOOL EXAMINATION

GLOBAL HISTORY AND GEOGRAPHY

Thursday, August 16, 2007 — 12:30 to 3:30 p.m., only

Student Name _Anna Demi_

School Name _Our Lady of Mercy_

Print your name and the name of your school on the lines above. Then turn to the last page of this booklet, which is the answer sheet for Part I. Fold the last page along the perforations and, slowly and carefully, tear off the answer sheet. Then fill in the heading of your answer sheet. Now print your name and the name of your school in the heading of each page of your essay booklet.

This examination has three parts. You are to answer **all** questions in all parts. Use black or dark-blue ink to write your answers.

Part I contains 50 multiple-choice questions. Record your answers to these questions on the separate answer sheet.

Part II contains one thematic essay question. Write your answer to this question in the essay booklet, beginning on page 1.

Part III is based on several documents:

Part III A contains the documents. Each document is followed by one or more questions. In the test booklet, write your answer to each question on the lines following that question. Be sure to enter your name and the name of your school on the first page of this section.

Part III B contains one essay question based on the documents. Write your answer to this question in the essay booklet, beginning on page 7.

When you have completed the examination, you must sign the statement printed on the Part I answer sheet, indicating that you had no unlawful knowledge of the questions or answers prior to the examination and that you have neither given nor received assistance in answering any of the questions during the examination. Your answer sheet cannot be accepted if you fail to sign this declaration.

The use of any communications device is strictly prohibited when taking this examination. If you use any communications device, no matter how briefly, your examination will be invalidated and no score will be calculated for you.

DO NOT OPEN THIS EXAMINATION BOOKLET UNTIL THE SIGNAL IS GIVEN.

Part I

Answer all questions in this part.

Directions (1–50): For each statement or question, write on the separate answer sheet the *number* of the word or expression that, of those given, best completes the statement or answers the question.

1 Which source of information is considered a primary source?

(1) travel diary of Ibn Battuta
(2) modern novel about the Golden Age of Islam
(3) textbook on the history of North Africa
(4) dictionary of English words adapted from Arabic

2 Which continent's economic and political development has been influenced by the Andes Mountains and the Amazon River?

(1) Asia   (3) Europe
(2) Africa   (4) South America

3 • Planting wheat and barley
  • Domesticating animals
  • Establishing permanent homes and villages

At the beginning of the Neolithic Revolution, the most direct impact of these developments was on

(1) religion and government
(2) transportation and trade
(3) diet and shelter
(4) climate and topography

4 • Kushites adapted Egyptian art and architecture.
  • Greeks adopted Phoenician characters for an alphabet.
  • Arabs used the Indian mathematical concept of zero.

These actions are examples of

(1) filial piety   (3) scientific research
(2) cultural diffusion   (4) ethnocentrism

5 Which belief system is most closely associated with the terms *Eightfold Path, Four Noble Truths,* and *nirvana*?

(1) Buddhism   (3) Judaism
(2) Christianity (4) Shinto

6 . . ."If a man has knocked out the teeth of a man of the same rank, his own teeth shall be knocked out. If he has knocked out the teeth of a plebeian (commoner), he shall pay one-third of a mina of silver.". . .

— Code of Hammurabi

Which statement is supported by this excerpt from Hammurabi's code of laws?

(1) All men are equal under the law.
(2) Fines are preferable to physical punishment.
(3) Law sometimes distinguishes between social classes.
(4) Violence must always be punished with violence.

7 Confucianism had a strong impact on the development of China mainly because this philosophy

(1) established a basic structure for military rule
(2) provided a basis for social order
(3) contained the framework for a communist government
(4) stressed the importance of the individual

8 The terms *masters, apprentices,* and *journeymen* are most closely associated with the

(1) encomienda system of Latin America
(2) guild system of Europe in the Middle Ages
(3) civil service system of China during the Tang dynasty
(4) caste system of India

Base your answers to questions 9 and 10 on the map below and on your knowledge of social studies.

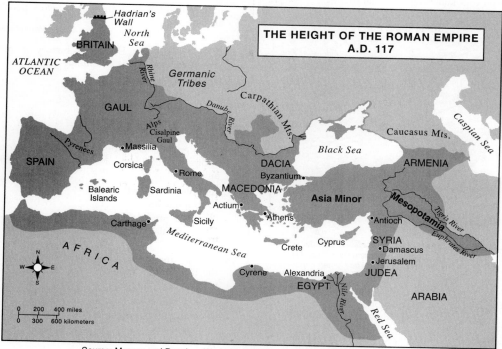

THE HEIGHT OF THE ROMAN EMPIRE A.D. 117

Source: Mazour and Peoples, *World History: People and Nations*, Harcourt Brace Jovanovich (adapted)

9 Which statement is best supported by the information on this map?

(1) The Roman Empire extended over three continents.

(2) Rivers kept invaders out of the Roman Empire.

(3) Alexandria served as the eastern capital of the Roman Empire.

(4) Carthage was eventually destroyed by the Romans.

10 Based on the information provided by this map, which body of water was most likely the center of Roman trade?

(1) Red Sea
(2) Black Sea
(3) Atlantic Ocean
(4) Mediterranean Sea

Base your answer to question 11 on the map below and on your knowledge of social studies.

Trade about A.D. 1000

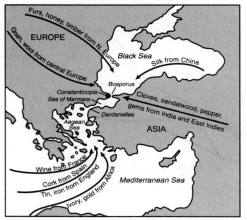

Source: Farah and Karls, *World History, The Human Experience*, Glencoe/McGraw-Hill (adapted)

11 Based on the information provided by this map, which statement about Constantinople is accurate?

(1) Africans traded more goods in Constantinople than in any other area.
(2) Constantinople was a city located on the Mediterranean Sea.
(3) Gold was the primary commodity that China sent to Constantinople.
(4) Constantinople was an important trading center.

12 One major characteristic of the Renaissance period is that the

(1) Catholic Church no longer had any influence in Europe
(2) manor became the center of economic activity
(3) classical cultures of Greece and Rome were revived and imitated
(4) major language of the people became Latin

13 ". . . Therefore those preachers of indulgences are in error, who say that by the pope's indulgences a man is freed from every penalty, and saved; . . ."
— Martin Luther

Which period in European history is most directly related to this statement?

(1) Age of Exploration
(2) Scientific Revolution
(3) Crusades
(4) Protestant Reformation

14 The economies of the western African civilizations of Ghana, Mali, and Songhai relied on

(1) industrial growth
(2) shipbuilding
(3) textile production
(4) trans-Saharan trade routes

15 A major reason for Zheng He's voyages during the 15th century was to

(1) promote trade and collect tribute
(2) establish colonies in Africa and India
(3) seal off China's borders from foreign influence
(4) prove the world was round

16 What was one effect of the Columbian exchange?

(1) rapid decline in European population
(2) economic instability in China and Japan
(3) introduction of new foods to both Europe and the Americas
(4) spread of Hinduism into Latin America

17 From the 15th to the 18th centuries, absolute monarchs of Europe and Asia sought to

(1) increase the power of the Catholic Church
(2) centralize their political power
(3) redistribute land to the peasants
(4) strengthen feudalism

Base your answer to question 18 on the map below and on your knowledge of social studies.

Asia — 1294

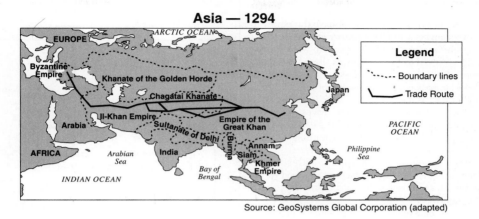

Source: GeoSystems Global Corporation (adapted)

18 Which group of people ruled much of Asia during the period shown on this map?

  (1) Mongol   (3) Japanese

  (2) Indian   (4) European

---

19 Which person is credited with saying "L'état, c'est moi" (I am the state)?

  (1) Louis XIV   (3) Karl Marx

  (2) John Locke   (4) Queen Isabella

20 Seventeenth-century scholars Galileo Galilei and René Descartes faced serious challenges to their scientific theories because their ideas

  (1) were based on the Bible

  (2) contradicted traditional medieval European beliefs

  (3) relied only on teachings from non-Christian cultures

  (4) were not supported by scientific investigations

21 Which statement expresses an idea of the Enlightenment?

  (1) The king is sacred and answers only to God.

  (2) History is a continuous struggle between social classes.

  (3) Those who are the most fit will survive and succeed.

  (4) All individuals have natural rights.

22 The breakdown of traditions, increased levels of pollution, and the expansion of slums are negative aspects of

  (1) militarism   (3) pogroms

  (2) collectivization   (4) urbanization

23 Which heading best completes this partial outline?

> I. _____
>
>   A. Rivalries between powerful countries over colonies
>
>   B. Breakup of large empires
>
>   C. Demand for self-determination by ethnic groups

  (1) Reasons For Communist Revolutions

  (2) Effects of Nationalism

  (3) Methods of Propaganda

  (4) Formation of Democratic Governments

Base your answer to question 24 on the passage below and on your knowledge of social studies.

. . . The factory owners did not have the power to compel anybody to take a factory job. They could only hire people who were ready to work for the wages offered to them. Low as these wage rates were, they were nonetheless much more than these paupers could earn in any other field open to them. It is a distortion of facts to say that the factories carried off the housewives from the nurseries and the kitchens and the children from their play. These women had nothing to cook with and [nothing] to feed their children. These children were destitute [poor] and starving. Their only refuge was the factory. It saved them, in the strict sense of the term, from death by starvation. . . .

— Ludwig von Mises, *Human Action, A Treatise on Economics*, Yale University Press

24 Which statement summarizes the theme of this passage?

(1) Factory owners created increased hardships.
(2) Factory owners preferred to use child laborers.
(3) The factory system allowed people to earn money.
(4) The factory system created new social classes.

25 What was one impact of industrialization on Japan during the Meiji Restoration?

(1) Japan became more isolated from world affairs.
(2) Demand for natural resources increased.
(3) Japan became a colonial possession of China.
(4) Traditional practices of Bushido were reintroduced.

Base your answer to question 26 on the map below and on your knowledge of social studies.

Eastern Asia in 1914

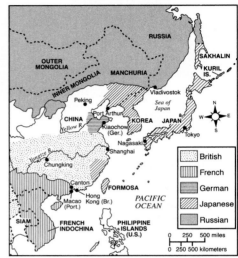

Source: Robert Feeney et al., *Brief Review in Global Studies*, Prentice Hall (adapted)

26 This map illustrates the concept of

(1) ethnocentrism   (3) containment
(2) socialism   (4) imperialism

27 Which region was described as "the powder keg of Europe" prior to World War I?

(1) Iberian Peninsula   (3) Balkan Peninsula
(2) British Isles   (4) Scandinavia

Base your answer to question 28 on the passage below and on your knowledge of social studies.

. . . In order to obtain Arab support in the War, the British Government promised the Sherif of Mecca in 1915 that, in the event of an Allied victory, the greater part of the Arab provinces of the Turkish Empire would become independent. The Arabs understood that Palestine would be included in the sphere of independence.

In order to obtain the support of World Jewry, the British Government in 1917 issued the Balfour Declaration. The Jews understood that, if the experiment of establishing a Jewish National Home succeeded and a sufficient number of Jews went to Palestine, the National Home might develop in course of time into a Jewish State. . . .

— Summary of the Report of the
Palestine Royal Commission, 1937

28 Which conclusion is best supported by this passage?

(1) The British made no promises to either the Arabs or the Jews.

(2) The Arab-Israeli conflict can be traced in part to British promises.

(3) The United Nations did not try to prevent conflict in the Middle East.

(4) Only the Jews were promised an independent state in Palestine.

---

29 • Led the Russians in a second revolution (1917)
• Promised "Peace, Land, and Bread"
• Established the New Economic Policy (NEP)

Which leader is being described by these statements?

(1) Czar Nicholas II   (3) Vladimir I. Lenin
(2) Nikita Khrushchev   (4) Mikhail Gorbachev

Base your answer to question 30 on the passage below and on your knowledge of social studies.

. . . A weary, exhausted, nerve-racked group of men it was indeed that, about noon November 1, assembled in a gully north of Sommerance [France] to rest and dig in for the night. The artillery was still firing furiously, but the enemy's barrage [bombardment] had ceased very suddenly about 10:00 a.m. and now only occasional shells from long-range rifles would explode in the vicinity. The weather was gloomy and the moist air chilled one to the bones. Yet it was with that meticulous [methodical] care that is characteristic of worn-out men, that we prepared our foxholes, carrying boards and iron sheeting from abandoned machine-gunners' dugouts in order to make our "houses" as comfortable as possible, even though only for one night. . . .

Source: William L. Langer, Gas and Flame in
World War I, Knopf/Borzoi

30 Which means of warfare is described in this passage?

(1) guerilla   (3) biological
(2) nuclear   (4) trench

31 A major goal of Joseph Stalin's five-year plans was to

(1) encourage communist revolutions in the colonies of the European powers

(2) transform the Soviet Union into an industrial power

(3) expand the Soviet Union's borders to include warm-water ports

(4) reduce the amount of foreign aid coming from the Western Hemisphere

Base your answer to question 32 on the chart below and on your knowledge of social studies.

NAZI RISE TO POWER

World War I
- German war debts
- Loss of German colonies
- Wish for revenge

Weak Government
- Doubts about Weimar Republic
- Quarrels among political groups
- Wish to return to strong leader like the Kaiser

Economic Problems
- Inflation
- Worldwide depression
- Unemployment

Source: *Guide to the Essentials of World History,*
Prentice Hall (adapted)

32 Based on the information in this chart, which situation gave rise to Nazi power in Germany?

(1) global prosperity and trade
(2) success of the Weimar Republic
(3) political and economic instability
(4) expansion of Germany's colonial empire

Base your answer to question 33 on the passage below and on your knowledge of social studies.

. . . "We may anticipate a state of affairs in which two Great Powers will each be in a position to put an end to the civilization and life of the other, though not without risking its own. We may be likened to two scorpions in a bottle, each capable of killing the other, but only at the risk of his own life.". . .

— J. Robert Oppenheimer, July 1953

33 This statement expresses concern about the

(1) threats to the environment by developed and developing economies
(2) differences between command and market economies
(3) economic costs of World War II
(4) dangers of the Cold War

Base your answer to question 34 on the cartoon below and on your knowledge of social studies.

Sending Forth Another Dove

Source: Herblock, May 13, 1941 (adapted)

34 The main idea of this 1941 cartoon is that Japan, Italy, and Germany

(1) had formed an alliance for peace
(2) were determined to defeat communism
(3) had supported a peaceful international solution
(4) were committed to aggression

35 At the end of World War II, the British decided to partition the Indian subcontinent into the nations of India and Pakistan. What was a primary reason for this division?

(1) India had adopted a policy of nonalignment.
(2) Religious differences had led to conflicts between Hindus and Muslims.
(3) Most of India's valuable resources were located in the south.
(4) British India's Muslim minority controlled most of India's banking industry.

Base your answer to question 36 on the graph below and on your knowledge of social studies.

World Petroleum Reserves

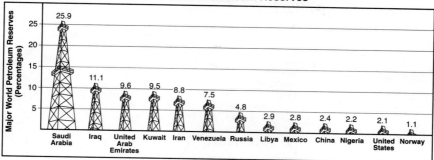

Source: John T. Rourke, *International Politics on the World Stage*, McGraw-Hill, 2003 (adapted)

36 Which conclusion is best supported by the information provided on this graph?

(1) The United States has adequate petroleum reserves to meet future needs.
(2) Nations lacking major petroleum reserves cannot industrialize.
(3) Overproduction of petroleum products has caused inflation in the Middle East.
(4) Most of the world's largest petroleum reserves are located in the Middle East.

Base your answer to question 37 on the cartoon below and on your knowledge of social studies.

Source: Clay Bennett, *Christian Science Monitor*, 2002

37 What does this cartoon suggest about the introduction of the EURO in Europe?

(1) Additional countries were created.
(2) Isolation among nations increased.
(3) Communist economic policies were adopted.
(4) Economic barriers between nations decreased.

38 The Four Modernizations of Deng Xiaoping in the 1970s and 1980s resulted in

(1) an emphasis on the Five Relationships
(2) a return to Maoist revolutionary principles
(3) a move toward increased capitalism
(4) the end of the communist system of government

39 One way in which Ho Chi Minh, Fidel Castro, and Kim Jong Il are similar is that each

(1) set up democratic governments
(2) used Marxist political principles
(3) overthrew a ruling monarch
(4) promoted Confucian principles

40 In the late 20th century, the Green Revolution had the greatest impact on

(1) grain production in India
(2) political freedom in Russia
(3) economic reforms in Cuba
(4) traditional customs in Japan

Base your answer to question 41 on the illustration below and on your knowledge of social studies.

A European View

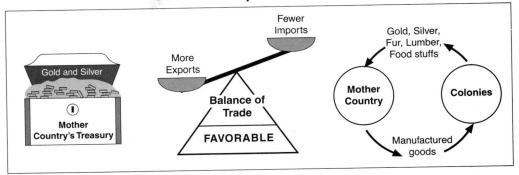

41 Which policy is portrayed in this illustration?

    (1) nonalignment

    (2) laissez-faire capitalism

    (3) perestroika

    (4) mercantilism

Base your answer to question 42 on the cartoon below and on your knowledge of social studies.

Source: Dana Summers, *The Orlando Sentinel* (adapted)

42 What is the main idea of this cartoon?

    (1) The original causes of apartheid have not been eliminated.

    (2) Apartheid improved race relations in South Africa.

    (3) Peace can be achieved by nonviolence.

    (4) Hate is caused by poverty.

43 Ethnic cleansing in Bosnia, the killing fields of Cambodia (Kampuchea), and the dirty war in Argentina are all examples of

    (1) nationalist revolts

    (2) human rights violations

    (3) international terrorism

    (4) religious conflicts

44 Studying the architectural features of the Parthenon, Notre Dame Cathedral, and the Taj Mahal provides information about the

    (1) beliefs and values of a given culture

    (2) climatic changes in an area

    (3) 19th-century use of technology

    (4) influence of Chinese design

45 Which geographic factor had the most influence on the development of Inca society and Japanese society?

    (1) frequent monsoons

    (2) large deserts

    (3) mountainous topography

    (4) tropical climate

Base your answer to question 46 on the diagram below and on your knowledge of social studies.

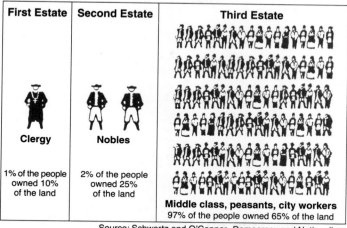

Source: Schwartz and O'Connor, *Democracy and Nationalism,* Globe Book Company (adapted)

46 Which revolution resulted from the division of society shown in this diagram?

(1) Puritan (1642)
(2) French (1789)
(3) Mexican (1910)
(4) Russian (1917)

47 The golden ages of the Roman, Byzantine, and Ottoman Empires can be attributed in part to

(1) cultural isolation
(2) stable governments
(3) command economies
(4) distinct social classes

48 One way in which Simón Bolívar, Jomo Kenyatta, and Mohandas Gandhi are similar is that each

(1) led a nationalist movement
(2) used nonviolent tactics
(3) supported imperialism
(4) opposed communism

49 Which factor most hindered the efforts of both Napoleon and Hitler to conquer Russia?

(1) climate
(2) fortifications
(3) advanced technology
(4) lack of ports

50 One way in which the Sepoy Mutiny in India, the Zulu resistance in southern Africa, and the Boxer Rebellion in China are similar is that each resulted from

(1) government policies of ethnic cleansing
(2) attempts by democratic forces to overthrow the monarchy
(3) native reaction to foreign interference in the region
(4) government denial of access to fertile farmland

This page left blank intentionally.

OK cool.

Answers to the essay questions are to be written in the separate essay booklet.

In developing your answer to Part II, be sure to keep these general definitions in mind:

(a) <u>describe</u> means "to illustrate something in words or tell about it"
(b) <u>discuss</u> means "to make observations about something using facts, reasoning, and argument; to present in some detail"

Part II

THEMATIC ESSAY QUESTION

Directions: Write a well-organized essay that includes an introduction, several paragraphs addressing the task below, and a conclusion.

Theme: Political Systems

> Political systems have affected the history and culture of nations and societies.

Task:

> Choose *two* different political systems and for *each*
> • Describe the characteristics of the political system
> • Discuss how the political system has affected the history *or* culture of a specific nation or society

You may use any political systems from your study of global history. Some suggestions you might wish to consider include absolute monarchy, constitutional monarchy, parliamentary democracy, direct democracy, theocracy, communism, and fascism.

You are *not* limited to these suggestions.

Do *not* use the United States as an example of a nation or society.

Guidelines:

In your essay, be sure to
• Develop all aspects of the task
• Support the theme with relevant facts, examples, and details
• Use a logical and clear plan of organization, including an introduction and a conclusion that are beyond a restatement of the theme

Democratic   Communism

In developing your answers to Part III, be sure to keep this general definition in mind:

> <u>discuss</u> means "to make observations about something using facts, reasoning, and argument; to present in some detail"

Part III

DOCUMENT-BASED QUESTION

This question is based on the accompanying documents. It is designed to test your ability to work with historical documents. Some of these documents have been edited for the purposes of this question. As you analyze the documents, take into account both the source of each document and any point of view that may be presented in the document.

Historical Context:

> Throughout history, natural resources such as water, coal, oil, and diamonds have both helped and hindered the development of nations and regions.

Task: Using information from the documents and your knowledge of global history, answer the questions that follow each document in Part A. Your answers to the questions will help you write the Part B essay, in which you will be asked to

> * Discuss how natural resources have helped **and/or** hindered the development of specific nations **or** regions

Do *not* use the United States as the specific nation or region.

Part A
Short-Answer Questions

Directions: Analyze the documents and answer the short-answer questions that follow each document in the space provided.

Document 1

Earliest Civilizations, 3500 – 1500 BC

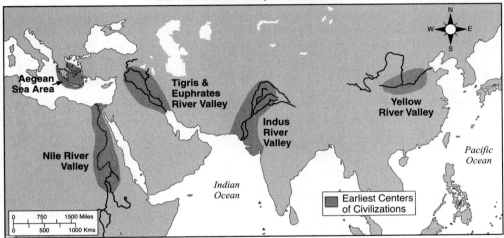

Source: *Historical Maps on File,* Revised Edition, Facts On File (adapted)

1 Based on this map, identify *one* geographic feature that influenced the location of early centers of civilization. [1]

_____

_____

Score [ ]

Document 2a

> ### "Farmers in India Await the Rains, and Despair"
>
> REWARI, India—When the monsoon rains that sweep across India every year failed to arrive in late June, the farmers here began to worry. Now, as they scan the empty blue skies for signs of clouds, their worry is turning to despair.
>
> Broad swaths [wide areas] of India are seeing the country's worst drought in 15 years. Here in the northern state of Haryana, the level of rainfall until July 24 was 70% below average; for the country as a whole, it was 24% below normal. Since July 24, there has been little relief for the hardest-hit areas.
>
> Under these parched [very dry] conditions, economists say, India's growth could wilt, since agriculture accounts for a quarter of gross domestic product [GDP] and sustains [supports] two-thirds of the nation's billion-strong population. Before the drought, economists were expecting agricultural expansion of around 2% and GDP growth of 4.5% to 6% in the current fiscal year, which began April 1. Now they are predicting that agricultural production will remain stagnant or even turn negative, shaving something like half a percentage point off overall economic growth. . . .

Source: Joanna Slater, *The Wall Street Journal*, August 6, 2002

2a Based on this excerpt by Joanna Slater, state **one** negative impact the lack of rain has had on the economy in India. [1]

_____

_____

Score ☐

Document 2b

"Indian Monsoon Drenches the Land; Marketers Drench the Consumer"

BOMBAY, India—One year after a crippling drought, plentiful rains are sweeping across India—and delivering a flood of good news for its economy.

Agriculture's contribution to India's gross domestic product [GDP], its total output of goods and services, has declined over the past decade as the service and industrial sectors have grown. Nevertheless, the showers are a relief for farmers, who depend on the monsoon to irrigate their crops. They are also a boon [benefit] to sales of everything from tractors to shampoo; a good harvest puts more money in the pockets of rural consumers, improving the fortunes of companies ranging from Anglo-Dutch Unilever to Honda Motor Co. of Japan to South Korea's Samsung Electronics Co.

Agriculture still sustains two-thirds of India's billion-strong population and contributes a quarter of its GDP, which economists predict will expand by as much as 6.5% in the fiscal year ending next March, partly because of the abundant rains and the resurgent [recovered] farm sector. . . .

Source: Joanna Slater, *The Wall Street Journal*, July 24, 2003

2b Based on this excerpt by Joanna Slater, state *one* positive impact that abundant levels of rain have had on the economy in India.   [1]

_____

_____

Score ☐

Document 3

Great Britain, 1750–1850

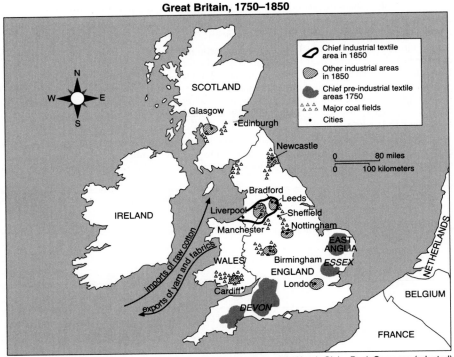

Source: Holt and O'Connor, *Exploring World History Workbook*, Globe Book Company (adapted)

3 Based on this map, state *one* way that coal affected the development of Great Britain between 1750 and 1850. [1]

_____

_____

Score [ ]

Document 4

> . . . The lives of factory workers in Manchester, and in the other new industrial cities rising up around Britain, were shaped by the burning of coal just as the coal miners' lives were shaped by the digging of it. Coal made the iron that built the machines the workers operated as well as the factories they worked in, and then it provided the power that made the machines and factories run. Coal gas provided the lights the workers toiled [worked] under, letting their work day start before dawn and end after dusk. When they left the factory doors, they would walk through a city made of coal-fired bricks, now stained black with the same coal soot that was soiling their skin and clothes. Looking up, they would see a sky darkened by coal smoke; looking down, a ground blackened by coal dust. When they went home, they would eat food cooked over a coal fire and often tainted with a coal flavor, and with each breath, they would inhale some of the densest coal smoke on the planet. In short, their world was constructed, animated, illuminated, colored, scented, flavored, and generally saturated by coal and the fruits [results] of its combustion. . . .

Source: Barbara Freese, *Coal: A Human History*, Perseus Publishing

4 According to Barbara Freese, what are *two* effects that coal had on factory workers in the industrial cities of Great Britain during the Industrial Revolution? [2]

(1)_____

_____

Score ☐

(2)_____

_____

Score ☐

Document 5

Kuwait became a major supplier of oil during the late 1940s and the 1950s. Kuwait made a deal with foreign oil companies in return for payments. This money changed the way many people earned a living in Kuwait and led to a change in Kuwait's economic infrastructure.

> . . .The government's efforts to modernize the City of Kuwait resulted in a construction boom, particularly in the period 1952 to 1965. Foreign planning consultants, architects, engineers, construction firms, and labor planned and created a city with the best material and technologies the industrial world could supply. In contrast to the land acquisition program, however, government outlays in this period to create social overhead capital did generate considerable economic activity. In addition to a great many public buildings, commercial centers, apartment blocks, and suburban community projects built in the period, the following were also constructed:
>
> 1. 176 government schools and 32 private schools.
>
> 2. 8 hospitals, 2 sanatoria [treatment centers], 37 dispensaries and health centers, 148 school dispensaries and 9 centers for preventive medicine.
>
> 3. 1,100 kilometers of paved roads.
>
> 4. A number of electric power stations and an expansive network for distribution and street lighting laid; between 1956 and 1965, installed capacity increased from 30,000 kwh to 370,000 kwh. . . .

Source: Jacqueline S. Ismael, "The Economic Transformation of Kuwait," *The Politics of Middle Eastern Oil*, Middle East Institute

5 According to Jacqueline S. Ismael, what are **two** ways Kuwait used its oil resources to improve the city of Kuwait? [2]

(1)_____

_____

Score ☐

(2)_____

_____

Score ☐

Document 6

"I can't see a reason to go to war with Iraq...."

Source: Michael Ramirez, *Los Angeles Times*, January, 2003 (adapted)

6 Based on Michael Ramirez's cartoon, in what way did Iraqi oil contracts influence the French government in 2003? [1]

_____

_____   Score ☐

Document 7

. . . When De Beers discovered diamonds in Botswana in 1969, the government had been independent for three years, and the men running it were traditional chiefs who owned cattle. They came from a desert culture where people have to scrimp and save to survive the long, dry season.

During three decades, Botswana's leaders have carefully guided what became the world's fastest-growing economy. They invested in roads, schools and clinics. In stark contrast to the rulers of Angola and Congo, they created an African nation devoted to improving the lives of its people. In 1965, only about half of primary school-aged children attended school. Today, 90 percent of that group is enrolled. Life expectancy, which was less than 50 at independence, is now near 70.*

Phones work in Botswana, potholes get repaired, garbage gets picked up, and a lively press pokes fun at the government without fear. At $3,600 per year, the gross national product per capita is seven times higher than the average for sub-Saharan Africa. The standard of living is higher than in South Africa, Turkey or Thailand.

"Diamonds are not devils," said Terry Lynn Karl, professor of political science at Stanford and author of "The Paradox of Plenty," (University of California Press, 1997), a book about the poisonous mix of natural resources, big money and thieving elites in developing countries. "What matters is that there be a tradition of good government and compromise in place prior to the exploitation of these resources.". . .

* Correction: The United Nations says that because of AIDS, the figure has fallen sharply and is 41, no longer close to 70.

Source: Blaine Harden, "Africa's Gems: Warfare's Best Friend," *New York Times*, April 6, 2000
Correction published April 17, 2000

7 According to Blaine Harden, what are **two** ways the sale of diamonds affected Botswana? [2]

(1)_____

_____

Score ☐

(2)_____

_____

Score ☐

Document 8

In 1980, diamonds were discovered at Gope in the Central Kalahari Game Reserve (CKGR). Since 1997, the government of Botswana has been removing the Bushmen from this area. Many wish to return to their traditional homelands.

> . . . In a recent court case concerning the Bushmen's right to return to their ancestral lands, Tombale assured the court that the evictions had nothing to do with diamonds. This was strange, because the bushmen's lawyers had never mentioned diamonds. They were just defending the Gana and Gwi Bushmen's right to live on lands they had occupied for thousands of years.
>
> And yet when Margaret Nasha said in February 2002 that the relocation of the Gana and Gwi was not unprecedented she cited an example of people being relocated 'to give way for projects of national interest' in Jwaneng. They were, in fact, relocated to make way for a diamond mine.
>
> As Botswana's foreign minister Mompati Merafhe has explained: 'Many Bushmen have been removed because of economic interests. In Orapa, my area, a great chunk of people were removed because of the mine. Botswana is where it is today because of this facilitation. These people are no exception.'. . .
>
> Meanwhile, back in the Kalahari the Botswana government has been parcelling up the CKGR into diamond concessions and sharing them out between De Beers, the Australian-based company BHP Billiton and the Canadian outfit Motapa Diamond Inc. And by November last year virtually the entire game reserve, bar [except for] a small bite-sized chunk in the northwest, had been dished out.
>
> So either the government has pulled off a fat scam by selling dud concessions to three unsuspecting multinationals — or it's lying. . . .

Source: "Why are the Bushmen being evicted?" *The Ecologist*, September 2003

8 Based on this excerpt from *The Ecologist*, state **one** impact the 1980 discovery of more diamonds has had on the people of Botswana. [1]

_____

_____

Score ☐

Part B
Essay

Directions: Write a well-organized essay that includes an introduction, several paragraphs, and a conclusion. Use evidence from at least *five* documents in your essay. Support your response with relevant facts, examples, and details. Include additional outside information.

Historical Context:

Throughout history, natural resources such as water, coal, oil, and diamonds have both helped and hindered the development of nations and regions.

Task: Using the information from the documents and your knowledge of global history, write an essay in which you

> • Discuss how natural resources have helped ***and/or*** hindered the development of specific nations ***or*** regions

Do *not* use the United States as the specific nation or region.

Guidelines:

In your essay, be sure to

- Develop all aspects of the task
- Incorporate information from *at least five* documents
- Incorporate relevant outside information
- Support the theme with relevant facts, examples, and details
- Use a logical and clear plan of organization, including an introduction and conclusion that are beyond a restatement of the theme

The University of the State of New York

REGENTS HIGH SCHOOL EXAMINATION

GLOBAL HISTORY AND GEOGRAPHY

Tuesday, January 22, 2008 — 9:15 a.m. to 12:15 p.m., only

Student Name _____

School Name _____

Print your name and the name of your school on the lines above. Then turn to the last page of this booklet, which is the answer sheet for Part I. Fold the last page along the perforations and, slowly and carefully, tear off the answer sheet. Then fill in the heading of your answer sheet. Now print your name and the name of your school in the heading of each page of your essay booklet.

This examination has three parts. You are to answer **all** questions in all parts. Use black or dark-blue ink to write your answers.

Part I contains 50 multiple-choice questions. Record your answers to these questions on the separate answer sheet.

Part II contains one thematic essay question. Write your answer to this question in the essay booklet, beginning on page 1.

Part III is based on several documents:

Part III A contains the documents. Each document is followed by one or more questions. In the test booklet, write your answer to each question on the lines following that question. Be sure to enter your name and the name of your school on the first page of this section.

Part III B contains one essay question based on the documents. Write your answer to this question in the essay booklet, beginning on page 7.

When you have completed the examination, you must sign the statement printed on the Part I answer sheet, indicating that you had no unlawful knowledge of the questions or answers prior to the examination and that you have neither given nor received assistance in answering any of the questions during the examination. Your answer sheet cannot be accepted if you fail to sign this declaration.

The use of any communications device is strictly prohibited when taking this examination. If you use any communications device, no matter how briefly, your examination will be invalidated and no score will be calculated for you.

DO NOT OPEN THIS EXAMINATION BOOKLET UNTIL THE SIGNAL IS GIVEN.

Part I

Answer all questions in this part.

Directions (1–50): For each statement or question, write on the separate answer sheet the *number* of the word or expression that, of those given, best completes the statement or answers the question.

Base your answer to question 1 on the map below and on your knowledge of social studies.

Selected World Climate Zones

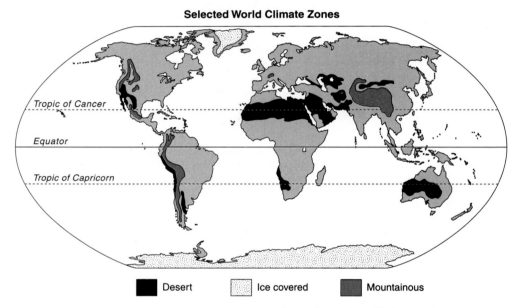

Source: *Geography on File,* Facts on File, 1994 (adapted)

1 Based on the information provided in this map, which statement is accurate?
  (1) The world's largest icecap is located in northern Europe.
  (2) Most mountainous climates are located on the eastern borders of the continents.
  (3) The largest desert area stretches from western Africa through much of southwestern Asia.
  (4) South America is connected to Antarctica by a narrow land bridge.

2 Slash-and-burn techniques are typically practiced by
  (1) people who live along rivers that deposit rich soil during floods
  (2) subsistence farmers who plant an area until the soil loses its fertility
  (3) farmers who rely on chemical fertilization and pesticides
  (4) nomads who use pastures for their livestock

3 Which feature would most likely be included in an economic system based on traditional agriculture and self-sufficiency?
  (1) banks   (3) gold standard
  (2) barter   (4) tariffs

4 Which geographic factor had a major influence on the development of both Egyptian and Babylonian civilizations?

(1) river valleys
(2) cool temperatures
(3) locations near a strait
(4) mountains

5 Which description accurately identifies Socrates, Plato, and Aristotle?

(1) rulers of the Roman Republic
(2) artists of the Italian Renaissance
(3) religious leaders of the Protestant Reformation
(4) philosophers of ancient Greece

Base your answer to question 6 on the passage below and on your knowledge of social studies.

... The actual journey to Mecca [Makkah] began on the fifth of *Dhu al-Hijjah*, 1393 (the 29th of December, 1973, according to the Gregorian calendar), at Beirut International Airport, but it was not until the afternoon of the seventh that I donned [put on] the *Ihram* [robe] and drove along on the road from Jiddah to Mecca. The road was crowded with cars, buses and trucks all packed with pilgrims chanting the Hajj refrain, the *Talbiyah*: ...

— Michael E. Jansen, *An American Girl on the Hajj*

6 This passage describes the experience of a follower of

(1) Christianity   (3) Hinduism
(2) Islam   (4) Judaism

7 In China, the development of civil service examinations and a belief in filial piety reflect the influence of

(1) Shinto   (3) Confucianism
(2) Jainism   (4) Buddhism

8 One way in which the Code of Hammurabi, the Twelve Tables, and the Justinian Code are similar is that each

(1) legalized monotheistic beliefs
(2) established legal standards
(3) provided records of economic activity
(4) supported republican governments

9 Which heading best fits the partial outline below?

I. _____

　A. People become more aware of the outside world.
　B. Merchant and craft guilds help commercial centers grow into cities.
　C. Trade routes develop to supply the growing demand for new products.
　D. Monarchs centralize control and increase their power.

(1) Seljuk Turks Dominate Europe
(2) Democracy Ends in Eastern Europe
(3) Feudalism Declines in Western Europe
(4) Religion Becomes Powerful Force in Europe

10 One way in which the African kingdoms of Ghana and Mali are similar is that they

(1) established their wealth through trade
(2) improved their military strength with the use of gunpowder
(3) opened trade routes to the Americas
(4) adopted Christianity as their major religion

11 One way in which the travels of Marco Polo and Ibn Battuta are similar is that they resulted in

(1) an increased interest in different cultures
(2) the development of slavery
(3) a reduction in trade
(4) the discovery of East Asia

12 • Classical Greco-Roman ideas were revived.
　• Wealthy patrons supported the arts and education.
　• Humanism spread throughout western Europe.

Which period in European history is most closely associated with these statements?

(1) Early Middle Ages   (3) Renaissance
(2) Industrial Revolution (4) Hellenistic Period

Base your answer to question 13 on the map below and on your knowledge of social studies.

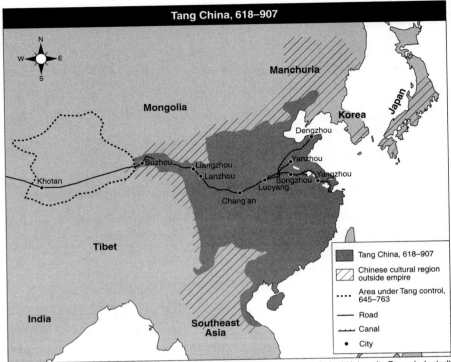

Tang China, 618–907

Manchuria

Mongolia

Korea

Japan

Dengzhou

Suzhou

Liangzhou
Lanzhou

Yanzhou

Khotan

Songzhou
Luoyang

Yangzhou

Chang'an

Tibet

India

Southeast
Asia

	Tang China, 618–907
	Chinese cultural region outside empire
	Area under Tang control, 645–763
	Road
	Canal
•	City

Source: Patrick K. O'Brien, general editor, *Oxford Atlas of World History*, Oxford University Press (adapted)

13 Which statement about the Tang dynasty is best supported by the information on this map?

(1) It experienced conflict in coastal areas.
(2) Its boundaries extended to India.
(3) It gained territory in Tibet and Korea.
(4) It exchanged goods using overland routes.

14 One similarity between Martin Luther and Henry VIII is that they

(1) argued against the establishment of a theocratic state
(2) protested against the ideas of the Enlightenment
(3) died during the Reign of Terror
(4) challenged the teachings of the Catholic Church

15 • Literacy rates rise.
• Shakespeare's sonnets circulated.
• Secular ideas spread.

Which innovation led directly to these developments?

(1) printing press   (3) paper currency
(2) astrolabe   (4) caravel

Base your answer to question 16 on the drawing below and on your knowledge of social studies.

A Typical Medieval Manor

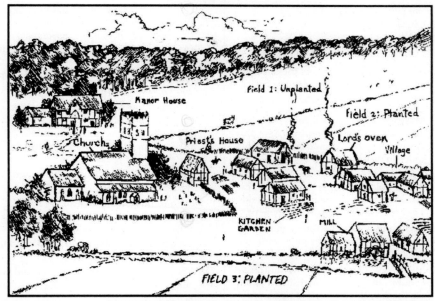

Source: James Killoran et al., *The Key to Understanding Global Studies*, 5th edition, Jarrett Publishing Company (adapted)

16 What inference can be drawn from the location of the church in this drawing?
  (1) The mill was managed by the church.
  (2) Religion played a significant role in the lives of the residents.
  (3) The church controlled trade within the manor.
  (4) The church played a limited role in education.

17 Which geographic feature had the greatest influence on the development of the Inca Empire?
  (1) deserts   (3) river valleys
  (2) irregular coastline   (4) mountains

18 What was one reason the Spanish conquistadors were able to conquer the Aztec Empire?
  (1) The Spanish soldiers made effective use of their military technology against the Aztecs.
  (2) Aztec religious beliefs promoted nonviolence.
  (3) Spain joined the Incas in their fight against the Aztecs.
  (4) The Spanish cavalry outnumbered the Aztec warriors.

19 Which statement describes an impact of the Columbian exchange on the lives of Europeans?
  (1) The combination of new products and ideas promoted economic growth.
  (2) Native Americans immigrated to Europe and competed with Europeans for jobs.
  (3) Millions of Europeans were killed by new American diseases.
  (4) Introduction of the Native American religions resulted in the decline of the Roman Catholic Church.

20 A common goal of Philip II of Spain and Louis XIV of France was to

(1) spread Calvinism
(2) promote political revolutions
(3) maintain absolute power
(4) isolate their nations

Base your answer to question 21 on the speakers' statements below and on your knowledge of social studies.

Speaker A: My king has brought together the best mapmakers and scientists to study navigation. The expeditions he has sponsored will increase Portugal's trade with the East and make us wealthy.

Speaker B: My people lost their land and were forced to work in the mines and fields. They received little economic benefit.

Speaker C: My queen has chartered joint-stock companies to control trade with our colonies.

Speaker D: My people were enslaved and have endured unspeakable hardships. Many died during the Middle Passage.

21 Which two speakers would most likely support mercantilism?

(1) A and B   (3) B and D
(2) A and C   (4) C and D

22 • Parliament offered the throne to King William and Queen Mary.
• Catholic King James II fled England for France.
• Parliament agreed to joint rule with the monarch.

These events are most closely associated with the

(1) Crusades
(2) French Revolution
(3) Glorious Revolution
(4) Reconquista

23 At the Congress of Vienna (1815), the governments of Europe reacted to the French Revolution and the rule of Napoleon by attempting to

(1) restore old regimes to power
(2) spread the idea of democracy
(3) encourage nationalist movements
(4) promote the European free-trade zone

24 One political objective of both Otto von Bismarck and Giuseppe Garibaldi was to

(1) overthrow divine right monarchies
(2) unify their nations
(3) establish communist systems
(4) form an alliance with Great Britain

25 Karl Marx predicted that laissez-faire capitalism would result in

(1) a return to manorialism
(2) a revolution led by the proletariat
(3) fewer government regulations
(4) an equal distribution of wealth and income

26 The Portuguese control of Macao and the British control of Hong Kong in China are examples of

(1) collectivization   (3) self-determination
(2) imperialism   (4) containment

27 Commodore Matthew Perry's visits to Japan in 1853 and 1854 resulted in the

(1) colonization of Japan by the United States
(2) transfer of spheres of influence to China
(3) introduction of Christianity to Japanese society
(4) opening of trade and diplomatic relations with Japan

28 The term *militarism* can best be defined as

(1) loyalty to a nation or ethnic group
(2) buildup of armaments in preparation for war
(3) avoidance of military involvement in civil wars
(4) control of territories for economic and political gain

516

29 A primary reason for Japan's involvement in the Sino-Japanese War and the Russo-Japanese War was to

(1) acquire natural resources in Manchuria and Korea
(2) control trade and markets in Southeast Asia
(3) end Japan's policy of isolationism
(4) remove foreign invaders from Japanese soil

Base your answer to question 30 on the passage below and on your knowledge of social studies.

. . . His Majesty's Government view with favour the establishment in Palestine of a national home for the Jewish people, and will use their best endeavours to facilitate the achievement of this object, it being clearly understood that nothing shall be done which may prejudice the civil and religious rights of existing non-Jewish communities in Palestine, or the rights and political status enjoyed by Jews in any other country. . . .

30 This 1917 passage is taken from a document known as the

(1) Truman Doctrine
(2) Marshall Plan
(3) Fourteen Points
(4) Balfour Declaration

31 Which slogan is associated with the Bolshevik (Russian) Revolution?

(1) "An Eye for an Eye"
(2) "Peace, Land, and Bread"
(3) "Liberty, Equality, Fraternity"
(4) "Take up the White Man's Burden"

32 Which action is most closely associated with Atatürk (Mustafa Kemal)?

(1) beginning the Zionist movement
(2) starting the Palestine Liberation Organization
(3) using Western practices to modernize Turkey
(4) enforcing Islamic law

33 Which aspect of the economy was emphasized in Joseph Stalin's five-year plans?

(1) heavy industry
(2) consumer goods
(3) famine relief
(4) private landownership

34 Mohandas Gandhi is most closely associated with the

(1) support of violence and terrorism to end British rule
(2) desire to strengthen the caste system
(3) use of civil disobedience to gain political freedom
(4) establishment of a national religion in India

35 ". . . Seventy thousand people were killed instantly, and many more would die — 60,000 by November and another 70,000 by 1950. Most of them would be victims of a new method of killing — radiation. . . ."

— Ronald Takai

The situation described in this passage was the direct result of which World War II event?

(1) blitz of London
(2) attack on Pearl Harbor
(3) D-Day invasion of Normandy
(4) bombing of Hiroshima

36 Between 1945 and 1947, the differences between the Hindus and the Muslims in India led to the

(1) Sepoy Mutiny
(2) Salt March
(3) policy of nonalignment
(4) partitioning of the subcontinent

37 What was a major reason for the formation of the North Atlantic Treaty Organization (NATO) in 1949?

(1) to control European trade
(2) to resist Soviet aggression
(3) to support the blockade of Berlin
(4) to strengthen communist governments

38 In Egypt, Gamal Abdel Nasser's seizure of the Suez Canal continued his policy of

(1) attracting investments from Western banks
(2) supporting the rights of British workers
(3) eliminating criticism of political opponents
(4) establishing national control of vital resources

Base your answer to question 39 on the cartoon below and on your knowledge of social studies.

Source: Arcadio Esquivel, Costa Rica, *La Nacion*; Panama, *La Prensa*

39 Which concept is illustrated in this cartoon?

(1) nonalignment   (3) nationalism
(2) interdependence   (4) socialism

40 The histories of Latvia, Estonia, Lithuania, and Finland have been greatly affected by their

(1) proximity to Russia
(2) abundant oil reserves
(3) aggressive foreign policies
(4) alliances with Israel

41 In 1989, the government of China responded to the challenge of protests in Tiananmen Square by

(1) halting trade with the West
(2) allowing democratic elections
(3) sending in tanks and troops to end the demonstrations
(4) calling for a special session of the United Nations Security Council

42 Which heading best completes the partial outline below?

I. _____

    A. Korea remains divided at the 38th parallel.
    B. East and West Berlin are split by a wall.
    C. Strategic arms limitation talks begin.

(1) Emerging Nations of the World
(2) Results of the Cold War
(3) Economic Benefits of World War II
(4) Ethnic Conflicts in the World

43 Which action occurred in the Soviet Union under Mikhail Gorbachev?

(1) Peasants were forced onto collective farms.
(2) Citizens experienced more personal freedoms under glasnost.
(3) The United States and the Soviet Union ended diplomatic relations.
(4) The Soviet government increased its control over the Orthodox Church.

44 Which statement is a fact rather than an opinion?

(1) The growing economy of Brazil threatens the economic power of the United States.
(2) Free trade will lower the standard of living for workers in developed nations.
(3) The European Union (EU) has issued a common currency called the euro.
(4) Developing nations will never be able to compete with developed nations.

Base your answer to question 45 on the cartoon below and on your knowledge of social studies.

"...after climbing a great hill, one only finds that there are many more hills to climb."
—Nelson Mandela in "The Long Walk to Freedom"

FREEDOM

RECONSTRUCTION

ELECTION
KEMPTON PARK
VICTOR VERSTER
POLLSMOOR
THE ISLAND
RIVONIA
ARMED STRUGGLE
TREASON TRIAL
DEFIANCE CAMPAI

Source: Jonathan Shapiro (Zapiro), *Sowetan*, 1994

45 What is the main idea of this cartoon?

(1) Nelson Mandela has completed South Africa's reconstruction.

(2) Although black South Africans have overcome many obstacles to achieve freedom, many struggles lie ahead.

(3) The mountains of South Africa have hindered black South African participation in national elections.

(4) The reconstruction of South Africa can only be achieved through violence, treason, and defiance.

46 A study of the fall of the Roman Empire (476) and of the collapse of the Soviet Union (1991) shows that powerful empires can

(1) lose strength when mercenaries enforce reforms

(2) be threatened only when directly attacked by outsiders

(3) conquer more than one continent and remain stable

(4) be weakened by both internal and external pressures

47 A comparison of the feudal system in Europe and the encomienda system in Latin America shows that both systems

(1) awarded land to the elite

(2) promoted religious tolerance

(3) relied on global trade for goods

(4) used a parliamentary system of government

Base your answer to question 48 on the cartoon below and on your knowledge of social studies.

Russian Economy

Source: Brian Gable, *The Globe and Mail*, Toronto, Canada (adapted)

48 The main idea of this 1990s cartoon is that Russia is

    (1) deciding between a capitalist or a communist system
    (2) attempting to restore military power
    (3) expressing concern about how the rest of the world views its government
    (4) maintaining a balance between a civilian and a military government

49 • Location — included lands surrounding the eastern Mediterranean Sea
    • People — Turks, Arabs, Greeks, Muslims, Christians, and Jews
    • Nickname during the 19th and early 20th centuries — "Sick Man of Europe"

    Which empire is described by these characteristics?

    (1) Gupta   (3) Roman
    (2) Mongol   (4) Ottoman

50 Which sequence of Russian events is in the correct chronological order?

    A. Catherine the Great westernizes Russia.
    B. Ivan III defeats the Mongols.
    C. Khrushchev places missiles in Cuba.
    D. Czar Nicholas II abdicates the throne.

    (1) $A \rightarrow B \rightarrow C \rightarrow D$ (3) $B \rightarrow C \rightarrow A \rightarrow D$
    (2) $B \rightarrow A \rightarrow D \rightarrow C$ (4) $D \rightarrow A \rightarrow C \rightarrow B$

Answers to the essay questions are to be written in the separate essay booklet.

In developing your answer to Part II, be sure to keep these general definitions in mind:

(a) <u>describe</u> means "to illustrate something in words or tell about it"
(b) <u>discuss</u> means "to make observations about something using facts, reasoning, and argument; to present in some detail"

Part II

THEMATIC ESSAY QUESTION

Directions: Write a well-organized essay that includes an introduction, several paragraphs addressing the task below, and a conclusion.

Theme: Change

> Not all revolutions are political. Nonpolitical revolutions have brought important intellectual, economic, and/or social changes to societies.

Task:

> Identify *two* nonpolitical revolutions that brought important intellectual, economic, and/or social changes to societies and for *each*
> - Describe *one* change brought about by this nonpolitical revolution
> - Discuss an impact this nonpolitical revolution had on a specific society or societies

You may use any nonpolitical revolution that brought important intellectual, economic, and/or social changes from your study of global history. Some suggestions you might wish to consider include the Neolithic Revolution (10,000–6,000 B.C.), the Commercial Revolution (11th–18th centuries), the Scientific Revolution (16th–18th centuries), the Enlightenment (17th–18th centuries), the Agricultural Revolution (18th–19th centuries), the Industrial Revolution in Europe (18th–19th centuries), and the Green Revolution (late 20th century).

You are *not* limited to these suggestions. However, do *not* choose a *political* revolution as one of your two revolutions.

Guidelines:

In your essay, be sure to
- Develop all aspects of the task
- Support the theme with relevant facts, examples, and details
- Use a logical and clear plan of organization, including an introduction and a conclusion that are beyond a restatement of the theme

In developing your answer to Part III, be sure to keep these general definitions in mind:

(a) <u>describe</u> means "to illustrate something in words or tell about it"

(b) <u>discuss</u> means "to make observations about something using facts, reasoning, and argument; to present in some detail"

Part III

DOCUMENT-BASED QUESTION

This question is based on the accompanying documents. The question is designed to test your ability to work with historical documents. Some of these documents have been edited for the purposes of this question. As you analyze the documents, take into account the source of each document and any point of view that may be presented in the document.

Historical Context:

Throughout history, governments have sometimes attempted to control the thoughts and actions of their people. Three such governments include **Russia under the rule of Peter the Great, Germany under the rule of Adolf Hitler,** and **China under the rule of Mao Zedong.** The efforts of these governments greatly affected their societies.

Task: Using the information from the documents and your knowledge of global history, answer the questions that follow each document in Part A. Your answers to the questions will help you write the Part B essay in which you will be asked to

> Choose *two* governments mentioned in the historical context and for *each*
> - Describe the efforts of the government to control the thoughts *and/or* actions of its people
> - Discuss an impact of this government's efforts on its society

Part A
Short-Answer Questions

Directions: Analyze the documents and answer the short-answer questions that follow each document in the space provided.

Document 1a

Peter the Great

Source: Chris Hinton, *What is Evidence?* John Murray, Ltd.

Document 1b

. . . A year later, in January 1700, Peter transformed persuasion into decree [law]. With rolling drums in the streets and squares, it was proclaimed that all boyars [Russian nobles], government officials and men of property, both in Moscow and in the provinces, were to abandon their long robes and provide themselves with Hungarian or German-style caftans. The following year, a new decree commanded men to wear a waistcoat, breeches, gaiters, boots and a hat in the French or German style, and women to put on petticoats, skirts, bonnets and Western shoes. Later decrees prohibited the wearing of high Russian boots and long Russian knives. Models of the new approved costumes were hung at Moscow's gates and in public places in the city for people to observe and copy. All who arrived at the gates in traditional dress except peasants were permitted to enter only after paying a fine. Subsequently, Peter instructed the guards at the city gates to force to their knees all visitors arriving in long, traditional coats and then to cut off the coats at the point where the lowered garment touched the ground. "Many hundreds of coats were cut accordingly," says Perry, "and being done with good humor it occasioned mirth [humor] among the people and soon broke the custom of wearing long coats, especially in places near Moscow and those towns wherever the Tsar came.". . .

Source: Robert K. Massie, *Peter the Great: His Life and World,* Alfred A. Knopf

1 Based on these documents, state *two* ways Peter the Great tried to control the actions of his people. [2]

(1) _____

_____

Score ☐

(2) _____

_____

Score ☐

Document 2

> . . . Peter's military reform would have remained an isolated incident in Russian military history had it not left a distinct and deep impression on the social and intellectual composition of all Russian society, and even influenced future political developments. The military reform itself made necessary other innovations, first to maintain the reorganised and expensive military forces, and then to ensure their permanency. The new recruiting methods, by spreading military obligations to classes hitherto [up to this time] exempt, and thus affecting all social classes, gave the new army a more varied composition, and completely altered existing social relationships. From the time that noblemens' serfs and servants joined the new army as ordinary recruits instead of only as menials or valets [servants], the position of the nobility, which had been preponderant [dominant] in the old army, was completely changed. . . .

Source: Vasili Klyuchevsky, translated by Liliana Archibald, *Peter the Great*, St. Martin's Press

2a According to Vasili Klyuchevsky, what was **one** way Peter the Great attempted to control the Russian people? [1]

_____

_____

Score ☐

b According to Vasili Klyuchevsky, what was **one** effect Peter the Great's reform had on the Russian nobles? [1]

_____

_____

Score ☐

Document 3

> **Emergence of "Dual Russia"**
>
> The Petrine [Peter's] Reform is often seen as the main cause and the starting point of the irrevocable [unalterable] split of Russian society into two parts. Peter's reforms transformed the upper levels of Russian society while the masses remained largely unaffected by them. Peter had forced the nobility to acquire technical knowledge of Western Europe and to adopt European styles of dress and manners. An increasingly Europeanized education of the upper classes brought with it a familiarity with the philosophies and theories of the Enlightenment. Soon many Russian nobles even preferred to speak the languages of Western Europe (particularly French and German) to Russian. By the nineteenth century their world was European in dress, manners, food, education, attitudes, and language, and was completely alien to the way of life of the Russian popular masses. . . .

Source: Alexander Chubarov, *The Fragile Empire: A History of Imperial Russia*, Continuum

3 According to Alexander Chubarov, what was **one** long-term effect Peter the Great's reform had on the upper classes of Russian society? [1]

_____

_____

Score ☐

Document 4a

> . . . On the night of May 10, 1933, thousands of Nazi students, along with many professors, stormed universities, libraries, and bookstores in thirty cities throughout Germany. They removed hundreds of thousands of books and cast them onto bonfires. In Berlin alone, more than twenty thousand books were burned. The book burnings were part of a calculated effort to "purify" German culture. Since April 12, the Nazi German Student Association had been purging libraries, working from lists of books deemed "un-German." The authors of some of the books were Jews, but most were not. . . .

Source: Michael Berenbaum, *The World Must Know: The History of the Holocaust as Told in the United States Holocaust Memorial Museum*, Little, Brown and Co.

4a According to Michael Berenbaum, what was **one** way the Nazi Party attempted to control the thoughts of the German people? [1]

_____

_____

Score ☐

Document 4b

> . . . The Hitler Youth movement was formed for the express purpose of creating loyal subjects to the state. By 1935, over three million boys and girls aged 10 and older were enrolled. "We were born to die for Germany" was one of their popular slogans. In addition to a strenuous physical fitness program, they received training in the use of weapons and heard lectures on Nazi ideology.

Source: Chartock and Spencer eds., *Can It Happen Again?*, Black Dog & Leventhal

4b According to the editors of *Can It Happen Again?*, what was **one** method used by the Nazi Party to influence the thinking of the young people of Germany? [1]

_____

_____

Score ☐

Document 5

In this excerpt Horst Krüger, a German author and prisoner of war, describes his reaction to reading a newspaper account of Hitler's death. He is reflecting on the state of the press while Hitler was in power.

> . . . When I first began to read the newspapers, he was already in power. I knew nothing but a subservient [obedient], bellicose [hostile], boastful press. I always felt it was a proven fact that Hitler had also conquered and occupied the German language, and my parents had always told me, "What you read in the papers isn't true, but you musn't say so. Outside, you must always act as if you believe everything." The German language and lies had become one and the same thing to me. Home was the only place where you could speak the truth. What you read in the papers was always a lie, but you weren't allowed to say so. And now I was holding a newspaper that was in German and that did not lie. How was it possible? How could language and truth coincide? How did it happen that you could believe something you saw in print? It was the first free German paper of my life. . . .

Source: Horst Krüger, *A Crack in The Wall: Growing Up Under Hitler,* Ruth Hein, tr., Fromm International Publishing Corporation

5 According to Horst Krüger, what was **one** impact of the Nazi government on German society? [1]

_____

_____

Score ☐

Document 6

This is an excerpt from the opening statement of Chief Prosecutor Robert H. Jackson at the trial of the major war criminals before the International Military Tribunal given on November 21, 1945.

> . . . Germany became one vast torture chamber. Cries of its victims were heard round the world and brought shudders to civilized people everywhere. I am one who received during this war most atrocity tales with suspicion and scepticism [doubt]. But the proof here will be so overwhelming that I venture to predict not one word I have spoken will be denied. These defendants will only deny personal responsibility or knowledge.
>
> Under the clutch of the most intricate web of espionage and intrigue that any modern state has endured, and persecution and torture of a kind that has not been visited upon the world in many centuries, the elements of the German population which were both decent and courageous were annihilated [reduced to nothing]. Those which were decent but weak were intimidated. Open resistance, which had never been more than feeble and irresolute, disappeared. But resistance, I am happy to say, always remained, although it was manifest in only such events as the abortive effort to assassinate Hitler on July 20, 1944. With resistance driven underground, the Nazi had the German State in his own hands.
>
> But the Nazis not only silenced discordant voices. They created positive controls as effective as their negative ones. Propaganda organs, on a scale never before known, stimulated the Party and Party formations with a permanent enthusiasm and abandon such as we, democratic people, can work up only for a few days before a general election. They inculcated [impressed upon] and practiced the Führerprinzip [leadership principle] which centralized control of the Party and of the Party-controlled State over the lives and thought of the German people, who are accustomed to look upon the German State, by whomever controlled, with a mysticism [a power to believe] that is incomprehensible to my people [the United States public]. . . .

Source: *Trial of the Major War Criminals Before the International Military Tribunal,*
Nuremberg, 14 November 1945–1 October 1946

6 According to Chief Prosecutor Jackson, what was **one** effect the Nazi government's actions had on the people of Germany? [1]

_____

_____

Score ☐

Document 7

This is an account of Nien Cheng's experiences during the Cultural Revolution. This excerpt describes what was happening the day she was sent to the Detention House.

> . . . The streets of Shanghai, normally deserted at nine o'clock in the evening, were a sea of humanity. Under the clear autumn sky in the cool breeze of September, people were out in thousands to watch the intensified activities of the Red Guards. On temporary platforms erected everywhere, the young Revolutionaries were calling upon the people in shrill and fiery rhetoric to join in the Revolution, and conducting small-scale struggle meetings against men and women they seized at random on the street and accused of failing to carry Mao's Little Red Book of quotations or simply wearing the sort of clothes the Red Guards disapproved of. Outside private houses and apartment buildings, smoke rose over the garden walls, permeating the air as the Red Guards continued to burn books indiscriminately. . . .

Source: Nien Cheng, *Life and Death in Shanghai*, Penguin Books

7 According to Nien Cheng, what were ***two*** actions taken by the Red Guards in an attempt to control the thoughts of the people during Mao's rule in China? [2]

(1) _____

_____

Score ☐

(2) _____

_____

Score ☐

Document 8

In Following the Revolutionary Road, Strive for an Even Greater Victory

Mao as the Reddest Red Sun in people's hearts, floating above Tiananmen Square. At the front of the huge, Little Red Book-waving crowd are the figures of a worker, peasant, and soldier, while representatives from other occupations stand just behind. The Book was compiled from Mao's Selected Works by Lin Biao in the early 1960s to be used for propaganda work in the People's Liberation Army. After the Cultural Revolution began, it became an integral part of the ritual of Mao worship. By 1970, this kind of orchestrated adulation [staged praise] and the power of Lin Biao were both at their zenith [height].

Source: *Picturing Power: Posters from the Chinese Cultural Revolution Exhibit*, Indiana University

8 According to this document, what was *one* way that Mao's government attempted to influence the people of China? [1]

_____

_____

Score ☐

Document 9

> . . . Between 1966 and 1976, a whole generation of teenagers failed to receive a real education; other Chinese came to call them "the lost generation." At least twenty thousand people lost their lives because of the Cultural Revolution.
>
> . . . Because of the Cultural Revolution, many Chinese young people grew up with no knowledge of traditional Chinese customs and beliefs. Needing to fill that gap, some of them began looking to the West — especially to the Western ideals of democracy, freedom, capitalism, and individualism. . . .

Source: *Great Events: The Twentieth Century 1960–1968,* Salem Press

9 Based on this excerpt from *Great Events*, state **one** impact the Cultural Revolution had on Chinese society. [1]

_____

_____

Score ☐

Part B
Essay

Directions: Write a well-organized essay that includes an introduction, several paragraphs, and a conclusion. Use evidence from *at least **four*** documents in your essay. Support your response with relevant facts, examples, and details. Include additional outside information.

Historical Context:

Throughout history, governments have sometimes attempted to control the thoughts and actions of their people. Three such governments include **Russia under the rule of Peter the Great, Germany under the rule of Adolf Hitler,** and **China under the rule of Mao Zedong.** The efforts of these governments greatly affected their societies.

Task: Using the information from the documents and your knowledge of global history, write an essay in which you

Choose *two* governments mentioned in the historical context and for *each*
- Describe the efforts of the government to control the thoughts *and/or* actions of its people
- Discuss an impact of this government's efforts on its society

Guidelines:

In your essay, be sure to
- Develop all aspects of the task
- Incorporate information from *at least **four*** documents
- Incorporate relevant outside information
- Support the theme with relevant facts, examples, and details
- Use a logical and clear plan of organization, including an introduction and a conclusion that are beyond a restatement of the theme

The University of the State of New York

REGENTS HIGH SCHOOL EXAMINATION

GLOBAL HISTORY AND GEOGRAPHY

Wednesday, June 18, 2008 — 1:15 to 4:15 p.m., only

Student Name _____

School Name _____

Print your name and the name of your school on the lines above. Then turn to the last page of this booklet, which is the answer sheet for Part I. Fold the last page along the perforations and, slowly and carefully, tear off the answer sheet. Then fill in the heading of your answer sheet. Now print your name and the name of your school in the heading of each page of your essay booklet.

This examination has three parts. You are to answer **all** questions in all parts. Use black or dark-blue ink to write your answers.

Part I contains 50 multiple-choice questions. Record your answers to these questions on the separate answer sheet.

Part II contains one thematic essay question. Write your answer to this question in the essay booklet, beginning on page 1.

Part III is based on several documents:

Part III A contains the documents. Each document is followed by one or more questions. In the test booklet, write your answer to each question on the lines following that question. Be sure to enter your name and the name of your school on the first page of this section.

Part III B contains one essay question based on the documents. Write your answer to this question in the essay booklet, beginning on page 7.

When you have completed the examination, you must sign the statement printed on the Part I answer sheet, indicating that you had no unlawful knowledge of the questions or answers prior to the examination and that you have neither given nor received assistance in answering any of the questions during the examination. Your answer sheet cannot be accepted if you fail to sign this declaration.

The use of any communications device is strictly prohibited when taking this examination. If you use any communications device, no matter how briefly, your examination will be invalidated and no score will be calculated for you.

DO NOT OPEN THIS EXAMINATION BOOKLET UNTIL THE SIGNAL IS GIVEN.

33/50
66%

Part I

Answer all questions in this part.

Directions (1–50): For each statement or question, write on the separate answer sheet the *number* of the word or expression that, of those given, best completes the statement or answers the question.

Base your answer to question 1 on the announcement below and on your knowledge of social studies.

Discovery
OF
Ancient Relics.

A Full, True, and Interesting Account of that Remarkable and Important Discovery made yesterday in taking down the old houses in the Castle-hill, when there was found a box containing several Ancient Coins, a Massy Gold Ring, an old fashioned Dirk, and a Wonderful Prophecy made in the year 1550, respecting great events which are to happen this present year.

Source: Broadside published in Edinburgh, Scotland, 1831 (adapted)

1 Which term best describes the items mentioned in this announcement?

  (1) icons   (3) artifacts
  (2) fossils   (4) replicas

2 One way in which South Korea, Saudi Arabia, and India are geographically similar is that each is located on

  (1) an island   (3) an isthmus
  (2) an archipelago (4) a peninsula

3 Which statement represents a characteristic of democracy?

  (1) Religious leaders control government policy.
  (2) Citizens are the source of power in government.
  (3) The government limits the thoughts and actions of the people.
  (4) The laws of the government are made by influential military officers.

4 The Bantu cleared the land, then fertilized it with ashes. When the land could no longer support their families, the Bantu moved further south. By 1110 B.C., the Bantu had spread their rich culture throughout central and southern Africa.

Which agricultural technique is described in this passage?

  (1) irrigation   (3) slash-and-burn
  (2) terrace farming (4) crop rotation

5 Which ancient civilization is associated with the Twelve Tables, an extensive road system, and the poets Horace and Virgil?

  (1) Babylonian   (3) Phoenician
  (2) Greek   (4) Roman

6 The term *feudalism* is best defined as a

  (1) holy war between Christians and Muslims
  (2) process in which goods are traded for other goods
  (3) division of political power between three separate branches
  (4) system in which land is exchanged for military service and loyalty

7 Which title best completes the partial outline below?

I. _____

  A. Incorporation of European and Arabic ideas in architecture
  B. Preservation of Greco-Roman ideas
  C. Spread of Orthodox Christianity into Russia
  D. Development of Justinian Code

  (1) Age of Discovery (3) Persian Empire
  (2) Byzantine Empire (4) Crusades

Base your answer to question 8 on the illustration below and on your knowledge of social studies.

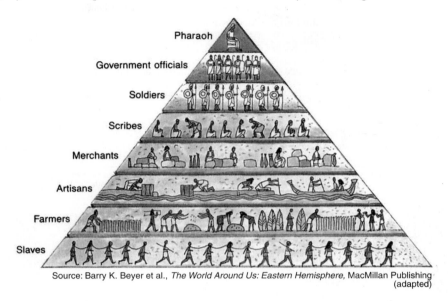

Source: Barry K. Beyer et al., *The World Around Us: Eastern Hemisphere*, MacMillan Publishing
(adapted)

8 Based on the information in this illustration, which statement about the society of ancient Egypt is accurate?

(1) The women had equal status to the men.
(2) The social structure was hierarchical.
(3) Social mobility was unrestricted.
(4) Soldiers outnumbered farmers.

9 Which statement about the Mongol Empire is accurate?

(1) The Mongols developed a highly technological society that emphasized formal education.
(2) European monarchies became a model for the early Mongol governments.
(3) Pax Mongolia led to regional stability, increasing trade on the Silk Road.
(4) The Mongols adopted Roman Catholicism as the official religion of the empire.

10 Which period in European history is most closely associated with Leonardo da Vinci, Michaelangelo, William Shakespeare, and Nicolaus Copernicus?

(1) Early Middle Ages   (3) Age of Absolutism
(2) Renaissance   (4) Enlightenment

11 What was one of the primary reasons for the spread of the bubonic plague?

(1) increase in trade
(2) colonization of the Americas
(3) development of the manorial system
(4) economic decline

12 Which situation is considered a cause of the other three?

(1) Religious unity declines throughout Europe.
(2) The Catholic Counter-Reformation begins.
(3) The power of the Roman Catholic Church decreases.
(4) Martin Luther posts the Ninety-five Theses.

Base your answer to question 13 on the table below and on your knowledge of social studies.

Population of the Largest Medieval Cities in 1250 and 1450

The 10 largest cities in 1250		The 10 largest cities in 1450	
1 Hangchow	320,000	1 Peking	600,000
2 Cairo	300,000	2 Vijayanagar	455,000
3 Fez	200,000	3 Cairo	380,000
4 Kamakura	200,000	4 Hangchow	250,000
5 Pagan	180,000	5 Tabriz	200,000
6 Paris	160,000	6 Canton	175,000
7 Peking	140,000	7 Granada	165,000
8 Canton	140,000	8 Nanking	150,000
9 Nanking	130,000	9 Paris	150,000
10 Marrakesh	125,000	10 Kyoto	150,000

Source: Tertius Chandler, *Four Thousand Years of Urban Growth*,
St. David's University Press (adapted)

13 Which statement can best be supported by the information in this table?

(1) The population of Paris increased between 1250 and 1450.
(2) The populations of Cairo and Nanking were higher in 1250 than in 1450.
(3) The population of most large cities exceeded one million people in 1450.
(4) The population of Peking increased more than the population of Canton between 1250 and 1450.

Base your answer to question 14 on the passage below and on your knowledge of social studies.

It would be wrong to call the Ottoman Empire a purely Islamic state. It was not. It was a state that claimed some kind of an attachment, some kind of allegiance to Islam, but combined it with other forms of heritage from the Byzantine tradition or from the Turkic tradition that did not really correspond to Islam. So they always had this very, very pragmatic approach to Islam.

— Professor Edhem Eldem, Bogazici University,
NPR News, *All Things Considered*,
August 18, 2004

14 This author is suggesting that during the Ottoman Empire

(1) religion was mingled with historic traditions
(2) most people belonged to minority religions
(3) rulers tried to separate politics from religion
(4) rulers operated under a strict set of laws

---

15 • Foreign rulers were overthrown.
• Admiral Zheng He established trade links.
• Civil service exams were reinstated.

These events in history occurred during the rule of the

(1) Mughal dynasty in India
(2) Abbasid dynasty in the Middle East
(3) Ming dynasty in China
(4) Tokugawa shogunate in Japan

16 What was the primary economic policy used by the Spanish with their Latin American colonies?

(1) embargoes
(2) tariffs
(3) boycotts
(4) mercantilism

17 In *Two Treatises of Government*, John Locke wrote that the purpose of government was to

(1) keep kings in power
(2) regulate the economy
(3) expand territory
(4) protect natural rights

Base your answer to question 18 on the map below and on your knowledge of social studies.

Source: Peter N. Stearns et al., *World Civilizations: The Global Experience*, Pearson (adapted)

18 Which generalization is best supported by the information on this map?

(1) No trade occurred between East Africa and the Persian Gulf region.

(2) The monsoon winds influenced trade between East Africa and India.

(3) Trading states developed primarily in the interior of East Africa.

(4) Trade encouraged the spread of Islam from East Africa to Arabia.

Base your answer to question 19 on the summaries of the "New Laws" quoted below and on your knowledge of social studies.

. . . Art. 31. All Indians held in encomienda by the viceroys, by their lieutenants, royal officers, prelates, monasteries, hospitals, religious houses, mints, the treasury, etc., are to be transferred forthwith to the Crown. . . .

Art. 38. Lawsuits involving Indians are no longer to be tried in the Indies, or by the Council of the Indies, but must be pleaded before the King himself. . . .

— New Laws issued by Emperor Charles V, 1542–1543

19 One purpose of these laws was to

(1) reduce local authority and increase central control

(2) increase religious authority and limit secular influences

(3) guarantee citizenship to Indians while supporting traditional practices

(4) promote economic development while expanding political rights for Indians

20 One major effect of Napoleon's rule of France was that it led to

(1) an increase in the power of the Roman Catholic Church

(2) massive emigration to the Americas

(3) trade agreements with Great Britain

(4) a restoration of political stability

21 Which idea is most closely associated with laissez-faire economics?

(1) communes

(2) trade unionism

(3) subsistence agriculture

(4) free trade

22 In the 19th century, a major reason for Irish migration to North America was to

(1) gain universal suffrage

(2) avoid malaria outbreaks

(3) flee widespread famine

(4) escape a civil war

23 A major goal of both the Sepoy Mutiny in India and the Boxer Rebellion in China was to

(1) rid their countries of foreigners
(2) expand their respective territories
(3) receive international military support
(4) restore an absolute monarch to the throne

24 Early exploration of Africa by Europeans was hindered by the

(1) lack of natural resources in Africa
(2) alliances between African kingdoms
(3) isolationist policies of European monarchs
(4) many different physical features of Africa

25 Which action taken by the Meiji government encouraged industrialization in 19th-century Japan?

(1) building a modern transportation system
(2) limiting the number of ports open to foreign trade
(3) forcing families to settle on collective farms
(4) establishing a system of trade guilds

26 One goal of the League of Nations was to

(1) promote peaceful relations worldwide
(2) stimulate the economy of Europe
(3) bring World War I to an end
(4) encourage a strong alliance system

27 • Five-year plans
• Collectivization of agriculture
• Great Purge

Which individual is associated with all these policies?

(1) Adolf Hitler   (3) Deng Xiaoping
(2) Joseph Stalin   (4) Jawaharlal Nehru

28 Japan's invasion of Manchuria, Italy's attack on Ethiopia, and Germany's blitzkrieg in Poland are examples of

(1) military aggression   (3) containment
(2) appeasement   (4) the domino theory

29 Which statement about the worldwide Depression of the 1930s is a fact rather than an opinion?

(1) Political leaders should have prevented the Depression.
(2) Germany was hurt more by the Treaty of Versailles than by the Depression.
(3) The economic upheaval of the Depression had major political effects.
(4) World War I was the only reason for the Depression.

30 Which group was accused of violating human rights in the city of Nanjing during World War II?

(1) Americans   (3) Japanese
(2) Chinese   (4) Germans

31 One way in which the Hitler Youth of Germany and the Red Guard of China are similar is that both organizations

(1) required unquestioning loyalty to the leader
(2) helped increase religious tolerance
(3) hindered imperialistic goals
(4) led pro-democracy movements

32 • French intent to recolonize Indo-China after World War II
• United States desire to prevent the spread of communism
• United States support for the French in Southeast Asia

These ideas are most closely associated with the

(1) causes of the conflict in Vietnam
(2) reasons for the Nationalist settlement of Taiwan
(3) factors that led to the Korean War
(4) results of the Marshall Plan

33 Which country is most closely associated with the terms *pass laws*, *homelands*, and *white minority rule*?

(1) El Salvador   (3) Iran
(2) South Africa   (4) Israel

Base your answer to question 34 on the photograph below and on your knowledge of social studies.

Mahatma Gandhi demonstrating cotton-spinning on his own *charka* in Mirzapur, 1925.

Source: Stanley Wolpert, *Gandhi's Passion: The Life and Legacy of Mahatma Gandhi*, Oxford University Press

34 During the Indian independence movement, the activity shown in this photograph inspired the Indian people to

(1) stop buying British goods
(2) reject Muslim rule
(3) join the Indian army
(4) expand British textile manufacturing

Base your answers to questions 35 and 36 on the passage below and on your knowledge of social studies.

. . . (1) Internally, arouse the masses of the people. That is, unite the working class, the peasantry, the urban petty bourgeoisie and the national bourgeoisie, form a domestic united front under the leadership of the working class, and advance from this to the establishment of a state which is a people's democratic dictatorship under the leadership of the working class and based on the alliance of workers and peasants.

(2) Externally, unite in a common struggle with those nations of the world which treat us as equals and unite with the peoples of all countries. That is, ally ourselves with the Soviet Union, with the People's Democracies and with the proletariat and the broad masses of the people in all other countries, and form an international united front. . . .

Source: Mao Tse-Tung [Mao Zedong], *Selected Works*, Volume Five, 1945–1949, New York International Publishers

35 In this passage, Mao Zedong is suggesting that China

(1) create a government under the leadership of industrialists
(2) give up its independence and become a part of the Soviet Union
(3) rely on the United Nations for economic aid
(4) join with the Soviet Union as a partner in communism

36 In this passage, Mao Zedong is using the ideas of

(1) Thomas Malthus
(2) Adam Smith
(3) Karl Marx
(4) Jiang Jieshi (Chiang Kai-Shek)

Base your answer to question 37 on the time line below and on your knowledge of social studies.

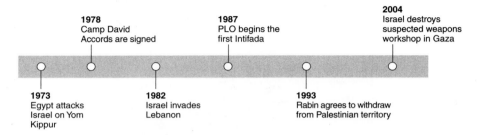

37 Which conclusion can be drawn from this time line?
   (1) Israel withdrew from the Camp David Accords.
   (2) The Palestinian army is superior to the Israeli army.
   (3) Long-lasting peace in the Middle East has been difficult to achieve.
   (4) Neighboring countries have not been involved in the Arab-Israeli conflict.

38 The destruction of the Berlin Wall and the breakup of the Soviet Union signify the
   (1) end of the Cold War
   (2) collapse of the Taliban
   (3) strength of the Warsaw Pact
   (4) power of the European Union

39 In the 20th century, urbanization affected the developing nations of Africa, Asia, and Latin America by
   (1) reducing literacy rates
   (2) weakening traditional values
   (3) strengthening caste systems
   (4) increasing the isolation of women

40 Which statement about the impact of the AIDS epidemic in both Africa and Southeast Asia is most accurate?
   (1) Life expectancy in both regions is declining.
   (2) The availability of low-cost drugs has cured most of those infected.
   (3) The introduction of awareness programs has eliminated the threat of the disease.
   (4) Newborn babies and young children have not been affected by the disease.

41 In August 1990, Iraq invaded Kuwait. The United Nations response led to the Persian Gulf War of 1991. This response is an example of
   (1) détente
   (2) empire building
   (3) totalitarianism
   (4) collective security

42 One similarity between the Roman Empire and the Ottoman Empire is that both
   (1) reached their height of power at the same time
   (2) developed parliamentary governments
   (3) ensured equality for women
   (4) declined because of corruption in government

43 Which statement regarding the impact of geography on Japan is most accurate?
   (1) Large plains served as invasion routes for conquerors.
   (2) Arid deserts and mountains caused isolation from Asia.
   (3) Lack of natural resources led to a policy of imperialism.
   (4) Close proximity to Africa encouraged extensive trade with Egypt.

Base your answer to question 44 on the map below and on your knowledge of social studies.

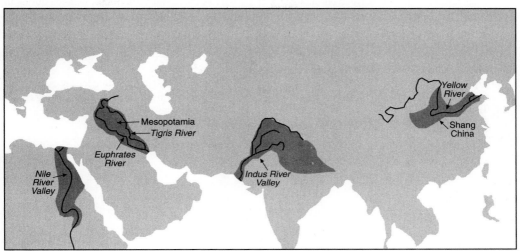

Source: Paul Halsall, ed., *Internet History Sourcebooks Project* (adapted)

44 Which revolution led to the development of these civilizations?

(1) Industrial   (3) Green

(2) Neolithic   (4) Commercial

45 The Age of Exploration led directly to the

(1) establishment of European colonies
(2) start of the Puritan Revolution
(3) invention of the magnetic compass
(4) failure of the Congress of Vienna

46 Which revolution was caused by the factors shown in this partial outline?

I. _____

    A. Bankruptcy of the treasury
    B. Tax burden on the Third Estate
    C. Inflation
    D. Abuses of the Old Regime

(1) Russian   (3) French
(2) Mexican   (4) Cuban

47 One way in which José de San Martín, Camillo Cavour, and Jomo Kenyatta are similar is that each leader

(1) made significant scientific discoveries
(2) led nationalist movements
(3) fought against British imperialism
(4) became a communist revolutionary

48 One way in which Vladimir Lenin's New Economic Policy and Mikhail Gorbachev's policy of perestroika are similar is that both

(1) allowed elements of capitalism within a communist economic system
(2) strengthened their country's military defenses
(3) supported censorship of news and of personal correspondence
(4) increased tensions during the Cold War

49 Which set of events in 19th- and 20th-century Chinese history is in the correct chronological order?

(1) Great Leap Forward → Opium Wars → Long March → Four Modernizations
(2) Four Modernizations → Long March → Opium Wars → Great Leap Forward
(3) Opium Wars → Long March → Great Leap Forward → Four Modernizations
(4) Long March → Four Modernizations → Great Leap Forward → Opium Wars

50 A study of Spain during the late 1400s, the Balkan States during the early 1900s, Rwanda during the 1990s, and Central Asia today shows that

(1) civil disobedience is an effective way to bring about change
(2) people have been encouraged to question tradition
(3) colonial rule has a lasting legacy
(4) ethnic conflicts have been a recurring issue in history

Answers to the essay questions are to be written in the separate essay booklet.

In developing your answer to Part II, be sure to keep these general definitions in mind:

(a) <u>explain</u> means "to make plain or understandable; to give reasons for or causes of; to show the logical development or relationships of"

(b) <u>discuss</u> means "to make observations about something using facts, reasoning, and argument; to present in some detail"

Part II

THEMATIC ESSAY QUESTION

Directions: Write a well-organized essay that includes an introduction, several paragraphs addressing the task below, and a conclusion.

Theme: Belief Systems

> The world has many different belief systems. Each is distinctive, but all greatly influenced the lives of their followers and the society in which the belief system was practiced.

Task:

> Choose *two* major belief systems and for *each*
> - Explain key beliefs *and/or* practices
> - Discuss an influence the belief system had on the lives of its followers or the society in which it was practiced

You may use any example from your study of global history. Some suggestions you might wish to consider include animism, Buddhism, Christianity, Confucianism, Daoism, Islam, Judaism, legalism, and Shinto.

You are *not* limited to these suggestions.

Do *not* use the United States as the focus of your answer.

Guidelines:

In your essay, be sure to
- Develop all aspects of the task
- Support the theme with relevant facts, examples, and details
- Use a logical and clear plan of organization, including an introduction and a conclusion that are beyond a restatement of the theme

In developing your answers to Part III, be sure to keep these general definitions in mind:

  (a) <u>describe</u> means "to illustrate something in words or tell about it"
  (b) <u>discuss</u> means "to make observations about something using facts, reasoning, and argument; to present in some detail"

Part III

DOCUMENT-BASED QUESTION

This question is based on the accompanying documents. The question is designed to test your ability to work with historical documents. Some of these documents have been edited for the purposes of this question. As you analyze the documents, take into account the source of each document and any point of view that may be presented in the document.

Historical Context:

> *Genocide, threats to the environment,* and *weapons of mass destruction* are problems that the world has had to face. Various attempts have been made by the international community and its members to address and resolve these problems.

Task: Using the information from the documents and your knowledge of global history, answer the questions that follow each document in Part A. Your answers to the questions will help you write the Part B essay in which you will be asked to

> Select *two* problems mentioned in the historical context and for *each*
> • Describe the problem
> • Discuss attempts made to address *and/or* resolve the problem

Part A
Short-Answer Questions

Directions: Analyze the documents and answer the short-answer questions that follow each document in the space provided.

Document 1

Raphael Lemkin created the term genocide. He sent a letter to the *New York Times* editor explaining the importance of the concept of genocide.

Genocide Before the United Nations

TO THE EDITOR OF THE NEW YORK TIMES:
    The representatives of Cuba, India and Panama to the United Nations Assembly have brought forth a resolution which calls upon the United Nations to study the problem of genocide and to prepare a report on the possibilities of declaring genocide an international crime and assuring international cooperation for its prevention and punishment and also recommending, among others, that genocide should be dealt with by national legislation in the same way as other international crimes. . . .

International Concept
    The concept of genocide thus is based upon existing and deeply felt moral concepts. Moreover, it uses as its elements well defined and already existing legal notions and institutions. What we have to do is to protect great values of our civilization through such accepted institutions adjusted to a formula of international law which is ever progressing. Because of lack of adequate provisions and previous formulation of international law, the Nuremberg Tribunal had to dismiss the Nazi crimes committed in the period between the advent of Nazism to power and the beginning of the war, as "revolting and horrible as many of these crimes were," to use the expression of the Nuremberg judgment.

    It is now the task of the United Nations to see to it that the generous action of the three member states should be transferred into international law in order to prevent further onslaughts [attacks] on civilization, which are able to frustrate the purposes of the Charter of the United Nations. . . .

Source: Raphael Lemkin, *New York Times*, Nov. 8, 1946 (adapted)

1 According to Raphael Lemkin, what is *one* way the world community can address the problem of genocide? [1]

_____

_____

Score ☐

Document 2a

... In 1948, the fledgling UN General Assembly adopted an international Convention on the Prevention and Punishment of the Crime of Genocide, which came into force in 1951. That convention defines genocide as "acts committed with intent to destroy, in whole or in part, a national ethnic, racial or religious group," including inflicting conditions calculated to lead to a group's destruction. ...

After the horrors of the Holocaust were revealed, the mantra [slogan] of the time became "never again." But it would take four decades, with the creation of the International Criminal Tribunal for the former Yugoslavia in 1994, before the international community would finally come together to prosecute the crime of genocide again.

Why did it take so long, despite atrocities and mass killings in Cambodia, East Timor, and elsewhere? ...

Source: Irina Lagunina, "World: What Constitutes Genocide Under International Law, and How Are Prosecutions Evolving?," Radio Free Europe/Radio Liberty, 9/10/2004

2a According to Irina Lagunina, what was **one** criticism of the international community's response to genocide? [1]

_____

_____

Score ☐

Document 2b

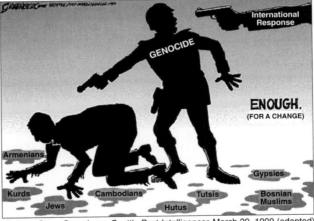

Source: Steve Greenberg, *Seattle Post-Intelligencer,* March 29, 1999 (adapted)

2b Based on this 1999 cartoon, identify **two** specific groups that have been victims of genocide. [1]

(1) _____

(2) _____

Score ☐

Document 3

> . . . Undeniably, there have been terrible human rights failures—in Cambodia, Bosnia, Rwanda. There, and elsewhere, national constitutions and international norms failed to deter; international institutions and powerful governments failed to respond promptly and adequately. (The expectation that they would fail to respond no doubt contributed to their failure to deter.) But international human rights may be credited with whatever responses there have been, however inadequate, however delayed; and international human rights inspired all subsequent and continuing efforts to address the terrible violations. The major powers have sometimes declared gross violations of human rights to be "threats to international peace and security" and made them the responsibility of the UN Security Council, leading to international sanctions (and even to military intervention, as in Kosovo in 1999). International tribunals are sitting to bring gross violators to trial; a permanent international criminal tribunal to adjudicate [judge] crimes of genocide, war crimes, and crimes against humanity is being created. Various governments have moved to support international human rights and made their bilateral and multilateral influence an established force in international relations. . . .

Source: Louis Henkin, "Human Rights: Ideology and Aspiration, Reality and Prospect," *Realizing Human Rights*, St. Martin's Press, 2000

3 Based on this document, state *one* attempt made to address the problem of genocide. [1]

_____

_____

Score ☐

Document 4

At the dawn of the twenty-first century, the Earth's physical and biological systems are under unprecedented strain. The human population reached 6.3 billion in 2003 and is projected to increase to about 9 billion in the next half century. The United Nations estimates that one-third of the world's people live in countries with moderate to high shortages of fresh water and that this percentage could double by 2025. Many of the world's largest cities are increasingly choked by pollution. As carbon dioxide and other greenhouse gases build in the atmosphere, the average surface temperature of the Earth has reached the highest level ever measured on an annual basis. The biological diversity of the planet is also under heavy stress. Scientists believe that a mass extinction of plants and animals is under way and predict that a quarter of all species could be pushed to extinction by 2050 as a consequence of global warming alone. Without question, the human impact on the biosphere will be one of the most critical issues of the century. . . .

Source: Norman J. Vig, "Introduction: Governing the International Environment," *The Global Environment: Institutions, Law, and Policy,* CQ Press, 2005 (adapted)

4 According to Norman J. Vig, what are **two** environmental problems that pose a threat to the world? [2]

(1) _____

_____

Score ☐

(2) _____

_____

Score ☐

Document 5

Desertification is a major environmental problem. Nearly one-quarter of the Earth's land is threatened by this problem. China is one of those areas.

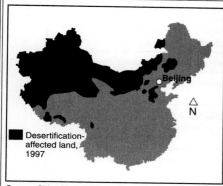

Desertification-affected land, 1997

Source: China National Committee for the Implementation of the U.N. Convention to Combat Desertification (adapted)

Whipped by the wind, sand from Sky Desert swept through this village [Longbaoshan] last month like sheets of stinging rain, clattering against dried corn husks and piling up in small dunes against buildings.

Longbaoshan, a farming community about 40 miles northwest of Beijing, stands on the front line of China's losing war against the country's advancing deserts. Driven by overgrazing, overpopulation, drought and poor land management, they are slowly consuming vast areas of the country in a looming ecological disaster.

Official figures tell a frightening story.

Between 1994 and 1999, desertified land grew by 20,280 square miles. Desert blankets more than a quarter of China's territory. Shifting sands threaten herders and farmers in a nation with one-fifth of the world's population and one-fifteenth of its arable land. Scientists warn of calamity if the government fails to stop the sands.

"Pastures, farmland, railroads and other means of transportation will be buried under sand," said Dong Guangrong, a research fellow in environmental engineering at the Chinese Academy of Sciences. "People will be forced to move."...

In March, the worst sandstorm in a decade blinded the capital, painting the sky yellow and engulfing 40-story buildings as visibility dropped to less than a football field. Beijingers gritted their teeth as a seasonal storm known as the Yellow Dragon dumped 30,000 tons of sand on the city. People on the street covered their mouths with surgical masks or their faces with scarves in a futile attempt to keep the sand out....

Officials here are trying to stop the sands by building green buffers. A project intended to protect Beijing in advance of the 2008 summer Olympic Games involves reclaiming desertified land in 75 counties....

Source: Frank Langfitt, "Desertification," *The Post-Standard*, May 13, 2002 (adapted)

5*a* Based on this document, state *one* problem desertification poses in China. [1]

_____

_____

Score ☐

b Based on this document, state *one* attempt the Chinese officials have made to address the problem of desertification. [1]

_____

_____

Score ☐

Document 6

Selected Efforts to Preserve the Environment

1972	Stockholm—United Nations Conference on Human Environment—beginning of organized international effort to safeguard the environment
1973	The Convention on International Trade in Endangered Species of Wild Fauna and Flora (CITES)—restricts trade in 5,000 animal and 25,000 plant species
1987	Montreal Protocol—binding agreement on protection of the ozone layer
1992	Rio de Janeiro "Earth Summit"—produced treaties on climate change and biodiversity
1994	The World Conservation Union (IUCN)—published a revised Red List of endangered and threatened species, creating a world standard for gauging threats to biodiversity
1997	Kyoto Protocol—negotiated an agreement on obligations to reduce green-house gases in the atmosphere
2004	European Union—issued its first-ever pollution register containing data on industrial emissions and representing a "landmark event" in public provision of environmental information
2006	United Nations General Assembly—declared the International Year of Deserts which led to the United Nations Convention to Combat Desertification

Source: "Environmental Milestones," World Watch Institute (adapted)

6 Based on this document, identify *two* ways the international community has attempted to address environmental problems. [2]

(1) _____

_____

Score ☐

(2) _____

_____

Score ☐

Document 7

The Twentieth Century's Deadly Yield

Weapons of mass destruction generally refer to biological, chemical, and nuclear weapons.

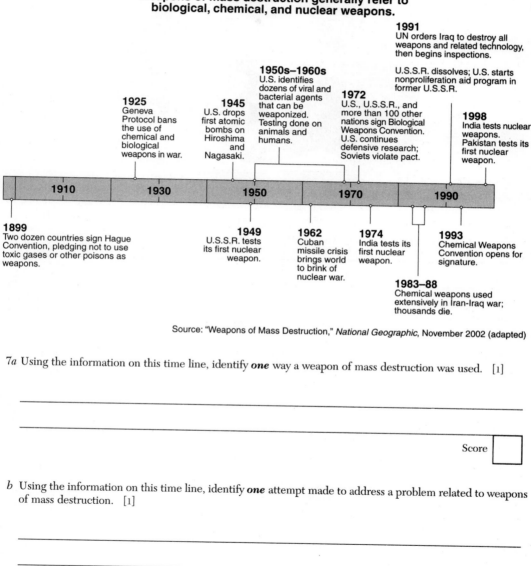

1991
UN orders Iraq to destroy all weapons and related technology, then begins inspections.

U.S.S.R. dissolves; U.S. starts nonproliferation aid program in former U.S.S.R.

1950s–1960s
U.S. identifies dozens of viral and bacterial agents that can be weaponized. Testing done on animals and humans.

1925
Geneva Protocol bans the use of chemical and biological weapons in war.

1945
U.S. drops first atomic bombs on Hiroshima and Nagasaki.

1972
U.S., U.S.S.R., and more than 100 other nations sign Biological Weapons Convention. U.S. continues defensive research; Soviets violate pact.

1998
India tests nuclear weapons. Pakistan tests its first nuclear weapon.

1910 | 1930 | 1950 | 1970 | 1990

1899
Two dozen countries sign Hague Convention, pledging not to use toxic gases or other poisons as weapons.

1949
U.S.S.R. tests its first nuclear weapon.

1962
Cuban missile crisis brings world to brink of nuclear war.

1974
India tests its first nuclear weapon.

1993
Chemical Weapons Convention opens for signature.

1983–88
Chemical weapons used extensively in Iran-Iraq war; thousands die.

Source: "Weapons of Mass Destruction," *National Geographic*, November 2002 (adapted)

7a Using the information on this time line, identify **one** way a weapon of mass destruction was used. [1]

_____

_____

Score ☐

b Using the information on this time line, identify **one** attempt made to address a problem related to weapons of mass destruction. [1]

_____

_____

Score ☐

Document 8

Source: Jeff Danziger, Tribune Media Services, January 4, 2002 (adapted)

8 Based on this cartoon, state **one** reason nuclear weapons pose a threat to the world community. [1]

_____

_____

Score ☐

Document 9

Civilian uranium is found at nonmilitary sites. It is used to conduct scientific and industrial research or to produce radioisotopes for medical purposes. This uranium can also be used to make highly enriched uranium (HEU), which is used in nuclear weapons.

Overview/Securing Civilian Uranium 235

- Terrorists who acquired less than 100 kilograms of highly enriched uranium (HEU) could build and detonate a rudimentary but effective atomic bomb relatively easily. HEU is also attractive for states that seek to develop nuclear weapons secretly, without having to test them.
- Unfortunately, large quantities of HEU are stored in nuclear research facilities worldwide—especially in Russia, often under minimal security.
- The U.S. and its allies have established programs to bolster security measures, convert reactors to use low-enriched uranium (which is useless for weapons) and retrieve HEU from research-reactor sites around the world. Dangerous gaps remain, however.
- High-level governmental attention plus a comparatively small additional monetary investment could go a long way toward solving the problem for good.

Source: Glaser and von Hippel, "Thwarting Nuclear Terrorism," *Scientific American,* February 2006

9 Based on this article by Glaser and von Hippel, state an attempt being made by the United States and its allies to improve the security of highly enriched uranium (HEU). [1]

_____

_____

Score ☐

Part B
Essay

Directions: Write a well-organized essay that includes an introduction, several paragraphs, and a conclusion. Use evidence from *at least **four*** documents in your essay. Support your response with relevant facts, examples, and details. Include additional outside information.

Historical Context:

> ***Genocide, threats to the environment,*** and ***weapons of mass destruction*** are problems that the world has had to face. Various attempts have been made by the international community and its members to address and resolve these problems.

Task: Using the information from the documents and your knowledge of global history, write an essay in which you

> Select ***two*** problems mentioned in the historical context and for ***each***
> * Describe the problem
> * Discuss attempts made to address ***and/or*** resolve the problem

Guidelines:

In your essay, be sure to
* Develop all aspects of the task
* Incorporate information from *at least **four*** documents
* Incorporate relevant outside information
* Support the theme with relevant facts, examples, and details
* Use a logical and clear plan of organization, including an introduction and a conclusion that are beyond a restatement of the theme

INDEX

1) 1
2) 3
3) 3
4) 2
5) 4
6) 1
7) 4
8) 4 1
9) 4 3
10) 4
11) 1
12) 3
13) 2
14) 1 2
15) 3 1
16) 2 3
17) 4
18) 1
19) 1 2
20) 4
21) 3
22) 3
23) 1
24) 2
25) 2

38/50
76%.

26) 1
27) 1 2
28) 3
29) 2 4
30) 4
31) 1
32) 3
33) 2
34) 3
35) 3
36) 1
37) 1 4
38) 3
39) 1
40) 4
41) 2
42) 4 1
43) 2
44) 1 3
45) 2
46) 4
47) 3 1
48) 1
49) 3
50) 4